DISPUTE RESOLUTION

ASPEN CASEBOOK SERIES

DISPUTE RESOLUTION

Beyond the Adversarial Model

Fourth Edition

Carrie J. Menkel-Meadow
Distinguished and Chancellor's Professor of Law (and Political Science) and Founding Faculty, University of California, Irvine Law School and A.B. Chettle Jr. Chair of Law, Dispute Resolution and Civil Procedure, Emerita, Georgetown University Law Center

Lela Porter Love
Emerita Professor of Law and Founding Director, Kukin Program for Conflict Resolution Benjamin N. Cardozo School of Law

Andrea Kupfer Schneider
Professor of Law and Director, Kukin Program for Conflict Resolution Benjamin N. Cardozo School of Law

Michael Moffitt
Philip H. Knight Chair, Professor University of Oregon School of Law

Kristen Blankley
Henry M. Grether, Jr., Professor of Law University of Nebraska-Lincoln College of Law

ASPEN PUBLISHING

To contact Customer Service, e-mail customer.service@aspenpublishing.com, call 1-800-950-5259, or mail correspondence to:

Aspen Publishing
Attn: Order Department
1 Wall Street
Burlington, MA 01803

Printed in the United States of America.

1 2 3 4 5 6 7 8 9 0

ISBN 978-1-5438-4713-0

Library of Congress Cataloging-in-Publication Data

Names: Menkel-Meadow, Carrie, author. | Love, Lela Porter, 1950- author. | Schneider, Andrea Kupfer, author. | Moffitt, Michael L., 1968- author. | Blankley, Kristen M., author.
Title: Dispute Resolution : Beyond the Adversarial Model / Carrie J. Menkel-Meadow, Chancellor's Professor of Law (and Political Science) and Founding Faculty, University of California, Irvine Law School and A.B. Chettle Jr. Chair of Law, Dispute Resolution and Civil Procedure, Emerita Georgetown University Law Center; Lela Porter Love, Professor of Law and Director, Kukin Program for Conflict Resolution and the Cardozo Mediation Clinic, Benjamin N. Cardozo Law School, Yeshiva University; Andrea Kupfer Schneider, Professor of Law and Director, Dispute Resolution Program, Marquette University Law School; Michael Moffitt, Philip H. Knight Chair, Professor, University of Oregon School of Law, Kristen Blankley, Henry M. Grether, Jr., Professor of Law, University of Nebraska-Lincoln College of Law.
Description: Fourth edition. | Burlington : Aspen Publishing, 2025. | Previous edition 2019. | Includes bibliographical references and index. | Summary: "Casebook on dispute resolution for law students"— Provided by publisher.
Identifiers: LCCN 2024043830 | ISBN 9781543847130 (hardback) | ISBN 9781543847147 (ebook)
Subjects: LCSH: Dispute resolution (Law)—United States. | LCGFT: Casebooks (Law).
Classification: LCC KF9084.A75 D57 2025 | DDC 347.73/9—dc23/eng/20240925
LC record available at https://lccn.loc.gov/2024043830

About Aspen Publishing

Aspen Publishing is a leading provider of legal educational content and digital learning solutions in the U.S. and around the world. Aspen provides best-in-class solutions through authoritative textbooks, written by renowned authors, and breakthrough products such as Connected eBooks, Connected Quizzing, PracticePerfect, and JD-Next.

The Aspen Casebook Series (famously known among law faculty and students as the "red and black" casebooks) encompasses hundreds of highly regarded textbooks in more than eighty disciplines, from large enrollment courses, such as Torts and Contracts, to emerging electives, like Sustainability and the Law of Policing. Study aids such as *Examples & Explanations* help law students master complex subject matter. Aspen's Paralegal, Criminal Justice, and Business Law series bring our hallmark publishing standards to undergraduate students. JD-Next is an innovative online law school prep course and admissions test that offers a realistic preview of law school, teaches underlying skills for academic success, and assesses applicants' academic readiness for law school.

Aspen Publishing is proud to be a UWorld company
Since 2003, UWorld has been a global leader in developing high-quality learning tools for students preparing for high-stakes exams. With a commitment to excellence, UWorld has helped millions of students in undergraduate, graduate, and professional programs in fields such as medicine, nursing, finance, and law achieve their academic and career goals.

Founded by Chandra S. Pemmasani, M.D., during his medical residency, UWorld began focusing on medical education and has since expanded into various academic fields, including law. In 2020, UWorld launched its Legal vertical, starting with its comprehensive Multistate Bar Exam (MBE®) Question Bank, followed by the acquisition of Themis Bar Review, which integrated resources to provide a complete bar exam preparation experience. In 2024, UWorld expanded its offerings by acquiring Aspen Publishing, enhancing its suite of legal education products.

Today, UWorld offers an unparalleled range of study materials that blend active learning methods with expert content, ensuring students and educators can access the most effective resources. From bar preparation to law school success, UWorld is committed to supporting the next generation of legal professionals. Learn more at uworld.com.

For Robert Meadow,
Peter, Nicole, Brad, Hunter, Miles and Dakota,
Rodd, Joshua, Noah, and Zachary Schneider,
Spencer and Sander Moffitt,
Michael, James, Billie, Corrinne, and Camden Douglass

Our partners and children whose support, love and dispute resolution talents we appreciate and cherish, and

For our many students, past, present, and future, whom we learn from and hope will use these materials to make the world a better place, with both peace and justice.

Summary of Contents

Contents

Preface to the Fourth Edition

Well, here we are twenty years after the first edition of this book, with a few personnel changes—Kristen Blankley joins Andrea Kupfer Schneider, Lela Love, Michael Moffitt, and Carrie Menkel-Meadow—to update our text to reflect the fact that twenty years on, conflict and disputes are still with us (as they are likely to be forever!). Despite the fact that not all disputes and conflicts have been "resolved," "managed," or "handled" (all different forms of dealing with conflicts and disputes), we do now have even more processes and methods to learn about—hybrid adaptations of the basic processes, online dispute resolution, artificial intelligence, dispute system design, and international and organizational processes that draw from different legal and cultural traditions. So, we still have plenty to teach and learn in our no longer "new" field.

We remain committed to the notion of "process pluralism," that no one method of dispute resolution will serve for all kinds of disputes and conflicts. Disputes—social, legal, familial, organizational, international, economic—all have contexts, different background rules or customs, varied parties, and varied sources of authority or legitimacy. This revised edition updates some of the conventional and older processes—negotiation, mediation, and arbitration, with new caselaw, new social science research, and new narratives of both successful and problematic efforts at conflict resolution, mostly, but not exclusively within (or adjacent to) the American legal system (with some treatment of international forms of dispute resolution). In addition, we look at the now expanding uses of online dispute resolution, artificial intelligence, and dispute system design (with obvious applications to the [we hope!] post-pandemic learning of dispute resolution by Zoom). We continue to question more conventional conceptions of disputes and conflicts as being about two contesting parties (with lawyers) using adversarial methods of argument and decision-making as an exclusive or most common form of dispute resolution, instead of the often more realistic and complex forms of multi-party and multiple issue forms of dispute resolution. Instead, we hope that students will learn to counsel clients (and themselves) to choose dispute resolution methods and processes that are most appropriate for the parties and the subject matter of any particular dispute.

In light of some recent conversations in our field, we note that this book was never called "Alternative" Dispute Resolution—but always Dispute Resolution, highlighting that even 20 years ago we didn't think negotiation, mediation and arbitration were just "alternatives" to one default form of legal problem solving—litigation. Whether the "A" stands for "alternative," "appropriate," "accessible," or "aspirational" dispute resolution, the processes of negotiation, mediation, and arbitration have long become far more "common" or normative for legal problem solving than litigation. This book then aims to teach students about the many processes, including transactional negotiation and negotiated rule-making, and large group facilitation for decision-making (e.g. zoning, legislation, and community dispute resolution), so that they may counsel their clients to make good decisions about how to deal with legal problems, create new entities, and structure constructive human decision making in a variety of contexts, as lawyers, leaders, facilitators, mediators, and yes, even judges!

We have once again streamlined the book (put it on a "diet") to make each chapter potentially teachable in a single week of class sessions for a full semester course. Our accompanying Teacher's Manual provides many simulations and role-plays (both short and extended) so that the book continues to focus on both theory and practice of each particular process. We continue to provide Problem Boxes in each chapter which can serve as classroom discussion prompts, homework assignments, policy discussions and yes, even exam questions or extended research topics for those using papers or projects in their teaching. We are all committed to the need for active participatory learning in this field and we also provide (in the Teacher's Manual) references to and suggestions for video, films, novels and literature (and dare we say "games" [e.g. Risk]) that provide examples of various forms of dispute resolution. Alas, Hollywood often distorts what really happens and students come to us with often preconceived (and often incorrect) conceptions of what each process is like. Sadly, even many practicing lawyers still don't know the difference between arbitration and mediation, so we suggest some "field" projects and activities so students can see how these processes really work in the real world. All of the authors have practiced in these fields, and we think education about Dispute Resolution works best with teachers who focus on both the big jurisprudential issues (e.g. is ADR privatizing justice?) and the practice issues (to caucus or not to caucus that is the question!) with attention to how practices affect the people using them and then the larger system in which they are embedded. What are the areas that need reform and who can reform dispute resolution—formal legislative processes or private creativity (e.g. the big case Mini-Trial of yore)?

★ ★ ★

Carrie thanks Andrea for taking over "management" of this edition—believe me, you are in better hands now. She especially thanks her research assistants, Alexandra Cadena and Celine Gruaz, and UCI librarians extraordinaire, Dianna Sahhar and Jeff Latta. Her assistant, Maria Gonzalez De Toro has been a problem solver, life saver, and friend. She thanks her students in courses including

"A"DR, Negotiation, International Dispute Resolution, Mediation, Complex Multi-Party Dispute Resolution, International Arbitration, and International Legal Analysis for always teaching her something new about her own field and the complexities of changing generational and legal cultures. The pandemic slowed down international teaching and lecturing, but not completely, and she thanks the Oxford Centre for Socio-legal Studies where much of these revisions were done in 2023, and Naomi Creutzfeldt and Horst Eidenmüller for inviting her to teach to an array of international and gifted students at Oxford and to online Zoom teaching in Belgium, Argentina, Chile, the UK, Israel, and Italy (where she prefers teaching in person!!). Carrie has mentored over 20 former students now teaching some of these materials in many countries and she especially thanks Kondi Kleinman, Peter Reilly, Clark Freshman, Michalyn Steele, Ana Carolina Viella, Orna Rabinovitz-Einy, Amy Cohen, Ana Silva, Hugo Rojas, Renzo Parodi, Alain Verbeke, Leticia Coppo, Rutger Metsch, Remy Gerbay, and others who continue to inspire her with teaching and practice ideas. Her service as Associate Editor of Harvard's Program on Negotiation, *Negotiation Journal* has kept her up to date on new research and teaching topics, and she thanks Joel Cutcher-Gershenfeld, Dan Druckman, Melissa Manwaring, and Silvia Glick for superb editorial meetings and symposia which continue to stretch the reach of the field. She sadly laments the loss of interactions of many former friends and leaders in the field who have departed this earth or their day jobs (retirement) including Frank Sander, Howard Raiffa, Roger Fisher, Margaret Shaw, Wallace Warfield, Michael Wheeler, Debbie Kolb, Robert Mnookin but a few of the field's leaders continue to hover and share their insights—Jim Sebenius, Larry Susskind, Howard Gadlin, Chris Honeyman, and the Senior Mediators Group. And most of all thanks to her very best student, Robert Meadow, problem solving negotiator for over fifty years.

Andrea thanks her co-authors for agreeing to "get the band back together" (with the excellent addition of Kristen), and arrive at a Fourth Edition to this textbook in record time. We are excited to bring this to you with all that has changed in the last few years. She thanks her research assistants Madison Gagne, Dighan Kelly, Matthew Kee and Alexa Miller for their excellent work. And Andrea is grateful to her new home, Cardozo Law School, for all of the support that the school has provided toward this book and, more importantly, in supporting the growth and development of the field of dispute resolution. And to the now thousands of students with whom she has explored these materials, she is eternally grateful for the best job in the world and the ability to continue to learn from you about dispute resolution—the good, the bad, and the ugly. She believes that we can find our best selves in how we approach conflict—she remains optimistic at the prospect of continuing to teach and build these skills.

Lela thanks Carrie for spearheading this project in the first place and Andrea for leading the charge on this 4th edition of book and for leading Cardozo's beloved dispute resolution program. She also thanks Robyn Weinstein for taking over Cardozo's Mediation Clinic and the care and keeping of the circle of alumni and friends who surround us there. She thanks her excellent Research Assistant, Corbin Gregg, for his most thoughtful work editing the manuscript.

Michael thanks the original co-authors of this casebook for their gracious invitation to join the team years ago. He thanks the University of Oregon and its leadership for many forms of conspicuous support for this project (for example funding through the Knight Chair in Law), and for the attitudinal support for this kind of work (a "good job!" now and then from a Dean or Provost or President goes an embarrassingly long way, and he is grateful to have received those). He also thanks the hundreds of practitioners and the thousands of disputants from and with whom he has worked over the years. Being invited (and being invited back!) to help disputants think through some of their hardest challenges has been a singular honor, and he hopes that students will learn not only the particulars of what seems to work, but also and perhaps more importantly, that one can (and perhaps must try?) to help when one can.

Kristen thanks her co-authors for the honor of being added to this Fourth edition of this text. She thanks them and all of the previous authors for their insight and excellent work on the First, Second, and Third editions. Her work on the Fourth edition was undoubtedly easier and smoother given the significant work put into the prior editions. She also thanks the University of Nebraska College of Law for supporting her dispute resolution work. She is extremely grateful for the opportunity to learn from her students and clients, and her experiences as a teacher and practitioner enrich her perspective on conflict and its resolution.

We thank The Froebe Group for fast, meticulous editing, especially Patrick Cline and Dena Kaufman for getting this to you all in almost record time for us busy law professors.

Mostly we thank each other for collaborations, including our former co-author, Jean Sternlight, now ongoing for decades as we continue to read, write, practice, think, and dream of a world that solves problems constructively and creatively. We certainly need it in these often-troubled times.

Please let us know what you think.

In peace,

Carrie Menkel-Meadow
Lela Love
Andrea Kupfer Schneider
Michael Moffitt
Kristen Blankley

November 2024

Preface to the Third Edition

The fact that we are writing a preface to a third edition of our Dispute Resolution text is evidence that the field is both now a consolidated field, and also that it is continually changing, requiring new materials, updates and reconceptualizations of some aspects of the field.

As we write this, both domestic and international dispute resolution issues remain at the foreground of legal, governmental, private and diplomatic activity. Negotiation (both in public diplomatic, legal, and private business settings) continues to be one of the most important human processes of conflict resolution and transaction planning (see *The Negotiator's Desk Reference,* Chris Honeyman and Andrea Kupfer Schneider, eds. 2017 DRI Press). Mediation is now often required by courts before litigation may proceed, and is chosen by many parties as the process with the most party control over both process and outcome. Increasingly international tribunals (including private commercial, trade and investment and public human rights) are also promoting mediation and more universities around the world are teaching mediation as an essential part of both a legal and a general education. The authors of this text now teach with these materials across the globe. Arbitration continues to be "required" as mandatory in a wide variety of contractual settings, including consumer and employment contracts, which makes the United States an outlier in the world. This text adds brand new chapters on arbitration, as our Supreme Court continues to favor arbitral processes over a wide variety of claims against it, and we add a new arbitration expert to our collaboration—thank you Michael Moffitt!

As the foundational processes covered in this book—negotiation, mediation and arbitration—continue to be combined and altered to produce new hybrid forms of dispute resolution, some hybrids have fallen off in use (e.g., summary jury trials and mini-trials) while new ones emerge (e.g., final offer mediation) and some hybrids (e.g., ombuds) are attracting more usage in private companies and government agencies. This text continues to reflect the new uses of various dispute processes in more settings and to ask questions about the "scaling up" of dispute resolution processes in our larger legal and democratic systems. This new edition focuses on perhaps the newest and most challenging form of dispute resolution "online dispute resolution" or ODR, which offers the potential for more access to justice (now called "ATJ"), as well as introducing concerns about "digital inequality." If Dispute Resolution (or ADR) is to continue to be "appropriate dispute resolution," we must always be mindful of its promises to deliver justice, fairness and good quality outcomes to those who participate in the processes.

The modern lawyer (and law student studying to be a modern lawyer) needs to understand and practice the many different ways of resolving clients' legal problems, using an ability to diagnose types of issues and problems and assessing the suitability of different processes for different kinds of legal problems and issues. The theme of "process pluralism" continues in this new version of the text, and we continue to focus on lawyers learning to counsel clients about appropriate process choices, from a perspective of knowing what each process offers, in terms of procedures used, party participation, choice, self-empowerment, creative solutions and achieving desired outcomes.

Assessment of what processes are appropriate for particular disputants, as well as for larger system choices, continue to be issues of both policy and ethics. As with our prior editions, each process is presented with a focus on skills, as well as the policy and ethical issues implicated in its use.

Any dispute resolution course works best with active participation by students in role-plays and simulations. These are available, both in the Teacher's Manuals to the texts we have written (*Dispute Resolution, Negotiation and Mediation)* and available online through WoltersKluwer for those who adopt this text. Each chapter contains "problem boxes" which ask students to actively engage in the materials. These problem boxes can be used for class discussion, as well as written assignments. Dispute resolution must be "practiced" to be learned and understood.

As in prior editions, we have tried to present a variety of materials, including general jurisprudential readings, skills prescriptions and exercises, cases, empirical studies, policy questions, and professional responsibility rules and questions to think about and discuss. We have heard the pleas of users (both students and professors) and have once again, trimmed our book, to make chapters shorter and more adapted to one chapter per class and or one chapter per week of a 14-week semester. We welcome your input and are all available to discuss pedagogic choices. Our revisions of the paperback "splits" for Negotiation and Mediation will follow shortly.

* * *

Carrie, Lela and Andrea thank Michael Moffitt for joining us on this edition as he concludes his service as Dean of the University of Oregon Law School and Jean Sternlight, our esteemed colleague, leaves us to pursue her interests in arbitration in other venues. Thanks to both of them for continuing to collaborate with us on all the issues in the field. We have all shared ideas and inputs on these revised materials—adding new materials, particularly the most recent case law in arbitration, new materials in negotiation and mediation and hybrids, and removing material that is now dated, as the uses of various forms of dispute resolution become more institutionalized. We still hope for more innovation and the development of new processes, as well as evaluative work on what is or is not working now. We welcome your input.

All of us remain grateful for the institutional support we receive from our institutions: Carrie thanks the University of California Irvine Law School (and the political science department), and Georgetown University Law Center for allowing her to teach a great variety of courses on the themes of this text (including Multi-Party and Advanced Dispute Resolution, Deliberative Democracy, as well as the basics, Negotiation, Mediation and ADR). She thanks Adelina Tomova for administrative assistance and generally helpful problem solving; and Caleb Nissley and Sarah Salvini for research assistance; Hagop Nazarian, Shunya Wade, Kevin Homrighausen and Tony Boswell for continued enthusiasm in studying dispute resolution and "youthifying" an old hand. In addition, she thanks students at the University of Torino, University of Hong Kong, the Center for Transnational Legal Studies (London), Queen Mary Law School, Haifa University, Leuven University (Belgium), and the University of Melbourne, as well as many other international venues where she has been able to use these materials and explore cultural variations in the uses of human dispute resolution systems. Lela Love thanks the Kukin Program for Conflict Resolution and the Benjamin Cardozo Law School for supporting her scholarship. Her wonderful colleagues at Cardozo have been so helpful—Donna Erez-Navot, the Assistant Director of the Kukin Program and Nicole Duke, the Program's RA. Also, Simeon Baum, Bob Collins, Brian Farkas, Tracey Frisch, Peter Halprin, Charlie Moxley, Glen Parker, Leslie Salzman, Robyn Weinstein, David Weisenfeld, Dan Weitz, and David White lend ongoing ideas and support—as well as Hal Abramson, Josh Stulberg, and Michael Tsur who come regularly to Cardozo and provide inspiration. Andrea Schneider (and the rest of us) continue to marvel at the ongoing contributions of Carrie Kratochvil who works to make all of this work come together. She is very appreciative of Marquette University Law School for its support of the Dispute Resolution Program and this book. She also thanks Ilena Telford, April Kutz, and Jad Itani for their research assistance on this edition. Michael Moffitt thanks the Appropriate Dispute Resolution Center at the University of Oregon School of Law, the Conflict and Dispute Resolution Master's Program at the University of Oregon, and Phil and Penny Knight for their continued support of his research and teaching. He thanks his research assistants from Oregon and Harvard: Haley Banks, Christopher Dotson, Deanna Goodrich, Christopher Groesbeck, Juhi Gupta, Ayoung Kim, Chantal Guzman-Schlager, Ben Pincus, Jordan Shapiro, Austin Smith and Elise Williard.

We continue to be grateful for our many mentors, noting with this edition the passing of Frank Sander, Howard Raiffa, Thomas Schelling, and Margaret Shaw, among the the founding fathers and mothers of our field. We continue to be inspired by them—to stretch their ideas into the 21st century, finding new uses of "varieties of dispute processing." Our students continue to inspire us and question us about when and how to use processes outside of courtrooms to resolve disputes. And, as we observe an increasingly polarized political world, both domestically and internationally, we are proud of our students, and yours, who are at the front line of using these materials to look for new ways to work together productively, across perceived differences in values and ideals.

We continue to be thankful for and indebted to John Devins at Wolters Kluwer who believes in us and this project and helps achieve "justice" in law school publishing. We thank the Troy Froebe Group for editing and production—thanks to Lori Wood, Maxwell Donnewald and Geoffrey Lokke.

We also want to thank each other for the continuing collegial and enriching relationships we have as we negotiate the words on these pages and engage happily and productively with our wider and wonderful "ADR" community in legal education and now, the growing interest in our field around the world. Despite the difficulties in world and domestic politics, we still hope that reading and working with these materials will increase well being and peace and justice in the world.

Carrie Menkel-Meadow
Lela Porter Love
Andrea Kupfer Schneider
Michael Moffitt

August 2018

Preface to the Second Edition

Since the publication of our first edition in 2005 there has been continued growth and diversification in the "process pluralism" we have described in both the older edition and now this new edition. Increasing use is being made of negotiation, mediation, and arbitration, and creative system designers are combining these processes in new ways in varied contexts. At the international level, more and more transnational disputes, conflicts, and transactions are drawing on dispute resolution processes,[1] which we hope soon to cover in a separate book on Transnational Dispute Resolution.

Nevertheless, since our last edition, the United States has been participating in two new wars and litigation and its concomitant fees and costs have continued to climb, even while an economic recession has altered the legal landscape. With the recession we have seen more housing foreclosures, a rise in financial fraud and complex business litigation, and additional banking, housing, employment, and consumer disputes that have caused many people great personal and financial harm. There has also been a major realignment in the market for legal services.

Thus, we think the process pluralism of ADR has gained even more importance in our daily and professional lives, and remains at the core of what all law students (and lawyers) should learn as part of their basic legal education and experience. We see ADR in the courts, out of the courts in a myriad of forms, and increasingly, in areas of aggregated disputes and conflicts, within organizations and among peoples and nations, spawning the new separate field of dispute system design. We report here, in the last chapter, some of the newest empirical and other research, designed to test claims about ADR's usefulness in our (and other) societies.

As in the first edition, we continue to center dispute resolution processes in a context of problem solving for clients, including individuals, governmental agencies, groups, private entities, organizations, corporations and nations. In order to

1. Carrie Menkel-Meadow, Why and How to Study Transnational Law, 1 UC Irvine L. Rev. 97 (2010).

negotiate, arbitrate, or mediate, lawyers need to understand their clients' needs and interests and those of the other parties, so interviewing, counseling, listening, communicating, and understanding are important constituent activities of dispute resolution which are also covered in this book.

In this new edition we have listened to our readers and students and streamlined (and shortened!) the materials we present to you. Instead of *Notes and Questions*, we now provide you with clearly demarcated *Problems* found, (somewhat ironically, in a book that is about "thinking outside of the box") inside grey boxes, which are easy to read (if not always easy to solve). These problem boxes can be used as out-of-class thinking and homework assignments or serve as discussion points for classes, whether in large group or smaller task groups. The Teacher's Manual for both the earlier edition (and this one too) continue to supply the largest collection of shorter role-plays and longer simulations for any ADR text, demonstrating our belief that the subjects of negotiation, mediation, arbitration, and dispute resolution generally are learned best *in action* where *theories in use*[2] can be tested for their efficacy, appropriateness, and ability to solve clients' problems. Both this book and the companion shorter "splits"—*Mediation: Practice Policy and Ethics* and *Negotiation: Processes for Problem Solving* can be used in both classroom (survey or specialized) courses or clinical settings, both within and outside of the United States.

This new edition adds new materials, including a number of recently decided cases, primarily on arbitration issues, from the highest courts in the land, and the latest in commentary and scholarship on dispute resolution issues. We have also edited some of the classic materials from our first edition to a more manageable length.

This book is presented in several sections. We offer two introductory chapters on the history and jurisprudence of dispute processes, as well as the importance and underlying value of problem solving for clients and the skills necessary to problem-solve. Then in three separate chapters for each primary process of negotiation, mediation, and arbitration we cover concepts and models of that process, skills needed to be both representatives and third party neutrals in that process, and the ethical, legal, and policy issues that are implicated in the use of those processes. Next, we provide a section of the book examining more complex issues in dispute resolution: variations and combinations of dispute resolution processes in both private and public settings; uses of dispute resolution in multi-party and transactional settings; and insights from dispute system design and related planning for dispute resolution processes. Finally, we survey some of the issues in assessing the past uses and future possibilities of dispute resolution, both for clients and for the larger society.

* * *

All of us remain grateful to our various institutions for support as teachers, scholars, and practitioners: Georgetown University Law Center, the Center for Transnational Legal Studies, and the University of California, Irvine Law School for Carrie Menkel-Meadow, Benjamin N. Cardozo Law School and its Kukin Program for Conflict Resolution at Yeshiva University for Lela Love, Marquette

2. Donald Schön, The Reflective Practitioner (1983).

University Law School and its Dispute Resolution Program for Andrea Kupfer Schneider and the University of Nevada, Las Vegas and its Saltman Center for Dispute Resolution for Jean Sternlight. We thank our deans, colleagues, and our many students who have worked with these materials and given us useful feedback.

We thank the many authors and publishers who have allowed us to reprint their materials (as formally acknowledged in the Acknowledgments). We are especially grateful to those who allowed us to use their materials without exorbitant permissions or royalty payments, in the interest of dissemination of learning and education. And we are grateful for the continued inspiration of both our intellectual mentors and seniors (a smaller group as we join the ranks of the "senior mentors" ourselves), and our enthusiastic students, many of whom want to make full-time careers in this field, which we all helped create and foster.

Individually and specifically we thank:

Carrie thanks Katherine M. Hayes (at Georgetown) and Jean Su (at UCI) for superb research assistance, manuscript preparation, and student insights; Maike Kotterba (CTLS) and Charlene Anderson (UCI) (for administrative support) and Peter Reilly, Clark Freshman, and Bob Bordone for mentees who have become true peers, colleagues, and friends in this work we all do.

Lela thanks Nicole and Peter for constant support (particularly Nicole's technical support) and research assistants Halley Anolik and Dan Liston who did excellent work with page proofs.

Andrea (and the rest of us) thanks Carrie Kratochvil who was there at the birth of this book and has been our constant star of minding, managing, and maneuvering this edition to completion. She also thanks research assistants Erica Hayden, Erin Naipo, Amanda Tofias, Ben Scott, and Andrea Thompson for their excellent work.

Jean thanks her family for their tolerance and research assistants Kimberly DelMonico, Kathleen Wilden, and Will Thompson for their excellent work.

All of us thank Aspen Publishers (again), especially Melody Davies who started with us, helped us with kindness and appreciation, and we hope is now enjoying retirement, John Devins who manages us, Troy Froebe who manages our manuscript, Tracy Metivier for permissions and related editorial work, and Enid Zafran for indexing.

We thank our students for teaching us, our colleagues for supporting and critiquing us, and most importantly, our families who continue to not only support us, but to love us, for which we are all eternally grateful.

Finally, all of us thank each other for continuing to work, learn, and collaborate with each other—often from scattered corners of the world as we continue to spread our hopes and dreams for a more peaceful and just world.

Carrie J. Menkel-Meadow
Lela Porter Love
Andrea Kupfer Schneider
Jean R. Sternlight

November 2010

Preface to the First Edition

This book is inspired by our conviction that study of a variety of different processes of dispute resolution, what we here call "process pluralism," will enable the lawyers of the future to be more creative and effective in their legal problem solving. We subtitle this book "Beyond the Adversarial Model" because we believe that while litigation, and the adversarial process that inspires it, has its place in the legal order, modern life requires additional processes that better meet the needs of parties in conflict, as well as of the larger societies within which legal and other disputes occur. We believe that these other processes will produce qualitatively better solutions, improve relationships between parties, and deliver both justice and peace, both effectively and meaningfully. We also care about efficiency, of course, but for us, that value must often bow to the others.

Two of us are of the founding generation of "alternative dispute resolution" (a field many now call "appropriate dispute resolution" or simply "dispute resolution"); the other two of us came fast behind with specialized knowledge of several of the processes we study in this book. We have all been teaching these processes for many years and thought it time to enter the field with a new textbook. (Note that we did not say "casebook," as "cases" are not all that our field is about.) This book is organized to provide a comprehensive treatment of the field of dispute resolution, whether taught with skills components (and use of the many simulations, role-plays, and problem sets found in the Teacher's Manual) or as a survey of the field's theoretical, practical, ethical, legal, or policy issues.

We begin with a theoretical and historical introduction to the field of dispute and conflict resolution, introducing readers to the basic concepts and their creative developers and pointing out innovations in social and legal problem solving. Important theorist and practitioner Professor Lon Fuller, whom we call "the jurisprude of ADR," introduces us to the idea of "process integrity"—the evaluation of each dispute resolution process for its own logic, function, purpose, and morality—a theme we follow throughout the book.

We then turn to the three foundational processes of dispute resolution: negotiation, mediation (as facilitated negotiation), and arbitration (party controlled adjudication). Each process is studied in three separate chapters. The first focuses on the concepts, frameworks, and approaches characterizing different conceptualizations of the process; another explores the skills and practices needed to conduct that process; and a third examines the legal, ethical, and policy issues the process raises. This section of the book is primarily concerned with how lawyers (whether as negotiators, mediators, representatives in mediation and arbitration, or arbitrators) can more effectively solve their clients' problems and the problems of those with whom their clients interact.

Each of these processes has become more complex, both in study and in practice, since the modern field was founded about thirty years ago. To help students cope with that complexity, we present materials for practice (role-plays and simulations are provided in the Teacher's Manual); for analysis (questions and problems are posed in the text's Notes and Questions sections, following each of the readings, drawn from law, social science, popular culture, and examples of the processes in use); and for speculation on future dispute resolution designs. Throughout these chapters, we focus on the multiple roles that lawyers can play and on the importance of the interaction, consultation, and participation lawyers should have with the parties and clients whose disputes and conflicts they are hoping to help resolve. We also suggest more active roles for parties and clients in participating with lawyers in the resolution of their own issues and problems. Our conception of these roles goes beyond what many have suggested before. We maintain that participation, empowerment, creativity, and self-determination are important values in the successful and satisfying resolution of disputes and conflicts.

Beyond the foundational processes, this book goes on to explore the sophisticated adaptations of these basic processes sometimes required by modern life. Beginning with Part III, we explore how the basic processes combine to form hybrid processes; how the addition of multiple parties and the introduction of more complex issues change our understanding of how these processes can be used; how we might anticipate and avoid disputes by using conflict resolution in transaction planning and contracts; and how international conflicts may differ from or require adaptation of the processes commonly used in domestic legal disputes.

Dispute resolution is no longer just about avoiding or settling lawsuits. It should be thought of before relationships are formed, throughout their duration, and then, if necessary, when things go bad. Since various forms of ADR have now been in use for at least three decades, we are in a position to present some important critiques of and challenges to ADR's use. A separate chapter in this text therefore asks practitioners and students to consider how the claims of dispute resolution processes in different fora can be properly assessed and evaluated. Our concluding chapter examines the issues involved in counseling clients on the most appropriate process to use to resolve their disputes and conflicts and to plan transactions.

Our goal in this book is to help you as lawyers and future lawyers to be as well educated and informed as possible about effective options for dispute resolution. From this basis, you will be better prepared to advise your clients about the many ways they can go about their dealings with others, both when putting things together and, sadly, when dealing with the consequences of relationships that fall apart.

★ ★ ★

This book is the culmination of many years of study, teaching, research, and writing by all of us, and we have many intellectual, personal, and work-related debts. We cannot begin to acknowledge all of those debts, but we would like to recognize a few.

First, our intellectual sources. In some ways, the field or "movement" of ADR is a continuation of earlier schools of legal thought, including both Legal Realism and the Legal Process school of the 1950s (see Henry M. Hart and Albert M. Sacks, The Legal Process: Basic Problems in the Making and Application of Law [1958, reissued in 1994, edited by Professors William N. Eskridge, Jr., and Philip P. Frickey]), both of which saw legal doctrine as insufficient to explain what lawyers did and how law is made, enforced, and lived. Both approaches sought to add people and processes to the study of law and its operations. The Law and Society field added empirical study of dispute processes by sociologists, anthropologists, psychologists, political scientists, and economists to the work of legal scholars, broadening the disciplinary reach of dispute processing studies during a period of both domestic and international conflict and ferment.

The 1960s and 1970s saw a tremendous explosion of legal rights, with many more laws added to the books than could easily be enforced in courts, no matter how actively managed. Those decades were further characterized by political movements that encouraged people with legal problems or issues to participate directly in the system, diminishing the involvement of professionals.

At the same time, two different schools of thought arose questioning the adequacy of lawsuits and traditional adversarialism to solve all social and legal problems. One group was concerned about finding qualitatively better solutions to conflicts and increasing parties' participation, while the other group was more concerned about efficiency and the costs in money and time of so much litigation. These two movements coalesced at a famous conference held in 1976—"Causes of Popular Dissatisfaction with the Administration of Justice"—and a speech delivered there by Professor Frank Sander officially launched the field of ADR. Concurrently, some of us (including the authors of this book) asked lawyers to learn to "problem solve" rather than to "beat or best the other side" in legal negotiations (Menkel-Meadow, 1984).

The study of negotiation was institutionalized as several law schools began to teach and study negotiation processes related to a variety of settings, producing a founding generation of negotiation scholars, many of whose works are cited and explored in the pages that follow. The concept of third party neutrals was added to facilitate negotiation, and two of us were early mediators when mediation found its place in the law school curriculum. The adaptation of the mediation process to legal disputes and conflicts is also chronicled in this book, with excerpts from those who founded and elaborated that field as well.

The study, practice, and teaching of first negotiation and then mediation were part of another important movement in legal education: clinical legal education, which seeks to teach law students how to behave as well as to think like lawyers. While litigation was the focus of most early clinical programs, frustration with enforcement of winning lawsuits or with the inefficacy of lawsuits to effect both individual and social change led some early clinicians to look for other methods of legal and social problem solving, all while teaching law students to understand that there are many ways to serve one's clients and solve legal problems. The clinical movement, like the study of ADR, is an "experiential" field, and we also owe intellectual debts to those, like Donald Schön and Chris Arygris, who developed, in professional education, the concepts and practices of "theories-in-use." This book elaborates theories of dispute resolution, in various forms, and asks students to put those theories into use immediately, while learning about them.

We have all been supported greatly by the institutions at which we teach, including Georgetown University Law Center (and before that UCLA); Benjamin N. Cardozo School of Law/Yeshiva University; Marquette University Law School; and the University of Nevada, Las Vegas, Boyd Law School (and before that the University of Missouri-Columbia School of Law). We thank our respective deans, colleagues, and disbursers of research funds for their ample support in producing this book, and, more importantly, for encouraging our teaching, scholarship, and practice in this field. The William and Flora Hewlett Foundation has done much to support the field and indirectly supported much of the work of this book (both the publications in it and the work described therein).

We thank the many authors and their publishers whose work we have reprinted (see Acknowledgments, following this Preface). Knowledge in dispute resolution is only partially reflected in reported cases; most of what we know comes from other sources, including articles, transcripts, rules, practice manuals, and empirical studies.

Carrie thanks James Bond, Jaimie Kent, Ellen Connelly Cohen, and, especially, David Mattingly for superb research assistance, editorial work, and manuscript preparation; Rada M. Stojanovich Hayes, Carolyn Howard, Sylvia Johnson, Ronnie E. Rease, Jr., and Toni Patterson for administrative and moral support; and Anna Selden and John Showalter for masterful manuscript management and computer feats beyond the call of duty. She thanks Robert Meadow, Susan Gillig, and Vicki Jackson for being the best dispute resolution role models a professor ever had, and Peter Reilly for being the best hope for the next generation of negotiation teachers and scholars.

Lela thanks Roger Deitz, for his painstaking edits; and her wonderful research assistants, Clymer Bardsley, Malte Pendergast-Fischer, Barry Rosenhouse, Michael Stone, and Chelsea Teachout, for their cheerful and energetic contributions.

Andrea thanks her amazing administrative assistant Carrie Kratochvil (as do the rest of us for organizing us all); her research assistants Amy Koltz, Deanna

Senske, Mindy Dummermuth, and Anna Coyer for their wonderful ideas and great work; and her colleague Joanne Lipo-Zovic.

Jean thanks and is grateful for the excellent research assistance of Alyson Carrel, Ann Casey, Jennifer Chierek, Michele Baron, and Mark Lyons.

We are all thankful for the wisdom, advice, guidance, and suggestions of Carol Liebman, Jennifer Gerada Brown, Michael Moffitt, Clark Freshman, and other anonymous reviewers of this book, long in birthing, and to a few more of you who ventured to teach this in page proofs and try it out.

We appreciate the Aspen team—Richard Mixter, who put us together, and Melody Davies, Elsie Starbecker, Lisa Wehrle, Elizabeth Ricklefs, Michael Gregory, Susan Boulanger, and Tracy Metivier, who kept us on track and together and worded and sewed and sold this book.

Most importantly, we want to publicly thank one another. We have been calling this "the girl" book, to mark the fact that still so few law casebooks are written by women, never mind totally written by women. (OK, so most of the authors in this edited volume are men. . . .) We hope this book will appeal to all genders, but still, we are proud that we have not only worked and played well together but that we also created life-time friendships and wonderful working relationships. We may have had some disputes (did we?), but we are proud to say that we have lived the words on these pages as we negotiated, mediated, and built consensus to bring you this book. We know this relationship will continue into many more editions (and the separate books on negotiation, mediation, and arbitration to be derived from this book).

Finally, we also want to thank our many students who worked with this book in draft and through its various stages of development. It is for you that this is written: May you all go forth and make the world a better place, using appropriate dispute processes to make more peace and justice in the world and to solve as many human problems as you possibly can.

Carrie J. Menkel-Meadow
Lela Porter Love
Andrea Kupfer Schneider
Jean R. Sternlight

October 2004

Acknowledgments

The authors wish to express their thanks to the following authors, periodicals, and publishers for their permission to reproduce materials from their publications:

"The ABCS of ADR: A Dispute Resolution Glossary." *Alternatives to the High Cost of Litigation*, vol. 13, no. 11, Nov. 1995. Copyright © 1995 John Wiley & Sons, Inc.

Aaron, Marjorie C. "Client Science: Advise for Lawyers on Initial Client Interviews." Copyright © 2013 Marjorie C. Aaron. Reprinted with permission.

Albin, Cecilia. "The Role of Fairness in Negotiation." *Negotiation Journal*, vol. 9, no. 3, July 1993. Copyright © 1993 John Wiley & Sons, Inc.

Aragaki, Hiro N. "Arbitration: Creature of Contract, Pillar of Procedure." *Yearbook on Arbitration and Mediation*, vol. 8, no. 5, 2016. Copyright © 2016 Penn State University Dickinson School of Law.

Arnold, Tom. "20 Common Errors in Mediation Advocacy." *Alternatives to the High Cost of Litigation*, vol. 13, no. 5, May 1995. Copyright © 1995 John Wiley & Sons, Inc.

Bordone, Robert C., and Michael L Moffitt. "Create Value out of Conflict." *Negotiation*, vol. 9, no. 6, 2006. Copyright © 2006 Harvard Business School Publishing. Reprinted by permission. All rights reserved.

Brown, Jennifer Gerarda. "Creativity: Creativity and Problem-Solving." *Marquette Law Review*, vol. 87, no. 4, 2004. Reprinted with permission.

Bush, Robert A. Baruch. "Mediation and Adjudication, Dispute Resolution and Ideology: An Imaginary Conversation." *Journal of Contemporary Legal Issues*, vol. 3, Jan. 1989. University of San Diego Law School. Reprinted with permission.

Cohen, Jonathan R. "Adversaries? Partners? How about Counterparts? On Metaphors in the Practice and Teaching of Negotiation and Dispute Resolution." *Conflict Resolution Quarterly*, vol. 20, no. 4, 2003. Copyright © 2003 John Wiley & Sons, Inc.

Cohen, Taya R., et al. "Honesty among Lawyers: Moral Character, Game Framing, and Honest Disclosures in Negotiations." *Negotiation Journal*, vol. 38, Apr. 2022. John Wiley & Sons, Inc. Reprinted with permission.

Dezalay, Yves, and Bryant G. Garth. *Dealing in Virtue*. Copyright © 1996 University of Chicago Press.

Fisher, Robert, et al. *Getting to Yes: Negotiating Agreement without Giving In*. Copyright © Roger Fisher and William Ury, 1981, 1991. Copyright © Roger Fisher, William Ury and Bruce Patton, 2011. Used by permission of HarperCollins Publishers.

Fisher, Roger, et al. *Beyond Machiavelli: Tools for Coping with Conflict.* Copyright © 1994 by the President and Fellows of Harvard College. Reprinted by permission of Harvard University Press. All rights reserved.

Fiss, Owen M. "Against Settlement." *Yale Law Journal*, vol. 93, no. 6, May 1984. Copyright © 1984 The Yale Law Journal Company, Inc.

Follett, Mary Parker. "Constructive Conflict." *Prophet of Management*, by Pauline Graham. Copyright © 1996 Harvard Business School Publishing. Reprinted by permission. All rights reserved.

Friedman, Gary, and Jack Himmelstein. *The Loop of Understanding.* Copyright © 2008 by the American Bar Association. Reprinted with permission. All rights reserved. This information or any portion thereof may not be copied or disseminated in any form or by any means or stored in an electronic database or retrieval system without the express written consent of the American Bar Association.

Fuller, Lon L. "The Forms and Limits of Adjudication." *The Principles of Social Order: Selected Essays of Lon L. Fuller*, edited by Kenneth Winston and Lon L. Fuller. Copyright © 2001 Hart Publishing, an imprint of Bloomsbury Publishing Plc.

Fuller, Lon L. "Mediation: Its Forms and Its Functions." *Southern California Law Review*, vol. 44, 1971. USC Gould School of Law. Reprinted with permission.

Gifford, Donald. "A Context-Based Theory of Strategy Selection in Legal Negotiation." *Ohio State Law Journal*, vol. 46, 1985. Reprinted with permission.

Golann, Dwight, and Eric E. Van Loon. "Legal Issues in Consensus Building." *The Consensus Building Handbook: A Comprehensive Guide to Reaching Agreement*, edited by Lawrence Susskind et al. Copyright © 1999 Sage Publications, Inc.

Harter, Philip J. "Negotiating Regulations: A Cure for the Malaise?" *Georgetown Law Journal*, vol. 3, no. 1, 1982. Reprinted with permission.

Heavin, Heather, and Michaela Keet. "Client-Centered Communication: How Effective Lawyering Requires Emotional Intelligence, Active Listening, and Client Choice." *Cardozo Journal of Conflict Resolution*, vol. 22, 2021. Reprinted with permission.

Hensler, Deborah. "A Glass Half Full, a Glass Half Empty: The Use of Alternative Dispute Resolution in Mass Personal Injury Litigation." *Texas Law Review*, vol. 73, 1995. Reprinted with permission.

Hinshaw, Art, et al. "Attorneys and Negotiation Ethics: A Material Misunderstanding?" *Negotiation Journal*, vol. 29, no. 3, 2013.

Hollander-Blumoff, Rebecca, and Tom R. Tyler. "Procedural Justice in Negotiation: Procedural Fairness, Outcome Acceptance, and Integrative Potential." *Law & Social Inquiry*, vol. 33, no. 2, May 2008. John Wiley & Sons, Inc. Reprinted with permission.

Korobkin, Russell B. "A Positive Theory of Legal Negotiation." *Georgetown Law Journal*, vol. 88, 2000. Georgetown University Law Center. Reprinted with permission.

Krieger, Stefan H., and Richard K. Neumann. *Essential Lawyering Skills: Interviewing, Counseling, Negotiation, and Persuasive Fact Analysis.* Wolters Kluwer, 2015.

Kruse, Katherine R. "Beyond Cardboard Clients in Legal Ethics." *Georgetown Journal of Legal Ethics*, vol. 23, 2010. Reprinted with permission.

Lehman, Warren. "The Pursuit of a Client's Interest." *Michigan Law Review*, vol. 77, no. 4, 2019. University of Michigan Law School.

Levin, Murray S. "The Propriety of Evaluative Mediation: Concerns about the Nature and Quality of an Evaluative Opinion." *Ohio State Journal on Dispute Resolution*, vol. 16, 2001. Ohio State University Moritz College of Law. Reprinted with permission.

Love, Lela P. "Glen Cove: Mediation Achieves What Litigation Cannot." *Consensus*, vol. 20, Oct. 1993. Copyright © 1993 by MIT-Harvard Public Disputes Program.

Love, Lela P. "Images of Justice." *Pepperdine Dispute Resolution Journal*, vol. 1, no. 1, 2000.

Love, Lela P. "Training Mediators to Listen: Deconstructing Dialogue and Constructing Understanding, Agendas, and Agreements." *Family Court Review*, vol. 38, no. 1, Mar. 2005.

Malin, Martin H. "Two Models of Interest Arbitration." *Ohio State Journal on Dispute Resolution*, vol. 28, 2013. Ohio State University Moritz College of Law. Reprinted with permission.

Martin Shapiro. *Courts: A Comparative and Political Analysis*. University of Chicago Press, 1981. Copyright © 1981 University of Chicago Press.

McAddo, Bobby, et al. "Institutionalization: What Do Empirical Studies Tell Us about Court Mediation?" *Dispute Resolution Magazine*, vol. 8, 2003. Copyright © 2003 by the American Bar Association. Reprinted by permission. All rights reserved.

McGovern, Francis E. "Toward a Functional Approach for Managing Complex Litigation." *University of Chicago Law Review*, vol. 53, no. 2, 1986. University of Chicago Law School. Reprinted with permission.

Menkel-Meadow, Carrie. "Aha? Is Creativity Possible in Legal Problem Solving and Teachable in Legal Negotiation?" *Harvard Negotiation Law Review*, vol. 6, 2001.

Menkel-Meadow, Carrie. "Alternative and Appropriate Dispute Resolution in Context: Formal, Informal, and Semiformal Legal Processes." *The Handbook of Conflict Resolution: Theory and Practice*, edited by Peter T. Coleman et al., 3rd ed., Jossey-Bass, 2017.

Menkel-Meadow, Carrie. "Conflict Theory." *Encyclopedia of Community, Vol. 1*, edited by Karen Christensen and David Levinson, Sage Publications, 2003.

Menkel-Meadow, Carrie. "Dispute Resolution." *The Oxford Handbook of Empirical Legal Research*, edited by Peter Cane and Herbert M. Kritzer, Oxford University Press, 2010.

Menkel-Meadow, Carrie. "Ethics Issues in Arbitration and Related Dispute Resolution Processes: What's Happening and What's Not." *University of Miami Law Review*, vol. 56, 2002.

Menkel-Meadow, Carrie. "Ethics, Morality and Professional Responsibility." *Dispute Resolution Ethics: A Comprehensive Guide*, by Phyllis Bernard and Bryant Garth, American Bar Association, 2002.

Menkel-Meadow, Carrie. "For and against Settlement: Uses and Abuses of the Mandatory Settlement Conference." *UCLA Law Review*, vol. 33, 1985.

Menkel-Meadow, Carrie. "Introduction." *Mediation: Theory, Practice and Policy*, edited by Carrie Menkel-Meadow, Routledge, 2000.

Menkel-Meadow, Carrie. "Introduction." *Multi-Party Dispute Resolution, Democracy and Decision-Making, Volume II*, edited by Carrie Menkel-Meadow, Routledge, 2012.

Menkel-Meadow, Carrie. "Is ODR ADR? Reflections of an ADR Founder from 15th ODR Conference, the Hague, the Netherlands, 22-23 May 2016." *International Journal of Online Dispute Resolution*, vol. 3, no. 1, 2016.

Menkel-Meadow, Carrie. "Modes of Conflict Resolution (Chart). Introduction: From Legal Disputes to Conflict Resolution and Human Problem Solving." *Dispute Processing and Conflict Resolution*, Routledge, 2003.

Menkel-Meadow, Carrie. "Mothers and Fathers of Invention: The Intellectual Founders of ADR." *Ohio State Journal on Dispute Resolution*, vol. 16, 2000.

Menkel-Meadow, Carrie. "Peace and Justice: Notes on the Evolution and Purposes of Legal Processes." *Georgetown Law Journal*, vol. 94, 2005.

Menkel-Meadow, Carrie. "Practicing "in the Interests of Justice" in the Twenty-First Century." *Fordham Law Review*, vol. 70, no. 5, 2002.

Menkel-Meadow, Carrie. "Pursuing Settlement in an Adversary Culture: A Tale of Innovation Co-Opted or "the Law of ADR."" *Florida State University Law Review*, vol. 19, no. 1, 1991.

Menkel-Meadow, Carrie. "The Lawyer's Role(S) in Deliberative Democracy." *Nevada Law Journal*, vol. 5, no. 2, 2004.

Menkel-Meadow, Carrie. "The Trouble with the Adversary System in a Postmodern, Multicultural World." *William & Mary Law Review*, vol. 38, no. 1, 2024.

Menkel-Meadow, Carrie. "Toward Another View of Legal Negotiation: The Structure of Problem Solving." *UCLA Law Review*, vol. 31, 1984.

Menkel-Meadow, Carrie. "Whose Dispute Is It Anyway? A Philosophical and Democratic Defense of Settlement (in Some Cases)." *Georgetown Law Journal*, vol. 83, 1995.

Menkel-Meadow, Carrie, and Michael Wheeler. *What's Fair: Ethics for Negotiators.* Jossey-Bass, 2004.

Moffitt, Michael. "Pleadings in the Age of Settlement." *Indiana Law Journal*, vol. 80, no. 3, 2005.

Menkel-Meadow, Carrie. "Settlement Malpractice." *University of Chicago Law Review*, vol. 86, no. 7, 2019.

Menkel-Meadow, Carrie. "Ten Ways to Get Sued: A Guide for Mediators." *Harvard Negotiation Law Review*, vol. 8, 2003.

Menkel-Meadow, Carrie. "Three Things to Be against ("Settlement" Not Included)." *Fordham Law Review*, vol. 78, no. 3, 2009.

Moffitt, Michael L., and Andrea Kupfer Schneider. *Examples & Explanations for Dispute Resolution.* Aspen Publishing, 2014.

Peppet, Scott R. "Six Principles for Using Negotiating Agents to Maximum Advantage." *The Handbook of Dispute Resolution*, edited by Michael L Moffitt and Robert C Bordone. Copyright © 2005 John Wiley & Sons, Inc.

Price, Marty. "Personalizing Crime: Mediation Produces Restorative Justice for Victims and Offenders." *Dispute Resolution Magazine*, vol. 7, 2000. Copyright © 2000 by the American Bar Association. Reprinted by permission. All rights reserved.

Reilly, Peter R. "Was Machiavelli Right? Lying in Negotiation and the Art of Defensive Self-Help." *Journal of Dispute Resolution*, vol. 24, no. 3, 2009. Ohio State Journal on Dispute Resolution. Reprinted with permission.

Reuben, Richard C. "Confidentiality in Arbitration: Beyond the Myth." *Kansas Law Review*, vol. 54, 2006. Reprinted with permission.

Riskin, Leonard L. "Mediator Orientations, Strategies and Techniques." *Alternatives to the High Cost of Litigation*, vol. 12, 1994. Copyright © 1994 John Wiley & Sons, Inc.

Riskin, Leonard L. "Mediation and Lawyers." *Ohio State Law Journal*, vol. 43, July 1982. Ohio State University Moritz College of Law. Reprinted with permission.

Rubin, Jeffrey Z., and Frank E. A. Sander. "Culture, Negotiation, and the Eye of the Beholder." *Negotiation Journal*, vol. 7, no. 3, July 1991. Copyright © 1991 John Wiley & Sons, Inc.

Rubin, Jeffrey Z., and Frank E. A. Sander. "When Should We Use Agents? Direct vs. Representative Negotiation." *Negotiation Journal*, vol. 4, no. 4, Oct. 1988. Copyright © 1988 by John Wiley & Sons, Inc. Reprinted by permission. All rights reserved.

Sander, Frank E. A. "Federal Rules Decisions." *Federal Rules Decisions*, vol. 70, 1976. Copyright © 1976 Thomson Reuters West. Reprinted with permission.

Sander, Frank E. A., and Stephen B. Goldberg. "Fitting the Forum to the Fuss: A User-Friendly Guide to Selecting an ADR Procedure." *Negotiation Journal*, vol. 10, no. 1, Jan. 1994. Copyright © 1994 John Wiley & Sons, Inc.

Sander, Frank E.A. "Varieties of Dispute Processing." *Federal Rules Decisions*, vol. 70, 1976. Thomson Reuters West. Reprinted with permission.

Scardilli, Frank J. "Sisters of the Precious Blood v. Bristol-Myers Co.: A Shareholder-Management Dispute." Harvard Faculty Seminar on Negotiation, 13 April 1982. The Program on Negotiation at Harvard Law School.

Schiltz, Patrick. "On Being a Happy, Healthy, and Ethical Member of an Unhappy, Unhealthy, and Unethical Profession." *Vanderbilt Law Review*, vol. 52, no. 4, May 1999. Vanderbilt University Law School. Reprinted with permission.

Schmitz, Amy J. "Untangling the Privacy Paradox in Arbitration." *Kansas Law Review*, vol. 54, 2006. Reprinted with permission.

Schneider, Andrea Kupfer. "Building a Pedagogy of Problem-Solving: Learning to Choose among ADR Processes." *Harvard Negotiation Law Review*, vol. 5, 2000. Copyright © 2000 by the Harvard Negotiation Law Review and the President and Fellows of Harvard College.

Schneider, Andrea Kupfer. "Negotiating While Female." *SMU Law Review*, vol. 70, 2017.

Schneider, Andrea Kupfer. "Shattering Negotiation Myths: Empirical Evidence on the Effectiveness of Negotiation Style." *Harvard Negotiation Law Review*, vol. 7, 2002.

Schneider, Andrea Kupfer, and Noah Ebner. "Social Intuition." *The Negotiator's Desk Reference*, edited by Andrea Kupfer Schneider and Chris Honeyman, Dri Press, 2017.

Schneider, Andrea Kupfer, and David Kupfer. *Smart & Savvy: Negotiation Strategies in Academia.* Meadows Communication LLC, 2017.

Schneider, Andrea Kupfer, and Sean MCarthy. "Modes of Communication." *The Negotiator's Desk Reference*, edited by Andrea Kupfer Schneider and Chris Honeyman, Dri Press, 2017.

Sebenius, James K. "Mapping Backward: Negotiating in the Right Sequence." *Negotiation*, vol. 7, no. 6, 2004. Reprinted as "A Better Way to Negotiate: Backward," in Harvard Business School Working Knowledge (July 26, 2004). Copyright © 2004 by Harvard Business Publishing. Reprinted by permission. All rights reserved.

Shapiro, Martin. *Courts: A Comparative and Political Analysis. University of Chicago Press*, 1981. Copyright © 1981 University of Chicago Press.

Shell, G. Richard. *Bargaining for Advantage: Negotiation Strategies for Reasonable People.* Copyright © 1999, 2006 by G. Richard Shell. Used by permission of Viking Books, an imprint of Penguin Publishing Group, a division of Penguin Random House LLC. All rights reserved.

Sternlight, Jean R. "ADR Is Here: Preliminary Reflections on Where It Fits in a System of Justice." *Nevada Law Journal*, vol. 3, 2003. UNLV William S. Boyd School of Law. Reprinted with permission.

Sternlight, Jean R. "Lawyerless Dispute Resolution: Rethinking a Paradigm." *Fordham Urban Law Journal*, vol. 37, no. 1, 2010. Reprinted with permission.

Sternlight, Jean R. "Lawyers' Representation of Clients in Mediation: Using Economics and Psychology to Structure Advocacy in a Non-Adversarial Setting." *Ohio State Journal on Dispute Resolution*, vol. 14, 1999. Ohio State University Moritz College of Law. Reprinted with permission.

Sternlight, Jean R., and Jennifer K. Robbennolt. "Good Lawyers Should Be Good Psychologists: Insights for Interviewing and Counseling Clients." *Ohio State Journal on Dispute Resolution*, vol. 23, May 2008. Reprinted with permission.

Stulberg, Joseph B. "Theory and Practice of Mediation - a Reply to Professor Susskind." *Vermont Law Review*, vol. 6, 1981. Vermont Law School. Reprinted with permission.

Stulberg, Joseph B., and Lela Porter Love. *The Middle Voice: Mediating Conflict Successfully.* Carolina Academic Press, 2009.

Sunstein, Cass R. "Deliberative Trouble? Why Groups Go to Extremes." *Yale Law Journal*, vol. 110, Oct. 2000. Copyright © 2000 The Yale Law Journal Company.

Susskind, Lawrence. "An Alternative to Robert's Rules of Order for Groups, Organizations and Ad Hoc Assemblies That Want to Operate by Consensus." *The Consensus Building Handbook: A Comprehensive Guide to Reaching Agreement*, edited by Lawrence Susskind et al. Copyright © 1999 Sage Publications, Inc.

Susskind, Lawrence. "Environmental Mediation and the Accountability Problem." *Vermont Law Review*, vol. 6, 1981. Reprinted with permission.

Ury, William L., et al. *Getting Disputes Resolved: Designing Systems to Cut the Costs of Conflict.* 1988. Copyright © 1988 John Wiley & Sons, Inc.

Watson, Lawrence M., Jr. *Effective Advocacy in Mediation: A Planning Guide to Prepare for a Civil Trial Mediation.* Copyright © Lawrence M. Watson, Jr. Reprinted with permission.

DISPUTE RESOLUTION

PART I INTRODUCTION

Chapter 1 Introducing the Fields of Conflict and Dispute Resolution

The skillful management of conflicts, [is] among the highest of human skills.
—Stuart Hampshire, *Justice Is Conflict* 35 (2000)

The core mission of the legal profession is the pursuit of justice, through the resolution of conflict or the orderly and civilized righting of wrongs.
—Howard Gardner, Mihaly Csiksentmihali & William Damon, *Good Work: When Excellence and Ethics Meet* 10 (2001)

Conflicts among human beings are as old as life itself. From the time we began to work and socialize with other people, we have had to learn how to resolve conflicts. Using approaches ranging from negotiation to violence, we have, in some eras, been more successful than in others in resolving our conflicts effectively and productively. Indeed, our degree of success in dealing with the conflicts inevitable to human interdependence is one mark of our success (or not) in achieving an advanced civilization.

In striving to deal with our differences, we often have focused on trying to establish fair processes to resolve these differences. Stuart Hampshire, the philosopher quoted above, has suggested that while we will never reach agreement about the substantive good in our culturally and politically diverse world, we can come close to achieving a human universal value by committing to "procedural fairness." Thus we have developed law, legal institutions, and other procedural mechanisms to try to regulate our conflicts or potential conflicts with one another. Both substantive law and legal processes are modes of conflict resolution. These processes include judicial, legislative, and executive entities. But it is also important to recognize that law and traditional legal institutions are not the only viable means for resolving human problems.

Because you are in law school, it probably now seems commonplace for you to think of all human problems as having a "legal" solution. Yet many problems, even when strictly legal, never go further than the lawyer's office. Instead, negotiation and drafting are used to resolve many problems, both small and complex, even when the disputes are bitterly contested. Sometimes such disputes are resolved in non-court settings, such as employee grievance systems, internal ombuds or complaint services, with privately contracted dispute resolution professionals, community action organizations or, these days, perhaps with an online customer service process. Even after a case has been filed with a court, the parties sometimes voluntarily choose some other means of dispute settlement or are assigned to one of the newer forms of dispute resolution you will study in this book. In addition, as both transactions and disputes increasingly transcend national boundaries, processes other than one nation's legal system may be needed to structure relationships and solve problems involving multiple parties of different legal systems. That is, the field of dispute resolution or alternative or "appropriate" dispute resolution (ADR) in law has grown out of recognition that the conventional legal systems of legislative enactments, litigation practices, trials, and court decisions are not always adequate to deal with all kinds of human problems.

This book uses the theory of "process pluralism" to explain why different kinds of matters may require different kinds of procedures or ways of dealing with the underlying conflict. If trial-by-court is an evolved form as compared to the trial-by-ordeal or trial-by-combat of medieval days, then our newer forms of dispute resolution may be thought of as an evolutionary improvement over trial-by-court. Empirical research has documented that, for many people, being treated fairly, by being heard and acknowledged, may be as important as achieving a good result or "winning" a dispute, known as the measure of procedural justice, as distinguished from a particular view of substantive justice.

Although not all disputes are legal, and not all legal disputes have to be "tried" in order to be resolved, lawyers play a key role in helping to resolve a broad array of conflicts in our society. To be effective in this role, you will need to expand your knowledge base and behavioral repertoires. That's why this book is called "beyond the adversarial model." This book presents a particular point of view that human relationships and well-being are improved by a greater number of choices about how to resolve human problems, and that some choices are better than others in particular cases. Usually (though not always) the maximum participation of parties in the decisions that affect their lives should be an essential part of any choice about how decisions should be made. While the adversary process has its place, modern life, with multiple parties and multiple issues present in almost every human endeavor, may not fit so easily in the casebook headings where often only one name appears on either side of the "v." Your job as a well-educated lawyer and citizen is to know about and assist others in making choices about what process is best for the particular matter at hand. During your lifetime, you have likely witnessed the failure of these processes at the international and national level as the United States has been engaged in a variety of armed conflicts (e.g., Afghanistan, Iraq) and has had more bellicose relations with some nations (North Korea and Iran), even while attempting diplomatic negotiations. The larger culture and changes over time often affect not only how nations and governments conduct themselves, but also how lawyers, clients, and ordinary citizens decide what processes to use.[1] But even war has its "rules" (*jus in bello*)[2]; and many new international organizations (e.g., United

1. Carrie Menkel-Meadow, The Historical Contingencies of Conflict Resolution, 1(1) Intl J. Conflict Resol. 32-55 (2013).
2. E.g., Geneva Conventions for Protections of War Victims (1949).

Nations; treaty monitoring committees) and processes (e.g., international mediation, fact-finding inquiries) now try to promote a variety of dispute prevention, avoidance, management, and resolution efforts.

To perform well in your job of assisting with process choices, you need to "*think outside of the box*," to be aware of many alternative modes of conflict resolution, and to communicate and consult well with your clients. In each chapter we will offer problems for you to solve (which, ironically, will sometimes appear "*inside the box*" to demarcate the problems from the text). Thus, this book exposes you to more varied forms of human problem solving (including negotiation, mediation, arbitration, and variants of these).

This book is organized to help you move from the simpler forms of conflict and dispute resolution to the more complex. This first chapter introduces some key concepts that describe the frameworks or theories human beings have developed to understand themselves and how they interact with each other, the history of these concepts, and the institutions and practices that have been built around them.

The second chapter will introduce the key skills needed to solve problems for clients, including interviewing clients about their needs and goals, and counseling them about available processes and potential outcomes. Subsequent sections of this book then examine particular forms of dispute resolution.

The focus initially is on the three foundational processes, other than litigation, that are most frequently used to resolve disputes in the United States and most parts of the world: negotiation, mediation, and arbitration. Later chapters explore the infinite possibilities of dispute resolution in our complex world. The chapter on hybrid processes shows how we can creatively combine aspects of negotiation, mediation, arbitration, and even adjudication to form other processes that may better serve the needs of disputants or society in particular situations.

Next you will examine particular processes that are used to deal with multi-party disputes, conflicts arising in the transactional context and developing systems of dispute resolution. Finally, we conclude with a few words about the future and potential of different means of dispute resolution.

As the book presents these various processes, it elaborates the *theories*, *frameworks*, *models*, *concepts*, and *basic premises* of a particular process; examines each process's *internal* or *institutional structures*; describes the *skills* and *practices* involved in each process; and explores the *policies*, *ethics*, and *issues* or *dilemmas* challenging the use of each particular process.

This book focuses on theory of process, with the hope that such a grounding will serve you in counseling clients, making and affecting policy and law, and structuring your own professional (and personal) life. In particular, the book is conceptualized to present "theories-in-use," as Donald Schön of MIT has defined that phrase in The Reflective Practitioner (1983). To practice good dispute resolution and problem solving, we need to have theories to inform our actions and assist the choices we make about what process is appropriate for a particular human problem. At the same time, our theories should be useful, so we should constantly test the assumptions on which we base our actions and correct them if they do not serve us well. If what we are doing cannot be understood or adequately explained, we need to refine our theories and practices.

To explore the theoretical underpinnings of process pluralism, this text looks to law and other disciplines, drawing at times from such fields as economics, game theory, political science, psychology, sociology, anthropology, philosophy, sociolegal studies, peace studies, communication, and urban planning and public policy studies.

As globalization increases our contacts with others—individuals, groups, organizations, nation-states, and cultures—we can see both the existence of other forms of conflict resolution embedded in other legal systems and cultures, and the need for different forms to deal with our many human problems and interactions, in varied regional and worldwide interdependent political, economic, and legal regimes. Perhaps you will develop your own new form of dispute resolution or process for some human, social, or legal problem we have yet to confront.

A. THEORETICAL UNDERPINNINGS OF CONFLICT AND DISPUTE RESOLUTION

Although law school focuses on disputes or cases, the disputes that make it into casebooks represent the tip of the iceberg of all the kinds of conflicts that people have. Lawyers are often called on not only to bring or defend lawsuits, but also to help prevent conflicts from arising or to deal with disputes other than in court. Thus, it is useful for lawyers to have a broad understanding of the types of conflicts that may exist. Scholars in a wide variety of the social sciences have attempted to define and develop taxonomies of different kinds of conflicts so as to better understand the different possible treatments or interventions available in conflict settings. At the same time, it is important to realize that not all conflict is bad or ought to be avoided. Professor Carrie Menkel-Meadow explores these multiple aspects of conflict.

Carrie Menkel-Meadow, CONFLICT THEORY

in Encyclopedia of Community: From the Village to the Virtual World 323-326 (Karen Christensen & David Levinson eds., 2003)

There are many reasons for conflicts to develop, at both the individual and at the group level. Some conflicts are based on belief systems or principles, some are based on personality differences, and others on conflicts about material goods or personal or group status or reputation. Because there are so many different reasons conflicts develop and because much conflict is dangerous and unproductive, the theory of conflict attempts to understand the different sources of conflict, the dynamics of how conflict develops, escalates or declines and how conflict can be managed, reduced or resolved.

At the same time, it must be recognized that conflict can have social utility as well. Many important changes in human society, many for the betterment of human life, have come from hard-fought conflicts that resulted in the change of human institutions, relationships or ideas. The United States Civil War, for example, was a bloody and painful war in which over a million Americans died, but this war eliminated slavery in the United States and ushered in a long period of change in race relations. . . . Even small interpersonal conflicts (like between a husband and wife or parent and child) can lead to important changes, not only in relationships between the people in conflict, but in larger social movements, such as the women's rights or feminist movement and the children's rights movement. Conflicts with outsiders often clarify and reinforce commitments and norms of one's own group. And internal conflict within the individual can lead to changed views and intellectual and emotional growth.

Conflict theory tries to explain the types of conflicts that exist and whether they are productive or destructive and then goes on to attempt to explain the ways in which conflict proceeds or is structured . . . and how it can be managed or resolved.

A conflict can be experienced as a simple disagreement, a feeling of discomfort or opposition, and a perception of difference from others, or a competition or incompatibility with others. Conflicts, then, can be perceptual, emotional or behavioral. When a conflict is actually acted on it becomes a dispute with someone or a group of others. In order for a conflict to fully develop into a dispute we have to experience some sense of wrong to ourselves, someone else to "blame" for that wrong and some way to take action against those we think caused our difficulty—what one set of scholars have called, "naming, blaming and claiming."[3] How the conflict turns into a dispute and how it is labeled ("framing") then may affect how it progresses and how it may either escalate and get worse, leading in extreme cases to war, or how it can be handled, managed or resolved.

TYPES OF CONFLICTS

Conflict can exist on many different levels, including the intrapersonal, interpersonal, intragroup, intergroup, and international. Conflicts can exist about different subject matters—ideational or beliefs, values, material and resources, emotions, roles and responsibilities. Conflicts vary in terms of the social contexts in which they are located (two old friends, family members, neighbors, strangers, consumers and merchants, distant nation-states) and in the time span in which they are located ("one-off" or "one-shot" encounters and conflicts, long-standing or "embedded" conflicts, temporary or "repeated" conflicts in on-going relationships like families and employment settings). Conflicts vary, even within the same social environment or subject matter by how the disputants treat the conflict, in the strategies, tactics and behaviors they employ (avoidance, self-help, peaceful negotiation, argument, escalation, physical violence, peace seeking, mediation or settlement) and how the strategies chosen interact with each other. And conflicts are often classified by how they affect the parties in the conflict (the consequences

3. William L.F. Felstiner, Richard Abel & Austin Sarat, The Emergence and Transformation of Disputes: Naming, Blaming and Claiming . . . , 15 L. & Socy. Rev. 631-654 (1980-1981).

of the conflict) and those outside of the conflict (the "externalities" of the conflict, like children in a marital argument or divorce and neighbors of warring states who accept refugees). . . .

Conflicts have also been classified by various social scientists and conflict theorists by virtue of what is at stake in the conflict such as:

> *Resources* (land, power, property, natural resources like water, oil, minerals, money);
> *Values or beliefs* (class, religious, nationality, political aspirations and codes that create systemic belief systems for groups or individual members);
> *Preferences or interests* (incompatible desires, wants or objectives of action);
> *Relationship* (differences in desires or objectives about relationships);
> *Identity* (concerns about recognition of and respect for group memberships).

The theory of such classifications is that if we can analyze different kinds of conflict, we can determine how they might enfold and whether a particular conflict is amenable to a positive outcome (whether harnessing the conflict to constructive solutions or processes) or whether it is likely to become destructive (for the parties or others affected by the parties). . . .

Problem 1-1. ***What Are the Conflicts?***

Look through a case reporter or one of your casebooks, or do a random search on a computer service, and choose a reported case. What dispute brought the parties to litigation? What underlying conflict(s) existed between the parties or between other people involved in or affected by the dispute? Where does their dynamic fit in the list of conflict types provided by Menkel-Meadow describing what is at stake?

Now, read a newspaper or magazine and find a conflict that is reported. How might the disputants (or possibly attorneys) have avoided such a conflict in advance? Do you think that the conflict you identified has positive or negative aspects, or both? What are they?

Conflicts will always exist. While we may prevent and avoid some, clearly we will never succeed in eliminating all of them. The remainder of this section examines how to deal with conflicts that already exist.

In focusing on conflict, it is critically important to examine what it means to "win" in a conflict. While many people assume that someone must lose when another person wins, the following readings show that this either-or mentality is often fallacious. The first excerpt is taken from the work of Mary Parker Follett, who was an important early theorist in the field of conflict resolution. She was trained as a political scientist and worked as a social worker, as well as working in labor-management relations, administrative "science," and business management. Follett urges that conflict can lead to a creative process that allows constructive solutions to come from the friction created by conflict. Yet the win-lose attitude toward conflict has permeated our culture in general, and our concept of the legal system in particular. Popular writer and professor of linguistics Deborah Tannen critiques the adversarial mindset of our society, arguing that it limits the possibilities for better alternatives and also makes for an uncomfortable civil society. Finally, Carrie Menkel-Meadow outlines some of the problems that arise when the legal system is envisioned in purely binary win-lose terms.

❖ *Mary Parker Follett*, CONSTRUCTIVE CONFLICT

in Prophet of Management: A Celebration of Writings from the 1920s, 67-69, 75, 77, 79, 82, 84-86 (Pauline Graham ed., 1995)

As conflict—difference—is here in the world, as we cannot avoid it, we should, I think use it. Instead of condemning it, we should set it to work for us. Why not? What does the mechanical engineer do with friction? Of course, his chief job is to eliminate friction, but it is true that he also capitalizes friction. The transmission of power by belts depends on friction between the belt and the pulley. . . . The music of the violin we get by friction . . . . We talk of the friction of the mind on mind as a good thing. So in business too, we have to know when to try to eliminate friction and when to try to capitalize it, when to see what work we can make it do. That is what I wish to consider here, whether we can set conflict to work and make it do something for us.

There are three main ways of dealing with conflict: domination, compromise and integration. Domination, obviously, is a victory of one side over the other. This is the easiest way of dealing with conflict, the easiest for the moment but not usually successful in the long run. . . .

The second way of dealing with conflict, that of compromise, we understand well, for it is the way we settle most of our controversies; each side gives up a little in order to have peace, or, to speak more accurately, in order that the activity which has been interrupted by the conflict can go on. . . .

Yet no one really wants to compromise, because that means a giving up of something. Is there any other method of ending conflict? There is a way now beginning to be recognized at least, and even occasionally followed: when two desires are integrated, that means that a solution has been found in which both desires have found a place, that neither side has to sacrifice anything. Let us take some very simple illustration. In the Harvard Library one day, in one of the smaller rooms, someone wanted the window open, I wanted it shut. We opened the window in the next room, where no one was sitting. This was not a compromise because there was no curtailing of desire; we both got what we really wanted. For I did not want a closed room, I simply did not want the north wind to blow directly on me; likewise the other occupant did not want that particular window open, he merely wanted more air in the room. . . .

[T]he revaluing of interests on both sides may lead the interests to fit into each other, so that all find some place in the final solution. . . . If the first step is to uncover the real conflict, the next is to take the demands of both sides and break them up into their constituent parts. . . . On the other hand, one often has to do just the opposite; find the whole demand, the real demand, which is being obscured by miscellaneous minor claims or by ineffective presentation. . . .

Finally, let us consider the chief obstacles to integration. It requires a high order of intelligence, keen perception and discrimination, more than that, a brilliant inventiveness. . . . Another obstacle to integration is that our way of life has habituated many of us to enjoy domination. Integration seems a tamer affair, it leaves no "thrills" of conquest. . . . Finally, perhaps the greatest of all obstacles to integration is our lack of training for it. In our college debates we try always to beat the other side. . . .

I should like to emphasize our responsibility for integration. . . . One test of business administration should be: is the organization such that both employers and employees, or co-managers, co-directors, are stimulated to a reciprocal activity which will give more than mere adjustment, more than equilibrium? Our outlook is narrowed, our activity restricted, our chances of business success largely diminished when our thinking is constrained within the limits of what has been called an "either-or" situation. We should never allow ourselves to be bullied by an "either-or." There is always the possibility of something better than either of two given alternatives.

Deborah Tannen, THE ARGUMENT CULTURE: MOVING FROM DEBATE TO DIALOGUE

3-4, 8, 10 (1998)

The argument culture urges us to approach the world—and the people in it—in an adversarial frame of mind. It rests on the assumption that opposition is the best way to get anything done: The best way to discuss an idea is to set up a debate; the best way to cover news is to find spokespeople who express the most extreme, polarized views and present them as "both sides"; the best way to settle disputes is litigation that pits one party against the other; the best way to begin an essay is to attack someone and the best way to show you're really thinking is to criticize. . . .

In a word the type of opposition I am questioning is what I call "agonism." I use this term, which derives from the Greek word for "contest," *agonia*, to mean an automatic war-like stance—not the literal fighting against an attacker or the unavoidable opposition that arises organically in response to conflicting ideas or actions. An agonistic response, to me, is a kind of programmed contentiousness—a prepatterned, unthinking use of fighting to accomplish goals that do not necessarily require it. . . .

Our determination to pursue truth by setting up a fight between two sides leads us to believe that every issue has two sides—no more, no less: If both sides are given a forum to confront each other, all the relevant information will emerge and the best case will be made for each side. But opposition does not lead to truth when an issue is not composed of two opposing sides but is a crystal of many sides. Often the truth is in the complex middle, not the oversimplified extremes.

Carrie Menkel-Meadow, THE TROUBLE WITH THE ADVERSARY SYSTEM IN A POSTMODERN, MULTICULTURAL WORLD

38 Wm. & Mary L. Rev. 5, 6-10 (1996)

Binary, oppositional presentations of facts in dispute are not the best way for us to learn the truth; polarized debate distorts the truth, leaves out important information, simplifies complexity and often obfuscates rather than clarifies. More significantly, some matters—mostly civil, but occasionally even criminal, cases—are not susceptible to a binary (i.e., right/wrong, win/lose) conclusion or solution. The inability to reach a binary resolution of these disputes may result because in some cases we cannot determine the facts with any degree of accuracy. In other cases the law may be conflicting, though legitimate, legal rights giving some entitlement to both, or all, parties. And, in yet another category of cases, human or emotional equities cannot be sharply divided.

Modern life presents us with complex problems, often requiring complex and multifaceted solutions. Courts, with what I have called their "limited remedial imaginations," may not be the best institutional settings for resolving some of the disputes that we continue to put before them.

Even if some form of the adversary system was defensible in particular settings for purposes of adjudication, the "adversary" model employed in the courtroom has bled inappropriately into and infected other aspects of lawyering, including negotiation carried on both in the "shadow of the court" and outside of it in transactional work. . . .

Furthermore, the complexities of both modern life and modern lawsuits have shown us that disputes often have more than two sides in the sense that legal disputes and transactions involve many more than two parties. Procedures and forms like interpleader, joinder, consolidation, and class actions have attempted to allow for more than just plaintiffs' and defendants' voices to be heard, all the while structuring the discourse so that parties must ultimately align themselves on one side of the adversarial line or the other. Multiparty, multiplex lawsuits or disputes may be distorted when only two sides are possible. Consider all of the multiparty and complex policy issues that courts contend with in environmental clean-up and siting, labor disputes in the public sector, consumer actions, antitrust actions, mass torts, school financing and desegregation and other civil rights issues, to name a few examples.

Finally, scholars have criticized modern adversarialism for the ways it teaches people to act toward each other.

Problem 1-2. ***What Do You Do About Conflict?***

For the next 24 hours, keep a list of all the conflicts, disputes, or disagreements in which you get (or could get) involved. What did you do? Argue, compromise, accommodate (give in), get your way, avoid, or "integrate"? How? Why?

Problem 1-3. *Framing Conflicts and Solutions*

Problem 1-1 asked you to examine a series of reported cases and consider what underlying conflicts brought the parties to litigation. Now consider the following with respect to these cases:

a. Who were the "real parties in interest," whether they were named in the reported case or not? Who else might be affected by a judicial resolution or settlement of the matter at issue?
b. How were the issues framed? In terms of perceived wrongs and rights? Legal entitlements? Were there any instances of cases in which both sides had legitimate claims to having been wronged?
c. Consider what solutions, other than those ordered by the court, might have resolved the conflict among all interested parties.

B. FRAMEWORKS FOR HANDLING CONFLICTS AND DISPUTES

Now that you have briefly examined the nature of conflict and some nonadversarial approaches to conflict resolution, we consider how disputants, lawyers, or others should choose the most appropriate process for resolving a particular dispute. In other words, as William Felstiner, Richard Abel, and Austin Sarat explain, once a "perceived injurious experience" (PIE) (or a potential conflict) with someone else occurs, the next question is what to do about that perception.[4] In the background, of course, are social processes and psychological factors that lead us to identify an "experience" as "injurious" or not, and that lead us to blame someone other than ourselves for what has happened. But, taking as given a body of PIEs, one can, in any social or legal culture, create a pyramid of possible ways in which such disputes are handled. The size and shape of the pyramid differs from culture to culture or legal system to legal system, but no system treats all conflicts the same; most have developed hierarchical systems for dealing with conflicts and disputes. In our U.S. legal system and culture, for example, despite all the claims that we are so litigious[5], most people avoid dealing with every little conflict they have. Imagine what your day would be like if you decided to file a lawsuit about everything that made you feel wronged.

Figure 1-1 shows our current U.S. legal system (which has been changing dramatically in the last few decades); at the top of the pyramid are those important disputes that go all the way to the Supreme Court and culminate in a reported decisional precedent. Note that most of your legal education has been about reading the reported cases from the top of the pyramid. From a social-scientific

4. Felstiner et al., supra note 3, at 633.

5. Marc S. Galanter, Reading the Landscape of Disputes: What We Know and Don't Know (and Think We Know) About Our Allegedly Contentious and Litigious Society, 31 UCLA L. Rev. 4-71 (1983).

perspective, this may be a very unrepresentative sample of the actual disputes or conflicts that people have, since the vast percentage of PIEs are resolved outside of courtrooms—whether through the choice not to pursue the claim, settlements, or third-party assisted processes such as mediation or arbitration.

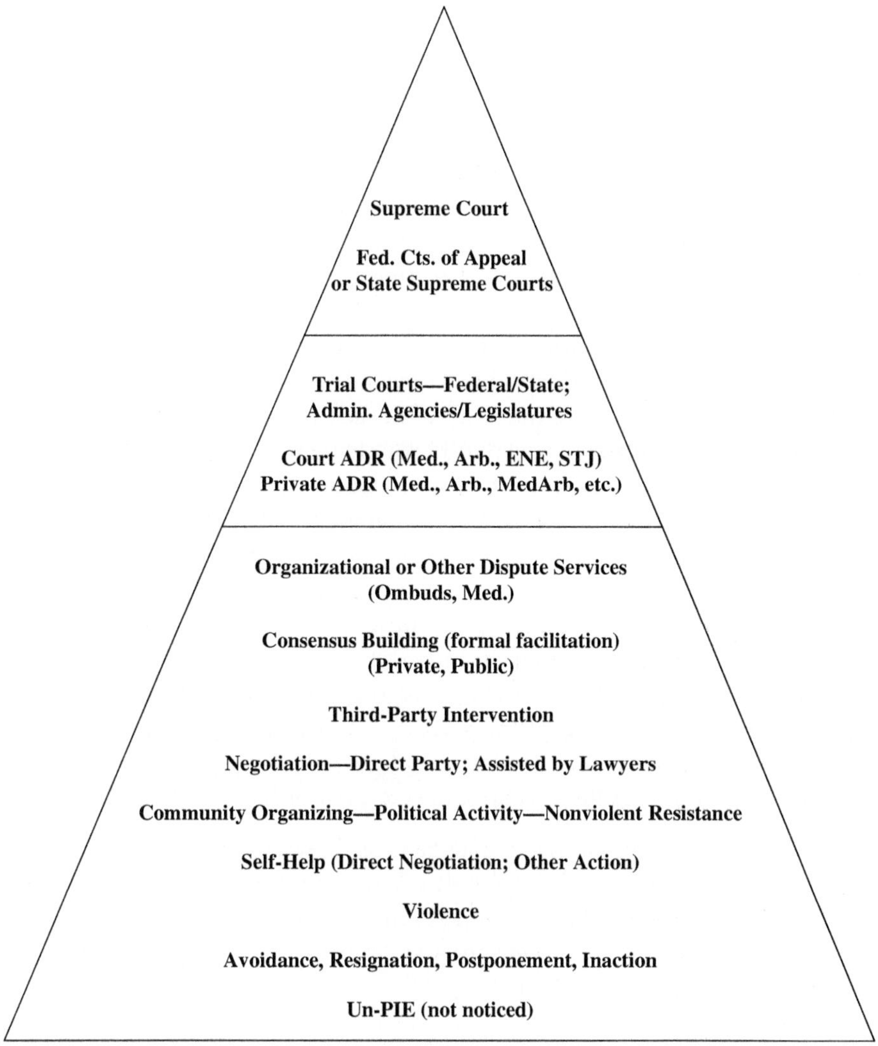

Figure 1-1
U.S. Legal System

The pyramid of dispute resolution is not a "given" in any society, but rather the result of choices made by policy makers and individuals in that society. Policy makers decide which dispute resolution mechanisms should be made available for which kinds of disputes, and policy makers choose whether and how to fund or subsidize particular dispute resolution tools. Disputants and their attorneys then make choices about how to approach a particular dispute, given the options provided in their society.

How should societies or individuals approach the question of what processes are most useful for resolving particular kinds of disputes? To use the phrase coined by one major negotiation theorist (and mathematician and decision scientist), Howard Raiffa,[6] there is both a science and an art to conflict resolution, problem solving, and decision-making. The science involves understanding and analyzing the nature of the problem in these categories:

1. Who are the parties? (And who speaks for them—principals, agents? Are they unified or divided?)
2. What issues do they have with each other (scarce or divisible resources, building or maintaining a relationship)?
3. How many parties? (Two? More than two? With or without representatives?)
4. How many issues are there?
5. How do the issues affect each other (intertwined, linked and dependent, or severable and independent)?
6. What are the relationships between the parties? (Formalized long-term relationships? Informal, episodic? One-off or one shot?)
7. How do the parties communicate with each other? Learn from each other? Signal to each other? (Directly? Through agents? Through the media?)
8. What kind of a solution do the parties require (a precedent; a fast, temporary, or permanent decision; a contingent agreement; a modifiable agreement; a public announcement; a private arrangement)?
9. Can the parties solve their own problems, or do they need help (either to assist in the seeking of a solution (process) or to fund or create the substantive solution ("external" resources))? Do they share norms, rules, or a culture to resolve the conflict, or do they need to look outside or create their own rules and norms of process or substance or both?
10. What are the stakes for the parties? (How seriously do they need to resolve the problem or conflict? Who stands to gain or lose what and how much?)

Only once a problem has been analyzed for these (and possibly other factors) can one consider what process might best effectuate the needs and interests of the parties in achieving their goals. (Of course, this becomes quite complicated when the parties don't agree on what their goals are, or if they each seek different things from the conflict before them.)

But the analysis does not stop there. The choice of a process itself shapes the outcomes. For example, the choice of an adjudicative process (litigation or binding arbitration) that results in a definitive ruling requires adversarial presentations and a win-lose result. The behaviors necessitated by such a process (presentation of evidence, witnesses, and arguments) reinforce the adversarial and competitive nature of the problem. Adversarial behaviors produce more conflict, making the likelihood greater that the parties will produce a competitive or zero- or negative-sum result. Similarly, if the parties choose negotiation but

6. Howard Raiffa, Negotiation Analysis: The Science and Art of Collaborative Decision Making (2002) (with John Richardson and David Metcalf).

use adversarial and competitive techniques (such as debate, argument, persuasion, and more extremely, lying, deception, threat, and intimidation) rather than a problem-solving approach, they may wind up either in a total loss or a stalemate (or at best, a coerced compromise or accommodation). Choosing a more cooperative process (explained in Chapters 3 and 4) can result in more joint gain, but it also presents the risk of one party being taken advantage of, for example, when it openly reveals information and the other party "uses" this information against it. Thus, behaviors and processes cannot be chosen for themselves; they must be related to an analysis of what the problem looks like and what goals and outcomes are possible. You can also see that choices about process or behavior are strategic, in the sense that they are necessarily affected by what the other parties do.

As individuals and policy makers choose appropriate dispute resolution processes, they must also consider the multiple ways in which people express themselves. One might call this the art of linking choice about process to particular behaviors so as to enhance the likelihood that desired goals and outcomes are achieved. Even in the traditional legal system and governmental institutions that you have studied, multiple "modes of discourse" are used. Political scientist Jon Elster,[7] for example, differentiates appeals to reason, argument, and principle (most familiar in law) from appeals to utilities, preferences, trading, and bargaining (which may be based on wants, needs, or interests but need not be principled). Added to this mix, other theorists suggest that claims of passion, including not only emotion but also religious, moral, and political beliefs, form yet a third mode of discourse that is presented in conflict situations. Jürgen Habermas,[8] an important social philosopher of the twentieth century, has spent his lifetime exploring the requirements for "ideal speech conditions" under which citizens could come together to achieve legitimate decisions about their joint lives, even where they don't share substantive values. But even Habermas privileges reason and persuasion as the most appropriate mode of discourse for proper political problem solving. What if others disagree and think that arguments based on passion are just as valid? Conflict-resolution professionals and political activists seeking to enact legitimate processes in the real world (such as in bitterly contested disputes about environmental justice, affirmative action, abortion, tax, and welfare policy) have had to confront these issues of different modes of discourse in a wide variety of settings.[9] Are some processes better than others at generating both innovative and acceptable "solutions" to difficult conflicts? Where do our ideas about problem-solving come from?

As you begin to think about which kinds of dispute resolution processes are best for resolving which kinds of disputes, or for engaging which kinds of "modes of discourse," it is appropriate to highlight the work of Lon Fuller. A legal scholar, philosopher and practitioner of law, and professor at Harvard Law School for many years, Fuller is considered by many the intellectual father of the jurisprudence of

7. Jon Elster, Strategic Uses of Argument in Barriers to Conflict Resolution (Kenneth Arrow et al. eds., 1995).

8. Jürgen Habermas, A Theory of Communicative Action (1984).

9. See, e.g., Amy Gutmann & Dennis Thompson, Democracy and Disagreement (1996).

ADR. He wrote a series of articles on each of several different legal processes, including adjudication, arbitration, mediation, contracting, and legislation, in which he discussed the special moralities and structures of each of these separate processes. Fuller also wrote more broadly about other types of processes, such as elections and administration, and called this entire project "eumonics"—the study of good social arrangements. Because Fuller saw each process as unique, he was very uncomfortable with some of the combinations of processes that are common today. (These are discussed at length in Chapter 12, Private and Public Hybrid Processes, where we return to the question of whether such combinations are a good idea jurisprudentially and ethically.) Carrie Menkel-Meadow introduces Fuller below.

Carrie Menkel-Meadow, MOTHERS AND FATHERS OF INVENTION: THE INTELLECTUAL FOUNDERS OF ADR

16 Ohio St. J. on Disp. Resol. 1, 15-21 (2000)

For Fuller, law was a "problem solving activity" purposively directed towards enabling voluntary transactions and contracts, preventing violence, defining ideals and standards for civic participation, as well as providing a means for settling disputes and preserving social harmony. Law was enacted in and enforced by a variety of different legal institutions, which is why some commentators refer to him as concerned, above all else, with "problems of institutional design," or as an "architect of social structure." Fuller saw that lawmaking and rulemaking occurred in the realms of private ordering—negotiating contracts and mediating solutions produced as much "law" as the public institutions of courts and legislatures. In his efforts to elaborate the different structures, functions, and moralities of different legal processes, Fuller wrote the first description of, and most sustained argument for, mediation. He said that this conciliatory process, which did not require a decision of state-made law, would "reorient the parties to each other" and "brin[g] about a more harmonious relationship between the parties, whether this be achieved through explicit agreement, through a reciprocal acceptance of 'social norms' relevant to their relationship or simply because the parties have been helped to a new and more perceptive understanding of one another's problems." Mediation, in Fuller's words, is for "the administration and enforcement of rules or social norms" between parties, not for the creation of state-made law. . . .

For Fuller, each process of decision making, or as he preferred to say, "problem solving," had its own logic, morality, and function. Fuller acknowledged that not all legal disputes or social problems were similarly structured. Where a problem was like a "spider web" in which unraveling one thread of a "polycentric" problem (such as deciding a single legal issue in a web of relationships such as occurred in a factory among labor and management or in a marriage) might destroy the whole web, mediation, with its ability to work on many issues at the same time and focus the parties on their relationship concerns, would be better. . . .

Lon L. Fuller, THE FORMS AND LIMITS OF ADJUDICATION

in The Principles of Social Order: Selected Essays of Lon L. Fuller (Kenneth I. Winston ed., rev. ed., 2001) 105-106, 113, 126-128, 133

It is customary to think of adjudication as a means of settling disputes or controversies. . . . More fundamentally, however, adjudication should be viewed as a form of social ordering, as a way in which the relations of men to one another are governed and regulated. . . . If . . . we start with the notion of a process of decision in which the affected party's participation consists of an opportunity to present proofs and reasoned arguments, the office of the judge or arbitrator and the requirement of impartiality follow as necessary implications. . . . Adjudication is, then, a device which gives formal and institutional expression to the influence of reasoned argument in human affairs. As such it assumes a burden of rationality not borne by other forms of social ordering. A decision which is the product of reasoned argument must be prepared itself to meet the test of reason. We demand of an adjudicative decision a kind of rationality that we do not expect of the results of contract or of voting. . . . The proper province of adjudication is to make authoritative determination of questions raised by claims of right and accusations of guilt. . . .

What kinds of tasks are inherently unsuited to adjudication? This . . . introduces a concept—that of the "polycentric" task. . . .

Some months ago a wealthy lady by the name of Timken died in New York leaving a valuable, but somewhat miscellaneous, collection of paintings to the Metropolitan Museum and the National Gallery "in equal shares," her will indicating no particular apportionment. When the will was probated the judge remarked something to the effect that the parties seemed to be confronted with a real problem. The attorney for one of the museums spoke up and said, "We are good friends. We will work it out somehow or other." What makes this problem of effecting an equal division of the paintings a polycentric task? It lies in the fact that the disposition of any single painting has implications for the proper disposition of every other painting. If it gets the Renoir, the Gallery may be less eager for the Cezanne but all the more eager for the Bellows, etc. If the proper apportionment were set for argument, there would be no clear issue to which either side could direct its proofs and contentions. Any judge assigned to hear such an argument would be tempted to assume the role of mediator or to adopt the classical solution: Let the older brother (here the Metropolitan) divide the estate into what he regards as equal shares, let the younger brother (the National Gallery) take his pick. . . .

We may visualize this kind of situation by thinking of a spider web. A pull on one strand will distribute tensions after a complicated pattern throughout the web as a whole. Doubling the original pull will, in all likelihood, not simply double each of the resulting tensions but will rather create a different complicated pattern of tensions. This would certainly occur, for example, if the double pull caused one or more of the weaker strands to snap. This is a polycentric situation because it is many centered—each crossing of strands is a distinct center for distributing tensions. . . . We are dealing with a situation of interacting points of influence and therefore with a polycentric problem beyond the proper limits of adjudication. . . . It may be said that problems in the allocation of economic resources present too strong a polycentric aspect to be suitable for adjudication. . . . When an attempt is made to deal by adjudicative forms with a problem that is essentially polycentric, what happens? . . . First, the adjudicative solution may fail. . . . Second, the purported arbiter ignores judicial proprieties—he "tries out" various solutions in posthearing conferences, consults parties not represented in the hearings, guesses at facts not proved and not properly matters for anything like judicial notice. Third, instead of accommodating his procedures to the nature of the problem he confronts, he may reformulate the problem so as to make it amenable to solution through adjudicative procedures.

One important theoretical question raised by students of conflict processes is the extent to which approaches to conflict resolution do or should cross cultural, temporal, or national lines. Do all humans have the same needs with respect to dispute resolution, or do different types of cultures and societies call for different dispute resolution processes? Social scientists such as anthropologists, historians, and sociologists have generally shed more light on this question than have legal scholars.

❖ *Martin Shapiro,* COURTS: A COMPARATIVE AND POLITICAL ANALYSIS

1-6, 9, 15-16 (1981)

Cutting across cultural lines, it appears that whenever two persons come into a conflict that they cannot themselves solve, one solution appealing to common sense is to call upon a third for assistance in achieving a resolution. So universal across time and space is this simple invention of triads that we can discover almost no society that fails to employ it. . . . [T]he triad for purposes of conflict resolution is the basic social logic of courts, a logic so compelling that courts have become a universal political phenomenon. The triad, however, involves a basic instability, paradox or dialectic that accounts for a large proportion of the scholarly quarrels over the nature of courts and the political difficulties that courts encounter in the real world. At the moment the two disputants find their third, the social logic of the court device is preeminent. A moment later when the third decides in favor of one of the two disputants, a shift occurs from the triad to a structure that is perceived by the loser as two against one. . . .

The most fundamental device for maintaining the triad is consent. . . . The almost universal reluctance of courts to proceed in the absence of one of the two parties is less a testimony to the appeal of adversary processes than it is a remnant of this emphasis on consent, of both parties choosing the triad as the appropriate device for conflict resolution. . . . Nearly every triadic conflict resolver adds another device to consent to avoid the breakdown into two against one. This device is the avoidance of the dichotomous, imposed solution. In examining triadic conflict resolution as a universal phenomenon, we discover that the judge of European or Anglo-American courts, determining that the legal right lies with one and against the other of the parties, is not an appropriate central type against which deviance can be conveniently measured. Instead, he lies at one end of a continuum. The continuum runs: go-between, mediator, arbitrator, judge. And placement on the continuum is determined by the intersection of the devices of consent and nondichotomous, or mediate, solution. . . . The key distinction between the mediator and arbitrator is that the arbitrator is expected to fashion his own resolution to the conflict rather than simply assisting the parties in shaping one of their own. . . . As societies become more complex, they tend to substitute law for the particular consent of the parties to a particular norm for their particular dispute. They also substitute office for their free choice of a particular third man to aid in resolution of their disputes. . . .

It would not be difficult to move about the world's legal systems endlessly multiplying the examples of the intermingling of mediation and judging. . . . In Western societies as well, firms that must maintain continuous relationships are not prone to litigation. . . . In short, if one were to review all societies, or even to confine oneself to modern industrial and commercial states where one would most expect to find the prototypic court, one discovers that legal processes are not necessarily or even entirely court processes, if we confine our definition to the prototype. For we frequently find intermediate rather than dichotomous resolutions. . . . A substantial share of the legal conflicts in most societies is resolved not by dichotomous but mediate decision, either rendered by a court itself or under the shadow of potential court proceedings. Much of what courts do is not adversarial in the sense of encouraging or requiring disputations between the two conflicting parties. It is enough that both parties present their views to one another with an option of going to a third. The style of interchange may be cooperative, benevolent, or even familial rather than one of ritualized trial by battle. Moreover, where courts preserve a more or less mediatory style, they may subtly mix preexisting legal rules with rules that emerge from the interaction of the parties. To the extent that there are preexisting rules, they may be ones created by the parties themselves in a contract. After the final settlement, less may depend on those rules than on a newly emerging agreement or understanding or set of subrules that is suggested or elicited in the very process of settling the dispute.

Problem 1-4. *Choosing an Appropriate Process*

What kind of dispute process do you think would be appropriate for each of the following conflicts?

a. Disagreement between the President and U.S. Congress over the federal budget;
b. A grade dispute between you and your professor;
c. A car accident between strangers involving only property damage;
d. A parent-child dispute about going to school;
e. A dispute between a fired high-tech employee and her former employer, when she takes the company source code with her, claiming she developed it and it is hers;
f. Whether and how much the federal government should pay victims of terrorism against the United States.

Do you think everyone involved in the conflicts would agree with your assessment about the most appropriate process?

C. INSTITUTIONS OF CONFLICT AND DISPUTE RESOLUTION

Now that you have examined theories of conflict and of dispute-resolution processes, you are ready to examine the institutions that our society and others have used to resolve disputes. In thinking about such processes as litigation, arbitration, mediation, negotiation, and the many other processes we discuss in the pages that follow, you may find it useful to consider where each process falls on a variety of continua, including the following:

Private ⟷ Public
Consensual/voluntary ⟷ Compelled/mandatory
Nonbinding ⟷ Binding
Informal ⟷ Formal
Oral-unwritten process and decision ⟷ Written rules, process, and decision
Temporary/contingent/variable outcome ⟷ "Permanent" decision or outcome
Parties only ⟷ Other participants, interested parties (representatives or third-party neutrals)
Dyadic (two-party) ⟷ Multiparty
Competitive (distributional) ⟷ Collaborative, integrative
Rights-based (public norms) ⟷ Interests-based (private norms; trades)
Commonsense/community norms ⟷ Expertise—science, technical process

"Pure" forms (e.g., facilitative mediation, adjudication) ⟷	"Hybrids" or combined process (e.g., evaluative mediation, court-hosted settlement conferences)
Pre-dispute contractual (ex ante commitment and consent) ⟷	Post-dispute election(ex post selection of DR process)

As societies or parties develop and choose different forms of conflict resolution, whether through laws or private contract, some of these forms become "institutionalized" and therefore formalized. Both public agencies (courts, administrative agencies, and even legislatures) and private organizations (such as the American Arbitration Association (AAA), the International Center for Conflict Prevention and Resolution (CPR), and the Judicial Arbitration and Mediation Services (JAMS)) offer (or, in some cases, require) particular forms of dispute resolution from a dispute resolution "menu." Thus, whether through public or private action, it seems inevitable that dispute resolution processes become institutionalized, or some say, "co-opted."[10] Consider the pros and cons of institutionalization as you study ADR.

Although most of your law school courses have focused until now on litigation, historically U.S. legal practice has included a variety of dispute institutions, beginning in pre-colonial times. Some of the root values of modern dispute-resolution ideology in the U.S. are found in early colonial "communitarianism." Early forms of mediation and arbitration generally were typically limited to culturally or religiously homogenous groups with presumedly shared values and goals. Many of these communities had different processes for resolving disputes with persons outside of the community and sometimes these were non-litigation processes as well. For example, the merchants of early America used commercial arbitration to resolve their disputes with one another.[11]

Modern dispute resolution in the United States began in the mid-1970s, as a host of complaints were leveled at the traditional legal system. These complaints can be divided into two categories: *efficiency* or "*quantitatively*" based arguments (that the legal system was overloaded, slow, inefficient, and often prohibitively expensive); and more "*qualitatively*" based arguments (that litigation outcomes were inadequate to solve social, human, and legal problems, and that the processes failed to permit parties to fully participate). Thus, attempts to develop new forms of dispute resolution in the legal system have emphasized speed, low cost, increased party participation, simplification of procedures, and more tailored and creative solutions. As new forms of dispute resolution were developed both outside of the formal legal system and eventually within the formal justice system itself, older forms of dispute resolution were also "rediscovered" and readapted for new uses (community mediation, industry-specific arbitration). Together, these

10. Carrie Menkel-Meadow, Pursuing Settlement in an Adversary Culture: A Tale of Innovation Co-opted or the Law of ADR, 19 Fla. St. U. L. Rev. 1 (1991) (suggesting that processes that were intended to create flexibility now offer complex systems of rules, process, and decision).
11. Jerold Auerbach, Justice Without Law? Resolving Disputes Without Lawyers (1983).

efforts eventually led to the development of new professions, including mediators, arbitrators, early neutral evaluators, and facilitators.[12]

The "modern dispute resolution movement" is often formally dated to the 1976 Pound Conference on the Causes of Popular Dissatisfaction with the Administration of Justice, at which Professor Frank Sander of Harvard Law School delivered an address on the "Varieties of Dispute Processing." This speech was so influential that a number of court systems received funding to develop the "Multi-Door Courthouse" to attempt to enact Professor Sander's ideas and make them a functional reality.

Frank E.A. Sander, VARIETIES OF DISPUTE PROCESSING

70 F.R.D. 79, 111-118, 120, 124-132 (1976)

[A] . . . way of reducing the judicial caseload is to explore alternative ways of resolving disputes outside the courts, and it is to this topic that I wish to devote my primary attention. By and large we lawyers and law teachers have been far too single-minded when it comes to dispute resolution. Of course, as pointed out earlier, good lawyers have always tried to prevent disputes from coming about, but when that was not possible, we have tended to assume that the courts are the natural and obvious dispute resolvers. In point of fact there is a rich variety of different processes, which, I would submit, singly or in combination, may provide far more "effective" conflict resolution.

Let me turn now to the two questions with which I wish to concern myself:

1. What are the significant characteristics of various alternative dispute resolution mechanisms (such as adjudication by courts, arbitration, mediation, negotiation, and various blends of these and other devices)?
2. How can these characteristics be utilized so that, given the variety of disputes that presently arise, we can begin to develop some rational criteria for allocating various types of disputes to different dispute resolution processes?

One consequence of an answer to these questions is that we will have a better sense of what cases ought to be left in the courts for resolution, and which should be "processed" in some other way. But since this inquiry essentially addresses itself to developing the most effective method of handling disputes it should be noted in passing that one by-product may be not only to divert some matters now handled by the courts into other processes but also that it will make available those processes for grievances that are presently not being aired at all. We know very

12. See, e.g., Carrie Menkel-Meadow, The Lawyer as Consensus-Builder: Ethics for a New Practice, 70 Tenn. L. Rev. 63 (2002); Carrie Menkel-Meadow, The Lawyer as Problem Solver and Third-Party Neutral: Creativity and Non-Partisanship in Lawyering, 72 Temple L. Rev. 785 (1999).

little about why some individuals complain and others do not, or about the social and psychological costs of remaining silent. It is important to realize, however, that by establishing new dispute resolution mechanisms, or improving existing ones, we may be encouraging the ventilation of grievances that are now being suppressed. Whether that will be good (in terms of supplying a constructive outlet for suppressed anger and frustration) or whether it will simply waste scarce societal resources (by validating grievances that might otherwise have remained dormant) we do not know. The important thing to note is that there is a clear trade-off: the price of an improved scheme of dispute processing may well be a vast increase in the number of disputes being processed.

THE RANGE OF AVAILABLE ALTERNATIVES

There seems to be little doubt that we are increasingly making greater and greater demands on the courts to resolve disputes that used to be handled by other institutions of society. Much as the police have been looked to to "solve" racial, school and neighborly disputes, so, too, the courts have been expected to fill the void created by the decline of church and family. Not only has there been a waning of traditional dispute resolution mechanisms, but with the complexity of modern society, many new potential sources of controversy have emerged as a result of the immense growth of government at all levels, and the rising expectations that have been created.

Quite obviously, the courts cannot continue to respond effectively to these accelerating demands. It becomes essential therefore to examine other alternatives.

The chart reproduced [in Figure 1-2] attempts to depict a spectrum of some of the available processes arranged on a scale of decreasing external involvement.

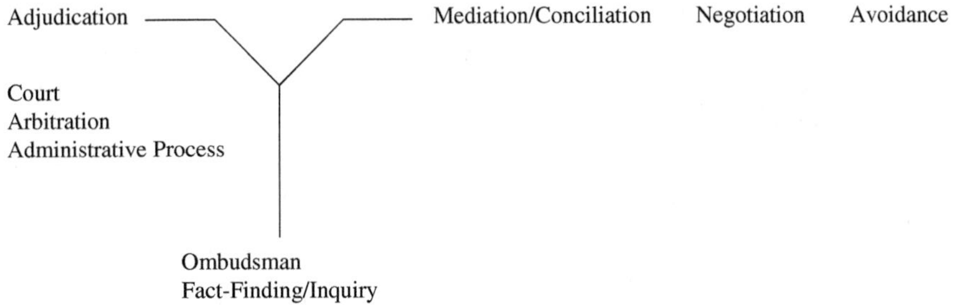

Figure 1-2
(Process Flow Chart)

At the extreme left is adjudication, the one process that so instinctively comes to the legal mind that I suspect if we asked a random group of law students how a particular dispute might be resolved, they would invariably say "file a complaint in the appropriate court." Professor Lon Fuller, one of the few scholars who has devoted attention to an analysis of the adjudicatory process, has defined adjudication as "a social process of decision which assures to the affected party a particular form of participation, that of presenting proofs and arguments for a decision in his favor." Although he places primary emphasis on process, I would like for present purposes to stress a number of other aspects—the use of a third party with coercive power, the usually "win or lose" nature of the decision, and the tendency of the decision to focus narrowly on the underlying relationship between the parties. Although mediation or conciliation also involves the use of a third-party facilitation (and is distinguished in that regard from pure negotiation), a mediator or conciliator usually has no coercive power and the process in which he engages also differs from adjudication in the other two respects mentioned.

Of course quite a variety of procedures fit under the label of adjudication. Aside from the familiar judicial model, there is arbitration, and the administrative process. Even within any one of these, there are significant variations. Obviously there are substantial differences between the Small Claims Court and the Supreme Court. Within arbitration, too, although the version used in labor relations is generally very similar to a judicial proceeding in that there is a written opinion and an attempt to rationalize the result by reference to general principles, in some forms of commercial arbitration the judgment resembles a Solomonic pronouncement, and written opinions are often not utilized. Another significant variant is whether the parties have any choice in selecting the adjudicator, as they typically do in arbitration. Usually a decision rendered by a person in whose selection the parties have played some part will, all things being equal, be less subject to later criticism by the parties.

There are important distinctions, too, concerning the way in which the case came to arbitration. There may be a statute (as in New York and Pennsylvania) requiring certain types of cases to be initially submitted to arbitration (so-called compulsory arbitration). More commonly arbitration is stipulated as the exclusive dispute resolution mechanism in a contract entered into by the parties (as is true of the typical collective bargaining agreement and some modern medical care agreements). In this situation the substantive legal rules are usually also set forth in the parties' agreement, thus giving the parties control not only over the process and the adjudicator but also over the governing principles.

As is noted on the chart, if we focus on the indicated distinctions between adjudication and mediation, there are a number of familiar hybrid processes. An inquiry, for example, in many respects resembles the typical adjudication, but the inquiring officer (or fact finder as he is sometimes called) normally has no coercive power; indeed, according to Professor Fuller's definition, many inquiries would not be adjudication at all since the parties have no right to any agreed-upon form of presentation and participation.

But a fact finding proceeding may be a potent tool for inducing settlement. Particularly if the fact finder commands the respect of the parties, his independent appraisal of their respective positions will often be difficult to reject. This is especially true of the Ombudsman who normally derives his power solely from the force of his position. These considerations have particular applicability where there is a disparity of bargaining power between the disputants (e.g., citizen and government, consumer and manufacturer, student and university). Although there may often be a reluctance in these situations to give a third person power to render a binding decision, the weaker party may often accomplish the same result through the use of a skilled fact finder.

There are of course a number of other dispute resolution mechanisms which one might consider. Most of these (e.g., voting, coin tossing, self-help) are not of central concern here because of their limited utility or acceptability. But one other mechanism deserves brief mention. Professor William Felstiner recently pointed out that in a "technologically complex rich society" avoidance becomes an increasingly common form of handling controversy. He describes avoidance as "withdrawal from or contraction of the dispute-producing relationship" (e.g., a child leaving home, a tenant moving to another apartment, or a businessman terminating a commercial relationship). He contends that such conduct is far more tolerable in modern society than in a "technologically simple poor society" because in the former setting the disputing individuals are far less interdependent. But, as was pointed out in a cogent response by Professors Danzig and Lowy, there are heavy personal and societal costs for such a method of handling conflicts, and this strongly argues for the development of some effective alternative mechanism. Moreover, even if we disregarded altogether the disputes that are presently being handled by avoidance—clearly an undesirable approach for the reasons indicated—we must still come to grips with the rising number of cases that do presently come to court and see whether more effective ways of resolving some of these disputes can be developed. . . .

CRITERIA

Let us now look at some criteria that may help us to determine how particular types of disputes might best be resolved:

1. Nature of Dispute

Lon Fuller has written at some length about "polycentric" problems that are not well suited to an adjudicatory approach since they are not amenable to an all-or-nothing solution. He cites the example of a testator who leaves a collection of paintings in equal parts to two museums. Obviously here a negotiated or mediated solution that seeks to accommodate the desires of the two museums is far better than any externally imposed solution. Similar considerations may apply to other allocational tasks where no clear guidelines are provided.

At the other extreme is a highly repetitive and routinized task involving application of established principles to a large number of individual cases. Here adjudication may be appropriate, but in a form more efficient than litigation (e.g., an administrative agency). Particularly once the courts have established the basic principles in such areas, a speedier and less cumbersome procedure than litigation should be utilized.

2. Relationship Between Disputants

A different situation is presented when disputes arise between individuals who are in a long-term relationship than is the case with respect to an isolated dispute.

In the former situation, there is more potential for having the parties, at least initially, seek to work out their own solution, for such a solution is likely to be far more acceptable (and hence durable). Thus negotiation, or if necessary, mediation, appears to be a preferable approach in the first instance. Another advantage of such an approach is that it facilitates a probing of conflicts in the underlying relationship, rather than simply dealing with each surface symptom as an isolated event.

3. Amount in Dispute

Although, generally speaking, we have acted, to date, in a fairly hit-or-miss fashion in determining what problems should be resolved by a particular dispute resolution mechanism, amount in controversy has been an item consistently looked to to determine the amount of process that is "due." The Small Claims Court movement has taken as its premise that small cases are simple cases, and that therefore a pared-down judicial procedure was what was called for. Next to the juvenile court, there has probably been no legal institution that was more ballyhooed as a great legal innovation. Yet the evidence now seems overwhelming that the Small Claims Court has failed its original purpose; that the individuals for whom it was designed have turned out to be its victims. Small wonder when one considers the lack of rational connection between amount in controversy and appropriate process. Quite obviously a small case may be complex, just as a large case may be simple. The need, according to a persuasive recent study, is for a preliminary investigative-conciliational stage (which could well be administered by a lay individual or paraprofessional) with ultimate recourse to the court. This individual could readily screen out those cases which need not take a court's time (e.g., where there is no dispute about liability but the defendant has no funds), and preserve the adjudicatory process for those cases where the issues have been properly joined and there is a genuine dispute of fact or law. Obviously such a screening mechanism is not limited in its utility to the Small Claims Court.

4. Cost

There is a dearth of reliable data comparing the costs of different dispute resolution processes. Undoubtedly this is due in part to the difficulty of determining what are the appropriate ingredients of such a computation. It may be relatively easy to determine the costs of an ad hoc arbitration though even there one must deal with such intangibles as the costs connected with the selection of the arbitrator(s). But determining the comparable cost of a court proceeding would appear to pose very difficult issues of cost accounting. Even more difficult to calculate are the intangible "costs" of inadequate (in the sense of incomplete and unsatisfactory) dispute resolution. Still, until better data become available, one can probably proceed safely on the assumption that costs rise as procedural formalities increase.

The lack of adequate cost data is particularly unfortunate with respect to essentially comparable processes, such as litigation and arbitration. Assuming for the moment that arbitration would produce results as acceptable as litigation—a premise that is even more difficult to verify—would cost considerations justify the transfer (at least in the first instance) of entire categories of civil litigation to arbitration, as has been done in some jurisdictions for cases involving less than a set amount of money? One difficulty in this connection is that we have always considered access to the courts as an essential right of citizenship for which no significant charge should be imposed, while the parties generally bear the cost of arbitration. Thus although I believe, on the basis of my own arbitration experience, that process is, by and large, as effective as and cheaper than litigation, lawyers tend not to make extensive use of it (outside of special areas such as labor and commercial law), in part because it is always cheaper for the clients to have society rather than the litigants pay the judges. Perhaps if arbitration is to be made compulsory in certain types of cases because we believe it to be more efficient, then it should follow that society should assume the costs, unless that would defeat the goal of using costs to discourage appeals. . . .

5. Speed

The deficiency of sophisticated data concerning the costs of different dispute resolution processes also extends to the factor of speed. Although it is generally assumed—rightly, I believe—that arbitration is speedier than litigation, I am not aware of any studies that have reached such a conclusion on the basis of a controlled experiment that seeks to take account of such factors as the possibly differing complexity of the two classes of cases, the greater diversity of "judges" in the arbitration group, and the possibly greater cooperation of the litigants in the arbitration setting.

Now that you have had some exposure to the animating theories and history implicated in the use of various forms of dispute resolution, we look at the different forms these processes can take and where they can be used. The following excerpt offers a glossary of basic dispute resolution processes. We will study them all in greater detail in the chapters that follow.

Center for Public Resources, THE ABC'S OF ADR: A DISPUTE RESOLUTION GLOSSARY

13 (11) Alternatives (to the High Cost of Litigation) 1 (1995)

Experts know that ADR encompasses a wide range of practices for managing and quickly resolving disputes at modest cost and with minimal adverse impact on commercial relationships. These processes, marked by confidentiality when desired, significantly broaden dispute resolution options beyond litigation or traditional unassisted negotiation.

Some ADR procedures, such as binding arbitration and private judging, are similar to expedited litigation in that they involve a third-party decision-maker with authority to impose a resolution if the parties so desire. Other procedures, such as mediation and the minitrial, are collaborative: a neutral third party helps a group of individuals or entities with divergent views to reach a goal or complete a task to their mutual satisfaction.

Arbitration, mediation and the minitrial tend to be the mechanisms most often used and, for many people, are synonymous with the term, "ADR." But to respond to specific needs, parties often craft hybrid procedures that combine elements of one or more dispute resolution methods.

The following glossary is designed to help parties communicate about this rapidly changing field. Definitions are not standardized, but flexible and creative like ADR itself. And with all aspects of ADR it is most important not that the parties use exactly the same term, but that they understand each other.

We have divided the glossary into private and court-related ADR processes.

PRIVATE ADR PROCESSES

Arbitration The most traditional form of private dispute resolution. It can be "administered" (managed) by a variety of private organizations, or "non-administered" and managed solely by the parties. It can be entered into by agreement at the time of the dispute, or prescribed in pre-dispute clauses contained in the parties' underlying business agreement. Arbitration can take any of the following forms:

Binding Arbitration A private adversarial process in which the disputing parties choose a neutral person or a panel of three neutrals to hear their dispute and to render a final and binding decision or award. The process is less formal than litigation; the parties can craft their own procedures and determine if any formal rules of evidence will apply. Unless there has been fraud or some other defect in the arbitration procedure, binding arbitration awards typically are enforceable by courts and not subject to appellate review.

Non-Binding Arbitration This process works the same way as binding arbitration except that the neutral's decision is advisory only. The parties may agree in advance to use the advisory decision as a tool in resolving their dispute through negotiation or other means.

"Baseball" or "Final-Offer" Arbitration In this process, used increasingly in commercial disputes, each party submits a proposed monetary award to the arbitrator. At the conclusion of the hearing, the arbitrator chooses one award without modification. This approach imposes limits on the arbitrator's discretion and gives each party an incentive to offer a reasonable proposal in the hope that it will be accepted by the decision-maker. . . .

"Bounded" or "High-Low" Arbitration The parties agree privately without informing the arbitrator that the arbitrator's final award will be adjusted to a bounded range. Example: P wants $200,000. D is willing to pay $70,000. Their high-low agreement would provide that if the award is below $70,000, D will pay at least $70,000; if the award exceeds $200,000, the payment will be reduced to

$200,000. If the award is within the range the parties are bound by the figure in the award. . . .

Fact-Finding A process by which the facts relevant to a controversy are determined. Fact-finding is a component of other ADR procedures and may take a number of forms.

In neutral *fact-finding,* the parties appoint a neutral third party to perform the function and typically determine in advance whether the results of the fact-finding will be conclusive or advisory only.

With expert *fact-finding,* the parties privately employ neutrals to render expert opinions that are conclusive or non-binding on technical, scientific or legal questions. In the latter, a former judge is often employed.

Federal Rules of Evidence 706 gives courts the option of appointing *neutral expert fact-finders.* And while the procedure was rarely used in the past, courts increasingly find it an effective approach in cases that require special technical expertise, such as disputes over high-technology questions. The neutral expert can be called as a witness subject to cross-examination.

In *joint fact-finding*, the parties designate representatives to work together to develop responses to factual questions.

Mediation A voluntary and informal process in which the disputing parties select a neutral third-party to assist them in reaching a negotiated settlement. Parties can employ mediation as a result of a contract provision by private agreement made when disputes arise, or as part of a court-annexed program that diverts cases to mediation. Unlike a judge or arbitrator, a mediator has no power to impose a solution on the parties. Rather, mediators assist parties in shaping solutions to meet their interests and objectives. The mediator's role and the mediation process can take various forms, depending on the nature of the dispute and the approach of the mediator. The mediator can assist parties to communicate effectively; can identify and narrow issues; crystallize each side's underlying interests and concerns; carry messages between the parties; explore bases for agreement and the consequences of not settling; and develop a cooperative problem-solving approach. By learning the confidential concerns and positions of all parties, the mediator often can identify options beyond their perceptions. The process is sometimes referred to as "facilitation" to structure participation in the mediation process, or "conciliation" in the international arena.

The mediator's role can take various forms. Some mediators, who favor a "facilitative" style, encourage parties to generate their own settlement options, and will not suggest settlement terms. At the other end of the spectrum are "evaluative" mediators, who will propose settlement options and try to persuade parties to make concessions.

To guide negotiations in major commercial disputes, parties sometimes ask the mediator to assume an evaluative role. The mediator might assess the merits of claims or defenses, liability or damages, or predict the likely outcome of the case in court. Generally, mediators need substantive law background or expertise to make sound assessments.

Med-Arb A short-hand reference to the procedure mediation-arbitration. In med-arb, the parties agree to mediate with the understanding that any issues not settled through the mediation will be resolved by arbitration asking the same mediator to act both as mediator and arbitrator. However, that choice may have a chilling effect on full participation in the mediation portion. A party might not believe that the arbitrator will be able to discount unfavorable information learned in mediation when making the arbitration decision. . . .

Multi-Step ADR Parties may agree, either when a specific dispute arises, or earlier in a contract clause between business venturers, to engage in a progressive series of dispute resolution procedures. One step typically is some form of negotiation, preferably face-to-face between the parties. If unsuccessful, a second tier of negotiation between higher levels of executives may resolve the matter. The next step may be mediation or another facilitated settlement effort. If no resolution has been reached at any of the earlier stages, the agreement can provide for a binding resolution—through arbitration, private adjudication, or litigation.

One form of multi-step ADR is the *wise man* procedure, typically used when problems arise in long-term partnerships such as those in the oil and gas industry. Sometimes called "progressive negotiation" or "mutual escalation," this procedure refers matters first to a partnership committee which oversees the day-to-day operations of the project. If the problem cannot be resolved at that level, the wise-man option—the next ADR step—is employed.

The wise men (or women) are respected senior executives of each company who are uninvolved in the project. These officials are given a fairly short time frame (sometimes just 30 days) to investigate the dispute. If that fails, the matter goes to a third step, usually binding arbitration. While pioneered in the oil industry, the wise man approach could also be useful in the high-technology field and other areas involving close and continuing business relationships.

Negotiated Rule-Making Also known as regulatory negotiation, this ADR method is an alternative to the traditional approach of U.S. government agencies to issue regulations after a lengthy notice and comment period. In reg-neg, as it is called, agency officials and affected private parties meet under the guidance of a neutral facilitator to engage in joint negotiation and drafting of the rule. The public is then asked to comment on the resulting, proposed rule. By encouraging participation by interested stakeholders, the process makes use of private parties' perspectives and expertise, and can help avoid subsequent litigation over the resulting rule.

Ombudsperson An organizational dispute resolution tool. The ombudsperson is appointed by an institution to investigate complaints within the institution and either prevent disputes or facilitate their resolution. The ombudsperson may use various ADR mechanisms such as fact-finding or mediation in the process of resolving disputes brought to his or her attention.

Partnering Typically used as a dispute-prevention method for large construction projects, this method is capable of being transposed in other settings, particularly in joint ventures. Before the work starts, parties to the project generally assemble for a several-day retreat away from their organizations. With the help of a third-party neutral, they get to know each other, discuss some of the likely rough spots in the project and even settle on a process to resolve misunderstandings and disputes as the project progresses.

Pre-Dispute ADR Contract Clause A clause included in the parties' business agreement to specify a method for resolving disputes that may arise under that agreement. It may refer to one or more ADR techniques, even naming the third party that will serve as an arbitrator or mediator in the case. Pre-dispute agreements requiring arbitration of consumer disputes, or entered into as a condition of employment, have generated substantial backlash lately from people who argue that these clauses are adhesion contracts.

Two-Track Approach Involves use of ADR processes or traditional settlement negotiations in conjunction with litigation. Representatives of the disputing parties who are not involved in the litigation are used to conduct the settlement negotiations or ADR procedure. The negotiation or ADR efforts may proceed concurrently with litigation, or during an agreed-upon cessation of litigation. This approach is particularly useful in cases when it may not be feasible to abandon litigation while the parties explore settlement possibilities; or as a practical matter, the specter of litigation must be present in order for the opposing party to consider or agree to an alternative mechanism. It also is useful when the litigation has become acrimonious, or when a suggestion of settlement would be construed as a sign of weakness.

COURT ADR PROCESSES

Court-Annexed Mediation In mediation, a neutral third party—the mediator—facilitates negotiations among the parties to help them settle. The mediation session is confidential and informal. Disputants clarify their understanding of underlying interests and concerns, probe the strengths and weaknesses of legal positions, explore the consequences of not settling, and generate settlement options. . . . A hallmark of mediation is its capacity to help parties expand traditional settlement discussions and broaden resolution options, often by going beyond the legal issues in controversy.

Mediation works much the same in courts and in private settings, with a few important differences. A court mediation program may be based in the court, or may involve referral by the court to outside ADR programs run by bar associations, nonprofit groups, other local courts, or private ADR providers. Some courts require litigants to use mediation in what are known as mandatory mediation programs. The purpose of the mediation session is unchanged whether litigants enter the program voluntarily, or by court mandate. The court mediator may be a lawyer trained in mediation and compensated by the parties, or serve as a volunteer. Judges, magistrate judges, or court ADR professionals also serve as mediators in some court programs. . . .

Early Neutral Evaluation Like mediation, ENE is applicable to many types of civil cases, including complex disputes. In ENE, a neutral evaluator—a private attorney expert in the substance of the dispute—holds a several- hour confidential session with parties and counsel early in the litigation to hear both sides of the case. Afterwards, the evaluator identifies strengths and weaknesses of the parties' positions, flags areas of agreement and disputes, and issues a non-binding assessment of the merits of the case. . . .

Originally designed to make both case management and settlement more efficient, ENE has evolved into a pure settlement device in some courts. Used this way, ENE resembles evaluative mediation, in which the mediator uses case evaluation as a settlement tool.

Court-Annexed Arbitration An adjudicatory dispute resolution process in which one or more arbitrators issue a non-binding judgment on the merits, after an expedited, adversarial hearing. The arbitrator's decision addresses only the disputed legal issues and applies legal standards. Either party may reject the non-binding ruling and proceed to trial.

Court-annexed arbitration is used mainly in small- and moderate-sized tort and contract cases when litigation costs are often disproportionate to the amounts at stake. . . . Once the premier court ADR process, it has lost popularity in recent years. Most court ADR development focuses on mediation.

Summary Jury Trial The summary jury trial is a non-binding ADR process used to promote settlement in ready cases headed for protracted jury trials. Usually, a judge or magistrate judge presides over the SJT; occasionally, a neutral attorney conducts the process. Part or all of a complex dispute may be submitted to a summary jury trial. After an abbreviated hearing in which counsel presents evidence in summary form, the jury renders a verdict. Non-binding, it becomes the basis for subsequent settlement negotiations. If the parties do not reach a settlement, the case proceeds to trial. Because they are costly, SJTs are used relatively rarely. Typically, the SJT is reserved for large cases when settlement efforts have failed and litigants differ significantly about jury outcome.

Appellate ADR Mediation programs have become increasingly popular among the nation's appeals courts. . . .[13]

In most programs, staff attorneys or outside lawyers conduct mandatory, preargument conferences in those cases that seem most likely to settle. Some appellate programs are geared exclusively toward settlement, while other programs also address case management and procedural issues.

Judge-Hosted Settlement Conferences The most common form of ADR used in federal and state courts is the settlement conference presided over by a judge or magistrate judge. Almost all of the 94 federal district courts use judicial settlement

13. All of the federal circuit courts of appeals now have appellate mediation programs, almost all of them using full-time staff mediators.

conferences routinely, and now, one third of the courts assign this role almost exclusively to magistrate judges.

The classic role of the settlement judge is to articulate judgments about the merits of the case and to facilitate the trading of settlement offers. Some settlement judges and magistrate judges also use mediation techniques and the settlement conference to improve communication among the parties, probe barriers to settlement, and assist in formulating resolutions. In some courts, a special judge or magistrate judge is designated as settlement judge. In others, the assigned judge (or another judicial officer who will not hear the case) hosts settlement conferences at various points during the litigation, often directly before trial.

Court Minitrial The minitrial is a flexible, non-binding settlement process primarily used out of court. During the past decade, some federal district judges have used their own version of the minitrial. Like the summary jury trial the court minitrial is a relatively elaborate ADR method generally reserved for large disputes.

In a typical court minitrial, each side presents a shortened form of its best case to settlement-authorized client representatives—usually senior executives. The hearing is informal, with no witnesses and a relaxation of the rules of evidence and procedure. A judge, magistrate judge or non-judicial neutral presides over the one- or two-day hearing. Following the hearing, the client representatives meet, with or without the neutral advisor, to negotiate a settlement. At the parties' request, the neutral advisor may assist the settlement discussions by acting as a facilitator or by issuing an advisory opinion. If the talks fail, the parties proceed to trial.

Multidoor Courthouse or Multi-Option ADR This term describes courts that offer an array of dispute resolution options or screen cases and then channel them to particular ADR methods. Some multidoor courthouses refer all cases of certain types to particular ADR programs, while others offer litigants a menu of options in each case. Multidoor courthouses have been established in state courts in New Jersey, Texas, Massachusetts, and the District of Columbia. On the federal level, courts in the Western District of Missouri, the Northern District of California, the District of Rhode Island, and others now have multi-option ADR.

Settlement Week In a typical settlement week, a court suspends normal trial activity and, aided by bar groups and volunteer lawyers, devotes itself to the mediation of long-pending civil cases. Mediation is the mainstay ADR method in a typical settlement week. . . .

Private Judging Private judging is a general term used to describe a private or court-related process in which disputing parties empower a private individual to hear and decide their case. The procedure may be exclusively a matter of contract between the parties or may be undertaken in connection with an authorizing statute. When authorized by statute, the process is sometimes referred to by the colloquial term, "Rent-a-Judge."

The remainder of this book examines these and other processes in detail. But it is important to emphasize from the outset that no list of dispute resolution processes is ever complete. Creative disputants and their attorneys will always think of new processes and new variations on existing processes. At the same time, it is also important to remember that parties may not have a "choice" about what process is best for them. Increasingly courts or legislatures may require them to use a particular form of dispute resolution. It is also possible that legislatures or courts may proscribe the use of certain dispute resolution procedures in particular contexts.

There are obviously many jurisprudential, policy, and practical issues to be explored here, from the perspective of both future policy makers and future attorneys. Thus, the final section of this introduction turns to some fundamental questions regarding where these alternative procedural approaches fit in a system of justice.

D. ANIMATING VALUES FOR CONFLICT AND DISPUTE RESOLUTION: OF PEACE AND JUSTICE

As you have now seen, many arguments, claims, and justifications can be made for the use of a wide variety of dispute processes in addition to litigation. At the same time, it is important to consider critiques. Social and legal change do not come easily. While the various procedural developments documented or urged by Professor Sander have occurred, criticisms of the new forms of dispute resolution have also emerged. The critics have challenged the "informalism," "de-legalization," "coercion," "privatization," and perceived unfairness of some of these new process innovations. You will explore these critiques more fully throughout this book, but below we present several of the classic critiques, including Owen Fiss's Against Settlement (1983). Although more flexible processes and more tailored solutions can seem to be more fair or just to particular disputants, critics claim that privatization of dispute resolution robs us of the ability to frame precedents from more public cases and thereby serve broader justice needs.

The tensions between formal legal systems and the alternatives to them likely will continue, since each type of system serves different but important goals.[14] Indeed, the debate between formal and informal procedures can be analogized to the age-old debate in jurisprudence about the relative value of clear, but often, rigid "rules," versus the need for more tailored and nuanced judgment, "standards" and legal "discretion." Some, including the authors of this book, are comfortable with this "creative" tension between formal and informal systems, believing that new developments in the alternatives that are responsive to critiques of the formal legal system may result in reforms in the formal justice system as well. Indeed, some have suggested that from a market perspective, the development of alternatives to the formal legal system provides an opportunity for "competition" in

14. Jean R. Sternlight, ADR Is Here: Preliminary Reflections on Where It Fits in a System of Justice, 3 Nevada L.J. 289 (2003).

the provision of dispute resolution services.[15] Others, however, are more fearful that growth of informal processes will lead to a degradation of traditional legal structures and processes.[16] In between formal and informal systems are now processes called "semi-formal" (like mediation and problem solving processes attached to courts, or highly formalized processes with many rules, outside of courts, like international arbitration).[17] This debate can be seen as another version of the "Fullerian" question as to whether it is important to preserve as sacrosanct the moral integrity of particular processes. This debate also implicates one of the major issues of conflict and dispute resolution: For whom is the dispute process intended? The parties in conflict? Or the larger society that may desire public pronouncements of norms and enforcement of legal "peace"? Carrie Menkel-Meadow and Owen Fiss address this issue below.

Carrie Menkel-Meadow, WHOSE DISPUTE IS IT ANYWAY? A PHILOSOPHICAL AND DEMOCRATIC DEFENSE OF SETTLEMENT (IN SOME CASES)

83 Geo. L.J. 2663-2665, 2669-2670 (1995)

In the last decade or so, a polarized debate about how disputes should be resolved has demonstrated to me once again the difficulties of simplistic and adversarial arguments. . . . David Luban and Jules Coleman, among other philosophers, have criticized the moral value of the compromises that are thought to constitute legal settlements. On the other side, vigorous proponents of alternative dispute resolution, including negotiation, mediation, arbitration and various hybrids of these forms of preadjudication settlement, criticize the economic and emotional waste of adversarial processes and the cost, inefficiency, and political difficulties of adjudication, as well as its draconian unfairness in some cases. . . . For me, the question is not "for or against" settlement (since settlement has become the "norm" for our system), but *when, how and under what circumstances* should cases be settled? When do our legal system, our citizenry, and the parties in particular disputes need formal adjudication, and when are their respective interests served by settlement, *whether public or private*?. . .

15. Bryant Garth, Privatization and the New Market for Disputes: A Framework for Analysis and a Preliminary Assessment, 12 Stud. L. Poly. & Socy. 367 (1992).
16. Deborah R. Hensler, Suppose It's Not True: Challenging Mediation Ideology, 2002 J. Disp. Resol. 81 (2002); Judith Resnik, Managerial Judges, 96 Harv. L. Rev. 76 (1982); Judith Resnik, Many Doors? Closing Doors? Alternative Dispute Resolution and Adjudication, 10 Ohio St. J. on Disp. Resol. 211 (1995).
17. Carrie Menkel-Meadow, Regulation ofDispute Resolution in the United States ofAmerica: From the Formal to the Informal to the Semi-Formal, in Regulating Dispute Resolution: ADR and Access to Justice at the Crossroads (F. Steffek, H, Unberath, H. Genn, R. Greger and C. Menkel-Meadow, eds., 2013).

Those who criticize settlement suffer from what I have called, in other contexts, "*litigation romanticism,*" with empirically unverified assumptions about what courts can and will do. More important, those who privilege adjudication focus almost exclusively on structural and institutional values and often give short shrift to those who are actually involved in the litigation. I fear, but I am not sure, that this debate can be reduced to those who care more about the people actually engaged in disputes versus those who care more about institutional and structural arrangements. I prefer to think that we need both adjudication and settlement. . . . Settlement can be justified on its own moral grounds—there are important values, consistent with the fundamental values of our legal and political systems that support the legitimacy of settlements of some, if not most, legal disputes. These values include consent, participation, empowerment, dignity, respect, empathy and emotional catharsis, privacy, efficiency, quality solutions, equity, access and, yes, even justice.

Though some have argued that compromise itself can be morally justified, I . . . argue here as well that compromise is not always necessary for settlement and that in fact, some settlements, by not requiring compromise, may produce better solutions than litigation. . . .

To summarize, it seems to me that the key questions implicated in the ongoing debate about settlement vs. adjudication are:

1. In a party-initiated legal system, when is it legitimate for the parties to settle their disputes themselves, or with what assistance from a court in which they have sought some legal-system support or service?
2. When is "consent" to settlement legitimate and "real," and by what standards should we (courts and academic critics) judge and permit such consent?
3. When, in a party-initiated legal system, should party consent be "trumped" by some other values—in other words, when should public, institutional, and structural needs and values override parties' desire to settle or courts' incentives to promote settlement?

In short, when is the need for "public adjudication . . . or public settlement" more important (to whom?) than what the parties may themselves desire?

❖ *Owen M. Fiss,* AGAINST SETTLEMENT

93 Yale L.J. 1073, 1075-1078, 1082-1083, 1085-1086, 1087-1088, 1089-1090 (1984)

The advocates of ADR. . . exalt the idea of settlement more generally because they view adjudication as a process to resolve disputes. They act as though courts arose to resolve quarrels between neighbors who had reached an impasse and turned to a stranger for help. Courts are seen as an institutionalization of the stranger and adjudication is viewed as the process by which the stranger exercises power. The very fact that the neighbors have turned to someone else to resolve their dispute signifies a breakdown in their social relations; the advocates of ADR acknowledge this, but nonetheless hope that the neighbors will be able to reach agreement before the stranger renders judgment. Settlement is that agreement. It is a truce more than a true reconciliation, but it seems preferable to judgment because it rests on the consent of both parties and avoids the cost of a lengthy trial.

In my view, however, this account of adjudication and the case for settlement rest on questionable premises. I do not believe that settlement as a generic practice is preferable to judgment or should be institutionalized on a wholesale and indiscriminate basis. It should be treated instead as a highly problematic technique for streamlining dockets. Settlement is for me the civil analogue of plea-bargaining: Consent is often coerced; the bargain may be struck by someone without authority; the absence of a trial and judgment renders subsequent judicial involvement troublesome; and although dockets are trimmed, justice may not be done. Like plea-bargaining, settlement is a capitulation to the conditions of mass society and should be neither encouraged nor praised.

THE IMBALANCE OF POWER

By viewing the lawsuit as a quarrel between two neighbors, the dispute-resolution story that underlies ADR implicitly asks us to assume a rough equality between the contending parties. It treats settlement as the anticipation of the outcome of trial and assumes that the terms of settlement are simply a product of the parties' predictions of that outcome. In truth, however, settlement is also a function of the resources available to each party to finance the litigation, and those resources are frequently distributed unequally. Many lawsuits do not involve a property dispute between two neighbors, or between AT&T and the government (to update the story), but rather concern a struggle between a member of a racial minority and a municipal police department over alleged brutality, or a claim by a worker against a large corporation over work-related injuries. In these cases, the distribution of financial resources, or the ability of one party to pass along its costs, will invariably infect the bargaining process, and the settlement will be at odds with a conception of justice that seeks to make the wealth of the parties irrelevant.

The disparities in resources between the parties can influence the settlement in three ways. First, the poorer party may be less able to amass and analyze the information needed to predict the outcome of the litigation, and thus be disadvantaged in the bargaining process. Second, he may need the damages he seeks immediately and thus be induced to settle as a way of accelerating payment, even though he realizes he would get less now than he might if he awaited judgment. All plaintiffs want their damages immediately, but an indigent plaintiff may be exploited by a rich defendant because his need is so great that the defendant can force him to accept a sum that is less than the ordinary present value of the judgment. Third, the poorer party might be forced to settle because he does not have the resources to finance the litigation, to cover either his own projected expenses, such as his lawyer's time, or the expenses his opponent can impose through the manipulation or procedural mechanisms such as discovery. It might seem that settlement benefits the plaintiff by allowing him to avoid the costs of litigation, but this is not so. The defendant can anticipate the plaintiff's costs if the case were to be tried fully and decrease his offer by that amount. The indigent plaintiff is a victim of the costs of litigation even if he settles. . . .

Of course, imbalances of power can distort judgment as well: Resources influence the quality of presentation, which in turn has an important bearing on who wins and the terms of victory. We count, however, on the guiding presence of the judge, who can employ a number of measures to lessen the impact of distributional inequalities. He can, for example, supplement the parties' presentations by asking questions, calling his own witnesses, and inviting other persons and institutions to participate as amici. These measures are likely to make only a small contribution toward moderating the influence of distributional inequalities, but should not be ignored for that reason. Not even these small steps are possible with settlement. There is, moreover, a critical difference between a process like settlement, which is based on bargaining and accepts inequalities of wealth as an integral and legitimate component of the process, and a process like judgment, which knowingly struggles against those inequalities. Judgment aspires to an autonomy from distributional inequalities, and it gathers much of its appeal from this aspiration. . . .

JUSTICE RATHER THAN PEACE

The dispute-resolution story makes settlement appear as a perfect substitute for judgment, as we just saw, by trivializing the remedial dimensions of a lawsuit, and also by reducing the social function of the lawsuit to one of resolving private disputes. In that story, settlement appears to achieve exactly the same purpose as judgment—peace between the parties—but at considerably less expense to society. The two quarreling neighbors turn to a court in order to resolve their dispute, and society makes courts available because it wants to aid in the achievement of their private ends or to secure the peace.

In my view, however, the purpose of adjudication should be understood in broader terms. Adjudication uses public resources, and employs not strangers chosen by the parties but public officials chosen by a process in which the public participates. These officials, like members of the legislative and executive branches, possess a power that has been defined and conferred by public law, not by private agreement. Their job is not to maximize the ends of private parties, nor simply to secure the peace, but to explicate and give force to the values embodied in authoritative texts such as the Constitution and statutes: to interpret those values and to bring reality into accord with them. This duty is not discharged when the parties settle. . . .

THE REAL DIVIDE

Someone like [former Harvard University President Derek] Bok sees adjudication in essentially private terms: The purpose of lawsuits and the civil courts is to resolve disputes, and the amount of litigation we encounter is evidence of the needlessly combative and quarrelsome character of Americans. Or as Bok put it, using a more diplomatic idiom: "At bottom, ours is a society built on individualism, competition, and success." I, on the other hand, see adjudication in more public terms: Civil litigation is an institutional arrangement for using state power to bring a recalcitrant reality closer to our chosen ideals. We turn to the courts because we need to, not because of some quirk in our personalities. We train our students in the tougher arts so that they may help secure all that the law promises, not because we want them to become gladiators or because we take a special pleasure in combat.

To conceive of the civil lawsuit in public terms as America does might be unique. I am willing to assume that no other country . . . has a case like *Brown v. Board of Education* in which the judicial power is used to eradicate the caste structure. I am willing to assume that no other country conceives of law and uses law in quite the way we do. But this should be a source of pride rather than shame. What is unique is not the problem that we live short of our ideals, but that we alone among the nations of the world seem willing to do something about it. Adjudication American-style is not a reflection of our combativeness but rather a tribute to our inventiveness and perhaps even more to our commitment.

In response to Fiss's article, Professor Michael Moffitt contrasts the views of "litigation romanticists" (like Fiss) and "ADR evangelists." He concludes that a more nuanced celebration and evaluation of both litigation and settlement is in order.

❖ *Michael Moffitt,* THREE THINGS TO BE AGAINST ("SETTLEMENT" NOT INCLUDED)

78 Fordham L. Rev. 1203, 1203-1205, 1223-1224, 1245 (2009)

Litigation and settlement do not merely co-exist. Instead, litigation and settlement have come to depend on each other in order to function properly. . . . The rules of civil procedure contemplate, and even encourage, settlement behavior at virtually every stage of litigation. Similarly, the prospect of litigation today shapes both settlement outcomes and settlement behaviors. I am not convinced, therefore, that it is possible to be wholly "for" one and "against" the other, given these intersections. . . .

I cautiously suggest that observers from all camps might endorse at least three of the fundamental principles Owen Fiss highlighted in his article. Ideal processes (1) deal appropriately with power imbalances, (2) minimize agency costs, and (3) ensure meaningful access to courts. Processes that consistently fail to protect these ideals deserve robust opposition. . . .

[For example,] power imbalances create problems in the real world. The on-the-ground practices of litigation and of settlement present pictures of sloppy, imperfect efforts at overcoming the worst aspects of power imbalances. We might reasonably compare the ideals of each process—ideals that largely assume away the persistence of power imbalances. We might also compare the sloppy reality of litigation with the sloppy reality of settlement.

The one thing we cannot responsibly do is compare the idealized vision of one practice against the sloppy reality of the other. Proponents of litigation must not present the question as, "Which is better, (a) having a judge protect the powerless litigant through the promotion of public values as articulated by the law, or (b) sending that powerless litigant alone into the hallway to compromise away her rights?" Proponents of settlement must not present the question as, "Which is better, (a) employing fully inclusive deliberative discourse to reach an elegant, fair, and creative resolution, or (b) sending disputants into a formalistic process navigable only by the rich?" The idealized visions of both processes are beautiful. The practices of both processes are flawed. If power imbalances skew one process, they skew the other, even if perhaps they do so in different ways. . . .

We should celebrate the beauty in each process's internal narrative of justice, of truth, of efficiency, of predictability, and even of morality. Proponents of settlement believe not merely in settlement's efficiency, but also in its ability to bring justice, to discover truth(s), and to provide stability. Proponents of litigation embrace the same values. We might usefully engage the empirical question of whether one process or the other does a better job of promoting each of these values. Both settlement and litigation fail on each of these measures with some reliability, and both processes continue to undergo reforms aimed at improving their performances as measured by these values. But to characterize either as unconcerned with any one of these values is simply false.

If we set out to compare settlement with litigation, we should do so responsibly. We should compare the idealized vision of settlement with the idealized vision of litigation. Or we should compare the sloppy reality of settlement in practice with the sloppy reality of litigation in practice. But more than anything, we should recognize that settlement and litigation are no longer separate—in practice or in theory. Because settlement and litigation are co-evolved, symbiotic processes, to stand against one is to stand against the other. I choose, instead, to be for litigation and for settlement.

Professor Nancy Welsh has summarized an important literature that suggests that the experience of a fair process (procedural justice) is critical to a perception of justice. According to Welsh, a fair process provides: (1) an opportunity for the disputants to express their views; (2) a third party who demonstrates that she has understood what is said; (3) a third party who treats the disputants in an even-handed way; and (4) a third party who treats the disputants with dignity and respect. Where disputants perceive they have been treated with procedural justice they are more likely to feel the outcome is fair (distributive justice) and to comply with the outcome. And, "if people perceive that a process was procedurally just, they are more likely to view the social institution that provided the process as *legitimate.*" Nancy A. Welsh, Remembering the Role of Justice in Resolution: Insights from Procedural and Social Justice Theories, 54 J. of Legal Educ. 49, 51-53 (2004).

The questions raised by Fiss and Moffitt are central concerns for this course. Is seeking peace and justice at the same time possible? Do we need justice to have peace? Must we have some kind of peace (or enough calm) to pursue peace?

Professor Carrie Menkel-Meadow takes on questions of justice and peace in the final excerpt.

Carrie Menkel-Meadow, PRACTICING "IN THE INTERESTS OF JUSTICE" IN THE TWENTY-FIRST CENTURY: PURSUING PEACE AND JUSTICE

70 Fordham L. Rev. 1761, 1764-1765, 1767-1770, 1773-1774 (2002)

In a recent address, . . . former President Clinton, upon accepting the Second Annual Cardozo International Advocate for Peace Award, said, "Throughout human history, tragically, we have seen more advances in tools for waging war than in the art of making peace." That comment, while certainly true of human behavior in general, is applicable to legal behavior as well. We have developed more and more sophisticated forms of legal warfare (discovery and the paper wars of attrition, and my personal favorite, the recent ad of the Los Angeles Intercontinental Hotel for a "litigation war room" available for lawyers planning strategy, taking depositions and developing their "battle plans," all in facilities with completely up to date technology and "close to the battlefield"—the courthouse). Fortunately, I think we have also seen some advances in developing some tools for "making peace" with the proliferation of mediation, problem solving and interest-based negotiation, negotiated rule-making and a variety of consensus building processes, as well as problem solving courts in a variety of substantive areas. These new tools are intended, in my view, to seek peace and justice simultaneously through the use of a variety of different forms of dialogue, policy-making, rule development, dispute settlement and conflict management. Peace, of at least some minimal sort, is a prerequisite to the search for justice. And to the extent that peace-seeking tools are part of what I would call "process consciousness," lawyers should be—but are not yet, by disposition or training—at the forefront of practicing justice by considering and shaping processes that are more likely to lead to peaceful and better outcomes. . . .

II. "PEACE WORK" AND PROBLEM SOLVING WITH CLIENTS

. . . The work of the lawyer as a conflict resolver is to explore not only legal, but also other needs and interests of the parties (including economic, social, psychological, political, religious, moral and ethical concerns). Utilizing theories, not only of law, but of human behavior (sociology, psychology and economics), lawyers as conflict professionals look for situations where these diverse needs and interests do not compete with each other (the assumption of the legal system that "money is proxy" for all other, often non-economic, interests) but complement each other (the "Homans principle"). Complementary needs permit "efficient trades" (pareto-optimal in economic parlance) or "log-rolling" (in the language of political scientists)—positive-sum, rather than zero-sum results. Thus, at the level of substantive problem solving, lawyers seeking to achieve both maximum gain for individual clients and joint gain for all involved in a particular situation must employ different kinds of cognitive processes and different technologies and techniques in order to fashion good and lasting solutions to disputes and conflicts. At the relational level, where legal disputes and conflicts either begin with or accumulate a large emotional "residue" of resentment, anger and a sense of injustice (and, therefore, demand for both compensation and retribution), skilled lawyers as peace-makers must develop different kinds of communication skills than the traditional forms of argument, debate and adversarial claiming. . . .

These new roles put lawyers in perhaps unfamiliar ways of functioning as they pursue justice. Focused not just on "winning" the case, but on meeting the needs of multiple sets of parties and affected third parties, and on looking for substantive solutions that will require marshaling new resources, drafting new regulations, creating new institutions (including public and private partnerships in some cases) and implementing and enforcing plans, lawyers will have to learn new skills and develop new conceptual frameworks. It will not be easy to do all of this, particularly in light of robust conventional frames and conceptual models through which we process the world, and because our system is more than several centuries old. It is clear we are living in a new world with new problems that will require new forms of processes and solutions if we are to achieve a peaceful and just world. If necessity is the mother of invention, we are certainly in need of the birth of some new ideas for pursuing justice, both at home and in the larger world we now all inhabit. Conventional approaches to pursuing "justice" like our "conventional" approaches of military solutions to international problems may destroy the very "res" we are fighting about (producing a "negative sum" game in negotiation parlance). Just as military solutions to "war" may not bring us peace, an exclusive focus on "legal" needs and interests may not bring us justice. This is true, whether we like it or not.

As you proceed to study the specific processes of dispute resolution in this book, ask yourself the following questions:

a. What is the purpose of this process?
b. What is the historical context of the development of this process? What problem was it created to solve? What new problems are created by it?
c. What is the relation of process to the substantive problem to be solved?
d. Who should have decision-making authority or power in this process—the parties, their representatives, courts, legislatures, other people affected by the conflict or dispute?
e. What are the relations or tensions between "justice" or "fairness" and "peace" in individual cases, and at the aggregate or system level?
f. How, if at all, has this process been institutionalized or formalized? What advantages or disadvantages are there to formalizing this process?

g. Why do we want and make process changes? What ills are we hoping to cure? What new problems do we create?
h. How should the success or effectiveness of a particular process be measured? What metrics are possible? Is party satisfaction enough, or should we look to some measures outside of the parties themselves?
i. What is the lawyer's proper role in dispute processes? As a representative of clients? As an officer of the court? Policy maker? Enacter?
j. What are the ethics of dispute resolution—both in the "macro" sense of systemic justice and in the "micro" sense of choosing particular processes and behaviors?

Further Reading

Jerold Auerbach. (1983). Justice Without Law? New York: Oxford University Press.

Jerome T. Barrett & Joseph Barrett. (2004). A History of Alternative Dispute Resolution: The Story of a Political, Social and Cultural Movement. San Francisco: Jossey-Bass Publishers.

Morton Deutsch. (1973). The Resolution of Conflict: Constructive and Destructive Processes. New Haven: Yale University Press.

Morton Deutsch & Peter T. Coleman (Eds.). (2000). The Handbook of Conflict Resolution: Theory and Practice. San Francisco: Jossey-Bass Publishers.

Mary Parker Follett. (1995). Prophet of Management: A Celebration of Writings from the 1920s (Pauline Graham, Ed.). Boston: Harvard Business School.

Lon L. Fuller. (Rev. ed. 2001). The Principles of Social Order: Selected Essays of Lon L. Fuller (Kenneth I. Winston, Ed.). Oxford: Hart Publishing.

Stuart Hampshire. (2000). Justice Is Conflict. Princeton: Princeton University Press.

Carrie Menkel-Meadow (2025). Advanced Introduction to Alternative Dispute Resolution. Cheltenham: UK; Northampton Mass: Edward Elgar.

Carrie Menkel-Meadow (2022). Very Short Introduction to Negotiation. Oxford University Press.

Carrie Menkel-Meadow. (2003). Dispute Processing and Conflict Resolution: Theory, Practice and Policy. Aldershot, UK and Burlington, VT.: Ashgate Press.

Michael L. Moffitt & Robert C. Bordone (2005). The Handbook of Dispute Resolution. San Francisco: Jossey-Bass Publishers.

Laura Nader, The Recurrent Dialectic Between Legality and Its Alternatives: The Limitations of Binary Thinking, 132 U. Pa. L. Rev. 621 (1984).

Joan C. Tonn. (2003). Mary Parker Follett: Creating Democracy, Transforming Management. New Haven: Yale University Press.

Chapter 2 The Lawyer as Problem Solver

In the Chinese language, the character for crisis is two different symbols—one means danger and the other means opportunity.

—John F. Kennedy

Discourage litigation. Persuade your neighbors to compromise whenever you can. As a peacemaker, the lawyer has superior opportunity of being a good man. There will still be business enough.

— Abraham Lincoln

This chapter focuses on the multiple roles that the lawyer may play in solving clients' problems and using various forms of dispute resolution to do so. In the first chapter, you read about conflict theory and frameworks for handling disputes in the United States and some of the issues these raise, as well as definitions of some of the processes available. You'll recall that some of what animated the creation of the ADR movement was a hope for justice, tailored to the parties' needs. In this chapter, we will introduce you to the skills you will need to be that kind of problem-solving lawyer. In order to try to accomplish both justice (for your clients and perhaps for the larger society as well) and satisfy your clients' instrumental and affective needs, you will have to have a deep repertoire of skills. Problem solvers are creative; thorough in discerning what their clients need and hope to accomplish; sensitive to what the other parties need and hope to accomplish; and considerate to what the situation permits (or, if altered, could allow). This creates a tension that some dispute resolution scholars and practitioners have called the need to both "create" and "claim" value.[1]

As a problem solver, you will have to consider the other side not only as a source of possible solutions to your problem, but also as someone with whom you will have to persuade and advocate. You will need to be creative

1. David A. Lax & James K. Sebenius, The Manager as Negotiator: Bargaining for Cooperation and Competitive Gain (1986).

and listen to the other side to find out what they want to accomplish and what they can offer as well. At the same time, you also have to be ready to express your clients' needs and goals firmly and clearly. How these conversations are conducted will be treated at length in this book in the chapters that follow. We begin with thoughts about learning how to listen, interview your own clients, listen to the other side, and then put on your "thinking caps" to come up with good, rigorous, and creative solutions to legal issues and disputes. Regardless of the dispute resolution process you ultimately engage in, this kind of understanding lays the foundation for you to be an effective advocate and problem-solver.

We will now turn to the skills that are essential for any good problem solver:

- considering client and social goals,
- listening to clients and parties,
- interviewing and counseling to determine interests, underlying needs, and goals under those interests, and
- effective communication with all those you interact with in solving legal problems through dispute resolution methods.

In the first section of this chapter, we look specifically at the reasons that clients may hire lawyers to deal with their problems. What are the advantages and the pitfalls of having an agent, such as a lawyer, working on a client's behalf and using approaches other than litigation? The second part of this chapter addresses the importance of understanding clients' interests in the pursuit of problem-solving. To adopt a problem-solving approach to their concerns, the lawyer needs to uncover more than the bases for a client's legal claims. Finally, the third section outlines the skill set needed to interview clients and discover their interests.

A. THE CLIENT/LAWYER RELATIONSHIP

Why do clients need attorneys in disputes that take place outside the courtroom? The first article, by Jeffrey Rubin and Frank Sander, uses agency theory to explain the potential benefit of having a lawyer represent a client in a negotiation. The second article, by Scott Peppet, explains how both lawyers and clients can better manage that relationship in a negotiation. The third article, by Jean Sternlight, continues and deepens the discussion of the role of attorneys in dispute-resolution settings. The final article, by Michael Moffitt, highlights the risks involved if clients' lawyers *fail* to provide this kind of professional assistance to their clients.

Jeffrey Z. Rubin & Frank E.A. Sander, WHEN SHOULD WE USE AGENTS? DIRECT VS. REPRESENTATIVE NEGOTIATION

4 Negot. J. 395, 396-398 (1988)

EXPERTISE

One of the primary reasons that principals choose to negotiate through agents is that the latter possess expertise that makes agreement—particularly favorable agreement—more likely. This expertise is likely to be of three different stripes:

Substantive knowledge. A tax attorney or accountant knows things about the current tax code that make it more likely that negotiations with an IRS auditor will benefit the client as much as possible. Similarly, a divorce lawyer, an engineering consultant, and a real estate agent may have substantive knowledge in a rather narrow domain of expertise, and this expertise may redound to the client's benefit.

Process expertise. Quite apart from the specific expertise they may have in particular content areas, agents may have skill at the negotiation process, per se, thereby enhancing the prospects of a favorable agreement. A skillful negotiator—someone who understands how to obtain and reveal information about preferences, who is inventive, resourceful, firm on goals but flexible on means, etc.—is a valuable resource. Wise principals would do well to utilize the services of such skilled negotiators, unless they can find ways of developing such process skills themselves.

Special influence. A Washington lobbyist is paid to know the "right" people, to have access to the "corridors of power" that the principals themselves are unlikely to possess. Such "pull" can certainly help immensely, and is yet another form of expertise that agents may possess, although the lure of this "access" often outweighs in promise the special benefits that are confirmed in reality. . . .

DETACHMENT

Another important reason for using an agent to do the actual negotiation is that the principals may be too emotionally entangled in the subject of the dispute. A classic example is divorce. A husband and wife, caught in the throes of a bitter fight over the end of their marriage, may benefit from the "buffering" that agents can provide. Rather than confront each other with the depth of their anger and bitterness, the principals . . . may do far better by communicating only indirectly, via their respective representatives. . . . Stated most generally, when the negotiating climate is adversarial—when the disputants are confrontational rather than collaborative—it may be wiser to manage the conflict through intermediaries than run the risk of an impasse or explosion resulting from direct exchange.

Sometimes, however, it is the agents who are too intensely entangled. What is needed then is the detachment and rationality that only the principals can bring to the exchange. . . .

Note, however, that the very "detachment" we are touting as a virtue of negotiation through agents can also be a liability. For example, in some interpersonal negotiations, apology and reconciliation may be an important ingredient of any resolution. Surrogates who are primarily technicians may not be able to bring to bear these empathetic qualities.

TACTICAL FLEXIBILITY

The use of agents allows various gambits to be played out by the principals, in an effort to ratchet as much as possible from the other side. For example, if a seller asserts that the bottom line is $100,000, the buyer can try to haggle, albeit at the risk of losing the deal. If the buyer employs an agent, however, the agent can profess willingness to pay that sum but plead lack of authority, thereby gaining valuable time and opportunity for fuller consideration of the situation together with the principal. Or an agent for the seller who senses that the buyer may be especially eager to buy the property can claim that it is necessary to go back to the seller for ratification of the deal, only to return and up the price, profusely apologizing all the while for the behavior of an "unreasonable" client. The client and agent can thus together play the hard-hearted partner game.

Conversely, an agent may be used in order to push the other side in tough, even obnoxious, fashion, making it possible—in the best tradition of the "good cop/bad cop" ploy—for the client to intercede at last, and seem the essence of sweet reason in comparison with the agent. Or the agent may be used as a "stalking horse," to gather as much information about the adversary as possible, opening the way to proposals by the client that exploit the intelligence gathered.

Problem 2-1. ***Why Hire a Lawyer?***

The passage above articulates potential reasons to use a lawyer.

As a lawyer, which reasons would you expect to most resonate with a skeptical client? Which are most resonant for you?

As a client, what concerns might you have about hiring a lawyer? How would you decide when to hire a lawyer? On what factors would your decision depend?

While we may want clients to hire lawyers for all of the reasons listed above, we also think that it is useful for lawyers to recognize some of the classic problems that may occur between lawyers and clients.

Scott R. Peppet, SIX PRINCIPLES FOR USING NEGOTIATING AGENTS TO MAXIMUM ADVANTAGE

In The Handbook of Dispute Resolution, 189-193 (Michael Moffitt & Robert Bordone eds., 2005)

Often, we do not negotiate for ourselves. Instead, we ask someone to represent us at the bargaining table. Agency—when someone else acts on our behalf—has advantages and disadvantages in negotiation. . .

OPPORTUNITIES AND PROBLEMS

We all have many agents working for us at any given moment. You entrust your safety to the pilot of a commercial airliner; you ask a physician to examine and heal you; you elect representatives to govern in the legislature; you hire employees to work for you; you cast votes for corporate officers running enterprises in which you hold stock; you trust the postman to carry your letters to faraway places; you have teachers educating your children; you beg your spouse to confront a frustrating neighbor on your behalf. Agency is a basic fact of life, not an occasional complicating factor. In a modern world, we each delegate to others constantly. This frees us to pursue our own interests and talents while giving us the benefits of others' time and expertise.

Agents provide many advantages and opportunities in negotiation. A negotiating agent—whether a lawyer, a sports agent, or a diplomat—may be able to assert his or her principal's interests more skillfully or forcefully than can the principal. Agents may have special training, such as a legal education, that equips them to argue for or defend a principal. And agents may be able to detach themselves from the emotional throes of a negotiation and gain perspective on the client's long-term interests. This may allow an agent to handle delicate issues that his or her principal might negotiate poorly.

There are also problems inherent in hiring a negotiating agent. Principal-agent theory focuses on three ways in which agents may differ from their principals. First, the agent may have different preferences than the principal. For example, the agent may not want to work as hard as the principal wishes him or her to work. Second, agents may have different incentives than the principal. They may have a different stake in the outcome, or may receive different rewards, than the principal. Third, an agent may have information unavailable to the principal, or vice versa. For example, the principal may not know how hard the agent is working. These divergences between agent and principal give rise to problems relating to monitoring, incentives, coordination, and strategy. The following sections consider each in turn.

THE MONITORING PROBLEM: A PRIMER ON PRINCIPAL-AGENT ECONOMICS

Principal-agent economics is concerned with situations in which a principal cannot directly observe an agent's actions and the principal cannot completely infer the agent's behavior by observing the outcome of the agent's activities. In other words, the principal depends on the agent, but the principal does not have sufficient information to judge the agent's performance perfectly. In these situations, an agent can take advantage of a principal—and vice versa. The most obvious example occurs when an agent pretends to work harder than he or she is actually working, otherwise known as "shirking." An employee might look busy while typing away at his computer, but he may actually be e-mailing a friend. Similarly, a lawyer negotiating for a client may bill for hours of unnecessary research or work done at a snail's pace.

Shirking can arise in various ways in the negotiation context. A negotiating agent may exaggerate the effort involved in negotiating a deal or dispute or skew her reports about what took place at the bargaining table. She might describe the intransigence of the other side, or how all of her skill and courage were needed to counter the other side's "hard bargaining" behavior. In reality, however, the agent may have faced a cooperative, efficient counterpart who posed no real challenge and demanded no extraordinary efforts.

The threat of an agent shirking or otherwise acting contrary to a principal's interests leads to agency costs. These are costs associated with attempting to control one's agent and minimize shirking or other troublesome behavior. For example, an employer may purchase software to monitor e-mail usage or spend time patrolling the halls to catch unwary employees. A client may pore over a lawyer's billing statement or hire a secondary attorney to monitor the first lawyer's performance. A principal may try to monitor the events unfolding in a negotiation by attending negotiation sessions that he or she could otherwise skip.

These attempts to monitor are inevitably imperfect. By definition, agency problems arise in those situations in which one cannot completely oversee an agent's behavior or infer the agent's actions from the outcome he or she produces. In addition, monitoring is expensive. A principal may not have the time, resources, or expertise to police her agent. In negotiation, for example, a principal may be unable to observe her agent once the agent leaves to bargain with the other side. The principal may never know exactly what words the negotiating agent chooses, how the agent's tone affects the negotiation, or whether the agent fully implements the principal's preferred strategy or tactics. There may be no efficient way for a principal or client to monitor her negotiating agent's behavior this closely.

THE INCENTIVE PROBLEM: NO PERFECT FEE STRUCTURE

In addition to monitoring, or in its place, a principal may use incentives to control an agent's behavior. Employers, for example, often structure employee compensation to align an employee's incentives with the employer's goals. Imagine that you are hiring an agent to negotiate several sales contracts for your business. If you want the agent to work quickly, you might pay "by the piece"—paying for each contract closed. . . . If you want the agent to work carefully and thoroughly, you might pay him or her by the hour. Or, if you want your agent to maximize the price received in each contract, you might structure a contingency fee that varies according to the negotiated outcome. Many negotiating agents, including lawyers, real estate brokers, investment bankers, and sports agents, work for contingency fees.

Unfortunately, no incentive structure can perfectly align the interests of a principal and an agent. Instead, each structure creates new incentive and monitoring problems. An hourly fee may induce an agent to delay. A flat fee or "by the piece" fee may create undesirable haste or impatience on the part of the agent. A contingency fee may lead to underinvestment of time or effort by the agent if the agent can settle the client's matter quickly and at very little cost for a reasonable amount. Put differently, under a contingency fee an agent may negotiate a mediocre but acceptable solution quickly rather than struggle to achieve an excellent (but more time-intensive) settlement, simply because the agent has only minor marginal gain from pushing for the better deal. In each case, although incentive structures can help to minimize agency costs, they are an imperfect solution.

THE COORDINATION PROBLEM: COMMUNICATION IS NOT FREE

Using a negotiating agent introduces a third type of problem: coordinating the agent's actions, goals, and strategies with those of the principal. If a negotiating agent perfectly understands her client's desires, she can negotiate most effectively on her principal's behalf. In reality, of course, an agent does not have all of this information. Even if a principal and an agent have aligned incentives and the desire to work well together (in other words, both are honorable and uninterested in shirking), the principal and agent must still coordinate their roles, responsibilities, and resources to maximum advantage.

This can become quite complicated. Should both principal and agent attend negotiation sessions? If so, who will say what? What role will each play? If not, what is the agent authorized to say or do on the principal's behalf? Does the agent have sufficient information from the principal about the latter's interests and priorities to be able to represent the principal in his absence?

These are particularly complicated questions for those interested in problem- solving, collaborative, or principled negotiation, as opposed to traditional positional or hard-bargaining negotiation. Rather than simply demanding a certain outcome, problem solving requires considering one's interests, needs, resources, and priorities. Problem solving also generally requires weighing considerations of fairness and comparing a proposed negotiated outcome to an available "walk-away" alternative. These tasks, however, are information-intensive. For a negotiating agent to carry out these tasks on a principal's behalf requires that the agent learn a great deal from the principal prior to setting out. What does the principal want? How does the principal reconcile his competing or contradictory interests? What are his relative priorities as between his interests? How does the principal see his walk-away alternative? What are the principal's risk preferences, and what resources and capabilities does he have available to trade?

To equip an agent to problem solve, a principal will have to answer at least some of these questions for his agent. In the absence of such information, a negotiating agent is likely to lack confidence about the principal's interests—and therefore may engage in more traditional forms of hard bargaining rather than in problem solving. And regardless of the principal's preferred approach to a negotiation, using an agent will require information exchange and coordination between the principal and that agent.

THE STRATEGY PROBLEM: AGENCY COMPLICATES NEGOTIATION STRATEGY

Hiring a negotiating agent also introduces several strategy problems vis-à-vis a principal's negotiation with the other side by increasing the likelihood of strategic misunderstanding. If a principal negotiates for herself, she can regulate how collaborative or adversarial she wishes to be, and she can monitor the other side's reactions. When she sends an agent to the bargaining table, however, the principal can no longer fine-tune her strategy and tactics. She must trust that the agent will not behave in ways that might be perceived as overly (or insufficiently) aggressive. And she must trust that the agent will recognize when his impact on the other side may be different from what he intended. For example, one common problem is giving the other side the impression that a principal and her agent are using "good cop-bad cop" tactics. Even if this is untrue, the other side may attribute such intentions to them and react accordingly. To further complicate matters, it may be true.

Involving an agent makes possible tactics otherwise unavailable to the principal alone. "Good cop-bad cop" is one such tactic. Authority tactics are another. An agent may reject a counterpart's offer (or threaten to do so) by claiming that his principal has not authorized him to accept such a small settlement. This may be an honest disclosure about the agent's authority, in which case the agent is trying to save the other side time. But the agent may be bluffing—trying to use deception about authority to convince the other side to revise its expectations. Similarly, an agent may try to pressure eleventh-hour concessions out of the other side by claiming that his principal has demanded those concessions in order to authorize a final settlement.

Introducing agents may cause other strategic problems. In some cases two agents simply may not get along. Their relationship may deteriorate during their negotiation as a result of bargaining behavior or strong emotions. They may grow overly suspicious of each other or overly defensive. As a result, their negotiations may become protracted and expensive as their fees mount and the promise of an agreement recedes. Principals may have to intervene in such circumstances. Two CEOs, for example, may decide to take a negotiation "back" from their lawyers because they fear that their attorneys will ruin the deal. In other words, the principals may intervene upon realizing that their agents have become unable to continue representing them effectively. Such a collapse negates the efficiency benefits that agents can provide if they can manage negotiation strategy effectively for their principals.

Problem 2-2. *Six Principles for Managing Agency in Negotiation*

How does negotiation magnify (or diminish) these tensions? Professor Peppet suggests six principles:

1. If possible, use agents (and work for principals) whose preferences are known and acceptable to you.
2. If possible, use agents (and work for principals) whose preferences are known to the other side.
3. If possible, change the structure of the negotiation to align the incentives of principal and agent.
4. Share information between principal and agent to the extent necessary to effect the principal's strategy.
5. Treat role coordination and authority delegation as an ongoing negotiation, not a one-time event.
6. Rely most heavily on an agent when psychological biases or emotional risks cloud the principal's decision-making.

Can you think of contexts in which one or more of these principles would be comparatively easier to uphold? Contexts in which it would be more challenging? (For example, how might these principles shape a criminal plea bargain? A commercial real estate purchase? A dispute involving you and multiple neighbors? A contested insurance claim?)

Problem 2-3. *Who Will You Trust?*

Even in high-profile contexts, parties do not always choose to be represented by counsel.

- In 2023, NFL quarterback Lamar Jackson represented himself in salary negotiations with the Baltimore Ravens that yielded a $260 million contract, which, at $52 million per year, was the highest salary ever negotiated. (He gave the typical 3% agent commission to his mom instead!)
- During the International War Crimes Tribunal for the Former Yugoslavia in the early 2000s, former Serbian leader Slobodan Milošević insisted on representing himself.

What might have motivated each of their decisions about using an agent?

Lawyers play (or can play) a number of different roles in their relationships with their clients. In the following two excerpts, Jean Sternlight provides five ways in which lawyers can be important to their clients in non-litigation processes, and Michael Moffitt provides a warning about what might happen if lawyers are ineffective in these representations.

Jean R. Sternlight, LAWYERLESS DISPUTE RESOLUTION: RETHINKING A PARADIGM

37 Fordham Urb. L.J. 1-2, 11-13, 26-31 (2010)

Do participants in mediation and arbitration have attorneys? Do they need them? Although the phenomenon of pro se litigation has received substantial attention in recent years, most commentators and policy makers have failed to focus on whether participants in mediation, arbitration, or other forms of alternative dispute resolution ("ADR") need legal assistance. Likely the failure to focus on the possible need for representation in proceedings is based on an often-unstated premise that because ADR is non-adversarial or at least less adversarial than litigation, the need for representation in ADR is necessarily or at least typically less than the need for representation in litigation. . . .

WHY MIGHT ATTORNEYS BE NEEDED IN ADR?

Some might suggest that one of the goals of ADR is to avoid the need for attorneys. One of the virtues of purportedly simpler less adversarial dispute resolution process would seem to be that disputants would be fully capable of representing themselves, and not have to rely on expensive attorneys. . . .

The other reason some may believe attorneys are not necessary in mediation or arbitration is their sense that the typically adversarial mindset of attorneys do not fit with less adversarial ADR processes. . . . Specifically, attorneys in mediation may focus unduly on narrow monetary interests, may be overly argumentative, or may discourage their clients from addressing opposing disputants directly. . . . Some jurisdictions have gone so far as to prohibit attorneys from participating in certain categories of court-connected mediation. . . .

Yet, particularly as ADR has become mandatory in many contexts in many jurisdictions, the question of whether individuals can effectively represent themselves has become more pressing. . . . Moreover, upon reflection most people would probably agree that lawyers at least potentially can be extremely helpful in ADR proceedings. . . .

[L]awyers add value through imparting their procedural and strategic knowledge regarding the various processes, gathering and presenting legal and factual information, assisting specifically in negotiation, and empowering their clients. Thus, even to the extent arbitration and mediation are relatively simple and non-adversarial, which is often not the case, lawyers can provide a great deal of assistance with regard to these processes.

1. Knowledge and Strategy re: Processes

Lawyers can be very useful in helping disputants decide whether arbitration or mediation might be desirable. . . . If an ADR process is to be used, lawyers can help select the neutral. In purely voluntary processes lawyers rely on their networks to find names of mediators and arbitrators who they think would or would not be appropriate. . . . Once the neutral is selected the lawyer can be very helpful in coaching the client in such matters as what to expect in mediation/arbitration, who to bring to the mediation/arbitration as participants or witnesses, or what strategic moves might be desirable in either process. . . . One additional way attorneys can help clients to succeed in mediation is to help them better understand their own situation and goals. . . .

2. Gathering and Presenting Factual Information

Gathering and presenting legal and factual information is often a key aspect of both mediation and arbitration. No matter how informal the process, disputants typically need to explain such matters as what happened, what relief they are seeking or seeking to avoid providing, and why they believe they are in the right and someone else is in the wrong. . . .

Lawyers are accustomed to ferreting out information . . . and may be very useful to help parties prepare for a mediation or arbitration. . . . Having gathered the facts the lawyer can help make strategic arguments regarding which facts to disclose, as well as when and how such facts should be disclosed. . . . And, assuming facts will be presented, lawyers can typically prepare both verbal and written versions of the facts that are much clearer, better organized, and more persuasive than the client might be able to manage on her own. . . .

3. Researching and Presenting Legal Arguments

Although some may assume that legal arguments have no place or less of a place in ADR proceedings than in court, they would be wrong. Mediations often occur in the shadow of litigation, with disputants quite cognizant that the case may proceed to litigation if it does not settle in mediation. Thus, the strength and weakness of legal arguments is highly relevant to determine whether a disputant ought to settle on particular terms. . . . Arbitrations, of course, typically turn on legal arguments, merely substituting the arbitrator's legal determinations for those of a judge. Thus, in both forms of ADR lawyers can help a great deal in researching and presenting legal arguments.

4. Empowering Clients

In addition to the tasks outlined above, lawyers are poised to help their clients . . .— specifically by providing emotional support and empowering their clients. Even in simpler ADR matters, that do not involve complex facts or law, it may be very important for clients to be accompanied and supported by a person who can help them emotionally to tell their own story. A large literature discusses this need as applied to minorities, women, and victims of domestic violence. But it seems that the empowerment issue is likely much bigger than that: many disputants can benefit substantially from the assistance of an attorney to help them tell their own story, even in matters that may seem relatively simple in terms of facts and law.

5. Drafting Agreements

If an agreement is reached in mediation the attorney can also help the client by drafting the actual mediation agreement. As with any contract, lawyers can add a great deal, ensuring that the terms of the contract are clear, fair and enforceable.

Michael Moffitt, SETTLEMENT MALPRACTICE

86 Chicago L. Rev. 1825, 1857-1858 (2019)

Properly understood, a lawyer has three distinct but related roles with respect to her client's decision-making about settlement. The lawyer must understand her client's interests—the "needs, desires, concerns, and fears" that motivate negotiators' decisions, akin to what the Model Rules describe as the "objectives of representation." She must communicate the implications of any potential settlement—what the negotiation literature refers to as "options"—with a specific eye toward the ways in which that settlement option intersects with the client's interests. And she must provide the client with a candid and accurate picture of litigation's risks, costs, and opportunities. A lawyer's mishandling of any of these represents—or at least should represent—both a breach of the lawyer's ethical duties and a clear instance of professional malpractice. . . .

In order to exercise informed choice, a client must understand the implications of a proposed settlement option, and in particular examine the ways in which it does or does not satisfy the client's interests. A number of dollars, a particular release or waiver clause, a confidentiality provision, a dispute resolution clause, a joint press statement, a contingent clause—any might be options that would take effect only if both parties agreed to them, and each might affect the client's interests. Assessing and articulating the implications of options, therefore, becomes central to the role of lawyer-as-settlement-advisor.

At a bare minimum, an attorney must convey the basic terms of an agreement accurately to the client. In the case underlying *Arnav Industries, Inc Retirement Trust v. Brown, Raysman, Millstein, Felder & Steiner*, 751 NE2d 936 (NY 2001), for example, the terms of a settlement were reached, but the next day, the plaintiffs' attorney sent a revised agreement for their signature, indicating that there had been a typographical error in the original. [The original agreement had noted the settlement amount as $2,800,000 rather than $2,080,000.] The plaintiffs signed the revised agreement without rereading it, only later to discover that the sheets they signed included a number of [other] changes resulting in a roughly $4 million reduction to what the plaintiffs would be owed upon the default of the opposing party to the settlement. The court in the subsequent malpractice lawsuit held—appropriately—that this plainly states a cause of action against the plaintiffs' original attorney. Attorneys must also accurately explain certain conspicuous deal terms, such as an amount of payment or the identities of the parties who will be bound.

More commonly, a client may not understand the implications of some inconspicuous deal term, particularly to the extent it may have an effect on the client's interests extending beyond the immediate case in question. For example, in the suit underlying *Ordon v. Karpie*, 425 F. Supp 2d 276 (D. Conn 2006), Dr. Andrew Ordon faced a complaint before the Connecticut Medical Examining Board. His attorney negotiated a potential settlement according to which Ordon would pay a $2,500 fine to the State of Connecticut but would face no restrictions on his practice. Indeed, Ordon's attorney "told Dr. Ordon that accepting the [o]ffer would have 'essentially no import' on him or his practice in Connecticut or any other jurisdiction." Relying on this advice, Ordon accepted and paid the fine. However, on the basis of the settlement's consent order, both California and New York subsequently instituted reciprocal discipline on Ordon that impaired his ability to establish practices in those states. . . .

Similarly, in *Collas v. Garnick*, 624 A2d 117 (Pa. Super. 1993), the plaintiff was injured in an automobile accident and brought a claim against the owner of the other vehicle involved. The plaintiff's attorney negotiated the terms of a potential settlement and presented it to his client, assuring her that "the release would have [no] impact upon her plan to sue the manufacturer of the vehicle in which she had been riding." The plaintiff signed the settlement and subsequently brought an action against the manufacturer of the seat belts in her car. The trial court barred that subsequent action on the basis of the general waiver she had already signed. She, therefore, brought a malpractice action against her attorney for breaching his duty to provide her with accurate counsel about the extent to which the proposed settlement would satisfy her interests.

Problem 2-4. *A Lawyer's Duties*

Based on the readings above, if you were a client hiring a lawyer, which of the duties do you think you would find most important? How would you know if your lawyer had fulfilled those duties properly?

As a lawyer, you will be providing a range of services to your clients. How do you imagine documenting your advice, or otherwise assuring that there is a record of having been effective as counsel? How will you guard against the risk of overly "defensive" practice?

B. CLIENT-CENTERED AND PROBLEM-SOLVING APPROACHES

Now that you have a better grasp of why a client might hire a lawyer, as well as some of the challenges presented by the lawyer-client relationship, consider what skills a lawyer should have to advance his client's interests. The client-centered approach outlined in this book tries to avoid the common trap that can occur when a "lay" story becomes a "law" story. Often, a client tells his lawyer a broad story about the event, a "lay" story, and the lawyer will narrow or rephrase the story in his efforts to seek remediation. The lawyer will construct a story which is recognizable to the other lawyer, so that he can demand a stock remedial solution, a "law" story. The "law" story can be likened to a legal cause of action with prescribed elements which must be pleaded in a particular way in the legal system. If negotiation fails and the lawyer begins to craft a lawsuit, the dispute may be even further narrowed by the special language requirements of the substantive law, pleading rules, and rules of procedure. The problem-solving approach, on the other hand, has a lawyer focus on the interests of the client, and work to accomplish them. The client's interests are key. The next excerpt tells us how to avoid treating our clients as "law" stories and to see beyond the law.[2]

❖ *Katherine R. Kruse*, BEYOND CARDBOARD CLIENTS IN LEGAL ETHICS

23 Geo. J. Legal Ethics 1, 20-22, 28, 31, 33-34, 36, 41, 44 (2010)

In the world of legal ethics, clients are most often constructed as cardboard figures interested solely in maximizing their own wealth or freedom at the expense of others. . . . The proliferation of these examples is no accident. Rather, it is a consequence of a choice by early legal ethicists to focus on the dilemma faced by a lawyer forced by professional duty to do something that would otherwise be wrong. To generate this kind of dilemma, legal ethicists had to posit hypothetical clients impervious to ordinary moral considerations, unconcerned with preserving their relationships with others and indifferent to their reputations in the community. . . .

The focus on moral lawyers and cardboard clients prevented the early ethicists from exploring the possibility that the real problems of legal professionalism might originate—not primarily from selfish clients who push their lawyers to the limits of the law—but primarily from lawyers who focus too narrowly on their clients' legal interests and fail to view their clients as whole persons with a myriad of non-legal concerns. . . .

The client-centered approach is directly responsive to the problem of legal objectification. It urges lawyers to unlearn the professional habit of "issue-spotting" their clients and to approach their clients as whole persons who are more than the sum of their legal interests. The hallmarks of the client-centered approach include understanding the client's problem from the client's point of view and shaping legal advice around the client's values. Under the client-centered approach, hearing clients' stories and understanding their values, cares and commitments is the first step—and a continuing duty—of legal representation. . . .

When clients come to lawyers for legal advice and representation, their legal issues are often entangled with values, projects, commitments, and relationships with others. Sometimes the client is getting legal help to start up a business a client has always

2. For more on the concept of "lay" versus "law" stories, see Carrie Menkel-Meadow, The Transformation of Disputes by Lawyers: What the Dispute Paradigm Does and Does Not Tell Us, 1985 Missouri J. Dispute Res. 25; G. Lopez, The Internal Structure of Lawyering: Lay Lawyering, 32 UCLA L. Rev. 1, 3 (1984); R. Nisbett & L. Ross, Human Inference: Strategies and Shortcomings of Social Judgment 32-41 (1980).

dreamed of having or helping a couple adopt a child. Sometimes legal action arises because a client has been harmed by the actions of others: the client has been fired from a job, hit by a car, or beaten by a spouse. Sometimes the client has been accused of treating others unjustly: sexually harassing an employee, reneging on a deal, negligently allowing harm to others, or committing a crime. Other times clients come to lawyers to overcome barriers to taking care of business as usual: a deal needs to be negotiated, property needs to be leased, or a permit needs to be obtained. . . .

The methods of client value clarification involve both actively listening to what the client wants and probing beneath the client's expressed desires. Client-centered interviewing literature, for example, suggests that the lawyer dedicate time early in a client's initial interview for open-ended questions and other active listening techniques that help the lawyer hear the client's problem in the client's own terms. Hearing the client's story—as the client chooses to tell it—is a key component of understanding what the client values and what it is about the legal representation that will threaten or further those values. . . .

The kind of moral neutrality that results from respect for another person's values helps to discipline lawyers' tendency to impose their own moral and value choices on their clients in the guise of legal advice. If we assume three-dimensional clients, it is respect for client values that ensures the good that moral activism hopes to achieve by importing moral considerations into legal representation without succumbing to the danger of moral overreaching. . . .

Lawyers, like clients, are morally complex three-dimensional persons who bring a mix of reputational interests, personal relationships, values, cares and commitments into the arena of legal representation. And, all of these factors may affect lawyers' decision making for better or for worse. . . .

In the arena of legal representation, lawyers and clients are thus differently situated, but it is difficult to conclude that one is better positioned than the other to engage in moral reasoning and decision making. The situations that lead clients to seek legal representation may incline clients to pursue their wants in favor of their values. Lawyers will generally have no particular investment in the situations in which their clients are embroiled. However, lawyers will inevitably have financial, reputational and personal interests that present their own form temptation to transgress moral and professional values. The principles of partisan loyalty and moral neutrality—redefined as attention to and deference to client value choices—can help check lawyers' own self-interested motivations in legal representation. . . .

Problem 2-5. ***Goals in Representing a Driver Charged with DUI***

You are a new associate in a firm and a partner whom you highly respect has just given you your first case. The case involves the daughter of a regular and important client. The daughter received a Driving Under the Influence citation, and you are to represent her as defense counsel. Describe the wants, values, and interests you, the daughter, and the parent might have regarding the case.

Some have urged that lawyers' perspectives and broader social values should be central to a representation, including at the interview stage. Laila Hlass and Lindsay Harris, for example, urge teaching law students not only client-centered interviewing, but also "critical interviewing," which they define as "using an intersectional lens to collaborate with clients, communities, interviewing partners, and interpreters in a legal interview. Critical interviewers identify and take into account historical and structural biases, privileges, and the role they play in the attorney-client relationship." Hlass & Harris, Critical Interviewing, 21 Utah L. Rev. 683 (2021).

Before moving to the question of what skills a lawyer needs in order to conduct an effective, client-centered interview, consider the stance you (or other lawyers) might bring to the conversation. If clients are supposed to control the overarching goals of the representation, does that mean that lawyers should be morally neutral? If yes, what are the broader implications in a world in which access to lawyers is concentrated among those with more resources? If no, what are the broader implications, particularly in contexts where clients are hiring lawyers because the clients cannot advocate for themselves? And in either event, must a lawyer be explicit about their views—about the social context and/or about the lawyer's role(s)? Similarly, what role should financial conditions and incentives play? To what extent should these considerations be an explicit part of the lawyer-client interview?

C. DISCOVERING THE CLIENTS' INTERESTS THROUGH INTERVIEWING

Interviewing skills are critical to learning what a case is about, helping clients choose a dispute resolution process and, once representation is underway, making sure client goals and needs are being met. An effective interview is essential to uncovering your client's understanding of what has already happened, their current interests, and their future needs. Without this knowledge, you may not be a good counselor, representative, or advocate for your client. In addition to initial interviewing, you can ensure that your client's goals, needs, and interests are being met through regular communication, as needs and interests may change during the course of representation. The lawyer who either assumes she knows what the client wants or, even more troublingly, substitutes her own judgment for the client's may be failing the client. Yet communication between lawyer and client does not always occur as often or go as well as it should. Our three excerpts in this section discuss, first, a general overview of how lawyers can use an interview. The second article discusses the benefits of the initial interview and ice-breaking. And the final excerpts, frame the purposes of the interview and provide perspective on the importance of non-legal considerations.

This article suggests that learning more about psychology can help attorneys be more effective at interviewing and counseling their clients.

❖ *Jean R. Sternlight & Jennifer Robbennolt*, GOOD LAWYERS SHOULD BE GOOD PSYCHOLOGISTS: INSIGHTS FOR INTERVIEWING AND COUNSELING CLIENTS

23 Ohio St. J. on Disp. Resol. 437, 437, 441-442, 538-544 (2008)

. . . To be effective in working with clients, witnesses, judges, mediators, arbitrators, experts, jurors, and other lawyers, attorneys must have a good understanding of how people think and make decisions, and must possess good people skills. . . . even experienced lawyers can improve their approach to interviewing and counseling by drawing on relevant psychology. . . . In general, interviewing and counseling sessions have three main components. First, the attorney uses an interview to obtain information from the client. Second, the attorney uses the counseling portion of the initial session to provide information to the client. Third, throughout the session the attorney is concerned with establishing rapport between attorney and client. . . .

A. PREPARING FOR THE INTERVIEW

1. Pre-Interview Information

. . . From a psychological standpoint, brief preliminary phone conversations can potentially be helpful in beginning to establish a relationship and build rapport. Conversely, the use of surveys or screening interviews with paralegals may give the impression that the attorney does not care enough about the client to participate in a conversation and may lead the attorney to pre-determine what kinds of issues are important. In-person interviews offer a better opportunity than phone conversations or certainly written surveys to impress the client, build rapport, learn from the client, minimize reliance on the attorney's prior conceptions, and assess the client's own credibility. If an attorney feels it is important to get a "heads up" on the subjects to be discussed, we suggest a brief and friendly phone call to probe the generalities of the problem. . . .

2. Setting the Stage

For an attorney [who] keeps a neat and comfortable office with diplomas or other awards on the wall, the intimate office setting can be appropriate. Alternatively, attorneys who have messy or otherwise unimpressive offices may want to conduct interviews in a nice conference room. In either setting, the attorney may want to offer the client a choice of seating options, and ensure that physical distance is sufficient for the client to feel comfortable

Lawyers who work as sports agents or who represent entertainers may well want to dress more flamboyantly than lawyers who do estate planning for elderly widows in the Midwest. So, while we cannot prescribe a particular set of clothes or hairstyle that is best for all situations, we can say that appearances do matter. . . .

B. CONDUCTING THE INTERVIEW

1. Importance of Open-Ended Questions[3]

. . . [Open-ended] questions are useful, from a psychological standpoint, for a variety of reasons. First, they allow clients to tell the story in the order that makes sense to them. This will encourage clients to tell a more complete story, aid clients' recall, allow clients to provide a level of detail with which they are confident, allow clients to explain their non-legal concerns, and deter attorneys from putting their clients' stories into pre-existing schema. Allowing clients to speak fully in response to open-ended questions will also speak to clients' desire for procedural justice. . . . [I]nterruptions may well cause clients to provide more limited information or to forget key details and is unlikely to make them feel respected.

2. Cultural Sensitivity and Avoidance of Stereotypes

As [an attorney] questions his clients he must be careful to avoid stereotypes. The mere fact that his client is dressed like a slob does not mean, for example, that his client is poor. Rather than make assumptions based on clients' appearance, race, ethnicity, gender, or other factors, the attorney should use his questions to allow his clients to tell their own stories. At the same time, the attorney should be attuned to the possibility that his clients' culture may lead them to have different preferences than might be natural to him. Some clients may, for example, be uncomfortable with the handshake, use of first names, and [a] straight gaze. . . .

3. Listening Effectively and Responding Encouragingly

In addition to asking appropriate questions of his clients, an attorney should . . . respond appropriately. Most people probably think they are fairly good listeners, but in fact many of us do not listen as effectively as we might. [We] may well be guilty of multi-tasking—letting [our] minds wander to other tasks while our clients describe their problems. Or, [we] may allow [ourselves] to be guided unduly by stereotypes and heuristics, placing [our] clients' problems into pre-determined categories. To battle these likely flaws [we] need to try to focus more attentively on [our] clients, and such effective listening includes not only hearing clients' words but also paying attention to their tone and body language.

[P]sychological studies have shown that interviewers can both obtain more information and also create better rapport by engaging in an effective and sympathetic back and forth with their clients. Similarly, [an attorney] must develop some comfort with interacting with his clients at an emotional level. If [he] attempts to completely avoid emotion, he will be unable to understand his clients' non-legal concerns, unable to build a solid rapport with his client, unable to encourage his client to provide all information pertinent to the legal issue, and unable to connect well to his client as a counselor.

---

3. Open-ended questions are those without a yes/no or even limited answer. Rather, these are broad questions where the questioner does not necessarily know where the answer will go.

4. Helping Clients Remember

. . . [An attorney] has at his disposal a number of helpful tools derived from the psychological literature that he can use to try to effectively trigger client memories. For example, he can use open-ended questions; ask his clients to retell their story in chronological or reverse chronological order; ask them to focus on details of the setting that may not be directly relevant to the legal problem; and try to get clients to focus more on facts. He also knows from the psychological literature that he will not have much success if he simply urges his clients to probe their memories better for all of the facts and understands that frequent interruptions can interfere with client memories.

Stefan Krieger and Richard Neumann explain that one of the marks of an effective person—in law and in almost any part of life—is the ability to ask the right question in the most productive way.

✓ Ask for all the important information.
✓ When asking questions, use the words that are most likely to produce valuable information.
✓ Ask at the right time and in the right context.
✓ Know when to ask narrow questions and when to ask broad questions.
✓ Know when to ask leading questions and when to ask non-leading questions.
✓ Be patient.
✓ Listen carefully to answers and ask thorough lines of questions.

Stefan H. Krieger & Richard K. Neumann, Jr. (eds.) (2015). Essential Lawyering Skills: Interviewing, Counseling, Negotiation, and Persuasive Fact Analysis (5th ed). Philadelphia: Wolters Kluwer.

5. Building Trust

. . . [T]he psychology literature shows that [an attorney] ought to care about creating trust because he will more readily obtain full information from a trusting client. Similarly, [an attorney] will be more effective as a counselor when his clients trust him. To gain his clients' trust, [an attorney] should not only continue to show clients that he is a competent and intelligent attorney, but also show clients that he cares about them as people and that he is willing to set aside his own personal interests, when necessary. Studies have shown that open communication, perspective taking, and willingness to explain can all be important to building a trusting relationship.

6. Being Aware of Clients' and One's Own Likely Cognitive Biases

. . . Both lawyers and clients tend to perceive the world through their schema and stereotypes, emphasize personal characteristics when they attribute causation, assume that others see the world the same way they do, are affected by an array of positive illusions, and show a tendency to do Monday morning quarterbacking. As clients report the "facts" as they understand them to their attorneys, the attorneys need to consider that their clients' discussions of these "facts" are undoubtedly affected by the psychology of cognition. Attorneys need to ask follow up questions and seek alternative perspectives to try to get beyond these biases. Similarly, attorneys need to be aware of the use of such heuristics in their own thinking.

7. Verifying Veracity

[An attorney] will be better off keeping an open mind and withholding judgment about veracity while seeking confirmation from other witnesses or documents. [He] also needs to remember that witnesses often report the same incident quite differently based on their different perceptions, construal, and memories, even though neither witness is lying.

8. Remembering the Interview

[An attorney's] own memory is no more infallible than that of his clients. [He] must take steps to ensure that he adequately recalls and records his discussions with his own clients, as absent special measures, surely his memory will fail.

This particular excerpt focuses on how we can make clients comfortable when first meeting. Our goals in the initial interview are to build rapport and trust while gathering information about their interests prior to selecting a process that best meets their needs.

Marjorie C. Aaron, CLIENT SCIENCE: ADVICE FOR LAWYERS ON INITIAL CLIENT INTERVIEWS

clientsciencecourse.com (2013)

ACTIVE, RESPONSIVE, AND EXPRESSIVE LISTENING

Many human resource department seminars and much literature are dedicated to the topic of "active listening." At a fundamental level, all good listening is active in that it is mindful and engaged. If you are entirely focused on the client's meaning, listening with full emotional as well as factual radar, that's active. So, one might say that good listening is active listening, and active listening is good.

Some articles and training programs use the term "active listening" to describe obvious discernible listener responses, often in the form of verbal interjections or interventions. Their purpose is to communicate to the speaker that the listener has, in fact, listened and understood the speaker's message and its meaning. . . .

The lawyer-listener's responses might be entirely non-verbal, or verbal. He might purse his lips, wince, frown, smile, wince again, look concerned, emit an audible sigh, as he hears the story, and he may adjust hand and body postures consistent with the emotions expressed as the story is told. That may be enough for the client to feel that his narrative and its full import have registered in the lawyer: he gets it. I'd call that expressive, responsive, and non-verbal.

Often, it's helpful and more effective to respond verbally. Some texts and articles use the term "active listening" to mean verbal responses in the form of paraphrase or some reflection back of the factual or emotional content of what was said.

Other sources consider only non-contentful but encouraging responses—"yes, go on"—"and so"—along with nods and other receptive signals to be active listening and "reflective listening" to require a verbal reflection back of factual and/or emotional content in what was said. This chapter and I are agnostic on the terminology. The point is that a listener can respond in a variety of ways to communicate that he or she is "with the client" and fully understands and appreciates the client's message and its meaning.

Here's a list of actions, all active, all responsive, some reflective:

- All non-verbal/inaudible: nodding, facial expressions, body language.
- No real words, but audible: sighs, ahhh, mmhmm, oh. . . .
- Encouragers: "yes, go on" . . . ,"and so" . . . , "that's okay" . . . "I see."
- Completers: And so you didn't expect that it . . . ? That's why you wanted to . . . ? Well, it's a big problem because. . . .
- Reflecting content, but short: "It was a complicated arrangement."
- Reflecting emotion, but short: "What a mess!" "Ouch, that was hurtful."
- Reflecting content, substantial restatement: Client: "The boss was an unfair, insensitive ogre to others in the office too. We all hated him." Lawyer: "Hmmm. . . . He was an ogre and everyone in the office hated him."
- Reflecting content, longer paraphrastic/interpretative: "In other words, the supervisor may indeed have humiliated her, but he did that to just about everyone so you're saying it wasn't about gender."
- Reflecting emotion, restatement: Client: "It was incredibly painful to watch this happen and feel helpless and unable to stop it." Lawyer: "I understand that you felt pained and helpless against it."
- Reflecting emotion, paraphrastic/interpretative: "I can hear that you were shocked by this. It came out of the blue, and it seemed like the others were making you the scapegoat. It's profoundly upsetting when people you trusted start to turn on you.". . .

ABOUT THAT ICE

Social convention generally makes us comfortable with the idea of starting a conversation with what's known as "ice breakers" or informal chitchat. Different cultures as well as different personalities within each culture tend to value this more than others. For example, in the southern U.S. states, the length of pleasantries and banter might make a northerner impatient. Regional stereotypes aside, we all know folks who just want to "get down to business" and others who tend toward social prologue.

When meeting a client for the first time—particularly where relationship and trust will be important—I recommend taking a bit of time and effort for conversation on commonalities outside of the legal problem. Neutral topics are best. So, if you know that a neighbor referred you, you might ask how the client knows your neighbor. Despite the cliché, weather or traffic work well, religion and politics are best avoided unless you both have matching political campaign buttons, or sit in adjacent church pews.

Do pay attention to small details that suggest a link or shared interest. Is the client carrying a tote bag with a symphony logo? "I notice your bag. Are you a symphony goer, or supporter?" Follow up with genuine, not fake curiosity. "Oh, so your teenager is the symphony goer in the family. Is he at Hill High School? I've heard they have a great music department." And so on. It's a good idea for your office to contain indicia of your own interests, whether baseball or ballet. These enable the client to spot commonalities as well.

Part of establishing relationship is attentiveness to the other's physical comfort. Thus, it is wise and kind to inquire about whether the client would like coffee, water, etc. Even if that's a task generally performed by the receptionist, it is wise to check: "Did they remember to offer you some water or a soft drink out there? If not, I'll be happy to." Even if the weather and parking seem too clichéd to raise, you can always talk about coffee. "Ahh. . . . I'm a coffee drinker too, but I wish I could offer you something better than that powdered creamer." Or, "yes, water is healthiest, how many glasses a day are we supposed to drink now? I always forget."

Two important caveats:

- First, if you hate chitchat because it seems so fake, there's no need to take on a ten-minute script. And if you are just going through the motions, checking off chitchat on your checklist, that will be obvious. For the not-naturally chatty, two pieces of advice: be genuinely curious—what little item could you learn about this client and she about you in this minute that you would not know otherwise? And it's okay to keep it short before turning to the business at hand.
- Second, never force chitchat on a client who's impatient, anxious, and entirely focused on talking about what brought him in. Imagine the client has said: "Hello, Ms. Jones, I really need your help with this subpoena and this thing the EEOC is saying my company did. I've been worried sick about it!" Would you really say: "Oh Mr. Smith, before we get to that may I say, I like your tie with the symphony logo, are you a subscriber?" Now, that would be foolish and bad practice! Again, take the client's lead.

For the most part, ice-breakers and chit chat are helpful first steps toward building trust and rapport. The potential client may be uncomfortable. He or she is soon to confide in you regarding a legal problem that is impacting personal, business, or professional spheres. If it weren't important to him, the client wouldn't be in your office. It's nice to have an opportunity to converse as human beings, to get used to speech patterns, physical presence, voice, and other human characteristics. . . .

In light of cognitive limitations in perception and memory, cognitive psychologists Edward Geiselman, Ronald Fisher and colleagues developed and named "cognitive interview" techniques. Their goal was a set of practical recommendations for interviewing techniques that incorporates current knowledge about what tends to enhance or distort memory and perception. Observing that an interview should occur in stages, they suggest:

(1) Begin by asking for an open-ended narrative, and don't interrupt. The technique for a cognitive interview here wholly overlaps with that stated earlier in this chapter. Do make the interviewee feel comfortable, try to establish rapport, and then don't interrupt the story as it's told. This is not the time to gather details, rather to listen and observe the way your witness (in this case, your potential client) relates his or her story.

(2) Move to the probing stage in which interviewee (client or witness) memory is called upon. The probing interviewer should direct the interviewee to each stage or topic in his story, using one or more of the four following cognitive interview techniques:

- Ask the interviewee to "reinstate the context" or remember as much as possible about everything he saw, heard, felt. Ask him to place himself back in the scene or circumstance as much as possible.
- Ask the interviewee to tell everything he remembers, even if it seems irrelevant or unimportant; these can help jog memory of things that are important. When asking for the full memory, the lawyer should specifically request that the interviewee refrain from guessing or inferring, or to explicitly differentiate from what he remembers and knows from what he believes or "figures" must have happened, or why. When the interviewee is talking, about a particular scene or event, the lawyer should avoid interrupting.
- If helpful to jog memory, suggest a change in order. People naturally try to remember and recount events in chronological sequence. Particularly if the interviewee is having trouble recalling detail or order, the lawyer can suggest that he try to remember what happened in reverse order, or by thinking about separate elements in what he considers their order of importance (or any other order). Sometimes, that will yield additional memory.
- If helpful, suggest a change in perspective. Again, when an interviewee is having trouble remembering, the lawyer might ask him to try to shift perspective on the scene, to think about what others present might have seen or heard.

In an interview informed by cognitive science, do NOT direct the interviewee's move from one observation to another, or from topic to topic. Do allow him to exhaust his memory on one topic first. For example, a skilled cognitive interviewer would NOT ask first: "How big is the corporate headquarters building?" Then, "you said you took the elevator. Did you see anyone else in the elevator? Then, "how far down the hall was the Vice President's office?" Then, "Where was the Vice President positioned in his office?"

This way of questioning too quickly distracts the interviewees mind from one image or memory cluster to another. First he has to think about the outside of the building—how big is it? Then he has to switch to people in the elevator (without having time to remember the whole elevator ride), then to the hall. Instead, the questioning should proceed in this fashion:

> "You said you approached the headquarters office. Can you tell me what you remember about the outside of the headquarters' building that day? Try to imagine you're there and remember whatever you saw."
> [After the interviewee has completed that description]
> "Okay, you said you walked into the lobby and went into the elevator,
> can you describe that in as much detail as you remember?"
> [After the interviewee has completed that description]
> "Okay, you got into the elevator: "What do you remember about the elevator ride?"
> . . . "Was there anyone else there? "Can you describe them and what they did?". . .

The "no interruption rule" still holds. Do not interrupt a description. And DO allow for hesitation and pausing. Recall can take time. Silence is not empty space; it is the sound of thinking and remembering. If the interviewee is struggling, you might use short encouragers . . . "that's okay" . . . "go on" . . . "whatever comes to mind." Only when nothing more comes to the client's or the witness's mind should you move to the next inquiry, noting that discussion can always go back if something is remembered later.

The final two excerpts circle back to the purpose(s) of the client interview and the importance of both listening and empathy in the lawyer-client context.

❖ *Stefan H. Krieger & Richard K. Neumann, Jr.*, ESSENTIAL LAWYERING SKILLS: INTERVIEWING, COUNSELING, NEGOTIATION, AND PERSUASIVE FACT ANALYSIS: FIFTH EDITION

97-106 (2015)

§8.1.1 YOUR PURPOSES IN INTERVIEWING CLIENTS

Client representation usually starts with an interview. A person who wants legal advice or advocacy calls to make an appointment. The secretary finds a convenient time and, to help the lawyer prepare, asks what the subject of the interview will be. The person calling says, "I want a new will drawn" or "I've just been sued" or "I signed a contract to buy a house and now the owner won't sell." At the time of the appointment, that person and the lawyer sit down and talk. If the visitor likes the lawyer and is willing to pay for what the lawyer might do, the visitor becomes a client of the lawyer.

During that conversation, the lawyer learns what problem the client wants solved and the client's goals in getting it solved; learns, factually, what the client knows about the problem; and tries to get to know the client as a human being and gives the client a reciprocal opportunity. Then or later, the lawyer and client also negotiate the retainer—the contract through which the client hires the lawyer—but here we focus on other aspects of the interview, especially fact-gathering.

These, then, are the lawyer's purposes in interviewing a client:

1. To Form an Attorney-Client Relationship.

That happens on three levels. One is personal, in that you and the client come to understand each other as people. To satisfy the client's needs, you have to understand the client as a person and how the problem matters in the client's way of thinking. If you and the client are to work together in a participatory relationship, you need to know each other fairly well. And the client cannot trust you without a solid feeling for the person you are. The second level is educational, in that you explain to the client (if the client does not already know) things like attorney-client confidentiality and the role the client would or could play in solving the problem. The third is contractual, in that the client agrees to hire you and pay your fees and expenses in exchange for your doing the work you promise to do.

2. To Learn the Client's Goals.

What does the client want or need to have done? Does the client have any feelings about the various methods of accomplishing those goals ("I don't want to sue unless there is no other way of getting them to stop dumping raw sewage in the river").

3. To Learn as Much as the Client Knows About the Facts.

This usually takes up most of the interview.

4. To Reduce the Client's Anxiety Without Being Unrealistic.

On a rational level, clients come to lawyers because they want problems solved. But on an emotional level, they come to get relief from anxiety. Even the client who is not in a dispute with anybody and wants something positive done, such as drafting a will, feels a reduction in anxiety when you are able to say—if you can honestly and prudently say it:—"I think we can structure your estate so that almost nothing would be taken in estate taxes and virtually everything would go to your heirs. It would take some work, but I think we can do it." Most of the time, you cannot offer even this much assurance in an initial interview because there are too many variables and, at the time of the interview, too many unknowns. When first meeting a client, you are almost never in a position to say, "If we sue your former employer, I think we will win." You need to do an exhaustive factual investigation before you can say something like that responsibly.

Most of the time, clients in initial interviews experience a significant degree of relief from anxiety simply from the knowledge that a capable, concerned, and likeable lawyer is committed to doing whatever is possible to solve the problem. When you help a client gain that feeling, you are reducing anxiety without being unrealistic. . . .

Heather Heavin & Michaela Keet, CLIENT-CENTERED COMMUNICATION: HOW EFFECTIVE LAWYERING REQUIRES EMOTIONAL INTELLIGENCE, ACTIVE LISTENING, AND CLIENT CHOICE

22 Cardozo J. Conflict Resol. 199, 199-202, 205-206, 208-210, 218-219 (2021)

While the lawyer must learn about the legally relevant facts that can impact the outcome of a negotiation, trial, or other disposition of a matter, lawyers also have ethical and professional obligations to understand their client's interests and goals in order to help the client make informed decisions about their case. This requires lawyers to engage in careful listening, questioning, and exploratory dialogue beyond the advice-giving realm. Here again, the educational literature widely discusses the centrality of psychological and "nonlegal" interests, and the benefits of active listening inside the negotiation and mediation of legal cases. We suggest that for methodical decision-making to occur, these skillsets need to be viewed as at the heart of the lawyer's engagement with the client. These skills need to be applied at the beginning of the lawyer-client relationship and used at key decision-making points in the litigation (or settlement) process.

In the traditional lawyer's office, this may not always be occurring. Although there is very little research about how lawyers and clients interact with one another, traditional images feature a hierarchical power dynamic between the lawyer and client, with clients being viewed as subordinates in the decision-making process. Such a power imbalance may silence or reshape client narratives. Anxious individuals are more likely to rely on the advice of others than on their own judgment. When lawyers cannot recognize a client's attempt to relate important information or simply view it as tangential, they unintentionally cut off the client's voice and inhibit responsive and inclusive legal decision-making. A lawyer's failure to truly hear a client impairs his or her ability to effectively collaborate, form a relationship, or grasp the full extent of information the client needs to share. Considering the stress clients face within any legal conflict, autonomous decision-making will not happen easily.

We suggest that a client-centered lawyering model (with its invitation to "reframe problems, question assumptions, shift perspectives. . .") is particularly effective when it comes to discussions about litigation risk. Such conversations require full and authentic client participation and collaborative decision-making, which can be difficult to deliver on against a backdrop of "old interview habits" and day-to-day pressures in a lawyer's practice. Transparency in the options and choices available to the client is critical. In approaching client interviews, interactions, and decision-making, we draw on ideas that will be familiar to most lawyers but may not be thought of as necessary skillsets to be employed by lawyers in their client interactions. We suggest that lawyers must understand how their own emotional intelligence and their clients' emotional intelligence impact their ability to understand and navigate the negotiation and litigation decisions that must be made. We also break down how a lawyer might use client-centered listening and questioning techniques to gather information, and then how that lawyer might offer information, in return, with an emphasis on client choice. Finally, we emphasize the benefits of these skills to *both the lawyer and the client* as options are generated and decisions are made about whether and how to proceed with litigation or opt for other alternatives such as negotiated or mediated settlements. . . .

Lawyers have been found to spend very little time on goal clarification with their clients. While lawyers in one study did discuss alternatives, they did not approach the interview as a chance for clients to make genuine choices among alternative courses of action. Rather, lawyers spent most of their time "explaining the law and advising the client *what* to do and *how* to do it." Trained to issue-spot in law school, lawyers have a tendency when gathering information to "troll for facts" in isolation from the context of clients' lives.

The instinct to information-gather in this way is understandable. It is deeply rooted in the focus inside legal education on legal analysis at the expense of understanding its backdrop. To view a client as a "bundle of legal rights and interests walking around in a human body." At a base level, clients want to be seen as more than "a file to get through." Lawyers who view themselves as problem-solving with the client, and who are open to dispute resolution processes other than litigation, naturally will seek a wider range of information from client narratives.

Research shows that clients tend to reveal critical information about themselves in their opening words of an interview. Unfortunately, much of this information is missed when the lawyer assumes the client's first responses are only part of the "icebreaking" stage, even in subsequent interviews with a client. Because there are conventions and learned greeting rituals within conversation, the lawyer will often assume nothing substantive is taking place. Instead of listening carefully to the client's words, the lawyer's mind may wander to formulating upcoming questions. Clients experiencing litigation stress may naturally skip over the "chit-chat" stage and immediately unburden themselves.

When lawyers listen to their clients and respond to them in a less directive approach, clients generally give more accurate and relevant information. Many clients prefer to present their issues in the form of a narrative, and it is through the client's narrative that a lawyer can see the situation through the client's eyes. Through a narrative, the lawyer can also draw meaning from what the client chooses to leave unsaid, explore whether two seemingly unrelated issues are in fact intertwined, and examine the relationship between the legal process and other important factors in their lives. Another advantage of narratives is that clients tend to perceive negative disclosures as less "face-threatening" when they are worked into a conversation.

When clients express themselves without interruption, it gives them a more active role in the interview process, resulting in partnership and co-participation. In contrast, when clients are interrupted, lawyers may end up actually losing relevant information. In a study of doctor-patient interviews, it was revealed that when patients were interrupted, only one in fifty returned to and completed what they were saying before they were interrupted. Interruptions result in doctors directing the conversation to the first issue raised, leaving patients unable to raise other serious concerns until late in the consultation.

Conversations about litigation risk can occur at different and even multiple stages in the lawyer-client relationship. In the early stages, this might involve posing broad questions: "Have you been involved in litigation before, or do you know friends or family who have?" "How do you expect the litigation process to work in your case?" "If you could have it your way, how would this matter proceed? What's the worst way this matter might proceed?" "Most people have some fears or concerns about litigation, whether or not they have been through litigation before. What are some of your fears and concerns?". . .

At the root of the skillset, what we are describing is empathy—the ability to understand others' emotions and situations, and then to convey and act on that understanding. Empathy fosters respect for others, and is seen as essential for rapport-building and for the effective management of relationships with clients. It is recognized as playing an important role in several aspects of legal practice, including dispute resolution and negotiation, as well as client counseling—and we suggest that it is equally important for decision-making about whether to litigate or settle.

Empathetic awareness allows lawyers to better understand their clients' situations and the backdrop of their lives. In their own legal clinic work, Marsden and Buhler have observed that when law students demonstrate empathy and sensitivity to clients' backgrounds, clients are more likely to trust students with relevant information. Research shows that clients do take note of whether their lawyers show genuine interest, and value corresponding lawyer attributes: "compassionate, understanding, interested, involved, human, accessible, personal, friendly, and nice."

While responding empathically may not come naturally to all lawyers, it is arguably a skill that can be taught and learned. During most interviews, a client's emotional reactions will surface, and at that point, it is important to recognize and acknowledge the emotional reactions, rather than ignore or avoid them. When a lawyer changes the topic, in response to a client's display of emotion, the lawyer inadvertently "takes back control" at a time when important information could be gathered. Emphatic responses—although affirming—are also neutral and nonjudgmental. Expressing empathy for the client's initial concerns will often lead to the disclosure of other concerns, and can therefore, be an effective step in information-gathering. Again, it may be helpful to draw a parallel to the medical field, where doctors are often having conversations with patients about risk and are taught to reflect concerns, as in the "NURS Quartet" for interviewing: Naming,

Understanding, Respecting, and Supporting. Naming the feeling is a way for doctors to signal to the patient that they have observed the emotion and that expressing emotions during the interview is acceptable. . . .

Within the realm of emotional intelligence, lawyers have not traditionally concerned themselves with the need to recognize client stress, nor do many lawyers think about how these stresses impact a client's decision-making ability. Because it is the norm for a lawyer to separate individual emotions from legal analysis the lawyer is precluded from fully understanding the impact of a client's emotions in their ability to understand the information that is being communicated to them, to assess options, and to make decisions. Instead, lawyers must engage in an active form of self-awareness. Without the capacity to clearly reflect on one's own experiences in litigation—and to communicate the implications of those experiences to a client, whether positive or negative—a lawyer can be at risk of "nudging," without transparency about her own values, beliefs, and preconceptions. The focus, we believe, ought to be on the client's freedom to make fully informed decisions guided by factors that have unique value to the client. The lawyer's job is to identify those factors through a lens which views emotions as clues for fears and priorities, and through a fulsome information-gathering process.

Active listening, open-ended questioning, and interviewing techniques are necessary skills for a lawyer to fully understand client narratives, interests, and goals. By employing these techniques, it is easier for the lawyer to provide *context-specific* information to the client, and to identify, through a collaborative process of discernment, what the risks and costs of litigation are likely to be. Generating and mapping out options will provide clear choices for clients. This will allow these clients to understand the risks and rewards of various options and enable them to make careful decisions about whether to pursue—or how to proceed with—litigation or settlement. Without such a client-centered approach, the promises embedded in negotiation and mediation—as well as the promises embedded in the lawyer-client relationship itself—cannot be fully realized.

Problem 2-6. ***Delivering Disappointing News***

A client comes to you and is insistent that he wants to go to court to sue his employer for discrimination. After carefully listening to your client and going over all the information, you conclude that he has a very weak case. (The specific comment his boss made, while awful and upsetting, probably does not alone constitute sufficient evidence of actionable discrimination. His sense that the workplace is "totally hostile in general," is clearly heart-felt, but you are concerned that you have not uncovered any specific employment decisions that would sustain a legal claim.) How do you present your client with your perspective on the risks and opportunities of litigating this case? What do you say to him if he still wants to pursue litigation?

With a fuller understanding of the client's needs, interests and goals—thanks to active listening skills and thoughtful interviewing and counseling techniques—lawyers often proceed to the most direct form of legal problem solving: negotiation. Negotiation is a process likely to be used in every transaction or dispute that comes to a lawyer. The next three chapters explore this process.

Further Reading

Marjorie Corman Aaron. (2012). Client Science: Advice for Lawyers on Counseling Clients Through Bad News and Other Legal Realities. Oxford: Oxford University Press.

John Barkai, How to Develop the Skill of Active Listening, 30 Prac. Law 73 (June 1984).

David A. Binder, Paul Bergman, Paul R. Tremblay & Ian S. Weinstein (2019). Lawyers As Counselors: A Client-Centered Approach (4th ed). Eagan, MN: West.

Robert F. Cochran, Jr., Introduction: Three Approaches to Moral Issues in Law Office Counseling, 30 Pepp. L. Rev. 592 (2003).

Stephen Ellmann, Robert D. Dinerstein, Isabelle R. Gunning, Katherine R. Kruse & Ann C. Shalleck. (2009). Lawyers and Clients: Critical Issues in Interviewing and Counseling. Eagan, MN: West.

Stephen Ellmann, Isabelle Gunning, Robert Dinnerstein & Ann Shalleck, Legal Interviewing and Counseling: An Introduction, 10 Clinical L. Rev. 281 (2003).

Cary Herman. (2021). Client Interviewing, Counseling, and Decision-Making: A Practical Approach (2d ed). Durham, NC: Carolina Academic Press.

Lauren Newell, Rebooting Empathy for the Digital Generation Lawyer, 34 Ohio St. J. on Disp. Resol. 1 (2019).

Oscar Salinas. (2016). A Short & Happy Guide to Effective Client Interviewing and Counseling. Eagan, MN: West.

Linda F. Smith, Was It Good for You Too? Conversation Analysis of Two Interviews, 96 Kentucky L.J. 579 (2007).

Paul R. Tremblay, "Pre-Negotiation" Counseling: An Alternative Model, 13 Clinical L. Rev. 541 (2006).

PART II THE BASIC PROCESSES: NEGOTIATION, MEDIATION, AND ARBITRATION

Chapter 3 Negotiation: Concepts and Models

When one door closes another door opens; but we so often look so long and so regretfully upon the closed door that we do not see the ones which open for us.

—Alexander Graham Bell

A pessimist sees the difficulty in every opportunity; an optimist sees the opportunity in every difficulty.

—Winston Churchill

If asked to draw a picture of a negotiation, many people likely would draw a table with two or more people sitting on opposite sides engaged in something akin to arm wrestling. This chapter expands upon and offers alternate pictures of negotiation. While it is true that many negotiations occur across large tables in conference rooms, many others occur in the hallways, via email, in the car, and at other everyday locations. Roger Fisher, author of the best-selling book *Getting to YES*,[1] says that a negotiation occurs every time that a person tries to influence someone else to do something. So, as you are reading this first chapter on negotiation, think about negotiations in which you have been regularly involved—with a parent, spouse, roommate, friend, neighbor, boss, or child. How do negotiations start? How do they proceed? What makes one successful and another the quintessential example of "if I had to do it again. . ."?

Negotiation is a process for resolving conflict and solving problems. It has conceptual and behavioral components, or, as negotiation scholar Howard Raiffa has described it, a "science" (of substantive ideas for solutions and outcomes) and an "art" (the behavioral and skill-based aspects of approaching others to jointly accomplish some goal). Before we turn to behavior, skills, and process (how to do negotiations), we need to spend some time thinking about how to analyze what we hope to accomplish. As many negotiation scholars and practitioners have suggested, and as we will elaborate on below, how we behave in negotiation (what model or approach we choose to use) will depend on what we are trying to accomplish (what goals we are hoping to achieve) in a particular negotiation. And,

1. Roger Fisher, William L. Ury & Bruce Patton, Getting to YES (1991).

in different kinds of negotiations, with different issues at stake or different kinds of parties, we might choose different models or approaches.

It is common for many to think of negotiation as an adversarial, competitive, or distributive (allocating scarce resources) exercise. Others prefer to see negotiation as an opportunity to resolve problems and seek joint gain while still being realistic about the stakes and about the parties, who may limit what is possible. It is useful to consider one's goals regarding both the process and the outcome of a negotiation, which will determine the orientation, mind-set, and behaviors chosen. These, in turn, will affect the outcomes produced. Some of the possibilities are illustrated below:[2]

Models of Negotiation

	Goal	Model	Behavior	Outcomes
I.	Win (Maximizing individual gain)	*Adversarial* *Distributive*	Competitive or positional debate Argue Hide information Make demands	Win/Lose Impasse
II.	Compromise (Relationship preserving)	*Soft* *Accommodative* *Sharing*	Cooperate Give in Make unnecessary concessions	Compromise Split the difference Lose
III.	Problem Solve (Maximizing joint gain)	*Integrative Problem Solving* *Principled* *Interest-based*	Collaborative Ask questions Listen Explore needs/ interests Find trades of complementary interests and needs Use objective criteria	Creative solutions Expanded issues and opportunities
IV.	Allocate created resources/ solutions	*Mixed*	Create, then "claim"	Pareto optimal sharing gain

This chapter explores some of these basic models and approaches to negotiation. First, you can think of negotiation as a process. You will conceptualize what the problem or dispute is about; what is at stake; what you might need to resolve the matter; and whom you might need to reach a good solution. Second, you will make choices about how to achieve those goals. The "art" of negotiation

2. This chart is derived from Carrie Menkel-Meadow, Toward Another View of Legal Negotiation: The Structure of Problem Solving, 31 UCLA L. Rev. 754 (1984) and ideas developed in Howard Raiffa, The Art and Science of Negotiation (1982) and David A. Lax & James K. Sebenius, The Manager as Negotiator: Bargaining for Cooperation and Competitive Gain (1986).

examines your – and your negotiation counterpart's – choices of behaviors and moves. Finally, if you reach an agreement, you must evaluate the outcome: does it satisfy your client's needs and goals and make the other side sufficiently satisfied ("joint gain"), so that all will comply with the agreement reached? Negotiation (whether direct, or as mediated by a third party in mediation) involves both cognitive and behavioral skills. As an effective negotiator, you should be able to analyze problems, plan for and prepare ideas for good resolutions, and choose behaviors that accomplish your goals.

Different descriptors of negotiation can be helpful to illustrate this process. We will examine negotiation as linear, cyclical and as a "game."

Professor Gerald Williams describes adversarial and distributive negotiation as proceeding in four stages: (1) orientation and positioning; (2) argumentation; (3) emergence and crisis; and (4) agreement or final breakdown.[3] Orientation involves the adoption of a basic approach and an examination of the style of the other negotiator. Orientation will dictate the approach, strategies, and tactics utilized by the negotiator and her counterpart. Positioning is establishing the negotiator's opening position (sometimes a dollar amount), which will be adjusted with further evaluations and information. During argumentation, stage two, legal and factual issues, as well as strengths and weakness, are outlined, and the parties usually go back and forth with offers. The third stage of emergence and crisis takes place as the deadline for settlement approaches. Parties often make a "final offer" to one another, leaving a choice of take it, leave it, or come up with something else. Finally, in stage four, the parties either reach a settlement or the matter must be resolved elsewhere—court, arbitration, or the like. In the case of an agreement, the parties must work out the always-important details of their agreement.

Another way of thinking about negotiation is as a cyclical process, as explained by Phillip Gulliver. The process is not always directly linear but may require several moves (or cycles) to move forward. As he writes, "In negotiation, . . . there is a cyclical process comprising the repetitive exchange of information between the parties, its assessment, and the resulting adjustments of expectations and preferences; there is also a developmental process involved in the movement from the initiation of the dispute to its conclusion—some outcome—and its implementation."[4]

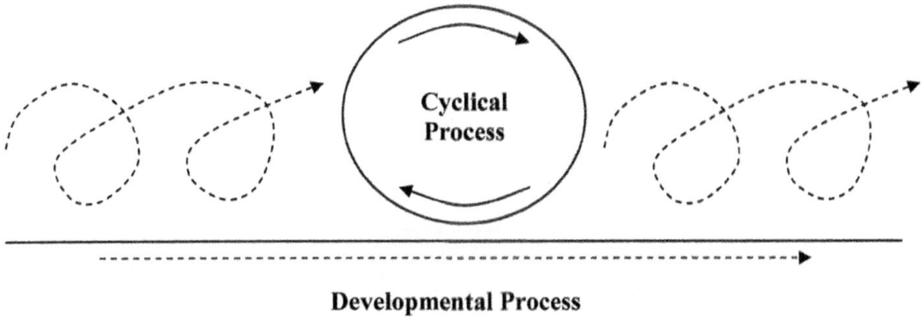

3. Gerald R. Williams, Legal Negotiation and Settlement 53 (1983).
4. Phillip H. Gulliver, Disputes and Negotiations: A Cross-Cultural Perspective 82 (1979).

Problem 3-1. *House Hunting*

Imagine that you are house hunting. You find a house that looks like it meets your needs and is priced fairly based on your looking at other houses in the neighborhood. It has the number of bedrooms you need and a lovely backyard. It is listed for $290,000, but your realtor thinks that it probably will go for less. You give an opening bid of $270,000. The realtor for the owners does not respond immediately but instead invites you to come back to see the house again. While there, the owner's realtor points out the newly refurbished kitchen with new appliances and a new floor. Also, he mentions that the owners recently redid much of the outdoor landscaping (which you cannot see because it is winter). You note, and point out to the realtor, that the driveway needs repaving soon. It also appears that the roof needs to be replaced within the next five years. When you ask for a response to your bid, the owners reply with a counteroffer of $285,000. You take your time to counteroffer and note that the house has been on the market for some time. You counteroffer at $280,000 and strongly let the realtor know this is your final bid. The owners accept.

Using Williams's stages, at which point does each stage commence in the above scenario? What issues are left for stage four? How does Gulliver's model help explain this negotiation?

Another well-known negotiation description often taught in economics and psychology classes is the Prisoner's Dilemma, a game-theory model of decision analysis. As Douglas Hofstadter described it:

> In case you're wondering why it is called "Prisoner's Dilemma," here's the reason. Imagine that you and an accomplice (someone you have no feelings for one way or the other) committed a crime, and now you've both been apprehended and thrown in jail and are fearfully awaiting trials. You are being held in separate cells with no way to communicate. The prosecutor offers each of you the following deal (and informs you both that the identical deal is being offered to each of you—and that you both know *that* as well!): "We have a lot of circumstantial evidence on you both. So, if you both claim innocence, we will convict you anyway and you'll both get two years in jail. But if you will help us out by admitting your guilt and making it easier for us to convict your accomplice—oh, pardon me, your *alleged* accomplice—why, then, we'll let you out free. And don't worry about revenge—your accomplice will be in for five years! How about it?" Warily you ask, "But what if we *both* say we're guilty?" "Ah, well, my friend—I'm afraid you'll both get four-year sentences, then."[5]

5. Douglas R. Hofstadter, Metamagical Themas: Questing for the Essence of Mind and Pattern 716 (1985).

Your choice in this scenario is limited to either trusting the other prisoner to also keep his or her mouth shut (and both get out of jail) or talk ("defect" in game theory parlance) and hope that the other prisoner was more trusting of you. Some have applied the Prisoner's Dilemma to all negotiations, arguing that each negotiator has the choice whether to work together or "defect."

Problem 3-2. *Prisoner's Dilemma Advice*

If one of the prisoners were your client, how would you advise him or her? If *both* of the prisoners were your clients, how would you advise them? Does your advice differ? Why or why not? Assume that the prisoners know each other. How would you advise your client now? Is this different advice than above? Why or why not?

What if the prisoners in the Prisoner's Dilemma were going to find themselves in the same situation next week? Does the idea of repeat interactions change behavior? In his work on game theory, famed political scientist Robert Axelrod discussed lessons from a computer tournament that was set up to test the best strategy for dealing with a Prisoner's Dilemma when the interactions were repeated over time (much like lawyers who operate in the same practice area or city). Axelrod's key lessons for a successful negotiation strategy from the tournament are:

1. Don't be envious—focus on how well you are performing, not compared to the other side, but to someone in the same position as you.
2. Don't be the first to defect—it pays to cooperate.
3. Reciprocate both cooperation and defection—work together but do punish for "bad" behavior.
4. Don't be too clever—be clear in your communication to the other side about your own behavior and expectations of their behavior.

Robert Axelrod, The Evolution of Cooperation (1984).

With these lessons in mind, how would you apply them to negotiation? Does it matter if this is the first time you've negotiated with your counterpart or the tenth? If you find yourself in a context with the hallmarks of a Prisoner's Dilemma, what options might you have to change the nature of the "game" in the real world?

Problem 3-3. ***Why We Cooperate***

Researchers have found a biological reason that people cooperate:

> What feels as good as chocolate on the tongue or money in the bank but won't make you fat or risk a subpoena from the [SEC]?
>
> Hard as it may be to believe in these days of infectious greed and sabers unsheathed, scientists have discovered that the small, brave act of cooperating with another person, of choosing trust over cynicism, generosity over selfishness, makes the brain light up with quiet joy.
>
> Studying neural activity in young women who were playing a classic laboratory game called the Prisoner's Dilemma, in which participants can select from a number of greedy or cooperative strategies as they pursue financial gain, researchers found that when the women chose mutualism over "meism," the mental circuitry normally associated with reward-seeking behavior swelled to life.
>
> And the longer the women engaged in a cooperative strategy, the more strongly flowed the blood to the pathways of pleasure.

Natalie Angier, Why We're So Nice: We're Wired to Cooperate, N.Y. Times, July 23, 2002, at F1.

The researchers had actually expected that the subjects would feel more emotion when one person cooperated and the other defected. In fact, the subjects were most responsive when patterns of cooperation occurred. Although the experiment was performed only on women, the researchers predicted that these findings would be the same for both genders. The researchers thought that this push to cooperate might explain why humans behave better than other species (assuming you think that). What do you think? If you have participated in a Prisoner's Dilemma game, how did you feel? For more on this biological need to cooperate, see also Frans de Waal's TED talk, Do Animals Have Morals? https://www.ted.com/talks/frans_de_waal_do_animals_have_morals.

Different descriptions of negotiation, and the assumptions behind them, can push us to make certain strategic choices as we negotiate. Consider how assuming you are in a Prisoner's Dilemma (with its one-shot assumptions) versus the repeat interactions in a cyclical process might nudge you toward a particular approach or model as outlined on page 78.

In addition, the models, or approaches, described below suggest other forms of process than those outlined above. These could include reciprocal questioning and sharing of information, time for non-evaluative brainstorming of new ideas and solutions; presentation of multiple "interests" and "needs" framed differently than single or rigid positions or demands; and either direct or facilitated trading and sharing of ideas, rationales and proposals for negotiated solutions. With negotiations varying in type and medium (whether in person, over email, on the telephone, or through written drafts of documents), there are likely to be great variations in how their stages and processes develop, whether in single, specially designated negotiation meetings, or in frequent, interrupted communications using a variety of media and negotiator representatives.

A. CHOOSING AMONG NEGOTIATION APPROACHES

As we delve into the different choices available in negotiation, we want to spend more time understanding how those choices should be made. Perhaps you feel you are in a prisoner's dilemma where it appears your only choice is to cooperate or defect. How would you know this? How could you assess the context, and what you might expect from your counterpart? This next excerpt focuses on how lawyers should choose their approach based on their goals in any negotiation.

❖ *Carrie Menkel-Meadow*, TOWARD ANOTHER VIEW OF LEGAL NEGOTIATION: THE STRUCTURE OF PROBLEM SOLVING

31 UCLA L. Rev. 755-762 (1984)

INTRODUCTION

When people negotiate, they engage in a particular kind of social behavior; they seek to do together what they cannot do alone. Those who negotiate are sometimes principals attempting to solve their own problems, or, more likely in legal negotiation, they are agents acting for clients, within the bounds of the law.

When lawyers write about this frequent social activity they join commentators from other disciplines in emphasizing an adversarial or zero-sum game approach to negotiation. In their view, what one party gains the other must lose. Resources are limited and must be divided. Information about one's real preferences must be jealously guarded. If the negotiation fails, the court will declare one party a winner, awarding money or an injunction. Successful negotiations represent a compromise of each party's position on an ordinal scale of numerical (usually monetary) values. This Article suggests that writers and negotiators who take such an adversarial approach limit themselves unnecessarily because they have not fully examined their assumption.

Recently, several analysts have suggested that another approach to negotiation, an approach I will call problem solving, might better accomplish the purposes of negotiation. This problem-solving model seeks to demonstrate how negotiators, on behalf of litigators or planners, can more effectively accomplish their goals by focusing on the parties' actual objectives and creatively attempting to satisfy the needs of both parties, rather than by focusing exclusively on the assumed objectives of maximizing individual gain. . . .

In order to contrast the adversarial model with the problem-solving model several key concepts must be defined and criteria for evaluation of the models made explicit. The negotiation models described here may seem unduly polarized, yet they represent the polarities of approach exemplified both by the conceptions of negotiation we construct as well as by the strategies and behaviors we choose. The models described here are based on orientations to negotiation, that is, how we approach our purpose in negotiation, rather than on the particular strategies or tactics we choose. It must be noted, however, that the tactics and strategies we choose may well be affected by our conception of negotiation. A general model demonstrates the relationship of negotiation orientations to negotiation results:

Orientation ⟶ Mind-set ⟶ Behavior ⟶ Results

The orientation (adversarial or problem solving) leads to a mind-set about what can be achieved (maximizing individual gain or solving the parties' problem by satisfying their underlying needs) which in turn affects the behavior chosen (competitive or solution searching) which in turn affects the solutions arrived at (narrow compromises or creative solutions).

The primary, but not exclusive, criterion for evaluation of a negotiation model is the quality of the solution produced. This includes the extent to which the process utilized contributes to or hinders the search for "quality" solutions.

In elaborating on approaches to negotiation I shall consider the following criteria of evaluation:

1. Does the solution reflect the client's total set of "real" needs, goals and objectives, in both the short and the long term?
2. Does the solution reflect the other party's full set of "real" needs, goals and objectives, in both the short and long term?
3. Does the solution promote the relationship the client desires with the other party?
4. Have the parties explored all the possible solutions that might either make each better off or one party better off with no adverse consequences to the other party?
5. Has the solution been achieved at the lowest possible transaction costs relative to the desirability of the result?
6. Is the solution achievable, or has it only raised more problems that need to be solved? Are the parties committed to the solution, so it can be enforced without regret?
7. Has the solution been achieved in a manner congruent with the client's desire to participate in and affect the negotiation?
8. Is the solution "fair" or "just"? Have the parties considered the legitimacy of each other's claims and made any adjustments they feel are humanely or morally indicated?

Criteria one through seven are all based on a utilitarian justification of negotiation. By satisfying these criteria, a negotiation may produce results which are more satisfactory to the parties, thus enhancing commitment to and enforcement of the agreement. The final criterion is applicable to those negotiators who wish to consider the effects of their solution on the other party from a humanitarian or ethical perspective.

In a further exploration, Carrie Menkel-Meadow suggested that the following factors might influence which model of negotiation we might choose in particular situations:

- *Subject matter* (Dispute vs. transaction, the material of the negotiation—is it limited, expandable, is there a need for a definitive, precedential ruling?)
- *Content of the issues* (What are the underlying interests of the parties—latent, manifest, short term, long term? Do the parties value the issues equally?)
- *Voluntariness* (Do the parties have a choice about negotiating?)
- *Visibility* (Will negotiations be conducted privately or publicly?)
- *Relationship* (Parties, negotiators, long term or one-shot)
- *Accountability* (To what constituencies is the negotiator responsible—a single client, an organizational client, a family, a labor union?)
- *Stake* (Who stands to "win or lose" most from the negotiation?)
- *Routineness* (How is the negotiation limited by frequency and norms of the problem, e.g. plea bargaining?)
- *Power* (How do parties assess their relative power in terms of fact, law, economic resources, and moral righteousness?)
- *Personal characteristics of the negotiator* (Psychological "orientations")
- *Medium of the negotiation* (Face-to-face encounter vs. telephonic or written or computer assisted negotiations)
- *Alternatives to negotiation* (Trial, transaction not consummated?)

From Carrie Menkel-Meadow, Legal Negotiation: A Study of Strategies in Search of a Theory, 1983 A.B. F. Res. J. 905, 927-928.

With these questions in mind, we can turn to an explanation of the classic negotiation approaches.

B. NEGOTIATION APPROACHES

Now that you've read about your mindset and orientation to negotiation (which often help determine how to approach a negotiation), we turn to elaborating the different approaches to legal negotiation. The readings that follow highlight differences among these various approaches and suggest criteria for choosing styles or behaviors that may be most effective in different contexts, participants, and kinds of issues. In short, there is no such thing as a single "negotiation" approach or style that will be appropriate in all situations.

> Trades would not take place unless it were advantageous to the parties concerned. Of course, it is better to strike as good a bargain as one's bargaining position permits. The worst outcome is when, by overreaching greed, no bargain is struck, and a trade that could have been advantageous to both parties does not come off at all.
>
> —Benjamin Franklin

The first approach (and one you are probably most familiar with from being a law student in our American culture) is called competitive bargaining or adversarial, distributive, or positional negotiating. Most of these labels refer to a negotiator who is primarily concerned with "winning" the negotiation for the client and themselves. A competitive negotiator is often seen as more likely to engage in negative tactics, less likely to be interested in the other side's point of view, and perhaps, but not always, more unpleasant. This approach is often used by those who assume that what is being bargained for must be distributed between the parties—such as in simply two-party, "pricing" situations. A higher price gives the seller additional gain at the expense of the buyer.[6]

The second approach is at the other end of the spectrum and called "soft" bargaining, also known as accommodating or cooperative bargaining. As the readings highlight, this approach focuses on relationships and on working with the other side. A cooperative negotiator is likely to be more pleasant and friendly. The risk for a cooperative negotiation approach is being taken advantage of by the competitive negotiator who values gain in the negotiation more than the relationship between the negotiators.

A third approach is problem solving, also called integrative, collaborative, or principled bargaining. A problem-solving approach to a negotiation is one in which the negotiator is interested in doing well for herself, her client, and in working with the other side to meet that party's interests. This model sees negotiation as an opportunity to "expand" the resources available and to search for creative solutions to negotiation problems and dilemmas. Some call this the "joint gain" model of negotiation.

Problem 3-4. ***Your Conflict Orientation***

Which orientation do you use when negotiating with your family? With your friends? With your romantic interest? With someone at work? Where someone has been very generous or very selfish in the past, would it influence your negotiation approach? Should your orientation change depending on what's at stake? What factors would you want to consider when determining which approach to apply?

6. An extreme form of distributive and competitive bargaining was popularized by Donald Trump in his ghost-written memoir, The Art of the Deal (1987). For a review of some disturbing experimental effects, after the 2016 election, on increased aggressiveness in communication leading to reduced gain, see Jennie Huang and Corinne Low, Trumping Norms: Lab Evidence on Aggressive Communication before and after the 2016 US Presidential Election 107 Am. Econ. Rev. 120-24 (2017).

The next excerpt provides a brief overview of the competitive approach and the motivations and attitudes of a competitive negotiator. Understanding this orientation, you may be better positioned to counter positional bargaining in the future.

1. Competitive Approaches to Negotiation

Gary Goodpaster, A PRIMER ON COMPETITIVE BARGAINING

1996 J. Disp. Resol. 325, 326, 341-342 (1996)

Competitive bargaining, sometimes called hard, distributive, positional, zero-sum or win-lose bargaining, has the purpose of maximizing the competitive bargainer's gain over the gain of those with whom he negotiates. He is, in effect, trying to "come out ahead of," or "do better than," all other parties in the negotiation. For this reason, we sometimes refer to this competitive bargaining strategy as a *domination* strategy, meaning that the competitive bargainer tends to treat negotiations as a kind of contest to win.

The competitive negotiator tends to define success in negotiation rather narrowly. It is simply getting as much as possible for himself: the cheapest price, the most profit, the least cost, the best terms and so on. In its simplest form, this strategy focuses on immediate gain and is not much concerned with the relationship between the negotiating parties. A more complex version of this strategy focuses on long-term gain. This focus usually requires some effort to maintain or further a relationship and usually moderates the competitive, often aggressive, behavior that jeopardizes relationships and possibilities of long-term gain. . . .

People bargain competitively essentially for three reasons, which often overlap. First, by inclination or calculation, they view the negotiation as a kind of competition, in which they wish to win or gain as much as possible. Secondly, they do not trust the other party. Where parties are non-trusting, they are non-disclosing and withhold information, which leads to further distrust and defensive or self-protective moves. Parties may be non-trusting because they are unfamiliar with the other party or because they are generally or situationally non-trusting. Finally, a party may bargain competitively as a defense to, or retaliation for, competitive moves directed at it.

---

2. Accommodating Approaches to Negotiation

A second approach to a negotiation when there are limited resources to divide is to be more concerned with the other sides' needs. Some authors describe this orientation as "accommodative," while other authors refer to this approach as "soft bargaining" or as "cooperative." While this approach is completely different from the adversarial approach, it often shares the assumption that a distributional negotiation exists.

This next excerpt from Donald Gifford explains the theory behind a cooperative strategy and the skills available to the cooperative negotiator working through a conflict.

Donald G. Gifford, A CONTEXT-BASED THEORY OF STRATEGY SELECTION IN LEGAL NEGOTIATION

46 Ohio St. L.J. 41, 52-54 (1985)

A view of human nature different than that upon which the competitive strategy is premised, with its emphasis on undermining the confidence of opposing counsel, underlies most collaborative interaction. In everyday events, even when they are deciding how to divide a limited resource between them, two negotiators often seek to reach an agreement which is fair and equitable to both parties and seek to build an interpersonal relationship based on trust. This approach to negotiation can be designated the cooperative strategy. The cooperative negotiator initiates granting concessions in order to create both a moral obligation to reciprocate and a relationship built on trust that is conducive to achieving a fair agreement.

The cooperative negotiator does not view making concessions as a necessity resulting from a weak bargaining position or a loss of confidence in the value of her case. Rather, she values concessions as an affirmative negotiating technique designed to capitalize on the opponent's desire to reach a fair and just agreement and to maintain an accommodative working relationship. Proponents of the cooperative strategy believe that negotiators are motivated not only by individualistic or competitive desires to maximize their own utilities, but also by collectivistic desires to reach a fair solution. Cooperative negotiators assert that the competitive strategy often leads to resentment between the parties and a breakdown of negotiations.

According to Professor Otomar Bartos, an originator of the cooperative strategy, the negotiator should begin negotiations not with a maximalist position, but rather with a more moderate opening bid that is both favorable to him and barely acceptable to the opponent. Once two such opening bids are on the table, the negotiators should determine the midpoint between the two opening bids and regard it as a fair and equitable outcome. External facts, such as how large a responsive concession the negotiator expects from the opponent, whether she is representing a tough constituency that would view large concessions unfavorably, and whether she is under a tight time deadline and wants to expedite the process by making a large concession, affect the size of the negotiator's first concession. According to Professor Bartos, the negotiator should then expect the opponent to reciprocate with a concession of similar size so that the midpoint between the parties' positions remains the same as it was after the realistic opening bids were made. The concessions by the parties are fair, according to Bartos, as long as the parties do not need to revise their initial expectations about the substance of the agreement.

The term *cooperative strategy* embraces a larger variety of negotiation tactics than Bartos' detailed model. Cooperative strategies include any strategies that aim to develop trust between the parties and that focus on the expectation that the opponent will match concessions ungrudgingly. Endemic to all cooperative strategies is the question of how the negotiator should respond if the opponent does not match her concessions and does not reciprocate her goodwill. The major weakness of the cooperative approach is its vulnerability to exploitation by the competitive negotiator. The cooperative negotiator is severely disadvantaged if her opponent fails to reciprocate her concessions. Cooperative negotiation theorists suggest a variety of responses when concessions are not matched. Professor Bartos recommends that the negotiator "stop making further concessions until the opponent catches up."

Because of its vulnerability to exploitation, the cooperative theory may not initially appear to be a viable alternative to the competitive strategy. As mentioned previously, in tightly controlled experiments with simulated negotiations, the competitive strategy generally produces better results. However, in actual practice, the competitive approach results in more impasses and greater distrust between the parties. Furthermore, most people tend to be cooperative in orientation and trusting of others. Professor Williams found that sixty-five percent of the attorneys he surveyed used a cooperative approach.[7] This, of course, means that in a majority of cases the cooperative negotiator will not be exploited by her opponent, because the opponent also uses a cooperative approach. Most cooperative negotiators probably would not feel comfortable using the competitive negotiators' aggressive tactics, which are designed to undermine the opponent and his case. Nor would they relish living and working in the mistrustful milieu which may result from the use of the competitive strategy.

Problem 3-5. *"Peace In Our Time"*

Many historians use British Prime Minister Neville Chamberlain's 1938 appeasement of Hitler as a worst-case example of the possible consequences of accommodating. To avoid war, Chamberlain agreed not to defend Czechoslovakia against a German invasion if Hitler agreed to end his territorial ambitions at that point. Although Chamberlain kept his promise, Hitler, as history tells us, did not.

The Russian invasion of the Ukraine in 2022 raised similar issues. Was the West too weak in its response to Russia's earlier invasion of Crimea and the Donbas region in 2014? Were different US Presidents being too "hard" or "soft" with Russian president Putin in response?

For a more positive example of hard bargaining, consider the US Women's Soccer team's filing of a lawsuit (and waging of a successful public relations campaign) against the US Soccer Federation for equal pay in 2022. (Or consider the Spanish women's soccer team's refusal to play until their coach was replaced in 2023.) Can you think of other positive or negative examples of hard or soft bargaining?

7. Gerald R. Williams, Legal Negotiation and Settlement 53 (1983).

3. Integrative or Problem-Solving Approaches to Negotiation

"It's not that I'm so smart, it's just that I stay with problems longer."
—Albert Einstein

Many beginner negotiators assume that the adversarial or cooperative approaches are the only choices of strategy in a negotiation. *This is a misconception.* Both strategies focus only on one part of the negotiation—dividing the "pie" of services or goods that are subject of negotiation—rather than on other activities that can expand the resources available to the parties before they may have to be allocated or divided. Problem solving, or integrative negotiation, looks for more creative solutions to problems that may lie outside of what the parties assume are available to them under a more distributive approach. This section discusses the various ideas and approaches that fall under integrative negotiation (also called "problem solving" and "principled negotiation").

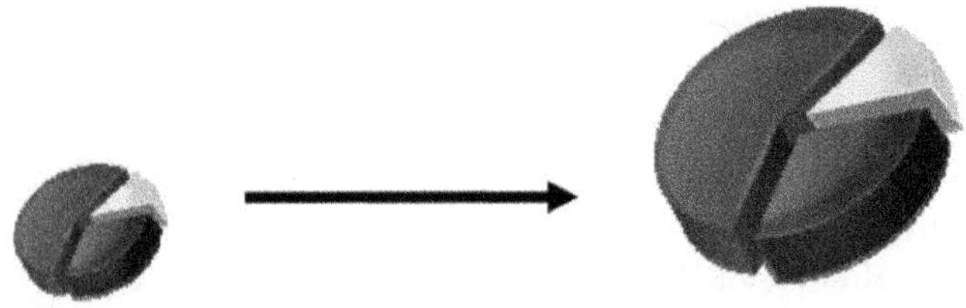

This first excerpt is from Carrie Menkel-Meadow's classic article on the problem-solving concept of negotiation, from which you already read at the beginning of this chapter.

❖ *Carrie Menkel-Meadow*, TOWARD ANOTHER VIEW OF LEGAL NEGOTIATION: THE STRUCTURE OF PROBLEM SOLVING

31 UCLA L. Rev. 794-801 (1984)

Problem solving is an orientation to negotiation which focuses on finding solutions to the parties' sets of underlying needs and objectives. The problem-solving conception subordinates strategies and tactics to the process of identifying possible solutions and therefore allows a broader range of outcomes to negotiation problems.

A.THE UNDERLYING PRINCIPLES OF PROBLEM SOLVING: MEETING VARIED AND COMPLEMENTARY NEEDS

Parties to a negotiation typically have underlying needs or objectives—what they hope to achieve, accomplish, and/or be compensated for as a result of the dispute or transaction. Although litigants typically ask for relief in the form of damages, this relief is actually a proxy for more basic needs or objectives. By attempting to uncover those underlying needs, the problem-solving model presents opportunities for discovering greater numbers of and better-quality solutions. It offers the possibility of meeting a greater variety of needs both directly and by trading off different needs, rather than forcing a zero-sum battle over a single item.

The principle underlying such an approach is that unearthing a greater number of the actual needs of the parties will create more possible solutions because not all needs will be mutually exclusive. As a corollary, because not all individuals value the same things in the same way, the exploitation of differential or complementary needs will produce a wider variety of solutions which more closely meet the parties' needs.

A few examples may illustrate these points. In personal injury actions courts usually award monetary damages. Plaintiffs, however, commonly want this money for specific purposes. For instance, an individual who has been injured in a car accident may desire compensation for any or all of the following items: past and future medical expenses, rehabilitation and compensation for the cost of rehabilitation, replacement of damaged property such as a car and the costs of such replacement, lost income, compensation for lost time, pain and suffering, the loss of companionship with one's family, friends and fellow employees and employer, lost opportunities to engage in activities which may no longer be possible, such as backpacking or playing basketball with one's children, vindication or acknowledgment of fault by the responsible party, and retribution or punishment of the person who was at fault. In short, the injured person seeks to be returned to the same physical, psychological, social and economic state she was in before the accident occurred. Because this may be impossible, the plaintiff needs money in order to buy back as many of these things as possible. . . .

Some of the parties' needs may not be compensable, directly or indirectly. For example, some injuries may be impossible to fully rehabilitate. A physical disability, a scar, or damage to a personal or business reputation may never be fully eradicated. Thus, the underlying needs produced by these injuries may not be susceptible to full and/or monetary satisfaction. The need to be regarded as totally normal or completely honorable can probably never be met, but the party in a negotiation will be motivated by the desire to satisfy as fully as possible these underlying human needs. Some parties may have a need to get "as much X as possible," such as in demands for money for pain and suffering. This demand simply may represent the best proxy available for satisfying the unsatisfiable desire to be made truly whole—that is to be put back in the position of no accident at all. It also may represent a desire to save for a rainy day or to maximize power, fame or love.

It is also important to recognize that *both* parties have such needs. For example, in the personal injury case above, the defendant may have the same need for vindication or retribution if he believes he was not responsible for the accident. In addition, the defendant may need to be compensated for his damaged car and injured body. He will also have needs with respect to how much, when and how he may be able to pay the monetary damages because of other uses for the money. A contract breaching defendant may have specific financial needs such as payroll, advertising, purchases of supplies, etc.; defendants are not always simply trying to avoid paying a certain sum of money to plaintiffs. In the commercial case, the defendant may have needs similar to those of the plaintiff: lost income due to the plaintiff's failure to pay on the contract, and, to the extent the plaintiff may seek to terminate the relationship with the defendant, a steady source of future business. . . .

To the extent that negotiators focus exclusively on "winning" the greatest amount of money, they focus on only one form of need. The only flexibility in tailoring an agreement may lie in the choice of ways to structure monetary solutions, including one shot payments, installments, and structured settlements. By looking, however, at what the parties desire money for, there may be a variety of solutions that will satisfy the parties more fully and directly. For example, when an injured plaintiff needs physical rehabilitation, if the defendant can provide the plaintiff directly with rehabilitation services, the defendant may save money and the plaintiff may gain the needed rehabilitation at lower cost. In addition, if the defendant can provide the plaintiff with a job that provides physical rehabilitation, the plaintiff may not only receive income which could be used to purchase more rehabilitation but be further rehabilitated in the form of the psychological self-worth which accompanies such employment. Admittedly, none of these solutions may fully satisfy the injured plaintiff, but some or all may be equally beneficial to the plaintiff, and the latter two may be preferable to the defendant because they are less costly.

Understanding that the other party's needs are not necessarily as assumed may present an opportunity for arriving at creative solutions. Traditionally, lawyers approaching negotiations from the adversarial model view the other side as an enemy to be defeated. By examining the underlying needs of the other side, the lawyer may instead see opportunities for solutions that would not have existed before based upon the recognition of different, but not conflicting, preferences.

An example from the psychological literature illustrates this point.[8] Suppose that a husband and wife have two weeks in which to take their vacation. The husband prefers the mountains and the wife prefers the seaside. If vacation time is limited and thus a scarce resource, the couple may engage in adversarial negotiation about where they should go. The simple compromise situation, if they engage in distributive bargaining, would be to split the two weeks of vacation time spending one week in the mountains and one week at the ocean. This solution is not likely to be satisfying, however, because of the lost time and money in moving from place to place and in getting used to a new hotel room and locale. In addition to being happy only half of the time, each party to the negotiation has incurred transaction costs associated with this solution. Other "compromise" solutions might include alternating

8. D.G. Pruitt & S.A. Lewis, The Psychology of Interactive Bargaining, in Negotiations: Social-Psychological Perspectives 169-170 (D. Druckman ed., 1977).

preferences on a year to year basis, taking separate vacations, or taking a longer vacation at a loss of pay. Assuming that husband and wife want to vacation together, all of these solutions may leave something to be desired by at least one of the parties.

By examining their underlying preferences, however, the parties might find additional solutions that could make both happy at less cost. Perhaps the husband prefers the mountains because he likes to hike and engage in stream fishing. Perhaps the wife enjoys swimming, sunbathing and seafood. By exploring these underlying preferences, the couple might find vacation spots that permit all of these activities: a mountain resort on a large lake, or a seaside resort at the foot of mountains. By examining their underlying needs, the parties can see solutions that satisfy many more of their preferences, and the "sum of the utilities" to the couple as a whole is greater than what they would have achieved by compromising.

In addition, by exploring whether they attach different values to their preferences they may be able to arrive at other solutions by trading items. The wife in our example might be willing to give up ocean fresh seafood if she can have fresh stream or lake trout, and so, with very little cost to her, the couple can choose another waterspot where the hikes might be better for the husband. By examining the weight or value given to certain preferences the parties may realize that some desires are easily attainable because they are not of equal importance to the other side. Thus, one party can increase its utilities without reducing the other's. This differs from a zero-sum conception of negotiation because of the recognition that preferences may be totally different and are, therefore, neither scarce nor in competition with each other. In addition, if a preference is not used to "force" a concession from the other party (which as the example shows is not necessary), there are none of the forced reciprocal concessions of adversarial negotiation.

The exploitation of complementary interests occurs frequently in the legal context. For example, in a child custody case the lawyers may learn that both parties desire to have the children some of the time and neither of the parties wishes to have the children all of the time. It will be easy, therefore, to arrange for a joint custody agreement that satisfies the needs of both parties. Similarly, in a commercial matter, the defendant may want to make payment over time and the plaintiff, for tax purposes or to increase interest income, may desire deferred income.

Getting to YES is a worldwide bestseller on principled or interest-based negotiation, also known as the integrative or problem-solving approach. Fisher and his co-authors explain below why adversarial and accommodating approaches produce agreements that are unwise, inefficient, or those that damage the parties' relationship. They then outline four points that will guide a negotiator to a better agreement.

Roger Fisher, William Ury & Bruce Patton, GETTING TO YES

4-7, 10-14 (2d ed. 1991)

Any method of negotiation may be fairly judged by three criteria: It should produce a wise agreement if agreement is possible. It should be efficient. And it should improve or at least not damage the relationship between the parties. (A wise agreement can be defined as one that meets the legitimate interests of each side to the extent possible, resolves conflicting interests fairly, is durable, and takes community interest into account.). . .

Taking positions, as the customer and storekeeper do, serves some useful purposes in a negotiation. It tells the other side what you want; it provides an anchor in an uncertain and pressured situation; and it can eventually produce the terms of an acceptable agreement. But those purposes can be served in other ways. And positional bargaining fails to meet the basic criteria of producing a wise agreement, efficiently and amicably.

ARGUING OVER POSITIONS PRODUCES UNWISE AGREEMENTS

When negotiators bargain over positions, they tend to lock themselves into those positions. The more you clarify your position and defend it against attack, the more committed you become to it. The more you try to convince the other side of the impossibility of changing your opening position, the more difficult it becomes to do so. Your ego becomes identified with your position. You now have a new interest in "saving face"—in reconciling future action with past positions—making it less and less likely that any agreement will wisely reconcile the parties' original interests.

ARGUING OVER POSITIONS IS INEFFICIENT . . .

Bargaining over positions creates incentives that stall settlement. In positional bargaining, you try to improve the chance that any settlement reached is favorable to you by starting with an extreme position, by stubbornly holding to it, by deceiving the other party as to your true views, and by making small concessions only as necessary to keep the negotiation going. The same is true for the other side. Each of those factors tends to interfere with reaching a settlement promptly.

ARGUING OVER POSITIONS ENDANGERS AN ONGOING RELATIONSHIP

Positional bargaining becomes a contest of will. . . . Anger and resentment often result as one side sees itself bending to the rigid will of the other while its own legitimate concerns go unaddressed. Positional bargaining thus strains and sometimes shatters the relationship between the parties.

THERE IS AN ALTERNATIVE . . .

The answer to the question of whether to use soft positional bargaining or hard is "neither." Change the game. At the Harvard Negotiation Project, we have been developing an alternative to positional bargaining: a method of negotiation explicitly designed to produce wise outcomes efficiently and amicably. This method, called *principled negotiation* or *negotiation on the merits*, can be boiled down to four basic points.

These four points define a straightforward method of negotiation that can be used under almost any circumstance. Each point deals with a basic element of negotiation and suggests what you should do about it.

People:	Separate the people from the problem.
Interests:	Focus on interests, not positions.
Options:	Generate a variety of possibilities before deciding what to do.
Criteria:	Insist that the result be based on some objective standard.

[E]motions typically become entangled with the objective merits of the problem. Taking positions just makes this worse because people's egos become identified with their positions. Hence, before working on the substantive problem, the "people problem" should be disentangled from it and dealt with separately. Figuratively if not literally, the participants should come to see themselves as working side by side, attacking the problem, not each other. Hence the first proposition: *Separate the people from the problem.*

The second point is designed to overcome the drawback of focusing on people's stated positions when the object of a negotiation is to satisfy their underlying interests. A negotiating position often obscures what you really want. Compromising between positions is not likely to produce an agreement which will effectively take care of the human needs that led people to adopt those positions. The second basic element of the method is: *Focus on interests, not positions.*

The third point responds to the difficulty of designing optimal solutions while under pressure. Trying to decide in the presence of an adversary narrows your vision. Having a lot at stake inhibits creativity. So does searching for the one right solution. You can offset these constraints by setting aside a designated time within which to think up a wide range of possible solutions that advance shared interests and creatively reconcile differing interests. Hence the third basic point: Before trying to reach agreement, *invent options for mutual gain.* . . .

[S]ome fair standard such as market value, expert opinion, custom, or law [should] determine the outcome. By discussing such criteria rather than what the parties are willing or unwilling to do, neither party need give in to the other; both can defer to a fair solution. Hence the fourth basic point: *Insist on using objective criteria.* . . .

PROBLEM Positional Bargaining: Which Game Should You Play?		**SOLUTION** Change the Game—Negotiate on the Merits
SOFT	**HARD**	**PRINCIPLED**
Participants are friends.	Participants are adversaries.	Participants are problem-solvers.
The goal is agreement.	The goal is victory.	The goal is a wise outcome reached efficiently and amicably.
Make concessions to cultivate the relationship.	Demand concessions as a condition of the relationship.	*Separate the people from the problem.*
Be soft on the people and the problem.	Be hard on the problem and the people.	Be soft on the people, hard on the problem.
Trust others.	Distrust others.	Proceed independent of trust.
Change your position easily.	Dig in to your position.	*Focus on interests, not positions.*
Make offers.	Make threats.	Explore interests.
Disclose your bottom line.	Mislead as to your bottom line.	Avoid having a bottom line.
Accept one-sided losses to reach agreement.	Demand one-sided gains as the price of agreement.	*Invent options for mutual gain.*
Search for the single answer: the one *they* will accept.	Search for the single answer: the one *you* will accept.	Develop multiple options to choose from; decide later.
Insist on agreement.	Insist on your position.	*Insist on using objective criteria.*
Try to avoid a contest of will.	Try to win a contest of will.	Try to reach a result based on standards independent of will.
Yield to pressure.	Apply pressure.	Reason and be open to reason; yield to principle, not pressure.

In contrast to positional bargaining, the principled negotiation (integrative/problem-solving) method of focusing on basic interests, mutually satisfying options, and fair standards typically results in a *wise agreement.* The method permits you to reach a gradual consensus on a joint decision *efficiently* without all the transactional costs of digging into positions only to have to dig yourself out of them. And separating the people from the problem allows you to deal directly and emphatically with the other negotiator as a human being, thus making possible an *amicable* agreement.

> **Problem 3-6.** ***Splitting an Orange***
>
> A classic example of value creation is the story of two siblings fighting over an orange. They agree to split it in half. One throws out the peel and eats her half of the orange. The other uses her half of the peel in a recipe and throws out the rest of the orange. How could these siblings have better resolved this dispute?

C. CHOOSING IN CONTEXT

In the excerpt below, two other approaches to negotiation are discussed in addition to the three outlined above. The fourth is a sharing or compromising approach—a style of negotiation in which you "split the difference." The fifth and final approach is avoiding. Avoiding is exactly what it sounds like: a negotiator who tries to avoid conflict. This person either does not engage with the conflict at all or at least tries to delay that engagement. Each of these approaches has advantages and disadvantages to consider when determining your choice. Thinking carefully about the questions posed at the beginning of the chapter, as well as your goals and those of your counterpart, will help make this choice proactive rather than reactive.

Andrea Kupfer Schneider & David Kupfer, SMART & SAVVY: NEGOTIATION STRATEGIES IN ACADEMIA

8-21 (2017)

Negotiation theorists have identified at least five key styles people use in a conflict or negotiation. For the purposes of this book, we first describe each style, its advantages, and its disadvantages, and then discuss what skills you need to implement each one. We also look at the role of goals—what you want to accomplish in the negotiation—and how that determines which style you select.

The following chart . . . details each style along three axes—level of assertiveness, level of empathy, and level of flexibility (or effort and creativity) needed to implement the style. . . .

COMPETING

Competing is probably the most commonly understood style of negotiation because it is the one most of us mastered at age 2 (and some of us never moved past). Because competing tends to be dramatic, it makes good theater and good stories. Because we so often see people competing—on the playing field, on the

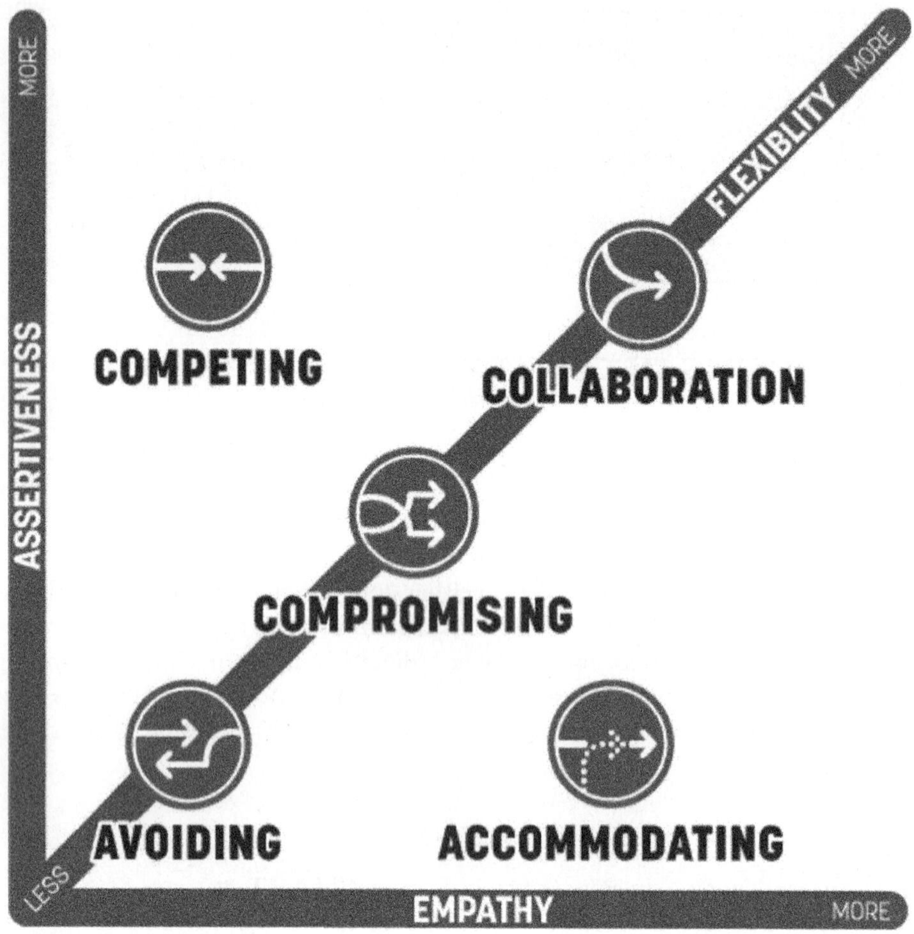

movie screen, and in the political arena, you might think, mistakenly, that this is how most conflicts are resolved. It's not. In real life, most disagreements are resolved through communication and problem-solving. But before celebrating or condemning competing, let's understand a little more about what it comprises.

A competing strategy is high in assertiveness and low in empathy, probably also low on flexibility. To compete effectively, you must make a strong case for yourself, you must be persuasive and firm, and you must often appear to be taking charge or controlling the conversation. The power of this style is the clarity of your position, and often the persuasiveness and the knowledge that goes along with being convinced that you are correct.

The advantages of competing are clear: if you come on strong, the other side might agree with you right off the bat and you might get your way with relatively little effort. Competing can be efficient: if you get your way within minutes, you don't waste much time. And in many cases, after a successful resolution, everyone understands who won and what was decided.

Of course, we all know the downsides of too much competing. If you approach a battle looking for a fight and convinced that you will win, the other side might not agree and might fight back even harder than he or she would if you took a softer approach, which can damage your relationship or lead to stalemate—or both. Some people might refuse to work with colleagues who are unceasingly competitive. And, less obvious but just as important, someone in power who is overly competitive, perhaps a team leader, could lose the valuable input of team members who tire of the "my-way-or-the-highway" style of decision-making.

Under what circumstances is competing a great choice? It's effective when important values (such as safety or reputation) are at stake, when a quick decision is needed (for example, when a deadline is approaching, or a decision is urgent), or when you know the other side is likely to give up easily.

ACCOMMODATING

At the opposite spectrum of behavior is the accommodating style of negotiation. This is low assertiveness and high empathy usually characterized by quickly agreeing to what the other side wants. This results in "giving in," agreeing and supporting the other side. The power behind this style is that if your greatest concern is making the other side happy, accommodating accomplishes that quickly and completely—as long as the other side approves.

Accommodating offers distinct advantages: If you give in, the other side will probably appreciate your bowing to his or her wishes, and that could improve your relationship. It also eliminates the conflict (at least in the short term) and can be efficient and easy to implement. You just say yes.

The big disadvantage to an accommodating style is that you don't get what you want. There are other drawbacks: other people might be frustrated by your lack of input, especially when they do want to work with you, or might lose respect for you and your interests. If you accommodate everyone all the time, a reputation of always giving in can damage your relationships and can make it increasingly difficult for you to stand up for yourself. It also denies you and your counterpart the opportunity to work through conflict in a productive manner.

An accommodating style is a good choice in several situations. If you really don't care about something (what movie to see, say, or where to go for dinner), giving in is simple. It works well when you care more about the relationship than the topic under discussion ("I have no interest in going to the opera, but if you want to go, I'll go with you.") Accommodating can also be used as part of a package of trade-offs. ("You decide this time. Next time, the choice is mine.") The catch in using accommodating as a relationship builder or as a trade-off is to be sure to communicate that accommodating now is connected to the future; if you fail to do that, the other person might not understand that sometime down the road, he or she must accommodate you.

AVOIDING

Moving to another corner, avoiding is low assertiveness and low empathy as well as low creativity and flexibility. It also has the lowest level of energy devoted to dealing with the conflict. Think of avoiding as both a long-term (stick your head in the sand) and short-term (don't answer the email until later) type of strategy.

You are delaying or avoiding a response to a conflict, trying to divert attention, not signaling how you really feel about a particular situation, and suppressing your personal emotion and position about this conflict.

The key advantage to avoiding is the lack of entanglement in issues that are trivial to you or relationships that are not sufficiently significant. Avoiding can freeze the status quo. And the conflict might be solved without your input. Most crucially, avoiding is a necessary component of time management and sanity maintenance (such as not answering your phone when caller ID shows it's from a marketing firm or long-winded friend). Not every problem needs you to solve it, and not every conflict is worthy of your energy. You might be wise, for example, to discuss with your department chair only the issues that are really hindering your research. Ignoring or avoiding other concerns allows both you and your negotiation partner to distinguish between the annoying and the important.

On the other hand, if you use this strategy too often or for too long, the disadvantages can be notable. People—you as well as others—might periodically explode from frustration. You could be frozen out from discussions on some matters, and others could feel negatively about your avoidance. If the problem gets solved without your input—and perhaps it will not be—you will not be participating in the solution that gets implemented.

So do think about when to avoid. For issues that you consider trivial or in situations where you know that others will take the lead and you will not mind, avoidance makes sense. Avoiding also is useful when you are not yet ready to negotiate. Perhaps you need more time to research the situation and figure out how to approach it. Perhaps you are too busy to really focus on the conflict. Perhaps you need to schedule the conversation for a time when you can be emotionally prepared. All of these are smart reasons for delaying your own engagement until you can be most effective.

COLLABORATION

At the last corner of the grid is collaborating, a strategy that engages the most energy by requiring assertiveness, empathy, and creativity for resolving the situation. If accommodating means "yes—we'll do it your way," collaborating is characterized by a "yes and. . ." style, one in which you clearly state your preference while also inquiring about the preference of the other side. The strategy is problem-focused, and multiple points of view are welcome in thinking about how to solve the dispute. The power of this style is in the complete involvement of everyone present—the ownership of the group—and potentially integrative, imaginative solutions.

The advantages to collaborating are primarily located in your relationship with the other party and in the substance of the solution. First, because the parties work together in creating the solution, they build trust between them. Because the dynamic of working together is often energetic and cooperative, collaborating increases the chances that the relationship will be improved and that the solution will be carried out. Second, because people's perspectives have been merged and they have probably shared more ideas in the collaborative process, any solution they devise is likely to be based on sound, relevant information and to be more durable than one that was decided unilaterally.

On the other hand, collaborating can be exhausting. Working with others takes time and motivation, can distract those involved from other pressing problems, and can bring on "analysis paralysis," a state in which too many people spend too much time analyzing and not enough time deciding. Especially when several parties are involved, just trying to enlist everyone in a collaborative process can take longer than the issue is worth.

In deciding when to collaborate, a negotiator needs to think about how important the issue is, how helpful information from the other side might be in figuring out a good solution, and how valuable the relationship with the other party or parties is. When done effectively, collaborating can merge the best of all possible worlds and is often the gold standard of how research and clinical work is done. At the same time, not every dispute is worth this level of attention.

COMPROMISING

Finally, in the middle of all of these styles is compromising, a strategy characterized by finding middle ground and using some empathy and creativity. A compromising style will urge moderation; use techniques like split-the-difference or trade-off, and move the parties toward finding a solution that offers something for everyone.

The advantages to compromising are numerous—it can be relatively fast, it can move things forward and give parties a way out of a stalemate, it is easy to understand and implement, and it appears reasonable. It is also familiar, because ever since childhood, when we had to take turns and share toys, most of us have long understood compromise as structurally fair.

On the other hand, when it is not moored to standards, compromising can feel like horse-trading. If we move to agreement and to creating a solution too quickly, it can be at the expense of better and more well-thought-out answers, and we may miss a chance to hear everyone's point of view. Compromising can also lead to patching up the symptoms of conflict without dealing with the causes, which can mean that the conflict will flare again.

Compromise is best used in two instances—when the issues are relatively unimportant to all concerned and an easy, efficient trade-off ("You pick the restaurant; I'll pick the movie") makes sense. Compromising is also an excellent "second-choice" style to conflict. At the end of a collaborating style, when few issues remain, compromising can get the deal done. And if competing is leading to what could be a stalemate, compromising can move the agenda forward.

Lawyers vary significantly on their approaches to negotiation. The excerpt below is based on an empirical study, conducted by Andrea Kupfer Schneider, which asked lawyers how they perceived the other side's negotiation strategy in their most recent negotiation. Lawyers rated their counterpart attorneys using 89 adjectives, 60 negotiation techniques, and 14 goals. The attorneys also rated their counterparts for effectiveness.

The excerpt discusses the division of attorneys into three groups: true problem solvers, cautious problem solvers, and adversarials. It outlines the differences among the groups, both in the description of the groups and each group's respective effectiveness. Note particularly the difference between true problem-solving negotiators—those who truly engage in the behavior described in the previous excerpts on integrative bargaining; "cautious" problem solvers—those who don't quite fully use the range of problem-solving behavior (and who might be closer to the compromise or accommodating approaches described above); and adversarial negotiators. Also, think about what adjectives most closely describe your approach to negotiation.

❖ *Andrea Kupfer Schneider*, SHATTERING NEGOTIATION MYTHS: EMPIRICAL EVIDENCE ON THE EFFECTIVENESS OF NEGOTIATION STYLE

7 HARV. NEGOT. L. REV. 143, 171-175 (2002)

[We] can separate negotiation styles into three clusters, which I have labeled true problem-solving, cautious problem-solving, and adversarial. . . . [L]awyers were divided far more evenly among the three clusters with approximately 36% in the true problem-solving group, 36% in the cautious problem-solving group, and 28% in the adversarial group. . . .

Top 20 Adjectives for Three Clusters

	TRUE PROBLEM-SOLVING	CAUTIOUS PROBLEM-SOLVING	ADVERSARIAL
1	Ethical	Ethical	Irritating
2	Personable	Experienced	Headstrong
3	Experienced	Confident	Stubborn
4	Trustworthy	Personable	Arrogant
5	Rational	Self-controlled	Egotistical
6	Agreeable	Rational	Argumentative
7	Fair-minded	Sociable	Assertive
8	Communicative	Dignified	Demanding
9	Realistic	Trustworthy	Quarrelsome
10	Accommodating		Confident
11	Perceptive		Ambitious
12	Sociable		Manipulative
13	Adaptable		Experienced
14	Confident		Hostile
15	Dignified		Forceful
16	Self-controlled		Tough
17	Helpful		Suspicious
18	Astute about the law		Firm
19	Poised		Complaining
20	Flexible		Rude

An interesting result in this analysis is the middle category. Clearly this middle group is comprised of "good" lawyers in that all of the adjectives are positive. Again, all nine are included in the true problem-solving group. In comparison, however, the true problem-solving group had forty-nine highly rated adjectives. Consequently, I have labeled the middle group "cautious problem-solvers" to highlight the fact that most of these traits are problem-solving, yet this group seems hesitant to utilize all of the problem-solving attributes. By "cautious," I do not mean to suggest that these negotiators are themselves cautious, but rather they are cautious about adopting a completely problem-solving approach to the negotiation.

The true problem-solving negotiator [understood] the case well (reasonable, prepared, accurate representation of client's position, did own factual investigation) and wanted to work with the other side (friendly, tactful, cooperative, facilitated the negotiation, viewed the negotiation process as one with mutual benefits, understood my client's interests). This negotiator was flexible (movable position, did not use take it or leave it) and did not engage in manipulative tactics (did not make unwarranted claims, did not use threats, avoided needless harm to my client). The true problem-solving negotiator believed in the good faith exchange of information (cooperative, forthright, trustful, sincere, shared information, probed). . . .

The cautious problem-solving group, as in the adjectives ratings, did not stand out in most of the characteristics and is only rated more than slightly characteristic in eight descriptions. These eight are all positive and also appear on the problem-solving list, but the cautious problem-solving category lacks twenty-two descriptions that true problem-solvers display. As described above, these absent characteristics describe negotiation qualities that add depth and breadth to a negotiator's skills. . . .

Number of Lawyers Per Group by Effectiveness

	Ineffective	Average	Effective
True Problem-Solving	1%	24%	75%
Cautious Problem-Solving	13%	62%	25%
Adversarial	58%	33%	9%

First, approximately 25% of the negotiators in the new cautious problem-solving group are effective, whereas 75% of the true problem-solvers are described as effective. The missing negotiation elements between the groups must cause this difference. Adjectives found in true problem-solving but not in cautious problem-solving highlight empathy (communicative, accommodating, perceptive, helpful), option creation (adaptable, flexible), personality (agreeable, poised), and preparation (fair-minded, realistic, astute about the law). These skills make the difference between average skills and truly effective skills. Contrary to popular belief, behaviors described by these adjectives are not risky at all. The traditional fear of problem-solving is that problem-solvers will be taken advantage of by more adversarial bargainers, yet only 1% of true problem-solving negotiators were considered ineffective.

Problem 3-7. ***Too Cautious?***

What seem to be the primary differences between true and cautious problem solvers? How do you think these differences matter in terms of effectiveness? Which of these do you think is the most important?

This final article makes the point that our views of the other side matter as we negotiate.

❖ *Jonathan R. Cohen*, ADVERSARIES? PARTNERS? HOW ABOUT COUNTERPARTS? ON METAPHORS IN THE PRACTICE AND TEACHING OF NEGOTIATION AND DISPUTE RESOLUTION

20 Conflict Resol. Q. 433, 433-436, 438-439 (2003)

A student of negotiation—or of its cousin, the assisted negotiation called mediation—will soon find herself awash in a sea of metaphors. Has she entered the animal kingdom, a dog-eat-dog world where hawks prey on doves and lions occasionally lie down with lambs? Or the kitchen, with pies to be baked and their slices cut, and oranges to be separated peel from fruit? Is she attending a music concert, where discord will be replaced by harmony, or embarking on a journey replete with speed bumps, road blocks, and detours, the negotiation "bicycle" at risk of falling if sufficient momentum is not maintained? Perhaps she is a carpenter carrying a toolbox of options, an engineer building bridges to span differences, or an architect designing a multidoor courthouse. . . .

If she is like most students, she will soon arrive at the competitive metaphors that dominate the field of negotiation, if not our culture. Negotiation is a game of poker in which players must hold the cards close to the chest. Negotiation is a sport like football, where a "level playing field" is required; mediators are thus "umpires" or "referees." Or like basketball, where "timeouts" are sometimes taken, or like baseball where parties sometimes play "hardball.". . .

The student may then realize that there is more to negotiation than competition. Although the adversarial metaphors capture an important piece of negotiation, they do not capture the whole of it. Competition is part of negotiation, but so is cooperation. Negotiation involves both give and take. As Schelling wrote, "the richness of the subject arises from the fact that . . . there is mutual dependence as well as opposition. Pure conflict, in which the interests of two antagonists are completely opposed, is a special case[.] . . . Concepts like . . . negotiation are concerned with the common interest and mutual dependence that can exist between participants in a conflict."

The student may now switch to a second set of metaphors within our field, those of cooperation. Whether through stumble or leap, she may well arrive at the metaphor of dance. The other party in the negotiation is not one's adversary, but one's *partner.* The dance occurs in steps and stages. As with empathy and assertiveness, skill in following one's partner is as important as skill in leading. It is essential to "put yourself in [the other side's] shoes," but hopefully without stepping on their toes. What is needed is to be shoulder to shoulder, side by side. Movement, balance, and trust are critical. Before an impasse is reached, perhaps a "trip to the balcony" can reveal new steps to be taken. As to third-party neutrals, the mediator is no longer an umpire at a sports event, but a choreographer.

Yet using solely cooperative metaphors is also problematic. Recall that when the dance metaphor is invoked, it is usually not the waltz but the aggressive and spicy tango, as in, "It takes two to tango." Schelling's point was that *both* competition and cooperation are present in negotiation. Disclosing one's interests, preferences, and resources may help to "expand the pie" (value creation), but it can also result in one getting a sliver (value distribution). On the other hand, if one refuses to disclose any information one may end up with the lion's share of a minuscule pie, also a poor outcome. Thus, most negotiation involves a blend of competition and cooperation.

How, then, is one to proceed? What language should be used to describe negotiation? If the goal is descriptive accuracy, since most negotiation is neither pure competition nor pure cooperation, I suggest using language that reflects the inherent tensions between competition and cooperation in negotiation and other forms of dispute resolution. Consider . . . what to call the other party to the negotiation. . . .

Parties to negotiations are often unsure of how to refer to one another. Those with largely competitive views of negotiation tend to label the other party as their "opponent" or "adversary." Those with largely cooperative views tend to label the other party their "partner." Yet what is needed is a word that captures the tension between these two roles. I suggest the word *counterpart.* As with competition, in negotiation the other party is against, or *counter* to, oneself. As with cooperation, the other party is in *partnership* with oneself. Negotiation involves an element of tension or paradox in one's relationship to the other party, and our language should reflect it. Using *counterpart* to describe such a mixed role has no less than biblical (though quite sexist) precedent. The second creation narrative in Genesis describes the creation of woman to be an "ezer c'negdo" to man. *Ezer* means "helper" and *c'negdo* means "against him." This term is sometimes well-translated as "counterpart." The language seems to suggest that being a good intimate partner involves both supportive and oppositional roles.

Problem 3-8. ***Mind-Sets and Behaviors***

Does Cohen's perception of the "counterpart" (and Carrie Menkel-Meadow's discussion of mindset early in this chapter) perhaps explain the variety of approaches that lawyers take in the Schneider study? How would someone more adversarial discuss their counterpart? Or someone engaged in more problem-solving?

Whatever choices you make as a negotiator about your approach, be sure to be mindful that different choices lead to different results. In the next chapter, we will look at the behaviors and skills that will also lead to being effective as a negotiator.

Further Reading

Hal Abramson, Fashioning an Effective Negotiation Style: Choosing Between Good Practices, Tactics, and Tricks, 23 Harv. Negot. L. Rev. 319 (2018).

Alexandra Carter. (2020). Ask for More. New York: Simon & Schuster.

David B. Falk, The Art of Contract Negotiation, 3 Marq. Sports L.J. 1 (1992).

Roger Fisher, William Ury & Bruce Patton. (2011). Getting to YES (3d ed.). New York: Penguin.

Roger Fisher, Elizabeth Kopelman & Andrea Kupfer Schneider. (1996). Beyond Machiavelli: Tools for Coping with Conflict. New York: Penguin.

P.H. Gulliver. (1979). Disputes and Negotiations: A Cross-Cultural Perspective (Studies on Law and Social Control). New York: Academic Press.

Russell Korobkin, A Positive Theory of Legal Negotiation, 88 Geo. L.J. 1789 (2000).

David A. Lax & James K. Sebenius. (1987). The Manager as Negotiator. New York: Free Press.

David A. Lax & James K. Sebenius. (2006). 3D Negotiation. Cambridge: Harvard Business Press.

Gary Lowenthal, A General Theory of Negotiation Process, Strategy and Behavior, 31 Kansas L. Rev. 96 (1982).

Avishai Margalit. (2010). On Compromise and Rotten Compromises. Princeton: Princeton University Press.

Michael Meltsner & Philip G. Schrag. (1974). "Negotiation." In Public Interest Advocacy: Materials for Legal Education. Boston: Little, Brown.

Carrie Menkel-Meadow. (2022). Very Short Introduction to Negotiation. Oxford: Oxford University Press.

Carrie Menkel-Meadow, Legal Negotiation: A Study of Strategies in Search of a Theory, 1983 A.B.F. Res. J. 905-937 (1983).

Robert H. Mnookin, Scott R. Peppet & Andrew S. Tulumello. (2000). Beyond Winning: Negotiating to Create Value in Deals and Disputes. Cambridge: Belknap Press of Harvard University Press.

Howard Raiffa, with John Richardson & David Metcalfe. (2007). Negotiation Analysis. Cambridge: Belknap Press of Harvard University Press.

Frank E.A. Sander & Jeffrey Rubin, The Janus Quality of Negotiation: Dealmaking and Dispute Settlement, 4 Negot. J. 109 (1988).

G. Richard Shell. (2006). Bargaining for Advantage (2d ed). New York: Viking.

Michael Wheeler. (2013). The Art of Negotiation: How to Improvise Agreement in a Chaotic World. New York: Simon & Schuster.

Chapter 4 Negotiation: Skills and Practices

Moderate your desire of victory over your adversary, and be pleased with the one over yourself.

—Benjamin Franklin, *The Morals of Chess* (1750)

In the first two chapters, you were introduced to different approaches toward conflict and processes for its resolution. Chapter 4 highlights approaches to negotiation, and delves further into the skills of a negotiator. As noted in Chapter 3, determining your approach to negotiation, and which skills are needed for a particular approach, depends on your goals.

The most effective negotiators are those who choose among different approaches depending on the context, the client, and the party on the other side. Each approach requires particular skills. In a competitive approach, for one example, the negotiator must persuasively present a client's most optimistic goals. In a cooperative approach, the lawyer must have the ability to listen carefully and understand the other side's interests. And a problem-solving negotiator needs both of those skillsets, together with the ability to find creative and flexible solutions that meet both sides' interests.

Below, skills are divided into key categories: assertiveness; empathy; creativity; social intuition; and cultural aptitude.

A. ASSERTIVENESS

Effective negotiators know how to ask for what they want and frame their arguments persuasively. Constructive assertiveness in negotiation is the ability to firmly and clearly ask for your optimistic goal and make appropriate concessions graciously. Assertiveness is explaining why what you want is fair. "Assertiveness is not being aggressive, negative, or threatening. It is *not* pounding the table or raising your voice. Nor is it sulking or pretending to agree—and later sabotaging whatever was agreed on. It is not passive-aggressive behavior. Bullies do sometimes get their way, but . . . in an arena where reputation is crucial, bullying is not a recipe for long-term success."[1]

Effective assertiveness begins with knowledge—fully understanding exactly what you want. Once you understand your goals, you need to determine which of your goals are the most important. You need to know why your position is fair so that you can persuade your counterpart. This next section outlines the component parts of assertiveness.

1. Set Your Parameters—Goals & Limits

a. Set Your Goals

In Chapter 2, we discussed the importance of interviewing your client to determine their goals. Goals may vary depending on what approach to the negotiation you choose. Regardless of approach, however, working with your client to set goals is an important first step in which to engage. Thinking about how to set optimistic and realistic goals—and why—is the subject of this first excerpt.

❖ *G. Richard Shell*, BARGAINING FOR ADVANTAGE: NEGOTIATION STRATEGIES FOR REASONABLE PEOPLE

31-34 (1999)

SET AN OPTIMISTIC, JUSTIFIABLE TARGET

When you set goals, think boldly and optimistically about what you would like to see happen. Research has repeatedly shown that people who have higher aspirations in negotiations perform better and get more than people who have modest or "I'll do my best" goals, provided they really believe in their targets.

In one classic study, psychologists Sydney Siegel and Lawrence Fouraker set up a simple buy-sell negotiation experiment. They allowed the negotiators to keep all the profits they achieved but told the subjects they could qualify for a second, "double-their-money" round if they met or exceeded certain specified bargaining goals. In other words, Siegel and Fouraker gave their subjects both concrete *incentives* for hitting a certain specified level of performance and, perhaps unintentionally, a hint that the assigned target levels were realistically attainable (why else would subjects be told about the bonus round?). One set of negotiators was told they would have to hit a modest $2.10 target to qualify for the bonus

1. Andrea Kupfer Schneider & David Kupfer, Smart & Savvy: Negotiation Strategies in Academia (2017).

round. Another set of negotiators was told they would have to hit a much more ambitious target of $6.10. Both sides had the same bottom line: They could not accept any deal that involved a loss. The negotiators with the more ambitious $6.10 goal achieved a mean profit of $6.25, far outperforming the median profit of $3.35 achieved by those with the modest $2.10 goal.

My own research has confirmed Siegel's and Fouraker's findings. In our experiment, unlike the one Siegel and Fouraker conducted, negotiation subjects set their own bargaining goals. And instead of letting everyone keep whatever profits they earned, we gave separate $100 prizes to the buyer and the seller with the best individual outcomes. The result was the same, however. Negotiators who reported higher prenegotiation expectations achieved more than those who entered the negotiation with more modest goals.

Why are we tempted to set modest bargaining goals when we can achieve more by raising our sights? There are several possible reasons. First, many people set modest goals to protect their self-esteem. We are less likely to fail if we set our goals low, so we "wing it," telling ourselves that we are doing fine as long as we beat our bottom line. Modest goals thus help us avoid unpleasant feelings of failure and regret.

Second, we may not have enough information about the negotiation to see the full potential for gain; that is, we may fail to appreciate the true worth of what we are selling, not do the research on applicable standards, or fail to note how eager the buyer is for what we have to offer. This usually means we have failed to prepare well enough.

Third, we may lack desire. If the other person wants money, control, or power more urgently than we do, we are unlikely to set a high goal for ourselves. Why look for conflict and trouble over things we care little about?

Research suggests that the self-esteem factor plays a more important role in low goal setting than many of us would care to admit. We once had a negotiation speaker who said that the problem with many reasonable people is that they confuse "win-win" with what he called a "wimp-win" attitude. The "wimp-win" negotiator focuses only on his or her bottom line; the "win-win" negotiator has ambitious goals. . . .

Once you have thought about what an optimistic, challenging goal would look like, spend a few minutes permitting realism to dampen your expectations. *Optimistic goals are effective only if they are feasible; that is, only if you believe in them and they can be justified according to some standard or norm. . . .* [N]egotiation positions must usually be supported by some standard, benchmark, or precedent, or they lose their credibility. No amount of mental goal setting will make your five-year-old car worth more than a brand-new version of the same model. You should also adjust your goal to reflect appropriate relationship concerns.

But do not let your ideas of what is appropriate or realistic take over completely. Simply note the reasons you come up with that explain why your optimistic goal may not be possible and look for the next highest, *defendable* target. Your old car may not be worth the same as a new one, but you should be able to find a used-car guide that reports the "average" price for your model. With that foundation, you can justify asking for a premium over that standard based on the tip-top condition of your vehicle.

One danger with being too realistic with your goals is that you may be making unwarranted assumptions about the values and priorities the other side will bring to the deal. Until you know for sure what *the other side* has for goals and what *the other side* thinks is realistic, you should keep your eyes firmly on your own defendable target. The other party will tell you if your optimistic deal isn't possible, and you will not offend him or her by asking for your goal so long as you have some justification to support it, you advance your ideas with courtesy, and you show a concern for his or her perspective.

BE SPECIFIC

The literature on negotiation goal setting counsels us to be as specific as possible. Clarity drives out fuzziness in negotiations as in many other endeavors. With a definite target, you will begin working on a host of psychological levels to get the job done. For example, when you land your new job, don't just set a goal to "negotiate a fair salary." Push yourself to take aim at a specific target—go for a 10 percent raise over what you made at your last job. Your specific goal will start you thinking about other, comparable jobs that pay your target salary, and you will begin to notice a variety of market standards that support a salary of that amount.

Be especially wary of goals such as "I'll do the best I can" or, worst of all, "I'll just go in and see what I can get." What we are really saying when we enter a negotiation with goals such as these is, "I do not want to take a chance on failing in this negotiation." Fear of failure and our natural desire to avoid feelings of disappointment and regret are legitimate psychological self-protection devices. But effective negotiators do not let these feelings get in the way of setting specific goals.

Problem 4-1. *Dealing with Regret*

In empirical experiments studying aspirations in negotiation, Russell Korobkin finds that setting aspiration levels can affect key "settlement levers," including reservation points; the definition of fairness; patience at the bargaining table; and rejection of barely-acceptable offers. At the same time, Korobkin writes, high aspiration levels can increase the likelihood of impasse and reduce satisfaction with the outcome. Russell Korobkin, Aspirations and Settlement, 88 Cornell L. Rev. 1 (2002).

Shell notes above that negotiators may set modest goals to avoid feelings of regret. Why might it be worth it to set high aspiration levels even if you are more likely to be disappointed?

b. Set Your Limits

Setting your limits—your walk-away point—requires knowing your own strengths and weaknesses, and your alternative to negotiating. Two key concepts are critical here: BATNA and Reservation Point. *Getting to YES* first introduced the idea of BATNA—"Best Alternative to a Negotiated Agreement." The phrase, now used widely in negotiation jargon, is a mechanism to ensure that you never make an agreement that is worse than what you would get if you did not negotiate at all—that is, if you walked away.

Using your BATNA to protect yourself from unwise agreements takes several steps. First, you must brainstorm all possible alternative actions to an agreement. This might include, for example, going to court, or making an agreement with another company, or buying a different house. Second, you choose your best alternative. Some BATNAs have no monetary equivalent (i.e., taking a vacation with one friend versus another), and so in those cases you have already completed your analysis. For those BATNAs you can convert to money, you would now convert your BATNA into a reservation price, or value. This number is the point at which you would be better off going to your BATNA and taking that action.

For example, assume you are purchasing a home. Your first-choice home is priced at $300,000. Your second choice is priced at $250,000, and you assume that you could probably purchase it for $240,000. How do you decide when buying your second choice makes more sense? You need to value the difference between the homes—what makes your first-choice home your preferred choice? List these out: (1) attached garage; (2) better school district; (3) larger back yard; (4) does not need to be painted before moving in. Next, attach values to each of these items. For some differences between the properties, like the garage and the back yard, you might check with your realtor to get a sense of how others might value particular items. For others, like the school district, you are attaching a tangible number to an intangible item. Ask yourself how much more you would pay for the exact same house in one neighborhood versus the other. For the last item, painting, you can price this with some research of your own.

Assume you've attached the following values for your items: (1) attached garage ($10,000); (2) better school district ($15,000); (3) larger back yard ($5,000); and (4) not having to paint ($5,000—for paint, the painter, and the inconvenience). The first-choice home is worth about $35,000 more to you. Therefore, your reservation price is $240,000 plus $35,000 = $275,000. This means that if you can't negotiate the price on the more expensive house down to $275,000 you would be better off, given your preferences, buying the less expensive home.

In negotiations, one of the largest difficulties that negotiators face is working without knowing the other party's BATNA or reservation values. To overcome this lack of information, negotiators often estimate the values after conducting more research about the other party, primarily by looking for past behaviors, interests, needs, and values.

The value created by the difference between each of the party's reservation values is the surplus available when the parties bargain. If the difference between the reservation values of the two parties is large, then there will be a relatively large amount of potential surplus to be divided between the parties. The parties lose this potential value if either side walks away.

The excerpt below provides advice on how to think about your BATNA to ensure you achieve a wise agreement. Your BATNA and reservation price (RP), as well as those of the other party, should set the parameters of the bargaining zone.

❖ *Russell Korobkin*, A POSITIVE THEORY OF LEGAL NEGOTIATION

88 Geo. L.J. 1789, 1794-1798 (2000)

INTERNAL PREPARATION

A negotiator cannot determine his RP without first understanding his substitutes for and the opportunity costs of reaching a negotiated agreement. This, of course, requires research. . . .

After identifying the various alternatives to reaching a negotiated agreement, the negotiator needs to determine which alternative is most desirable. Fisher and his coauthors coined the appropriate term "BATNA"—"best alternative to a negotiated agreement"—to identify this choice. The identity and quality of a negotiator's BATNA is the primary input into his RP.

If the negotiator's BATNA and the subject of the negotiation are perfectly interchangeable, determining the reservation price is quite simple: the reservation price is merely the value of the BATNA. For example, if Esau's BATNA is buying another catering business for $190,000 that is identical to Jacob's in terms of quality, earnings potential, and all other factors that are important to Esau, then his RP is $190,000. If Jacob will sell for some amount less than that, Esau will be better off buying Jacob's company than he would pursuing his best alternative. If Jacob demands more than $190,000, Esau is better off buying the alternative company and not reaching an agreement with Jacob.

In most circumstances, however, the subject of a negotiation and the negotiator's BATNA are not perfect substitutes. If Jacob's business is of higher quality, has a higher earnings potential, or is located closer to Esau's home, he would probably be willing to pay a premium for it over what he would pay for the alternative choice. For example, if the alternative business is selling for $190,000, Esau might determine he would be willing to pay up to a $10,000 premium over the alternative for Jacob's business and thus set his RP at $200,000. On the other hand, if Esau's BATNA is more desirable to him than Jacob's business, Esau will discount the value of his BATNA by the amount necessary to make the two alternatives equally desirable values for the money; perhaps he will set his RP at $180,000 in recognition that his BATNA is $10,000 more desirable than Jacob's business, and Jacob's business would be equally desirable only at a $10,000 discount. . . .

The relationship between a party's BATNA and his RP can be generalized in the following way. A party's RP has two components: (1) the market value of his BATNA; and (2) the difference to *him* between the value of his BATNA and the value of the subject of the negotiation. A seller sets his RP by calculating (1) and either *subtracting* (2) if the subject of the negotiation is more valuable than his BATNA (and therefore he is willing to accept less to reach an agreement) or *adding* (2) if the BATNA is more valuable than the subject of the negotiation (and therefore, he would demand more to reach an agreement and give up his BATNA). A buyer sets his RP by calculating (1) and either *adding* (2) if the subject of the negotiation is more valuable than his BATNA (and therefore he would pay a premium to reach an agreement) or *subtracting* (2) if his BATNA is more valuable than the subject of the negotiation (and therefore he would demand a discount to give up the BATNA). . . .

By investigating an even wider range of alternatives to reaching agreement, and by more thoroughly investigating the value of obvious alternatives, the negotiator can alter his RP in a way that will shift the bargaining zone to his advantage. . . .

EXTERNAL PREPARATION

External preparation allows the negotiator to estimate his opponent's RP . . . [t]o accurately predict Jacob's RP and therefore pinpoint the low end of the bargaining zone. This information will also prepare Esau to attempt to persuade Jacob during the course of negotiations to lower his RP. . . .

It is worth noting that in the litigation context both parties often have the same alternatives and the same BATNA. If plaintiff Goliath determines that his BATNA is going to trial, then defendant David's only alternative—and therefore his BATNA default—is going to trial as well. In this circumstance, internal preparation and external preparations merge. . . .

Problem 4-2. *BATNA Research*

Assume that a local sandwich shop is negotiating with a national coffee franchise, Morebucks, to serve Morebucks coffee. The sandwich shop is interested in serving Morebucks so that it can bring in more customers and make more money.

- What else can the sandwich shop do to improve its financial situation? Your answers are all alternatives to a negotiated agreement, and some of these alternatives may make sense to do anyway.
- What type of research would you perform in advance of the negotiations with Morebucks? Based on your research and your alternatives to this agreement, you can choose your BATNA. The BATNA is an action plan.
- Next, if possible, translate this BATNA into a reservation price. For example, assume you find out that (1) the other national coffee franchise, Coffeebest, usually charges $3 per pound of coffee to its franchisees; (2) the standard price from Morebucks to outside

vendors is usually $4 per pound; and (3) Morebucks has been known to give discounts for long-term contracts, for large volume, and in new areas where it is trying to create a niche. How do you set your reservation price?

Dealing with Regret: A Redux

Now that you've learned about aspiration levels and BATNA, we can combine learnings to manage regret in both lawyers and clients. To avoid regret in negotiations, the best practice is to set high aspirations but measure achievements with your BATNA.

2. Speak Persuasively

After setting your goals and limits, it is time to make your case for trying to solve the problem in a way that best meets your client's objectives. This is the other key component of assertiveness. It is when all of the knowledge you have gets put into action. This section discusses some of the communication techniques that can make you persuasive. Before making your presentation to your counterpart in the negotiation, you need to think about how to make the most persuasive case. This is not unlike a trial lawyer's task when preparing to make arguments in front of a jury. What is likely to convince them that you are making good suggestions for a good resolution of a negotiation problem or set of issues?

a. Appeal to Justice and Fairness

A crucial part of setting your limits and goals—and of convincing others to respect them—depends on establishing relevant criteria for assessing possible negotiation claims and outcomes. The excerpt that follows focuses on different types of fairness in a negotiation.

❖ *Cecilia Albin*, THE ROLE OF FAIRNESS IN NEGOTIATIONS

9 Negot. J. 223, 225-228, 233-239 (1993)

[T]he actual practice of negotiation . . . suggests that concepts of fairness are often an influential factor. They influence the "give-and-take" in the bargaining process, help parties to forge agreement, and help to determine whether a particular outcome will be viewed as satisfactory, and thus be honored in the long run. Notions of fairness may create a motivation to resolve a particular problem through negotiation in the first place, and thus have an impact on the positions and expectations which parties bring to the table. . . .

This study identifies and analyzes four types of fairness which have an impact on negotiation: structural fairness, process fairness, procedural fairness, and outcome fairness. In any one case, all four types of fairness will not necessarily be significant nor even present. While concerns about outcome fairness are commonly thought to dominate negotiations, in some contexts no outcome can be quite fair—e.g., in the allocation of a single indivisible good or burden for which there is no adequate compensation, such as a death mission or a child in a custody dispute. Parties may then agree to use a procedure viewed as fair for settling the issue, and to accept whatever (unfair) solution it produces. Similarly, when a negotiation process cannot be fair in important respects (e.g., permit participation by all parties or public scrutiny), greater demands will often be advanced regarding the fairness of its outcome.

STRUCTURAL FAIRNESS

We commonly think of fairness as relating to the outcome, and perhaps also the process, of negotiations. Yet an important class of fairness issues concerns the overarching structure of the negotiation process which, in turn, reflects more or less the structure of the dispute and overall relations between parties. . . .

A major set of structural components concerns the parties to the negotiations, including any third parties: their identity; number; attributes (e.g., interests, amount of resources); representation; and relations, including the distribution of resources between them. . . . The idea that every major party to a conflict, or groups most affected by the outcome should be given a genuine opportunity to be represented in the negotiations is regarded as a key element of fairness which significantly influences perceptions of the legitimacy of the outcome and the chances of its implementation.

A second group of structural elements concerns the issues to be negotiated—their number and grouping as they appear on the agenda when negotiations begin; their complexity and "sums" (degree to which they are, or are perceived as, zero-sum or positive sum); and relationships between them (e.g., degree to which they are separate or intertwined) . . . .

Another category of structural fairness elements is the rules and codes of conduct to govern the negotiations, and ways in which these are established. These elements include agenda-setting (e.g., issues to be negotiated, their order on the agenda, and time allowed for each issue); communication procedures between parties and with the outside world (e.g., use of press conferences to report on progress or deadlocks); voting procedures; and the use of deadlines and other time limits. A common notion of fairness is that parties, whether equal or not in power, should have an *equal* chance to determine the agenda, equal control over the use of deadlines, and so forth.

> ***Mind Your Manners***
>
> A study of libel litigation found that the primary goals of plaintiffs—restoring reputation, correcting a falsehood, and vengeance—had little to do with money or even their chance of success. The way that plaintiffs were treated when they called to complain of libel was directly connected to whether they chose to sue. The Iowa study of libel litigation found that some plaintiffs who were initially unsure about whether to sue only initiated lawsuits after being treated rudely by the media defendant. Randall Bezanson, et al., Libel Law and the Press: Myth and Reality, 29-53 (1987).

Finally, a major set of structural elements involving fairness issues concerns the physical features of the negotiations: the location; the presence and degree of access of various audiences to the negotiations; the availability of communication channels between parties; and access to information and technical support. . . .

PROCESS FAIRNESS

Process fairness concerns two broad issues: the extent to which parties in the process of negotiating relate to and treat each other "fairly"; and how parties' notions of (outcome) fairness influence the dynamics of the negotiation process, including their choice of procedures for arriving at an agreement.

"Fair behavior" in negotiations can be defined as the extent to which parties actually honor agreements reached on many structural issues before the process began and the degree to which they use procedures without deception in the effort to find a solution.

PROCEDURAL FAIRNESS

Procedural fairness concerns specific mechanisms used for arriving at an agreement. These mechanisms are considered fair because of some intrinsic value (e.g., they give parties an equal chance to "win" or demand equal concessions from them), because they tend to produce fair outcomes, or because of both of the qualities. Thus procedural fairness concerns the features of the mechanisms themselves, while process fairness refers to larger issues, such as how the mechanisms are actually used in the negotiation process (e.g., if in good faith, without bluffing) and the substance of parties' concessions.

These kinds of procedures are often used when parties cannot agree on a fair solution; when no solution can be quite fair (e.g., the allocation of a mission involving high risks of death); when a solution is needed quickly; when the stakes are relatively low so that it is not worth using a more time consuming procedure; when the stakes are so high that full-fledged bargaining would seem inappropriate or involve too many pressures and pain; and when the greater ambiguity or manipulability of other procedures are to be avoided.

OUTCOME FAIRNESS

Outcome fairness refers to the principles underlying the allocation (exchange or division) of benefits and burdens in negotiated agreements, and the extent to which parties actually consider that allocation fair after the fact.

Three major principles will be discussed, with brief references to ethnic conflict in which outcome fairness issues figure prominently: equity, equality, and need.

Equity. Originating in Aristotle's notion of justice as rooted in "balance" and "proportion," the equity principle holds that resources (rewards) should be distributed proportionally to relevant contributions (inputs). Fairness is achieved when each party's ratio of inputs to rewards is the same, and injustice is experienced in relation to these ratios rather than in absolute terms. Relevant contributions may be qualities and endowments (e.g., status, power, skills, wealth, intelligence), or actions and efforts (e.g., hours worked, tasks completed, leadership exercised). . . .

Equality. The principle of equality, also termed "impartial justice," holds that parties should receive the same or comparable rewards, irrespective of their contributions or needs. The norm finds its origins in the Enlightenment and the philosophy of Jean-Jacques Rousseau, which regarded individual differences as environmental products and equal treatment of all people as the natural and preferred type of human relationships. . . .

Need. A third major principle of outcome fairness is need, also termed compensatory or redistributive justice. This principle stipulates that resources should be allocated proportionally based on the strength of need alone, so that the least endowed party gets the greatest share.

Problem 4-3. ***The Cold Shoulder***

Assume your landlord failed to repair your broken heater in the dead of winter after you made multiple calls to him. Would it matter to you if you later found out that the landlord had left the country for a family emergency rather than just ignored your calls?

Start Walking!

A favorite story about the phenomenon of valuing respect over money comes from Steve Lubet's story of his family trip to Petra in Jordan. Tourists can either walk over a mile to the ruins at Petra or hire a Bedouin guide and horse for the ride. Tourists can either hire a horse round-trip (for 7 dinars) or one way (guides would demand 7 dinars and would reluctantly lower to 4 dinars). In an experiment over three days, Professor Lubet tried unsuccessfully to negotiate a lower price than 4 dinars for just the return trip each day from Petra. His theory was that (a) by the end of the day there were more horses than tourists and that (b) guides would prefer to use their horses as much as possible in order to make money. As he wrote, "So we walked. Four of us. Three times. . . . The result was clearly suboptimal. My family walked instead of riding; the horses idled instead of working." Why did the Bedouin horse owners refuse to bargain lower with Lubet? Lubet asked his children why. "'Because you didn't offer them enough money Daddy, and they thought that you didn't respect them.' 'But they still should have preferred the money to just standing around not working.' 'No, Daddy, they would rather stand around than take less than they thought they were worth.'" The moral of the story: how you treat people can affect your negotiation outcomes! Steven Lubet, Notes on the Bedouin Horse Trade or "Why Won't the Market Clear, Daddy?," 74 Tex. L. Rev. 1039 (1996).

b. Framing, Narrative, and Talking to Help Others Listen

One of the ways to make your presentation more persuasive is to tell a coherent story about what your client desires. For example, in addition to your legal arguments, you might also base your argument on good policy; a principle to be upheld; the better consequences of your agreement; an appeal to justice or morality; the needs and interests of the other side; or the general custom in that type of business or situation.

Additional methods to deepen your presentations and suggestions include framing and analogy. Negotiators sometimes use metaphors and labeling to make their arguments more persuasive. In a negotiation, are we *partners* or *opponents*? Are people in this country without papers illegal immigrants taking American jobs, or important contributors to the growth of the American economy? Were the Founding Fathers "freedom fighters," or were they traitors to the Crown? The use of labels simplifies a complex situation to convince and persuade the recipient. How you view the situation clearly affects what action you think is appropriate.

Other framing occurs using specifics and detail. You can use statistics or expert authority to provide specific support for your argument. Sometimes this experience is personal or "anecdotal," appealing to notions of justice, emotion, empathy, or morality—if you can tell a heartfelt story about how your motorcycle helmet saved your life, you might be better able to persuade a legislator to change the law. Many congressional hearings focus on this type of framing. Other times you can tell a story using vivid detail to describe what happened and bring the listener into the situation. Excellent trial attorneys often use this type of framing with a jury. In fact, in a study comparing the use of pallid information ("The defendant staggered against a serving table, knocking a bowl to the floor") versus vivid information ("The defendant staggered against a serving table, knocking a bowl of guacamole to the floor and splattering guacamole on the white shag carpet"), members of the mock jury were more likely to find the latter defendant guilty.[1]

---

1. R.M. Reyes, W.C. Thompson & G.H. Bower, Judgmental Biases Resulting from Differing Availabilities of Arguments, 39 J. Personality & Soc. Psychol. 2 (1980), cited in Scott Plous, The Psychology of Judgment and Decision Making 127-128 (1993).

Reader's Report from the Parent of a College Coed

Dear Mother and Dad:

Since I left for college I have been remiss in writing and I am sorry for my thoughtlessness in not having written before. I will bring you up to date now, but before you read on, please sit down. You are not to read any further unless you are sitting down, okay?

Well, then, I am getting along pretty well now. The skull fracture and the concussion I got when I jumped out the window of my dormitory when it caught on fire shortly after my arrival here is pretty well healed now. I only spent two weeks in the hospital and now I can see almost normally and only get those sick headaches once a day. Fortunately, the fire in the dormitory, and my jump, was witnessed by an attendant at the gas station near the dorm, and he was the one who called the Fire Department and the ambulance. He also visited me in the hospital and since I had nowhere to live because of the burnt-out dormitory, he was kind enough to invite me to share his apartment with him. It's really a basement room, but it's kind of cute. He is a very fine boy and we have fallen deeply in love and are planning to get married. We haven't got the exact date yet, but it will be before my pregnancy begins to show.

Yes, Mother and Dad, I am pregnant. I know how much you are looking forward to being grandparents and I know you will welcome the baby and give it the same love and devotion and tender care you gave me when I was a child. The reason for the delay in our marriage is that my boyfriend has a minor infection which prevents us from passing our pre-marital blood tests and I carelessly caught it from him.

Now that I have brought you up to date, I want to tell you that there was no dormitory fire, I did not have a concussion or skull fracture, I was not in the hospital, I am not pregnant, I am not engaged, I am not infected, and there is no boyfriend. However, I am getting a "D" in American History, and an "F" in Chemistry and I want you to see those marks in their proper perspective.

Your loving daughter,
Sharon

Sharon may be failing chemistry, but she gets an "A" in psychology. The author of the preceding letter, sent to author Robert Cialdini, masterfully frames her message. The context, placing, and timing of information become critical to how the listeners receive the information. Robert B. Cialdini, Influence: The Psychology of Persuasion 15-16 (1993).

Problem 4-4. *Reciprocity*

Robert Cialdini explains that the rule of reciprocity says that we should try to repay, in kind, what another person has provided us. If someone does us a favor, we should do her one in return; if someone sends us a birthday present, we should remember their birthday with a gift of our own; if a couple invites us to a party, we should be sure to invite them to one of ours. By virtue of the reciprocity rule, we are *obligated* to the future repayment of favors, gifts, invitations, and the like. The reciprocity technique is used in hundreds of different contexts.

1. Have you seen this technique yourself? Did you feel compelled to reciprocate (the invitation, the gift, help on homework, the free address labels, and so on)?
2. How can the concept of reciprocal concessions be used in a negotiation?
3. How can you protect yourself against conceding too much if this is used unfairly?

Although not every negotiation ends up being difficult, negotiators need a set of tools to deal with more challenging situations as they arise. In the next excerpt, three negotiation trainers and researchers advise how to talk in a manner that helps others to listen.

❖ *Douglas Stone, Bruce Patton & Sheila Heen*, DIFFICULT CONVERSATIONS: HOW TO DISCUSS WHAT MATTERS MOST

195-200 (1999)

TELLING YOUR STORY WITH CLARITY: THREE GUIDELINES

Obviously, how you express yourself makes a difference. How you say what you want to say will determine, in part, how others respond to you, and how the conversation will go. So when you choose to share something important, you'll want to do so in a way that will maximize the chance that the other person will understand and respond productively. Clarity is the key.

1. Don't Present Your Conclusions as the Truth

Some aspects of difficult conversations will continue to be rough even when you communicate with great skill: sharing feelings of vulnerability, delivering bad news, learning something painful about how others see you. But presenting your story as the truth—which creates resentment, defensiveness, and leads to arguments—is a wholly avoidable disaster. . . .

Some words—like "attractive," "ugly," "good," and "bad"—carry judgments that are obvious. But be careful with words like "inappropriate," "should," or "professional." The judgments contained in these words are less obvious, but can still provoke the "Who are you to tell me?!" response. If you want to say something is "inappropriate," preface your judgment with "My view is that . . ." Better still, avoid these words altogether.

2. Share Where Your Conclusions Come From

The first step toward clarity, then, is to share your conclusions and opinions as *your* conclusions and opinions and not as the truth. The second step is to share what's beneath your conclusions—the information you have and how you have interpreted it. . . .

3. Don't Exaggerate with "Always" and "Never": Give Them Room to Change

In the heat of the moment, it's easy to express frustration through a bit of exaggeration: "Why do you *always* criticize my clothes?" "You *never* give one word of appreciation or encouragement. The only time anyone hears anything from you is when there's something wrong!"

"Always" and "never" do a pretty good job of conveying frustration, but they have two serious drawbacks. First, it is seldom strictly accurate that someone criticizes *every* time, or that they haven't at some point said *something* positive. . . .

"Always" and "never" also make it harder—rather than easier—for the other person to consider changing their behavior. In fact, "always" and "never" suggest that change will be difficult or impossible. The implicit message is, "What is wrong with you such that you are driven to criticize my clothes?" or even "You are obviously incapable of acting like a normal person." . . .

The key is to communicate your feelings in a way that invites and encourages the recipient to consider new ways of behaving, rather than suggesting they're a schmuck and it's too bad there's nothing they can do about it. . . .

The secret of powerful expression is recognizing that you are the ultimate authority on you. You are an expert on what you think, how you feel, and why you've come to this place. If you think it or feel it, you are entitled to say it, and no one can legitimately contradict you. You only get in trouble if you try to assert what you are *not* the final authority on—who is right, who intended what, what happened. Speak fully from the range of your experience and you will be clear. Speak for yourself and you can speak with power.

3. Avoid Getting Stuck

Chapter 2 already discussed the importance of gathering information to prepare for the negotiation and the key roles that listening and understanding play in seeking information from the client and the other side. What happens when negotiators do not share useful information? What happens when negotiators get too wedded to the information they already have? Awareness of barriers, such as anchoring, overconfidence, and reactive devaluation, will help you identify roadblocks when you encounter them with yourself or others. This awareness will help you navigate these barriers in future negotiations. These next problems each explain the theory behind a barrier to constructive negotiation and then challenge you to understand how it works. Think about how each of these errors can either make you more assertive or more prone to mistake in setting your goals and limits in a negotiation.

Anchoring is the phenomenon where people are heavily influenced by the initial figure encountered when estimating the value of an item. The initial figure, whether high or low, "anchors" our estimation of the item's value, influencing our decision making. For example, if we asked you whether the average temperature in San Francisco is higher or lower than 558 degrees, and then asked you to estimate the average temperature, your answer to the second question would likely be influenced by the first question.[2]

Problem 4-5. ***Anchors Aweigh***

Studies have shown that first numbers such as statutory damage caps, insurance policy caps, opening offers and demands, and negotiator aspirations can influence negotiation outcomes.

- If parties can become anchored by information, should you make the first offer in a negotiation? What are the risks? What are the benefits?
- How does the concept of setting aspirations tie in with the concept of anchoring? Can you also anchor yourself?
- How can you protect yourself from the anchoring phenomenon? How can lawyers assist their clients in this?

Reactive devaluation is the tendency to undervalue a proposal because it was offered by an adversary. It is often a knee-jerk overreaction that can inhibit the ability to exploit tradeoffs on issues each side prioritizes differently. See Richard Birke & Craig R. Fox, Psychological Principles in Negotiating Civil Settlements, Acad. of Mgmt. Rev. 23-24, 48-50 (Oct. 1981).

2. Scott Plous, The Psychology of Judgment and Decision Making 127-128 (1993).

> **Problem 4-6. *Bowing to Authority***
>
> - Can you think of an instance where, in negotiating with a parent or other authority figure, you automatically dismissed an otherwise "good" offer?
>
> A phenomenon related to reactive devaluation is an elevated willingness to accept proposals—regardless of their objective or rational value or cost—if the proposal comes from someone loved or admired.
>
> - Are there some people to whom you say "yes" before hearing even what they propose? Knowing that negotiators can gain power from being liked and trusted, how would that influence your strategy as a negotiator?

It is human nature to overestimate our own achievements and capabilities. We focus on the "facts that are consistent with our desired outcomes" and discount the inconsistent facts. For example, overconfidence causes soon-to-be-married couples, who know the divorce rate is 40-50 percent, to estimate their chances of later divorcing at zero. Why is *overconfidence* a problem? In a negotiation context, overconfidence leads us to overestimate our trial alternatives. We focus on the strengths of our case and underappreciate the weaknesses. Studies have shown that participants in final-offer arbitration overestimated the chance of their offer being chosen by 15 percent. We can combat our tendency towards overconfidence by preparing alternative scenarios that will cover the range of potential outcomes, rather than focusing on a single outcome. See Donald R. Philbin, Jr., The One Minute Manager Prepares for Mediation: A Multidisciplinary Approach to Negotiation Preparation, 13 Harv. Negot. L. Rev. 249, 281-283 (Winter 2008).

> **Problem 4-7. *Overconfidence***
>
> What else can you, as the lawyer, do to help combat overconfidence in your client? In yourself? How can we use other types of criteria (e.g., fairness) to keep us from being too confident in our approach? Consider the advice from Chapter 2 about sharing risks and opportunities with the client candidly.

B. WORKING WITH THE OTHER SIDE

In the following excerpt, Andrea Schneider and David Kupfer explain the concept of empathy and why it is an important skill for negotiators to have.

Andrea Kupfer Schneider & David Kupfer, SMART & SAVVY: NEGOTIATION STRATEGIES IN ACADEMIA

38-39 (2017)

Putting this in very simple terms, when you are negotiating, you are trying to change someone's mind. Empathy helps you figure out what the other person is thinking, and that insight into his or her mind can greatly improve your chances of changing it. Think of the other person's interests, positions, and wishes as the map of the territory you are trying to navigate: When you understand what the other side thinks—and why he or she thinks it—you can start factoring that into your journey to reaching your own goals.

If you take time to consider the other person's (or the other side's) perspective, you will be more likely to be able to frame arguments in the way that will be persuasive to him or her. And empathizing with someone makes it more likely that he or she will empathize—or at least listen—to you. Finally, empathy helps build relationships through trust and respect. With that improved relationship, you will get more information and better, lasting outcomes.

Empathy has long been considered crucial to relationships. Almost every culture has a saying about empathy. In Russia, people note that everyone views the world from his or her own bell tower. In the novel *To Kill a Mockingbird*, Atticus Finch tried to explain it to his daughter. You never really understand someone, he told Scout, until "you climb into his skin and walk around in it."

What does empathy mean? Webster's defines it as "the action of understanding, being aware of, being sensitive to, and vicariously experiencing the feelings, thoughts, and experience of another of either the past or present without having the feelings, thoughts, and experience fully communicated in an objectively explicit manner." So, it is the real understanding of the other side's perspective—why he or she thinks a certain way, and how that makes him or her feel.

Empathy is *not* sympathy or agreement, and therein lies the challenge. To accomplish your goal, you want to understand where the other person you're negotiating with is coming from—*and* at the same time still recognize the importance of your own interests. Some negotiators have difficulty continuing to think of their own view as "right" when they are working hard to understand the perspective of the other party, but the most successful negotiators manage this balance, recognizing that effective empathy gives them the ability to be more persuasive in asserting their own perspective and also makes it more likely that the other side will respond well to their assertiveness. If you understand what really matters to your chair, your colleague, or anyone else sitting across the table or the desk, you will be better able to persuade that person on his or her own terms.

True empathy consists of both cognitive and emotional understanding—understanding both *what* the other's person perspective is and *how* that perspective makes that person feel. Effective negotiators can build skills in both these arenas to improve their empathy.

This next excerpt demonstrates several tools we can use to expand our empathy for our negotiation counterpart, including role reversal—literally sitting in the other side's seat.

❖ *Roger Fisher, Elizabeth Kopelman & Andrea Schneider*, BEYOND MACHIAVELLI: TOOLS FOR COPING WITH CONFLICT

32-35 (1996)

OBSERVE FROM DIFFERENT POINTS OF VIEW

To understand a conflict in which we are a party, we will want to observe it from at least three points of view. First, we want to be aware of ourselves (Are we angry? Losing control? Reacting? Drifting?) and to consider the conflict from our own point of view (What are our goals? What are our interests? What risks do we see? And so forth). Our point of view is an important starting point. It is, however, only a starting point.

We will also want to observe the situation from the point of view of the other parties to this conflict. Putting ourselves hypothetically in their shoes, what would we see? How does everything look from that vantage point? If we were there, what would be our goals, our interests, our concerns? Would we feel justifiably angry? How does the conflict look from there?

And finally, to gain a more balanced view, how would the situation look from the point of view of a neutral third party? How would a "fly on the wall" describe things? How are the parties behaving? Do they seem to be quarreling, debating, scoring points, bickering, and attacking each other, or are they jointly attacking the problem? Are they wasting time or using it well?

To understand conflict well we want to observe it from all three positions. (If there are several parties to a conflict, we will want to understand how each sees it.) One who is skilled at dealing with conflict is likely to be adept at jumping back and forth, observing what is going on from each of these three positions, even "on line," while participating in a discussion. . . .

Three Positions for Observing a Conflict
First Position (Mine): How I see the problem, from my own perspective.
Second Position (Theirs): How I see the problem when I stand in the shoes of the other party to the dispute.
Third Position ("Fly on the Wall"): How a neutral third party would assess the conflict.
These three distinct points of view illuminate a variety of dimensions of a conflict.

TO GAIN EMPATHY, REVERSE ROLES

Understanding is not simply an intellectual activity. Feeling empathetically how others may feel can be as important as thinking clearly about how others may think.

There is a lot of truth in the old saying that "where you stand depends upon where you sit." Another way of trying to understand the other side's perceptions is literally to sit in a different chair, pretend to be someone on the other side, and try to see the situation from that vantage point.

The chairman of a company held liable for a patent infringement had called in a consultant to advise about the negotiation of a possible settlement on the dollar amount of damages. The case had been in litigation for years. The chairman had been told that if the worst happened, and he should be held liable, he could always settle—but he had little appreciation of how much the other side would expect.

Encouraged by the consultant, the executive agreed to switch seats, moving from his own chair to a chair the consultant had designated as that of the president of the plaintiff company. While the executive initially resisted "playing games," he was eventually persuaded to assume the role of that president and to state the plaintiff's case in the first person as forcefully as he could. Within a few minutes he was playing the role well. Asked how much he might accept in settlement (an amount that, in real life, would be paid out by this executive's own company) he replied (still in his role as the opposing company's president), "Why, I wouldn't take their whole damn company!" Shaken by this experience, and with new insight into what might be required to settle this case, his company raised its settlement offer by one hundred-fold. It was rejected, and the judgment was ultimately for even more. An earlier attempt to appreciate the other side's partisan perceptions would no doubt have led him to pursue a wiser strategy from the outset. . . .

To gain insight by reversing roles, we first identify the person whom we expect to be attempting to persuade (the "absent party") and find a friend or colleague to help us. Our helper is someone who either already knows our side of the conflict or will quickly learn the points we currently plan to make. Then we sit in the chair labeled "absent party," and with the assistance of the helper, come to think of ourselves as being that person. Finally, our helper sits in our chair, assumes our role, and presents our side of the case. While playing the part of someone on the other side of a conflict, we hear our own arguments come back at us. Through such role reversal we can often gain insight and empathy for the other side—sometimes dramatically so—in a way that helps us tailor our arguments to make them more persuasive.

> **A Note on Listening**
>
> Empathy is virtually impossible without finding out what is important to the other side. In many ways, this is like interviewing your client. We have outlined this skill in interviewing in Chapter 2 and will also return to this in Chapter 6 on Mediation Skills.

C. CREATIVITY AND FLEXIBILITY

Effective negotiators understand the different approaches to a negotiation and know how to choose a style suitable for the context and the counterpart. They are flexible and can change styles during the negotiation as the situation evolves. Effective negotiators also recognize that they can meet their interests in several ways. They are flexible in terms of what goes into a settlement because they recognize that some opportunities might create new value and get them more than what they thought was available.

As parents of young children know, children are far better at being creative than their parents. What adults may see as a basic shoebox is actually a house for dinosaurs, a bookcase for baby books, the first block in a tower, or a hat, all depending on how you look at it. After years of being told to color in the lines, and that the grass should be green and the sky should be blue, to answer only the question asked, and to play games only by the rules printed on the box, we all lose much of our natural creativity. Yet the need to be creative hardly decreases with age. In fact, certain successful companies incorporate "creative conflict" into the very structure of the company.[3] Procter & Gamble, for example, fosters competition among its various brands. Nissan uses this method for designing new car models. Other companies use the model of brain teaser questions in their interviewing process to find creative people.[4]

Lehman Brothers used to follow this methodology of asking interviewees tough questions. In response to an interviewer's request to open a window in an office on the 43rd floor, the interviewee tossed a chair through the window![5] While we don't recommend this approach, we do appreciate the ability of this particular person to let no barrier to creativity stand in their way.

The value of creative thinking also applies to effective negotiation where the ability to "think outside the box" is quite valuable. Without this skill—often overlooked in legal education—problem-solving or integrative solutions to negotiation become far more difficult. Often, the difference between simple compromise

3. Sy Landau, Barbara Landau & Daryl Landau, From Conflict to Creativity 97-98 (2001).
4. Microsoft's brainteaser methodology not only has spawned a book, William Poundstone's *How Would You Move Mount Fuji?* (2003), but also multiple Web sites to help potential employees prepare for their interview.
5. Michael Lewis, Liar's Poker (1989).

(splitting the orange) and a more collaborative or integrative solution (separating the peel and fruit) is being sufficiently creative and flexible. This section focuses on the advantages that creative thinking brings to a negotiation and then provides some specific ideas to increase creativity.

The following excerpt by Carrie Menkel-Meadow starts with the importance of creativity in successful problem-solving, and then highlights past examples of legal creativity and what that means.

Carrie Menkel-Meadow, AHA? IS CREATIVITY POSSIBLE IN LEGAL PROBLEM SOLVING AND TEACHABLE IN LEGAL EDUCATION?

6 Harv. Negot. L. Rev. 97, 106, 122-123, 125, 127-128, 131, 133, 135-136 (2001)

Dispute negotiation too often looks for its solutions among legal precedents or outcomes thought likely in the "shadow of the courthouse" (these days most often [a] compromise of some monetary values), and deal negotiations too often seek solutions in the boilerplate language of form contracts for transactions. Ironically, these litigated outcomes and boilerplate clauses were once the creative ideas of some lawyers who developed a new reading of a statute, a novel argument before a common law or Constitutional court, developed a new scheme of risk allocation, or found a new source of capital or drafted a new clause for a deal document. . . .

In this literature, the following techniques are suggested as formal ways of enhancing creativity, solving problems and suggesting new ideas, some as separate individual cognitive processes, and others as structured processes to be used in multiparty settings.

1. Uses of analogy (direct, fanciful) and use of metaphor;
2. Aggregation/disaggregation/re-combination of elements of a problem;
3. Transfer (cross-disciplinary use of concepts, ideas, information, solutions from other fields);
4. Reversal (either extreme polarization or gradual modification of ideas)—which is done both in cognitive and in personal forms (as in role-reversal efforts to understand the point of view of others in the situation);
5. Extension—extending a line of reasoning, principle or solution beyond its original purpose;
6. Challenging assumptions—re-examining givens or problem statements and unpacking clichéd, conventional solutions or stereotypes;
7. Narrative—fully describing facts and problems to elaborate on complexity, and producing alternative endings;
8. Backward/forward thinking—focusing on how we came to a particular situation (reasons why, causes) in order to figure out how we get to desired end-state(s);
9. Design—plan for desired future end-state, structures, means;

10. Random stimulation/brainstorming—separation of idea generation, randomly generated, from judgment and evaluation. . . .
11. Visualization—use of different competencies and modes of thinking and processing information; this includes efforts at altered states (e.g., retreats and meditations);
12. Entry points—explicit reframing of problems and solutions from different perspectives. . . .

Lawyers work with words, so most of our creative acts involve the construction of new language and interpretation of existing language, creating new concepts from whole cloth or from the interstices of statutory, regulatory or contractual gaps. Our words have the force of law behind them, however, so that powerfully creative words in law have been known to create whole new institutions. Examples of new legal and real entities that have been created are corporations, trusts, regulatory agencies, condominiums, unions and tax shelters. In addition, our words have created new legal rights and constructs like leases, sexual harassment, probation—and also have recognized (sometimes from conflicting ideologies) new claims like civil rights, privacy, free speech and emotional distress. . . .

Law's creativity may be somewhat limited by the bounds of law and legal ethics rules, but there still remains a fair amount of problem space to be manipulated within our adversarial culture. At the same time, the adversarial culture may also constrain and cabin our thinking unnecessarily by structuring it in polarized and oppositional terms. Are transactional lawyers more creative by being less constrained? Corporations and trusts, for example, were created legally to accomplish many different goals, some adversarial (tax delay, minimization or avoidance), but also to permit different power and control arrangements and to bundle and unbundle interests of wealth, time and assets to permit great flexibility of action. . . .

Legal creativity is necessarily limited by its need to work within the law, or at least within the foreseeable boundaries of legal change, but for optimal problem solving it would seem we should try to push the boundaries of little "c" creativity as much as we can to produce at least a greater number of choices about how best to accomplish legal results.

In this next excerpt, Professor Brown explains several different techniques for negotiation creativity.

❖ *Jennifer Gerarda Brown*, CREATIVITY AND PROBLEM-SOLVING

87 Marq. L. Rev. 697-705 (2004)

Negotiation experts seem to agree that creative solutions are often the key to reaching value-maximizing outcomes in integrative, interest-based bargaining. Sticking to the problem as it is initially framed and considering only the solutions that most readily present themselves will sometimes yield the optimal result, but more often the situation will require the parties and their representatives to think more expansively. This process of thinking more expansively—thinking "that ventures out from the accustomed way of considering a problem, to find something else that might work"—is often referred to as creativity or creative thinking. Some commentators distinguish creative thinking from creativity, arguing that creativity "is more value-laden and tends to be often linked with art (in its broad sense)." Creativity might seem to resemble any other artistic quality, something people lack or possess as much as a matter of genetics as anything else. And yet, like other artistic qualities (observation, hand-eye coordination, vocabulary, or writing skills), creativity may be teachable—or at least, whatever quantity one has as a matter of natural endowment might be enhanced with the right training. On the theory that both creativity and creative thinking can be enhanced with some training and work, this essay will use the terms interchangeably. . . .

I. BEYOND BRAINSTORMING

Most teachers and trainers of interest-based negotiation will spend some time teaching creative thinking. Following the template set forth in *Getting to YES*, they will encourage their students to "brainstorm." Brainstorming . . . is a somewhat formalized process in which participants work together to generate ideas. I say that it is formalized because it proceeds according to two important ground rules: participants agree not to evaluate the ideas while they are brainstorming, and they agree not to take "ownership" of the ideas. They strive to generate options and put them on the table, no matter how wacky or far-fetched they may seem. The "no evaluation" rule encourages participants to suspend their natural urge to criticize, edit, or censor the ideas. Evaluation can come later, but the notion here is that solutions will flow more easily if people are not assessing even as they articulate them. The "no ownership" rule also facilitates innovation because participants are encouraged to feel free to propose an idea or solution without endorsing it—no one can later attribute the idea to the person who proposed it, or try to hold it against that person. People can therefore propose ideas that might actually disadvantage them and benefit their counterparts without conceding that they would actually agree to such proposals in the final analysis. The ground rules for brainstorming constrain the natural inclination to criticize, so that participants are free to imagine, envision, and play with ideas, even though these processes come less easily to them.

Why is brainstorming so popular, both in practice and in negotiation training? Perhaps the answer lies not so much in what it activates, but in what it disables. What I mean is that it may be easier to teach people what *not* to do—rather than what to do affirmatively—in order to enhance their creative thinking. We may not know much about how to unleash new sources of creativity for negotiators, but we are pretty sure about some things that impede creative thinking. Theory and practice suggest that creative thinking is difficult when people jump to conclusions, close off discussion, or seize upon an answer prematurely. Indeed, the very heuristics that make decisionmaking possible—those pathways that permit people to make positive and sometimes normative judgments—can also lead people astray. One of the ways they may be led astray is that the heuristic prompts them to decide too quickly what something is or should be. Once judgment has occurred, it is tough to justify the expenditure of additional energy that creative thinking would require. Creativity could be considered the "anti-heuristic"; it keeps multiple pathways of perception and decision-making open, even when people are tempted to choose a single, one-way route to a solution. If we do nothing else, we can attempt to delay this kind of judgment until negotiators have considered multiple options. Brainstorming provides the structure for this kind of delay. . . .

A. Wordplay

Once an issue or problem is articulated, it is possible to play with the words expressing that problem in order to improve understanding and sometimes to yield new solutions.

1. Shifting Emphasis

To take a fairly simple example, suppose that two neighbors are in a dispute because cigarette butts and other small pieces of trash, deposited by Mr. Smith in his own front yard, are blowing into Mr. Jones's yard, and those that remain in Mr. Smith's yard are detracting from the appearance of the neighborhood (at least as Mr. Jones sees it). Mr. Jones might ask himself (or a mediator at the neighborhood justice center), "How can I get Mr. Smith to stop littering in his yard?" Shifting the emphasis in this sentence brings into focus various aspects of the problem and suggests possible solutions addressing those specific aspects. Consider the different meanings of the following sentences:

"How can *I* get Mr. Smith to stop littering in his yard?"
"How can I get Mr. *Smith* to stop littering in his yard?"
"How can I get Mr. Smith to stop *littering* in his yard?"
"How can I get Mr. Smith to stop littering in *his* yard?"
"How can I get Mr. Smith to stop littering in his *yard*?"

As the focus of the problem shifts, so too different potential solutions might emerge to address the problem as specifically articulated.

2. Changing a Word

Sometimes changing a word in the sentence helps to reformulate the problem in a way that suggests new solutions. In the example above, Mr. Jones might change the phrase "littering in his yard" to something else, such as "neglecting his yard" or "hanging out in his yard." It may be that something besides littering lies at the root of the problem, and a solution will be found, for example, not in stopping the littering, but in more regularized yard work.

3. Deleting a Word

Through word play, parties can delete words or phrases to see whether broadening the statement of the problem more accurately or helpfully captures its essence. Mr. Jones might delete the phrase "Mr. Smith" from his formulation of the problem, and thereby discover that it is not just Mr. Smith's yard, but the entire street, that is looking bad. Focusing on Mr. Smith as the source of the problem may be counterproductive; Mr. Jones might discover that he needs to organize all of the homeowners on his block to battle littering in order to make a difference. Deleting words sometimes spurs creativity by removing an overly restrictive focus on the issue or problem.

4. Adding a New Word

A final form of word play that can spur creative thinking is sometimes called "random word association." Through this process, participants choose a word randomly and then think of ways to associate it with the problem. Suppose Mr. Jones and Mr. Smith were given the word "work" and asked how it might relate to their dispute. Here are some possible results:

Work (time, effort): Mr. Smith will try to work harder to keep his yard looking nice, and he will check Mr. Jones's yard every Saturday to make sure there are no cigarette butts or other pieces of trash in it.

Work (being operational or functional): What the neighborhood needs is a sense of cohesion; Mr. Jones and Mr. Smith will organize a neighborhood beautification project to try to instill a sense of community among their neighbors.

Work (job): Although Mr. Smith's odd working hours sometimes lead him to smoke on his front porch and chat with his friends or family late at night (after Mr. Jones has gone to bed), Mr. Smith will stay in the back of his house after 10 P.M., further from Mr. Jones's bedroom window.

As the different meanings and resulting associations of "work" are explored by the parties, they discover new ways to solve their shared problem. Other seemingly unrelated words might trigger still more associations and more potential solutions. . . .

D. Atlas of Approaches

Another technique for stimulating creative ideas about a problem from a variety of perspectives is called the "Atlas of Approaches." Roger Fisher, Elizabeth Kopelman and Andrea Kupfer Schneider propose this approach in *Beyond Machiavelli*, their book on international negotiation.[9] Using the Atlas of Approaches technique, participants adopt the perspectives of professionals from a variety of fields. By asking themselves, for example, "What would a journalist do?," "What would an economist do?," "How would a psychologist view this?," and so on, negotiators are able to form a more interdisciplinary view of their problem. With this more

9. Roger Fisher et al., Beyond Machiavelli: Tools for Coping with Conflict 67 (1996).

complete picture of the issues and potential outcomes, they might be able to connect disciplines in ways that give rise to creative solutions. . . .

F. "WWCD": What Would Croesus[10] Do?

This process requires a participant to take the perspective of an unconstrained actor. What solutions suggest themselves if we assume no limit to available money, time, talent, technology, or effort? In some ways, one could think of the WWCD method as a more specific application of brainstorming. As the proponents of brainstorming are quick to point out, creativity and the free flow of ideas can be impeded by criticism or assessment. WWCD takes off the table any assessment based on constraints—financial, technological, etc. If we assume that we can afford and operationalize any solution we can come up with, what might we discover?

A second phase of this approach requires participants to think about the extent to which their unconstrained solution might be modified to make it workable given the existing constraints. . . .

This final excerpt explores how conflict itself can lead to ideas for resolution.

Robert C. Bordone & Michael Moffitt, CREATE VALUE OUT OF CONFLICT

9 Negot. 1 (June 2006)

In this article, we present six different ways to find value when you're in the throes of a seemingly intractable business dispute.

1. CAPITALIZE ON SHARED INTERESTS

Disputes highlight the ways in which we differ from the other side. After all, without differences, there would be no disputes. Yet these conspicuous differences often mask the *noncompetitive similarities* that also exist between those involved in a dispute—similarities that can add value for both sides.

Consider a dispute between a high-tech manufacturer and a small company that licenses a critical piece of intellectual property to the manufacturer. The two sides bitterly disagree about the appropriate method for calculating royalties under the license—but this isn't their only set of relevant interests. Both are interested

10. Nalebuff and Ayers explain: "Croesus (rhymes with Jesus) was the supremely rich king of Lydia (modern Turkey), reigning from 560 to 546 B.C. His wealth came from mining gold . . . His lavish gifts and sacrifices made his name synonymous with wealth. Even today we say 'rich as Croesus.'" Barry Nalebuff & Ian Ayres, Why Not? How to Use Everyday Ingenuity to Solve Problems Big and Small (2003).

in sustaining the market's confidence in the new product, and they're aware that suppliers, creditors, and prospective customers might shy away from deals with feuding business partners. Given this shared interest, the two sides could agree to keep certain aspects of the dispute confidential. They could also put the proceeds from the new product into escrow, pending resolution of the dispute according to a specified timeline. . . .

2. EXPLORE DIFFERENCES IN PREFERENCES, PRIORITIES, AND RESOURCES

Important disputes typically involve more than one issue—including disputes that appear to be "just about the money." Who pays and when? In what form is payment made, with what level of confidentiality, and with what effect on future dispute?

In the heat of the moment, disputants too often focus on one conspicuous issue (such as money), a mistake that risks masking other important concerns. Whenever more than one issue is on the table, it's likely that parties will value certain issues more than others. You may be able to resolve the dispute by capitalizing on differences in relative preferences, priorities, or resources. . . .

3. CAPITALIZE ON DIFFERENCES IN FORECASTS AND RISK PREFERENCES

One common source of conflict arises from diverging expectations about what will happen in the future. And when it comes to predicting the future, disputants tend to behave less than ideally. The overconfidence bias can lead both sides to overestimate the likelihood of achieving their desired outcomes. Similarly, egocentrism can cause people to have an inflated perception of the fairness of their own position. Such biases can easily lead to impasse.

One value-creating antidote may be *contingent agreements*—deal structures that permit parties to "bet" on their predictions by specifying different payoffs based on future events. Take the example of a developer disagreeing, citing data that suggest that property values near luxury malls actually rise faster than average. . . .

If the developer is highly confident in his assessment and if the homeowners truly fear declining property values, the parties can structure a contingent agreement that protects them all. . . .

4. STRUCTURE AN AGREEMENT THAT RECOGNIZES VARYING TIME FRAMES

. . . Suppose that a Web design firm has performed design and hosting work for a small but growing business. The Web design firm added a sizable charge for "scope change," citing several requests the small business made during the construction and maintenance of the site. The small company disputes that the changes were significant enough to warrant the extra charges and refuses to make an additional payment.

By haggling back and forth, the parties may (or may not) find a payment amount acceptable to both sides. But they might find that both parties would benefit by exploring possible time frame differences. Is the small business facing a relatively tight cash-flow situation? If so, it might consider structuring payments over time, rather than arguing about a lump-sum figure. Is the Web design firm concerned about its ability to retain long-term clients? Perhaps it should consider counting part of the monthly payment as an ongoing retainer fee. The small business would gain ongoing services, and the Web design firm would convert a one-time customer into a revenue stream similar to an annuity. Clearly, capitalizing on differences in the implicit calendars each disputant envisions can be the key to an efficient resolution.

5. ADDRESS POTENTIAL IMPLEMENTATION

Problems Up Front

Resolving a significant dispute typically requires more than a onetime exchange of dollars. Implementation often occurs over time, raising reasonable fears that one or more parties will violate the agreement's explicit provisions or its spirit. The fear of misbehavior can be so great that it prevents disputants from reaching a resolution.

Successful negotiators explicitly address implementation difficulties by crafting resolution terms that manage risk. . . .

6. MINIMIZE TRANSACTION COSTS

Sometimes creative solutions to a dispute are simply not possible. Perhaps emotions are too high, the relationship has become too bitter, or the issues on the table don't lend themselves to elegant trade-offs. One or more parties may perceive litigation to be the best option. . . .

Problem 4-8. ***Medicine for Cheesecake***

There once was a law student with chronic medical problems. Unfortunately, she was also uninsured. The good news was that she was a fabulous cook. The first time she saw the doctor she explained her financial situation. The doctor had plenty of money, but he loved cheesecakes. The law student was able to work out with her doctor a payment plan for services over time. What kind of solution is this? After they negotiated the first time, she delivered a chocolate chip cheesecake to the doctor in appreciation for his understanding. The next time she needed the doctor, the doctor requested payment in cheesecakes! What kind of solution is this?

In Dean Pruitt's book chapter, *Achieving Integrative Agreements*, he discusses five methods for achieving integrative agreements. These are ways to take the parties' initially opposing demands and transforming them into alternatives that reconcile their interests. These five methods (with examples from his chapter) are:

Expanding the Pie: Creating an integrative agreement by increasing the available resources.

> If the husband rejects the seashore because it keeps him away from the mountains and the wife rejects the mountains because they deny her the pleasure of the seashore, where do they go on vacation? Our married couple might solve their problems by persuading their employers to give them four weeks of vacation, so they can take two in the mountains and two at the seashore.

Nonspecific Compensation: One party gets what he or she wants and the other is repaid in an unrelated way.

> The wife may agree to go to the mountains, even though she finds them boring, if her husband promises her a fur coat.

Logrolling: Each party concedes on low priority issues in exchange for concessions on issues of higher priority to itself. Logrolling is used in situations where several issues are under consideration and the parties have differing priorities among these issues. Each gets that part of its demands that it finds most important.

> Suppose that in addition to disagreeing about where to go on vacation, the wife in our example wants to go to a first-class hotel while her husband prefers a tourist home. If accommodations are a high priority issue for the wife and location for the for the husband, they can reach a fairly integrative solution by agreeing to go to a first-class hotel while in the mountains.

Cost Cutting: One party gets what he or she wants, and the other's costs are reduced or eliminated. The result is high joint benefit, not because the first party has changed his or her demands but because the second party suffers less. Cost cutting often takes the form of specific compensation in which the party who concedes receives something in return that satisfies the precise values frustrated.

> Suppose that the husband . . . dislikes the beach because of the hustle and bustle. He may be quite willing to go there on vacation if his costs are cut by renting a house with a quiet inner courtyard where he can read while his wife goes out among the crowds.

Bridging: Here, neither party achieves its initial demands, but a new option is devised that satisfies the most important interests underlying these demands. Bridging typically involves a reformulation of the issue.

> Suppose that the husband in our vacation example is mainly interested in fishing and hunting and the wife in swimming and sunbathing. Their interests might be bridged by finding an inland resort with a lake and a beach that is close to woods and streams.

Dean Pruitt, "Achieving Integrative Agreements," in Negotiation in Organizations 36-41 (Max Bazerman & Roy Lewicki eds., 1983).

D. SOCIAL INTUITION

The final skill in this chapter brings in social intuition. We define this overarching term as encompassing both emotional intelligence and nonverbal communication skills. Social intuition in negotiation is the skill that helps us determine how to approach our counterpart, when to take a break in a negotiation, and to gauge how persuasive our arguments might be, among other choices. The first excerpt outlines how we can use social intuition in negotiation, and the second then focuses on how modes of communication (email, video, text, etc.) impact our ability to utilize this negotiation skill.

❖ *Andrea Kupfer Schneider & Noam Ebner*, SOCIAL INTUITION

in Christopher Honeyman & Andrea Kupfer Schneider, The Negotiator's Desk Reference 127-142 (2017)

To fully understand the notion of social intuition, and to consider its practical implementations in negotiation, one must assess it from three different angles:

Self*:* This aspect might be best introduced as self-awareness with regard to our own emotions, cognitive patterns, biases and attributions, and typical responses and reactions. Studies have long shown that people with more self-control, to delay gratification for example, are more successful. Similarly, as we monitor our emotional tenor during a negotiation, we can control better how we come across. This part of social intuition might be measured by examining our tone, our pace of conversation, how we carry ourselves physically in the negotiation, and even how our emotions are shown on our faces. Does our content match up with our conduct? Do the substantive words we say flow congruently with the process actions we are taking? Or are there emotional "gaps" between what we intend, what we say, and what we do? The first step in social intuition is the ability to be aware of your own emotional tenor.

Negotiators who have this awareness are likely to be more effective in projecting clear and congruent messages. They are able to recognize the effects that the other, the situation, or other factors are having on their own internal resources of energy, motivation and focus. Finally, they are also able to recognize when their own emotional states are likely to support their negotiation efforts, and when they are likely to undermine them.

Other: The second aspect might be best captured as the ability to read your counterpart. Can you note, and understand, their signals—in body language or in verbal nuance? Can you measure their attention span, identify and understand the different laughs they emit, and register and understand the meaning of different volume levels they use? Does their behavior seem consistent with what they are saying substantively, and with what you understand to be their interests? In this aspect, you are working to be attuned to their emotional state and to how that state is reflected through their signals.

Negotiators who are able to "read" their counterpart in such a detailed and comprehensive manner are likely to gain an abundance of information that can be helpful in a negotiation. They might be able to separate their counterpart's core concerns from tangential issues; they might recognize when their counterpart is aiming high rather than approaching their reservation point. At a very attuned level, they might be able to discern truth from lies, or recognize manipulative tactics, cloaked in politeness or affability, for what they truly are.

Each of these two aspects of social intuition is valuable to negotiators in its own right. Combined, they are even more valuable. Negotiators who are attuned to themselves, and who are able to read others, enjoy the ability to recognize mutual effects of these two elements. They will notice how the sound of their counterpart's voice (or, further nuanced, its particular sound at a particular volume) impacts them emotionally. They will notice how their counterpart's actions in the interaction do not exist in a vacuum, but are reactive to their own words and actions (e.g., "She raises her voice and talks over me every time I use the word 'no'"). Such recognition is not only helpful for contributing to negotiators' overall understanding of the situation—it also sets the stage for their ability to implement a third element of social intuition, which we call bridging.

Bridging: This third aspect involves action you take in order to form connections with the other through the interactional exchange—connections that support you in affecting the other. For example, suppose that you have sensed that your counterpart is feeling ill-at-ease about a particular issue. Your actions—whether to help them feel more at ease, or less so—are likely to affect how they handle negotiating this issue. Bridging actions will likely include all sorts of micro-responses of which we might not even be aware as we are performing them. When this bridging works well, both negotiators look and feel as if they are moving together, even though substantive differences might still remain. The elements of situational awareness—the ability to read ourselves, read our counterpart, and read the situation—all come together as we take bridging actions.

Social intuition in negotiation is, therefore, the convergence of three areas of capacity: The negotiator's capacity for self-awareness, the negotiator's capacity to focus attention on the other and elicit information beyond what is being conveyed explicitly, and the negotiator's capacity to be in tune with, and affect, their counterpart through intentional acts of bridging.

Problem 4-9. ***Social Intuition***

Elements of social intuition can be found in non-verbal, para-verbal, and verbal exchanges:

Nonverbal:	Para-verbal:	Verbal:
• Body language and mirroring	• Pace	• Humor
• Proximity	• Tone	• Metaphors
• Eye contact		
• Physical contact (i.e., handshakes)		

Consider how each of these elements are managed through the self, the other, and bridging. How do you manage these elements in a negotiation? Which of these do you think is the easiest for you? The most challenging?

Andrea Kupfer Schneider & Sean McCarthy, MODES OF COMMUNICATION

in Christopher Honeyman & Andrea Kupfer Schneider, The Negotiator's Desk Reference (2017)

DIFFERENCES IN MODES OF COMMUNICATION

It is helpful to outline the differences between the modes of communication, and then to think about how they operate in a negotiation. First, different modes permit varying levels of social intuition as well as perception of nonverbal language. Face to face conversations are considered media "rich" because they allow tracking of multiple social cues. In face to face conversations (in person and online via video), you can interpret body language, tone, eye contact, and facial expressions in addition to hearing the content of the conversation. Phone conversations provide some of this; through the tone, pauses, and inflections of even a verbal conversation, we can learn a lot about how the other party is feeling, in addition to the content. Email (or texting), on the other hand, does not incorporate those contextual elements. We will discuss below how to add "e-empathy" to your communication to try to bring that media richness into all of your communications.

The difference between modes of communication is also reflected in the content that comes across. In face to face conversations, the conversation often rapidly switches between the personal and the professional, the mundane (think the weather) and the more on point. In email communications, the content tends to be more task-oriented. What do we need to get done? What is the answer to X? This is less personal, unless we take the time in the email (often at the beginning or end, or both) to add the personal touches. We are more trained (at least in U.S. culture) to schmooze automatically at the beginning of a face to face negotiation; this same impulse does not necessarily occur online. Another noticeable difference is the timing of conversations. Face to face conversations are, by their very nature, synchronous conversations. In other words, both parties are engaged at the same time. Even when one side is talking, the other person is interacting through their body language and responses. Online communication may occur simultaneously, particularly with texting, but only if both parties happen to be on their devices at the same time and choose to engage that way. Often, our emails are sent without direct knowledge of whether the other party is available to read one at that time (or even within a short period of time.) In face to face conversations, also, we often take turns—question, response, follow-up question, response, etc. Via email, particularly when one of the parties is at meetings or otherwise unavailable, the communication can stack up . . . [T]he situation has evolved over the course of time, and you are reading the fifth email about a particular issue that arose several hours ago. . .

Finally, the asynchronicity of email also means that while our "work" hours might be over for the day, our work communication via email or text can continue (for better and worse) throughout our waking hours. And this flexibility impacts the level of distraction as well as on what device we typically read. We might be reading email about important subjects over dinner in the evening, while watching television, or in the midst of putting kids to sleep . . . Not surprisingly, this opportunity to read email or texts into the night can also affect the quality of our reading.

WHY THE DIFFERENCES IN MODES MATTER FOR NEGOTIATION

Negotiation experts regularly discuss the importance of building trust and a relationship in a negotiation. Much of your ability to create rapport comes from the ability to see or at least hear the other party. Our mirroring skills in body language, the level of eye contact, even nodding, are all impossible via email. And so when we send and receive email messages, there is much less context for the content of the email. Is the other party joking when they say that they are crushed not to receive a draft of the report today? How about their disappointment at our missing a meeting? In face to face communication, we would immediately know if someone was sad or happy, joking or snarky. Over email, we have to make guesses. In work situations, in more formal contexts, or when dealing with superiors, we are more likely to assume bad intentions or worry that something is wrong. Our reading of the emails is more analytical and literal, since that is the only information in front of us (Ebner 2014). The content of the information exchange is also different. Without the ability to explain in real time, ask questions, and clarify ambiguities, we often make assumptions about the content of the email. Even when we ask questions, these might not be answered directly. Or we ask several questions and the response might only cover one or two of the questions.

Finally, developing relationships and trust over email is more challenging. Several studies have shown that parties are more adversarial with each other via email (and even over the phone) compared to face to face negotiations. Parties tend to share less information and cooperate less in the process of negotiation via email, resulting in lower levels of trust and higher potential for deceptive practices. And without the facial and verbal cues of face to face communication, we have higher levels of negative attribution. In other words, we assume the worst and are more likely to attribute poor motives to our counterpart. . . .

This links to social intuition, in which you need to stay attuned to how the communication is occurring. The choice of communication mode should be highly influenced by your attention to the emotional tenor of the negotiation. Email negotiations—and the fact that we don't know when someone received the email, when they are going to respond, or what they are thinking—can be fraught with miscommunication. Part of social intuition is managing your own anxiety as well as theirs. What are the expectations for responding to emails? Do others in your workplace seem to respond within twenty-four hours, or is a more leisurely rate acceptable? Different assumptions operate in different environments.

The chart below is now updated to consider these modes of communication in light of our extensive use of video conferencing post-Covid:

Differences in Modes of Communication[6]

	Content	**Nonverbal Cues**	**Timing**	**Trust/ Relationship**
Face-to-Face	All things personal and/or professional	High level of verbal and nonverbal cues	Simultaneous	Easy to build rapport
Phone	All things personal and/or professional	Paraverbal only	Simultaneous	More challenging

6. This chart is adapted from the Singapore Mediation Week Keynote address. August 30, 2023.

	Content	Nonverbal Cues	Timing	Trust/ Relationship
Email	Tends to be more task-oriented	Only if added deliberately	Dependent on access and promptness of reply	More challenging
Text	Tends to be more personal but that is changing	Easy to add emojis to language; and lots of casual language	Can be simultaneous	More challenging if professional
Video Conferencing	Depends on platform expectations (i.e., FaceTime v. Zoom)	High in verbal and nonverbal cues (but technologically dependent)	Simultaneous	Can be easier, but technologically dependent

E. CULTURE

Many of the elements of social intuition (eye contact, proximity, body language) are highly related to culture. Advice on dealing with cultural differences in negotiation runs the risk of either being too simplistic (don't cross your legs in certain cultures) or being so general that it is not helpful (there may be different assumptions about how negotiations are conducted). This next excerpt will point out some common cultural differences in negotiation while also reminding negotiators that cultural differences may or may not explain any one individual's approach to negotiations. Much like gender and race, culture can be an obvious difference between negotiators, but perhaps not the determining one in how each party approaches the negotiation. The second excerpt focuses on gender stereotypes, with advice for how to respond to them.

❖ *Jeffrey Z. Rubin & Frank E.A. Sander,* CULTURE, NEGOTIATION, AND THE EYE OF THE BEHOLDER

7 Neg. J. 249, 251-253 (1991)

The purpose of this brief column is to draw attention to several considerations that should be borne in mind in any analysis of culture and negotiation. Our thesis is that, although differences in culture clearly *do* exist and have a bearing on the style of negotiation that emerges, some of the most important effects of culture are felt even before the negotiators sit down across from one another and begin to exchange offers. Culture, we believe, is a profoundly powerful organizing prism, through which we tend to view and integrate all kinds of disparate interpersonal information. . . .

The label of culture may have an effect very similar to that of gender or intellectual aptitude; it is a "hook" that makes it easy for one negotiator (the perceiver) to organize what he or she sees emanating from that "different person" seated at the other side of the table. To understand how culture may function as a label, consider the following teaching exercise, used during a two-week session on negotiation. . . . During one class session, the fifty or so participants were formed into rough national groups and were asked to characterize their national negotiating style—as seen by others. That is, the task was *not* to describe true differences that may be attributable to cultural or nationality, but to characterize the stereotypic perceptions that others typically carry around in their heads.

This exercise yielded a set of very powerful, albeit contradictory, stereotypic descriptions of different nationalities. To give a couple of examples, British participants characterized others' stereotypic characterization of the British as "reserved, arrogant, old-fashioned, eccentric, fair, and self-deprecating." . . . And a cluster of Central Americans listed others' stereotypes of them as negotiators as "idealistic, impractical, disorganized, unprepared, stubborn in arguments, and flowery in style."

Now imagine that you have begun to negotiate with someone from another culture, who at some point in the proceedings simply insists that he or she can go no further and is prepared to conclude without an agreement if necessary; in effect, says this individual, his BATNA has been reached, and he can do just as well by walking away from the table. How should you interpret such an assertion? If you share the general cluster of stereotypes described by the students, your interpretation will probably depend on the other person's culture or nationality. Thus, if the other negotiator is British, and (among other things) you regard the British as "fair," you may interpret this person's refusal to concede further as an honest statement of principle. The same behavior issuing from a Central American, however (someone you suspect of being "stubborn in arguments"), may lead you to suspect your counterpart of being stubborn and perhaps deceitful. Wouldn't you therefore be more likely to strike an agreement with a British than a Central American negotiator—despite the fact that each has behaved in the identical way?

If there is any truth to our surmise, you can see how powerful the effects of culture may prove to be, leading us (even before we have had a chance to gather information about our counterpart) to hold a set of expectations that guide and inform our judgments. Moreover, once our "hypotheses" about others are in place, it becomes very difficult to disprove them. We tend to gather interpersonal information in such a way that we pay attention only to the "facts" that support our preconceived ideas, ignoring or dismissing disconfirming data. . . .

[P]robably the wisest thing any of us can do to prepare for such negotiations is to: be aware of our biases and predispositions; acquire as much information as possible about our counterpart as an individual; and learn as much as we can about the norms and customs (of all kinds) that are to be found in our counterpart's home country.

Problem 4-10. ***Negotiating Within Cultures***

Do you think that it will be easier in your career to negotiate with lawyers who have gone to the same law school as you? Who have taken negotiation courses? How might these types of professional cultures be the same or different than other types of "culture"?

The following excerpt examines common stereotypes for women in negotiation. For women lawyers, these differences have not been seen in the representation of clients nor in their own salary negotiations upon graduation. Nonetheless, it is useful to consider how these stereotypes might show up in the workplace, or when negotiating on behalf of oneself, or could be magnified (or mitigated) by other cultural, racial, ethnic and professional differences.

Andrea Kupfer Schneider, NEGOTIATING WHILE FEMALE

70 SMU L. R. 695 (2017)

"[W]omen don't negotiate." Where does this myth come from? Studies have shown that men initiate salary negotiations four times as often as women; and that when women do negotiate, they ask for thirty percent less money than men. Yet, there is a disconnect between the artificial experimental settings in which we typically study negotiation and the reality of negotiation in the workplace. While this disconnect does not explain the entire misperception, it can help put the perception into context as we examine the other myths later in this article.

A. WE BASE OUR MYTH ON LIMITED STUDIES

Conceptual and methodological problems in the study of negotiation have contributed to this myth in three ways. First, we study the wrong thing: we only measure confidence and competitiveness rather than a host of other equally important negotiation skills . . . Second, we study the wrong time frame: we study one-off interactions in which quick decisions are required without the ability to research or reflect—the workplace rarely operates that way. Third, we study the wrong people: we examine undergraduate or young graduate students and draw conclusions for how adults in the workplace negotiate.

1. We Study the Wrong Thing

Negotiation research has, in the past, tended to use settings with low stakes and a competitive model to assess how people react to short-term, material gains. These studies often focus on what are traditionally seen as masculine characteristics of negotiation—aggressiveness and confidence (or overconfidence)—which often translate into an ask for something, whether or not one is qualified or deserving of it. Since these characteristics are the variables that are being measured, the games themselves are rigged to show men as more effective . . . Furthermore, these studies often only focus on salary negotiations and then treat salary as the sole measure of success, thus ignoring other elements that could be measured. There are other components of a job besides salary that are negotiated, and women, not surprisingly, are much more likely to negotiate about family issues than men. This ability to negotiate the myriad of issues that contribute to worker satisfaction could make women more satisfied with their jobs in the long run. The underlying point here is that gender differences in negotiation may be context specific . . . The framing of the negotiation matters.

2. We Study the Wrong Time Frame

Since simulations often are limited in their time frame, they miss longer-term, ongoing negotiation interactions between the parties. These scenarios tend to test quick response versus long-term thinking. Researchers have noted that women's natural inclination to spend more time thinking about the impact on relationships and connection means that women will spend more time thinking about problems and process before arriving at a solution. . .

So why are these negotiation studies problematic in terms of drawing lessons for women? First, the age and experience of the negotiator matters. Second, the professional training of the negotiator matters. And, finally, the context of the negotiation matters.

B. REALITY IS MORE NUANCED THAN A LAB

1. Age and Experience Matter

These college-age studies fail to recognize the difference that age and experience make. More recent negotiation research utilizes online and other techniques to analyze adults. For most of us—male or female—we presumably mature between college and adulthood. Therefore, in all likelihood, we are able to bring more nuanced and effective skills to the table by the time we are in a position to negotiate on behalf of our companies, clients, and ourselves. . . .

2. Assumptions and Training Matter

These assumptions about negotiation can be changed. Perhaps women do not negotiate for salary in equal numbers to men because they have been socialized not to . . . However, when women are trained to negotiate, evidence shows that differences between men and women evaporate. The undergraduate management students, who, in the Babcock studies above did not negotiate, started to negotiate in equal rates after being trained . . . Another interesting element of negotiation to follow is the expectations around negotiation (we return to this subject in the next section). In situations where it is clear that the salary is negotiable, studies show no gender differences in the person's likelihood to negotiate. Interestingly, these differences in propensity to negotiate, even salary, might be changing over time. To whatever extent we think there might be differences in older generations on which some of these stereotypes are based, these differences may be evaporating. In a study of the workplace from Australia conducted in 2013-2014, there is no difference in the likelihood to ask for a raise based on gender. This study also showed that when women did not negotiate, it was not based on the fear that asking would harm the relationship.

3. Context Matters

As we assess negotiation skills, we should understand that "the meaning of conflict to the various parties, the nature of the parties' relationships, the gender of the negotiators or representatives as distinct from the principals, the parties' relative social status or perceived power, their expectations, and their feelings about third parties" all impact behavior. As outlined above, these negotiation games that are written about in academic studies do not mirror real world negotiations in which skills such as preserving the relationship and problem-solving techniques are seen as important. Leadership guides and business bestsellers, for example, often focus on the importance of relationships, emotional intelligence, and integrity. Indeed, many have argued that women actually excel in real negotiation settings where other skills are valued. Women in the workplace tend to exhibit cooperative behavior, to contribute to collective knowledge, and display high ethical standards. We will return to these skills in the section below. These strengths are eclipsed by the current negotiation paradigm which either ignores these assets or considers them irrelevant or unproductive. Perhaps more experiments that better replicate adult reality would showcase the importance of women's strengths. We need to examine situations where long-term relationships matter. If done that way, women's strengths, such as communal sharing, would be evident. Finally, we need to note the dearth of research regarding gender differences in the long-term context, other than in representing clients. For example, in studies of attorneys, which implies repeated interactions with another attorney, women had equal skills. Additional studies in other areas would give us a broader set of tools to measure effectiveness . . . .

A. WHAT INDIVIDUAL NEGOTIATORS CAN DO

1. Recognize the Stereotype

Studies have shown that when women recognize the fallacy that they cannot negotiate on their own behalf they will do better in the negotiation. Showing women that this is a mistaken stereotype may help them find the strength and give them the confidence to not conform to that view. In particular, when women mentally reframe negotiation as a way of advocating for all women, they see themselves as more powerful . . . Additional studies on how women view themselves—and how, when women view negotiation as part of their job, they are more effective negotiators—show that this self-view of negotiation skills is crucial. Finally, recognizing the harmful stereotype that money is "masculine" will help dismantle this.

2. Work Within the Stereotype

While this might sound counterintuitive, there are elements of the female negotiation stereotype that can assist women in making their case. Women inspire paternalistic attitudes in negotiation, a hallmark of benevolent sexism. First, there is the expectation of "communalism"—that women work for the team and for others. A woman may reduce the likelihood of backlash and be assertive by framing her requests (for increased budget, for example) as a benefit to the whole group. Furthermore, when presenting herself as a team-player, a woman's negotiation skills are seen as legitimate and necessary. . . .

4. Be Pleasant and Assertive

When negotiating, both men and women still should follow best practices in terms of balancing assertiveness with other more collaborative negotiation skills. Too much agreeableness can be inversely related to income and earnings unless balanced with assertiveness. Women should utilize their comparative strengths in empathy and social intuition to read the situation and understand when to be assertive and when not to. This combination of assertiveness with empathy, and social intuition is often what is needed to be more effective. . . .

V. CONCLUSION

Out of five key negotiation skills, there is only one skill in which women, in some instances and in some studies, are rated lower than men. Yet, we do not worry that men, comparatively lacking empathy or social intuition, cannot negotiate as well as women. Overall, we know that the most effective negotiators—the most effective leaders—bring all of these skills to the table and utilize them as needed . . . Women can work to minimize backlash, change expectations, and utilize all other negotiation skills in order to be effective. At the same time, society, companies, and the law should continue to support and encourage negotiation as one way that equality can be reached.

Race, Gender, and the Perception of a Bad BATNA

In the mid-1990s, a study was performed concerning negotiations for a new car.

"More than 180 independent negotiations at ninety dealerships were conducted in the Chicago area to examine how dealerships bargain. Testers of different races and genders entered new car dealerships separately and bargained to buy a new car, using a uniform negotiation strategy. The study tests whether automobile retailers react differently to this uniform strategy when potential buyers differ only by gender or race.

The tests reveal that white males receive significantly better prices than blacks and women. . . . [W]hite women had to pay forty percent higher markups than white men; black men had to pay more than twice the markup, and black women had to pay more than three times the markup of white male testers. Moreover, the study reveals that testers of different race and gender are subjected to several forms of nonprice discrimination. Specifically, testers were systematically steered to salespeople of their own race and gender (who then gave them worse deals) and were asked different questions and told about different qualities of the car." Ian Ayres, Fair Driving, 104 Harv. L. Rev. 817, 818-819 (1991).

One hypothesis suggested by the author was that in making offers to white women, and to black men and women, salespeople assumed that these groups of people had poor BATNAs because these negotiators were unwilling or unable to negotiate and had less ability to search and find a better deal. See Ian Ayres, Further Evidence of Discrimination in New Car Negotiations and Estimates of Its Cause, 94 Mich. L. Rev. 109 (1995).

Decades later, the adverse effects of race in negotiations persist in car loans, eBay transactions, and elsewhere. See 1 Michael Z. Green, Negotiating While Black, The Negotiator's Desk Reference 563 (2017). Consider how the structure of private negotiations could or should be changed to mitigate the impacts of differences and discrimination. One helpful advantage of technology could be the increased transparency and speed in which these discriminations are discovered. (Consider that Lilly Ledbetter, who sued for wage discrimination, was blocked in her court case by the statute of limitations since it took her 20 years to discover the discrimination.) In contrast, as Orly Lobel has highlighted in *The Equality Machine*,[7] companies (and those who want to push companies) can access and mine thousands of transactions and search for patterns in individual transactions. For example, AirBNB changed its process after finding patterns of individual negotiations that were discriminatory. As we turn to ethics in the next chapter, we should continue to consider both our individual and societal responsibility to fairness and justice in legal disputes.

Further Reading:

Ian Ayres, Fair Driving, 104 Harv. L. Rev. 817 (1991).

Ian Ayres, Further Evidence of Discrimination in New Car Negotiations and Estimates of Its Cause, 94 Mich L. Rev. 109 (1995).

Linda Babcock & Sara Laschever (2003). Women Don't Ask: Negotiation and the Gender Divide. Princeton: Princeton University Press.

Max H. Bazerman & Margaret A. Neale. (1992). Negotiating Rationally. New York: The Free Press.

7. Orly Lobel, *The Equality Machine* (2022).

Steven J. Brams & Alan D. Taylor. (1996). Fair Division. Cambridge: Cambridge University Press.

Jeanne Brett. (2001). Negotiating Globally. San Francisco: Jossey-Bass Publishers.

Jennifer Gerarda Brown. (2006). Creativity and Problem-Solving. In Andrea Kupfer Schneider & Christopher Honeyman (eds.), The Negotiator's Fieldbook (pp. 407-414). Washington, DC: ABA Section on Dispute Resolution.

Daniel Del Gobbo, The Feminist Negotiator's Dilemma, 33 Ohio St. J. on Disp. Resol. 1 (2018).

Clark Freshman, Adele Hayes & Greg Feldman, The Lawyer-Negotiator as Mood Scientist: What We Know and Don't Know About How Mood Relates to Successful Negotiation, J. Disp. Resol. 1, 55 (2002).

Bee Chen Goh. (2017). Typical Errors of Westerners. In Andrea Kupfer Schneider & Christopher Honeyman (eds.), The Negotiator's Desk Reference (pp. 583-593). St. Paul, MN: DRI Press.

Dwight Golann, Grieving over Settlement: The Role of Loss in Settlement Negotiations, 34 St. J. Disp. Resol. 333 (2019).

Sheila Heen & Douglas Stone. (2017). Perceptions and Stories. In Andrea Kupfer Schneider & Christopher Honeyman (eds.), The Negotiator's Desk Reference (pp. 351-363). St. Paul, MN: DRI Press.

Loretta Kelly. (2006). Indigenous Experiences in Negotiation. In Andrea Kupfer Schneider & Christopher Honeyman (eds.), The Negotiator's Fieldbook (pp. 301-314). Washington, DC: ABA Section on Dispute Resolution.

Russell Korobkin & Chris Guthrie. (2006). Heuristics and Biases at the Bargaining Table. In Andrea Kupfer Schneider and Christopher Honeyman (eds.), The Negotiator's Fieldbook (pp. 351-359). Washington, DC: ABA Section on Dispute Resolution.

Russell Korobkin & Chris Guthrie, Psychological Barriers to Litigation Settlement: An Experimental Approach, 93 Mich. L. Rev. 107, 144-146 (1994).

Yair Livneh, Overcoming the Loss Aversion Obstacle in Negotiation, 25 Harv. Negot. L. Rev. 187 (2020).

Michelle LeBaron and Maged Senbel, Conflicts with Religious or Worldview Dimensions: Why They Matter and How to Engage Them, 23 Cardozo J. Confl. Resol., 301 (2022).

Roy J. Lewicki & Barbara Benedict Bunker. (1995). Trust in Relationships: A Model of Development and Decline. In Barbara Bunker, Jeffrey Rubin et al. (Eds.), Conflict in Cooperation and Justice (p. 133). San Francisco: Jossey-Bass Publishers.

Carrie Menkel-Meadow, Aha? Is Creativity Possible in Legal Problem Solving and Teachable in Legal Education, 6 Harv. Neg. L. Rev. 97 (2001).

Robert Mnookin, Why Negotiations Fail: An Exploration of Barriers to Conflict Resolution, 8 Ohio St. J. on Disp. Resol. 235 (1993).

Barry Nalebuff & Ian Ayres. (2003). Why Not? Boston: Harvard Business School Press.

Dan Orr & Chris Guthrie, Anchoring, Information, Expertise, and Negotiation: New Insights from Meta-Analysis, Ohio St. J. on Disp. Resol. 597-598, 608-609 (2006).

Linda L. Putnam. (2006). Communication and Interaction Patterns. In Andrea Kupfer Schneider & Christopher Honeyman (eds.), The Negotiator's Fieldbook (pp. 385-394). Washington, DC: ABA Section on Dispute Resolution.

Lee Ross. (1995). Reactive Devaluation in Negotiation and Conflict Resolution. In Kenneth Arrow et al. (eds.), Barriers to Conflict Resolution. New York: W.W. Norton & Co.

Andrea Kupfer Schneider. (2017). Productive Ambition. In Andrea Kupfer Schneider & Christopher Honeyman (eds.), The Negotiator's Desk Reference (pp. 321-329). St. Paul, MN: DRI Press.

Andrea Kupfer Schneider & Sean McCarthy. (2018). Choosing Among Modes of Communication, Negotiator's Desk Reference (ed. C. Honeyman & A.K. Schneider) St. Paul, MN: DRI Press 2018.

Andrea Kupfer Schneider et al., Likeability v. Competence: The Impossible Choice Faced by Female Politicians, Evaded by Lawyers, 17 Duke J. Gender L. & Pol'y 363 (2010).

Andrea Kupfer Schneider, Negotiating While Female, 70 SMU L. Rev. 695 (2017).

Jeffrey M. Senger, Decision Analysis in Negotiation, 87 Marq. L. Rev. 721 (2004).

Jeff Seul, Negotiating Across Worldviews, 38 Negot. J. 357 (2022).

Daniel L. Shapiro. (2006). Untapped Power: Emotions in Negotiation. In Andrea Kupfer Schneider & Christopher Honeyman (eds.), The Negotiator's Fieldbook (pp. 263-269). Washington, DC: ABA Section on Dispute Resolution.

Donna Shestowsky. (2017). Psychology and Persuasion. In Andrea Kupfer Schneider & Christopher Honeyman (eds.), The Negotiator's Desk Reference (339-350). St. Paul, MN: DRI Press.

Chapter 5 Negotiation: Law and Ethics

This chapter examines the intersection of law, ethics and reputation in negotiation. Beyond keeping your license and avoiding a malpractice case when your settlement is overturned for fraud, your behavior in negotiation, and the reputation you build over time, are possibly the most important elements of your practice. In studies of lawyers negotiating, the adjective "ethical" was most highly correlated with effectiveness. Why is this the case? Your reputation impacts whether others can share information with you and trust you to implement agreements, as well as the likelihood that you can work out the integrative settlements that often serve your client's needs. Your reputation for ethicality in the legal community—the combination of reputation, trustworthiness, and truthfulness—community overall often determines business referrals, repeat customers, and economic success.

A. HOW TO BUILD A REPUTATION

The first question concerns your view of negotiation. The excerpt that follows asks you to explore your fundamental beliefs about ethics in negotiation in light of three common stances.

G. Richard Shell, BARGAINING FOR ADVANTAGE: NEGOTIATION STRATEGIES FOR REASONABLE PEOPLE

215-220 (1999)

I want to challenge you to identify what your beliefs are. To help you decide how you feel about ethics, I will briefly describe the three most common approaches to bargaining ethics I have heard expressed in conversation with literally hundreds of students and executives. See which shoe fits—or take a bit from each approach and construct your own.

As we explore this territory, remember that nearly everyone is sincerely convinced that they are acting ethically most of the time, whereas they often think others are acting either naively or unethically, depending on their ethical perspective and the situation. Thus, a word of warning is in order. Your ethics are mainly your own business. They will help you increase your level of confidence and comfort at the bargaining table. But do not expect others to share your ethics in every detail. Prudence pays.

THREE SCHOOLS OF BARGAINING ETHICS

The three schools of bargaining ethics I want to introduce for your consideration are (1) the "It's a game" Poker School, (2) the "Do the right thing even if it hurts" Idealist School, and (3) the "What goes around, comes around" Pragmatist School.

Let's look at each one in turn. As I describe these schools, try to decide which aspects of them best reflect your attitudes. After you figure out where you stand today, take a moment and see if that is where you ought to be. My advice is to aim as high as you can, consistent with your genuinely held beliefs about bargaining. In the pressured world of practice, people tend to slide down rather than climb up when it comes to ethical standards.

The "It's a Game" Poker School

The Poker School of ethics sees negotiation as a "game" with certain "rules." The rules are defined by the law. . . . Conduct within the rules is ethical. Conduct outside the rules is unethical.

The modern founder of the Poker School was Albert Z. Carr, a former Special Consultant to President Harry Truman. Carr wrote a book in the 1960s called, appropriately enough, *Business as a Game*. In a related article that appeared in the *Harvard Business Review*, Carr argued that bluffing and other misleading but lawful negotiation tactics are "an integral part of the [bargaining] game, and the executive who does not master [these] techniques is not likely to accumulate much money or power."

People who adhere to the Poker School readily admit that bargaining and poker are not exactly the same. But they point out that deception is essential to effective play in both arenas. Moreover, skilled players in both poker and bargaining exhibit a robust and realistic distrust of the other fellow. Carr argues that good players should ignore the "claims of friendship" and engage in "cunning deception and concealment" in fair, hard bargaining encounters. When the game is over, members of the Poker School do not think less of a fellow player just because that person successfully deceived them. In fact, assuming the tactic was legal, they may admire the deceiver and vow to be better prepared (and less trusting) next time.

We know how to play poker, but how exactly does one play the bargaining "game"? Stripped to its core, it looks like this: Someone opens, and then people take turns proposing terms to each other. Arguments supporting your preferred terms are allowed. You can play or pass in each round. The goal is to get the other side to agree to terms that are as close as possible to your last proposal.

In the bargaining game, it is understood that both sides might be bluffing. Bluffs disguise a weak bargaining hand, that is, the limited or unattractive alternatives you have away from the table, your inability to affect the other side's alternatives, and the arguments you have to support your demands. Unlike poker players, negotiators always attempt to disclose a good hand if they have one in a bargaining game. So the most effective bluffs are realistic, attractive, difficult-to-check (but false) alternatives or authoritative (but false) supporting standards. Experienced players know this, so one of the key skills in the bargaining game is judging when the other party's alternatives or arguments are really as good as he or she says. If the other side calls you on your bargaining bluff by walking away or giving you a credible ultimatum, you lose. Either there will be no deal when there should have been one, or the final price will be nearer to their last offer than to yours.

As mentioned above, the Poker School believes in the rule of law. In poker, you are not allowed to hide cards, collude with other players, or renege on your bets. But you are expected to deceive others about your hand. The best plays come when you win the pot with a weak hand or fool the other players into betting heavily when your hand is strong. In bargaining, you must not commit outright, actionable fraud, but negotiators must be on guard for anything short of fraud.

The Poker School has three main problems as I see it. First, the Poker School presumes that everyone treats bargaining as a game. Unfortunately, it is an empirical fact that people disagree on this. For a start, neither the idealists nor the pragmatists (more on these below) think bargaining is a game. This problem does not deter the Poker School, which holds that the rules permit its members to play even when the other party disagrees about this premise.

Second, everyone is supposed to know the rules cold. But this is impossible, given that legal rules are applied differently in different industries and regions of the world. Finally, . . . the law is far from certain even within a single jurisdiction. So you often need a sharp lawyer to help you decide what to do.

The "Do the Right Thing Even if It Hurts" Idealist School

The Idealist School says that bargaining is an aspect of social life, not a special activity with its own unique set of rules. The same ethics that apply in the home should carry over directly into the realm of negotiation. If it is wrong to lie or mislead in normal social encounters, it is wrong to do so in negotiations. If it is OK to lie in special situations (such as to protect another person's feelings), it is also OK to lie in negotiations when those special conditions apply.

Idealists do not entirely rule out deception in negotiation. For example, if the other party assumes you have a lot of leverage and never asks you directly about the situation as you see it, you do not necessarily have to volunteer the information weakening your position. And the idealist can decline to answer questions. But such exceptions are uncomfortable moments. Members of the Idealist School prefer to be candid and honest at the bargaining table even if it means giving up a certain amount of strategic advantage.

The Idealist School draws its strength from philosophy and religion. For example, Immanuel Kant said that we should all follow the ethical rules that we would wish others to follow. Kant argued that if everyone lied all the time, social life would be chaos. Hence, you should not lie. Kant also disapproved of treating other people merely as the means to achieve your own personal ends. Lies in negotiation are selfish acts designed to achieve personal gain. This form of conduct is therefore unethical. Period. Many religions also teach adherents not to lie for personal advantage.

Idealists admit that deception in negotiation rarely arouses moral indignation unless the lies breach a trust between friends, violate a fiduciary responsibility, or exploit people such as the sick or elderly, who lack the ability to protect themselves. And if the only way you can prevent some terrible harm like a murder is by lying, go ahead and lie. But the lack of moral outrage and the fact that sometimes lying can be defended does not make deception in negotiations right.

Idealists strongly reject the idea that negotiations should be viewed as "games." Negotiations, they feel, are serious, consequential communication acts. People negotiate to resolve their differences so social life will work for the benefit of all. People must be held responsible for all their actions, including the way they negotiate, under universal standards.

Idealists think that the members of the Poker School are predatory and selfish. For its part, the Poker School thinks that idealists are naïve and even a little silly. When members of the two schools meet at the bargaining table, tempers can flare.

Some members of the Idealist School have recently been trying to find a philosophical justification for bluffs about bottom lines. There is no agreement yet on whether these efforts have succeeded in ethical terms. But it is clear that outright lies such as fictitious other offers and better prices are unethical practices under idealist principles.

The big problem for the idealist is obvious: Their standards sometimes make it difficult to proceed in a realistic way at the bargaining table. Also, unless adherence to the Idealist School is coupled with a healthy skepticism about the way other people will negotiate, idealism leaves its members open to exploitation by people with standards other than their own. These limitations are especially troublesome when idealists must represent others' interests at the bargaining table.

Despite its limitations, I like the Idealist School. Perhaps because I am an academic, I genuinely believe that the different parts of my life are, in fact, whole. I aspire to ethical standards that I can apply consistently. I will admit that I sometimes fall short of idealism's strict code, but by aiming high I am leaving myself somewhere to fall that maintains my basic sense of personal integrity.

I confess my preference for the Idealist School so you will know where I am coming from in this discussion. But I realize that your experience and work environment may preclude idealism as an ethical option. That's ok. As I hope I am making clear, idealism is not the only way to think about negotiation in ethical terms.

The "What Goes Around Comes Around" Pragmatist School

The final school of bargaining ethics, the Pragmatist School, includes some original elements as well as some attributes of the previous two. In common with the Poker School, this approach views deception as a necessary part of the negotiation process. Unlike the Poker School, however, it prefers not to use misleading statements and overt lies if there is a serviceable, practical alternative. Uniquely, the Pragmatist School displays concern for the potential negative effects of deceptive conduct on present and future relationships. Thus, lying and other questionable tactics are bad not so much because they are "wrong" as because they cost the user more in the long run than they gain in the short run.

As my last comment suggests, people adhere to this school more for prudential than idealistic reasons. Lies and misleading conduct can cause serious injury to one's credibility. And credibility is an important asset for effective negotiators both to preserve working relationships and to protect one's reputation in the market or community. The latter concern is summed up in what I would call the pragmatist's credo: What goes around comes around. The Poker School is less concerned with reputation and more focused on winning each bargaining encounter within the rules of the "game."

What separates the Pragmatist School from the Idealist School? To put it bluntly, a pragmatist will lie a bit more often than will an idealist. For example, pragmatists sometimes will draw fine distinctions between lies about hard-core facts of a transaction, which are always imprudent (and often illegal), and misleading statements about such things as the rationales used to justify a position. A pragmatic car salesman considers it highly unethical to lie about anything large or small relating to the mechanical condition of a used car he is selling. But this same salesman might not have a problem saying "My manager won't let me sell this car for less than $10,000" even though he knows the manager would sell the car for $9,500. False justifications and rationales are marginally acceptable because they are usually less important to the transaction and much harder to detect as falsehoods than are core facts about the object being bought and sold.

Pragmatists are also somewhat looser within the truth when using so called blocking techniques—tactics to avoid answering questions that threaten to expose a weak bargaining position. For example, can you ethically answer "I don't know" when asked about something you do know that hurts your position? An idealist would refuse to answer the question or try to change the subject, not lie by saying "I don't know." A pragmatist would go ahead and say "I don't know" if his actual state of knowledge is hard to trace and the lie poses little risk to his relationships.

Regardless of which of Shell's schools you belong to, there are many questions each negotiator must answer about their approach. The excerpt below summarizes those important questions.

Carrie Menkel-Meadow, WHAT'S FAIR IN NEGOTIATION? WHAT IS ETHICS IN NEGOTIATION?

in What's Fair: Ethics for Negotiators xiii-xvi (Carrie Menkel-Meadow & Michael Wheeler, eds., 2004)

"What's fair" in negotiation is a complex and multifaceted question, asking us to consider negotiation ethics on many different levels simultaneously. First, there are the concerns of the individual negotiator: What do I aspire to? How do I judge my own goals and behavior? What may I do? How will others judge me (my counterpart in a two-party negotiation, others in a multi-lateral negotiation, those with whom I might do business in the future, those who will learn of and judge my behavior or results in any negotiation that might become more public than the involved parties)? How do I calibrate my actions to those of the others with whom I am dealing? (Should I have a relative ethics that is sensitive, responsive, or malleable to the context, circumstances, customs or personalities of the situation at hand?) What limits are there on my goals and behavior, set from within (the "mirror" test—how do I appear to myself at the end of the day) or without, either informally, (the "videotape test"—what would my mother, teacher, spouse, child or clergy person think of me if they could watch this?) or formally (rules, laws, ethics standards, religious or moral principles to which I must or choose to adhere)? With what sensibility should I approach each negotiation I undertake?

For those who negotiate as agents, there is the added dimension of what duty is owed a client or principal. When do agent and principal goals properly align? When are they different . . . and how are differences to be reconciled? When do legal rules (like the creation of fiduciary relationships) define the limits and obligations of negotiator-principal interactions?

Third, there is the question of duty, responsibility or relationship to the Other (call him "counterpart," "opponent," "adversary," "partner," "boss" or "subordinate," spouse or lover, child or parent). . . . Do we follow some version of the Golden Rule and treat others as we would hope to be treated by them (a norm of aspirational reciprocity), or does the Golden Rule tarnish a bit on application in particular contexts?. . .

How do those outside of a negotiation judge its ethical externalities, or social effects? Has a particular negotiation done more good than harm? For those inside the negotiation? Those affected by it: employees, shareholders, vendors and clients, consumers and the public? And, to what extent must any negotiation be morally accountable for impacts on third parties (children in a divorce, customers in labor-management negotiation, similarly situated claimants in mass torts, employees in an acquisition) and for its intergenerational effects (future generations in environmental disputes)?

The provision of procedural justice, explained in the next excerpt, is also important to perceptions of fairness, to reputation building, and to success as a negotiator.

❖ *Rebecca Hollander-Blumoff & Tom R. Tyler*, PROCEDURAL JUSTICE IN NEGOTIATION: PROCEDURAL FAIRNESS, OUTCOME ACCEPTANCE, AND INTEGRATIVE POTENTIAL

33 Law & Soc. Inquiry 473, 474, 492-494 (2008)

What does procedural justice in negotiation entail? Procedural justice literature has identified four factors that typically play an important role in assessment of procedural justice: input, neutrality, respect/politeness, and trust. First, it is important to allow parties opportunities to state their arguments and to make clear that those arguments are being listened to by acknowledging them. Second, people value having an unbiased and factual decision-making process in which the rules are applied in a consistent manner. Third, they want to be treated with dignity and courtesy and to have their rights acknowledged. Finally, people want to deal with people whose motives they trust. That is, they value people who act in good faith.

The findings suggest that when negotiators act in procedurally fair ways, they lose nothing at all in their "bottom line" in a zero-sum setting, expand the negotiation pie in a setting in which there is integrative potential, and in fact gain other important advantages in terms of agreement acceptance. . . . Thus, the wise negotiator, to achieve successful outcomes, may want to act in procedurally just ways when dealing with others in order to foster greater acceptance of the agreement and more disclosure of value-creating opportunities.

First, in order to obtain the best potential negotiation outcomes (settlement over nonsettlement, . . . or value-creating integrative over nonintegrative bargaining. . .), a rational actor should treat others in a fair manner. Second, and perhaps more striking, this research challenges the premise at the heart of the rational actor model: what drives people in their assessments of outcome is not just the gain maximizing/loss minimizing analysis of the economic results that they achieve, but also how fairly they feel they have been treated in the negotiation process. Thus, the real-world negotiator evaluates his or her outcome not in purely economic terms of gain and loss but in process terms of fairness.

The other side of building trust in a negotiation often depends on your ability to work with others who might have different approaches. When both negotiators operate in the same school (for example, you both are pragmatists according to Shell's taxonomy), negotiations tend to proceed smoothly. But what if you are an idealist negotiating with a poker player? Is all hope lost for working together? This next excerpt gives advice on how to remain true to your own approach while protecting yourself and your client. Consider this your "defense against the dark arts."

Peter Reilly, WAS MACHIAVELLI RIGHT? LYING IN NEGOTIATION AND THE ART OF DEFENSIVE SELF-HELP

24 Ohio St. J. on Disp. Resol. 3, 483-484, 486-493, 496-497, 499, 502-503 (2009)

[I]nformation is the lifeblood of any negotiation, and therefore, the mindsets, strategies, and techniques that influence if, when, and how information is obtained and/or exchanged (and that influence how complete and accurate that information will be) are extremely important in the process of defending one's self (or one's client) against lying and deception. . . .

A. CONDUCT THOROUGH BACKGROUND RESEARCH

Conducting a search on various Internet search engines (such as Yahoo! or Google) can often yield large amounts of information about other parties to the negotiation. Websites established by private companies, government entities, and various non-profit groups are available for criminal, financial, and other background checks. If possible, speaking with groups or individuals who have previously worked with or negotiated with one's potential negotiation counterparts can be very illuminating. It can be surprising how much of a "reputation" people develop, sometimes favorable and sometimes unfavorable, based on previous negotiation behavior. . . .

B. NETWORK FOR POTENTIAL NEGOTIATION COUNTERPARTS

There are times when one has no control over who will sit on the other side of the negotiation table. However, in those instances when one can play a role in selecting negotiation counterparts, one should attempt to do so through referrals, recommendations, or outside introductions. This is a compliment to the party being approached, which can generate feelings of goodwill and help solidify new working relationships should the negotiation process move forward. Initial meetings through referrals and introductions also signal that there is a greater prospect for the development of long-term relationships. Research suggests that, in general, even the prospect of a long-term relationship raises people's ethical standards and reduces exploitative conduct such as lying. . . .

C. CREATE RAPPORT

A cordial and supportive environment (one infused with sincerity, understanding, impartiality, empathy, and expressions of genuine concern for the other party) will probably not magically prevent lies or encourage people to disclose their deceitful behavior. However, research suggests that such an environment can lead to these individuals relaxing their defenses and providing information that may be used to secure the truth in the future. . . . Research shows that people are more inclined to lie by omission (not revealing the whole truth) than by commission (falsely answering a question when asked), so when they are asked to elaborate and thereby make direct statements that are lies, some people cannot do it and will back away from earlier statements. Finally, one can neutralize the harshness of asking a negative question by implying the question is a playful one. For example, "May I play the devil's advocate for a moment?" is one way to blunt the harshness of a request for information. . . .

D. DEMAND THE USE OF OBJECTIVE STANDARDS—BUT AVOID BEING HAMSTRUNG BY THEM

Asking questions such as, "What do you base that number on?" or "Is that according to industry standard?" is essentially asking the other party to justify their position using objective standards. People will be less likely to attempt to lie and deceive if they know from the start of the negotiation that objective criteria and standards will constantly be sought from other parties, as well as outside sources. . . .

E. STRATEGICALLY LIMIT INFORMATION REVELATION

Before the negotiation, one should brainstorm and list specific questions that will likely be asked by the other party. With enough preparation, many (if not most) questions can be anticipated. One might practice aloud how specific questions will be responded to and addressed, especially difficult and controversial questions. Practicing aloud can make it easier to arrive at word and phrase choices that will prevent or limit the revelation of strategic information. Preparation should also include deciding upon which tactic to employ in responding to questions about information that one does not wish to disclose. For example, should one decide to ignore the question all together? Or pretend to misconstrue the question and answer a less intrusive, specific, or direct question?. . .

F. RECOGNIZE AND THWART TACTICS OF EVASION

The simplest way to get information is to ask for it, yet it is sometimes the most obvious (and crucial) questions that do not get asked (or answered) during a negotiation. Prior to negotiating, one should write out a list of all the questions he or she wants answered, in order of importance. During the negotiation, one should listen carefully to the responses provided; many will be mere attempts to evade answering the question. Evasion techniques are abundant and varied (ignoring the question; offering to return to the question later; answering only part of the question; answering a related but less intrusive, specific, or direct question; calling the question unfair or inappropriate and therefore not entitled to a response, etc.). These or similar evasion techniques will likely be employed throughout the negotiation, and the most effective antidote is careful listening to determine if one's question is being addressed in full, in part, or not at all. One must continue grilling until the information being sought is either revealed or protected in a very different manner. Thus, one might continue asking the same question (along with reasonable follow-up questions to probe even deeper) until the question (1) can be "checked off" as having been responded to in a (reasonably) complete and forthcoming manner, or (2) is met by the other party saying something to the effect of, "I simply cannot tell you that," or "I cannot speak about that issue at all."

G. ESTABLISH LONG-TERM RELATIONSHIPS AND WATCH FOR SIGNS OF DECEPTION

If one were skilled at detecting liars upon meeting them, one could simply walk away from the negotiation. Unfortunately, research indicates that people are very poor at such immediate detection. This is true even among the so-called "experts" (such as police investigators) who are more confident, but not more accurate, in their determinations of who is lying and who is not. . . . This conclusion underscores the importance of developing long-term relationships with potential negotiation partners, where baseline behaviors can be established, where changes in those normal behaviors can be observed, and where possible deception can thereby be detected.

H. USE "COME CLEAN" QUESTIONS STRATEGICALLY

Used at critical moments in the negotiation (often toward the conclusion of covering an important topic within the context of a larger negotiation), one can ask the "come clean" question: "Is there something known to you, but not to me, that needs to be revealed at this point?". . . .

A Trust Land Mine

In any negotiation, you're likely to have information about the other party or about the deal (industry facts, economic health, new products, and so on) that he might not know you have. To gain some measure of your counterpart's trustworthiness, plant a "trust land mine": Ask some questions to which you already know the answers. If someone avoids your information requests, or if he lies outright, that's one sign that you should be careful about what you reveal—or even call off talks altogether. Of course, someone who answers a few questions truthfully might not always behave honestly. Nonetheless, trust land mines offer a reasonably good way of determining if a person is leveling with you.

Carrie Menkel-Meadow, Know When to Show Your Hand, 10 Negotiation Newsletter 1 (June 2007).

B. WHY DOES UNETHICAL BEHAVIOR HAPPEN (ANYWAY)?

The excerpt below reflects on the tension for a lawyer in deciding how truthful to be in negotiation.

❖ *James J. White*, MACHIAVELLI AND THE BAR: ETHICAL LIMITATIONS ON LYING IN NEGOTIATION

1980 Am. B. Found. Res. J. 926-928, 931-935 (1980)

[I]n negotiation, more than in other contexts, ethical norms can probably be violated with greater confidence that there will be no discovery and punishment. Whether one is likely to be caught for violating an ethical standard says nothing about the merit of the standard. However, if the low probability of punishment means that many lawyers will violate the standard, the standard becomes even more difficult for the honest lawyer to follow, for by doing so he may be forfeiting a significant advantage for his client to others who do not follow the rules. . . .

On the one hand the negotiator must be fair and truthful; on the other he must mislead his opponent. Like the poker player, a negotiator hopes that his opponent will overestimate the value of his hand. Like the poker player, in a variety of ways he must facilitate his opponent's inaccurate assessment. The critical difference between those who are successful negotiators and those who are not lies in this capacity both to mislead and not to be misled.

Some experienced negotiators will deny the accuracy of this assertion, but they will be wrong. I submit that a careful examination of the behavior of even the most forthright, honest, and trustworthy negotiators will show them actively engaged in misleading their opponents about their true positions. . . . To conceal one's true position, to mislead an opponent about one's true settling point, is the essence of negotiation.

Of course there are limits on acceptable deceptive behavior in negotiation, but there is the paradox. How can one be "fair" but also mislead? Can we ask the negotiator to mislead, but fairly, like the soldier who must kill, but humanely?. . .

Problem 5-1. *What's My (Bottom) Line?*

Assume that the defendant has instructed his lawyer to accept any settlement offer costing less than $100,000. Having received that instruction, how might the lawyer respond to the plaintiff's question, "I think $90,000 will settle this case. Will your client give $90,000?"

What would you do? Is a negative response a lie? What kind of response can you craft without lying or giving away your client's bottom line?

More recent studies find deviations and variations in following the Model Rules of Professional Conduct and norms of truthful behavior.

Do Lawyers Do the Right Thing in Practice?

[A] certain degree of dissembling and misdirection is to be expected in the negotiation realm. Consistent with these expectations, Model Rule 4.1 legitimizes some deceitful negotiation techniques and only prohibits fraudulent misrepresentations about material matters. Rule 4.1's truthfulness standard has been a fertile topic of discussion since its adoption. . . .

[W]e surveyed 734 practicing lawyers and asked them what they would do if a client asked them to assist him in a fraudulent pre-litigation settlement scheme [The plaintiff first asked the lawyer to not reveal his current healthy status when the other side wrongly assumed that she was responsible for infecting him with a deadly disease or, second, not to reveal it unless directly asked.] Nearly one-third indicated they would agree to one of the client's two requests to engage in the fraudulent scheme. Half of the respondents indicated that they would refuse both of the client's overtures. And the remaining twenty percent of respondents either indicated that they were not sure how to respond to both requests or refused one request and indicated that they were not sure how they would respond to the other request. . . .

[T]he study explored the respondents' reasons for agreeing or disagreeing with the client's requests. . . . First, there appears to be substantial misunderstanding as to what constitutes a misrepresentation, the standard that sets the boundary between acceptable and unacceptable negotiation behavior under the Rule. Second, the findings suggest substantial confusion surrounding the rule's operative term "material fact." Third, the respondents who agreed to the client's most egregious request appear to believe that other legal rules, including other portions of the Model Rules, either gave them permission or required them to engage in the fraudulent scheme.

Art Hinshaw & Jess K. Alberts, Doing the Right Thing: An Empirical Study of Attorney Negotiation Ethics, 16 Harv. Negot. L. Rev. 95 (2011).

❖ *Art Hinshaw, Peter Reilly & Andrea Kupfer Schneider,* ATTORNEYS AND NEGOTIATION ETHICS: A MATERIAL MISUNDERSTANDING?

29 Negot. J. 265 (2013)

Helping students develop their professional judgment, which includes a solid grounding in ethics, is no easy task. Law students come to us in various stages of professional development. In our negotiation classes, law students engage in behavior that runs the gamut of ethical and unethical practices. Naturally this is to be expected as they make mistakes trying to master the professional conduct rules and apply them in real time. What troubles us is the surprising number of students who engage in patently fraudulent conduct but have absolutely no idea that what they are doing is in the least bit wrong. This happens every semester, and our concerns are not based on the behavior of just one or two individuals. We believe this behavior reflects a number of different phenomena:

- the attorney rules of professional conduct governing negotiation, which instruct that deceit, misdirection, dissembling, and lying are "ethical" in some circumstances;
- the lack of understanding that personal relationships and reputations are an important aspect of the legal profession;
- an insufficient focus on fraud in the law school curriculum; and
- the hypercompetitive environment of law school and legal practice. . . .

[Two of us surveyed practicing lawyers using the questions below.]

QUESTION ONE: SETTLEMENT AUTHORITY

The first survey question involves the issue of settlement authority. Questions of settlement authority in a negotiation can be difficult. If the attorney reveals the amount at which she is authorized to settle, she is effectively settling for that amount. The pressure to lie is thus clear, particularly if the attorney is not adept at deflecting this type of question. On the other hand, straightforward denial of explicit authority is not permitted. Here is how the American Bar Association's Rules on Professional Responsibility parse this issue. Generally speaking, an attorney's valuation of a claim and a party's settlement intentions, while important in a negotiation, are enumerated exceptions from consideration of what constitutes a material statement in negotiations. The specific limits of the authority that a client has given a lawyer to settle a case, however, is considered a material fact (ABA Committee on Ethics and Professional Responsibility 2006).

Question One in each study asked: Your clients, the defendants, have told you that you are authorized to pay $750,000 to settle the case. In settlement negotiations, after your offer of $650,000, the plaintiff's attorney asks, "Are you authorized to settle for $750,000?" Can you say, "No, I am not."

The correct answer to this question is "No" according to the ABA Opinion 06-439. . . .

QUESTION TWO: MATERIAL FACTS

Questions Two and Three each deal with the representation of material facts in a negotiation. The definition of "material" is crucial to any analysis because only "material" facts fall under the requirement of truthfulness. (Attorneys may lie about other facts in a negotiation that are not considered "material" without violating the rules.) Materiality is generally understood as information a reasonable negotiator would find important in deciding what course of action to take in the negotiation. This includes the particulars of the issue in dispute, the damages claimed, and any other facts upon which the deal is structured. (For example, in a negotiation for the purchase of a business, that firm's financial records are material facts.). . .

Question Two in each study asked: You represent a plaintiff who claims to have suffered a serious knee injury. In settlement negotiations, can you say that your client is "disabled" when you know she is out skiing?

In this scenario, the health of the client's knee is the critical issue; thus, descriptions of the knee's health are material to the negotiation. Saying that the client is disabled suggests that the injury is much more serious than it actually is. The proper answer is "no." . . .

QUESTION THREE: FACTS TO A CLAIM

Question Three also deals with the issue of material facts and which facts are necessary in order to make a claim of emotional distress (a particular claim under tort law).

Question Three in each study asked: You are trying to negotiate a settlement on behalf of a couple who charge that the bank pulled their loan, ruining their business. Your clients are quite upbeat and deny suffering particularly severe emotional distress. Can you tell your opponent, nonetheless, that they did?

For reasons similar to the correct answer to Question Two, the correct answer in this scenario is "no." The clients' state of mind is the critical issue for the emotional distress claim, so statements describing their mental distress are material to the negotiation. Stating that they have severe emotional distress would be impermissible lying. . . .

QUESTION FOUR: CORRECTING MISIMPRESSIONS

Finally, Question Four concerns omission, which receives a slightly more nuanced treatment in the Rules of Professional Responsibility. According to those rules, an omission of a material fact can also be unethical in certain cases. But more importantly, the law of fraud for both tort and contract law requires correction of a misimpression. . . .

The final question in each study was:

> In settlement talks over the couple's lender liability case, your counterpart's comments make it clear that he thinks the plaintiffs have gone out of business, although you didn't say that. In fact, the business is continuing, and several important contracts are in the offing. You are on the verge of settlement; can you go ahead and settle without correcting your opponent's misimpression?

Generally speaking, a lawyer is not responsible for an opposing counsel's misunderstanding of the facts surrounding a negotiation, and there is no duty to correct that misunderstanding. However, the erroneous statement is the only reason why the other party is making this particular contract offer. In this situation, silence in the face of the mistaken statement effectively confirms that the statement is true. The correct answer to the question is thus "no.". . .

BUT TOO MANY LAWYERS FAIL TO HONOR THE NORM

In these studies, we sought to determine how attorneys would apply the ethical negotiation standards in context. A disturbing number of our study respondents answered the various queries incorrectly. What makes these numbers troubling is that only one of the scenarios, Question Four. . . . (whether the attorney needed to correct the bank's belief that the plaintiffs had gone out of business), can be considered anything near to being a close call. The degree of confusion or misunderstanding we uncovered is disconcerting. The standard at issue is low: to refrain from engaging in fraudulent misrepresentations. That such a high number of lawyers report they would engage in dubious conduct should concern us all. . . .

THE EMPHASIS ON COMPETITION HAS AN IMPACT ON ETHICS

Based on our findings, we conclude that practicing lawyers who simply make mistakes when applying these standards (as opposed to those who consciously make the deliberate decision to break the rules and lie) do so for one of two reasons. Either they overthink the professional rules because they can be confusing, or they have only a superficial understanding of the ethical requirements. In either case, these errors reflect a tension inherent in the legal profession's two most cherished values: a commitment to the client and a commitment to justice.

The importance of being loyal to clients is consistently inculcated in law students. Concepts such as zealous advocacy ("make your best argument") and confidentiality (the sanctity of attorney–client privilege) are emphasized and scrutinized in course after course that teach students "how to think like a lawyer." Concepts of justice and ethics are emphasized, but usually in the abstract and not in conjunction with concepts of client centered advocacy.

In legal practice, business demands have pushed achieving the best possible results for the (usually paying) clients to the forefront, resulting in an emphasis on a lawyer's total commitment to the client. In fact, many lawyers now believe that loyalty to their clients is their "first and only" responsibility. Particularly in harder economic times when they fear losing clients, lawyers may be more willing to lie on a client's behalf than they would on their own. (Studies have shown that threat perception increases the likelihood of deceptive behavior.) One scholar has even suggested that dishonesty is so prevalent among attorneys in negotiation that all attorneys owe it to their clients to assume that the other party's attorney will not be truthful in a negotiation.

Every step of participation in the legal profession, from getting into law school to landing one's first job, to achieving visible professional success, is decided through competition. And the profession tends to attract competitive individuals. Add negotiation—which can bring out anybody's more competitive inclinations—to this mix and the result is the quintessential competitive lawyering activity.

For lawyers, the competitive pressures of bargaining can push ethical concerns into the background, sharpening the attorney's focus on such values as zealous advocacy. This is most apparent in lawyer discipline cases when attorneys defend their egregious behavior by claiming it is condoned in the rules of professional conduct. Recently, in an attempt to dismiss a fraud case against him, a lawyer claimed that under attorney confidentiality rules, he had no duty to reveal his client's ongoing fraud—a serious misunderstanding of the current rules (Braga 2011).

PSYCHOLOGY AND ETHICS

. . . Unless lawyers are primed to consider ethics as part of the decision-making process in any given case, ethical concerns may not factor into the decision at all. . . .

Similarly, lawyers make *forecasting errors*, in which they fail to recognize that the pressures of law practice can create ethical dilemmas. . . .

Additionally, many unethical actions may reflect *self-control depletion*. According to this theory, a person has reserves of self-control, but as one engages in self-control tasks throughout the day (or throughout the representation of the client), those reserves are depleted and one's ability to recognize and respond appropriately to ethical challenges decreases. Thus, the likelihood of unethical behavior increases.

Finally, people may find themselves sliding down ethical "slippery slopes" in which an early ambiguous decision is used to justify later unethical actions. Gaining a better understanding of how seemingly ethical lawyers may make unethical decisions could help law students make more ethical decisions when they become practicing attorneys.

NEGOTIATION STRATEGIES

As our three studies show, the primary norm is consistently to obey the rules governing attorney negotiation conduct. That said, too many lawyers make simple mistakes when applying the rules, some because of confusion and others because of competitive norms or cognitive errors. To strengthen adherence to the rules, we suggest some strategies for both negotiators and negotiation instructors.

For negotiators, the most important steps are to learn the rules regarding truthfulness and to create rapport, essentially a positive professional relationship, with one's counterpart. These strategies work to prevent the lawyer from lying (unless she or he consciously chooses to lie) and to prevent his or her counterpart from lying as well.

Learning and understanding how the rules work is painless, but changing one's subconscious responses and reactions is difficult. As outlined above, the structural and psychological encouragements to lie are important to comprehend and to counter. Becoming a reflective and thoughtful negotiator is one way to address these semi-automated systems, as is understanding how one's actions reflect and form our values. Consciously acknowledging that there is an ethical component in most decision making makes the ethical implications of one's decisions more difficult to ignore. Most individuals do not enter a negotiation intending to be unethical.

Furthermore, attorneys need to recognize that their own affirmative statements are made in context—and that contexts can change. They also need to remember that different lawyers interpret actions and the rules differently—others might view one's actions as unethical even when one is convinced otherwise. A common strategy we have taught our students is to "gut check" their actions by contemplating whether they would be comfortable with their behavior being reported on the front page of the New York Times, being posted on Facebook, or being described to their grandmother.

Earlier, Richard Shell described three schools of bargaining ethics, including the Poker game school. The culture of law schools may add to developing competitive mindsets. The excerpt below expands on the impact of a gaming mindset or "game framing" on negotiation behavior.

Taya R. Cohen, Erik G. Helzer, and Robert A. Creo, HONESTY AMONG LAWYERS: MORAL CHARACTER, GAME FRAMING, AND HONEST DISCLOSURES IN NEGOTIATION

38 Negot. J. 199–234 (2022)

. . . Games have many elements and have been notoriously difficult to define precisely. We focus here on two key features of games to make the argument that game framing of negotiation is associated with less honesty. First, prototypical games are adversarial; they have winners and losers, and the goal is to win. It is not necessary that a game be adversarial, but typically they are experienced as such. . . . An implication of prototypical games being adversarial is a strategic, competitive motivation to achieve one's goals and beat opponents. We know from prior work that people who approach negotiation as a chance to win or compete versus collaborate are more likely to engage in competitive negotiation behavior, both ethical and unethical. An adversarial mindset is likely to be particularly prevalent among lawyers in the United States because the U.S. legal system is an adversary system, and law schools train students accordingly. However, just because a system is adversarial in structure does not necessarily imply that behavior within that system will be unethical or dishonest. Rather, an adversarial system can be set up to encourage fair competition. This view is highlighted in the Comment to Rule 3.4, Fairness to Opposing Party and Counsel:

> [1] The procedure of the adversary system contemplates that the evidence in a case is to be marshaled competitively by the contending parties. Fair competition in the adversary system is secured by prohibitions against destruction or concealment of evidence, improperly influencing witnesses, obstructive tactics in discovery procedure, and the like. (Rule 3.4, American Bar Association 2020)

Note that the limited application of "fair competition" in this Rule only prohibits dishonest misconduct related to improper tactics to conceal facts; it does not necessarily require promotion of mutual understanding and affirmative disclosure of all the factual elements underlying the matter. While competitive beliefs about negotiation on their own might not be sufficient to elicit unethical or dishonest behavior, we propose that when such beliefs are combined with a perspective that the rules governing negotiation are arbitrary and artificial, and by implication that one's behavior when negotiating does not carry implications for one's character outside of the negotiation, they create a mindset that allows for dishonesty and other morally questionable negotiation tactics. This brings us to a second key feature of games. Game rules are arbitrary and artificial in that they do not carry over outside the specific game and could easily be different. . . . The expression "it's just a game" captures this sentiment. Situations that are viewed as game-like are perceived to be artificial, with rules for behavior that are arbitrary and constrained narrowly to the specific game setting, rather than broadly applicable or generalizable outside that setting. The perceived arbitrariness of the rules governing "games" can allow for psychological bracketing of the meaning of choices in the game—behaviors that test or cross moral boundaries can be cordoned off from negotiators' beliefs about character and values. Accordingly, viewing a negotiation through a game frame allows a negotiator to believe, "How I behave when negotiating is not a reflection of who I am, it is just how the 'game' is played." While this construct in and of itself may not necessarily give rise to dishonest behavior, we expect it will indeed be associated with dishonesty when it is combined with a competitive motivation to win. In this way, our conceptualization of game framing of negotiation bears similarities to what Shell has labeled the "Poker School" of bargaining ethics. To summarize, we argue that the opposite of an ethical decision frame is a game frame. A game frame of negotiation holds that negotiation is an adversarial context with arbitrary and artificial rules. We hypothesize that game framing will be inversely associated with moral character and also inversely associated with honest disclosure. That is, the more that lawyers view negotiation through a game frame, the less forthcoming they will be in situations in which honest disclosure is not mandated by law or professional rules of conduct. . . .

Educators, mentors, and negotiators themselves should be mindful of the various ways they can invite game framing of negotiation. Game norms can be reinforced informally through language that likens real-world, consequential decisions to games and game-playing. . . . [W]e contend that ethical framing (rather than game framing) is overall beneficial for negotiations and other business dealings. Consistent with our argument, Schneider surveyed lawyers about the effectiveness of different negotiation styles and found that the single adjective (out of 89 included for study) most closely linked with lawyers' perceptions of effective problem solving was "ethical." Along similar lines, negotiation textbooks, reference books, and popular press books overwhelmingly encourage negotiators to honestly disclose information about their interests and priorities to create value, build trust, and enhance their reputations. Questions remain about what characteristics might make negotiators more versus less willing to honestly share information. Our study suggests that moral character and game framing of negotiation are both likely to play a role. . . .

To the extent that teaching law students to "think like a lawyer" encourages them to adopt a game frame of negotiation, we can expect such training to reduce the likelihood of honest disclosure, which could temper their effectiveness at problem solving and may adversely impact their mental health as well. If students enter law school with high moral character and an ethical frame of negotiation but are later encouraged through their law school training to adopt a game frame and/or behave in ways that run counter to their own sense of right and wrong, it could lead to a Person X Situation mismatch resulting in ethical conflict, psychological distress, emotional exhaustion, and worse. The same case could be made for training business students to think of business as a game—doing so could adversely affect their ethics, effectiveness, and well-being. We encourage longitudinal studies of law students and business students that investigate how moral character, game framing, honesty, and well-being may change over the course of law school and business school, and as students' careers progress post-graduation.

Understanding why well-meaning attorneys make unethical mistakes is crucial to avoiding them. In the next excerpt, former big firm partner and now judge Patrick Schlitz provides advice to law students about to enter the profession about dealing with the ethical landmines awaiting them.

❖ *Patrick J. Schlitz*, ON BEING A HAPPY, HEALTHY AND ETHICAL MEMBER OF AN UNHAPPY, UNHEALTHY, AND UNETHICAL PROFESSION

52 Vand. L. Rev. 871, 906-912, 915-918 (1999)

THE ETHICS OF LAWYERS

[T]he legal profession is widely perceived—even by lawyers—as being unethical. Only one American in five considers lawyers to be "honest and ethical," and "the more a person knows about the legal profession and the more he or she is in direct personal contact with lawyers, the lower [his or her] opinion of them." This should concern you.

There are many reasons why ethics courses are so unpopular, but the most important is probably that law students do not think that they will become unethical lawyers. Students think of unethical lawyers as the sleazeballs who chase ambulances (think Danny DeVito in *The Rainmaker*) or run insurance scams (think Bill Murray in *Wild Things*) or destroy evidence (think Al Pacino's crew in *The Devil's Advocate*). Students have a hard time identifying with these lawyers. When students think of life after graduation, they see themselves sitting on the 27th floor of some skyscraper in a freshly pressed dark suit (blue, black, or gray) with a starched blouse or shirt (white or light blue) doing sophisticated legal work for sophisticated clients. Students imagine—wrongly—that such lawyers do not have to worry much about ethics, except, perhaps, when the occasional conflict of interest question arises.

If you think this—if you think that you will not have any trouble practicing law ethically—you are wrong. Dead wrong. In fact, particularly if you go to work for a big firm, you will probably begin to practice law unethically in at least some respects within your first year or two in practice. This happens to most young lawyers in big firms. It happened to me, and it will happen to you, unless you do something about it.

A. PRACTICING LAW ETHICALLY

Let's first be clear on what I mean by practicing law ethically. I mean three things. First, you generally have to comply with the formal disciplinary rules—either the Model Rules of Professional Conduct, the Model Code of Professional Responsibility, or some state variant of one or the other. As a law student, and then as a young lawyer, you will often be encouraged to distinguish ethical from unethical conduct solely by reference to the formal rules. Most likely, you will devote the majority of the time in your professional responsibility class to studying the rules, and you will, of course, learn the rules cold so that you can pass the Multi-State Professional Responsibility Exam ("MPRE"). In many other ways, subtle and blatant, you will be encouraged to think that conduct that does not violate the rules is "ethical," while conduct that does violate the rules is "unethical.". . .

I don't have anything against the formal rules. Often, they are all that stands between an unethical lawyer and a vulnerable client. You should learn them and follow them. But you should also understand that the formal rules represent nothing more than "the lowest common denominator of conduct that a highly self-interested group will tolerate." For many lawyers, "[e]thics is a matter of steering, if necessary, just clear of the few unambiguous prohibitions found in rules governing lawyers." But complying with the formal rules will not make you an ethical lawyer, any more than complying with the criminal law will make you an ethical person. Many of the sleaziest lawyers you will encounter will be absolutely scrupulous in their compliance with the formal rules. In fact, they will be only too happy to tell you just that. . . .

The second thing you must do to be an ethical lawyer is to act ethically in your work, even when you aren't required to do so by any rule. To a substantial extent, "bar ethical rules have lost touch with ordinary moral intuitions." To practice law ethically you must practice law consistently with those intuitions. . . .

The third thing you must do to be an ethical lawyer is to live an ethical life. Many big firm lawyers—who can be remarkably "smug[] about the superiority of the ethical standards of large firms"—ignore this point. So do many law professors who, when writing about legal ethics, tend to focus solely on the lawyer at work. But being admitted to the bar does not absolve you of your responsibilities outside of work—to your family, to your friends, to your community, and, if you're a person of faith, to your God. To practice law ethically, you must meet those responsibilities, which means that you must live a balanced life. If you become a workaholic lawyer, you will be unhealthy, probably unhappy, and, I would argue, unethical. . . .

B. BIG FIRM CULTURE

. . . Because practicing law ethically will depend primarily upon the hundreds of little things that you will do almost unthinkingly every day, it will not depend much upon your thinking. You are going to be busy. The days will fly by. When you are on the phone negotiating a deal or when you are at your computer drafting a brief or when you are filling out your time sheet at the end of the day, you are not going to have time to reflect on each of your actions. You are going to have to act almost instinctively.

What this means, then, is that you will not practice law ethically—you cannot practice law ethically—unless acting ethically is habitual for you. You have to be in the habit of being honest. You have to be in the habit of being fair. You have to be in the habit of being compassionate. These qualities have to be deeply ingrained in you, so that you can't turn them on and off—so that acting honorably is not something you have to decide to do—so that when you are at work, making the thousands of phone calls you will make and writing the thousands of letters you will write and dealing with the thousands of people with whom you will deal, you will automatically apply the same values in the workplace that you apply outside of work, when you are with family and friends. . . .

C. BECOMING UNETHICAL

. . . Unethical lawyers do not start out being unethical; they start out just like you—as perfectly decent young men or women who have every intention of practicing law ethically. They do not become unethical overnight; they become unethical just as you will (if you become unethical)—a little bit at a time. And they do not become unethical by shredding incriminating documents or bribing jurors; they become unethical just as you are likely to—by cutting a corner here, by stretching the truth a bit there. . . .

Problem 5-2. ***Schlitz School***

Schlitz gives some specific advice: "[D]o not pad your time sheets—even once. And do not tell lies to partners or clients or opposing counsel. And do not misrepresent legal authority to judges. And do not break your promises. And do not do anything else that is contrary to the values you now hold. And finally, when you screw up—as I did, as every lawyer does—pick yourself up, dust yourself off, and try that much harder to develop the habit of acting ethically."

How would you translate this into negotiation advice for yourself?

Wise Master

A wise master once wanted to test his students. The temple where they studied was run down, and students normally begged for food in the nearby town. One day the master told the students that each of them was to go into the town and steal something they could sell to raise money. "In order not to defile our excellent reputation by committing illegal and immoral acts, please be certain to steal when no one is looking. I do not want anyone to be caught." After some hesitation, the group of students set out except for one young boy. When the master asked him why he did not go, the boy responded, "I cannot follow your instructions to steal where no one will see me. Wherever I go, I am always there watching. My own eyes will see me steal." The boy was the only one who passed the test. Adapted from Heather Forest, The Wise Master, *Wisdom Tales from Around the World* 15-16 (1996).

C. ETHICAL RULES

As the studies above show, not all lawyers even understand the ethical rules that provide guidelines for how lawyers should behave in negotiations. Below, we have excerpted a selection from the Delaware Lawyers' Rules of Professional Conduct, which mirror the Model Rules of Professional Conduct—but please refer to the applicable rules in your own state. In the excerpt that follows, Carrie Menkel-Meadow reviews the most important of these rules and explains the impact of these ethical rules on negotiation conduct.

RULE 1.2 Scope of Representation

(a) [A] lawyer shall abide by a client's decisions concerning the objectives of representation and . . . shall consult with the client as to the means by which they are to be pursued. . . . A lawyer shall abide by a client's decision whether to settle a matter. . .

(d) A lawyer shall not counsel a client to engage, or assist a client, in conduct that the lawyer knows is criminal or fraudulent, but a lawyer may discuss the legal consequences of any proposed course of conduct with a client and may counsel or assist a client to make a good faith effort to determine the validity, scope, meaning or application of the law.

RULE 1.4 Communication

(a) A lawyer shall:

(3) keep the client reasonably informed about the status of the matter;

(b) A lawyer shall explain a matter to the extent reasonably necessary to permit the client to make informed decisions regarding the representation. . . .

RULE 1.6 Confidentiality of Information

(a) A lawyer shall not reveal information relating to the representation of a client unless the client gives informed consent, the disclosure is impliedly authorized in order to carry out the representation or the disclosure is permitted by paragraph (b).

(b) A lawyer may reveal information relating to the representation of a client to the extent the lawyer reasonably believes necessary:

(1) to prevent reasonably certain death or substantial bodily harm;. . .

(2) to prevent the client from committing a crime or fraud that is reasonably certain to result in substantial injury to the financial interests or property of another and in furtherance of which the client has used or is using the lawyer's services;

(3) to prevent, mitigate, or rectify substantial injury to the financial interests

or property of another that is reasonably certain to result or has resulted from the client's commission of a crime or fraud in furtherance of which the client has used the lawyer's services;. . . .

RULE 4.1 Truthfulness in Statements to Others

In the course of representing a client a lawyer shall not knowingly:

(a) make a false statement of material fact or law to a third person; or

(b) fail to disclose a material fact when disclosure is necessary to avoid assisting a criminal or fraudulent act by a client, unless disclosure is prohibited by Rule 1.6. . . .

COMMENT

Misrepresentation

[1] A lawyer is required to be truthful when dealing with others on a client's behalf, but generally has no affirmative duty to inform an opposing party of relevant facts. A misrepresentation can occur if the lawyer incorporates or affirms a statement of another person that the lawyer knows is false. Misrepresentations can also occur by partially true but misleading statements or omissions that are the equivalent of affirmative false statements. For dishonest conduct that does not amount to a false statement or for misrepresentations by a lawyer other than in the course of representing a client, see Rule 8.4.

Statements of Fact

[2] This Rule refers to statements of fact. Whether a particular statement should be regarded as one of fact can depend on the circumstances. Under generally accepted conventions in negotiation, certain types of statements ordinarily are not taken as statements of material fact. Estimates of price or value placed on the subject of a transaction and a party's intentions as to an acceptable settlement of a claim are ordinarily in this category, and so is the existence of an undisclosed principal except where nondisclosure of the principal would constitute fraud. Lawyers should be mindful of their obligations under applicable law to avoid criminal and tortious misrepresentation.

Crime or Fraud by Client

[3] Under Rule 1.2(d), a lawyer is prohibited from counseling or assisting a client in conduct that the lawyer knows is criminal or fraudulent. Paragraph (b) states a specific application of the principle set forth in Rule 1.2(d) and addresses the situation where a client's crime or fraud takes the form of a lie or misrepresentation. Ordinarily, a lawyer can avoid assisting a client's crime or fraud by withdrawing from the representation. Sometimes it may be necessary for the lawyer to give notice of the fact of withdrawal and to disaffirm an opinion, document, affirmation or the like. In extreme cases, substantive law may require a lawyer to disclose information relating to the representation to avoid being deemed to have assisted the client's crime or fraud. If the lawyer can avoid assisting a client's crime or fraud only by disclosing this information, then under paragraph (b) the lawyer is required to do so, unless the disclosure is prohibited by Rule 1.6.

RULE 8.4 Misconduct

It is professional misconduct for a lawyer to:

(a) violate or attempt to violate the Rules of Professional Conduct, knowingly assist or induce another to do so, or do so through the acts of another; . . .

(c) engage in conduct involving dishonesty, fraud, deceit or misrepresentation;

(d) engage in conduct that is prejudicial to the administration of justice;

Carrie Menkel-Meadow, ETHICS, MORALITY AND PROFESSIONAL RESPONSIBILITY IN NEGOTIATION

in Dispute Resolution Ethics 131-139 (Phyllis Bernard & Bryant Garth, eds., 2002)

Most discussions of negotiation ethics begin with Model Rule of Professional Conduct 4.1(a) and (b), which provides that a lawyer shall not, in the course of representing a client,

> Make a false statement of material fact or law to a third person; or fail to disclose a material fact to a third person when disclosure is necessary to avoid assisting a criminal or fraudulent act by a client, unless disclosure is prohibited by Model Rule 1.6 [client confidentiality rule].

What the black-letter rule appears to require (a fair amount of candor) is in fact greatly modified by the Comments. For example, Comment 2 states that this rule applies only to "statements of fact," and "whether a particular statement should be regarded as one of fact can depend on the circumstances." "Opinions" (of value, of interpretations of facts or of case law) are not considered "facts" under this rubric. Most significantly, the Comment goes on to exempt from the operation of the rule three particular kinds of statements made in negotiation. According to the Comment, there are "generally accepted conventions in negotiation" (a nod to the sociological phenomenology of negotiation) in which no one really expects the "truth" because these statements are not "material" statements of fact. These are (1) estimates of price or value placed on the subject of the transaction, (2) a party's intentions as to an acceptable settlement of a claim and (3) the existence of an undisclosed principal, except where non-disclosure of the principal would otherwise (by other law) constitute fraud.

Thus, the exception in the Comment defines away, as not material, several key notions of how negotiations are conducted, including inflated offers and demands (otherwise known as "puffing" and "exaggeration"), failure to disclose "bottom lines" or "reservation prices," and non-disclosure of a principal (say Donald Trump or Harvard University) where knowledge of who the principal is might raise a price or demand, on the assumption that the principal has deep pockets. In addition, as discussed more fully below, Comment 1 suggests that while a negotiating lawyer "is required to be truthful when dealing with others on a client's behalf," a lawyer does not have an affirmative duty to inform an opposing party of relevant facts (subject to some further qualifications that failure to act or to correct may sometimes constitute a misrepresentation and that substantive law may, in fact, sometimes require affirmative disclosure—see Comment 3).

A simple reading of these provisions demonstrates how indeterminate and unhelpful the formal rules of professional responsibility are. First, the claim that there are "generally accepted conventions" is an empirical one, without substantiation in the text of the Comments. Who, in fact, generally "accepts" these conventions? All lawyers? Lawyers who subscribe to the conventional, adversarial and distributive models of negotiation? Many lawyers would probably "accept" even more classes of "untruthful" or less-than-full-disclosure statement in negotiations. . . .

In an important test of these "generally accepted conventions," Larry Lempert asked 15 legal and ethics experts how—under these rules—they would resolve several important disclosure dilemmas, including lying about authorized limits given by the client, lying about the extent of a personal injury as a plaintiff's lawyer during a litigation negotiation, exaggerating an emotional distress claim in a torts negotiation, and failing to correct the other side's misimpression about the extent of injuries. Not surprisingly, there was relatively little consensus among the experts about how far a lawyer-negotiator could go in lying about, deceiving or misrepresenting these issues, all of which could be argued to be within the three "generally accepted conventions" excluded from the general non-misrepresentation rule.

Recently, I have added to this list the following negotiator's ethical dilemmas in a variety of lawyer-negotiator ethics CLE programs. Consider what you would do in the following situations, in addition to those four listed above.

1. Just before the closing of a sale of a closely held business, a major client of the business terminates a long-term commercial relationship, thereby lessening the value of the firm being purchased—and you represent the seller. Do you disclose this information to the buyer?
2. On the morning of a scheduled negotiation about a litigation matter, you receive notice that your request for a summary judgment has been denied. The lawyer for the other side is coming to your office and clearly has no notice of the judge's ruling. Do you disclose it before negotiating or seek to "close the deal" quickly with an offer before the other side finds out about the summary judgment decision?
3. You receive, by mistake, a fax addressed to all of the counsel on the other side of a multi-party litigation. It contains important and damaging-to-the-other-side information that would enhance your bargaining position. What do you do?. . .
7. In a hotly contested contractual negotiation the other side demanded the inclusion of a particular clause that your client did not want to agree to but finally did when it was made a "deal-breaker." The final draft of the contract, prepared by the other side, arrives at your office without the disputed clause, which you know the other side really wants included in the final deal. What do you do?. . .

Remarkably, time after time, use of these hypotheticals reveals exactly the opposite of what Comment 2 to Model Rule 4.1 so baldly states. In my experience, there are virtually no "generally accepted conventions" with respect to what should be done in these situations. Different negotiators bring to the table different assumptions of what they are trying to do, and with those assumptions come different ethical orientations.

Thus, for those who are "tough negotiators" or who see legal negotiation as an individual maximization game, whether in the litigation or transactional context, most of the deceptions above can be justified by reference either to "expectations" about how the legal-negotiation game is played, or to the lawyer's obligation to be a zealous advocate and not to "do the work" of the other side. For those lawyers who are concerned about making a good agreement "stick"—the instrumentalists—some disclosure is considered desirable (for example, in the scenarios above that describe the omission of a contract provision or the failure to correct misimpressions) because of a concern that some failures to disclose might lead to a post-hoc attack on the agreement (fraud, negligent misrepresentation, unilateral mistake).

Still others regard negotiations as opportunities for problems to be solved and so are more likely to thoughtfully consider the later impact of doing some of the things suggested above. These lawyers ask questions such as these: What would be gained or lost by revealing to the landlord's lawyer that you know he is lying? How can you honestly return the helpful fax and honestly disclose what you now know, but perhaps shouldn't use? When should clients be consulted about these ethical choices, as Model Rule 1.2 suggests they should be, at least about some matters? And those who value their reputations and/or see negotiations as a method for achieving some modicum of justice outside of courtrooms or in deals would disclose (as some ethics opinions and fraud cases say they must) the omitted contract clause and the diminished value of the purchased company (is it a material matter?).

Thus, there are no "generally accepted conventions" in negotiation practice, especially as more and more lawyers and law students are trained in the newer canon of Getting to Yes, collaborative, integrative and problem-solving negotiation models. Who decides what "generally accepted conventions" are? The drafters of the ethics rules, without empirical verification? And, more importantly, why should "generally accepted conventions" prevail in an ethics code? Are we looking at "generally accepted conventions" in other areas of the Rules? . . . The answer is usually "no"—we require lawyers appearing before tribunals to reveal adverse authority without regard to what "accepted conventions" of advocacy might suggest, e.g. that each side should do its own research and it is up to the judge or her clerk to find the cases. . . .

Model Rule 4.1, however, is not the only rule that might be seen to govern negotiation ethics. Model Rule 1.2, defining the scope of legal representation, has implications for negotiation behavior in several respects. First, Model Rule 1.2 provides for allocation of decision-making responsibility between lawyers and clients in any representation. Clients are to make decisions about the "objectives of representation," and lawyers, in consultation with clients, may make decisions about the "means" of representation. Some states now require, and others recommend, that this consultation about "means" should include counseling about and consideration of the forms of dispute resolution that should be considered in any representation, including negotiation, mediation, arbitration or other forms of "appropriate dispute resolution." Some might think that such consideration of "means" should extend to the different models of negotiation or different strategies now possible within the growing sophistication about different approaches to negotiation.

Second, and most importantly, Model Rule 1.2 requires the lawyer to "abide by a client's decision whether to settle a matter" and thus requires the lawyer to transmit settlement offers to the client, especially in conjunction with the requirements of Model Rule 1.4(a) that a lawyer "shall keep the client reasonably informed about the status of the matter" and Model Rule 1.4(b) that a lawyer "shall explain a matter to the extent reasonably necessary to permit the client to make informed decisions regarding the representation." Model Rule 1.2(d) also admonishes lawyers not to counsel a client to engage in and not to assist the client in conduct the lawyer knows is fraudulent or criminal, and thus, once again, the Rule implicates the substantive law of fraud and crimes. Lawyers may not assist clients in such activities, and thus, what constitutes a misrepresentation in a negotiation is dependent on tort and criminal law, outside the rules of professional responsibility. The lawyer may, then, be more restricted in 1.2(d) by what other laws prohibit clients from doing than by what the lawyer might be restricted from in 4.1.

Beyond these more specific requirements, Model Rule 8.4 can be and has been invoked with respect to the lawyer's duty to be honest and fair in negotiation. Model Rule 8.4 states that "it is professional misconduct for a lawyer to ". . . (c) engage in conduct involving dishonesty, fraud, deceit or misrepresentation," once again incorporating by reference not only substantive standards of legal fraud and misrepresentation, but also suggesting that certain forms of dishonesty or breach of interference with the administration of justice (especially when a "pattern of repeated offenses" exists) may subject a lawyer to discipline for his deceptive or other fraudulent actions in negotiations.

Problem 5-3. ***Zealous Advocate or Diligent Negotiator?***

The article above outlines how lawyers believe that they have a purported duty to be a zealous advocate. Yet, the actual phrase "zealous advocacy" is no longer used in the Model Rules. This used to be the requirement under the Model Code of Professional Responsibility Canon 7 entitled "A Lawyer Should Represent a Client Zealously Within the Bounds of the Law," adopted in 1969 but was taken out with the adoption of the Model Rules in 1983. The closest language to the requirement for zealous advocacy is found in current Rule 1.3 on Diligence, Comment 1: "A lawyer should pursue a matter on behalf of a client . . . and take whatever lawful and ethical measures are required to vindicate a client's cause or endeavor. A lawyer must also act with commitment and dedication to the interests of the client and with zeal in advocacy upon the client's behalf. . . .".

Do you think that the change away from the phrase zealous advocacy represents a shift in a lawyers' actual obligation toward their client? The language in the Comment still uses "zeal in advocacy"!

Problem 5-4. When Can You Lie?

A district attorney was sanctioned by the Colorado state disciplinary board for deception when, during a hostage negotiation, the district attorney pretended that he was a public defender and acted on behalf of a murder suspect to encourage him to surrender. In affirming the sanctions, the Colorado Supreme Court held that "Purposeful deception by an attorney licensed in our state is intolerable. . . ." In the Matter of Paulter, 47 P.3d 1175, 1176 (Colo. 2002). If the Colorado Supreme Court would not condone deceiving a murder suspect during a hostage negotiation, do you think there is any lying of which it might approve?

D. THE COMMON LAW OF ETHICS

This next section examines the common law treatment of negotiation ethics. Why not have a good faith standard in negotiations to regulate lawyer behavior? Good faith could require that lawyers show up for a scheduled meeting, exchange reasonable offers, and treat each other with some amount of courtesy. The problem with suggesting a good faith standard is two-fold. First, in the negotiation context (as well as in the mediation context discussed in Chapter 8), good faith is difficult to define.[1] While it is true that courts have found violations of good faith in specific instances where parties have unreasonably delayed negotiations, failed to seek approval of an agreement, and breached an agreement, these cases are more rarities than the norm and definitions of good faith remain vague. Second, even if we could define good faith, it is unclear if there really is any duty to engage in good faith negotiations. Although both the UCC and Restatement of Contracts refer to a duty of good faith in performance, neither specifies a duty of good faith in negotiations. In one of the more famous cases finding a violation of good faith (Hoffman v. Red Owl Stores, 26 Wis. 2d 683, 1965), the plaintiff, Mr. Hoffman, relied on and acted upon Red Owl's negotiated promises of a franchise—selling his previous business, gathering his savings, and moving to a new town—and the court found sufficient reliance on Red Owl's promises to find a violation of good faith on their part. However, only in certain narrow contexts—[2] for example, after preliminary agreements are made, or when negotiations are conducted under court order, or in the labor-management context—can we generally expect that

1. See Robert S. Summers, The General Duty of Good Faith—Its Recognition and Conceptualization, 67 Cornell L. Rev. 810 (1982).
2. See NLRB v. Katz, 369 U.S. 762 (1962); NLRB v. American Nat. Ins. Co., 343 U.S. 395 (1952).

a duty to negotiate in good faith exists. So instead of good faith, the common law has focused on misrepresentations, omissions and misstatements of material facts. We examine each of these.

1. Misrepresentation

RESTATEMENT (SECOND) OF TORTS §525 (1977)
§525 Liability for Fraudulent Misrepresentation

One who fraudulently makes a misrepresentation of fact, opinion, intention or law for the purpose of inducing another to act or to refrain from action in reliance upon it, is subject to liability to the other in deceit for pecuniary loss caused to him by his justifiable reliance upon the misrepresentation.

RESTATEMENT (SECOND) OF CONTRACTS §§161, 164 (1981)
§161 When Non-Disclosure Is Equivalent to an Assertion

A person's non-disclosure of a fact known to him is equivalent to an assertion that the fact does not exist in the following cases only:

a. where he knows that disclosure of the fact is necessary to prevent some previous assertion from being a misrepresentation or from being fraudulent or material.

b. where he knows that disclosure of the fact would correct a mistake of the other party as to a basic assumption on which that party is making the contract and if non-disclosure of the fact amounts to a failure to act in good faith and in accordance with reasonable standards of fair dealing.

c. where he knows that disclosure of the fact would correct a mistake of the other party as to the contents or effect of a writing, evidencing or embodying an agreement in whole or in part.

d. where the other person is entitled to know the fact because of a relation of trust and confidence between them.

§164 When a Misrepresentation Makes a Contract Voidable

(1) If a party's manifestation of assent is induced by either a fraudulent or a material misrepresentation by the other party upon which the recipient is justified in relying, the contract is voidable by the recipient. . . .

Understanding the definition of a fraudulent statement is useful, but what does this mean for a practicing attorney? Examining court cases can further clarify and define the elements of misrepresentation, material fact, reliance, and damages.

A misrepresentation clearly includes a deliberate lie. The law, however, goes further so that uncorrected mistakes are also included under knowing misrepresentation.

STARE v. TATE

21 Cal. App. 3d 432, 98 Cal. Rptr. 264 (1971)

Justice KAUS delivered the Opinion of the Court. . . .

FACTS

The agreement in question was signed by both parties on February 21, 1968. . . .

In the negotiations both sides apparently agreed that the community property was to be evenly divided. They did not agree, however, on the value of certain items and on the community property status of certain stocks which stood in the husband's name alone.

These disagreements centered principally on items which, it was understood, were to be retained by the husband. . . .

In January, 1968, Joan's attorney prepared a document entitled "SECOND PROPOSAL FOR A BASIS OF SETTLEMENT—TATE v. TATE" which, among other things, arrived at a suggested figure of $70,081.85 for the value of Joan's share in the Holt property. This value was arrived at by a computation set forth in the proposal. It is copied in the footnote.[3]

It is obvious that Joan's attorney arrived at the figure of $70,081.85 for the community equity in the property only by making two substantial errors. First, the net value after deducting the encumbrances from the asserted gross value of $550,000 is $241,637.01, not $141,637.01; second, one-half of $141,637.01 is substantially more than $70,081.85. The correct figure for the equity should have been $120,818.50[,] or roughly $50,000 more.

The mistake did not escape Tim's accountant who discovered it while helping Tim's attorney in preparing a counter-offer. He brought it to the attention of the attorney who, in his own words, reacted as follows:

> "I told him that I had been arguing with [the wife's attorney] to use the value that was on the . . . real property tax statement, but I knew that that was low and [he] would never go for it, that the appraisal had been $425,000.00 when the building had been purchased by said owners, and I thought that until we got it, that we would use something like a $450,000.00 value, and he said, 'Fine.' It is my recollection that I said to him, 'You know, you might as well use the figure that Walker has there because his mistake is a hundred thousand dollars and we value it at a hundred thousand dollars less, so it is basically the same thing, so give it a $70,000.00 equity,' and that is what he did and that is how it came about."

3. "888 East Holt Avenue, Pomona (Note: value as per previous offer)

Total value	$ 550,000.00
Less encumbrance	– 308,362.99
Net value	$ 141,637.01
One-half community	$ 70,081.85"

A counter-offer was then submitted to Joan and her lawyer. It lists all of the community assets, with the property in question being valued at $70,082.00, rounding up the erroneous figure in Joan's offer to the nearest dollar. There can be no reasonable doubt that the counter-offer was prepared in a way designed to minimize the danger that Joan or her attorney would discover the mistake. . . .

On February 16, 1968, the parties and their attorneys had a settlement conference. The counter-offer was the basis for the discussion. There was no mention that the figure of $70,082 for the equity in the Holt property was based on an agreed value of $550,000 or any other figure. . . .

The mistake might never have come to light had not Tim desired to have that exquisite last word. A few days after Joan had obtained the divorce he mailed her a copy of the offer which contained the errant computation. On top of the page he wrote with evident satisfaction: "PLEASE NOTE $100,000.00 MISTAKE IN YOUR FIGURES. . . ." The present action was filed exactly one month later. . . .

DISCUSSION

There is really no substantial conflict in the evidence and it is hard to understand how the trial court could do anything but grant Joan's prayer for relief.

Section 3399 of the Civil Code provides:

> "When, through fraud or a mutual mistake of the parties, *or a mistake of one party, which the other at the time knew or suspected*, a written contract does not truly express the intention of the parties, it may be revised on the application of a party aggrieved, so as to express that intention, so far as it can be done without prejudice to rights acquired by third persons, in good faith and for value." (Emphasis added.)"

Clearly there was a mistake, Joan and her attorney thinking that a $550,000 value resulted in a community equity about $70,000. . . . Inasmuch as the error was discovered by Tim's attorney, it is, of course, no defense that it was negligently made by Joan's attorney. . . .

The case was fully tried and, as we said at the outset of our discussion, the record supports nothing but a judgment for the plaintiff as prayed.

The judgment is reversed with directions to make findings and conclusions and to enter a judgment in conformity with this opinion.

Problem 5-5. *Misrepresentation & Mistake*

What if the mistake in Stare v. Tate had been a mistake of law rather than of math? Is there a duty to correct this? What about a situation when one side intentionally shields itself from the truth so that it does not "know"?

2. Omissions

Many negotiators' instinct may be that they can't be found liable for misrepresentation if they merely remain silent. However, omissions can be fraudulent, as outlined in Restatement Second (Contracts) §161. This next excerpt walks through the Restatement and further explains a lawyer's duties in negotiation.

G. Richard Shell, BARGAINING FOR ADVANTAGE: NEGOTIATION STRATEGIES FOR REASONABLE PEOPLE

208-209 (1999)

Surprisingly, there are circumstances when it may be fraudulent to keep your peace about an issue even if the other side does not ask about it. When does a negotiator have a duty to voluntarily disclose matters that may hurt his bargaining position? American law imposes affirmative disclosure duties in the following four circumstances:

1. *When the negotiator makes a partial disclosure that is or becomes misleading in light of all the facts* If you say your company is profitable, you may be under a duty to disclose whether you used questionable accounting techniques to arrive at that statement. You should also update your prior statement if you show a loss in the next quarter and negotiations are still ongoing.

2. *When the parties stand in a fiduciary relationship to each other.* In negotiations between trustees and beneficiaries, partners in a partnership, shareholders in a small corporation, or members of a family business, parties may have a duty of complete candor and cannot rely on the "be silent and be safe" approach.

3. *When the nondisclosing party has vital information about the transaction not accessible to the other side.* A recent case applying this exception held that an employer owed a duty of disclosure to a prospective employee to disclose contingency plans for shutting down the project for which the employee was hired. In general, sellers have a greater duty to disclose hidden defects about their property than buyers do to disclose "hidden treasure" that may be buried there. Thus, a home seller must disclose termite infestation in her home,[4] but an oil company need not voluntarily disclose that there is oil on a farmer's land when negotiating to purchase it.[5] This is a slippery exception; the best test is one of conscience and fairness.

4. See, e.g., Miles v. McSwegin, 388 N.E.2d 1367 (Ohio 1979).
5. See, e.g., Zaschak v. Travers Corp., 333 N.W.2d 191 (Mich. App. 1983).

4. *When special codified disclosure duties, such as those regarding contracts of insurance or public offerings of securities, apply.* Legislatures sometimes impose special disclosure duties for particular kinds of transactions. In the United States, for example, many states now require home sellers to disclose all known problems with their houses.

Problem 5-6. *Sellers or Buyers Beware?*

Do you think home buyers should carefully inspect and inquire or that sellers with "superior information" should inform regarding non-obvious defects connected with house sales?

If your neighbors are unpleasant, are you required to reveal this to potential purchasers of your house? If your neighbors belong to a rock band that practices late into the night, are you required to disclose this? If you are selling a home in which a murder occurred, are you required to reveal this?

In Reed v. King, 145 Cal. App. 3d 261 (1983), the court found that the seller of a house who represented it as fit for an elderly woman living alone had a duty to disclose that the house was the site of a multiple murder 10 years before!

If none of these four exceptions applies, neither side is likely to be found liable for fraud based on a nondisclosure. Each party can remain silent, passively letting the other proceed under its own assumptions.

An example of an omitted fact deemed a material misrepresentation arose in the case of Kentucky Bar Ass'n v. Geisler, 938 S.W.2d 578 (Ky. 1997). Geisler represented a pedestrian who was struck by an automobile. In the course of Geisler's negotiations with defense counsel, Geisler's client died. The attorneys eventually reached a settlement, but only following the settlement did the defendants learn that Geisler's client had died. When she faced a Bar disciplinary action, Geisler argued that she was under no affirmative duty to disclose the information and that the information was immaterial. The Supreme Court of Kentucky was unmoved by these arguments. It found the client's death to be plainly material to the settlement of a tort claim for injuries to the client. Citing the Kentucky equivalent of Model Rule 4.1, it also pointed out that "misrepresentations can occur by failure to act." In issuing its order publicly reprimanding Geisler and ordering her to pay the costs associated with her reprimand, the Kentucky Supreme Court wrote:

> [T]his Court fails to understand why guidelines are needed for an attorney to understand that when their client dies, they are under an obligation to tell opposing counsel such information. This seems to be a matter of common ethics and just plain sense. However, because attorneys such as respondent cannot discern such matters and require written guidelines so as to figure out their ethical convictions, this Court [affirms the ABA Formal Opinion on this matter].

3. Material Facts

In examining whether action or inaction amounts to fraud, it is also important whether the facts under discussion are material. In negotiations in which puffing and bluffing are seen as part of the game, could a lawyer get in trouble for stretching too far? The answer is that it depends on what you are talking about in the negotiation. When the parties are of equal bargaining power, courts have permitted a certain amount of puffing and (over-)predictions of quality. The following case highlights some traditional ways that courts have examined sales promises.

❖ VULCAN METALS CO. v. SIMMONS MANUFACTURING CO.

248 F. 853, 856-857 (2d Cir. 1918)

Judge Learned HAND delivered the Opinion of the Court.

The first question is of the misrepresentations touching the quality and powers of the patented machine. These were general commendations, or, in so far as they included any specific facts, were not disproved; e.g., that the cleaner would produce 18 inches of vacuum with 25 pounds water pressure. They raise, therefore, the question of law how far general "puffing" or "dealers' talk" can be the basis of an action for deceit.

The conceded exception in such cases has generally rested upon the distinction between "opinion" and "fact"; but that distinction has not escaped the criticism it deserves. An opinion is a fact, and it may be a very relevant fact; the expression of an opinion is the assertion of a belief, and any rule which condones the expression of a consciously false opinion condones a consciously false statement of fact. When the parties are so situated that the buyer may reasonably rely upon the expression of the seller's opinion, it is no excuse to give a false one. And so it makes much difference whether the parties stand "on an equality." For example, we should treat very differently the expressed opinion of a chemist to a layman about the properties of a composition from the same opinion between chemist and chemist, when the buyer had full opportunity to examine. The reason of the rule lies, we think, in this: There are some kinds of talk which no sensible man takes seriously, and if he does he suffers from his credulity. If we were all scrupulously honest, it would not be so; but, as it is, neither party usually believes what the seller says about his own opinions, and each knows it. Such statements, like the claims of campaign managers before election, are rather designed to allay the suspicion which would attend their absence than to be understood as having any relation to objective truth. It is quite true that they induce a compliant temper in the buyer, but it is by a much more subtle process than through the acceptance of his claims for his wares. . . .

In the case at bar, since the buyer was allowed full opportunity to examine the cleaner and to test it out, we put the parties upon an equality. It seems to us that general statements as to what the cleaner would do, even though consciously false, were not of a kind to be taken literally by the buyer. As between manufacturer and customer, it may not be so; but this was the case of taking over a business, after ample chance to investigate. Such a buyer, who the seller rightly expects will undertake an independent and adequate inquiry into the actual merits of what he gets, has no right to treat as material in his determination statements like these. . . . We therefore think that the District Court was right in disregarding all these misrepresentations.

Problem 5-7. ***Types of Lies***

1. What type of lie was the lie about whether the vacuum cleaners had been marketed? Do you agree with the court that this type of lie should be illegal? What was the court's reasoning?
2. What type of lie was the lie about the performance of the vacuum cleaners? Do you agree with the court that this type of lie should be permitted (and expected)? What was the court's reasoning?

As respects the representation that the cleaners had never been put upon the market or offered for sale, the rule does not apply; nor can we agree that such representations could not have been material to Freeman's decision to accept the contract. The actual test of experience in their sale might well be of critical consequence in his decision to buy the business, and the jury would certainly have the right to accept his statement that his reliance upon these representations was determinative of his final decision. . . .

Courts have distinguished between opinion and fact as a way to determine when there is material misrepresentation of fact. A demand—"my client will only accept X"—is not deemed to be material as a matter of law. This type of statement is seen as an opinion rather than fact. Similarly, the reservation price—"my client won't settle for less than X"—is also viewed as an opinion unless tied to a specific material fact (like an insurance policy limit or a board of directors' settlement authorization vote; see ABA Ethics Opinion 06-439). Similarly, other types of tactics in a negotiation could be problematic if you start to inflate your own alternatives. The following case is a good example of what can happen with too much bluffing.

BEAVERS v. LAMPLIGHTERS REALTY

556 P.2d 1328, 1329-1331 (Okla. Ct. App. 1976)

BRIGHTMIRE, Judge.

It was sometime in January 1974 plaintiff saw a Lamplighters' for sale sign in front of an attractive Spanish style house at 4912 Larissa Lane. He liked the storybook looks of the abode, called the telephone number printed on the sign, and eventually was shown the house by agent Norma Ray. Shortly thereafter, on February 11, 1974, plaintiff's offer of $34,500 for the dwelling was rejected.

Plaintiff still wanted the place, however. He let a day or two pass and again called Lamplighters. This time a "Mr. Taylor came on the phone" and asked if plaintiff was still interested in the home. "Yes," said plaintiff, "but doggone it . . . they were asking too much."

"If you are going to do anything, you had better do it pretty quick, because I've got a buyer for it," said the realtor.

"You do?" responded plaintiff.

"Yes," said Taylor, "it [is] the original builder and he is coming in."

"Paul Good?" asked plaintiff.

"Yes," answered Taylor, adding that Good was coming in with a check right away.

"How much is it?" plaintiff asked concerning the check.

"Thirty-seven thousand dollars" was the answer.

"Well, he's bought it."

"No," retreated Taylor, "[i]f you want to put in a bid, he's going to be here within the hour. I just talked to him."

The high pressure tactic worked. Said plaintiff, "I [don't] know whether 'panicked' [is] the [right] word or not, but I figured . . . that [if] the original builder would pay thirty-seven thousand for the home, that maybe . . . it absolutely should be worth that much to me . . . and I just increased it [the fictitious offer] two hundred and fifty dollars. And the next thing I know I bought myself a home" for $37,250 by executing a contract dated February 15, 1974.

It was a while before plaintiff found out he had been a victim of a gross deception. One day, after he had moved into the house—and found, incidentally, that the agent Ray had made false representations about the condition of the house, requiring him to expend about $6,000 for repairs—he chanced to meet builder Paul Good at a neighbor's home, got to talking to him about plaintiff's house and came upon some interesting facts. Good said he had earlier looked at the house "but it was out of the ball park as far as he was concerned" and that he "would have given in the . . . lower thirties."

"Well," said plaintiff, "I'd offered thirty-four five to start."

"That should have bought it," said Good.

"Didn't you offer thirty-seven thousand?" plaintiff asked Good.

"No," he answered. . . .

In the instant case the evidence so far adduced establishes that realtor Taylor, upon becoming aware of plaintiff's desire for the Spanish villa, undertook to bring about a rather rapid resolution of the price problem by using, as it were, a dynamite sales technique to blast an immediate positive response out of plaintiff. The deliberate lie did indeed achieve the intended and expected effect and induced plaintiff to purchase the property for a figure higher than he would have had to pay absent the fraud. [The court held that this was fraudulent inducement.]

Problem 5-8. ***Going Too Far, or Right On?***

Do you agree with the court in *Beavers*? In Kabatchnick v. Hanover-Elm Bldg. Corp., 103 N.E.2d 692 (Mass. 1952), another court held that a landlord's lie that he had another, much higher, offer to rent was fraud. If you were selling a home and wanted to make it look like it was very popular and likely to be sold soon, what might you say to a potential buyer without risking violating the law?

E. ADDITIONAL LAW REGARDING SETTLEMENTS

1. Duty to Inform and Gain Approval of Settlements

A lawyer is required to inform her client of any settlement offer in a negotiation and, according to Model Rule 1.2, also must educate the client sufficiently so that the client can make an informed decision about whether to accept the offer. Model Rule 1.2 states that the lawyer must abide by the client's decisions concerning the objectives of representation, but the requirement to inform the client about settlement and to gain approval of any settlement is much more specific. In fact, lawyers have faced sanctions, including disbarment, when this particular requirement of client representation is overlooked. For example, in In re Brown (453 P.2d 958, Ariz. 1969), Attorney Brown failed to communicate a settlement offer to his client for $600 in a dog bite case. After the client lost (and had to pay costs and jury fees), Brown was disbarred for this and a collection of other problematic law practices. (The great movie *The Verdict* portrays Paul Newman turning down an offer on behalf of his clients without communicating it to them, but note, this is only acceptable in the movies.)

An attorney is similarly only able to accept an offer on the client's behalf when he or she has specific authorization from the client to do so. A general authorization as part of an agreement to retain the lawyer's services, for example, is insufficient. "An attorney who is clothed with no other authority than that arising from his employment as attorney has no implied authority by virtue of his general retainer to compromise and settle a claim of his client." Cross v. State, 643 P.2d 39, 43 (1982). Clients also retain the right to change their mind. Restatement (Third) on the Law Governing Lawyers §22(3) says the client can revoke any authorization he or she previously had given the lawyer. In re Lewis (463 S.E.2d 862, Ga. 1995) is an example of a client revoking the broad authorization she had previously given Lewis, her attorney, to act in her best interest. When Lewis accepted a settlement without consulting her, she repudiated the settlement and filed a complaint against Lewis. The court held that a broad authorization is not adequate; there must be specific authorization to accept a settlement offer.

2. Keeping the Terms of Settlements Confidential

Another relevant body of law covering negotiation is confidentiality. As discussed further in Chapter 8, settlement discussions must be kept confidential, unless there is an evidentiary exception or contrary legal policy.

A combination of four basic mechanisms provides confidentiality protections in the context of dispute resolution (all of these are discussed in more detail in Chapter 8):

1. Evidentiary exclusions ("If the only place you heard it was during our settlement efforts, you can't use it in court.")
2. Contract ("We have a deal to keep our mouths shut.")
3. Privilege ("You can't make me testify. You can't even make me produce information in discovery.")
4. Protective order ("Under penalty of contempt, you have to keep your mouth shut.")

Each of these mechanisms sometimes assures disputants that their conversations in negotiations will remain confidential.

The most pertinent law regarding settlement offers and confidentiality is Federal Rule of Evidence 408, which states that settlement discussions cannot be revealed in litigation to demonstrate liability. Settlements themselves can also impose confidentiality as part of the agreement. In some cases, such as consumer safety, sexual harassment, and similar situations in which others might face the same danger as a settling plaintiff, this confidentiality could be troubling for public policy reasons. A recent case in California highlights this dilemma. A court reviewed (and remanded) a settlement agreement that included a "fake arbitration" in which the arbitrator would rule for the defendant and the defendant could issue a press release claiming innocence from the sexual harassment claims. After the arbitrator and the plaintiff refused to participate in the sham arbitration, the court remanded some claims back to arbitration. See Nelson v. American Apparel, (Cal App. LA County, No. BC333028) (remanding for arbitration on some issues, but not to be published in official reports, as per California's unique "de-publication" procedure) Some jurisdictions' laws limit the enforceability of confidentiality provisions in certain contexts. We return to confidentiality in Chapter 8.

Problem 5-9. ***I Want to Know!***

As a response to the #MeToo movement, the issue of confidential settlements in sexual harassment cases received intense focus. States have responded in different ways with some proposals including the possibility of confidentiality being eliminated by law. For example, California has prohibited any clause in a settlement agreement that restricts the disclosure of "factual information" regarding any harassment or assault claim. New York has prohibited any settlement of harassment or discrimination from requiring the plaintiff to pay damages to the defendant in the event the plaintiff violates a nondisclosure clause. Why might parties in these cases want confidentiality? Why might the public interest override this private interest? How about claims regarding consumer safety? What should arguably remain confidential—or be public?

3. Enforcement of Settlements

Most negotiated settlement agreements are enforced just like any other contract. Settlements, however, incorporated into court decrees (antitrust violation settlements, mass torts, class actions, and institutional reforms such as school desegregation, environmental regulation, and housing reform), as well as all cases involving minors and others who are legally incapacitated, often receive judicial oversight of their enforcement. For example, in the well-known case of Spaulding v. Zimmerman (263 Minn. 346, 116 N.W.2d 704, 1962), the judge overturned a settlement on behalf of a minor where the defendant's doctor had not disclosed his discovery of the plaintiff's aneurysm to the plaintiff prior to settlement.

Settlements can also be overturned by a court using typical contract defenses like coercion, duress, unconscionability, and mutual mistake. These familiar contract doctrines apply in a negotiation context as well. This section just highlights two of these—duress and unconscionability—for a brief review of what you learned in your Contracts class.

Duress in a negotiation has been found when there is an illegitimate use of power by one side to coerce the other side into an agreement. Coercion might derive from a threat of physical power, a threat of criminal prosecution, or even a threat to reveal unpleasant information.

Generally, unconscionability is found in situations of unequal bargaining power resulting in grossly unfair settlement terms. As the court outlined in Williams v. Walker-Thomas Furniture (350 F. 2d 445, D.C. Cir. 1965), where a furniture store's credit agreement with its customer was voided, "Unconscionability has generally been recognized to include an absence of meaningful choice on the part of one of the parties together with contract terms which are unreasonably favorable to the other party." Unconscionability is typically reviewed in two parts—procedural unconscionability and substantive unconscionability—and a court will usually look for evidence of both kinds to overturn a contract.

When it is difficult to negotiate directly, the parties often seek help, for their substantive, process and ethical problems, from a third-party neutral. The next few chapters explore how mediators can facilitate negotiation and help the parties resolve their problems.

Further Reading

Arthur Isak Applbaum. (1999). Ethics for Adversaries. Princeton: Princeton University Press.

Phyllis Bernard & Bryant Garth (eds.). (2002). Dispute Resolution Ethics: A Comprehensive Guide. Washington DC: American Bar Association Section on Dispute Resolution.

Warren Burger, The Necessity for Civility, 52 F.R.D. 211 (1971).

Jonathan Cohen, When People Are the Means: Negotiating with Respect, 14 Geo. J. Legal Ethics 739 (2001).

David Luban. (1988). Lawyers and Justice. Princeton: Princeton University Press.

Carrie Menkel-Meadow, The Evolving Complexity of Dispute Resolution Ethics, 30 Geo. J. Legal Ethics 389 (2017).

Carrie Menkel-Meadow & Michael Wheeler. (2004). What's Fair: Ethics for Negotiators. San Francisco: Jossey-Bass Publishers.

Richard C. Reuben, Rethinking the Law of Legal Negotiation: Confidentiality Under Federal Rule of Evidence 408 and Related State Laws, 59 B.C. L. Rev. 523 (2018).

Deborah L. Rhode. (2000). In the Interests of Justice: Reforming the Legal Profession. New York: Oxford University Press.

Chapter 6 Mediation: Concepts and Models

Summum ius. Summa iniuria. (The strictest following of the law can lead to the greatest injustice.)

—Marcus Tullius Cicero

There is no intractable problem.

—Desmond Tutu

Conflicts are created and sustained by human beings. They can be ended by human beings.

—George J. Mitchell (referring to conflicts in Northern Ireland and the Middle East)

This chapter explores the foundations of mediation, the historical context for current perspectives on different types of mediation, and the place mediation holds in the array of dispute resolution processes. As mediation has developed, different orientations, goals, and strategies relating to the process have been propounded and debated. Using stories of actual mediations as background, a sampling of major approaches and varying descriptions of the mediation process are presented. The chapter concludes by reflecting on the direction that mediation will or should take as it becomes more central to human problem solving, legal practice, and courts.

A. INTRODUCTION TO MEDIATION

1. What Is Mediation?

Mediation is a process in which an impartial third party acts as a catalyst to help others constructively address and perhaps resolve a dispute, plan a transaction, or define the contours of a relationship. A mediator facilitates negotiation between the parties to enable better communication, encourage problem solving, and develop an agreement or resolution by consensus among those parties.

Mediators intervene in a wide array of disputes—from family and community to commercial and international. Mediation is useful for parties facing an actual dispute, trying to reconcile competing interests, or planning for the possibility of conflict. For example, a mediator can help divorcing couples determine parenting arrangements and asset division, or help people who are contemplating marriage negotiate a prenuptial agreement. A mediator can help settle a controversy over liability and damages related to an environmental disaster such as an oil spill, or can help a community determine a site for a highway or garbage facility.

In mediation, as in negotiation, the parties retain control over the outcome of their dispute, in some cases through their attorneys. This central feature of mediation—self-determination by the parties—is a facet of the promise of democratic process—that the voice and wisdom of people can shape novel outcomes responsive to particular situations. In this respect, mediation is fundamentally different from adjudication, where power to determine the outcome is ceded to a judge, jury, or arbiter.

2. Comparing Adjudication and Consensus-based Processes

Adjudication and the rule of law clarify and develop public norms. In adjudicative processes, like litigation and arbitration, a neutral decision maker—a judge, jury, arbiter, or panel of arbiters—determines the outcome of a dispute in accord with legal rules or industry (or other) norms. Adjudication supports the stability and predictability inherent in having laws and methods of evenhanded application of published rules or community norms. Litigation can give society precedents that promote order by guiding similarly situated actors.

Mediation, on the other hand, enhances communication, fosters collaboration, and encourages problem solving. While negotiation can also do these things, negotiation lacks the assistance of an impartial professional charged with making the process constructive. Mediation processes are suitably tailored to particular, not general, situations.

These different goals of consensus-based processes are also important to achieving individual and community well-being. If, for example, landlords and tenants, teachers and school boards, or employers and employees can resolve an existing controversy through mediation, they not only can achieve a creative resolution tailored to their specific situation, but also can bank their success in problem solving to help resolve, if not prevent, future disputes. The very success of their ability to problem solve together can provide a process precedent for resolving other issues that may arise.

In comparing and contrasting adjudication and mediation, two very different approaches to addressing disputes, it is important to note that they serve different goals and objectives and have their own logic and integrity. In adjudication, with ideals embedded in concepts of evolving law and precepts for ordering society, a decision maker (whether judge, jury or arbiter) determines facts and applies rules to determine rights and liabilities with respect to past acts. In mediation, a structuring of the future is possible to avoid past pitfalls and build new opportunities. The spotlight moves from evidence of past conduct and historic facts to parties' interests and possibilities for optimal balancing of those interests. Where, for example, a supplier and a customer have taken a matter to court to determine damages for a shipment that was nonconforming under a contract, those same parties in mediation might adjust their differences by arrangements in future contracts, making allowances for wrongs experienced by parties with respect to past conduct.

3. The Advantages of Mediation

Jarndyce v. Jarndyce

Jarndyce v. Jarndyce . . . has, in the course of time, become so complicated, that no man alive knows what it means. The parties to it understand it least; but it has been observed that no two Chancery lawyers can talk about it for five minutes, without coming to a total disagreement as to all the premises. Innumerable children have been born into the cause; innumerable young people have married into it; innumerable old people have died out of it. Scores of persons have deliriously found themselves made parties in Jarndyce v. Jarndyce, without knowing how or why; whole families have inherited legendary hatreds with the suit. The little plaintiff or defendant, who was promised a new rocking-horse when Jarndyce and Jarndyce should be settled, has grown up, possessed himself of a real horse, and trotted away into the other world. . . . [T]here are not three Jarndyces left upon the earth perhaps, since old Tom Jarndyce in despair blew his brains out at a coffee-house in Chancery Lane; but Jarndyce and Jarndyce still drags its dreary length before the Court, perennially hopeless.

—Charles Dickens, Bleak House

To understand the various rationales for mediation, examine the fictional case of Jarndyce v. Jarndyce, the focal point of Charles Dickens' novel, *Bleak House*. The case involves a will contest that consumes several generations in a family. The family members become so obsessed and absorbed by the legal contest that they lose their way in life and become divided one against the other. The legal issues in the fictional case are so complicated that even the lawyers cannot explain or agree on them. Ultimately, the legal costs consume the estate, and the lawsuit ends with everyone (except the lawyers who retain their fees) a loser.

In a variety of ways, the story illustrates many of the common shortcomings of litigation: prohibitive expense, heart-breaking delay, a lack of party participation and control of the process, unsatisfactory outcomes from a party's perspective, and an adversarial orientation that makes parties enemies. Mediation can address each of these shortcomings by providing the benefits described here.

a. Settlement: Avoiding the Expense, Delay, Adversarial Dynamic, and Risks of Adjudication; Benefits to Courts

The success mediators have in settling cases in a satisfactory and efficient manner is a key reason that many lawyers advise clients to mediate even though there is always the chance that mediation will not resolve the situation. Compared to the risky undertaking of adjudication—whether litigation or arbitration—mediation offers parties the possibility of an acceptable conclusion that they have crafted and endorsed themselves. In litigation, a judge or jury decides the matter, checked only by the appeal process. In binding arbitration, an individual decision maker (or a panel of decision makers), chosen by the parties, renders a final decision. Whenever a party gives another person the power to decide a controversy, the outcome is inherently unpredictable and may produce an unhappy surprise.

The benefits of speedy closure to conflict are financial, practical, and psychological. Litigation tends to be slow and expensive. Centuries ago William Shakespeare's Hamlet complained about "the law's delay." The parties in Jarndyce v. Jarndyce grew old before the litigation whimpered to an end. In Jarndyce v. Jarndyce any settlement—before the estate was exhausted—would have provided greater benefit to the parties (viewed as a group) than the failed litigation. While the procedural aspect of the arbitration process, created by the parties in their agreement to arbitrate, can be fast, arbitration can also be crafted to resemble litigation, in which case it too becomes slow and costly. Many disputes need prompt address. At least one side will want to resolve a patent dispute before the patent expires or someone begins to profit from abusing someone else's intellectual property. A benefit to resolving an allegation of discrimination in the workplace through prompt mediation is that it may prevent the employee from becoming embittered and infecting others in the office, or before a similar act of discrimination occurs. Solutions different from those courts can order, such as transfer to another job in the same company, can solve the problem without the need to adjudicate the legal claim. Businesses embroiled in conflict are diverted from the pursuit of business goals. A mediation can be scheduled quickly, and sessions can take as little as a few hours or one to two days to complete, preserving time, profit, and ongoing relationships.

Mediation can temper unrealistic positions, unwarranted assumptions, and demonization of another party. Overblown and overconfident views of a case and the dynamics of adversarial behavior can box parties into unproductive assertions and claims. Face-to-face interaction between the parties can allow each side to hear the presentation of one another and to consider the other's perspectives.

> Justice delayed is justice denied.
>
> —Attributed to William E. Gladstone

Finally, settlement benefits the court system. While there is no consensus among scholars or administrators regarding the ability of alternative dispute resolution processes to relieve court dockets, in offering a variety of methods to resolve disputes, courts can serve the various interests of disputing parties and may unclog their dockets as well.

b. Participation and Self-Determination: Giving Parties Voice and Choice

A central value of mediation is self-determination by the parties. Self-determination, in this context, means that parties retain control over both their participation in the process of dispute resolution and the outcome of their dispute.

Parties in adjudicative processes must fit their story within the narrow frame of a legal "cause of action" or an allowable arbitral claim, confine themselves to evidence that the decision maker will consider probative and persuasive, and give control over both process and outcome to a judge, jury, or arbiter. Because of these constraints, parties often do not feel they have had a chance to express themselves and be heard. In Jarndyce v. Jarndyce, both parties and lawyers were confused about the legal case, and no one seemed capable of controlling the delay (which exceeded the lives of many of the disputants) or the costs (which exceeded the assets being contested). A fundamental lack of control—or self-determination—can be the price of obtaining a third-party decision. Similarly, remedies in adjudicative processes are those prescribed by the forum, rather than remedies tailored for and by parties.

Mediators, at least ideally, promote party empowerment and self-determination by carving out space and time for each side to tell their story and be heard in a meaningful way. This feature alone can be important to clients. Mediators also seek party involvement in crafting proposals that are responsive to each side's needs. Participation in finding and power in choosing the solution means the parties are invested in the outcome, and hence the resolution is more durable when the parties have been properly involved. Apologies and other amends, and benefits that will "satisfy the heart," can be both more valuable and less costly than outcomes dictated by third parties.

If only the family in *Bleak House* had talked through their perspectives and explored what they could do for one another, the family members may have found some satisfactory resolution to their differences that would have benefited someone other than the attorneys.

c. Better Outcomes: Generating Creative Problem Solving

Many proponents of mediation emphasize its ability to engage participants in a forward-looking exercise of developing options and optimal outcomes. Many mediators try to get parties out of an adversarial contest and into the exercise of creating a better future. Custom-tailored outcomes, developed to maximize benefits for all sides, can create more value for parties than the standardized remedies provided in adjudicative forums. Agreements can be finely calibrated to balance out equities arising from past (mis)conduct and thus be reparative from a justice perspective. At the same time, the outcome must be better than the litigation (or other) alternatives of each party, since either party can "veto" the agreement (of course, this assumes that the parties are adequately informed and not strong-armed into settlement). Such "quality" solutions will likely be perceived as fairer by the parties. From a societal perspective, community value flows from maximizing individual benefit and from reducing the disaffection costs of conflict, such as poor health, social friction, and aggression.

Mediation can produce outcomes that litigation or arbitration cannot. For example, in commercial settings, compensatory damages can be replaced by profitable deals that take into account past wrongs. Agreements to communicate in a certain way, to write letters of reference, or to refrain from contact or conduct can be valuable. Apologies can allow parties to "let go" and move on with their lives. Such results are not generally part of the remedies available to an arbitrator or judge.

Additionally, party-crafted and voluntary agreements that are responsive to the interests and values parties articulate are more durable than judgments that the "losing" party may find unfair and attempt to avoid by using an appeals process or simply making it difficult to collect the judgment. Parties in mediation can also create procedures for resolving whatever new conflicts they might have and for resolving issues that can occur when interpretations differ on what agreements mean.

No efforts to find a creative and consensual outcome were made in Jarndyce v. Jarndyce. An infinite array of possibilities might have worked in that case had mediation been tried. Unfortunately, as the estate in Jarndyce v. Jarndyce shrank because of the litigation, so did the set of possible beneficial outcomes.

d. *Relationship, Community, and Harmony: Building Bridges Between People*

Many societies see conflict as a potential threat to the social fabric. These cultures value processes that rebuild connection between parties and bring both individual well-being and community harmony. Navajo peace-making tribunals and mediation in China and Japan are examples. Any process such as mediation that allows parties to recognize each other's perspectives and interests—even when these parties are strangers to each other—has a significant value in a world where strife and conflict threaten to tear families, communities, and nations apart. Society's interest in promoting healing relationships is measured, in part, by the costs of disaffection evident in depression, crime, productivity loss, and, ultimately, war.

> **A Contempt for His Own Kind**
>
> The receiver in the cause has acquired a goodly sum of money by it, but has acquired too a distrust of his own mother, and a contempt for his own kind.
>
> —Charles Dickens, Bleak House

The benefit of using mediation radiates beyond a single dispute to the larger system. In the context of a family, school, agency, workplace, or industry, mediation is used not only to resolve specific disputes, but also to promote understanding and collaboration, for example, among parents and children, students from different ethnic groups, supervisors and employees, or customers and suppliers. As parties sit down and listen to each other, stereotypes can be shattered and more responsible, responsive, and profitable citizens, communities, and governments can emerge.

Problem 6-1. ***The Relation Between Case Type and Process***

Are the benefits discussed above relevant to all case types? For example, are relationship and community as important in a construction case as they might be in a probate matter? Can you make an argument that all these advantages might be useful aspirations in a variety of case types?

Problem 6-2. ***It's All About Money!***

In the context of civil litigation, some commentators believe that disputes are "all about money." Do you agree? Do you think that lawyers and their clients might have a different perspective on this question? See Tamara Relis, Perceptions in Litigation and Mediation: Lawyers, Defendants, Plaintiffs and Gendered Parties (2009); Hal Abramson, Birgit Sambeth Glasner, Bill Marsh, Bennett G. Picker, & Jerry Weiss, Are Legal Disputes Just About Money? Answers from Mediators on the Front Line, 19 Cardozo J. Conflict Resol. 1 (2017).

4. The History of the U.S. Mediation Movement

a. Roots

The resolution of conflict by both adversarial contest and peace-making activities has ancient origins. History chronicles parallel movements of, as well as tension between, justice as embodied in the imposition of law backed by force, and justice inherent in voluntary agreement and reconciliation. Various religious groups have long traditions of mediation, from Jewish rabbinical courts to mediative mechanisms used by Puritan, Quaker, Muslim, and other religious groups.

Professor David Luban describes an early reported settlement of a case that could have become an adversarial contest among the gods:

> The first trial in Greek literature occurs in the Homeric *Hymn to Hermes.* The infant Hermes, on the night of his birth, steals the cattle of Apollo, who eventually tracks him down. Hermes in the meantime has climbed back into his crib and donned his swaddling clothes. He indignantly denies the deed and swears mighty oaths of innocence: "I will swear the great oath on my father's head. I vow that I myself am not the culprit and that I have seen no one else stealing your cows—whatever these cows are." . . . Apollo takes Hermes before Zeus for judgment. Zeus is more amused than angered at Hermes' prodigious theft; he commands the two gods "to come to an accord and search for the cattle." Hermes shows Apollo where he has hidden them, then he placates Apollo with the gift of a splendid tortoise shell lyre, together with the secret of playing it. The delighted Apollo reciprocates by granting Hermes "a beautiful staff of wealth and prosperity"; and the two gods become eternal allies. This delightful comic poem inaugurates a theme of profound

> importance. It is noteworthy that Zeus is concerned above all with harmony and friendship among the Olympians, and not with punishment for Hermes' crime or for his violation of a sacred oath. The dispute between Apollo and Hermes is resolved by an amicable settlement and not a judgment.[1]

Mediation is not a new approach to dispute resolution. What follows is an examination of some recent developments in the United States.

b. Labor

Formal institutionalization of mediation in the United States first occurred in the labor field. The U.S. Department of Labor created a panel in 1913 to handle labor-management conflicts. In 1947, this panel evolved into the Federal Mediation and Conciliation Service, which was charged with maintaining stability in industries through mediation.

Two types of mediation characterize labor and employment disputes: collective bargaining mediation, and the mediation of individual employee grievances. In collective bargaining mediation, where the terms and conditions of employment are negotiated, participants are generally experienced professionals representing large constituencies. Mediators often have knowledge about workplace issues and special bargaining dynamics. Where mediators help to address individual employee grievances—including claims of discrimination—the parties describe the issues that have affected them personally. The discussion can be therapeutic insofar as parties feel heard, and indirectly the workplace may be improved by individuals getting responsive treatment to their concerns or reparations for their injuries.

c. Community

The Civil Rights Act of 1964 created the Community Relations Service (CRS) of the U.S. Department of Justice to help resolve disputes involving discrimination through negotiation and mediation, and to restore disrupted racial and ethnic harmony. The CRS has intervened in a variety of controversies, including disruptions around desegregation orders, marches of the Ku Klux Klan, and tensions resulting from a lack of cultural awareness of, for example, Arab and Muslim cultural and religious practices. Today, mediation programs in state and federal agencies still respond to disputes concerning discrimination.

Neighborhood justice centers (also called community dispute resolution centers), where volunteer mediators intervene in community cases or "minor disputes," have been funded by state and federal budgets since the 1960s. Community centers receive case referrals both from the courts and from other agencies and institutions, as well as serving "walk-in" clients. These centers typically address disputes between landlords and tenants, neighbors, family members, persons involved in love triangle or workplace situations, and a variety of other

1. David Luban, Some Greek Trials: Order and Justice in Homer, Hesiod, Aeschylus and Plato, 54 Tenn. L. Rev. 279, 280 (1987).

matters. Developed to be responsive to disputes that the litigation system could not handle effectively, community mediation centers have thrived on the simple premise that parties can solve their problems with the help of trained interveners and, in so doing, achieve better outcomes and alleviate the tensions that conflict engenders in communities.

d. Family

One of the major growth areas for mediation has been in family disputes. The acrimony and expense surrounding divorce and the breakup of families has had such an adverse impact on parents, children, extended families, and society generally that courts, clients, and practitioners have sought "a better way" than litigation. Many states now mandate mediation in cases involving child custody and visitation before litigation is permitted. Some courts mandate or encourage mediation of property and partner support issues, sometime separately and sometimes in conjunction with custody issues. Private practitioners, as well as court programs, provide mediation services to families. Success in divorce mediation has encouraged the development of mediation programs in other family situations, such as probate disputes and mediation between parents and children in PINS (persons in need of supervision) proceedings.

Family mediators come to the field from a variety of backgrounds, including psychology, mental health, social work, as well as law. It is not uncommon for co-mediation teams to work with divorcing parties. One mediator may be expert in psychology and the other in law and financial issues. Such teams are often gender-balanced as well.

e. Civil Cases

In 1976 many eminent jurists and scholars gathered at the Pound Conference on the Causes of Popular Dissatisfaction with the Administration of Justice. As Chapter 1 explores in more detail, at the conference, Professor Frank Sander described a different vision of a justice system in which courts "have many doors," some leading to litigation and others leading to alternative processes. Many legal scholars trace the modern U.S. alternative dispute resolution (ADR) movement to this event.

A "litigation boom" in the late 1970s and 1980s spurred on overloaded judges to find ways to reduce court dockets. By 1988, Florida authorized civil trial court judges to refer almost any civil case to mediation. Other state and federal courts followed suit, and today mediation is a predictable step in the pre-litigation process in many venues.

f. Online Mediation

Online mediation has increased dramatically as both the number of online transactions grows and the technology continues to improve. Vendors like eBay regularly use online dispute resolution mechanisms, including mediation, to resolve their disputes. Such online platforms will likely continue to expand. In addition, traditional mediators now also use technology, such as online video, to bring parties who are at too great a distance from the mediation site into the room.

The era of COVID, which curtailed in-person meetings and travel, saw the rapid expansion of mediation by Zoom and other virtual meeting rooms technology. The convenience and comfort of virtual mediations has led to many mediators continuing a practice of remote mediation even beyond the necessity for it. In that case, the mediator may need to guide parties on how to use the technology, if necessary.

g. Other Arenas

It is hard to find an area where mediation is not used for resolving disputes. Mediation is an important resolution tool today in organizations, schools, government agencies, the criminal and civil justice system, and for environmental, construction, police-civilian, international, and intellectual property disputes.

In business matters, the International Institute for **C**onflict **P**revention and **R**esolution (CPR) has obtained commitments from many Fortune 500 companies to use mediation and other ADR processes rather than (or at least before) litigation. Mediation, with its forward-looking aspect, appeals to businesspeople who want to avoid the costs and risks of litigation.

5. Mediation's Core Values

The following two excerpts capture critical features of the essence and origins of mediation. Note how mediation does not lend itself to a simple description.

❖ *Carrie Menkel-Meadow*, INTRODUCTION

in Mediation: Theory, Practice and Policy xiii-xiv, xvi-xvii, xxix (2000)

Mediation is both a legal process and more than a legal process, used for thousands of years by all sorts of communities, families and formal governmental units. . . . [It] has become a sort of aspirational ideology for those who see its promise in promoting more productive ways of expressing and dealing with human conflict. . . . Mediation, in this larger sense, represents a political theory about the role of conflict in society, the importance of equality, participation, self-determination and a form of leaderless leadership in problem-solving and decision-making. Mediation, as a theory, is aspirational and utopian. In its most grandiose forms, mediation theorists and proponents expect mediation, as a process, to achieve the transformation of warring nation-states, differing ethnic groups, diverse communities, and disputatious workplaces, families and individuals and to develop new and creative human solutions to otherwise difficult or intractable problems. For some, it is a process for achieving interpersonal, intrapersonal and intrapsychic knowledge and understanding. . . .

Mediation, as a structured form of conflict resolution, challenges the Anglo-American idea of adversarial dispute resolution, which presumes that two sides must argue their case to a third-party neutral who will make rule-based, often binary, decisions about who is right and wrong. Instead, it offers the possibility of party-crafted solutions to problems, disputes, conflicts, transactions and relationships, which are facilitated by a third party with no authority to decide anything or to impose any rules. . . .

The forms that mediation takes are themselves subject to debate. While most definitions of mediation conclude that a third-party *neutral* should facilitate the negotiation among parties, many mediation processes—historically and with cultural variations—in fact involve a third party who is quite enmeshed in the community as a "wise elder" or, in more recent times, as a substantive expert who may promise *impartiality* to the parties but who may know quite a bit about the disputants or the subject matter of the dispute. Mediation's forms, then, are variable across cultures, times and different political systems. . . . To the extent that mediation privileges certain forms of communication ("talking cures") its use and its forms may be varied in different settings by culture, nationality, ethnicity, gender, race and class. . . . As anthropologists and other scholars have discovered, there is no cultural uniformity to the practice or form of mediation, and different social groupings and political configurations may re-form or deform the mediation mode to respond to their particular interests. Some have suggested that mediation, with its focus on words, communications and interpersonal competence, may be ethnocentrically based in cultures that privilege such forms of problem-solving. . .

THE FUTURE HOPE AND PROMISE OF MEDIATION

Theorists and practitioners of mediation claim a central core of functions for mediation:

1. that it is a consensual process, both in participation and in agreements reached;
2. that it is, at its core, voluntarily engaged in (subject to recent efforts to mandate mediation in some contractual or court settings);
3. that it is participatory by the principals engaged in whatever problem or issue is presented at the mediation (who may have representatives who appear as well);
4. that it is "facilitated" by a third party "outside" the immediate dispute or conflict (the "neutrality" principle reframed to reflect some of the recent developments in use of expert facilitators);
5. that it seeks to develop solutions to problems or resolutions of conflicts or disputes on terms of mutual agreement and fairness to the parties;
6. that it seeks to facilitate mutual understanding and apprehension of the other parties' needs, interests and situations.

These core functions are located within an ideology or belief system, held by most theorists and practitioners of mediation, that such a process will reduce unnecessary conflict or acrimony among and between people in conflict, will lead to increased learning and knowledge about others and, where possible, will facilitate the creation of mutually satisfactory solutions to problems or resolutions of conflict that are better than what the parties might have achieved in other fora.

Problem 6-3. ***Was King Solomon a Mediator or Arbitrator?***

Many people know the story about King Solomon and the two mothers—two women claiming they were the mother of the same child. King Solomon offers to settle the dispute by cutting the baby in two with his sword, each woman receiving half. When he lifts his sword to do so, one of the women cries out "No, don't cut the baby—give it to her" (the other woman). "Ah," says King Solomon, "then you must be the real mother for you do not want harm to come to the child." If you see this as a clever way for an arbiter to get evidence, what might a mediator have done?

The excerpt that follows also analyzes the central values of mediation. Lon Fuller focuses on how mediation builds a different relationship among parties and hence affects the resolution of future controversies—emphasizing the more expansive potential of mediation beyond settlement of specific controversies.

❖ *Lon L. Fuller,* MEDIATION—ITS FORMS AND FUNCTIONS

44 S. Cal. L. Rev. 305, 307-309, 325-327 (1971)

Casual treatments of the subject in the literature of sociology tend to assume that the object of mediation is to make the parties aware of the "social norms" applicable to their relationship and to persuade them to accommodate themselves to the "structure" imposed by these norms. From this point of view the difference between a judge and a mediator is simply that the judge orders the parties to conform themselves to the rules, while the mediator persuades them to do so. But mediation is commonly directed, not toward achieving conformity to norms, but toward the creation of the relevant norms themselves. This is true, for example, in the very common case where the mediator assists the parties in working out the terms of a contract defining their rights and duties toward one another. In such a case there is no pre-existing structure that can guide mediation; it is the mediational process that produces the structure.

It may be suggested that mediation is always, in any event, directed toward bringing about a more harmonious relationship between the parties, whether this be achieved through explicit agreement, through a reciprocal acceptance of the "social norms" relevant to their relationship, or simply because the parties have been helped to a new and more perceptive understanding of one another's problems. . . .

But at this point we encounter the inconvenient fact that mediation can be directed, not toward cementing a relationship, but toward terminating it . . . [O]ne of the most dramatically successful uses of mediation I ever witnessed involved a case in which an astute mediator helped the parties rescind a business contract. Two corporations were entrapped by a long-term supply contract that had become burdensome and disadvantageous to both. Canceling it, however, was a complicated matter, requiring a period of "phasing out" and various financial adjustments back and forth. For some time the parties had been chiefly engaged in reciprocal threats of a lawsuit. On the advice of an attorney for one of the parties, a mediator (whose previous experience had been almost entirely in the field of labor relations) was brought in. Within no time at all a severance of relations was accomplished and the two firms parted company happily.

Thus we find that mediation may be directed toward, and result in, discrepant and even diametrically opposed results. This circumstance argues against our being able to derive any general structure of the mediational process from some identifiable goal shared by all mediational efforts. We may, of course, indulge in observations to the effect that the mere presence of a third person tends to put the parties on their good behavior, that the mediator can direct their verbal exchanges away from recrimination and toward the issues that need to be faced, that by receiving separate and confidential communication from the parties he can gradually bring into the open issues so deep-cutting that the parties themselves had shared a tacit taboo against any discussion of them and that, finally, he can by his management of the interchange demonstrate to the parties that it is possible to discuss divisive issues without either rancor or evasion. . . . [This] analysis . . . has dealt only inferentially and indirectly with what may be said to be the central quality of mediation, namely, its capacity to reorient the parties toward each other, not by imposing rules on them, but by helping them to achieve a new and shared perception of their relationship, a perception that will redirect their attitudes and dispositions toward one another.

This quality of mediation becomes most visible when the proper function of the mediator turns out to be, not that of inducing the parties to accept formal rules for the governance of their future relations, but that of helping them to free themselves from the encumbrance of rules and of accepting, instead, a relationship of mutual respect, trust and understanding that will enable them to meet shared contingencies without the aid of formal prescriptions laid down in advance. Such a mediational effort might well come into play in any of the various forms of mediation between husband and wife associated with "family counseling" and "marriage therapy." In the task of reestablishing the marriage as a going concern the mediator might find it essential to break up formalized conceptions of "duty" and to substitute a more fluid sense of mutual trust and shared responsibility. In effect, instead of working toward achieving a rule-oriented relationship he might devote his efforts, to some degree at least, in exactly the opposite direction.

. . . The negotiation of an elaborate written contract, such as that embodied in a collective bargaining agreement between an employer and a labor union, does indeed present a special set of problems for the mediator. . . . [I]t should be remembered that the primary function of the mediator in the collective bargaining situation is not to propose rules to the parties and to secure their acceptance of them, but to induce the mutual trust and understanding that will enable the parties to work out their own rules. The creation of rules is a process that cannot itself be rule-bound; it must be guided by a sense of shared responsibility and a realization that the adversary aspects of the operation are part of a larger collaborative undertaking. The primary task of the arbitrator [sic] is to induce this attitude of mind and spirit, though to be sure, he does this primarily by helping the parties to perceive the concrete ways in which this shared attitude can redound to their mutual benefit.

It should also be noted that the benefits of a collective bargaining agreement do not lie simply in the aptness of the numbered paragraphs that appear over the parties' signatures, but derive also from the mutual understanding produced by the process of negotiation itself. I once heard an experienced and perceptive lawyer observe, speaking of complex business agreements, "If you negotiate the contract thoroughly, explore carefully the problems that can arise in the course of its administration, work out the proper language to cover the various contingencies that may develop, you can then put the contract in a drawer and forget it." What he meant was that in the exchange that accompanied the negotiation and drafting of the contract the parties would come to understand each other's problems sufficiently so that when difficulties arose they would, as fair and reasonable men, be able to make the appropriate adjustments without referring to the contract itself.

Problem 6-4. ***The Relation Between Values and Approach***

As you consider the story of Zeus's intervention in the dispute between Hermes and Apollo, what values were served by the approach Zeus took? What arguments could you make that judgment and punishment of Hermes would be a more prudent approach?

Problem 6-5. ***Providing a Fish or Making Fishermen***

After studying Fuller's excerpt, what are the prime benefits of mediation? Is it more important that the process settle a given dispute—or that it realign relationships so that parties can resolve disputes themselves, without the need for outside intervention?

Problem 6-6. *The Effect of Means on Ends*

In light of the benefits that Fuller articulates, consider some case you have studied or participated in. In what ways might mediation have served the parties differently than litigation?

6. Mediation's Place in the Justice System

Although mediation may be an excellent dispute resolution process for many disputes, it is just one among an array of processes that complement each other and serve different goals. The following excerpts illuminate how mediation fits into the landscape of major processes comprising our justice system. In the first, an idealized, simplified description of litigation, arbitration, and mediation illustrate how each of these processes has a legitimate claim to justice delivery. The second article delineates various rationales a court might consider when including a mediation component, and explores the contrasting purposes of litigation and mediation.

❖ *Lela P. Love*, IMAGES OF JUSTICE

1 Pepp. Disp. Resol. L.J. 29, 29-32 (2000)

. . . In an effort to capture the vision behind the three major dispute resolution processes, this essay will present an image of a judge, an arbiter and a mediator. . . .

LITIGATION

Standing straight and tall in public places, a blindfolded woman holds up scales. Since she is blindfolded, she cannot be swayed by gender, race, wealth, or other influences or advantages that one party might hold. On her scales, disputing parties rest their case: the best they can muster for themselves and the worst they can present about the other side. The matter is weighed on these scales in public view, and the balance resolves the matter.

The scales themselves get more precisely balanced after each weighing, after each case. The weight and moment of precise and particular factors are calibrated, and the blindfolded lady announces how much factors weigh, this time, and for all time.

Should a party suspect that the scales were out of balance or the blindfold had been lifted, he may appeal to higher authorities to test the integrity of the process.

This lady is accessible to all, rich and poor alike. . . . And if one party invokes her aid, the other must answer and counterweight the scale, or risk an unfavorable verdict. He must also risk the power behind this blindfolded figure—the power of the state to take and give property and liberty. . . .

ARBITRATION

Wise, sophisticated, trusted, and honored in his community, the arbitrator is chosen by the parties who can agree that whatever such a person decides is just. The arbitrator does not wear blindfolds because the parties trust his discretion. On the other hand, the arbitrator cannot meet privately with a party, because the parties do not trust each other.

The arbitrator stands, aloof from the parties, arms folded in skepticism, but listening attentively for each clue which will piece together the puzzle of facts he must see clearly.

The gift the arbitrator gives the parties is a prompt decision informed by his expertise in the particular arena. His decision is bound to favor one party over the other, but his quick and precise award will allow the parties to move on with their lives and their businesses.

There is no appeal from this arbitrator because, in choosing him, the parties chose to live with what he decides. Thus, the power of the arbitrator is immense, once conferred by the parties, and is further bolstered by the blindfolded lady who will ensure that his awards are honored. . . .

MEDIATION

In this image one sees a figure sitting with the parties, her hands reaching towards each of them as if to support them in telling their tale or to caution them in listening to each other to weigh the matter more carefully. It is also possible that her outreached hands are pointing to the parties to remind them of their responsibility for dealing thoughtfully with their situation and each other, understanding the opportunities and risks inherent in various choices, and summoning their creativity in addressing the conflict.

The figure is not alone or aloof. Her outstretched arms form a bridge between the parties, so that communication and positive energy can flow again. Her presence is a catalyst setting in motion the potential that the parties hold.

Unlike the blindfolded lady, the mediator sees all that is offered unprotected by formal procedure or rules of evidence. Unlike the arbitrator or the judge, the mediator may meet with the parties together or listen to them privately so that each nuance of meaning and each atom of possibility are captured and offered back, in their most palatable form, for the parties.

The mediator's features are hazy, since the focus and light remains on the disputing parties. Her presence, however, exudes optimism, respect, and confidence in the parties' capacity. She brings an energetic and urgent sense that justice can be done by the parties' own hands.

In the following excerpt, Professor Robert Baruch Bush explores the underlining rationale for litigation and mediation and examines whether and how mediation should become part of court-sponsored dispute resolution.

Robert A. Baruch Bush, MEDIATION AND ADJUDICATION, DISPUTE RESOLUTION AND IDEOLOGY: AN IMAGINARY CONVERSATION

3 J. Contemp. Legal Issues 1, 1-6, 12 (1990)

. . . The setting for the conversation is as follows. A judge has been empowered by a state statute to refer cases from his civil docket to mediation. The statute says that he can, in his discretion, refer any and all cases; the decision is his, and the parties cannot refuse mediation without showing good cause. The judge can send all his cases to mediation on a blanket basis, or certain categories of cases, or individual cases on a case by case basis, whichever he decides. This is what the statute empowers him to do, and the Supreme Court has set up rules enabling him and other judges to do it. The problem is that the judge is uncertain how to exercise this new power. He has no clear idea which cases, if any, he should refer to the mediation process.

So, he picks six representative cases from his civil docket: a divorce case with a custody question, a complex commercial litigation, a landlord-tenant case, a discrimination suit, a consumer case, and a personal injury litigation. He sends copies of the case files, with names deleted, to four individuals who are friends or associates: his law clerk, his court administrator, his former law professor, and a practicing mediator who is a friend of his. The judge asks each of them for their advice. Should he send any of these cases to mediation? All of them? None of them? What should he do?

He is a bit startled when he gets back the results of this survey, because he gets four completely different recommendations. From the law professor, he gets the recommendation that he should send no cases to mediation; all the cases should stay in court. The law clerk gives him a more complex recommendation. He says that the discrimination case, the consumer case, and the personal injury case should be kept in court, but the divorce, the landlord-tenant, and the commercial cases should go to mediation. The court administrator says he should send them all to mediation, unless both parties to the dispute object; if both parties object, he shouldn't refer them to mediation, whatever the type of case. Finally, the mediator tells him that he should send all the cases to mediation, whether or not the parties object.

The judge is puzzled by this set of responses [and] . . . does what judges are very good at doing. He calls all four advisors and says, "I'd like you to argue this out in front of me. I want to hear what you have to say in the presence of one another. That way you can present the reasons for your recommendations, and I can hear some kind of response from you towards one another."

So, the four advisors come together with the judge in an informal meeting over lunch. The court administrator goes first. "Judge," she begins, "I'll tell you the reason for my recommendation. As far as I'm concerned, the most important goal we have here is saving time and money. That's the main goal that we want to keep in mind in using your powers under this new mediation statute. I suspect that was the legislature's main reason for enacting this law. The courts are heavily backlogged, delay is epidemic, and adding new judges and courtrooms appears fiscally—and politically—impossible. Settlements are the only solution. Settling cases is going to save public and private expense. It's also going to increase public satisfaction with the system. Now, since all cases have some potential to settle," she continues, "and we don't know which ones will and which ones won't, it makes sense to refer them all to mediation, unless we have a clear indication in advance that there's no real settlement possibility. For example, if both parties show a clear desire not to go to mediation, not to negotiate, then in that case it makes no sense to waste the time." She concludes, "That is the reason for my recommendation. Refer to mediation, unless it's clear that there's opposition on both sides to settlement."

The law clerk then is called upon. He says, "Judge, as you know, I disagree, and the reason for my recommendation is the following. In my view, the main goal is not saving time and money, regardless of what the legislature may have had in mind. There are other goals of dispute resolution that are much more important.

"Generally, it, seems to me," the law clerk continues, "protecting individual rights and ensuring some kind of substantive fairness to both sides in the resolution of the dispute are the most important goals. And when rights and substantive fairness are most important, adjudication in court is the best tool we have to accomplish those goals. However, there are cases, where rights and fairness are not the only or the most important goals. For example, if there is an ongoing relationship between the parties, preserving that relationship may be very important both to the parties and to the public. In that case, mediation would be desirable, because preserving relationships is something that mediation does much better than the adjudication process. Therefore, I think that you can distinguish between cases on the basis of the ongoing relationship factor. When you have such a relationship, refer to mediation; otherwise, keep the case in court. That's the way I've split up the cases you sent us. I'm not sure that it's immediately obvious from the way I've divided them, but that was my criterion, and I think it's the best one for you to use."

Next it is the mediator's turn. "I both agree and disagree with the administrator and the law clerk, your Honor," she explains. "Saving time and money must be considered important, and preserving relationships, in certain cases, is also a very important goal. But both of these are really just part of a more general goal that I consider the most important aim of dispute resolution: that is, to reach the best possible substantive result or solution to the parties' problem. Sometimes the best solution will be one that saves the parties time and money; sometimes it will be one that preserves the relationship. Sometimes it will be one that does neither of these. That will depend on many details of the case."

"But whatever the details, there is plenty of evidence now that, in terms of achieving the best results for the individual case in question, mediation is a process that has tremendous advantages over adjudication. The process is flexible, issues can be framed more effectively and discussed more fully, a greater variety of possible solutions can be considered, and unique, innovative and integrative solutions are possible, even likely. Therefore, mediation ought to be tried first in all cases because the potential to arrive at superior substantive results is always greater in mediation than in adjudication. If mediation doesn't work, if there's no resolution, then the parties can go back to court. But, in the first instance, achieving superior results is the most important goal to strive for in every single case. And mediation is the best vehicle we have for doing this. That's why I recommended referring all your cases to mediation, without exceptions."

Finally the law professor speaks. "Your Honor," he begins, "I'm sorry to have to disagree. But all of your other friends here have missed the point. I say this because they're all talking about goals that don't really pertain to your function, the function of a court. A court is a public institution, and the goal of a court as a public institution is not to save time and money; nor is it to help private parties secure private benefits in individual cases. Your goal as a public institution is to promote important public values. That ought to be your primary concern: the promotion and the securing of important public values through the dispute resolution process. That is what distinguishes your function from that of a mere private arbitrator, and justifies the public support—legal and fiscal—given uniquely to the courts."

"I submit to you, your Honor, that the most important public values at stake in dispute resolution are basically four. There may be others; but I think that these four have widely been recognized as the most important ones. First is the protection of the fundamental civil rights of the parties as individuals. Second is the pursuit of substantive or social justice, as between different classes represented by the parties in the case, and especially as between rich and poor, strong and weak, haves and have-nots. Third is the promotion of what the economists call efficiency—that is, the greatest possible level of aggregate societal welfare—through encouragement of activities that make the best use of our limited societal resources. And fourth is the establishment and articulation of public values that give us a sense of social solidarity in our society as a whole, which is of course a very pluralistic one and therefore requires the cement of shared values. . . ."

"Your Honor," the professor continues, "adjudication serves every one of these values. It does so because it operates by using and generating both procedural and substantive rules—using them in the instant case, and generating them for future cases. Indeed the rules themselves are often related to and based upon these values. Substantive rules promote economic welfare by signaling economic actors how to use resources efficiently. Substantive and procedural rules promote social justice by reducing the advantage of the powerful, in the aggregate and in the individual case. Procedural rules protect directly against violations of fundamental civil rights. And substantive rules foster solidarity by giving meaning to shared public values. Therefore, the rule-based, public adjudication process is an excellent—an unparalleled—instrument for accomplishing these values. Mediation, on the other hand, weakens and undermines every single one of these values. Why? Because, simply, it neither uses in the instant case nor generates for the future rules, whether procedural or substantive, based on these values or any other values. Mediation rests solely on the expedient of compromise. Therefore it cannot help but undermine all of these important, rule-dependent values."

"This brings me to the heart of my argument, your Honor," says the professor. "First, we can't sacrifice public values of this stature solely to save time and money. Certainly, we can't do so as a matter of public policy. If, as a matter of necessity, the courts can't handle all cases, that's one thing. But to adopt a public policy saying that values like rights protection and social justice are less important than saving money and judicial economy would be inexcusable. Second, there's no way of neatly dividing up cases on the basis that some involve these public values and others do not. That simply isn't true. All six of the kinds of cases that you submitted to us involve one or more of these public values. Indeed, most of them involve several. The same would be true for any other disputes we might examine." Here the professor went into a lengthy analysis of how this was so, which for the sake of brevity we will not reproduce. "Therefore," he concluded, "'channeling' of different cases to different processes is undesirable."

"Finally, you cannot, as the mediator suggested, consider the value of better results for the parties in the individual case superior to these *public* values. You cannot do so, your Honor, as a matter of public policy. Why not? Because this would be to put private benefit over public values, over the public good, and as a public servant you cannot legitimately do so. . . . Therefore, your Honor, I say all of these cases should remain in court, unless perhaps a petition is submitted by both parties to adjourn pending voluntarily initiated settlement discussions or mediation." . . .

Before the judge has a chance to adjourn and consider arguments more thoroughly, however, the mediator asks the judge for one more minute. "Judge," she says, "I have another point to make. The reason I didn't make it before is that it's a little hard to articulate. But I see I will have to try. The truth is that the concern for better results in individual cases is not all that makes mediation important, in my view, even though I admit that most advocates of mediation emphasize this as the primary advantage of mediation. But there's more involved, and it goes far beyond expediency and private benefit. When I say mediation ought to be used in all these cases, my reason is also based on promoting public values, public values which are important to all of the cases you sent us, public values, different from and more important than the ones that the professor mentioned. In other words, like the professor's argument for adjudication, my argument for mediation is also a public values argument, but it is based on a different view of public values than the view he presented."

"Now, my problem is that it is hard to articulate clearly what these different public values are. I think they're evoked or implied by concepts like reconciliation, social harmony, community, interconnection, relationship, and the like. Mediation does produce superior results, as I argued earlier. But it also involves a non-adversarial process that is less traumatic, more humane, and far more capable of healing and reconciliation than adjudication. Those are the kinds of concerns that make me feel that these cases ought to be handled in mediation, not for private benefit reasons and not for expediency reasons, but because of these reconciliatory public values promoted by mediation. . . ."

"How can I define this public value? Simply put, it is the value of providing a moral and political education for citizens, in responsibility for themselves and respect for others. In a democracy, your honor, that must be considered a crucial public value and it must be considered a public function. As far as I'm concerned, there's the potential for that kind of direct and experiential education in every single one of these cases that you sent to us; and that potential can only be realized in mediation. It cannot be accomplished in adjudication. . . . In my view, this civic education value is more important than the values that the professor is concerned about. . . . Finally, I just want to clarify an important connection between my argument here and our earlier discussion. On reflection, I've realized that the 'superior results' argument that I mentioned at our first meeting is also based, at least in part, on the public value I'm talking about here. That is, many of us place value on the integrative, 'win/win' solutions that mediation helps produce precisely because such solutions embody in concrete terms the kind of respect for others that is the essence of the civic education value. So the 'superiority' of results we speak of is not only, or primarily, that the results better serve the individual interests of the parties—a private benefit—but that they express each individual's considered choice to respect and accommodate the other to some degree—a democratic public value. In short, both the experience of the mediation process and the kind of results it produces serve the public value of civic education in self-determination and respect for others."

Problem 6-7. ***You Be the Judge***

If you were the judge, what would you decide? What would be your rationale for choosing to refer or not refer cases (and certain case types) to mediation? Why were some of the characters more persuasive to you than others?

Problem 6-8. ***Promoting Law or Fostering Relationship***

Returning to the case of Hermes and Apollo, Zeus missed an opportunity to underline and elaborate on the importance of honoring sacred oaths and not stealing. If you were Zeus, does what happened between Hermes and Apollo after your intervention illustrate the values described by Bush's mediator? As you read the case examples that follow, keep asking which of Bush's characters—the law clerk, court administrator, law professor, or mediator—becomes more persuasive.

B. EXAMPLES OF MEDIATIONS

The following accounts of actual mediations illustrate practices and outcomes possible in the mediation of real cases. The first case is an appeal by shareholders against a large corporation, which was mandated into the mediation program of the U.S. Court of Appeals for the Second Circuit. The second case involves a minority group, a town, and a litigation that raised constitutional questions.

These cases provide a window into mediation. The examples illustrate that mediation can address a broader range of issues and achieve outcomes more custom-tailored than litigation, while leading parties to a deeper appreciation of one another's perspective and a higher level of collaboration. As you read about these situations, imagine how the stories would have come out differently if mediation had not been used.

1. Sisters of the Precious Blood and Bristol-Myers

Frank J. Scardilli, SISTERS OF THE PRECIOUS BLOOD v. BRISTOL-MYERS CO.: A SHAREHOLDER-MANAGEMENT DISPUTE

Presentation at a Harvard Faculty Seminar on Negotiation on April 13, 1982

This case was on appeal to the U.S. Court of Appeals for the Second Circuit from a grant of summary judgment in favor of Bristol-Myers Co., defendant-appellee (hereinafter "Bristol") and against the Sisters of the Precious Blood, plaintiff-appellant (hereinafter "Sisters"). The latter, who owned 500 shares of Bristol stock, started a lawsuit against Bristol under the proxy solicitation section of the Securities Exchange Act of 1934 alleging that a shareholder resolution they proposed was defeated because Bristol's stated opposition to the resolution in the proxy materials distributed to the shareholders was based on serious misrepresentations of fact.

The Sisters were concerned that the company's sales practices in the third world of its infant baby formula were contributing to serious illness, malnutrition and death of infants because of the unsanitary conditions often prevailing there. Frequently the formula is mixed with contaminated water, there is no refrigeration and its use discourages breastfeeding which is clearly healthier in most instances than is the formula.

The Sisters' proposed resolution requested that management report to the shareholders the full extent of its marketing practices of the infant formula in the third world to alert other shareholders to what they perceived was irresponsible business behavior. Their lawsuit was aimed at getting the company to come up with a corrected proxy solicitation to be submitted to a special meeting of the shareholders to be called specifically for that purpose rather than await the next annual meeting of shareholders.

The court declined to grant the relief sought by the Sisters. . . .

MEDIATION EFFORTS ON APPEAL

The first of four conferences seeking to mediate this dispute was held on July 19, 1977. . . . Apparently because they believed no amicable resolution was possible, counsel who appeared for the parties were very able but had virtually no settlement authority. . . .

As is customary, I first explored the arguments of counsel relative to the strengths and weaknesses of their legal positions on appeal. The parties seemed genuinely far apart in their assessment of the likely outcome in our court. The issue on appeal involved some complexity because of the rather technical requirements for suits under Section 14 of the Securities Exchange Act of 1934. While generally appellees have a distinct advantage, if for no other reason than that only about one out of eight cases is reversed on appeal in our court, the outcome of this particular case was hard to predict. Even if the district court decision were deemed technically correct, this could have disturbing policy implications because the decision appeared to create a license for management to lie with impunity whenever it sought to defeat a proposed shareholder resolution. . . . The SEC was apparently disturbed by this implication and advised me it was seriously considering filing a brief amicus curiae urging our court to reverse the decision below. . . .

Predictably, the parties' respective positions on what might constitute a satisfactory settlement were far apart. The Sisters were adamant on the principle that no settlement terms could be discussed unless Bristol openly admitted that it had lied in its earlier proxy solicitation and that this fact had to be communicated through new proxy solicitations at a special meeting of the shareholders to be convened solely for that purpose. Bristol, of course, insisted it had been truthful all along. It offered, however, to permit the Sisters to make any written statement they wished at the next annual shareholders' meeting, and Bristol would simply state its opposition to the proposal without elaboration. This was unacceptable to the Sisters. Because it was clear I needed parties with more authority and flexibility, I set up a second conference requiring senior counsel to come in with their clients.

The second conference, held in the middle of August, 1977, was attended by senior counsel for both sides, the inside General Counsel of Bristol, and a representative of the Advisory Committee of the Interfaith Group for Corporate Responsibility, which was the real moving force behind the Sisters' litigation.

It soon became apparent that there was very deep hostility and profound distrust between the parties. Each was convinced the other was acting in bad faith. The Sisters were outraged by Bristol's insistence that it had not lied. Its distrust of Bristol was total and uncompromising. At this conference, the Sisters, for the first time, insisted that they would have to be reimbursed for their litigation expenses of approximately $15,000 before any settlement could be effected. After checking with top management, counsel for management flatly refused to pay anything at all to the Sisters. . . .

It became clear that the respective parties' self-image was significantly at variance with the image each had of the other.

Bristol regarded itself as by far the most responsible marketer of infant formula in the third world, far more so than its three major American competitors and the giant Swiss company Nestle. It claimed it put out a quality nutritional product that was very useful when mothers either could not or chose not to breast feed their infants; that it did not advertise its infant formulas directly to consumers in the third world; that the company policy already sought to minimize the danger of improper use by its labeling. In short, it was convinced that its business practices were both prudent and responsible. Therefore, they were furious that they had been singled out as "baby killers" by the Sisters, who had so testified before a Congressional committee and who had lost few opportunities to criticize them in the media. It was clear they viewed the Sisters as wild-eyed, misguided religious fanatics who were themselves engaging in a distortion of the facts and reckless character assassination.

The Sisters, on the other hand, had spent years accumulating data in affidavits taken throughout the world regarding the enormous peril to infants created by the indiscriminate use of infant formula in the third world. They had witnessed suffering and death and were suffused with the self-righteousness of avenging angels. To them Bristol was a monster who cared only about profits and not at all about the lives and health of infants. . . .

As negotiations proceeded, it became apparent that no meaningful communication could take place until each of the parties realized that its view of the other was a grossly distorted caricature and counter-productive.

I struck often at the theme that it was dangerous to assume that one with whom you disagree violently is necessarily acting in bad faith. Moreover, I stressed to both that I had become fully and firmly convinced that each of the parties was acting in complete good faith, albeit from a different perspective. I strove to get each to view the matter through the eyes of the other. . . .

It was necessary to convince each that its interests were not nearly as incompatible as they perceived them and that the interest of each would be best served by a cooperative problem-solving attitude rather than a litigious one.

I stressed that neither party's true interest would be served by "winning" the appeal. A "win" by Bristol would not be likely to stop the public attacks in the media which so angered and disturbed them. Likewise, a "win" by the Sisters could mean a remand for an expensive trial with no assurance whatever thereafter that Bristol's marketing practices would be altered in any way.

The point was made forcibly to the Sisters that their insistence that Bristol admit that it had lied was totally unrealistic and that progress was impossible so long as they insisted on humiliating the company's management. They were reminded that their real interest lay in effecting marketing changes in the third world and they could best achieve this in a climate of cooperative good will with management. So long as management perceived them as vindictive it was likely to simply dig in its heels and refuse to budge. I urged that a softening of their attitude would in turn create a more flexible attitude in management.

Bristol in turn was forced to concede that, notwithstanding what they viewed as the distasteful stridency of the Sisters, there was indeed a real moral issue to be faced, and they had a real interest in being perceived as highly ethical, responsible businessmen who were not insensitive to the human tragedy which could result from the improper use of their product in the third world. . . .

After considerable negotiation in four face-to-face conferences supplemented by numerous telephone conferences over a period of nearly six months, in the course of which Bristol voluntarily changed some of its marketing practices, the parties finally agreed to resolve their differences as follows:

1. The Sisters were satisfied that Bristol had already changed some of its marketing practices which the Sisters had regarded as particularly offensive.
2. The Sisters would be given direct access to Bristol's Board of Directors and other representatives of the company at various times for the purpose of maintaining a first-hand continuing dialogue on the problems of marketing infant formula in the third world.
3. Bristol and the Sisters would each prepare a separate written statement of its views not to exceed 1500 words to be presented to the shareholders in the next quarterly report of the Company. This would be preceded by an agreed-upon joint preamble which would recite the background of the litigation, its resolution by the parties and that the Sisters and Bristol planned to continue to exchange views in an atmosphere of mutual respect for each other's good faith.

To insure that the statements would not be inflammatory, each side was given the right to veto the statement of the other. Agreeing on the principle, however, was easier than its implementation. Numerous drafts were exchanged and when appropriate I mediated between their respective versions. The final agreement on language was arrived at as a result of a 4.5 hour drafting session involving 8 people sitting around a conference table in the court in the afternoon of Christmas Eve of 1977. In a sense of relief and elation, the Chairperson of the Interfaith Group for Corporate Responsibility stated: "It is fitting and perhaps prophetic that we have finally resolved our differences on how best to protect tender infants on this [Christmas] eve. . . ."

Problem 6-9. ***Private v. Public Benefit?***

It is usually easy to see how a settlement achieves private benefit, as parties do not usually settle unless the settlement is better than the anticipated legal outcome and its related costs. Using this case as an example, is there *public* benefit from private parties settling a case? And, if something is gained for the public, what is lost? How do you think the professor in the imaginary conversation by Professor Baruch Bush above would react to this mediation description? Remember that the professor is concerned about litigation's role in protecting individual rights, promoting social justice for the poor and weak, maximizing aggregate societal welfare, and articulating public norms.

2. Glen Cove

Lela P. Love, GLEN COVE: MEDIATION ACHIEVES WHAT LITIGATION CANNOT

20 Consensus 1, 1-2 (Oct. 1993)

The city of Glen Cove, Long Island, and Central American refugees who sought day labor at a "shaping point" (a locale in the city where employers go to find day workers) experienced a bitter and protracted controversy with no end in sight—despite nearly two years of litigation—when the parties decided to attempt to work out their differences in mediation. Mediation resolved not only the issues which were being litigated, but also many other issues that, although not causes for legal action, were nonetheless extremely important to the individuals and groups involved in the controversy. . . .

BACKGROUND: TENSIONS BUILD

In 1988 tensions began to build between Glen Cove officials and the Central American immigrants (some of whom were undocumented aliens) who congregated in front of Carmen's Deli to find employment. More than 100 men, many from other towns, would gather on a given day to seek odd jobs from landscapers and other contractors.

Local merchants and neighbors expressed concerns about disorderly and noisy behavior at the shaping point, including cat-calling to women, and littering and urinating in public. City officials were also concerned about traffic safety, since employers would stop on a major road to negotiate with and pick up day workers. There also was a sentiment that it was illegal for those who were undocumented to seek employment.

Salvadoran workers, on the other hand, were interested in their survival, since the day labor was their means of livelihood, and a "shaping point" was essential for finding work. Many who gathered were political refugees from El Salvador, to whom a return home might mean a death sentence. There were those who felt that, since the laborers serviced the lawns and country clubs of the wealthy, the effort to remove them from gathering in public was unfair.

In addition to issues about the shaping point itself, the perception among the Hispanic community that the City—particularly the police—were hostile, created problems for both sides: poor channels of communication to cope with the host of problems; and a lack of resources for Central Americans when they were preyed upon by criminal elements in the community (a pressing problem).

ORDINANCES PROPOSED TO DEAL WITH PROBLEM

Tensions heightened in 1989 when the city, in an effort to curb the size of the gatherings, successfully urged the Immigration and Naturalization Service to round up and detain illegal aliens gathering in front of Carmen's Deli. This was followed by the city's proposing first an ordinance making it illegal for groups of five or more persons to assemble publicly to seek employment and later an ordinance which prohibited any "illegal undocumented alien" from soliciting work in a public or private place. These ordinances engendered a strident debate, although neither was adopted. In 1990, the City Council did adopt an ordinance which prohibited standing on a street or highway and soliciting employment from anyone in a motor vehicle and also prohibited occupants of a stopped or parked motor vehicle from hiring or attempting to hire workers.

The Hispanic community and civil libertarians saw the ordinance(s) as specifically targeted against Hispanics, as well as unconstitutional. Several months after the ordinance was adopted, advocacy groups for Central American refugees filed a three million dollar class action suit against Glen Cove, alleging violation of Hispanic persons' First Amendment right of freedom of speech and 14th Amendment right of equal protection.

WHAT MEDIATION ACHIEVED

Two full days of mediation, spaced a week apart to give the parties time to come up with innovative proposals to address the concerns raised the first day, were sufficient to achieve consensus on an outline of an acceptable accord. This agreement was refined over several months and adopted in late 1992, providing for the dismissal of the lawsuit and the enforcement of the terms of the agreement by the federal court.

The significant achievements of the mediation process in this case were:

- The parties recognized their mutual interest in improving communications with each other.
- Greater accessibility to the city soccer field for the Salvadoran community was arranged.
- The City agreed to help find alternative sites for a shaping point (including possible use of Industrial Development Agency funds) or to support alternatives to meet the Hispanic community's employment needs. The Central American Refugee Center (CARECEN) agreed to educate day laborers who congregate in public places about their responsibilities to the community.
- Relations between the police and the Salvadoran community were addressed by CARECEN's agreement to host community meetings giving the police a platform to educate Salvadorans about community interests and concerns and undertaking such education themselves. The police in turn agreed to: cultural awareness training for all city police officers; appointing a liaison to the Salvadoran community who would attend CARECEN-organized community meetings; training two officers in conversational Spanish; taking ability in Spanish into account in hiring officers; adopting a policy barring officers from inquiring about immigration status under certain circumstances; and instituting a written protocol (in consultation with CARECEN) for the police handling of situations where a party does not speak English.

- The Ordinance was amended to a form acceptable to all parties and designed to promote the City's interest in traffic safety without singling out the Salvadoran Community or infringing upon Constitutional rights.

Perhaps most importantly, the mediation created a respectful dialogue between the parties, which should result in an enhanced ability to confront new problems as they arise . . . Alan Levine, the Director of the Hofstra Constitutional Law Clinic, which represented CARECEN, was quoted as saying, "If everyone lives up to their obligations under this agreement, it promises to establish the kinds of relationships between a municipal government and a minority population that one would hope for."

The town of Glen Cove enjoyed improved relations between town officials and the Salvadoran community as a byproduct of the mediation. A shaping point, with toilet facilities provided by the city and a variety of supportive services for day laborers, was ultimately put into place. If mediation can set new precedents with respect to community interaction and constructive problem solving, do those results counterbalance the loss of a legal precedent in a case with important constitutional issues?

Problem 6-10. ***What's at Stake?***

Compare the issues addressed in the litigation and mediation of the Glen Cove case:

LITIGATION	MEDIATION
Constitutionality of the town ordinance	*Constitutionality of the town ordinance*
Discrete incidents of *alleged police misconduct* at the shaping point	*Communication* between town officials and Salvadorans
	Police interactions with non-English-speaking individuals and groups (protocols when language barriers are present, cultural awareness and sensitivity, and opportunities for communication)
	Concerns regarding *public conduct of Salvadorans* ("cat-calling," public urination, blocking entryways)
	Use of the *city soccer field*
	A shaping point for day laborers and employers

Is a case about the legal causes of action it presents or all the concerns the parties have? What public utility derives from addressing the parties' concerns?

In this situation, the plaintiffs' lawyers—prominent civil rights attorneys—had their own agenda regarding creating legal precedent with respect to a constitutional issue. Would it be ethical for lawyers to ignore their clients' concerns in pursuit of such a goal?

C. APPROACHES TO MEDIATION

Mediation takes various forms depending on variables such as culture, context, mediator goals and strategies, and party participation and preferences. This section explores a variety of different approaches that arguably fall within the family group of mediation and examines the need for transparency about approach. As Chapters 7 and 8 will reveal, a lively debate about the proper boundaries of the mediation process itself exists. Also consider that the variety and flexibility of mediator approaches are cited as among the strengths of the mediation process.

1. Narrow or Broad Problem Definition, Evaluative or Facilitative

The various mediator orientations described by Professor Leonard Riskin below on his grid are often-cited descriptors of important differences in mediator orientations.

❖ *Leonard L. Riskin*, MEDIATOR ORIENTATIONS, STRATEGIES AND TECHNIQUES

12 Alternatives 111, 111-113 (1994)

Almost every conversation about "mediation" suffers from ambiguity. People have disparate visions of what mediation is or should be. Yet we lack a comprehensive system for describing these visions. This causes confusion when people try to choose between mediation and another process or grapple with how to train, evaluate, regulate, or select mediators.

I propose a system for classifying mediator orientations. Such a system can help parties select a mediator and deal with the thorny issue of whether the mediator should have subject-matter expertise. The classification system starts with two principal questions: 1. Does the mediator tend to define problems *narrowly* or *broadly*? 2. Does the mediator think she should *evaluate*—make assessments or predictions or proposals for agreements—or *facilitate* the parties' negotiation without evaluating?

The answers reflect the mediator's beliefs about the nature and scope of mediation and her assumptions about the parties' expectations.

PROBLEM DEFINITION

Mediators with a *narrow* focus assume that the parties have come to them for help in solving a technical problem. The parties have defined this problem in advance through the *positions* they have asserted in negotiations or pleadings. Often it involves a question such as, "Who pays how much to whom?" or "Who can use such-and-such property?" As framed, these questions rest on "win-lose" (or "distributive") assumptions. In other words, the participants must divide a limited resource; whatever one gains, the other must lose.

The likely court outcome—along with uncertainty, delay and expense—drives much of the mediation process. Parties, seeking a compromise, will bargain adversarially, emphasizing positions over interests.

A mediator who starts with a *broad* orientation, on the other hand, assumes that the parties can benefit if the mediation goes beyond the narrow issues that normally define legal disputes. Important interests often lie beneath the positions that the participants assert. Accordingly, the mediator should help the participants understand and fulfill those interests—at least if they wish to do so.

THE MEDIATOR'S ROLE

The *evaluative* mediator assumes that the participants want and need the mediator to provide some direction as to the appropriate grounds for settlement—based on law, industry practice or technology. She also assumes that the mediator is qualified to give such direction by virtue of her experience, training and objectivity.

The *facilitative* mediator assumes the parties are intelligent, able to work with their counterparts, and capable of understanding their situations better than either their lawyers or the mediator. So the parties may develop better solutions than any that the mediator might create. For these reasons, the facilitative mediator assumes that his principal mission is to enhance and clarify communications between the parties in order to help them decide what to do.

The facilitative mediator believes it is inappropriate for the mediator to give his opinion, for at least two reasons. First, such opinions might impair the appearance of impartiality and thereby interfere with the mediator's ability to function. Second, the mediator might not know enough—about the details of the case or the relevant law, practices or technology—to give an informed opinion.

Each of the two principal questions—Does the mediator tend toward a narrow or broad focus? and Does the mediator favor an evaluative or facilitative role?—yield responses that fall along a continuum. Thus, a mediator's orientation will be more or less broad and more or less evaluative.

STRATEGIES AND TECHNIQUES OF EACH ORIENTATION

Each *orientation* derives from assumptions or beliefs about the mediator's role and about the appropriate focus of a mediation. A mediator employs *strategies*—plans—to conduct the mediation. And he uses *techniques*—particular moves or behaviors—to effectuate those strategies. Here are selected strategies and techniques that typify each mediation orientation. . . .

The following grid shows the principal techniques associated with each mediator orientation, arranged vertically with the most evaluative at the top and the most facilitative at the bottom. The horizontal axis shows the scope of problems to be addressed, from the narrowest issues to the broadest interests.

EVALUATIVE

	• Urges/pushes parties to accept narrow (position-based) settlement • Develops and proposes narrow (position-based) settlement • Predicts court outcomes • Assesses strengths and weaknesses of legal claims	• Urges/pushes parties to accept broad (interest-based) settlement • Develops and proposes broad (interest-based) settlement • Predicts impact (on interests) of not settling • Probes parties' interests	
NARROW Problem Definition	Litigation Issues Other Distributive Issues	Business (Substantive) Issues Business Interests Personal Interests Societal Interests	**BROAD** Problem Definition
	• Helps parties evaluate proposals • Helps parties develop narrow (position-based) proposals • Asks parties about consequences of not settling • Asks about likely court outcomes • Asks about strengths and weaknesses of legal claims	• Helps parties evaluate proposals • Helps parties develop broad (interest-based) proposals • Helps parties develop options • Helps parties understand issues and interests • Focuses discussion on underlying interests (business, personal, societal)	

FACILITATIVE

While the terminology of the original Riskin grid has been widely used and debated, in a more recent article, Professor Riskin replaces the "facilitative-evaluative" dichotomy with "elicitive-directive."[2] The new terminology has proven less controversial, though Riskin expresses reservations about the static quality of the grid and its oversimplification as an accurate "map" of the mediation process.

2. Leonard L. Riskin, Decisionmaking in Mediation: The New Old Grid and the New New Grid System, 79 Notre Dame L. Rev. 1 (2003).

Problem 6-11. ***Subject-Matter Expertise?***

Imagine you are called on to recommend a mediator for a client. If the client wants the mediator to give evaluative input, would you require that the mediator have subject-matter expertise in lieu of process expertise? Or would you find someone with both? If your client cares about his relationship with his counterpart, how would you strike the balance between process and subject-matter expertise?

2. Facilitative Mediation: Problem-Solving, Understanding-Based, or Transformative

a. Problem-Solving Approach

The problem-solving approach to mediation, most clearly aligned with what has been called facilitative-broad mediation in Riskin's grid above, seeks to assist parties in understanding their interests, the issues, and each other more fully, and to generate options and ultimately solutions or agreements.

b. Understanding-Based Model

The understanding-based model incorporates knowledge of law by inviting lawyers to bring legal perspectives into the mediation while retaining an emphasis on parties working together to find a resolution ideal for them—and doing that using joint sessions only where all parties and their attorneys participate. This use of joint session only is a marked departure from other models that use a caucus (private meetings with fewer than all participants) on either an as-needed or an exclusive basis. In this model, on Riskin's grid, the mediator is facilitative, urging the lawyers to be evaluative, and broad, going where the parties go with the issues to be examined.

Gary Friedman & Jack Himmelstein, CHALLENGING CONFLICT: MEDIATION THROUGH UNDERSTANDING

xxvii, xxviii (2008)

Understanding-based mediation offers people in conflict a way to *work together* to make decisions that resolve their dispute. This non-traditional approach to conflict is based on a simple premise: *The people ultimately in the best position to determine the wisest solution to a dispute are those who created and are living the problem.* They may well need support, and we seek to provide them support in helping them find a productive and constructive way to work together, to understand their conflict and the possibilites for resolving it, and to reach a resolution. . . .

To pursue this path, we work from a base of four interrelated core principles.

- First, we rely heavily on the power of **understanding** rather than the power of coercion or persuasion to drive the process.
- Second, the primary **responsibility** for whether and how the dispute is resolved needs to be with the parties.
- Third, the parties are best served by **working together** and making decisions together.
- Fourth, conflicts are best resolved by **uncovering what lies under** the level at which the parties experience the problem.

Two special features of the understanding-based model flow from its core principles: first, the non-caucus approach, as it is the parties, not the mediator, who should gain the fullest picture of their problem; and second, the invitation to lawyers to participate, so that parties can understand possible legal outcomes and decide themselves what importance to give to the law. In other forms of facilitative mediation, the caucus is a tool that can be used for specific purposes, and, in some cases, is used to the exclusion of joint sessions. In some mediation programs and approaches, lawyers are excluded to make the process less adversarial, and, in others, lawyers become the central participants, speaking for their clients, rather than being present to enhance party understanding as in the Friedman-Himmelstein model.

c. Transformative Model

While problem-solving and understanding-based mediation include creative problem-solving, along with enriched understanding, as a goal of mediation, Robert Baruch Bush and Joseph Folger, in their transformative mediation model, reject problem-solving as a goal of mediation and add party empowerment to that of enhanced understanding between parties. This model of mediation aims not at solving the problem or finding a resolution, but rather at changing the parties amid conflict—making the parties stronger themselves ("empowerment") and more open to an understanding of each other ("recognition"). Since transformative mediation facilitates empowerment and recognition—rather than resolution—it is arguably not on Riskin's Grid at all.

❖ *Robert A. Baruch Bush & Joseph P. Folger*, THE PROMISE OF MEDIATION: THE TRANSFORMATIVE APPROACH TO CONFLICT

45-46, 65-66 (Revised ed. 2005)

. . . The transformative theory of conflict starts by offering its own answer to the foundational question of what conflict means to the people involved. According to transformative theory, what people find most significant about conflict is not that it frustrates their satisfaction of some right, interest, or pursuit, no matter how important, but that it leads and even forces them to behave toward themselves and others in ways that they find uncomfortable and even repellent. More specifically, it alienates them from their sense of their own strength and their sense of connection to others, thereby disrupting and undermining the interaction between them as human beings. This crisis of deterioration in human interaction is what parties find most affecting, significant—and disturbing—about the experience of conflict.

. . . [I]n the transformative model [m]ediation is defined as a process in which a third party works with parties in conflict to help them change the quality of their conflict interaction from negative and destructive to positive and constructive, as they explore and discuss issues and possibilities for resolution. The mediator's role is to help the parties make positive interactional shifts (empowerment and recognition shifts) by supporting the exercise of their capacities for strength and responsiveness, through their deliberation, decision making, communication, perspective taking, and other party activities. The mediator's primary goals are (1) to support empowerment shifts, by supporting—but never supplanting—each party's deliberation and decision making, at every point in the session where choices arise (regarding either process or outcome) and (2) to support recognition shifts, by encouraging and supporting—but never forcing—each party's freely chosen efforts to achieve new understandings of the other's perspective.

The goals of a transformative mediator—empowerment and recognition—are, to some degree, at odds with the goals of a problem-solving mediator and of an understanding-based mediator. However, to solve a problem or understand a situation, it is helpful to have the parties be both strong individually (empowerment) and responsive to each other (recognition). Consequently, there may be some overlap between the purposes, strategies, and techniques of transformative, understanding-based, and facilitative mediators. On the other hand, if the mediator has "problem-solving" in mind, she may be less inclined to keep the focus on empowerment and recognition and more inclined to solve the problem.

Providing a living laboratory for a particular mediation model, the U.S. Postal Service, one of the largest employers in the United States, adopted a transformative model for workplace disputes involving allegations of discrimination. The program, REDRESS, which is probably the largest employment mediation program in the world, uses outside mediators with specialized training in transformative mediation and provides a forum for supervisors and employees to mediate during their working hours. Noted scholar Professor Lisa Bingham (now Amsler) collected data from the program's inception in 1994 until 2006. Her findings include high levels of participant satisfaction with both the mediation process (91.2 percent for complainants and 91.6 for management) and the mediators (96.5 percent for complainants to 96.9 for management), high levels of satisfaction with the mediation outcome (from 64.2 percent for complainants to 69.5 percent for management), a significant drop in the number of formal discrimination complaints at the Postal Service, and evidence of improved communication between employers and supervisors during mediation. The program is ongoing (https://about.usps.com/what-we-are-doing/redress/about.htm). Perhaps most significantly, findings suggest there is a positive impact on the workplace itself because of the transformative mediation program.[3]

3. Directive and Evaluative Mediation

A number of approaches to mediation envision a central role for the mediator of importing information that will influence, if not determine, the outcome.

a. Trashing and Bashing

Studying mediator approaches in civil court cases, including personal injury, construction, commercial, contract, and real estate, Professor James Alfini describes two approaches that place the mediator in a role of considerable outcome influence. A "**trasher**" tears apart the case of each party "to get them to a point where they will put realistic settlement figures on the table." In other words, the trasher will point out weaknesses that each side will face at trial. A "**basher**" does not engage in case evaluation but spends "most of the session bashing away at . . . [parties'] initial offers in an attempt to get the parties to agree to a figure somewhere in between."[4]

b. Norm-educating and Norm-advocating

Professor Ellen Waldman describes forms of mediation she calls "**norm-educating**" and "**norm-advocating**." The norm-educating mediator ensures that party decision-making is informed by relevant legal and social norms—either by educating parties himself or making sure that each party's lawyer does that. While a norm-educating mediator would allow the parties to make decisions contrary to prevailing norms (once they were properly educated), a norm-advocating mediator would not. A norm-advocating mediator "provide[s] information about legal and ethical norms to secure their implementation." Professor Waldman asserts that the norm-advocating model is used in "a variety of conflicts, including bioethical, environmental, zoning, and, in some instances, discrimination disputes."[5]

---

3. See Lisa Blomgren Bingham, Cynthia J. Hallberlin, Denise A. Walker & Won-Tae Chung, Dispute System Design and Justice in Employment Dispute Resolution: Mediation at the Workplace, 14 Harv. Negot. L. Rev. 1, 46 (2009).
4. James J. Alfini, Trashing, Bashing, and Hashing It Out: Is This the End of "Good Mediation"?, 19 Fla. St. U. L. Rev. 47 (1991).
5. Ellen A. Waldman, Identifying the Role of Social Norms in Mediation: A Multiple Model Approach, 48 Hastings L.J. 703, 734, 745-746 (1997).

c. Community-enhancing and Community-enabling

Similarly, Professor Clark Freshman describes two forms of mediation that place responsibility on the mediator to import information about community values. In "**community-enhancing mediation**," a mediator helps "individuals order their activities and resolve their disputes consistent with the values of some relevant community." As examples of this, Professor Freshman cites mediation in rabbinical courts and the Islamic community. In "**community-enabling mediation**," assisted by the mediator, individuals "make informed choices about the kinds of communities they value and what weight, if any, to give to the norms such individuals may associate with that community." . . . The mediator has responsibility to discuss the norms of relevant communities—for example, the norms of same-sex couples, or Jewish couples, or simply the legal norms. "[C]ommunity-enabling mediation should be designed to allow individuals to make informed decisions about how to organize their lives and intimate relationships by exposing them to competing norms, including competing communities."[6]

Problem 6-12. ***What Is Mediation?***

The central aspects of mediation, outlined by Carrie Menkel-Meadow earlier in this chapter, are that it is: (1) consensual; (2) voluntary; (3) participatory; (4) facilitated by a third party outside the dispute; (5) seeking solutions and resolutions acceptable to all parties; and (6) seeking enhanced understanding among parties. Do all the variants described above comport with those core aspects? If your answer is no, would you amend the list or exclude the variant from the mediation family? Consider particularly whether evaluative-narrow mediation (Riskin), transformative mediation (Bush and Folger), "trashing" and "bashing" (Alfini), norm-advocating mediation (Waldman), and community-enhancing mediation (Freshman) arguably fall outside at least one of Menkel-Meadow's parameters.

4. Transparency About Approaches

In teaching about models generally, Professor Michael Moffitt has suggested that mediators falling into almost any of the categories above vary amongst themselves in the degree to which they are transparent about their own approaches and interventions. To what degree does or should a mediator: (1) communicate explicitly to the parties what process and steps she intends to pursue with them

6. Clark Freshman, Privatizing Same-Sex "Marriage" Through Alternative Dispute Resolution: Community-Enhancing Versus Community-Enabling Mediation, 44 UCLA L. Rev. 1687, 1692-1697 (1997).

next? And (2) communicate explicitly to the parties the impacts or effects she hopes to have on the parties with her actions? One can imagine a mediator using almost any model varying on either of these answers. Even something as simple as a mediator's decision about how to respond to a party's asserted position (when the mediator judges that she should dig into the party's interests) can illustrate assumptions about whether to be transparent on either of these questions. The box that follows, from Michael Moffitt, Casting Light on the Black Box of Mediation: Should Mediators Make Their Conduct More Transparent?, 13 Ohio State J. on Disp. Resol. 1, at 48 (1997), illustrates transparency in action.

Examples of Different Kinds of Transparency in Interest-Exploration

Sample responses to one party's statement: "I want a guarantee that I'll have a check for $10,000 in my office by the end of the week or else we have no deal."

	Non-Transparent About Impact	Transparent About Impact
Transparent About Process	I'd like to ask you some questions about the needs and concerns which underlie that position. For example, why is the timing of the payment an issue for you?	I'd like to find a way for you to assert your needs and concerns productively. To that end, I'd like to ask you some questions about the interests which underlie your position. Can you explain to me, for example, why you are concerned about the timing of the payments?
Non-Transparent About Process	Why is the timing of the payment important to you?	I'd like to find a way for you to assert your needs and concerns in a way which will help the mediation progress rather than creating a process of demands and counter-demands. Can you help me understand what it is about the timing of the payments that is important to you?

D. TRENDS: THE FUTURE OF MEDIATION IN THE LEGAL ARENA

1. Challenges Ahead

a. *The Demise of Party Participation and a Broad Problem-Definition in Court Contexts*

Professor Nancy Welsh suggests that the powerful and simple vision of mediation as a process to foster party participation and self-determination is "thinning." To put the concern more boldly, mediation may be gutted in the process of its adoption into the adversarial world of attorneys and courts. Mediators, many of them attorneys and retired judges, may have a conception of mediation built on judicial settlement conferences, where the neutral often provides reasoned evaluation. Parties (as clients) take the back seat, "largely limited to selecting from among the settlement options developed by their attorneys," allowing their attorneys to drive the mediation. Caucusing, rather than joint sessions, dominates the process.[7] What this means is that mediation may shift towards an adversarial and lawyer-focused process—at least in court-based contexts.

In more recent research examining mediation in court-oriented, civil (non-family) cases, Professors Welsh and Riskin found that mediations are tending to focus very narrowly on the legal claim. The bargaining revolves around the likely court outcome and discounts off the litigation prediction that each side might accept to avoid litigation costs and risks. While this narrow focus might serve repeat players—attorneys and other court regulars, like insurance adjusters—it can ignore the interests of "one shot" participants in the legal system who can have broader interests and concerns than a "cause of action" encompasses.[8] Recall Riskin's Grid, presented earlier in this chapter. One of the exciting potentials of mediation is a party-centered problem definition where the process addresses all negotiable concerns raised, including personal, business and societal issues that go beyond the legal cause of action.

b. *Mediator Conduct*

Professor James Coben, who has done exhaustive studies on lawsuits involving mediation, writes: "mediation's dirty little secret is the degree to which mediators . . . routinely and unabashedly engage in manipulation and deception to foster settlements, albeit under the rationale of fostering self-determination. Sophisticated consumers have come to know and expect it. Unsophisticated consumers are not so lucky."[9] As examples of mediator manipulation, Coben points to: skipping

---

7. Nancy A. Welsh, The Thinning Vision of Self-Determination in Court-Connected Mediation: The Inevitable Price of Institutionalization?, 6 Harv. Negot. L. Rev. 1 (2001).

8. Leonard L. Riskin & Nancy A. Welsh, Is That All There Is? "The Problem" in Court-Oriented Mediation, 15 Geo. Mason L. Rev. 863 (2008).

9. James R. Coben, Mediation's Dirty Little Secret: Straight Talk About Mediator Manipulation and Deception, 2 J. Altern. Disp. Resol. Emp. 4 (2000).

or delaying meals to increase pressure, conveying false demands, reframing, the use of neuro-linguistic programming to increase party comfort, over-reporting progress—or the opposite, overly pessimistic predictions of stalemate—to generate movement, strategically setting out Kleenex to encourage emotional expression, and the like.

Some of these "manipulations" are arguably part of a mediator's job; others are unethical. In any case, the regulation of mediator conduct is one of the issues for the field that lie ahead.

2. The Promise of Mediation

We return, however, to the simple vision of mediation: enabling parties to work together to resolve their dispute as they see best. How can we ensure that that vision stays vital?

> **Problem 6-13.** ***What Type of Mediation?***
>
> At various junctures, mediators, parties, and programs choose the type of mediation they want to embrace. Those junctures include: when novices sign up for mediation training; when programs and courts develop requirements to serve on their mediator panel; when attorneys choose a mediator for their clients and when individual mediators, programs and courts determine how to evaluate "success" in mediation. What direction will you, the reader, take at those junctures?

The next chapter asks: what is the role—the tasks and skills—of the mediator and the attorney in mediation? What practical challenges does the mediator face? If the incoming generation of lawyers and mediators attends to those questions, then mediation can keep its simple promise of party self-determination.

Further Reading

James Alfini, Sharon Press & Joseph Stulberg. (3d ed. 2013). Mediation Theory and Practice. Durham, NC: Carolina Academic Press.

Robert A. Baruch Bush & Joseph P. Folger. (2d ed. 2005). The Promise of Mediation. San Francisco: Jossey-Bass Publishers.

Nadja M. Alexander, James R. Coben, Sarah R. Cole, Craig A. McEwen, Nancy H. Rogers & Peter N. Thompson. (2024). Mediation Law Policy and Practice. Thomson Reuters Trial Practice Series.

Nancy Dubler & Carol Liebman. (2011). Bioethics Mediation: A Guide to Shaping Shared Solutions. New York: United Hospital Fund.

Douglas Frenkel & James Stark. (2018). The Practice of Mediation: A Video-Integrated Text. Burlington, MA: Aspen Publishing.

Gary Friedman & Jack Himmelstein. (2009). Challenging Conflict: Mediation Through Understanding. Washington, DC: ABA Publishing.

Amos Gabrieli, Nourit Zimerman & Michal Alberstein, Authority-Based Mediation, 20 Cardozo J. Confl. Resol. 1 (2018).

Eric Galton & Lela Love (Eds.). (2012). Stories Mediators Tell. Washington, DC: ABA Publishing.

David Hoffman. (2013). Mediation: A Practice Guide for Mediators, Lawyers, and Other Professionals. Boston: MCLE New England.

Kolb & Associates. (1997). When Talk Works: Profiles of Mediators. San Francisco: Jossey-Bass Publishers.

Kimberlee Kovach. (3d ed. 2004). Mediation: Principles and Practice. Eagan, MN: Thomson West.

Lela Love & Glenn Parker (Eds.). (2017). Stories Mediators Tell—World Edition. Washington, DC: ABA Publishing.

Lela P. Love & Thomas J. Stipanowich, Dear 1L: Five Guideposts for Your Future Professional Practice, 22 Cardozo J. Conflict Resol. 529 (2021).

Carrie Menkel-Meadow (Ed.). (2001). Mediation: Theory, Policy and Practice. Farnham, UK and Burlington, VT: Ashgate Press.

Carrie Menkel-Meadow. (2016). Mediation and Its Applications for Good Decision Making and Dispute Resolution. Cambridge, Antwerp, Portland: Intersentia.

Christopher Moore. (4th ed. 2014). The Mediation Process: Practical Strategies for Resolving Conflict. San Francisco: Jossey-Bass Publishers.

Joseph B. Stulberg & Lela P. Love. (3d ed. 2019). The Middle Voice: Mediating Conflict Successfully. Durham, NC: Carolina Academic Press.

Chapter 7 Mediation: Skills and Practices

Leaders must . . . create an attitude of success, the belief that problems can be solved, that things can be better. Not in a foolish or unrealistic way, but in a way that creates hope and confidence.

—George Mitchell

Our task now is not to fix the blame for the past, but to fix a course for the future.

—John F. Kennedy

The very first requirement in a hospital is that it should do the sick no harm.

—Florence Nightingale

A mediation is successful if it accomplishes any of the following goals: giving disputing parties a better understanding of their dispute and of each other's perspective, enabling parties to develop options responsive to issues raised by the dispute, and bringing closure to the dispute on terms that are mutually agreeable. Conversely, the mediation process should not make negotiations more difficult, nor should it generate an outcome worse than outcomes available elsewhere. In other words, at a minimal level, the process should do no harm. This chapter explores skills mediators and any attorneys involved in mediation should possess to achieve success.

Both the mediator and any attorney representatives share the goal of helping disputants advance their interests. This chapter first examines mediator skills and strategies to enable parties to achieve a successful outcome. Even if you have no intention of practicing as a mediator, attorneys need to understand what a mediator does and how mediators think in order to utilize their services to best advantage. It then identifies best practices—and practices to avoid—for the attorney representative who wants to maximize the good that mediation might do for his client.

A. THE MEDIATOR

[C]areful as someone crossing an iced-over stream.
Alert as a warrior in enemy territory.
Courteous as a guest.
Fluid as melting ice.
Shapeable as a block of wood.
Receptive as a valley.
Clear as a glass of water.
—Tao Te Ching 15 (Steven Mitchell trans., 1991)

The *Tao Te Ching* describes Masters who lead in subtle ways so people believe they have achieved results on their own. This invisible leadership that supports parties in determining an appropriate outcome is one vision of the mediation process.

An Endless Supply of Patience

[T]here must be an endless supply of patience and perseverance. Sometimes the mountains seem so high and rivers so wide that it is hard to continue the journey. . . . Seeking an end to conflict is not for the timid or the tentative. . . . We had 700 days of failure and 1 day of success.

— George J. Mitchell (describing negotiations in Northern Ireland)

1. Mediator Traits

What personality traits serve a mediator? Generally, a mediator must be able to stay in the middle —that is, be neutral, impartial, and nonjudgmental. Other often-cited attributes of a good mediator include being a good listener; displaying intelligence; having the ability both to take charge and to recede into the background when the parties are engaging in constructive conversation; and having the energy, optimism, and dogged perseverance to press on when hope fades. Confidence, decisiveness, flexibility, creativity, reliability, nondefensiveness, a sense of humor, and empathy are other important traits. Some mediators are naturally more blessed with these traits than others. However, nurture and support, training and mentoring, and self-reflection can go a long way in developing these qualities.

Working with these traits, what tasks do mediators perform?

2. Mediator Tasks

Organization: Imagine a *host* who provides for your comfort and safety and a meeting *chair* who convenes the meeting and organizes the discussion so it is efficient and meaningful.

Communication: Picture a master *communicator* who helps parties speak clearly and listen to each other, who clarifies, summarizes, translates, and reframes so everyone understands what is said, and who captures and records understandings and agreements.

Education: Envision a *teacher* who explains the process and encourages parties to get helpful information and advice, a *coach* and *model* who demonstrates effective negotiation behaviors and attitudes, and a *strategist* who urges evaluation and reality-testing of every attitude and option.

Negotiation: Consider a master *negotiator* who elicits common interests, frames negotiable issues, inspires the parties to develop options, conveys offers and counteroffers, and makes sure that agreements are clear and doable.

Protection: Think about a *sentinel* who prevents misuse of process, and a *referee* who ensures an equal place at the table.

If the mediator accomplishes these tasks and fulfills these roles, the parties will have the best chance of success in the process.

3. Who Can Be a Mediator?

With these traits and tasks framing some of the challenges for mediators, keep in mind that there is no universal consensus on one correct method for mediation practice. This means there are considerable questions about how to assure the quality of mediators' services. What, if any, limits ought there to be on those who can be mediators? Should their conduct be regulated or constrained in some way?

As Professor Michael Moffitt explains, mediators are not easily subject to the kinds of licensure requirements that exist as to other practices or professions like law and medicine:

> Part of the reason no state has exclusive control over entry into the mediation marketplace relates to . . . a definitional problem. Unless the state can say with precision what a practice entails, it cannot draw boundaries around a practice. Without boundaries, there is no way to establish exclusive control. . . . If, for example, mediation is defined as assisting disputing parties, does anything distinguish mediation from therapy? Even defining mediation in terms of specific practices does not cure the problem. I cannot imagine, for example, that we will ever see the day that a private citizen will face state sanction for the Unauthorized Asking of an Open-Ended Question.[1]

Short of a general licensure system, some courts and other institutions have tried to determine how to measure competence and qualify persons for mediation service on their rosters or panels. A typical formula includes: a certain number of

1. Michael Moffitt, The Four Ways to Assure Mediator Quality (and why none of them work), 24 Ohio State J. on Disp. Resol. 191, 205-206 (2009).

hours of training; experience observing and co-mediating cases under supervision; and continuing education requirements. Some court-annexed panels also rely on educational degree requirements, mandating a college degree or, in some cases, a law (or other graduate) degree, or, in a few cases, having been a practicing member of the bar in a particular state for a number of years.[2]

4. Mediator Strategies and Skills for Stages in the Mediation Process

A variety of ways can be used to describe the stages of the mediation process and the major skills associated with each. Here we will look at the following: (1) getting started; (2) listening; (3) organizing the conversation; (4) encouraging movement; (5) using private meetings; and (6) closing. While this description of stages might suggest that mediation proceeds in a linear fashion, this is not always or even usually the case. We use the stages as a helpful map of the process, knowing that sometimes conversation is circular rather than linear.

a. Getting Started

The mediator must consider and help the parties resolve a variety of issues prior to the start of a mediation session. Among those issues are choosing participants, assessing whether participants have special needs, deciding what preliminary and procedural issues need to be addressed, and setting the stage.

i. Who Should Participate in the Mediation?

Although many of the final decisions rest with the parties, mediators commonly help to assess questions about who might play what role(s) during a mediation. The following chart outlines some potential mediation participants, generalizes about whether they should participate in mediation, and suggests a rationale for inclusion.

PARTICIPANT	INCLUDE?	RATIONALE FOR INCLUSION/EXCLUSION
Party	Yes	The parties are in the best position to examine underlying interests, to develop creative proposals, and to determine whether commitment to a proposal is possible and optimal.
Attorney(s) or other representative	Yes	If a party to the dispute wants a representative—to help articulate the legal case or some other aspect of the situation, to be a negotiation coach or protector, to assist in listening, persuading, and developing and analyzing options—then she should be allowed such support.

2. For a critique of the current lack of regulation, see Art Hinshaw, Regulating Mediators, 21 Harv. Negot. L. Rev. 163 (2016).

PARTICIPANT	INCLUDE?	RATIONALE FOR INCLUSION/EXCLUSION
Interpreter	Yes, if needed	Since understanding is a central goal of mediation, an interpreter is critical if there are language issues.
Expert	Maybe	An expert may be needed to inform or educate the parties or to expand settlement options. Mutually acceptable experts can be particularly helpful to provide information where data is lacking.
Witness	Maybe	Another voice may be helpful to persuade a party to consider another perspective. Sometimes a witness can have more impact than a party, who may be mistrusted. Additionally, the cumulative impact of another voice—particularly a credible voice—can be powerful.
Support person	Maybe	A general rule is "to keep it simple" where possible. On the other hand, some parties cannot operate effectively without a support person—for example, a spouse, significant family member, or business partner.
The public/the media/observers	Maybe	Although many aspects of the mediation process are best accomplished with the fewest number of participants, and the process is most often described as confidential, there are some contexts in which outsiders' presence may be important for legal reasons, for reasons of legitimacy, or for reasons of implementation.

General guidelines, however, do not answer all questions. For example, situations arise where a party cannot be present and an attorney or other representative attends as a surrogate negotiator. Additionally, unlike litigation, where parties are named in the papers filed with the court, in mediation it is sometimes hard to tell who the parties are. For example, a litigated custody dispute typically has as the parties those persons—often the parents—named in the complaint. However, in the mediation of a situation concerning parenting arrangements, the parties may include a much broader potential array—grandparents, aunts, uncles, or the children themselves.

Although the same people may participate in mediation and adjudication, their role in each process is quite different. In adjudication, parties, attorneys, experts, and witnesses all work for "their" side to persuade a neutral decision maker. In mediation, on the other hand, participants increase the common information base and operate to shift parties' perspective and develop proposals responsive to the situation.

Problem 7-1. ***Who Should Participate?***

Recall a dispute with which you have been involved. To have a successful mediation, whom would you want to attend the mediation? Does it depend on your goals? If the same dispute had been brought to court,

> who would have been the named parties? Now examine a case you have studied in other law school courses—Brown v. Board of Education, for example. Who might the participants be in a mediation of that situation?

ii. What Procedural Issues Must Be Addressed?

In addition to the participant mix, issues about allocating mediation costs, determining necessary information EXCHANGE, and deciding the nature of pre-mediation submissions, if any, must be addressed. The excerpt that follows discusses the challenges of setting the procedural framework for a mediation.

❖ *Joseph B. Stulberg and Lela P. Love*, THE MIDDLE VOICE, 3d ed.

53-54 (2019)

Where will people meet? How many will be there? When will they meet? How long will the session last? Will there be food? Who will talk first? Who will sit where?

The mediator wants to ensure that meeting arrangements and procedures do not disrupt the discussions. She wants them handled well so that people feel comfortable as they start to talk with one another.

The mediator begins by taking care of these important details. Usually, after having consulted with the parties, she simply announces the framework and makes appropriate arrangements. Sometimes, however, these matters become issues of fierce debate among the parties and end up as the first topic for mediated discussion. In any event, no mediator thinks they are trivial. The procedural framework creates a space within which people must feel safe, and the mediator must construct it with care. Like any host, the mediator will receive no compliments for handling arrangements well but will invite interminable haggling and destructive exchanges for botching them. . . .

Although these seem straightforward enough, they can be devilishly complicated. If a mediator schedules a meeting for 11:00 A.M., does that mean the meeting will last only until lunch at noon? If only one party has to travel seventy miles to attend a meeting in the city where all of the other parties live and work, should the mediator change the meeting site so that everyone must travel thirty-five miles, or should she alternate meeting sites so as not to favor one group? If one group has only two negotiators, but the other has five negotiating team members and thirty "observers and supporters," should the mediator arrange a meeting site that accommodates eight or thirty-eight persons? The mediator must develop guidelines with a keen sensitivity to the impact that choices will have on the parties' interaction and the way in which the guidelines might affect her own image as neutral.

---

iii. How Is the Stage Set?

Sometimes when I consider what tremendous consequences come from little things . . . I am tempted to think . . . there are no little things.

—Bruce Barton, in Stephen R. Covey, *The Seven Habits of Highly Effective People*, 287 (1989)

We shape our buildings: thereafter they shape us.

—Winston Churchill

Israel-PLO Agreement Ceremony

Sometimes getting the atmosphere right is the most important thing. When we signed the Israel-PLO agreement in 1993 on the White House lawn, I had a tough time. First Arafat wanted to bring his gun—he said he didn't go anywhere without his gun. Well I said, "This isn't about guns. If you want to walk away from a televised audience of a billion people because you won't leave your six-shooter at the door, I'll be happy to tell them that." So he left his gun.

Then I said to Rabin, "He left his gun. You've got to shake hands with him." He said, "I am signing the agreement, I have to shake his hand?" We are laughing today, but this was a tough thing for him. These guys had fought for decades. How many young Israelis had Rabin put in body bags? He lived and they died. . . . He was considering all that. Finally I said to him, "Yitzhak, you have made all these steps and you have taken all these risks and the whole world will be looking at you. And I have to shake hands with Arafat; so you do too." And he looked at me and he said, "Well I suppose you do not make peace with your friends." And then he smiled at me and said, "but no kissing."

—William J. Clinton, Acceptance Speech, International Advocate for Peace Award, Benjamin N. Cardozo School of Law, Mar. 19, 2001.

In determining how to choose and arrange a room for a mediation, key mediation goals must be kept in mind: to enhance communication between the parties, to ensure safety, to maximize comfort, to support mediator neutrality, and to set a stage or create an atmosphere that is conducive to creativity and to inspiration.

Mediators must consider what artwork to place on the walls to create a positive atmosphere, what sort of furniture would be most helpful—a round, rectangular, square, or some other shaped table? No table? And, of course, the mediation space should have extra rooms for private meetings, kitchen facilities, telephones, computers, copiers, internet access, and printing capabilities.

Food and beverages are inextricably linked to the success of meetings. In setting the stage for a mediation that may go all day, food will play an important role. Keep in mind that hunger is related to energy, creativity, irritability, and patience, and consequently the mediator should keep a sharp eye on parties' needs for food and drink. What opportunities and dangers lie in arranging opportunities for parties to "break bread together"? For example, cultural differences may dictate that certain foods not be served or that there be "comfort" food for particular groups. Delicious food and drink—and good coffee—can be inspirational!

Problem 7-2. *How Should You Seat the Parties?*

Assuming there are two parties and one mediator, would you sit parties side by side to emphasize that they are facing a common problem and must work together, or sit them across the table from each other, where direct eye contact is easy and the security of a table between them may provide safety and psychological comfort? Draw a diagram showing the seating arrangement. The drawing should display the type of table you have chosen and where the parties and mediator are seated in relation to the door. If the parties bring representatives, should an attorney be seated nearest the mediator, or should the party be given that place with his attorney by his side (on the side away from the mediator)? Add attorneys to your drawing. How might differences in the nature of the dispute, or in the personalities or backgrounds of the disputants, affect your handling of these issues?

iv. How Does the Mediator Open the Session?

Typically, the mediator begins the session by making opening remarks. The goals in making these remarks include: developing trust and rapport with the parties, educating the parties about the mediation process, ensuring that everyone (mediator and parties) have compatible goals, and developing consensus about guidelines for the process.

What follows is a sample opening statement by a mediator in a community mediation center, which primarily handles neighbor, landlord-tenant, and family-related disputes. In this context, unlike some others, it is common for mediators to meet with parties together without much (or any) background information about the underlying dispute. Keep in mind that the statement might look very different in other contexts, but it would still address the goals set out above.

> *Good morning. Welcome to mediation. My name is Corbin Gregg, and I have been assigned to assist you.*
>
> *Please check that I have your names and addresses recorded correctly. Am I pronouncing your names correctly? [The mediator will place the parties' names on his note pad—spelled correctly and also phonetically, if necessary—in a configuration that provides a seating chart.]*
>
> *I want you both to know that I have never met either of you before [Confirm that is correct], and I know very little about the concerns that brought you here today. [Summarize any information received or conversations had ahead of time.] I look forward to your explaining this matter to me. I am telling you this because it is my job not to take sides, but rather remain in the middle, as a neutral—both as we begin and throughout the session. I am not a judge. A judge would decide who was wrong or right with respect to what happened in the past. I am here to help you work out how you want the future to be.*
>
> *Before you tell me what brought you here, I want to explain the goals of this process and suggest some guidelines for our conversation. My first job is to understand your concerns and to be sure that you understand each other. To do that, it is important that each person has the*

opportunity to speak without being interrupted. I know you will want to comment about what the other person says and perhaps remember some points that are new to you, so I have given you paper and a pen to make notes. When it is your turn to speak, you will have a full opportunity to explain your concerns and respond to one another. Can you agree not to interrupt each other and not to interrupt me? Are there other conversation guidelines that might be helpful?

After we explore the situation and your goals, I will encourage you to work together to come up with proposals to address the concerns you raised. If you are able to reach an agreement that resolves your concerns, if you wish and at your request, I will assist you in writing up your commitments to each other.

I will be taking notes as we proceed to help me remember the concerns you raise and the understandings you reach. However, I will destroy my notes at the end of this session. I am telling you this so you will feel comfortable to speak freely here. This session is private and confidential. That means I am under a duty not to reveal what is said in this room to anyone outside this room. There are some exceptions to confidentiality, however. [Review here any pertinent exceptions, e.g., child abuse.] The only record of what happened in this session will be the agreement you make to resolve your concerns; that document will not be confidential.

There may come a time when it would be helpful to meet individually with each of you. If that happens, I will explain that process—which is called caucusing—in more detail.

Sessions here generally take two hours. They can also be shorter or longer as you require. I am committed to work with you as long as necessary. What are your time constraints?

Do you have any questions?

Ms. Weinstein, since you brought this matter to the attention of the Center, would you please begin and relate what brought you here?

Observe the language in the opening. The mediator refers to *concerns*, *interests*, *priorities*, *proposals*, *options*, and *agreements*, rather than using adversarial or potentially abrasive words such as *parties*, *allegations*, *claim*, *position*, or *problem*.

Problem 7-3. ***Practice Preparing and Delivering an Opening***

How would you change this opening if attorneys were present? If you were conducting a mediation between fellow law students? Note that every opening statement should include the following: introductions, disclaiming of mediator partiality or bias, explanation of the mediation process and the mediator's role, development of ground rules (including understandings regarding courtesy), note taking, confidentiality, the length of the session, the use of separate meetings or caucuses, and an opportunity to ask questions.

Choose a context and in groups of three, prepare and then practice giving an opening statement to your colleagues as they play parties. In turn, each student in the group should be the mediator and the other students should be parties. Note that even if three people use the same words, their openings may have very different impacts. After each opening, the mediator should reflect on their performance and the parties should give the mediator feedback on their body language and eye contact (which should not favor either party), whether they created a tone of trust and optimism, and whether they conveyed confidence and competence.

b. Listening to Understand the Conflict

Once the mediator has set the stage and delivered an opening statement, she asks the parties to describe the matter that brought them to mediation. As the mediator listens to the parties and urges them to listen to each other, she is looking for elements of the conflict that may be constructive in developing a better understanding among them and be helpful in generating ideas for resolutions. You have seen that listening is a critical skill for the negotiator. The excerpts that follow show how a mediator will (or should) help advance good listening.

i. "Looping"

One mediator technique for listening is called "looping," which is taught in the understanding-based model of mediation introduced in Chapter 6. Looping is both a skill and a method of inculcating a genuine commitment in the mediator to understand each disputant that comes before them and demonstrate that understanding.

Gary Friedman & Jack Himmelstein, THE LOOP OF UNDERSTANDING

(2004)

Central to the Understanding-Based approach to mediation is the search for understanding. The "Loop of Understanding," as we have come to call it, gives form and substance to that effort. "*Looping*" is a technique, but it is also much more than a technique. The goal is to *Develop Understanding* systematically, authentically and compassionately throughout the mediation.

Looping builds on the mediator's intention. Just as successful mediation ultimately must build on the parties' intention to work through their conflict together, looping proceeds from the mediator's intention to understand the parties and to build a ground of understanding between the mediator and the parties.

THE STEPS OF LOOPING

Although the approach is similar to and borrows much from what others have referred to as "active listening," "looping" captures a fuller sense of it for us. We term it the "loop" of understanding because the goal is to complete a loop.

For the mediator, the simple steps are to try within him or herself to understand each party, to try to express that understanding to that party, and to seek and receive confirmation from the party that he/she feels understood. The last step is crucial. When a party confirms that the mediator understands what he or she has been trying to express, that loop is complete. Until then, it is not.

Step 1:	**M inquires of**	→	**P**
Step 2:	**P responds, asserts**	→	**M**
Step 3:	**M demonstrates and confirms understanding**	→	**P**
Step 4:	**P responds**	→	**M**

If yes, loop is complete.If no, go back to Step 1 and ask: "What am I missing?"

By bringing *looping* to the exchange between him/herself and each of the principal antagonists to the conflict, the mediator has begun to understand each of them. And while they likely do not feel understood by each other, they feel at least somewhat understood by the mediator. He has also begun to clarify the essence of the dispute.

The goal is to understand the speaker *and* to demonstrate that you understand. Already this is much more than many mediators (and others) will do in the effort to listen. Even when we make a sincere effort to understand another, that effort is often evidenced by silent attention, a nod of agreement, or a statement such as: "I understand what you are saying." These are not bad. But when it comes to the goal of resolving conflict through understanding, much more is possible. Stating what you hear the other to have said goes further. It shows that you understand (if you do).

So far we have a partial loop—statement by the loopee and response (restatement) by the looper. The next step begins to close the loop. If done with the intent of fostering understanding, it tests whether the mediator has truly understood. The mediator asks the party whether the response captured the meaning of what he was trying to communicate.

The loopee's response can close the loop. If "yes"—if the speaker confirms that he/she feels understood—this one loop is complete. If the speaker does not feel fully understood by the looper's words (whether because the looper missed something or simply because the speaker has the need to clarify what he/she meant), the loop is not complete. The party can then clarify what he/she meant), the mediator loops back and again seeks confirmation. When the party confirms that the mediator correctly has understood, that loop is complete.

The point is not to convince, nor to contradict, nor to take exception to, nor explain away. The point is to understand. . . .

The honest attempt by the mediator to understand each party begins to point to an alternative to the confines of a most basic element that keeps people ensnared in a Conflict Trap. For when people are locked in conflict, they typically tend to want to defend their position, blame the other, and try to convince a third party that they are right and the other wrong. The mode is one of defense, persuasion, coercion.

When conflict takes that form, understanding is at a minimum. Misunderstanding prevails. The more the parties to conflict feel blamed or vilified by the other, the more they feel misunderstood. The more that they feel misunderstood, the more they tend to justify, blame and vilify. The cycle is well known and yet, once within its grasp, very powerful. Understanding, from the get-go, can help begin to soften the strictures and be the beginning of pointing the way out.

A caution: our recommendation for looping from the start applies to the mediator looping the parties, not to asking the parties to loop each other. Many mediators, drawn by the desire to increase understanding, will turn to the parties early on and ask: what did you understand the other to say? Our advice, generally, is: NOT YET. People are much more willing and able to understand another when they feel understood themselves. To put it another way, being mired in feelings of being misunderstood is not a good place from which to be asked to understand another. And parties to conflict are often mired in just such feelings. By establishing some understanding at the start (by the mediator of the parties), the mediator can begin to help break the cycle of misunderstanding. The invitation to the parties to loop each other can also prove essential, but it rarely comes at the start.

LOOPING FROM THE INSIDE OUT

As the description we have been giving about *looping* may suggest, it is both a skill and much more than a skill. To understand *looping* and its place in this approach to mediation is to realize that understanding has an inner life. And it is in that inner life that the essential spirit of looping is grounded. The mediator needs to want to loop (and learn to loop) as more than a useful skill. The hard work is to truly want to understand the people before you—to reach inside oneself when each speaker is speaking and make the effort to understand how the other (each of them) really experiences the situation—even (and particularly) when you find it difficult to understand them. That inner desire to understand is key.

Focusing too much on the outer skill, on getting the words right, on learning to rephrase or reframe (which are important skills to learn) can miss the essential point. *That point* is truly *to want to* understand—to connect within oneself to one's own intention to do that. If the inner intent is there, you may at times miss some of the basic steps and still move toward understanding.

---

ii. Reframing

In the next excerpt Professor Lela Love describes another listening skill—that of reframing. Love urges mediators to translate accusations, put-downs, and threats into "building blocks" for moving forward and helping parties shift their perspectives.

Lela P. Love, TRAINING MEDIATORS TO LISTEN: DECONSTRUCTING DIALOGUE AND CONSTRUCTING UNDERSTANDING, AGENDAS, AND AGREEMENTS

adapted from 38 Fam. & Concil. Cts. Rev. 27 (2000)

Much as a miner looks for gold, a mediator listens to the often hostile, accusatory, and adversarial dialogue between parties, gleaning the constructive elements—the "heart of gold"—that are being expressed. Amidst the put-downs, insults, and threats that are frequently exchanged by people in conflict, the mediator must extract solid building blocks, which will allow disputants to construct different perspectives, clearer understandings and ultimately agreements. The mediator must hear and identify those elements, and also enable the parties to hear each other. This task is difficult because parties in conflict typically experience fear, confusion, anger, hate, frustration, and hopelessness, and the expression of these feelings can be so loud that other elements are drowned out. The mediator must be optimistic that "gold" exists and be able to selectively and thoughtfully frame constructive components at appropriate times in the session.

What are the building blocks of constructive dialogue and how would the mediator translate these building blocks into language that might reorient the parties toward the dispute and toward each other? The "heart of gold," or building blocks of constructive dialogue, are each discussed below.

INTERESTS AND NEEDS

Interests are the underlying and inescapable human motivators that press us into action. When interests are frustrated by actions or inactions of others, frequently a conflict ensues. Examples of interests include: survival, security, reputation, financial well-being, respect, career, and health. Recognition of these important matters at stake can be motivating.

In many cases, mediators find common interests among the disputants. In an employment scenario, frequently both a supervisor and an employee share an interest in their respective reputations, careers and financial security. In a landlord-tenant situation, both disputants often have a common interest in: a safe, clean and serviceable dwelling and responsive and respectful treatment. Divorcing parents usually share an interest in the well-being, health, and happiness of their children. A common interest provides a useful foundation upon which to build.

ISSUES

Issues are those distinct and negotiable matters or behaviors that are frustrating a party's interests. Issues are the critical components of the negotiating agenda. Since mediators are generally charged with helping craft a discussion agenda that is right "on target" with respect to concerns raised, a mediator's ability to mine the conversation for issues and to label them in neutral language is key. One of the unique strengths of mediation, compared to litigation or arbitration, is its ability to address the infinitely wide range of concerns that disputing parties have with each other.

Legal issues or causes of action are distinct from negotiable issues. In a probate dispute, for example, the litigated issues might be: whether undue influence was exerted on the testator or whether the testator had testamentary capacity. These legal questions might never be resolved in mediation. Rather, though parties might discuss the legal cause of action, the negotiable issues, often broader than the legal ones, would be targeted for resolution: the disposition of the art collection; the division of the residuary estate; the division of photographs, albums and family memorabilia; the hosting of holiday events; interaction between aunts, uncles, nieces and nephews; and so on.

The mediator pays attention to how issues are framed. In a labor-management context, frequent issues that arise include: wages, benefits, vacations, and overtime. Note that those descriptions of the issues do not take sides. In a divorce context, financial and parenting arrangements are frequently central. In a litigation context, the negotiable issue of "parenting arrangements" would be described as "custody" and "visitation"—a framing that invites adversarial positioning rather than problem-solving. In a landlord-tenant situation where back rent is contested, if the mediator framed the issue as "the delinquent rent owed by the tenant" she is inviting a hostile reaction from the tenant. Identifying the issue simply as "the rent" serves better.

PROPOSALS

Proposals are offers or suggestions for the resolution of particular issues or of the dispute. Like other elements which require mining, proposals are rarely neatly and attractively packaged by the parties. Disputants frequently embed a proposal in a threat or insult, and mediators must be attuned to extract and display the proposal. A supervisor might say to an employee, for example: "If you didn't have such a nasty attitude, the company might help you. As it is, you're going to walk." From a mediator's perspective, that may be a proposal! The mediator would want to know what specifically the employee might do to display a different attitude and what sort of "help" might ensue.

> LEGEND: Common interests → **Bold**;
> Issues → <u>underscore</u>;
> Mutually Acceptable Proposals → *italics*
>
> **Employer and Employee want to end their employment relationship in an amicable manner.**
>
> To that end, they agree:
>
> 1. <u>Employment Relationship</u>.
>
> A. <u>Employee's Employment Status</u>. **Both Employer and Employee would like to facilitate Employee's smooth transition to a new job. Consequently, they agree:**
>
> *i. that Employee shall remain at the company for 3 months with full pay and benefits, retaining her current office, telephone and e-mail privileges, and job title. During that period Employee shall look for other employment and shall have no job-related responsibilities. At the end of that period, Employee shall resign; and*
>
> *ii. that Employer shall provide Employee with outplacement services at a provider chosen by Employee for one year or until Employee is hired (whichever occurs sooner). . . .*

Opening proposals (often called "positions") tend to be extreme and unworkable, since workable proposals would have led to resolution and avoided the need for a mediator. However, they are nonetheless an important indication of what each party sees as an interest-satisfying outcome.

Consequently, a mediator must be encouraged to pay sharp attention to proposals, even though he may not relay or reframe each proposal, as some may be so extreme that they would result in further alienation of the parties.

The relationship of interests, issues and proposals to agreements is the following. Agreements begin with a purpose clause (common interests), they employ headings (the issues in dispute) and they entail understandable and precise arrangements and undertakings between the parties (proposals that are mutually acceptable). Hence the mediator, even as he listens to the opening presentations of the parties, is actually beginning to construct an agreement from the articulated interests, issues and proposals he hears (see box on previous page).

FEELINGS

Both recipients of and witnesses to put-downs and insults tend naturally to react with alarm, heightened adrenaline and, especially for the recipient, an attack response. Mediators must hear, and at appropriate points reframe, the feelings that generate such statements: the speaker is angry; the speaker is scared; the speaker is frustrated. It is often the case that all parties to a conflict have similar feelings of anger and frustration. In many cases, a vitriolic insult is the tip of an iceberg of a history of hurt feelings, waiting to be heard and acknowledged. Sometimes the venting and acknowledgment alone can shift the feelings themselves. Mediators should be trained to hear insults and reframe the statement to acknowledge the feelings underneath.

PRINCIPLES, VALUES AND RULES

Parties govern themselves in accordance with certain principles and values they hold dear. A sense of entitlement and need for "justice" and setting things right grows out of parties' understanding of family, industry, community, religious or legal rules and norms. Exposing and clarifying the parties' (and sometimes their attorneys' or other experts') operating principles, values, norms, and rules are part of the mediator's task. This is so for several reasons: (1) behavior becomes more understandable when the parties understand the important principles, values and rules governing the other party's behavior; and (2) proposals generally will not work for a party unless they comport with the party's operating norms.

In court-annexed settings or for disputes involving legal claims and lawyers, the law, and the parties' perceptions and positions with respect to their legal rights and obligations, may play a critical role. If counsel are present in the mediation session, their presentations regarding the legal posture of the case will be a key element in framing the parties' perceptions of legal norms. Such presentations will assist the parties re-evaluate their understanding of the litigation alternative. The mediator should encourage a discussion and analysis of the weaknesses and strengths of elements of each party's case. Risk assessment (or conversely, opportunity analysis) with respect to litigation may provide a key piece to the puzzle of what would provide a meaningful settlement in court-connected cases. It is up to the mediator to encourage the attorneys to make presentations about legal norms, risks and opportunities, which are persuasive in terms of making the other side re-evaluate their litigation option, but are not personally offensive to the other side such that a climate for constructive negotiation is undermined.

Lawyers, however, can overemphasize the importance of the role of law. Remember that it is usual for legal analysis to result in widely different assessments of likely litigation outcomes. Also, other values and interests come into play for many parties. The power of an apology, for example, and the recognition it entails, is typically underestimated by lawyers. Moral, religious, family or community values can play a more decisive role, in some cases, than legal norms.

VISIONS

A vision in this context is a picture that a party may have of an ideal state. Often the frustration and high tension in a conflict setting is due to the fact that the status quo is so far from where a party would like it to be. Interestingly, "visions" often do not conflict, and sometimes are complementary. For example, in disputes between neighbors parties often say: "I just want peace when I come home"; or "I want my building to feel welcoming"; or "I want to be left alone, not bothered." In an employment situation, parties might say: "I want a friendly workplace"; or "I want co-workers who pull together"; or "I want my employees to care about the business." The mediator can explore these pictures by asking: "Tell me more about how you would like your building to be"; or "Describe how you would like the office to be" (asking both parties, of course). Such an exploration can result in a target status quo that is appealing to both parties. Having some clarity about the ideal makes it easier to dream up intermediate steps to achieve such an ideal.

STORIES

Allowing parties to tell their stories (often a story of a wrong they have experienced) is critical to each party being able to move beyond that experience of wrong and to listen to the other party's story, frequently a quite different story or viewpoint on the same "facts," and invariably expanding the picture or "reality" which informs each individual party's perception of events. Mediators need to understand that they must listen to each party's story and be able to see how that party views events, but—unlike a judge or an arbitrator—they need not judge or determine which version of events constitutes "facts." By preserving for each party an uninterrupted platform for speech, the mediator gives each party voice and respect and encourages a heightened level of understanding. Unlike an arbitrator or neutral expert who must find "facts," a mediator gives each party the storytelling floor so that the parties can be shifted by the power of the other's narrative (sometimes assisted by advocates and the translating function of the mediator). The telling of the story may shift the speaker; the hearing of the story may shift the listener; from a mediator's perspective, the parties, as first-hand participants, are in the best position to judge the "truth" around the events related to their conflict.

BATNAS (BEST ALTERNATIVE TO A NEGOTIATED AGREEMENT)

A party's BATNA represents their favored or default option if mediation is unsuccessful in resolving the conflict. How the mediator uses BATNAs can be very important. BATNAs are frequently expressed as a threat, for example: "I will pursue this all the way to the Supreme Court"; "I have friends" (sometimes meaning "my friends will injure you"); "we will send in troops"; or "I will tell Mom." Such statements may be expressions of options a party may have, and the mediator will urge the parties to explore and evaluate the realistic costs and opportunities available through each option. Each party's perspective will be informed by the evaluation of the other side. In that manner, the process enables decision-making to take place in an environment providing enriched information. In its least ambitious form, mediation can be seen as an opportunity to "beat the BATNA" of each party through the negotiation process.

Problem 7-4. ***Finding the Gold!***

Ask a colleague to describe a conflict that is distressing him. As you listen, identify and reframe for the speaker the interests, issues, feelings, proposals, principles, rules/laws, visions, and any BATNA expressed.

If these elements are not described, ask questions to elicit them. So, for examples, you might say: "Why is that important to you?" "Is there anything else that concerns you?" "Tell me more about where that idea came from?" "Can you help us understand what you mean by 'fair'?" "What would a good relationship with your co-worker look like?"

c. Organizing the Conversation

As any chair of a meeting would do, the mediator must help the parties build a constructive discussion agenda. The negotiation agenda items—the issues—are those matters that require negotiation. After identifying those matters and framing them in a neutral manner, the final challenge is to order the agenda in a way most conducive to collaboration, which Professor Joseph Stulberg discusses in the excerpt below.

Joseph B. Stulberg, THE THEORY AND PRACTICE OF MEDIATION: A REPLY TO PROFESSOR SUSSKIND

6 Vt. L. Rev. 85, 99-103 (1981)

An important consideration for the mediator when trying to structure effective communication is the order in which the parties will discuss the issues. To those unfamiliar with the negotiation-mediation process, this matter might appear to be a trivial house-keeping point. Frequently, however, stalemates and impasses occur not because parties disagree on all matters but because they have failed to structure discussions so that they can distinguish those matters on which they agree from those on which they do not.

. . . A mediator could adopt one of several approaches in structuring the discussion of issues. He could start by discussing the easy issues first. Everyone can assess matters in terms of degree of importance. If the mediator focuses discussions on those less important matters (i.e., the matters perceived as enhancing the parties' relationship without in any way jeopardizing their substantive interests), then he can help the parties begin to forge some agreements.

Using this approach serves two purposes. First, it begins to develop a pattern of agreement and momentum of progress between the parties. Confidence in the talks grows as agreement is reached on some items, and the parties obtain a limited basis for believing it possible to resolve the more difficult issues. Second, by building a series of small agreements, the mediator has laid a settlement foundation. As the parties reach more difficult issues, the cost of not settling increases since that cost would include relinquishing all agreements which had been reached. That fact alone might give the parties a strong incentive to reconsider any resistance to the remaining matters.

Another approach would involve dividing issues and proposals according to their common subject-matter. The mediator could categorize the proposals [in a labor dispute] into such subjects as vacation, wages, hours of work, and the like and then discuss each party's proposal(s) that falls within that category. The starting point of the discussion would be the category of issues that seems most susceptible to prompt resolution. . . .

[T]he mediator could approach the discussion of the issues and proposals according to existing time constraints. The mediator could suggest that the parties first address those matters requiring prompt attention and defer discussion on the other matters until they could be addressed at a more leisurely pace. . . .

The most effective approach depends on the context of the discussions and the individual parties. What must be underscored is that the approach to the discussion of issues can be deliberate rather than haphazard; it is the mediator's job to ensure that the discussions are intelligently ordered.

Problem 7-5. ***How Do You Structure the Agenda?***

Another approach is to allow the parties to negotiate about the order of the agenda. The mediator might, for example, lay out issues heard, check that the list fully represents the topics that must be addressed, and then ask, "What would you like to talk about first?" What are the advantages of the more directive approach that Stulberg suggests? The disadvantages?

Imagine that you are a mediator faced with parties disputing over the amount of damages a defendant will pay, the timing of the payment, the method of payment, and the type of release that plaintiff will give. In what order would you address these issues? Analyze the advantages and disadvantages of different choices. Wherever you start, having the ability to shelve an issue and get movement elsewhere by moving to another issue can keep the mediation dynamic.

d. Encouraging Movement Towards Options and Agreements

"Generating movement" and overcoming impasse is frequently portrayed as the use of strategies to find a compromise between two extreme positions that disputants take. For example, if one party demands "$1 million" to compensate for damaged reputation, and the response is "I've done nothing wrong. I'll give you nothing. Everything I said was true!", a "compromise" might be the payment of any amount between $0 and $1 million.

However, the idea of movement—and strategies for achieving movement—is a much richer study than simply techniques to encourage compromise, accommodation, and trade-off. Movement of any sort can engender movement of every sort. Consequently, it is helpful to think of movement from a variety of angles.

Mediators are responsible for creating a safe space where both listening and being heard can encourage softening of extreme positions, lessen demonization of the other party, and abate some of the blame and anger disputing parties often experience. Sometimes parties need to be understood before they can move on. Any movement towards understanding and "letting go" is potentially impasse-breaking movement. Other times disputants need to confront the cost of being stuck in blame, recriminations, and extreme, unworkable positions before they can move into a collaborative posture to attempt to find mutually acceptable resolutions.

Former President Bill Clinton describes accompanying Nelson Mandela to the South African prison cell where Mandela slept on the floor for the final 14 years of his incarceration without heat, toilet, or faucet. Clinton asked whether Mandela was bitter and angry as he walked away from that cell after 27 years of imprisonment. Mandela replied that he felt anger rising up, but he said to himself: "Mandela, they had you 27 years. If you are still angry with them when you get out the gate, they will still have you. . . . I wanted to be free, and so I let it go."[3] Mandela thoughtfully weighed the cost of carrying his anger, and he moved beyond it. This internal movement of "letting go" of anger can have powerful consequences, as Mandela's career exemplifies. When negotiating parties relinquish some of their bitterness and animosity, possibilities for resolution emerge.

In your study of negotiation, you learned methods of generating flexibility, creativity and "out-of-the-box" thinking in the context of negotiation. You also examined psychological barriers to "rational" resolutions and methods to address such barriers. The mediator—really a negotiation moderator—must be aware of and use those same strategies and skills. The mediator is charged with

3. William J. Clinton, Acceptance Speech, International Advocate for Peace Award, Benjamin Cardozo School of Law, Mar. 19, 2001.

jump-starting the process of option generation and tries to bring negotiators up to speed, with respect to both a constructive perspective and awareness of productive strategies. The mediator has the advantage of being impartial, providing a lightning rod for frustration, and having a fresh outlook on the situation.

Where substantive resolutions cannot be found, the mediator can assist with a search for procedural resolutions. For example, if disputants agree that Party A should compensate Party B for a piece of antique furniture but cannot agree on the value of the furniture, they might agree to accept the valuation of a neutral expert. Tossing a coin to decide an issue is another example of a procedural resolution.

What follows is a short list of techniques to generate movement that are specifically targeted at mediators. They are divided into three categories. The first and second categories highlight strategies that strengthen the individual negotiating parties and enable them to understand each other's perspective. The third category highlights techniques that may be helpful in developing agreements. Even though this list was developed for mediator training, see how the ideas for effective mediator strategies parallel approaches for negotiators.

Lela P. Love & Joseph B. Stulberg, TARGETS AND TECHNIQUES TO GENERATE MOVEMENT

in Training Materials (2004)

POSITIVE PSYCHOLOGICAL STANCE. EMPOWERMENT. STRENGTH.

1. Compliment productive behavior. ("Thank you both for coming to mediation." "You did a good job explaining your concerns, Ms. A, and you in listening patiently, Mr. B." "I'd like to commend you both for developing a variety of options. Let's try to find one that works for both of you.") Behavior that is commended tends to be repeated. Sincere praise is empowering. As well as being empowering, this move is aimed at educating parties about constructive conduct.

2. Use a "paradoxical intervention." Offer the parties a choice. ("It seems as if you keep returning to the question of who was at fault for the project's failure. We can certainly spend our time together exploring that question if you think that discussion would be useful. Or, in the hour we have remaining today, we could examine how you would like to structure future arrangements to address what happened. It's up to you. How would you like to spend the time?") This intervention is "paradoxical" because typically when people are offered the choice as to whether they would like to continue attacking and blaming each other or to move on, they will choose the latter, while, absent the offer, they will continue to attack and blame.

3. Appeal to principles and ideals. If disputants both agree that, for example, avoiding unnecessary harm or dividing a family's assets so that children share equally or treating men and women equally are shared principles or ideals, then those common goals can shape various elements of the discussion.

UNDERSTANDING. RECOGNITION. PERSPECTIVE TAKING.

1. Highlight common interests, common values and common feelings. ("You both seem to care deeply about the happiness of your child." "If I understand you correctly, you both would like to find a way to end your partnership while preserving the value of the business you have created and also preserving your reputations.") Interests, values and feelings are powerful. When parties discover they share an interest or value or feeling it can become a common motivator and bridge.

2. Build information base regarding each party's interests, assumptions, aspirations, values, priorities, legal analysis and past practices. (*"Tell me more about...."*) Information is frequently the lever that shifts parties in meaningful ways.

3. Try role reversal. This technique comprises a variety of methods to challenge a party to see the situation from the point of view of another party or person. A mediator could actually ask the parties to switch seats or to imagine how the other person is feeling or conceive a solution that the other party would find desirable. (*"Putting yourself for a moment in X's chair and considering what he has said here this morning about . . . how would you see this situation?" "Can you propose a solution that might be regarded favorably by X?"*)

BUILDING SETTLEMENTS AND AGREEMENTS.

1. Explore the costs of no agreement on both quality of life ("What will it be like going home this evening and facing the same situation?") **and process costs** ("Have you explored the costs—in terms of time, money and stress—of litigation?"). Using decision tree formulas, for example, a mediator can assist parties to develop an analysis of the expected value of a litigated outcome (likely court outcome times % likelihood of that court outcome minus costs of litigation and discounted by the time it will take to get outcome) and to compare that figure to proposals on the table.

2. Use deadlines to move participants. ("The building closes at midnight. Up to this point we have achieved x, y, and z. Would you like to bring closure to this in this session? Any ideas?") One reason deadlines may be effective is that loss aversion comes into play. That is, the opportunity to bring closure may be lost forever if movement does not occur.

3. Seek accommodations to priority proposals of the other side. ("Ms. A, you have said you need money immediately, and Ms. B you are most concerned about the amount of the payment, is there any amount between $10,000, Ms. B's first offer, and $100,000, requested by Ms. A, that, Ms. A, you would be willing to accept if the money was paid immediately?").

Problem 7-6. ***Should You Be Transparent?***

Do you think mediators should explain *why* they are using a particular strategy or technique? (Recall our grid of transparency from the end of Chapter 6.) Professor Michael Moffitt explores the advantages of a transparent approach. One example he uses is that a mediator, instead of simply asking a party why the party is making a proposal that the lease run for no more than three years, might say: "I'm hoping you'll change the way you're thinking about your demands. Right now, you seem to be fixed on the idea that there is only one way you can be satisfied in this dispute, and that seems unlikely to me. I think it would be more productive for you and for this process if you (and the rest of us) were better able to understand the things that are motivating you to make these demands. Why is the duration of the lease important to you?" Michael Moffitt, Casting Light on the Black Box of Mediation: Should Mediators Make Their Conduct More Transparent?, 13 Ohio State J. on Disp. Resol. 1, 34 (1997). Or, what if you follow Joseph Stulberg's suggestion to start with easy issues before tackling harder ones, and, in response, a party says, "No, I'm here to talk about the $500,000 he owes"? The mediator, being transparent, might say, "I thought starting with an easier issue might create some momentum for the conversation. We will certainly address all the issues today—including the monetary issue." What are the potential benefits and dangers of a transparent approach? Try it out as you explore the role of a mediator in a roleplay.

e. Using the Caucus

Among the strategies to build a richer information base, encourage perspective taking, and promote a more creative approach to dispute resolution is to invite parties to meet separately with the mediator. After the mediator and each side give an opening statement—and at each juncture for the remainder of the mediation—a choice can be made about whether to stay in joint session or move to caucus. A joint session is where all the participants meet together with the mediator. A caucus is where the mediator meets individually with one side or some subset of the entire participant group (for example, one side only, lawyers only, clients only, kids without parents). In a caucus, parties are invited to speak openly with the assurance that the mediator will not share information conveyed unless given permission to do so. Practically speaking, this means that once a caucus is used, the mediator must keep track of what is said and where it is said, and whether the mediator has permission to share private information with other participants.

Different philosophies guide mediators in determining their preferred approach to using the caucus. Four dominant approaches are followed: never caucus, caucus selectively, mostly caucus, or only caucus. As you read about each of these, consider what goals each approach is most likely to advance: understanding, problem-solving, or settlement?

i. Never Caucus

Mediators using a never caucus approach believe that private meetings can taint the mediator's neutrality, create undue reliance on the mediator, cut off the parties' direct communication, and undermine the opportunity for collaboration. The Understanding-Based model, discussed in Chapter 6, follows this "non-caucus" approach:

> The mediator holds all matters confidential as to outsiders, but holds nothing confidential between the parties. If the mediator speaks with either of the parties separately, which we believe is not the preferred way to proceed, that information is available to the other party. . . . [T]he goal [is] that all parties understand all relevant information rather than the mediator putting him or herself in the position of being the only one who has the whole picture. The mediator will also not speak with the parties' lawyers unless both parties give permission.[4]

ii. Caucus Selectively

In the caucus selectively approach, most meetings are conducted in joint session unless there is a particular reason to caucus. Mediators following this approach might conduct an entire mediation without ever using a caucus. Such mediators view the caucus as a tool used only for particular applications. Reasons *not* to caucus include the belief that direct communication between parties is superior to using an intermediary and that parties benefit from working out matters themselves. A "selective caucus" mediator might suggest a caucus when, for example, communication becomes so heated or the parties so volatile that constructive progress is threatened; an apparent power imbalance suggests that individual explorations of the underlying dynamic is necessary; the mediator believes that more information is available, but it will not be shared with all present; the parties need space to reflect about existing proposals; the parties need space in which to be creative about new proposals about which they are not yet sure; or the mediator wants to "reality check" that proposals being considered are doable and optimal.

iii. Mostly Caucus

In the mostly caucus approach, parties typically meet jointly at the beginning of the mediation and at the end when a resolution is reached. In the middle, the mediator conducts a series of caucuses. Proceeding in this manner ensures that hostilities between the parties do not escalate the dispute and maximizes mediator control over the flow of information and over the way proposals are developed and presented. The caucus, to the extent parties share information

4. Gary Friedman & Jack Himmelstein, Center for Mediation in Law, Memo No. 2, Elements of Mediator-Parties Contract (2003).

about their bottom line, also maximizes the potential benefit of mediation in preventing impasse where there is a positive zone of agreement. However, the approach also takes power and control away from the parties, as the mediator becomes the source of information and the person who holds the key to movement.

iv. Always Caucus

In the always caucus approach, even the joint opening session is eliminated and the mediator shuttles back and forth between the parties for the entire mediation. This approach, which shares many of the benefits and down sides of the mostly caucus approach, eliminates harsh exchanges between the parties, replacing them with the diplomacy of the mediator. Keeping adversarial parties away from one another may be more comfortable for all involved. However, the approach does not have the benefit of allowing the parties to learn directly from each other or to develop a creative synergy in exploring a satisfactory resolution.

Problem 7-7. ***Should You Use a Caucus?***

As a mediator moves along the spectrum from never caucus to always caucus, what is lost and gained? In answering, consider the potential impact on: party understanding and relationship; the possibility of generating creative outcomes; and the goal of achieving a settlement.

f. Drafting Agreements and Closing the Session

Sessions can end without an agreement; with a written agreement; with a verbal agreement; with a partial agreement regarding substantive issues; with an agreement to return for another session; or with an agreement to use some other procedure to address the dispute. One of the final tasks of a mediator is to help parties capture and memorialize their commitments to each other if they have been able to resolve their dispute, and, in every case, formulate a plan going forward. This is an important mediator function for several reasons. First, the mediator must ensure the parties have the same, clear understanding about the agreement so that a dispute does not arise about its terms. Reviewing the terms of agreement (if it is verbal) or reducing the agreement to a writing (if the parties want a written agreement) can aid that task. Second, helping bring closure with an agreement can be important both psychologically and practically. Psychologically, leaving mediation with an agreement means that the matter is put to rest, and that closure is achieved. The internal debate about agreement terms can cease. Practically speaking, the parties can move on with their lives, and the momentum achieved in the session will not be lost by the passage of time and intervening events. If the matter is in litigation, the litigation can end.

Drafting agreements, however, is a task closely connected with the practice of law. Some mediators hesitate to draft agreements or even memoranda of understanding for fear they are engaging in the unauthorized practice of law or may otherwise expose themselves to liability. In business and employment cases where parties have their own attorneys, a mediator may well avoid drafting a detailed and comprehensive agreement. In such instances, the mediator leaves that to the parties' attorneys. Many mediators, however, will draft a "bare-bones" memorandum of understanding at the parties' request, capturing essential features of the agreement.

In situations where the parties do not have lawyers and ask the mediator to draft an agreement, the mediator can provide a valuable service by capturing agreement terms. In community cases, for example, mediators routinely draft agreements, as agencies and parties expect this service to bring effective closure to the mediation.

To avoid a charge of engaging in the unauthorized practice of law, the safest posture for the mediator is to view herself as a scribe, capturing the parties' undertakings, using the parties' exact words, avoiding additional provisions, and advising the parties to get legal advice prior to signing the agreement.

Principles of good agreement drafting include being sure that agreement terms are understandable and precise. This can be achieved by using the parties' own words and "plain English," as well as making sure that payment terms, the time frame and other methods of performance are clear. Mediators also want to make an agreement appealing. To that end, many mediators will begin with a statement of common interests and goals (like a purpose clause in a contract); put mutual obligations first; and balance the agreement (for example, if party A agrees to pay money, then Party B agrees to provide a receipt). An agreement, until it is signed, is merely a draft or proposal. Whether or not it matures into an agreement that is durable will depend in part on the quality of the drafting.

Some research suggests that agreements made by the parties are more likely to be complied with than judgments of a court.[5] To the extent that the parties understand and have endorsed their own agreement, this outcome seems logical.

In every case, whether or not any agreement is achieved, the mediator must end on as positive a note as possible, commending the parties for their efforts and acknowledging any constructive movement that has been made. The mediator will want both parties to leave the session at the same time, avoiding the appearance of partiality that may be created where one side lingers for a private conversation with the mediator. The mediator will also want to ensure there is an exit strategy so that parties who are still uncomfortable in each other's presence do not find themselves together in a small elevator.

5. Roselle L. Wissler, The Effectiveness of Court-Connected Dispute Resolution in Civil Cases, 22 Conflict Res. Q. 55 (2004).

Problem 7-8. *Should the Mediator—or One of the Attorneys—Draft the Parties' Agreement?*

If the mediator is not a lawyer, one concern with drafting an agreement is whether that is the practice of law. In response to the unauthorized practice of law issue, the ABA Section of Dispute Resolution adopted a resolution on Mediation and the Unauthorized Practice of Law on February 2, 2002 (available at https://mediate.com/mediation-and-the-unauthorized-practice-of-law/). With respect to agreement drafting, the resolution advises:

> When an agreement is reached in a mediation, the parties often request assistance from the mediator in memorializing their agreement. The preparation of a memorandum of understanding or settlement agreement by a mediator, incorporating the terms of settlement specified by the parties, does not constitute the practice of law. If the mediator drafts an agreement that goes beyond the terms specified by the parties, he or she may be engaged in the practice of law. However, in such a case, a mediator shall not be engaged in the practice of law if (a) all parties are represented by counsel and (b) the mediator discloses that any proposal that he or she makes with respect to the terms of settlement is informational as opposed to the practice of law, and that the parties should not view or rely upon such proposals as advice of counsel, but merely consider them in consultation with their own attorneys.

Note, however, that this resolution is not controlling on courts or local Bar associations.

If you were a divorce mediator without legal training with a background in psychology, would you feel comfortable drafting an agreement in light of this resolution? If you were an attorney-mediator authorized to practice in the relevant jurisdiction, would you feel comfortable adding "boiler plate" terms to the parties' agreement?

On the other hand, if you are a lawyer and draft the settlement agreement, you could be engaging in a conflict of interest by representing both parties to a divorce (and many jurisdictions do not permit a lawyer to represent both sides in litigation). Some states have directly addressed this concern by noting that drafting the agreement is not considered a conflict as it does not create a lawyer-client relationship. Other states have suggested that this dual representation is permitted.

What if your jurisdiction has a form, and your job is largely to fill in the blanks on a form provided by the appropriate jurisdiction?

5. Other Mediator Approaches

The models and strategies presented above assume that the mediator is chairing a negotiation process where negotiable issues are targeted, and the parties are accompanied and supported in a problem-solving quest to find resolutions to those issues. As Chapter 6 discusses, there are other approaches to mediation. For example, transformative mediation rejects problem-solving as a goal, exclusively seeking instead party empowerment and recognition. Since the goals of transformative mediation differ, at least in some respects, from other types of mediation, practitioner skills also vary. The transformative mediator will focus on practices that empower parties and support recognition between them. The opening statement of a transformative mediator will lay out these goals, indicating that settlement is only one of the possible outcomes of the mediation. All critical choices about process and outcome will be strictly left to the parties, and the mediator will consistently follow, rather than lead, the parties.

The evaluative mediator, mentioned in Riskin's grid in Chapter 6, uses many of the facilitative skills discussed above and *also* must be adept at evaluation—skills more akin to those of an arbitrator. In addition to finding facts and applying legal rules or industry customs—or determining what might be the most acceptable or the most likely court outcome—mediators who evaluate must do it in a way that, ideally, makes parties feel non-defensive and that is least likely to impact the parties' perception of the mediator's neutrality. This is particularly important if the mediator plans to continue mediation if the evaluation does not result in an agreement.

B. THE ATTORNEY REPRESENTATIVE

> *If lawyers are not leaders in marshaling cooperation and designing mechanisms that allow it to flourish, they will not be at the center of the most creative social experiments of our time.*
>
> —Derek Bok, former president of Harvard University

In Section A, above, you examined how a mediator prepares for and strategizes about various steps in the mediation process. Now change your perspective to an attorney representing a client in mediation. All the negotiation skills you studied, and many of the mediator skills, are relevant for the attorney representative too. We will look now at add-on considerations for the attorney operating in a mediation context. Professor Harold Abramson offers attorneys a framework for representing clients in mediation that he labels the Mediation Representation Triangle. The three elements of the Triangle are: (1) negotiating effectively in the mediation process; (2) enlisting the assistance of the mediator; and (3) developing a representation plan that focuses on: selecting a suitable mediator, preparing pre-mediation submissions, participating in pre-mediation conferences, presenting opening statements, and switching strategically between joint sessions and caucuses. For each of these opportunities for representation, Abramson recommends that attorneys figure out how to advance their client's interests through problem-solving choices.[6]

---

6. Harold Abramson, Mediation Representation: Advocating in a Problem-Solving Process (3d ed., 2013).

What follows is an analysis of the problem-solving perspective, followed by advice about how to put the perspective into action—as well as what actions the attorney representative should avoid.

1. The Problem-Solving Perspective

In the excerpt that follows, Professor Leonard Riskin describes an attitude and perspective shift—a new orientation that lawyers must adopt to be constructive mediation advocates.

Leonard L. Riskin, MEDIATION AND LAWYERS

43 Ohio St. L.J. 29, 43-45 (1982)

E.F. Schumacher begins his Guide for the Perplexed with the following story:

> On a visit to Leningrad some years ago, I consulted a map . . . but I could not make it out. From where I stood, I could see several enormous churches, yet there was no trace of them on my map. When finally an interpreter came to help me, he said: "We don't show churches on our maps." Contradicting him, I pointed to one that was very clearly marked. "That is a museum," he said, "not what we call a 'living church.' It is only the 'living churches' we don't show." It then occurred to me that this was not the first time I had been given a map which failed to show many things I could see right in front of my eyes. All through school and university I had been given maps of life and knowledge on which there was hardly a trace of many of the things that I most cared about and that seemed to me to be of the greatest possible importance to the conduct of my life.

The philosophical map employed by most practicing lawyers and law teachers, and displayed to the law student—which I will call the lawyer's standard philosophical map—differs radically from that which a mediator must use. What appears on this map is determined largely by the power of two assumptions about matters that lawyers handle: (1) that disputants are adversaries—i.e., if one wins, the others must lose—and (2) that disputes may be resolved through application, by a third party, of some general rule of law. These assumptions, plainly, are polar opposites of those which underlie mediation: (1) that all parties can benefit through a creative solution to which each agrees; and (2) that the situation is unique and therefore not to be governed by any general principle except to the extent that the parties accept it.

In addition to the perspective shift that Riskin describes, the lawyer must be comfortable with appropriate strategies and skills for a consensual process.

2. Strategies and Skills of the Attorney Representative

a. Prescriptions for the Attorney

Larry Watson, a former litigator and seasoned mediator of civil trial cases, provides practical guidance.

Lawrence M. Watson, Jr., EFFECTIVE ADVOCACY IN MEDIATION: A PLANNING GUIDE TO PREPARE FOR A CIVIL TRIAL MEDIATION

prepared for various Continuing Legal Education programs

. . . With the expansion of mediation as the leading ADR process, it is clear that the civil trial counsel's role must thus also expand to include proficiency in reaching acceptable mediated settlements for their clients. The growth of ADR is redefining the role of the American trial lawyer. . . .

STEP ONE: PREPARING THE CLIENT FOR THE MEDIATION EXPERIENCE

It is critically important to have the clients understand that the outcome of the mediation process contemplates "win-win," not "win-lose." Mediation is a process that seeks to *reconcile* disputes. Mediation is not a process that seeks to *adjudicate* disputes. The outcome of reconciliation is an *agreement* with the other side. The outcome of adjudication is a *judgment* against the other side. There are big differences between the two. . . .

Clients should therefore understand that the mediation program does not dwell on who may be proven right or wrong in court—it is a factor, but not a controlling factor. To be successful at mediation, the client must understand the focus must ultimately come to mutually satisfying the interests of all parties to the dispute. Simply stated, the process involves compromise—giving as well as getting. . . .

Bear in mind, one salient difference between resolving disputes through adjudication and resolving disputes through reconciliation is the range of settlement options available to the parties. With the exception of some limited equitable relief that might [be] available in some cases, the judicial resolution of a dispute will be restricted to money judgments. An important benefit offered to parties agreeing to reconcile their differences is the broad range of settlement options that can be deployed. Thinking through and developing contingent plans to utilize these options in advance, doing feasibility research on settlement alternatives before the mediation starts, can dramatically increase the potential for a successful outcome. . . .

STEP TWO: DEFINING THE OVERALL GOALS OF MEDIATION

The first step of any journey is to decide where you want to go. In a civil trial mediation, that step is taken by simply sitting down with the client and mutually agreeing, in concept, on a range of acceptable outcomes to the mediation process. As noted above, every effort should be made to avoid "bottom line" dollar amount absolutes. To the contrary the client should be impressed and thinking about the wide range of objectives which could become available through a well-structured and prepared mediation session. . . .

STEP THREE: DECIDING WHEN, WHERE, WHO AND HOW WE WILL MEDIATE THIS CASE

Although a bit dated, an attitude still exists among many trial lawyers (and litigation clients) that being the first one to suggest mediation—or any settlement process—is a sign of weakness to be avoided. A "macho mind set" about the case would suggest that even discussing reconciliation signals a lack of confidence in the merits of one's position, and involves an immediate loss of face. There are a number of ways to get past this problem.

In jurisdictions where mediation is mandatory, the problem can be avoided by simply noting that going to mediation is an inevitable circumstance and both sides would be better off attempting to take the initiative to control the process. The argument that both parties are better served by deciding on a mutually agreeable mediator, picking a time and location of their choosing, and defining the format for the process themselves rather than allowing the judge or a court administrator to do it for them is compelling. . . .

Another approach is to attribute the idea to the economics. Once a litigation plan is roughly sketched, it is natural for both sides to note the costs involved in legal fees and expenses.

A. Selection of the Mediator

In preparing the initial list, or in making the final selection from the list, it is wise to take the time to complete some level of research on each mediator under consideration. Ask the mediators under consideration to submit resumes and, more importantly, the names of other counsel with whom they have worked in the past. Contact those lawyers and ask about the proposed mediator's style, energy, creativity and success rate. Network with other lawyers in your own firm or in the field to see if they have had any experience with the proposed mediator as well. Prepare a short report on each and include the client in the final determination. In particularly significant cases where the proposed mediators are unknown, arrange for a short interview session to meet with the proposed mediators in advance. Again, including the client in those sessions will go a long way to help determine the best person for the job.

The overall goal in selecting the mediator should be to find an individual who can truly serve as a neutral, who demonstrates a capacity to work hard, and who will command the respect of both sides.

B. Location, Duration and Timing

The choice of location for a mediation session should be driven solely by the physical requirements necessary to stage the event. Appropriate considerations would thus include reasonable travel accessibility, ample room for attendees in joint and caucus sessions, adequate secured storage space for files and materials, overnight lodging opportunities and some separation from other distractions. Choice of location should never be allowed to become a positional issue involving a "home court" advantage of one party or another.

The duration and timing for a mediation is, perhaps, more important than the location. Sufficient time should be allotted for a mediation to allow for adequate presentations by all parties followed by ample time to privately caucus and develop alternative resolution options. Obviously, the number of parties, complexity of issues, and dollar amounts involved will play into defining an appropriate time to reserve for the mediation. The decision-making temperament of the parties—the amount of time the individuals involved in the dispute will need to make up their minds—is also an important factor in scheduling mediations. Creating situations in which the parties are rushed to judgment, or forced to endure exhausting marathon sessions into the late hours of the night can compromise the validity of the agreement reached. Scheduling or conducting a mediation in a manner that adversely affects the parties' self determination is tantamount to abusing the process. "Mediation remorse" should be carefully avoided. . . .

STEP FOUR: PREPARATION FOR MEDIATION

The presentation of the client's case in the opening phase of a mediation is a task that must meet two, often conflicting, needs.

First, the client must feel his or her story has been told. Any anger, frustration, and discontent stemming from the events leading to the dispute must be relieved before focused attention can be given to reconciliation considerations. To one extent or another, therefore, the client must be given the chance to vent. In all occasions, the client must feel that the merits of . . . his or her position in the debate have been fairly presented and understood.

Secondly (and often in contradiction of satisfying the client's "venting" needs) there is a need for the opening presentations to clearly and effectively communicate the "other side of the story" to the opposition. Many clients to a dispute might be quite pleased with a lawyer that relieves built up feelings and relates their positions in ominous, scolding, or even threatening terms. An overly aggressive tone or demeanor to an opening presentation in a mediation, however, can serve to "turn off" the opposition and the critical task of expanding their understanding of the dispute is not achieved. . . .

One acceptable method of satisfying both needs is to simply allow the client an opportunity to participate in the opening presentations to satisfy whatever venting needs exist. In that event, counsel would prepare and execute an opening presentation geared toward communicating the reality of the dispute to the opposition in a tone and manner best suited to complete that task. The client could then add the emotive element to the presentation while satisfying his or her need to vent.

Accordingly, the best overall theme and tone of opening presentation in mediation would probably be a matter of fact description of the case to be presented at trial—firmly and unequivocally stated. It should clearly set forth the principal contentions underlying the position asserted, and the facts, principal documents, and expert opinions that support those contentions. There should be minimal argument—let the facts do the arguing. . . .

STEP FIVE: SOMETHING OTHER THAN MONEY—PREPARING SETTLEMENT OPTIONS

. . . In commercial cases, a systematic search for settlement options other than money should be conducted before the mediation commences. . . . If there is any way to convert a business dispute to a business opportunity, careful consideration should be given to that option in advance. The objective of any advance consideration of "other than money" settlement options is to make sure that they are potentially doable—that there are no legal, contractual, political or physical barriers to including such terms to the final agreement. The ultimate decision whether or not to include these terms in a final arrangement can be made later. The settlement negotiations themselves should be entered with an, "anything is possible" frame of mind. . . .

An example of a settlement that is a "win-win" and goes beyond a financial payment is the following. Two musicians named Ben Gibbard and Jimmy Tamborello collaborated by sending materials back and forth to each other as they worked on songs, and eventually chose the name "Postal Service" for their band. The United States Postal Service ("USPS") sent them a cease-and-desist letter, alleging a trademark infringement. The USPS and the musicians eventually entered negotiations to avoid litigation and settled with a relatively straightforward licensing arrangement. Stemming from the same initial set of negotiations, however, they also struck a set of business arrangements in which the band performed for the USPS's National Executive Conference and the USPS website sold copies of the band's music.[7] The two stories in Chapter 6—The Sisters and Glen Cove—provide other examples of "win-win" possibilities.

In the next excerpt, Jean Sternlight suggests a case-by-case approach to attorney strategy for representation in mediation, sensitive to the particular client and to each situation.

---

7. Robert Bordone & Michael Moffitt, Create Value out of Conflict, 9 Negot. 1 (2006).

Problem 7-9. *Non-Monetary Settlements and Legal Fees*

Attorneys tend to assume that most disputes turn on money, whereas studies suggest that clients' interests are often much broader. One of the difficulties of other-than-money settlements can be the fee arrangements between lawyers and clients. If the plaintiff's lawyer's fee is based on a percentage of the settlement, then that lawyer has a built-in incentive to maximize settlement dollars. An apology, for example, provides no tangible benefit to a lawyer operating with a contingency fee. If the defense attorney's fee is based on an hourly charge, the defense attorney may have an incentive to allow the dispute to continue rather than resolve. How might lawyers, clients and mediators deal with these potential conflicts of interest?

Jean R. Sternlight, LAWYERS' REPRESENTATION OF CLIENTS IN MEDIATION: USING ECONOMICS AND PSYCHOLOGY TO STRUCTURE ADVOCACY IN A NONADVERSARIAL SETTING

14 Ohio St. J. on Disp. Resol. 269, 274, 291-292, 295-296 (1999)

While no single lawyer's role in mediation is always proper, lawyers need to be particularly vigilant in guarding against their own tendencies to behave in mediation exactly as they would in litigation. Instead, to serve their clients' interests, and in light of the conflicts of interest and perception between lawyers and their own clients, attorneys should often encourage their clients to play an active role in the mediation, allow the discussion to focus on emotional as well as legal concerns, and work toward mutually beneficial rather than win-or-lose solutions. Those lawyers who, seeking to advocate strongly on behalf of their clients, take steps to dominate the mediation, focus exclusively on legal issues, and minimize their clients' direct participation, will often ill serve their clients' true needs and interests. Such overly zealous advocates are frequently poor advocates. . . .

If advocacy is defined broadly as supporting or pleading the cause of another, there is no inconsistency between advocacy and mediation. Permitting an attorney to act as an advocate for her client simply allows that attorney to speak and make arguments on her client's behalf and to help her client achieve her goals. . . . Nor is it clear why "adversarial" behavior, at least broadly defined, is necessarily inconsistent with mediation. To the extent that acting adversarially means advocating only on behalf of one's own client and not on behalf of any other party or on behalf of the process or system, the conduct is easy to reconcile with mediation. The problem-solving that works well in mediation does not require sacrifice of one's self-interest, but rather allows parties to search for solutions that are mutually beneficial. . . .

Yet, while attorneys may appropriately advocate for their clients in mediation, it is certainly true that those attorneys who attempt to employ traditional "zealous" litigation tools when representing their clients in mediation may frequently (but not always) fail either to fulfill their clients' wishes or to serve their clients' interests. Those who would hoard information, rely solely on legal rather than emotional arguments, or refuse to let their clients speak freely will often have little success in mediation. This is not because attorneys ought not to advocate for their clients, but rather because attorneys ought not to advocate *poorly* on behalf of their clients.

---

b. Avoiding Mistakes as a Representative in Mediation

With advice in hand on what you should do as an attorney in mediation, the following excerpt highlights some things you should *not* do.

Tom Arnold, 20 COMMON ERRORS IN MEDIATION ADVOCACY

13 Alternatives 69, 69-71 (1995)

Trial lawyers who are unaccustomed to being mediation advocates [make] common errors. . . .

WRONG CLIENT IN THE ROOM

CEOs settle more cases than vice presidents, house counsel or other agents. Why? For one thing, they don't need to worry about criticism back at the office. Any lesser agent, even with explicit "authority," typically must please a constituency which was not a participant in the give and take of the mediation. That makes it hard to settle cases.

A client's personality also can be a factor. A "Rambo," who is aggressive, critical, unforgiving, or self-righteous doesn't tend to be conciliatory. The best peace-makers show creativity, and tolerance for the mistakes of others. Of course, it also helps to know the subject. . . .

ADDRESSING THE MEDIATOR INSTEAD OF THE OTHER SIDE

Most lawyers open the mediation with a statement directed at the mediator, comparable to opening statements to a judge or jury. Highly adversarial in tone, it overlooks the interests of the other side that gave rise to the dispute.

Why is this strategy a mistake? The "judge or jury" you should be trying to persuade in a mediation is not the mediator, but the adversary. If you want to make the other party sympathetic to your cause, don't hurt him. . . .

FAILURE TO USE ADVOCACY TOOLS EFFECTIVELY

You'll want to prepare your materials for maximum persuasive impact. Exhibits, charts, and copies of relevant cases or contracts with key phrases highlighted can be valuable visual aids. A 90-second video showing key witnesses in depositions making important admissions, followed by a readable size copy of an important document with some relevant language underlined, can pack a punch.

TIMING MISTAKES

Get and give critical discovery, but don't spend exorbitant time or sums in discovery and trial prep before seeking mediation.

Mediation can identify what's truly necessary discovery and avoid unnecessary discovery. One of my own war stories: With a mediation under way and both parties relying on their perception of the views of a certain vice president, I leaned over, picked up the phone, called the vice president, introduced myself as the mediator, and asked whether he could give us a deposition the following morning. "No," said he, "I've got a Board meeting at 10:00." "How about 7:30 A.M., with a one-hour limit?" I asked. "It really is pretty important that this decision not be delayed." The parties took the deposition and settled the case before the 10:00 board meeting. . . .

HURTING, HUMILIATING, THREATENING, OR COMMANDING

Don't poison the well from which you must drink to get a settlement. That means you don't hurt, humiliate or ridicule the other folks. Avoid pejoratives like "malingerer," "fraud," "cheat," "crook," or "liar." You can be strong on what your evidence will be and still be a decent human being.

All settlements are based upon trust to some degree. If you anger the other side, they won't trust you. This inhibits settlement.

The same can be said for threats, like a threat to get the other lawyer's license revoked for pursuing such a frivolous cause, or for his grossly inaccurate pleadings.

Ultimatums destroy the process, and destroy credibility. Yes, there is a time in mediation to walk out—whether or not you plan to return. But a series of ultimatums, or even one ultimatum, most often is very counterproductive.

FAILURE TO TRULY CLOSE

Unless parties have strong reasons to "sleep on" their agreement, to further evaluate the deal, or to check on possibly forgotten details, it is better to get some sort of enforceable contract written and signed before the parties separate. Too often, when left to think overnight and draft tomorrow, the parties think of new ideas that delay or prevent closing.

LACK OF PATIENCE AND PERSEVERANCE

The mediation "dance" takes time. Good mediation advocates have patience and perseverance.

Simeon Baum, another accomplished attorney and mediator, urges advocates in mediation not to balk at emotion.[8] Seasoned mediator Jeff Kichaven chastises attorneys representing clients in mediation for failure to recognize the importance of civility, acknowledgment, and apology.[9] One study concludes that a full apology that accepts responsibility will have a more favorable impact on willingness to settle than a partial, "safe" apology that expresses sympathy.[10] A full apology, however, may be risky if the case does not settle. Nonetheless, given the data, attorneys should help their clients weigh the likely costs and benefits of a partial or full apology.

C. THE IMPACT OF DIFFERENCES AND DIVERSITY

> Culture is a product of "groupness" including practices, beliefs, norms, rules, behaviors and customs which are often further identified with race, nationality, ethnicity, religion, gender and social groups (e.g., self-identifying non-binary, LGBTQ+) and even voluntary associations and affiliations (e.g., political parties, gangs) and "status" cultures (e.g., student, academic, legal, professional, "business" capitalist culture, working class). Culture affects the way we see and process the world, with language, images, assumptions, norms, and the choices we see as acceptable and viable in particular situations.
>
> —Carrie Menkel-Meadow, (2002). Cross-cultural Disputes and Mediator Strategies, in Routledge Handbook of Intercultural Mediation, (Dominic Busch, ed.). New York and London: Routledge Taylor Francis Group.

A thread running through all discussions of skills and strategies—for both neutrals and attorneys—is the importance of differences and diversity. Gender, age, ethnicity, religion, education, social standing, profession, nationality, and a variety of other factors will all impact the conduct of negotiation. They play an equal role in mediation. Psychological differences among parties (for example, extroverts versus introverts) and cultural norms of different groups will require different approaches to mediation. The mediator's cultural and other norms can also be a factor.

Choice of mediator may be influenced by culture. Certain cultures have specific requirements and preferences with respect to mediators and the process generally. A North American view of mediator qualifications typically focuses on neutrality, training, and experience. Other cultures might prefer a "wise elder" who is inextricably linked to the community, is not a stranger to the parties, and will lead—rather than follow—the parties to a resolution. Professor Isabelle Gunning teaches us that other cultures—Navajo peacemakers and the

8. Simeon H. Baum, Top 10 Things Not to Do in Mediation, N.Y. L.J., Apr. 25, 2005, at 510.

9. Jeff Kichaven, Apology in Mediation: Sorry to Say, It's Much Overrated, Int'l Risk Mgmt. Inst. (2003).

10. See, generally, on apology, Jennifer K. Robbennolt, Apologies and Legal Settlement: An Empirical Examination, 102 Mich. L. Rev. 460, 469 (2003).

Filipino Katarungang Pambarangay system—prefer mediators who are not strangers to the parties and who intervene more actively than many American mediators, injecting community values.[11] A student from Ghana, when asked what key mediator trait would engender confidence and acceptability in his country, answered "old."

Every feature of the mediation process—when and where parties meet, how the session is opened, how the seating is arranged, and who attends—is shaped by culture. Attorneys, like mediators, must be skilled in understanding and adapting to cultural differences, both with their clients and across the table in mediation.

In addition to understanding the culture of others, a mediator must understand her own cultural (and other) biases to act impartially. In fact, many scholars point out that neutrality and impartiality—while something to be strived for—are not, in any pure form, attainable. Consider these examples of mediator bias from Professor Trina Grillo:

> George, a Black man, is in the process of divorcing Michelle, a white woman. During the course of the mediation, the mediator asks a number of times whether there is a history of domestic violence. She seems not to believe George or his wife when each insists that although Michelle occasionally has attacked George, he has never fought back.
>
> Elaine is a Black woman, who has worked herself up in the ranks of the local telephone company from an entry level position to her new job, in which she supervises a number of employees. She handles herself with calm and poise, but also a certain coolness. Joe, her husband, who is also Black, is a friendly, gregarious man who has not been reliable in meeting his support obligations or in taking regular responsibility for their two sons. In mediation, Elaine immediately senses that the mediator favors her husband and does not like her. This intuition is confirmed when the mediator permits her husband to interrupt her constantly, but quickly stops her with a sharp lecture when she tries to interrupt him. At one point, the mediator turns to her and says, "I was a single parent too, and I did not have the luxury of an ex-husband who was willing to help me with the children." Five minutes later, the mediator repeats the same statement. When Elaine mentions her debilitating health problems, the mediator laughs and says, "You don't have to act sick to get what you want."[12]

Professor Grillo concludes that while these examples are extreme, questionable mediator impartiality remains a troublesome aspect of any mediation.

Some scholars have concluded that formal processes, like litigation, are more advantageous for minority disputants because more formality deters prejudice by—among other factors—putting people on their best behavior.[13] Additionally, serious questions have been raised about whether minority or female disputants

11. Isabelle R. Gunning, Diversity Issues in Mediation: Controlling Negative Cultural Myths, 1995 J. Disp. Resol. 55.

12. Trina Grillo, The Mediation Alternative: Process Dangers for Women, 100 Yale L.J. 1445, 1586 (1991).

13. Richard Delgado, Chris Dunn, Pamela Brown, Helena Lee & David Hubbert, Fairness and Formality: Minimizing the Risk of Prejudice in Alternative Dispute Resolution, 1985 Wis. L. Rev. 1359.

fare as well in mediation in terms of the monetary outcome as white male participants, particularly if the mediator is not of the same ethnicity as the minority disputant.[14] Another generation of research is needed to address these critical concerns. In the meantime, mediators and attorneys must be acutely aware of these issues and make appropriate adjustments where necessary. They must also strive to understand their own personal and cultural biases and to act impartially.

Problem 7-10. *Know Thyself!*

Reflect on your family of origin—an important aspect of your identity. Recall meals and gatherings. Were they begun with prayer or animated discussion? Did family members interrupt each other or wait for a turn to speak? Recall conflicts in the family. What was the process for resolving conflicts? Whatever your answers, you are probably describing biases you will need to appreciate to serve as either an impartial mediator or an effective representative.

One way to test your biases is to take an online implicit bias test. Go to https://implicit.harvard.edu and try.

Whether you are serving as a mediator or an attorney in mediation, the combination of attention to best practices and constant self-reflection are the keys to improving your practice. We turn now to policy issues, confidentiality, and legal and ethical questions.

Further Reading

ABA Section of Dispute Resolution. (June 12, 2017). Report of the Task Force on Research on Mediator Techniques.

Harold I. Abramson. (3d ed. 2013). Mediation Representation: Advocating in a Problem-Solving Process. New York: Wolters Kluwer Law and Business.

Laurence J. Boulle & Nadja Alexander. (3d ed. 2019). Mediation: Skills and Techniques. Chattswood, NSW: Lexis Nexis Butterworths.

Alyson Carrel & Noam Ebner, Mind the Gap: Bringing Technology to the Mediation Table, 2019 J. Disp. Resol. (2019).

John W. Cooley. (2005). Creative Problem Solver's Handbook for Negotiators and Mediators (Volumes 1 and 2). Washington, DC: ABA Section of Dispute Resolution.

Joseph P. Folger & Robert A. Baruch Bush, Transformative Mediation and Third-Party Intervention: Ten Hallmarks of a Transformative Approach to Practice, 13 Mediation Q. 263 (1996).

14. Gary LaFree & Christine Rack, The Effects of Participants' Ethnicity and Gender on Monetary Outcomes in Mediated and Adjudicated Civil Cases, 30 L. & Soc'y. Rev. 767 (1996).

Gary Friedman & Jack Himmelstein. (2008). Challenging Conflict: Mediation Through Understanding. Washington, DC: ABA Section of Dispute Resolution.

Eric Galton & Lela Love (Eds.). (2012). Stories Mediators Tell. Washington, DC: ABA Section of Dispute Resolution.

Dwight Golann. (2d ed. 2021). Mediating Legal Disputes: Effective Strategies for Neutrals and Advocates. ABA Book Publishing.

John Haynes. (1994). The Fundamentals of Family Mediation. Albany, NY: State University of NY Press.

Carol Izumi, Implicit Bias and the Illusion of Mediator Neutrality, 34 Wash. U. J.L. & Pol'y 71 (2010).

Lela P. Love & Glenn Parker (Eds.). (2017). Stories Mediators Tell—World Edition. Washington, DC: ABA Publishing.

Carrie Menkel-Meadow. (2022). Cross-cultural Disputes and Mediator Strategies, Chapter 2 in Routledge Handbook on Intercultural Mediation (Dominic Busch, ed.). New York and London: Routledge Taylor Francis Group.

Sharon Press and Ellen E. Deason, Mediation: Embedded Assumptions of Whiteness?, 22 Cardozo J. of Conflict Resol. 453 (2021).

J. Edward Russo & Paul J.H. Schoemaker. (1990). Decision Traps: The Ten Barriers to Brilliant Decision-Making and How to Overcome Them. New York: Simon & Schuster.

Andrea Kupfer Schneider & Christopher Honeyman. (2d ed. 2017). The Negotiator's Desk Reference. St. Paul, MN: DRI Press.

Joseph B. Stulberg & Lela P. Love. (3d ed. 2019). The Middle Voice: Mediating Conflict Successfully. Durham, NC: Carolina Academic Press.

Ellen Waldman (Ed.). (2011). Mediation Ethics: Cases and Commentaries. San Francisco: Jossey-Bass Publishers.

Robyn Weinstein & Lance Bond, Visions for the Future: Diversity and Inclusion Initiatives in Court-Annexed ADR Program, 22 Cardozo J. Conflict Resol. 499 (2021).

Roselle L. Wissler & Art Hinshaw, The Initial Mediation Session: An Empirical Examination, 27 Harv. Negot. L. Rev. 1 (2021).

Chapter 8 Mediation: Law, Policy, and Ethics

It must be remembered that there is nothing more difficult to plan, more doubtful of success, nor more dangerous to manage, than the creation of a new system. For the initiator has the enmity of all who would profit by the preservation of the old institutions and merely lukewarm defenders in those who would gain by the new ones.

—Niccolo Machiavelli

Many innovations that start as a simple idea become more complex as their use grows. This natural process of maturation has affected mediation as well. As mediation moves into the courts, the more familiar adversarial paradigm has exerted a gravitational pull, shifting mediation towards litigation with less party participation and interaction, more attorney control, and greater influence of legal norms, sometimes overriding party interests and values. While studying this chapter on legal, policy, and ethical questions, keep in mind that mediation springs from the simple—yet radical—idea of assisting disputing parties to resolve their conflict or construct a deal themselves. Part A examines the interaction between law and mediation and the development of law about mediation. In Part B, four policy issues that continue to be regularly debated are explored. Part C looks at ethical questions for mediators, parties, and their representatives in mediation.

A. MEDIATION AND THE LAW

1. The Relationship Between Law and Mediation

a. The Law's Long Shadow

Particularly where mediation is taking place under the roof of a courthouse or in the context of a litigated case, there can be tension between the rule of law and party choice. For example, when a mediator helps an employer and employee negotiate in the context of a Title VII discrimination claim, should a mediator allow an employee to trade his right to freedom from discrimination for some other benefit the employer offers? Should the mediator at least raise the law's prohibition on discrimination? Or, if a contract claim is being pursued and the statute of limitations has run, should the mediator alert the parties to the fact that a legal claim is barred? Would it make a difference if the mediator were operating in a court-sponsored or mandated program? If the agreement were subject to court approval?

Even where legal principles are not explicitly raised, public values and norms may influence the process. And certainly, where a litigated case is mediated, parties bargain in "the shadow of the law."[1] Law, then, plays a significant role in mediation, as do other norms, even without the mediator being charged with injecting such norms or ensuring a "fair" settlement. Legal and other norms affect the assumptions, expectations, BATNAs, and proposals of bargaining parties and hence shape negotiated outcomes.

Problem 8-1. ***The Shadow of the Law***

When you bargain with a landlord over repairs or with a merchant over defective goods you have purchased, does your understanding of the law affect your negotiation? Are there other situations where the law—or your belief about the law—has an impact on your negotiations?

b. Informed Consent

What if the law's shadow does not reach all parties, and some bargain in ignorance of legal norms? Should parties to a court-mandated mediation negotiate without knowledge of the relevant law? This issue is less troubling when parties are represented by attorneys because the attorneys have the responsibility of informing their clients about the law and legal entitlements. With respect to *pro se* parties, however, Professor Jacqueline Nolan-Haley states that courts requiring unrepresented parties to mediate should ensure that those parties have a basic knowledge of their legal rights.[2] If you agree with this proposition, how could courts or administrative tribunals sponsoring mediation programs ensure that parties have knowledge of their rights? Some courts, for example, make a court attorney available for that service. Others offer literature explaining basic legal information. Many mediators would inquire whether parties would prefer to adjourn a session until they have legal—or other expert—representation or advice.

1. Robert Mnookin & Lewis Kornhauser, Bargaining in the Shadow of the Law: The Case of Divorce, 88 Yale L.J. 950 (1979).

2. Jacqueline M. Nolan-Haley, Informed Consent in Mediation: A Guiding Principle for Truly Educated Decisionmaking, 74 Notre Dame L. Rev. 775, 780 (1999); but see, Joel Kurtzberg & Jamie Henikoff, Freeing the Parties from the Law: Designing an Interest and Rights Focused Model of Landlord/Tenant Mediation, 1997 J. of Disp. Resol. 53.

Another solution for parties who do not understand their legal rights is placing the burden on mediators to provide "simple legal information" without engaging in unauthorized practice of law.[3] This may be fraught with problems. Such a task risks impinging on a mediator's neutrality since legal information often favors one party over another. Parties with information about the law often ask how the law applies to them. If the mediator begins to interpret the law, such conduct quickly becomes the practice of law and the mediator risks liability for engaging in that activity. The mediator may not be an attorney, and, even if she is, she may not have expertise in the law at issue or be positioned to do appropriate research.

Clearly, informed parties are preferable to ignorant ones. However, assuring that parties have full information may not be possible, even if it were desirable. Different counselors, after all, have different opinions, and considerations of the psychological, economic, and social impacts of various options might be as important as the relevant legal norms. Lawyer mediators may overrate the importance of law. Therapist mediators may focus on theories of healing and group dynamics that they use in therapy. Mediators with multiple professions are well advised not to confuse their professional roles. Arguably, the principle of self-determination requires the parties to determine the amount and type of information they wish to obtain when making a decision.

Problem 8-2. ***Legal Information***

Imagine that free or low-cost legal aid and public defenders were readily available to all—analogous to free health care. Would the concern about informed consent evaporate? Does the availability of information on the Internet change the calculus? Or, is it that when people go to court—like when the sick go to a hospital—we expect a higher level of informed consent?

c. Sources of "Law" and Justice

Lawyers tend to think of law—and the related concept of justice—as the body of legal precedents and legislation that govern legal entitlements and duties. In adjudication, justice norms come from these public pronouncements.

In regulating conduct in every sphere of life, however, there are many more norms and expectations that govern an individual's idea of proper conduct. These norms include, for instance, family and community values, religious and moral codes, and practical considerations. Robin Hood was said to be a champion of distributive justice—a belief that resources should be allocated among people in a way that is fair. And he was a criminal in the eyes of the law. In considering distributive justice, principles such as equality, equity, and need come into play. All of those notions might justify Robin Hood's "illegal" conduct in stealing

3. Sandra E. Purcell, The Attorney as Mediator—Inherent Conflict of Interest?, 32 UCLA L. Rev. 986, 1009-1010 (1985).

from the rich to give to the poor. At both an individual and societal level, good relationships, peace, harmony, and the maintenance of stability are values that can impact the outcome of a dispute, but these values may not be reflected in legal doctrine or a court-governed outcome.

Whether or not we assume that parties consider their legal rights as they bargain, there are contexts where even the courts prefer that the parties determine their own outcome regardless of legal entitlements. For example, in Card v. Card, 706 So. 2d 409, 410 (Fla. Dist. Ct. App. 1998), the court articulated a preference for party self-determination over third-party decision making for parenting decisions:

> When divorcing parents cede to the judicial branch of government the duty to decide the most intimate family issues, it is not unlikely that one or both parents will be less than satisfied with the decision. The bench and bar have for years now encouraged divorcing parents to resolve their differences through mediation. In effect, parents have been urged to make their own law, in the hope that they can better live with a decision that is their own, rather than a decision that is externally imposed. Where attempts at mediation or other settlement fail, or are not seriously undertaken, a court must decide.

This proposition is in keeping with the notion that in mediation, the fair outcome is that which the parties themselves find fair and best for their circumstances. According to this view, the application of public norms and the use of public processes is the fallback option when parties cannot agree. When developing their own agreement, parties are not guided solely by those values articulated by courts and legislatures. Rather, they may aspire to guide their conduct by values that the public does not require—values of generosity, forgiveness, and connection, for example. Or they may be driven by practical considerations: their priorities, personal cost-benefit analysis, and the like.

Problem 8-3. ***What Drives Decisions?***

Examine an important decision you have made about a dispute in which you were (or are) involved. What influenced your decision? How important was "the law"?

2. Litigation About Mediation

In some ways, the proliferation of issues and case law surrounding mediation is an alarming development. If mediation is, at its heart, about parties finding a way to resolve their own dispute, often supported by their lawyers and with the help of a mediator, why is this effort to avoid the costs and limited outcomes of lawsuits spawning its own litigation? The answer is probably that growth and use breed complexity. Below is a short, and not exhaustive, survey of issues unique to mediation—that is, questions that arise because mediation has been chosen by or imposed upon the parties, or because a neutral intervener has been added to the negotiation process. Section 3 that follows also examines law but focuses on one issue—confidentiality—a legal issue that dwarfs others in the mediation context in sheer volume of statutes and cases.

a. The Effect of a Duty to Mediate

Generally, courts will enforce obligations to mediate as a prerequisite to allowing access to arbitration or litigation—whether the obligation arises from a court order, a statutory mandate, or a pre-dispute agreement of the parties. A variety of rationales support courts' power to compel mediation. In In Re Atlantic Pipeline Corp., 304 F.3d 135, 140 (1st Cir. 2002), the court lays out the sources of court authority to compel mediation—court rule, applicable statutes, the rules of civil procedure, and the court's inherent power—and affirms the court's power to do so. In an unusual opinion, Annapolis Professional Firefighters Local 1926 v. City of Annapolis, 642 A.2d 889, 895 (Md. Ct. Spec. App. 1994), the court noted that it would enforce an agreement to mediate "to the same extent that it would be enforced if the chosen method were arbitration." In an amusing footnote, the opinion said the court might not enforce an agreement to resolve a dispute by trial by combat or ordeal, but that it did not "wish to put a straightjacket on the creative development of new forms of alternative dispute resolution that individual parties, or industries, find useful and preferable to litigation." Id.

Non-compliance with a contractual duty to mediate could result in a stay of proceedings or a dismissal of the claim, as courts will keep the door shut to arbitration and litigation if parties do not comply with agreements to mediate. For example, in In Re Pisces Foods, LLC, 228 S.W.3d 349 (Tex. App. 2007), where mediation was a precondition to arbitration and neither party had submitted the dispute to mediation, the trial court refused to compel arbitration. The lesson is that dispute resolution clauses that obligate parties to engage in mediation are likely to be enforced—drafters should take note, and should consider defining the contours of the duty they impose, and the mechanism to enforce it!

Courts, legislators, and lawyers in preparing contracts must weigh the possible burden of adding a mediation obligation against the benefits that might follow from the use of mediation.

b. The Enforceability of Mediated Agreements

Once an agreement has been reached in mediation, will it be enforced? In many cases, a mediated agreement is simply a contract between the parties, enforceable like other contracts but with no special standing by virtue of the mediator's participation. In some situations, however, where mediation is part of the court process, a judge or arbitrator will enter the mediation agreement as an order of the court or an arbitral award.

You will see in the section on confidentiality below that confidentiality and privilege intersect with the enforcement of mediated agreements in multiple ways. For example, if mediation is confidential and communications are privileged, how can a party prove a contract defense like fraud, duress, or mistake when challenging an agreement? With respect to enforceability, are oral agreements enforceable if you cannot prove them due to confidentiality? While these questions are explored in the material on confidentiality, take note that the assertion of an oral agreement or a contract defense may have a different outcome where an agreement arises from mediation.

However, while confidentiality can pose challenges to enforceability of mediated agreements, also realize that mediated agreements have their own strengths where they are the product of an exploration of parties' interests, a thoughtful weighing of options, and mediator-driven reality testing. Those features of the mediation process arguably make mediation agreements more durable than many contracts, and more durable than court awards, in situations where one side seeks to avoid judgment.

Increasingly, legislation is being developed that makes mediation agreements easier to enforce, like arbitration awards. For example, the European Union Directive on Mediation requires that: "Member States shall ensure that . . . the parties, or for one of them with the explicit consent of the others, [can] request that the content of a written agreement resulting from mediation be made enforceable . . . by a court or other competent authority in a judgment or decision or in an authentic instrument in accordance with the law of the Member State where the request is made."[4]

In 2018, the Singapore Convention on Mediation was adopted by the United Nations General Assembly. The Singapore Convention, developed by the U.N. Commission on International Trade Law (UNCITRAL), was created to promote international trade and commerce by enabling disputing parties to easily enforce cross-border settlement agreements arising out of international commercial mediation. As of June 2024, 57 countries have signed the Singapore Convention and 14 countries have ratified it. Its sister document, the New York Convention on the Recognition and Enforcement of Foreign Arbitral Awards, adopted in 1958 and now ratified by 172 countries, enables the ready enforcement of cross-border arbitral awards and has given arbitration a serious boost as the international dispute resolution process of choice. The Singapore Convention should help boost mediation's international use and popularity, just as the New York Convention did for arbitration.

c. Special Requirements of Mediated Agreements

Sometimes it is unclear whether a memorandum of understanding or an agreement entered into during a mediation session was intended to bind the parties in the same way as a contract. Particularly where mediation is compelled by courts, scholars and legislatures have worried that the momentum created by the process would unduly pressure parties into agreements. Wanting to ensure that mediated agreements are entered into with care, some legislatures have imposed special requirements on mediated agreements. For example, in Haghighi

4. Directive 2008/52/EC of the European Parliament and of the Council of 21 May 2008 on Certain Aspects of Mediation in Civil and Commercial Matters.

v. Russian-American Broadcasting Co., 173 F.3d 1086, 1087 (8th Cir. 1999), because a settlement agreement did not contain the magic words required by Minnesota statute that it "was binding," the courts refused to enforce an otherwise fair agreement signed by the parties and their attorneys. The lesson of *Haghighi* is that drafters of mediated agreements must be on guard for special requirements imposed by legislatures to make agreements binding in the mediation context.

3. Confidentiality in Mediation

Since the beginning of the modern mediation movement, confidentiality offered to the parties has often been a hallmark of mediation. The promise of confidentiality, in turn, has created complex legal and policy issues, some of which remain unsettled. This section explores those issues.

Like speaking with an attorney, a priest, a psychiatrist, or a doctor, most people expect that their conversation with a mediator will be kept in confidence. In most cases, such special relationships are protected by legal privileges that are created by statute and evidence rules. Additionally, many professionals may have ethical duties, imposed by professional standards of conduct, not to disclose those communications where privacy is expected or promised. Contracts can also protect communications between parties and professionals from disclosure.

Confidentiality is deemed necessary in relationships where parties might not otherwise share information, and where furthering the particular relationship, activity, or service is important to society. Settling disputes is important to both courts and communities. Since, arguably, parties would not be candid with mediators without confidentiality protections, confidentiality is thought by many to be critical to mediation. Further, calling mediators to testify raises issues about their neutrality, since the mediator's testimony will most likely favor one party over another. Proponents of confidentiality point out that confidentiality also helps protect mediators and mediation programs from being bombarded by subpoenas. Fairness considerations also weigh in favor of confidentiality, as a more sophisticated party might use mediation to obtain information and then use the information to harm or take advantage of the more forthcoming party.

However, opponents of blanket confidentiality raise important concerns. There is always tension between the public's right to obtain the "truth" or "every person's testimony" in adjudicative proceedings and the public good furthered by confidentiality. Where important matters are being resolved out of public view, concerns arise about coercion, misconduct, and a loss of societal protections for the less powerful. Confidentiality interferes with public oversight. Some have argued that confidentiality is not necessary for mediation to succeed, and indeed programs have operated successfully without confidentiality protections.

Different balances have been struck between the need for mediation confidentiality and the need for disclosure about what occurred in mediation. In striking that balance, both common law and statutes have been used, both to protect confidentiality as well as to delineate exceptions. The discussion that follows outlines the legal sources of confidentiality protections and exceptions to confidentiality laws and privileges. In doing so, this section reviews decisions applying statutory and common law. However, state-by-state variation in the law (not to mention international differences) and conflicting court opinions make this area murky. At the end of this section, you will see an attempt to bring coherence: the Uniform Mediation Act.

a. Sources of Confidentiality

i. Common Law and Evidentiary Exclusions

Traditionally, evidence concerning offers of settlement and compromise of disputed claims has been excluded in judicial proceedings on the grounds of it being not probative as an admission with respect to the amount or validity of a claim. Parties, for example, might make a settlement offer simply to get rid of a claim, or perhaps out of sympathy for the other side even where they do not feel legally responsible. However, statements of fact—"I am to blame because I was texting when I crossed into your lane"—made in settlement discussions would be admissible under the common law.

Federal Rule of Evidence 408 and similar state counterparts broaden the common-law protection. In addition to settlement offers, Rule 408 protects evidence of conduct or statements made in compromise negotiations as well. While Rule 408 provides more protection for settlement discussions, the protection is still quite limited. Evidence from settlement discussions may be introduced to show bias or prejudice, impeach credibility, or prove a material matter other than liability. To be excluded, the evidence must have a sufficient relationship to discussions of settlement. Furthermore, the rule applies only to subsequent litigation (not administrative or legislative

> **Federal Rule of Evidence 408**
>
> COMPROMISE AND OFFERS TO COMPROMISE
>
> (a) Prohibited uses. Evidence of the following is not admissible on behalf of any party, when offered to prove liability for, invalidity of, or amount of a claim that was disputed as to validity or amount, or to impeach through a prior inconsistent statement or contradiction:
>
> (1) furnishing or offering or promising to furnish—or accepting or offering or promising to accept—a valuable consideration in compromising or attempting to compromise the claim; and
>
> (2) conduct or statements made in compromise negotiations regarding the claim, except when offered in a criminal case and the negotiations related to a claim by a public office or agency in the exercise of regulatory, investigative, or enforcement authority.
>
> (b) Permitted uses. This rule does not require exclusion if the evidence is offered for purposes not prohibited by subdivision (a). Examples of permissible purposes include proving a witness' bias or prejudice; negating a contention of undue delay; and proving an effort to obstruct a criminal investigation or prosecution.

hearings or other types of public disclosure), and there must be a disputed civil claim (that is, negotiations over matters that are not a legal cause of action may not be protected).

Given the many complexities and exceptions included in Rule 408, if a mediator were to explain the law thoroughly to the parties, what level of confidence do you think they would have about the confidentiality of the process? Do you think Rule 408, standing alone, is a sufficient protection for statements made in mediation?

ii. Discovery Limitations

In addition to Rule 408, mediation communications might receive protection under the Federal Rules of Civil Procedure and comparable state rules. Discovery Rule 26(c) has been invoked to protect a party from harm that might be caused by divulging information learned in mediation. That rule would allow a party to seek, and a court to issue, a protective order to protect a party "from annoyance, embarrassment, oppression, or undue burden or expense."

iii. Contracts

In agreements to mediate, parties can, and frequently do, agree not to disclose information conveyed in the mediation and not to subpoena the mediator to testify about what happened. Mediators, both in their opening statements to parties and in agreements to mediate, typically promise not to disclose information that arises in the mediation. Such agreements may provide additional protection for confidentiality.

For example, in Princeton Insurance Company v. Vergano, 883 A.2d 44 (Del. Ch. 2005), where medical malpractice defendants sought the mediator's testimony that plaintiff's representations in

A Sample Confidentiality Provision from an Agreement to Mediate

Confidentiality. The parties and mediator agree to the following confidentiality provisions:

a. Without the consent of all parties and an order of the court, no evidence that there has been a mediation or any fact concerning the mediation may be admitted in a trial de novo or in any subsequent proceeding involving any of the issues or parties to the mediation.
b. Statements made and documents produced in this mediation which are not otherwise discoverable are not subject to discovery or other disclosure and are not admissible into evidence for any purpose, including impeachment.
c. The mediator will not discuss the mediation process or disclose any communications made during the mediation process except as authorized by the parties or required by law or other applicable professional codes. If either party seeks to subpoena the mediator or the mediator's records, that party shall be liable for, and shall indemnify the mediator against, any liabilities, costs, or expenses, including reasonable attorneys' fees, which the mediator may incur in resisting such compulsion.

Agreement provision provided by Professor James Coben.

mediation about her pain and suffering were inconsistent with surreptitious post-mediation surveillance videos, the court refused to force the mediator to testify. The Court pointed both to public policy and to the terms of the parties' own mediation agreement. Their agreement specified that the mediator would not be called on to testify, and that statements at the mediation would remain confidential and could not be used in any judicial proceeding.

However, courts may refuse to enforce a confidentiality agreement because suppression of evidence needed in litigation is contrary to public policy. Hence, legal protection for such agreements is not certain. Even if the confidentiality agreement is upheld for those signing it, third parties may have access to the information through discovery and subsequent use in trial.

iv. Statutory and Judicially Created Privileges

A privileged communication is protected from being divulged in court. Privileges, the strongest protection of confidentiality in mediation, can be created by statutes or by court decisions.

An example of a statutory privilege is in the box to the right. Yet even such seemingly clear statutes do not necessarily yield predictable answers regarding mediation privilege. Cases construing this California statutory privilege reach different outcomes. In the *Foxgate* case, which follows in the policy section on "good faith," the privilege is upheld. Following *Foxgate*, in Eisendrath v. Superior Court, 134 Cal. Rptr. 2d 716 (Cal. Ct. App. 2003), the court also upheld the privilege in the context of mediation communications between a husband and wife, holding that no evidence of such communications was admissible even if the communications were made outside the presence of the mediator, as long as they were materially related to the mediation. However, the *Olam* case below creates an exception to the confidentiality privilege, holding that the statutorily created privilege yields to a claim of undue influence

California Evidence Code §703.5. Judges, arbitrators or mediators as witnesses; subsequent civil proceeding

No person presiding at any judicial or quasi-judicial proceeding, and no arbitrator or mediator, shall be competent to testify, in any subsequent civil proceeding, as to any statement, conduct, decision, or ruling, occurring at or in conjunction with the prior proceeding, except as to a statement or conduct that could (a) give rise to civil or criminal contempt, (b) constitute a crime, (c) be the subject of investigation by the State Bar or Commission on Judicial Performance, or (d) give rise to disqualification proceedings.

California Evidence Code §1119. Written or oral communications during mediation process; admissibility

(a) No evidence of anything said or any admission made for the purpose of, in the course of, or pursuant to, a mediation or a mediation consultation is admissible or subject to discovery, and disclosure of the evidence shall not be compelled, in any arbitration, administrative adjudication, civil action, or other noncriminal proceeding in which, pursuant to law, testimony can be compelled and given. . . .
(c) All communications, negotiations, or settlement discussions by and between participants in the course of a mediation . . . shall remain confidential.

where there is an express waiver of confidentiality by the parties. Reading these cases together, you will see a struggle to balance various public policy interests.

In addition to statutory privileges, some courts have created common law privileges for mediation communications. The case of Folb v. Motion Picture Industry, 16 F. Supp. 2d 1164 (1998), explores the costs and benefits of a mediation privilege and the essential elements in the creation of a privilege. In *Folb*, the plaintiff (Folb), in a discrimination action against his former employer (the Plans), seeks information from a mediation session between the Plans and another employee (Vasquez) whom Folb allegedly sexually harassed. Applying the federal common law of privilege, the court denied Folb access to mediation information—information that might have exonerated him from the charge by his employer—and created a federal mediation privilege—at least in those federal courts bound by this decision. The court cited the following factors as critical to the creation of a common law privilege:

> (1) whether the asserted privilege is "rooted in the imperative need for confidence and trust[;]" (2) whether the privilege would serve public ends; (3) whether the evidentiary detriment caused by exercise of the privilege is modest; and (4) whether denial of the federal privilege would frustrate a parallel privilege adopted by the states. Id. at 1171.

v. Ethical Norms

Finally, ethical norms about confidentiality are yet another source of confidentiality regulation. The Model Standards of Conduct for Mediators (2005), sponsored by the American Bar Association, the American Arbitration Association, and the Association for Conflict Resolution, provide that: "A mediator shall maintain the confidentiality of all information obtained by the mediator in mediation, unless otherwise agreed to by the parties or required by applicable law." This code of conduct, and others like it, mean that mediators could be challenged in ADR provider proceedings and professional license and discipline proceedings (if they are lawyers or other professionals with disciplinary bodies), and that parties can try to use ethical rules to protect confidentiality in other settings, like malpractice lawsuits.

b. Exceptions to Confidentiality

While several exceptions to confidentiality are discussed below, perhaps the biggest exception is the fact that mediation evidence is regularly considered by courts without confidentiality being raised either by the court or the participants, leading to the conclusion that "the walls of the mediation room are remarkably transparent."[5]

5. James R. Coben & Peter N. Thompson, Disputing Irony: A Systematic Look at Litigation About Mediation, 11 Harv. Negot. L. Rev. 43, 59 (2006).

i. Criminal or Quasi-Criminal Cases

In criminal or quasi-criminal cases, where the defendant's constitutional rights and personal liberty are at stake, there is more momentum to admit mediation communications. In Florida v. Castellano, 460 So. 2d 480 (Fla. Dist. Ct. App. 1984), the court held that privileges in Florida had to be established by the legislature and could not be judicially created. In that case, a criminal defendant in a murder case, to support a contention of self-defense, sought the testimony of a community mediator that the murder victim had made life-threatening statements to the defendant during a mediation. Despite the mediator's assurance to the parties of confidentiality, the court ordered the mediator to testify and stated that: "If confidentiality is essential to the success of the CDSP [Citizens Dispute Settlement Program] program, the legislature is the proper branch of government from which to obtain the necessary protection." Id. at 482. In addition to rejecting the privilege argument, the court rejected an argument that the mediation communications were protected under the Federal Rules of Evidence as "offers to compromise," noting that the "plain language of the provision only excludes evidence of an offer of compromise presented to prove liability or the absence of liability for a claim or its value . . . [which is] simply not relevant to the situation where a mediator testifies in a criminal proceeding regarding an alleged threat made by one party to another in a prior CDSP setting." Id. at 481.

However, courts have also upheld confidentiality in criminal contexts. In People v. Snyder, 492 N.Y.S.2d 890 (Sup. Ct. 1985), where a defendant in a murder case also sought the testimony of a community mediator to support his claim of self-defense, confidentiality was upheld. A New York Supreme Court held that the statute establishing the Community Dispute Resolution Center's program provided for confidentiality, which could not be waived by parties. Similarly, in State v. Williams, 877 A.2d 1258 (N.J. 2005), where a defendant sought to support his self-defense claim in an assault action with testimony from a mediator, the court held that the state's interest in protecting mediation confidentiality outweighed the defendant's need for evidence, particularly where the defendant had other evidence to support his self-defense claim and there were concerns about mediator neutrality.

In juvenile cases, courts are more likely to pierce confidentiality to protect the youth, rather than the mediation process. In Rinaker v. Superior Court of San Joaquin County, 62 Cal. App. 4th 155 (3d Dist. 1998) (discussed in *Olam* below), a California appellate court found that inconsistent statements made by a witness in a confidential mediation proceeding could be admitted when balanced against the competing goals of preventing perjury and preserving the integrity of the truth-seeking process of a juvenile delinquency hearing. In this context, the *Rinaker* court found that:

> neither the witness nor the mediator had a reasonable expectation of privacy in inconsistent statements made by the witness during confidential mediation because it has long been established that, when balanced against the competing goals of preventing perjury and preserving the integrity of the truth-seeking process of a juvenile delinquency proceeding, the interest in promoting settlements (in this case through confidential mediation of a civil harassment action

against the minors) must yield to the minors' constitutional right to effective impeachment. Id. at 161.

Inconsistencies like this gave rise to the Uniform Mediation Act (UMA), discussed below. In Section 6 of the UMA, court proceedings involving a felony are exceptions to a confidentiality privilege if the need for the evidence substantially outweighs the interest in protecting the privilege.

Outside of the use of mediation communications in court, questions arise about whether confidentiality may be breached for health and safety purposes. In particular, exceptions may arise if there is a credible threat of harm to self or others at the mediation session. Mediators may also be mandatory reporters of child abuse and neglect.

ii. Mediation Documents

Will documents produced in or for mediation be usable in later litigation? The answer is unclear and will vary by jurisdiction.

In In re Grand Jury Proceedings, 148 F.3d 487 (5th Cir. 1998), the court held that mediation documents could be subpoenaed for grand jury investigation. Construing the Agricultural Credit Act, which provides that mediation sessions shall be confidential to qualify for federal funding, the court declined to infer a privilege for documents sought by a grand jury.

However, in Rojas v. Los Angeles Superior Court, 93 P.3d 260 (Cal. 2004), the California Supreme Court decided that evidence prepared for a mediation in an action for construction defects, including photographs, expert witness reports, and raw test data, was not discoverable in a subsequent action even though the repairs in question had been made so the evidence was otherwise unobtainable. In the first suit, owners of an apartment complex sued contractors and settled in mediation. In the second suit, residents of the apartments sued the building owners and sought to obtain evidence the owners had compiled while securing their settlement in mediation with the contractors. The Supreme Court held that the evidence was not discoverable, pursuant to California's Evidence Code, section 1119(b), which provides: "No writing, as defined in section 250, that is prepared for the purpose of, in the course of, or pursuant to, a mediation . . . is admissible or subject to discovery. . . ." Id. at 265. Citing *Foxgate*, the Court gave great deference to the statutory confidentiality privilege and the importance of the legislative policy protecting mediation confidentiality, noting that the legislature, not the courts, should create exceptions to mediation confidentiality or privilege.

This section may well encourage you to consider stamping documents used in mediation "For mediation only," to attempt to preserve an objection to the use of the documents in subsequent litigation.

iii. Contract Defenses

Recall the prior section on the enforceability of agreements arising in mediation. Since mediation is a negotiation process that most often moves towards an agreement, or contract, traditional contract defenses—mistake, duress, fraud, undue influence, technical failings of the document—are raised in the context of enforcing mediated settlement agreements. Courts resolve these cases using general contract law principles. However, confidentiality protections could make such cases difficult, if not impossible, to prove. Consequently, many courts are reluctant to impose bright-line rules regarding confidentiality that would result in unfairness.

So, for example, a contract defense of mutual mistake might open the door to mediation communications. In DR Lakes Inc. v. Brandsmart U.S.A., 819 So. 2d 971, 972 (Fla. Dist. Ct. App. 2002), where a party claimed that a settlement agreement entered after mediation contained a $600,000 clerical error, the court allowed evidence as to what transpired in the mediation, holding that the privilege for mediation confidentiality must yield in such instances.

The defense of incapacity has, at least in one jurisdiction, pierced confidentiality. The Georgia Supreme Court, in Wilson v. Wilson, 282 Ga. 728, 732 (2007) created an exception to confidentiality where a party contended that he was incompetent to sign an agreement, allowing the mediator to testify as to whether a party had the mental capacity to enter a settlement agreement.

The contract defense of duress has opened the door to breaching mediation confidentiality. In FDIC v. White, 76 F. Supp. 2d 736 (N.D. Tex. 1999), a party tried to avoid a mediation settlement agreement by alleging that threats of criminal prosecution made in mediation were coercive. Considering these allegations of duress, a federal district court in Texas allowed into evidence otherwise privileged mediation communications, ultimately finding that the written settlement agreement was not the result of duress. Or consider McKinlay v. McKinlay, 648 So. 2d 806 (Fla. Dist. Ct. App. 1995), where a wife in a divorce action, to avoid a mediation settlement agreement, alleged she was badgered and intimidated by her husband's counsel, given inaccurate information, and pressured by the mediator, and also pressured by her own counsel to settle. The wife also asserted she was under severe emotional distress at the time of the mediation. The court held that these allegations waived her statutory privilege to preclude mediation communications and testimony from the mediator and that it was "a breach of fair play to deny husband the opportunity to present rebuttal testimony." Id. at 810.

In the *Olam* case below, despite the mediation privilege created by the California Evidence Code (see box on page 280), the court admits evidence of mediation communications. The plaintiff, who was 65 years old and suffering from high blood pressure, was represented by an attorney in a court-sponsored, voluntary mediation. She asserted that she had signed a Memorandum of Understanding (MOU) under duress and hence sought to avoid its enforcement. Both parties expressly waived their statutory mediation privilege. After finding that the parties' waiver of confidentiality was not a sufficient basis to order the mediator to testify, the court conducted a two-stage balancing analysis and concluded that the mediator should testify. Judge Brazil, a noted scholar in the ADR field, thoughtfully lays out pertinent considerations in the opinion and finds the need for mediator testimony trumps the need to protect mediation confidentiality.

OLAM v. CONGRESS MORTGAGE CO.

68 F. Supp. 2d 1110, 1118, 1131-1134, 1136-1139 (N.D. Cal. 1999)

. . . [P]laintiff alleges that at the time she signed the MOU she was suffering from physical pain and emotional distress that rendered her incapable of exercising her own free will. She alleges that after the mediation began during the morning of September 9, 1998, she was left *alone* in a room *all* day and into the early hours of September 10, 1998, while all the other mediation participants conversed in a nearby room. She claims that she did not understand the mediation process. In addition, she asserts that she felt pressured to sign the MOU—and that her physical and emotional distress rendered her unduly susceptible to this pressure. As a result, she says, she signed the MOU against her will and without reading and/or understanding its terms. . . .

We turn to the issue of whether, under California law, we should compel the mediator to testify—despite the statutory prohibitions set forth in sections 703.5 and 1119 of the Evidence Code. The most important opinion by a California court in this arena is Rinaker v. Superior Court, 62 Cal. App. 4th 155 (3d Dist. 1998). In that case the Court of Appeal held that there may be circumstances in which a trial court, over vigorous objection by a party and by the mediator, could compel testimony from the mediator in a juvenile delinquency proceeding (deemed a "civil" matter under California law). The defendant in the delinquency proceeding wanted to call the mediator to try to impeach testimony that was expected from a prosecution witness. That witness and the delinquency defendant had earlier participated in a mediation—and the delinquency defendant believed that the complaining witness had made admissions to the mediator that would substantially undermine the credibility of the complaining witness's testimony—and thus would materially strengthen the defense. In these circumstances, the *Rinaker* court held that the mediator could be compelled to testify if, after in camera consideration of what her testimony would be, the trial judge determined that her testimony might well promote significantly the public interest in preventing perjury and the defendant's fundamental right to a fair judicial process.

In essence, the *Rinaker* court instructs California trial judges to conduct a two-stage balancing analysis. The goal of the first stage balancing is to determine whether to compel the mediator to appear at an in camera proceeding to determine precisely what her testimony would be. In this first stage, the judge considers all the circumstances and weighs all the competing rights and interests, including the values that would be threatened not by public disclosure of mediation communications, but by ordering the mediator to appear at an in camera proceeding to disclose only to the court and counsel, out of public view, what she would say the parties said during the mediation. At this juncture the goal is to determine whether the harm that would be done to the values that underlie the mediation privileges simply by ordering the mediator to participate in the in camera proceedings can be justified—by the prospect that her testimony might well make a singular and substantial contribution to protecting or advancing competing interests of comparable or greater magnitude.

The trial judge reaches the second stage of balancing analysis only if the product of the first stage is a decision to order the mediator to detail, in camera, what her testimony would be. A court that orders the in camera disclosure gains precise and reliable knowledge of what the mediator's testimony would be—and only with that knowledge is the court positioned to launch its second balancing analysis. In this second stage the court is to weigh and comparatively assess (1) the importance of the values and interests that would be harmed if the mediator was compelled to testify (perhaps subject to a sealing or protective order, if appropriate), (2) the magnitude of the harm that compelling the testimony would cause to those values and interests, (3) the importance of the rights or interests that would be jeopardized if the mediator's testimony was not accessible in the specific proceedings in question, and (4) how much the testimony would contribute toward protecting those rights or advancing those interests—an inquiry that includes, among other things, an assessment of whether there are alternative sources of evidence of comparable probative value. . . .

Here . . . all parties to the mediation want the mediator to testify about things that occurred during the mediation—so ordering the testimony would do less harm to the actual relationships developed than it would in a case where one of the parties to the mediation objected to the use of evidence from the mediator. . . .

That conviction is reinforced by another consideration. As we pointed out above, under California law, and this court's view of sound public policy, there should be no occasion to consider whether to seek testimony from a mediator for purpose of determining whether the parties entered an enforceable settlement contract unless the mediation produced a writing (or competent record) that appears on its face to constitute an enforceable contract, signed or formally assented to by all the parties. Thus, it is only when there is such a writing or record, and when a party nonetheless seeks to escape its apparent effect, that courts applying California law would even consider calling for evidence from a mediator for purposes of determining whether the parties settled the case. Surely these circumstances will arise after only a tiny fraction of mediations. . . .

[A discussion follows in which the judge describes, first, the interests harmed by ordering the mediator to testify under seal, including preserving mediators' capacity to create an environment of trust by offering confidentiality; compromising a mediator's ability to remain neutral in the eyes of the parties since his testimony will take sides; and the psychic burden on mediators of promising confidentiality and not delivering that and thus compromising the mediator's professional integrity. He then examines the interests advanced by ordering the mediator to testify, including: doing justice by having the mediator's probative testimony about the central factual issue in the case; assuring the court about the integrity of its mediation program (since allegations included that the process was unfair to a party); and signaling to the public that mediation agreements are serious and will be enforced.]

The ultimate outcome in the *Olam* case, after Judge Brazil examined the mediator *in camera*, was admission of the mediator's testimony and a finding that the agreement was not the product of duress. The mediator's testimony substantially and critically differed from Ms. Olam's account of events and was particularly probative to the court.

However, subsequent cases, while not overruling *Olam*, have limited the reach of its holding. In In re Marriage of Kieturakis, 41 Cal. Rptr. 3d 119 (Cal. Ct. App. 2006), the court held that a party seeking to set aside a mediated settlement agreement on the grounds of fraud or duress must waive confidentiality to proceed (as the parties in *Olam* did), which could mean that a challenge based on fraud, duress, or undue influence would fail if the other side refused to waive the confidentiality privilege, thereby preventing a mediated settlement from being effectively challenged.

iv. The Terms of Settlement Agreements

Even in contexts in which mediation communications *leading* to settlement may be deemed confidential, the terms of the parties' agreements themselves are not usually protected. Parties sometimes seek to shield even the terms of their agreements through specific contract provisions, with mixed success.

But what happens if the parties' (alleged) agreement was not reduced to writing? If one party seeks to introduce evidence of that agreement, will it be treated as a mediation communication (and therefore confidential) or as a term of a settlement (and therefore admissible)? Courts are divided.

Under contract law, oral agreements are generally enforceable—with exceptions for Statute of Frauds scenarios (for example, agreements to transfer an interest in land or agreements that cannot be performed in one year). Confidentiality protections could effectively make an oral agreement reached in mediation impossible to prove. The Indiana Supreme Court, in Vernon v. Acton, 732 N.E.2d 805 (Ind. 2000), concluded that confidentiality—the protection of Indiana Rule of Evidence 408—would encompass oral agreements and therefore testimony about such agreements would be precluded. Similarly, in Simmons v. Ghaderi, 44 Cal. 4th 570 (2008), the California Supreme Court held the statutory mediation confidentiality precluded the plaintiffs from proving an oral settlement agreement. The Utah Supreme Court also refused to enforce an oral mediated settlement agreement in Reese v. Tingey Construction, 177 P.3d 605 (Utah 2008). In GLN Compliance Group v. Aviation Manual Solutions, 203 P.3d 595 (Colo. App. 2008), the Colorado Court of Appeals held that despite there being a written transcript made of a mediated oral settlement agreement, the written transcript was not admissible and hence the contract was not enforceable. The result of this line of cases is that, to be enforceable, mediation agreements must be written and signed.

However, in Kaiser Found. Health Plan of the Northwest v. Doe, 903 P.2d 375 (Or. Ct. App. 1995), an oral settlement agreement reached in mediation was enforced, creating an exception to mediation confidentiality. Similarly, in Few v. Hammack Enters., 511 S.E.2d 665 (N.C. Ct. App. 1999), testimony and other evidence arising in a mediation was found admissible solely for purposes of determining if a settlement was reached and, if so, what the terms of that settlement were.

Sometimes parties develop a Memorandum of Understanding in mediation with the intention that this understanding will subsequently be expanded into a detailed agreement. The effect of such a memorandum—whether it is a binding contract—depends on party intent but will be influenced by confidentiality restrictions too. Also, the agreement must be sufficiently detailed and complete. In Chappell v. Roth, 548 S.E.2d 499 (N.C. 2001), the court held that the failure of the parties to reach agreement on specific terms of a release precluded enforcement of the agreement because a valid agreement requires a meeting of the minds on all terms.

v. Mediator Misconduct

Allegations of mediator misconduct have resulted in "opening the door" shut by confidentiality to allow a mediator to defend himself. In Allen v. Leal, 27 F. Supp. 2d 945 (S.D. Tex. 1998), the court held that a mediator could testify to defend himself against charges of misconduct. In that case, the mother of a child shot by a police officer was attempting to avoid the settlement agreement, which she claimed was coerced by the mediator. The court noted that the plaintiffs "'opened the door' by attacking the professionalism and integrity of the mediator and the mediation process, [hence] the Court was compelled, in the interests of justice, to breach the veil of confidentiality." Id. at 947.

vi. Other Issues Surrounding Exceptions to Confidentiality

Many other questions arise in the complicated arena of confidentiality exceptions. For example:

- What is mediation itself, for purposes of analyzing whether a privilege applies? Some statutes require a court order to mediate; others require that a "mediator" have a certain amount of training and experience; others require a written agreement to mediate. Are other professionals functioning in a mediator-like role, like ombuds, "mediators" for purposes of confidentiality?
- When does mediation begin? Is the "beginning" the first formal session or the first point of contact between a party and mediator's office staff? When does mediation end? Does the "end" of mediation include post-mediation communications, including questions relating to the agreement if the mediation results in an agreement?
- Who is covered by the mediation privilege? Typically, statements by parties, their attorneys, and the mediator are covered, but what about the statements of witnesses, support persons, and other types of advocates?
- Are the protections of a privilege limited to court proceedings, or are they broader?
- Who holds the privilege, and who can waive the privilege? Parties only? Does the mediator independently hold the privilege?

Case law and statutes give various, sometimes conflicting, answers to these questions. As you will see immediately below, the creation of the Uniform

Mediation Act (UMA) was a response to this lack of consistency. As you read the UMA, see whether you can answer these questions. A simple lesson to be taken away from this section on confidentiality is that confidentiality in mediation is not simple, and the answers may vary by jurisdiction!

c. The Uniform Mediation Act

As is evident from the questions above and the different views of mediation confidentiality, this subject is riddled with confusion and controversy. To promote uniformity, in 2001 the National Conference of Commissioners on Uniform State Laws and the American Bar Association approved and recommended for enactment in all states the Uniform Mediation Act (UMA), after a lengthy and careful process. The purpose of uniform laws is to bring coherency, consistency, and predictability to an area of practice, but, as of 2024, only thirteen states have adopted the UMA. As you read selected sections of the UMA that follow, consider why it has not been more universally embraced.

THE UNIFORM MEDIATION ACT, SECTIONS 2-6

Section 2. Definitions.

In this [Act]:

(1) "Mediation" means a process in which a mediator facilitates communication and negotiation between parties to assist them in reaching a voluntary agreement regarding their dispute.

(2) "Mediation communication" means a statement, whether oral or in a record or verbal or nonverbal, that occurs during a mediation or is made for purposes of considering, conducting, participating in, initiating, continuing, or reconvening a mediation or retaining a mediator.

(3) "Mediator" means an individual who conducts a mediation. . . .

Section 3. Scope.

(a) Except as otherwise provided in subsection (b) or (c), this [Act] applies to a mediation in which:

(1) the mediation parties are required to mediate by statute or court or administrative agency rule or referred to mediation by a court, administrative agency, or arbitrator;

(2) the mediation parties and the mediator agree to mediate in a record that demonstrates an expectation that mediation communications will be privileged against disclosure; or

(3) the mediation parties use as a mediator an individual who holds himself or herself out as a mediator, or the mediation is provided by a person that holds itself out as providing mediation. . . .

[Section 3 goes on to note mediations where the Act does not apply: collective bargaining, judicial, school or correctional institution mediations.]

Section 4. Privilege against disclosure; admissibility; discovery

(a) Except as otherwise provided in Section 6, a mediation communication is privileged as provided in subsection (b) and is not subject to discovery or admissible in evidence in a proceeding unless waived or precluded as provided by Section 5.

(b) In a proceeding, the following privileges apply:

(1) A mediation party may refuse to disclose, and may prevent any other person from disclosing, a mediation communication.

(2) A mediator may refuse to disclose a mediation communication, and may prevent any other person from disclosing a mediation communication of the mediator.

(3) A nonparty participant may refuse to disclose, and may prevent any other person from disclosing, a mediation communication of the nonparty participant.

(c) Evidence or information that is otherwise admissible or subject to discovery does not become inadmissible or protected from discovery solely by reason of its disclosure or use in a mediation.

Section 5. Waiver and preclusion of privilege

(a) A privilege under Section 4 may be waived in a record or orally during a proceeding if it is expressly waived by all parties to the mediation and:

(1) in the case of the privilege of a mediator, it is expressly waived by the mediator; and

(2) in the case of the privilege of a nonparty participant, it is expressly waived by the nonparty participant.

(b) A person that discloses or makes a representation about a mediation communication which prejudices another person in a proceeding is precluded from asserting a privilege under Section 4, but only to the extent necessary for the person prejudiced to respond to the representation or disclosure.

(c) A person that intentionally uses a mediation to plan, attempt to commit or commit a crime, or to conceal an ongoing crime or ongoing criminal activity is precluded from asserting a privilege under Section 4.

Section 6. Exceptions to privilege

(a) There is no privilege under Section 4 for a mediation communication that is:

(1) in an agreement evidenced by a record signed by all parties to the agreement;

(2) available to the public under [insert statutory reference to open records act] or made during a session of a mediation which is open, or is required by law to be open, to the public;

(3) a threat or statement of a plan to inflict bodily injury or commit a crime of violence;

(4) intentionally used to plan a crime, attempt to commit a crime, or to conceal an ongoing crime or ongoing criminal activity;

(5) sought or offered to prove or disprove a claim or complaint of professional misconduct or malpractice filed against a mediator;

(6) except as otherwise provided in subsection (c), sought or offered to prove or disprove a claim or complaint of professional misconduct or malpractice filed against a mediation party, nonparty participant, or representative of a party based on conduct occurring during a mediation; or

(7) sought or offered to prove or disprove abuse, neglect, abandonment, or exploitation in a proceeding in which a child or adult protective services agency is a party. . . .

(b) There is no privilege under Section 4 if a court, administrative agency, or arbitrator finds, after a hearing in camera, that the party seeking discovery or the proponent of the evidence has shown that the evidence is not otherwise available, that there is a need for the evidence that substantially outweighs the interest in protecting confidentiality, and that the mediation communication is sought or offered in:

(1) a court proceeding involving a felony [or misdemeanor]; or

(2) except as otherwise provided in subsection (c), a proceeding to prove a claim to rescind or reform or a defense to avoid liability on a contract arising out of the mediation.

(c) A mediator may not be compelled to provide evidence of a mediation communication referred to in subsection (a)(6) or (b)(2).

(d) If a mediation communication is not privileged under subsection (a) or (b), only the portion of the communication necessary for the application of the exception from nondisclosure may be admitted. Admission of evidence under subsection (a) or (b) does not render the evidence, or any other mediation communication, discoverable or admissible for any other purpose.

Problem 8-4. ***The* Olam *Case Under a UMA Regime?***

If the *Olam* case (above) had been decided in a jurisdiction that had adopted the UMA, what would the outcome have been?

Problem 8-5. ***Does the UMA Make It All Come Clear?***

Professor Scott Hughes opined that some of the UMA's provisions would "decimate predictability." Can you now answer the questions that precede the UMA above? Imagine a mediation participant asks you to explain confidentiality in a state where the UMA is adopted. What would you say? For one very amusing answer to this question, see https://open.mitchellhamline.edu/dri_mclvideo/40.

d. Sanctions for Breach of Confidentiality

Breaches of confidentiality have yielded an array of outcomes in different courts ranging from monetary sanctions (attorney's fees, mediator's fees and costs) to the dismissal of an action.

Monetary sanctions were awarded in Bernard v. Galen Group, 901 F. Supp. 778 (S.D.N.Y. 1995), where the plaintiff's lawyer, in an unsolicited letter to the judge, divulged specific terms of settlement offers. The lawyer was fined $2,500.

Courts have split on whether a new trial is necessary where confidential information is divulged. In Hudson v. Hudson, 600 So. 2d 7 (Fla. Dist. Ct. App. 1992), the court held that admitting evidence about an oral mediation agreement taints the subsequent judgment and ordered a new trial where this error was made. However, in Enterprise Leasing Co. v. Jones, 789 So. 2d 964 (Fla. 2001), the Florida Supreme Court held that where a party reveals mediation settlement offers to a judge, it does not automatically disqualify the judge, absent proof that the confidential communication results in actual prejudice.

The severe sanction of case dismissal with prejudice is also possible. In Paranzino v. Barnett Bank, 690 So. 2d 725 (Fla. Dist. Ct. App. 1997), where the plaintiff breached mediation confidentiality by divulging to a newspaper specific terms of the defendant's settlement offer, the court dismissed her case with prejudice.

B. FOUR POLICY QUESTIONS AT THE INTERSECTION OF LAW, JUSTICE, AND MEDIATION

Judges and juries rely on law—the complex web of statutes and decided cases—to decide cases. Arbitrators apply whatever norms—law, custom, tradition, contractual and legal rules—parties dictate in their agreement to arbitrate. Mediators, however, elicit principles and standards from the parties and cannot prescribe the governing norms or determine the outcome. Given these fundamental differences among processes, the relationship of law and justice to mediation raises challenging questions. This section explores four questions that generate vigorous debate about mediation among scholars and practitioners.

1. Mandatory Mediation

Given the benefits of mediation both to parties and society, mediation is now routinely required as a preliminary step to getting into court. Benefits of mandating mediation include disposing of matters clogging court dockets, overcoming the hurdle that a party proposing mediation may be perceived as weak by the other side, educating parties and attorneys about mediation, creating a body of skilled neutrals, providing parties who are uneducated about mediation the benefits the process can provide, and encouraging the voluntary use of mediation.

However, since mediation is often described as a voluntary and consensual process that promotes party self-determination, mandated participation seems contradictory. Despite the contradiction, studies suggest that mandating mediation does not reduce the rate of settlement as compared to voluntary mediation (or does so only marginally), nor does it adversely impact the parties' experience in mediation.

The next two excerpts examine this issue. Roselle Wissler addresses some concerns about mandatory mediation and concludes that, on balance, it is worthwhile. Trina Grillo raises serious concerns about mandating mediation in the context of divorce and custody cases, which is one of the arenas where mediation has been regularly required as a prerequisite to court action.

❖ *Roselle L. Wissler*, THE EFFECTS OF MANDATORY MEDIATION: EMPIRICAL RESEARCH ON THE EXPERIENCE OF SMALL CLAIMS AND COMMON PLEAS COURTS

33 Willamette L. Rev. 565-566 (1997)

Although parties tend to be satisfied with their experience in mediation, voluntary mediation programs consistently report low rates of utilization. In order to divert more cases from the courts and to expose more parties to the benefits associated with mediation, many states have adopted mandatory mediation programs for a variety of disputes. Critics have raised the concern that coercion into the mediation process translates into coercion in the mediation process, creating undue settlement pressures that produce unfair outcomes. In cases involving an imbalance of power, the weaker party is thought to be particularly vulnerable to such pressures. However, studies of divorce mediation that examine the effects of mandatory mediation and that explore gender differences in evaluations of the process tend not to support such concerns.

This Article reports research on the effects of mandatory mediation in two different court settings: small claims courts and common pleas courts. . . . [I]t reports the findings of two studies that compare mandatory and voluntary mediation in terms of case outcomes and parties' and attorneys' evaluations. These studies reveal few differences between mandatory and voluntary mediation and between the assessments of male versus female litigants and white versus nonwhite litigants in mandatory mediation. Thus, there is little support for concerns about pressures to accept unfair settlements in mandatory mediation. The findings of these and prior studies suggest that costs associated with mandatory mediation are relatively few, compared to the benefits that mediation provides as an alternative to adjudication.

❖ *Trina Grillo*, THE MEDIATION ALTERNATIVE: PROCESS DANGERS FOR WOMEN

100 Yale L.J. 1545, 1549-1550, 1582-1583 (1991)

. . . [M]andatory mediation provides neither a more just nor a more humane alternative to the adversarial system of adjudication of custody, and, therefore, does not fulfill its promises. In particular, quite apart from whether an acceptable result is reached, mandatory mediation can be destructive to many women and some men because it requires them to speak in a setting they have not chosen and often imposes a rigid orthodoxy as to how they should speak, make decisions, and be. This orthodoxy is imposed through subtle and not-so-subtle messages about appropriate conduct and about what may be said in mediation. It is an orthodoxy that often excludes the possibility of the parties' speaking with their authentic voices.

Moreover, people vary greatly in the extent to which their sense of self is "relational"—that is, defined in terms of connection to others. If two parties are forced to engage with one another, and one has a more relational sense of self than the other, that party may feel compelled to maintain her connection with the other, even to her own detriment. For this reason, the party with the more relational sense of self will be at a disadvantage in a mediated negotiation. Several prominent researchers have suggested that, as a general rule, women have a more relational sense of self than do men, although there is little agreement on what the origin of this difference might be. Thus, rather than being a feminist alternative to the adversary system, mediation has the potential actively to harm women.

. . . Proponents of [mandatory mediation] seldom recognize that, even though an agreement might not be required, a person might agree to something because of the pressures of the situation; or that, even if no agreement is reached, the process itself might be traumatic.

It is presumptuous to assume that the state has a better idea than the parties themselves about whether mediation will work in their particular case. A party may know something the mediator does not: that her spouse is a pathological, but convincing, liar; that years of living with a man have resulted in a pattern in which the woman consistently accommodates him, even when she does not want to; that the woman will lose sight of her own needs in the attempt to appear a cooperative female; or that the woman will sacrifice many of her interests in order to end what may be a psychologically painful process. In sum, there may be an internal wisdom, one that needs to be honored, that mediation is inappropriate in a particular situation. It is true that mandatory mediation may serve the interests of women who do not wish to enter the adversary process; if opting out of mediation is permitted, some women (as well as some men) will be forced to litigate when their preference would have been to mediate. There is no way around this unfortunate situation. Either some women will be forced to litigate against their will, or some women will be forced to mediate against their will. Mediation poses such substantial dangers, and provides so few benefits to unwilling female participants, however, that to my mind it is indefensible to require mediation, notwithstanding that such a requirement would help women who do want to mediate. . . .

Problem 8-6. ***Would You Welcome an Order to Mediate?***

Imagine that you have been married for 10 years and have two young children. Your spouse tells you that he or she will seek custody of the children in court. Would you welcome a mandate to mediate? Would it make a difference if you were the victim of domestic violence?

If you are running a court program, how should the court screen for domestic violence? And what if the victim still wants to proceed with mediation because she believes that it will be more beneficial for her and her family to proceed through mediation than through litigation? How should lawyers be trained to handle these cases? How might the mediation process itself be adjusted to protect victims of domestic violence? For a discussion of domestic violence and mediation, see Lisa Lerman, Mediation of Wife Abuse Cases: The Adverse Impact of Informal Dispute Resolution on Women, 7 Harvard Women's L.J. 57 (1984).1

What level of participation does mandatory mediation require? Do Trina Grillo's concerns seem less pressing if a woman is free to leave once she finds mediation will not serve her needs? How does the answer to this question affect your views on the relative advantages and disadvantages of a court-annexed program? As you read the section below on good faith participation, keep these questions in mind.

2. A "Good Faith" Requirement

Connected to the growth of court-ordered mediation and of contracts that require the use of mediation prior to adjudication, commentators have advocated, and some legislatures and courts have required, "good faith" participation in mediation. The call for good faith in mediation is premised on the need to ensure that the court-ordered process is not a waste of time, that it is at least possible to achieve a collaborative resolution, and that mediation is not misused. Furthermore, some suggest that to the extent that courts order participation and parties devote resources to it, society should protect the integrity of the process.

One of the problems with a good faith requirement is the difficulty in defining "good faith." It is easier to identify what is indicative of bad faith than to define good faith. A list of such indicators might include: failure to attend mediation; failure to bring the client or an organizational representative with settlement authority to mediation; failure to exchange information, bring data, or bring a key expert; failure to prepare a requested pre-mediation memorandum; and failure to participate seriously or to make suitable offers in mediation. Some items on the list are objective, and others are highly subjective. Attendance arguably falls into the objective category; serious participation is certainly open to differences of opinion and thus harder to enforce.

There are other challenges with a good faith requirement. Placing the burden on mediators to report bad faith can compromise their facilitative role and neutral posture. It could create an incursion into mediation confidentiality, since allegations or evidence of bad faith would require disclosure of otherwise confidential mediation proceedings and mediator testimony. This could increase adversarial behavior of the parties—who would have a new weapon to use against each other—and undermine confidence in the mediator. Similarly, creating a cause of action for bad faith participation could encourage satellite litigation and spawn more procedural costs and delay for litigants—an ironic outcome, since mediation ideally reduces costs and delays.

In Foxgate Homeowners' Assn. v. Bramalea, 25 P.3d 1117 (Cal. 2001) the court struggled between upholding a good faith standard in court-ordered mediation on the one hand and maintaining mediation confidentiality on the other. In that case, the mediator's report indicated that the defendant appeared late at the mediation and brought no experts despite the court's notice that they should bring experts. The report concluded that the defendant's attorney "spent the vast majority of his time trying to derail the mediations." Id. at 1121. Plaintiff, who brought nine experts to the mediation, sought sanctions against the defendant for bad faith conduct. The court ruled that a mediator cannot report to the court bad faith conduct of mediation participants, as the legislative mandate about confidentiality was clear.

a. Tests for Good Faith

Professor John Lande, in an exhaustive summary of the status of good faith cases, concludes that courts have consistently found bad faith where a party failed to attend mediation or to provide a required pre-mediation memorandum; have split in cases involving allegations that organizational parties, such as corporations, have provided representatives without sufficient settlement authority; and have rejected a finding of bad faith in other types of cases involving more subjective allegations of bad faith.[6]

However, no generalization is without exceptions. In In re A.T. Reynolds & Sons, Inc., 424 B.R. 76 (Bankr. S.D.N.Y. 2010), the United States Bankruptcy Court of the Southern District of New York, after ordering parties to mediate, found the creditor in bad faith, despite it sending a representative with full settlement authority to the mediation, because it refused to engage in risk analysis. The Court sanctioned the creditor the amount of the mediation's costs. In Carlsbad Hotel v. Patterson-Uti Drilling Company, 199 P.3d 288 (2008), a defendant was

6. John Lande, Using Dispute System Design Methods to Promote Good-Faith Participation in Court-Connected Mediation Programs, 50 UCLA L. Rev. 69 (2002).

sanctioned for bad faith because he came to a mediation with no intent of settling, made an offer of $1,000 only after the mediator threatened him with sanctions, then refused to make a higher offer. In *Carlsbad*, the defendant was ordered to pay plaintiff's costs, including attorney's fees, for the mediation, because defendant put all parties through "an exercise in futility." Id. at 294.

b. Corporate Representatives and Good Faith

With respect to corporate parties, it is sometimes difficult to ascertain who is best fitted to participate in mediation to satisfy a requirement that a representative "with settlement authority" attend. In G. Heileman Brewing Co. v. Joseph Oat Corp., 871 F.2d 648 (7th Cir. 1989), the court affirmed the district court's conclusion that the company had failed to send a representative in an appropriate position to the settlement conference. In that case, a corporate representative was sent with authority to speak for a party, but the only instruction he had was to make no offer. The court ruled that the corporate representative attending a pretrial conference must "hold a position within the corporate entity allowing him to speak definitively and to commit the corporation to a particular position in the litigation." Id. at 653. Similarly, in Nick v. Morgan's Foods, 99 F. Supp. 2d 1056 (E.D. Mo. 2000), aff'd. 270 F.3d 590 (8th Cir. 2001), the defendant was sanctioned for sending a corporate representative (the regional manager) who had no independent knowledge of the case, nor the authority to reconsider Morgan Food's position on settlement. The manager's authority was limited to $500, after which the general counsel, who was not present, had to be consulted.

Of course, beyond the minimum necessary for "good faith," the more authority the corporate representative has, the more flexible and creative they can be. Having someone high on the corporate ladder can make a critical difference in terms of a good settlement.

c. Is Attendance by Telephone in Good Faith?

The meaning of "attendance" has also been challenged. In Raad v. Wal-Mart Stores, 1998 U.S. Dist. LEXIS 11881 (D. Neb. 1998), Wal-Mart was sanctioned—ordered to pay $4,950 representing plaintiff's costs for the mediation—for failing to bring a corporate representative to a court-ordered mediation, even though the representative was available by phone. In a similar case, another court said:

> There are several reasons for requiring the presence of authorized representatives at a settlement conference. During the conference, counsel for both sides are given an opportunity to argue their clients' respective positions to the court, including pointing out strengths and weaknesses of each party's case. In this discussion, it is often true that client representatives and insurers learn, for the first time, the difficulties they may have in prevailing at a trial. They must, during the conference, weigh their own positions in light of the statements and arguments made by counsel for the opposing parties. It is often true that as a result of such presentations, the clients' positions soften to the extent that meaningful negotiation, previously not seriously entertained, becomes possible. This dynamic is not possible if the only person with authority to negotiate is located away from the courthouse and can be reached only by telephone, if at all. The absent decision-maker learns

> only what his or her attorney conveys by phone, which can be expected to be largely a recitation of what has been conveyed in previous discussions. At best, even if the attorney attempts to convey the weakness of that client's position as they have been presented by opposing counsel at the settlement conference, the message, not unlike those in the children's game of "telephone," loses its impact through repetition, and it is simply too easy for that person to reject, out of hand, even a sincere desire on the part of counsel to negotiate further. At worst, a refusal to have an authorized representative in attendance may become a weapon by which parties with comparatively greater financial flexibility may feign a good faith settlement posture by those in attendance at the conference, relying on the absent decision-maker to refuse to agree, thereby unfairly raising the stakes in the case, to the unfair disadvantage of a less wealthy opponent. In either case, the whole purpose of the settlement conference is lost, and the result is an even greater expenditure of the parties' resources, both time and money, for naught. Dvorak v. Shibata, 123 F.R.D. 608, 609-10 (D. Neb. 1988).

Note that the courts decided these cases prior to Nebraska's adoption of the UMA. The UMA permits a mediator to report to the court "whether the mediation occurred or has terminated, whether a settlement was reached, and attendance." Neb. Rev. Stat. 25-2936. This statute may change the court's analysis regarding telephone attendance.

As technology makes "virtual" meetings more readily available, the meaning of "attendance" may shift! For example, in video conference mediations, must the camera be on for a party to be deemed present?

d. *Sanctions for Bad Faith*

Sanctions for bad faith can range from the award of the other side's costs of participation in mediation, including attorneys' fees, to an ordered apology or remedial education, or to a default judgment or dismissal against the party acting in bad faith. In Brooks v. The Lincoln Nat'l. Life Ins. Co., 2006 U.S. Dist. LEXIS 61114 (D. Neb. 2006), an attorney was ordered to send letters of apology to all participants, complete an educational course on representation in mediation and notify his client of this sanction. The attorney in *Brooks* had rejected his opponent's initial settlement offers, refusing to give the mediator an opportunity to explain the opponent's reasoning, and demanded a serious offer "in five minutes." Id. at 4. Not getting an offer he thought serious, he peremptorily left the mediation.

Problem 8-7. ***The Court Gone Wild?***

In a civil action against Joseph Francis (and his companies), Doe v. Francis, No. 5.03cv260-RS-WCS, 2003 WL 24073307 (N.D. Fla. 2003), the founder of the lucrative soft porn videos *Girls Gone Wild*, alleging the enticement of underage girls to perform sexual acts on film, the parties were ordered to mediation by U.S. District Judge Smoak.

Francis' actions at the court-ordered mediation included: arriving four hours late and keeping out-of-town plaintiffs waiting; wearing sweat shorts, a backwards baseball cap, and no shoes; placing his bare, dirty feet on the table facing plaintiffs' counsel; interrupting plaintiff's counsel to yell repeatedly, "Don't expect to get a fucking dime—not one fucking dime!"; threatening, as the plaintiffs and their counsel left the room, "We will bury you and your clients! I'm going to ruin you, your clients, and all of your ambulance-chasing partners!"; and, as a farewell, saying to plaintiffs' counsel: "Suck my dick." Pitts v. Francis, 2007 WL 4482168 (N.D. Fla. 2007) at 11-12. After this outburst, the mediation continued for 13 hours.

The sanctions for Francis' conduct included paying plaintiffs' attorneys fees and costs and serving time in jail until he mediated in good faith. The Judge, finding that the mediation was essentially a sham, specified that proper participation in mediation would include Francis arriving on time, dressed and groomed appropriately. The Court elaborated that Francis would wear "a business suit and a tie, business shoes and socks and he will conduct himself and communicate in a manner during the mediation with the demeanor and courtesy expected in serious business transactions and appearances before the court." Id. at 6. Upon the mediator's certification that Francis participated in good faith, Francis would be released from incarceration.

Is this an example of a good case making bad law? Or, was Judge Smoak correct to find Francis in civil contempt and to order him to be jailed until he mediated in good faith?

3. Mediator Evaluation and Assessment

Another heated debate is whether a mediator should offer the parties assessments about positions parties are taking, the likely adjudicated outcome, or other matters in dispute. This evaluative function is clearly the domain of neutral experts, arbiters, and judges. Should it also be a service provided by mediators? As mediation has been brought into the courts, the practice of evaluative mediation has grown, perhaps because lawyers and clients are most comfortable in adversarial processes and with neutrals who give opinions. The Riskin Grid shown in Chapter 6 depicts a mediation universe split into evaluative and facilitative spheres. An evaluative mediator, according to Riskin, has an evaluative orientation and does some or all of the following: develops and proposes settlement terms, urges parties to accept a particular settlement, predicts court outcomes, and assesses strengths and weaknesses of legal claims. While a facilitative mediator may be very energetic in urging parties to reevaluate their positions and legal analysis, she would not give her own opinion of the merits of claims or defenses or of the likely outcome of a case. Some scholars claim that evaluative mediation is an oxymoron, just as facilitative arbitration would be.[7] In the excerpt that follows, Murray Levin reflects on this question.

7. Kimberlee K. Kovach & Lela P. Love, "Evaluative" Mediation Is an Oxymoron, 14 Alternatives 31 (1996).

Murray S. Levin, THE PROPRIETY OF EVALUATIVE MEDIATION: CONCERNS ABOUT THE NATURE AND QUALITY OF AN EVALUATIVE OPINION

16 Ohio St. J. on Disp. Resol. 267, 270-271 (2001)

. . . Proponents of evaluative mediation assert that disputants [need] help in understanding the law and how their case is affected by the law, and that lawyers want mediators to provide direction regarding appropriate settlement figures. Additionally, proponents claim that because settlement negotiation takes place in the context of the alternative of litigation, the alternative outcome is highly relevant and therefore evaluation should be considered a valuable and proper component of mediation. Included within this group of proponents are commentators who do not advocate evaluative mediation, per se, but believe it should be available when chosen by the disputants.

Opponents of evaluative mediation counter that the tenor of the mediation process changes dramatically when the mediator assumes an evaluative role, because evaluation reduces mediator impartiality and disputant self-determination. When the mediator interjects an opinion, the disputant's ability to fashion a resolution based on their own needs is compromised. Understanding that the mediator will be evaluative, the disputants will not be as forthright with the mediator. A foremost goal will be a favorable mediator evaluation, and a disputant will not be willing to share information that could have an adverse effect on that evaluation. Under these circumstances it is more likely that the mediator will not learn about important information that could be relevant to assisting the disputants and should be relevant to forming a valid evaluation. This is especially likely if the mediation occurs at an early point in time prior to discovery. Evaluation turns the process away from problem solving toward an adversarial contest—sharing turns to posturing. Facilitative mediators view the potential for sharing of information through mediation as a chief means to assist the parties in recognizing opportunities to create new value and find win-win solutions. Moreover, too much emphasis on a likely legal outcome overlooks the possibility that the legal solution is not necessarily the best solution. Critics also express concern about the directive and coercive nature of the process when evaluation occurs. Some have gone so far as to characterize evaluative mediators as "Rambo mediators" who are out to "knock some sense" into the disputants by "banging their heads together" or "twisting their arms." Even if the evaluative mediator does not pressure, but merely opines, it is hard to deny a preferential effect, for there is a natural tendency to rely on the ideas, opinions, and predictions of the mediator. Undeniably, any opinion or evaluation will favor one side and disfavor the other. One may then ponder whether this influence is justified—whether the evaluative mediator's evaluation is valid and proper.

Elsewhere in his article, Levin notes the lack of empirical research testing the quality or validity of mediator evaluative opinions. He points to data from studies regarding negotiation outcomes between highly regarded lawyer negotiators, case evaluations by lawyers and claims adjusters, and mock jury experiments displaying—with remarkable ranges of outcomes—the difficulty of predicting negotiation or litigation outcomes. This difficulty is compounded by the fact that mediation takes place under the umbrella of confidentiality, and consequently the protections of a public process and the right of appeal are absent. Concerns about mediator opinions are allayed to some extent by the fact that such opinions are not binding on the parties.

Proponents of mediators being able to give a neutral assessment when requested by the parties point to its value in providing a reality check to reduce unrealistic expectations and bridge final gaps. Its use may be particularly appropriate as a last step when all else has failed.

Problem 8-8. *Does Case Type Matter?*

Is evaluation appropriate in some cases but not others? If you think so, what cases would call for evaluative mediation? Cases involving constitutional or statutory rights? Commercial cases? Divorce cases? Personal injury cases? Environmental cases?

There is agreement that combining evaluative and facilitative dispute resolution services can be useful in particular cases when requested by informed parties.

Indeed, the principle of self-determination suggests that parties should be free to pursue the approach to dispute resolution that best suits their needs. Nonetheless, the debate continues about what to call a combination of facilitation and evaluation. Should evaluative mediation be called mediation or mediation *plus* neutral evaluation?

Proponents of careful labeling of processes argue that calling evaluative mediation "mediation *plus* neutral evaluation" would: make the services to be provided by the neutral clearer (a benefit both for providers and participants); help educate consumers about choices with respect to dispute resolution options; and forewarn advocates and parties about the best approach to information sharing and advocacy in a blended process where the neutral's opinion might have a decisive impact on negotiations. Furthermore, insuring a meaningful array of processes—rather than one process labeled "mediation" but consisting of a variety of approaches—is more likely to generate thoughtful choice about process options. In New York, qualification requirements for neutrals are different for those serving as mediators, arbitrators, and neutral evaluators—indicating that distinct processes have significant differences in practice and training norms and cannot be blended unless all criteria for insuring quality are met.[8] Finally, the benefits of a multi-door courthouse may be lost if the courthouse has only two doors: litigation and "mediation"—an amorphous process that means whatever works to resolve the dispute.

8. Part 146.4, Rules of the Chief Administrative Judge, New York State Unified Court System.

On the other hand, as you have seen from Riskin's grid in Chapter 6, since a considerable portion of the mediation world is already evaluative, the word "mediation" has come to include this blended process. Advocates of mediator flexibility note that mediation has been characterized by fluidity and creativity, and mediators should not be constrained by excessive rules or constricting labels.

Problem 8-9. ***Impacts of a Blended Process?***

If you were responsible for a panel of mediators where evaluative mediation was the norm, what impact would that have on the qualification criteria for panelists? The description of the panel's services? Accountability for erroneous conclusions of mediators? Training for panelists? Whether the program encouraged—or allowed—the use of caucuses and ex parte communications? Ethical rules?

4. Mediator Responsibility for the Quality of the Parties' Agreement

Self-determination by the parties is the hallmark of mediation. This means that the parties' sense of fairness usually trumps other arguably applicable norms. The following two excerpts explore mediator accountability for the quality of mediated outcomes. Does a high-quality outcome mean that the parties' agreement is in keeping with applicable norms—law, industry norms, best practices, and the interests of third parties and future generations? Or, is a high quality agreement in the mediation context one with which the parties are satisfied, and to which they are committed? Two prominent professors reach remarkably different conclusions about the nature and scope of the mediator's job with respect to mediated outcomes.

❖ *Lawrence Susskind*, ENVIRONMENTAL MEDIATION AND THE ACCOUNTABILITY PROBLEM

6 Vt. L. Rev. 1, 6-8, 18, 42, 46-47 (1981)

. . . The success of most mediation efforts tends to be measured in rather narrow terms. If the parties to a labor dispute are pleased with the agreement they have reached voluntarily, and the bargain holds, the mediator is presumed to have done a good job. In the environmental field, there are reasons that a broader definition of success is needed—one that is more attentive to the interests of all segments of society.

If the parties involved in environmental mediation reach an agreement, but fail to maximize the joint gains possible, environmental quality and natural resources will actually be lost. If the key parties involved in an environmental dispute reach an agreement with which they are pleased, but fail to take account of all impacts on those interests not represented directly in the negotiations, the public health and safety could be seriously jeopardized. If the key parties to a dispute reach an agreement, but selfishly ignore the interests of future generations, short term agreements could set off environmental time bombs that cannot be defused. Although the key stakeholders in an environmental dispute may pay only a small price for failing to reach an agreement, their failure could impose substantial costs on many groups, who may be affected indefinitely. Finally, the parties to environmental disputes must be sensitive to the ways in which their agreements set precedents; even informal settlements have a way of becoming binding on others who find themselves in similar situations. . . .

[E]nvironmental mediators ought to accept responsibility for ensuring (1) that the interests of parties not directly involved in negotiation, but with a stake in the outcome, are adequately represented and protected; (2) that agreements are as fair and stable as possible; and (3) that agreements reached are interpreted as intended by the community-at-large and set constructive precedents. . . .

Effective environmental mediation may require teams composed of some individuals with technical backgrounds, some specialized in problem-solving or group dynamics and some with political clout. . .

Environmental mediators ought to be concerned about (1) the impacts of negotiated agreements on underrepresented or unrepresentable groups in the community; (2) the possibility that joint net gains have not been maximized; (3) the long-term or spill-over effects of the settlements they help to reach, and (4) the precedents that they set and the precedents upon which agreements are based. To be effective, an environmental mediator will need to be knowledgeable about the substance of disputes and intricacies of the regulatory context within which decisions are embedded. An environmental mediator should be committed to procedural fairness—all parties should have an opportunity to be represented by individuals with the technical sophistication to bargain effectively on their behalf. Environmental mediators should also be concerned that the agreements they help to reach are just and stable. To fulfill these responsibilities, environmental mediators will have to intervene more often and more forcefully than their counterparts in the labor-management field. Although such intervention may make it difficult to retain the appearance of neutrality and the trust of the active parties, environmental mediators cannot fulfill their responsibilities to the community-at-large if they remain passive.

Joseph B. Stulberg, THE THEORY AND PRACTICE OF MEDIATION: A REPLY TO PROFESSOR SUSSKIND

6 Vt. L. Rev. 85, 85-88, 108-109, 112-115 (1981)

. . . Paradoxically, while the use of mediation has expanded, a common understanding as to what constitutes mediation has weakened. . . . It is important . . . to identify and clarify the principles and dynamics which together constitute mediation as a dispute settlement procedure. . . . Susskind's argument is novel in that he asserts that the mediator of environmental disputes, unlike his counterpart in labor management, community, or international disputes, should not be neutral and should be held accountable for the mediated outcome. Since most mediators believe that a commitment to impartiality and neutrality is the defining principle of their role, Susskind's argument carries significant consequences for mediation.

. . . Susskind's demand for a non-neutral intervenor is conceptually and pragmatically incompatible with the goals and purposes of mediation. The intervenor posture that Susskind advocates is not anchored by any principles or obligations of office. The intervenor's conduct, strategies or contribution to the dispute settlement process is, therefore, neither predictable nor consistent. It is precisely a mediator's commitment to neutrality which ensures responsible actions on the part of the mediator and permits mediation to be an effective, principled dispute settlement procedure. . . .

On a substantive level, Susskind argues that the mediator must ensure that the negotiated agreements are fair. The most dramatic example of the difference between the traditional neutral mediator and Susskind's environmental mediator is the person Susskind describes and endorses as a mediator with "clout." For Susskind, the term "clout" applies to a mediator publicly committed to a particular substantive outcome with the power to move the contesting parties toward an agreement. In contrast, the traditional mediator would view that public commitment as the signal reason for disqualifying himself from service.

It is more than a mere terminological quibble to analyze whether a mediator must be someone who is committed to a posture of neutrality. Such a commitment enables both the mediation process and the mediator to operate effectively. A commitment of neutrality provides the mediator with a principled rather than opportunistic basis for service. As a result, the parties will use his services in ways that would be foreclosed to the "mediator with clout." Susskind's analysis has practical implications for mediator selection, training, scope of service, and financing of services. Clarifying this matter is of no small moment for those interested in the continued experimentation and use of mediation.

One disclaimer is in order. Arguing that a mediator's role requires a commitment to impartiality and neutrality is not to claim that Susskind's "mediator with clout" could not be an effective intervenor. There are many types of "intervenors with clout," a police officer, parent, government regulatory agency, psychologist, marriage counselor, meeting facilitator, corporate executive, and school principal. For certain kinds of dispute settings, those persons intervene with clout in much the same way that Susskind proposes for his environmental dispute mediator. Such a description does not make these persons mediators nor does it make their intervention ineffective or less effective than service rendered by a mediator. It simply constitutes a different kind of intervention posture from that of a mediator. One purpose served by conceptual analysis is to distinguish among different functions served by various types of intervenor postures, allowing those involved to become more sensitive to the types of intervention which are appropriate to different disputes.

. . . At issue is an understanding of, and respect for, what the parties to the mediation session are entitled to expect from the intervenor. Will confidences be honored? Who sets the agenda in terms of issues to be discussed? Will the order in which the issues are discussed be skewed so as to insure the mediator's desired outcome? Will meeting times be scheduled for the convenience of the parties or might they be arranged by the intervenor in order to make it difficult for some (i.e. "obstreperous") parties to attend and voice objections to the intervenor's preferred position? Will the mediator refuse to schedule meetings if the one party whose position the mediator supports demands that future meetings be conditional upon the other parties having made particular concessions?

. . . Is it appropriate, for example, for the "mediator with clout" to threaten a recalcitrant party with political retaliation? If not, why not?. . . . To suggest that an environmental mediator assume the responsibility of protecting the public's interest within the mediation context is comparable to suggesting that the way to avoid impasses in mediation is to authorize the mediator to impose dispositive, enforceable decisions on the parties.

Such a proposal is not simply adding a different twist to the mediation process; it is converting it from mediation to arbitration in the interest of promoting finality. Susskind has yet to meet the burden of justifying how the environmental mediator can assume this particular responsibility to the "public" without simultaneously converting the dispute settlement procedure into something other than mediation.

. . . Susskind suggests that "environmental mediators ought to be concerned . . . about . . . the possibility that joint net gains have not been maximized [and about] . . . the long-term or spillover effects of the settlements they help to reach." Susskind proposes that it is the mediator's responsibility as an objective observer to insure that the final solution secures the greatest overall net benefits for each party, without leaving any party worse off than it was in its original configuration (the Pareto-optimal principle). He further suggests that the solution agreed upon should have the least possible adverse impact on other aspects of present or future community life. Simply stating the proposed responsibility for the mediator in this way reveals how awesome the task is that Susskind is proposing for the environmental mediator. To insure that the Pareto principle is met, the environmental mediator must be able to generate, or at least guarantee, consideration of every possible technical solution to the environmental problem. He must secure demographic information on all persons affected by the dispute and factor their interests, desires, aspirations, preferences and values into the solution. He must project alternative development plans for jobs, tax bases, population trends, aesthetic values, school development and recreational needs for each possible solution. He must calculate the advantages and disadvantages of each solution against retaining the status quo, including the costs involved in using alternative dispute settlement procedures. And the list goes on.

Although these tasks might constitute a city planner's dream, they [raise] the serious possibility that Pareto-optimal outcomes in the context of an environmental dispute are not, in principle, possible. As such, Susskind's proposal that the mediator ought to insure such an outcome must, charitably speaking, be held in abeyance.

A more troublesome question arises, however, regarding the justification for a mediator to block an agreement that fails to meet the requirements of the Pareto principle. Who authorized the mediator to design or insure the attainment of the "optimal" outcome so conceived? Clearly, it is preferable for persons to act as rational agents and do the "right" thing. Even conceding, however, the dubious proposition that the mediator could identify the "right" course of action as defined by the Pareto principle, on what basis does the mediator assume as an obligation of office that he help parties do only what is "right" and not necessarily that which is possible?. . .

If we were to accept the obligations of office that Susskind ascribes to the environmental mediator with regard to insuring Pareto-optimal outcomes, then the environmental mediator is simply a person who uses his entry into the dispute to become a social conscience, environmental policeman, or social critic and who carries no other obligations to the process or the participants beyond assuring Pareto-optimality. It is, in its most benign form, an invitation to permit philosopher-kings to participate in the affairs of the citizenry. . . .

The potential range of services for Susskind's environmental mediator, versus that of a traditional mediator committed to a posture of neutrality, is so importantly different that it is seriously misleading to use the same label to describe these respective intervention postures.

Problem 8-10. ***Achieving Pareto Superior Outcomes***

A "Pareto superior" outcome (based on the Pareto principle, named after an Italian economist) means that an agreement maximizes the available utilities or good for the parties involved. Said another way, Pareto efficient situations are those in which it is impossible to improve one person's outcome without making someone else's worse. For example, in a case involving the termination of an employee, the employer may agree to provide a positive reference for the employee, which costs the employer nothing and provides an enormous benefit to the employee. This is Pareto superior to a severance package without provision for a reference, assuming the employer has positive things to say. While Stulberg rejects placing responsibility on the mediator for insuring a Pareto superior result, what mediator tools have you studied that encourage movement in a Pareto superior direction? Should a mediator work to ensure parties reach Pareto superior outcomes?

Problem 8-11. ***What's Your Opinion?***

With a group of five colleagues, consider one of the questions posed from the point of view of a mediator, a judge, a participant in mediation, a legislator and a member of a bar committee. How would you answer these questions?

1. Should mediation be mandatory?
2. Should courts enforce a "good faith" requirement?
3. Should the mediator provide evaluations or assessments for the parties?
4. Should the mediator bear responsibility for the quality of the parties' agreement?

At the end of this chapter, there are suggestions for further readings on some of these topics.

C. ETHICS IN MEDIATION

Like all professionals, mediators face many ethical choices in their practice. Ethical dilemmas often result from conflicting obligations or aspirations. As you have seen in the discussions above, conflicts abound between the rule of law and the goal of party choice, or the aspiration of good faith conduct and the promise of confidentiality. Michael Moffitt describes different scenarios below that raise ethical issues for mediators and possibly could lead to mediator liability. Read these examples in light of the 2005 Model Standards of Conduct for Mediators.[9]

The Model Standards provide guideposts that articulate the fundamental values and mediator duties associated with mediation. Those values are: party self-determination, mediator impartiality, mediator disclosure and avoidance of conflicts of interest, mediator competence, mediator maintenance of the confidentiality and quality of the process, truth in advertising, disclosure of fees, and the mediator's duty to improve the practice of mediation. However, ethics codes rarely give bright-line boundaries and indisputable answers. Rather, they help develop a moral compass for reflective practitioners and a guide to the outer limits of permissible conduct. Pinpoint for each scenario what, if anything, about the mediator's conduct arguably violates a duty to the process or parties or society. Then, double-check your answers against the prescriptions in the Model Standards.

9. Model Standards of Conduct for Mediators, American Bar Association, American Arbitration Association, and Association for Conflict Resolution (2005).

Michael Moffitt, TEN WAYS TO GET SUED: A GUIDE FOR MEDIATORS

8 Harv. Negot. L. Rev. 81, 86, 95-96, 111, 113-114, 116-117, 120, 122, 125 (2003)

[Eight of ten dilemmas posed by Moffitt follow.]

1. Melissa Mediator is a member of a small consulting firm specializing in corporate dispute resolution. One of the firm's clients is a large, multinational conglomerate. Unlike most of her colleagues, Melissa has never done work for the conglomerate. A dispute arises between one of the subsidiaries of the conglomerate and a local business. Melissa agrees to mediate the dispute and discloses nothing about the relationship between the conglomerate and her firm.
2. After considerable efforts to facilitate an agreement, and at the request of the disputants, Marjorie Mediator examines the evidence each side has compiled and develops her best assessment of a court's likely disposition of the case. The parties then quickly agree to basic settlement terms. Again at the parties' request, Marjorie drafts a formal contract to capture the terms of the parties' agreement.
3. Plaintiffs brought suit seeking injunctive relief to force a change in a particular policy at the defendant corporation and seeking modest monetary damages. During a private caucus, Marsha Mediator learns that the defendant has already decided to change the policies in question, in a way the plaintiffs will embrace. When Marsha asks defense counsel why they have not told the plaintiffs about the corporation's plans, they indicate that they hope to use the change in policies as a "trade-off concession" in order to minimize or eliminate any financial payment. In a subsequent private meeting with the plaintiffs, without the consent of the defendant, Marsha says, "Look, the defendants have already told me that they're going to make the policy change, the only issue is money."
4. Maurice Mediator learns during a conversation with a divorcing couple that the children are regularly subjected to living arrangements tantamount to abuse or neglect. Maurice mentions his concern, but both of the parents swear that the circumstances will change once they can finalize the divorce. Maurice says nothing to anyone outside of the mediation and proceeds to assist the parties in finalizing the terms of the divorce.
5. Mitchell Mediator's website touts his mediation services as "expert." In part, it says, "Over 1,000 cases of experience. Certified and sanctioned by the State and by prominent national mediation organizations." Mitchell is a former judge who presided over more than a thousand civil cases during his years on the bench. He has formally mediated, however, only a few dozen cases. Furthermore, neither the state nor the national mediation organizations to which Mitchell belongs certifies or sanctions

mediators. Mitchell is simply a member of the mediation rosters each body maintains.

6. During the mediation, Muriel Mediator adopts an aggressive approach to creating settlement. As always, she had told the parties, a divorcing couple, "Bring your toothbrushes when you show up to my mediation." The divorcing wife, unrepresented by counsel, is visibly worn down by Muriel's relentless efforts at "persuasion." When the wife protests and indicates a desire to leave, Muriel threatens to report to the judge that the wife did not participate in mediation in good faith. Muriel further indicates that such a report would "all but guarantee that you'll lose your claim for custody of the children."
7. In a private caucus, the plaintiffs tell Manuel Mediator that they would be able to break this case wide open if only they could get some cooperation from a few important executives in the defendant corporation. They admit, however, that they have had no luck so far in their efforts. Manuel then sits down privately with the general counsel for the defendant and says, "Look, I spoke with the plaintiffs. They have just lined up some key insider witnesses, including a couple members of your management team. It's time for you to end this." The general counsel looks surprised but increases the defendants' offer considerably. The mediator takes the new offer to the plaintiffs, who quickly agree to it.
8. Michael Mediator misses an opportunity to improve the parties' understanding of each other and of the relevant issues. Michael creates an unhelpful agenda and refuses to adapt his approach. Michael misreads the parties' primary concerns. He makes inappropriate suggestions. Michael is unprepared. He listens horribly. Michael oversees a lengthy process that produces no agreement and worsens the parties' relationship.

Wrestling with these eight scenarios should develop an appreciation of major dilemmas that have informed the development of mediation ethical codes. Recurring issues, many of which have no definitive resolution, include: conflicts of interest that impact mediator neutrality or create the appearance of mediator bias; mediator evaluation and agreement drafting that raise questions about unauthorized practice of law; mediator responsibilities to maintain party confidences and simultaneously promote settlement; mediator duties to endangered third parties, as such duties impact mediation confidentiality; consumers' rights to truthfulness in advertising and parties' rights to honesty and integrity from the mediator; the line between energizing parties to move forward and improperly pressuring them into settlement; and the contours of minimal competence. These issues have been at the center of scholarship and debate and have puzzled thoughtful practitioners. Sometimes there are no bright line answers. In other cases, there are clear sources of ethical guidance from rules or the ethics committees of bar associations and organizations serving neutrals.

Problem 8-12. ***What Would You Advise?***

Imagine a situation where a colleague asks you whether she can accept an appointment as an estate administrator where, after serving as a mediator, the parties to the mediation ask the mediator to take on this role. The mediation parties are both beneficiaries of the estate.

What happens to a mediator who breaches an ethical duty? Mediators operating under the umbrella of a court-annexed or court-sponsored ADR program may be protected by quasi-judicial immunity. In Wagshal v. Foster, 28 F.3d 1249 (D.C. Cir. 1994), the court held that a mediator's actions in communicating to the judge—and breaching the confidentiality prescribed for his role—when he recused himself from a case were within the scope of his official duties and hence entitled to absolute immunity. Some scholars and practitioners feel that mediators should not enjoy immunity; rather, like other professionals, they should be liable for malpractice. Professor Michael Moffitt argues that "a mediator who engages in egregious behavior, violates contractual or statutory obligations, or breaches separately articulated duties should enjoy no legal or de facto immunity from lawsuits."[10]

Even absent immunity, there are other ways in which mediators are virtually immune from liability. Because there are no bright line standards for mediator conduct, it is difficult to prove that a mediator has been negligent. A party may not be able to establish that an unfavorable settlement amounts to an actionable injury or appropriate damages for that injury. Further, parties often agree in their agreements to mediate to hold mediators harmless from future actions. Finally, these hurdles are compounded by the evidentiary restrictions related to confidentiality discussed earlier in this chapter.

For the most part a lawyer representative's ethical duties in mediation will track his duties as a negotiator when there is no mediator. A lawyer cannot misrepresent material fact, but there remains room for "puffing and bluffing" in mediated negotiations. Lawyers must be as diligent in mediation as they are in other areas of legal service and follow the Code of Professional Conduct. For example, an attorney was found in violation of the rules of professional conduct where he arrived an hour late at two mediation sessions and was unprepared. Attorney Grievance Comm'n of Md. v. Steinberg, 910 A.2d 429 (Md. 2006). Can you think of any other ethical responsibilities a lawyer representing a party in a mediation should have that might be different from a representative role in litigation?

Multiple models of mediation and mediation's rapid growth raise concerns about maintaining a core consistency to the process and safeguarding consumers. At the same time, proponents of mediation want to preserve its flexibility and creativity. For one attempt to specify some general principles of "ethical practice" in this new field, Professor Carrie Menkel-Meadow has proposed a "credo" of

10. Michael Moffitt, Suing Mediators, 83 B.U. L. Rev. 147, 207 (2003).

basic principles for mediators and neutral consensus builders or facilitators. She suggests that all third-party neutrals should:

- ensure broad party and "stakeholder" participation;
- provide opportunities for participants to agree on procedural and ground rules, as well as on decision rules for agreements;
- encourage participant recognition of both individual and joint needs and interests;
- encourage parties to express reasons and justifications for their views, needs, and offers;
- facilitate creative and tailored solutions to meet parties' needs and objectives;
- provide a place of fair hearing and respect for all parties;
- facilitate capacity-building of parties to negotiate on their own behalf;
- consider the practicality and enforceability of agreements reached;
- be themselves free from bias and conflicts of interests; and
- avoid unjust, unfair, or unconscionable agreements, wherever possible.[11]

While grappling with perplexing ethical questions, keep in mind the enormous promise of mediation—a process geared towards helping parties communicate more effectively, tap into human creativity, and bring about consensual and durable resolutions.

Further Reading

Law and Mediation

James R. Coben & Peter N. Thompson, Disputing Irony: A Systematic Look at Litigation About Mediation, 11 Harv. Negot. L. Rev. 43 (2006).

Jonathan M. Hyman & Lela P. Love, If Portia Were a Mediator: An Inquiry Into Justice in Mediation, 9 Clinical L. Rev. 157 (2002).

Singapore Mediation Convention Reference Book, 20 Cardozo J. Conflict Resol.1001 (2019).

Joseph B. Stulberg, Fairness and Mediation, 13 Ohio St. J. on Disp. Resol. 909 (1998).

Evaluative Mediation

Marjorie Corman Aaron, ADR Toolbox: The Highwire Art of Evaluation, 14 Alternatives 62 (1996).

Deborah R. Hensler. (2000). In Search of "Good Mediation." In Joseph Sanders & V. Lee Hamilton (Eds), Handbook of Justice Research in Law (p. 231). New York: Kluwer Academic/Plenum Publishers.

11. Carrie Menkel-Meadow, The Lawyer as Consensus Builder: Ethics for a New Practice, 70 Tenn. L. Rev. 63, 106-110 (2002).

Lela P. Love & Kimberlee K. Kovach, ADR: An Eclectic Array of Processes, Rather Than One Eclectic Process, 2000 J. Disp. Resol. 295 (2000).

Lela P. Love, The Top Ten Reasons Why Mediators Should Not Evaluate, 24 Fla. St. U. L. Rev. 937 (1997).

Lela P. Love & John W. Cooley, The Intersection of Evaluation by Mediators and Informed Consent: Warning the Unwary, 21 Ohio St. J. on Disp. Resol. 45 (2005).

Jeffrey W. Stempel, The Inevitability of the Eclectic: Liberating ADR from Ideology, 2000 J. Disp. Resol. 247 (2000).

Mandatory Mediation

Giuseppe De Palo, Mediating Mediation Itself: The Easy Opt-Out Model Settles the Perennial Dispute Between Voluntary and Mandatory Mediation, 22 Cardozo J. Conflict Resol. 543 (2021).

Mary G. Marcus, Walter Marcus, Nancy A. Stilwell & Neville Doherty, To Mediate or Not to Mediate: Financial Outcomes in Mediated Versus Adversarial Divorces, 17 Mediation Q. 143 (1999).

Good Faith

Carol L. Izumi & Homer C. La Rue, Prohibiting "Good Faith" Reports Under the Uniform Mediation Act: Keeping the Adjudication Camel Out of the Mediation Tent, 2003 J. Disp. Resol. 67 (2003).

Kimberlee K. Kovach, Good Faith in Mediation – Requested, Recommended or Required? A New Ethic, 38 S. Tex. L. Rev. 575 (1997).

ABA Section Council, Resolution on Good Faith Requirements for Mediators and Mediation Advocates in Court-Mandated Mediation Programs, available at: *http://www.abanet.org/dispute.*

Edward Sherman, Court Mandated Alternative Dispute Resolution: What Form of Participation Should Be Required?, 46 SMU L. Rev. 2079 (1993).

Maureen A. Weston, Checks on Participant Conduct in Compulsory ADR: Reconciling the Tension in the Need for Good-Faith Participation, Autonomy, and Confidentiality, 76 Ind. L.J. 591 (2001).

Michael Young, Mediation Gone Wild: How Three Minutes Put an ADR Party Behind Bars, 25 Alternatives 97 (2007).

Confidentiality

Ellen E. Deason, Enforcing Mediated Settlement Agreements: Contract Law Collides with Confidentiality, 35 U.C. Davis L. Rev. 33 (2001).

Scott H. Hughes, The Uniform Mediation Act: To the Spoiled Go the Privileges, 85 Marq. L. Rev. 9 (2001).

Pamela A. Kentra, Hear No Evil, See No Evil, Speak No Evil: The Intolerable Conflict for Attorney-Mediators Between the Duty to Maintain Mediation

Confidentiality and the Duty to Report Fellow Attorney Misconduct, 1997 BYU L. Rev. 715 (1997).

Ethics

CPR-Georgetown Model Rule 4.5.4: Conflicts of Interest (2002) at *www.cpradr.org.*
Phyllis Bernard & Bryant Garth (Eds.). (2002). Dispute Resolution Ethics: A Comprehensive Guide. American Bar Association Section of Dispute Resolution.
Mary B. Culbert, Proposal: A New Unified Canon of Mediator Ethics, 29 Ohio St. J. on Disp. Resol. 1 (2023).
Carrie Menkel-Meadow, The Evolving Complexity of Dispute Resolution Ethics, 30 Geo. J. Legal Ethics 389 (2017).
Carrie Menkel-Meadow, Ethics and Professionalism in Non-Adversarial Lawyering, 27 Fla. St. U. L. Rev. 153 (1999).
Carrie Menkel-Meadow, Ethics in ADR: The Many "Cs" of Professional Responsibility and Dispute Resolution, 28 Fordham Urb. L.J. 979 (2001).
Carrie Menkel-Meadow, Is Mediation the Practice of Law?, 14 Alternatives 57 (1996).
Robert B. Moberly, Ethical Standards for Court-Appointed Mediators and Florida's Mandatory Mediation Experiment, 21 Fla. St. U. L. Rev. 701 (1994).
Scott Peppet, ADR Ethics, 54 J. Legal Educ. 72 (2004).
Scott Peppet, Contractarian Economics and Mediation Ethics: The Case for Customizing Neutrality Through Contingent Fee Mediation, 82 Tex. L. Rev. 227 (2003).
Charles Pou Jr., "Embracing Limbo": Thinking About Rethinking Dispute Resolution Ethics, 108 Penn. St. L. Rev. 199 (2003).
Leonard Riskin, Toward New Standards for the Neutral Lawyer in Mediation, 26 Ariz. L. Rev. 329 (1984).
Ellen Waldman. (2011). Mediation Ethics: Cases and Commentaries. San Francisco: Jossey-Bass Publishers.

Mediator Immunity

Scott H. Hughes, Mediator Immunity: The Misguided and Inequitable Shifting of Risk, 83 Or. L. Rev. 107 (2004).
Judith Maute, Public Values and Private Justice: A Case for Mediator Accountability, 4 Geo. J. Legal Ethics 503 (1991).
Michael Moffitt, Suing Mediators, 83 B.U. L. Rev. 147 (2003).
Michael Moffitt, The Four Ways to Assure Mediator Quality (and why none of them work), 24 Ohio State J. on Disp. Resol. 191 (2009).

Regulating Mediation

Felix Steffek, Hannes Unberath, Hazel Genn, Reinhard Greger & Carrie Menkel-Meadow (Eds.). (2013). Regulating Dispute Resoluiton: ADR and Access to Justice at the Crossroads. Oxford and Portland: Hart Publishing.

Chapter 9 Arbitration: Concepts and Models

Equity bids us: to settle a dispute by negotiation and not by force; to prefer arbitration to litigation—for an arbitrator goes by the equity of a case, a judge by the strict law, and arbitration was invented with the express purpose of securing full power for equity.

—Aristotle

Arbitration is a process in which a third party who is not acting as a judge renders a decision in a dispute, following a contested presentation of evidence and arguments by the disputants or their representatives. Disputants have used arbitration for thousands of years. Before societies created the kinds of the modern system of courts and judges with which we are today familiar, disputants often brought their problems to others to reach a resolution. In some cases, the third party might have been a wise elder or other expert who was able to offer a perspective that formed the basis of a resolution. In other cases, the third party might have occupied a position of authority such that her or his decision offered the prospect of enforcement and accompanying resolution.[1]

In most contemporary contexts, arbitration occupies a space somewhere between formal litigation and the kinds of purely consensual dispute resolution processes described elsewhere in this book. At the most fundamental level, arbitrators—like judges—render decisions in cases brought before them. However, unlike litigation, in most cases all other aspects of arbitration are subject to the contractual arrangements between the disputants. How does one bring a claim? What powers will the decision-maker have to compel discovery, to issue sanctions, to issue awards, to receive motions, or to hear evidence? What opportunities will the

1. The story of King Solomon officiating over perhaps the most famous maternity suit in history is likely an illustration of this principle. In response, to hearing Solomon's declaration that the child should be split in two, one of the two claimants backed down, agreeing that the other woman should have the baby. Solomon then deemed the woman who refused to permit the baby to be divided to be the true mother. Perhaps the dispute was brought to Solomon because he was "wise." At least as likely, although less apocryphal, such dispute would have been brought before him because he was King (and any of his decisions were, therefore, enforceable). Was this an arbitration or an artful "evaluative" mediation?

parties have to shape the parameters of the award, to raise issues on appeal, or to enforce the award? These are all questions to which our civil litigation system supplies pre-made answers. Whether civil litigants should be permitted to change the default procedural rules of litigation is a matter of some debate. See, e.g., Michael Moffitt, Customized Litigation: The Case for Making Civil Procedure Negotiable, 75 Geo. Wash. L. Rev. 461 (2007); Jaime Dodge, The Limits of Procedural Private Ordering, 97 Va. L. Rev. 723 (2011); Kevin E. Davis & Helen Hershkoff, Contracting for Procedure, 53 Wm. & Mary L. Rev. 507 (2011); Robert G. Bone, Party Rulemaking: Making Procedural Rules Through Party Choice, 90 Tex. L. Rev. 1329 (2012); H. Allen Blair, Promise and Peril: Doctrinally Permissible Options for Calibrating Procedure Through Contract, 95 Neb. L. Rev. 787 (2017). But there is no serious debate about whether parties should be able to customize arbitration agreements. Indeed, this is among the most fundamental aspects of arbitration. In arbitration, the parties have the opportunity to craft the process answers to these and most other questions.

Given the opportunity for customization based on the parties' interests, arbitration comes in a great variety of flavors. This diversity of processes, all under the umbrella of "arbitration," is both a strength and a challenge of arbitration. On the positive side, the chance to use customized procedures narrowly tailored to particular kinds of disputes, dispute contexts, or disputants creates an opportunity for efficiency and justice. On the negative side, the infinite variability, without significant constraints or parameters, creates an opportunity for contractual mischief in the creation of arbitration agreements.

The breadth of the umbrella under which various procedures all qualify as "arbitration" also creates a challenge for students because generalizations are difficult and are almost always laden with caveats. For example, while one often hears arbitration is quicker and cheaper than litigation, this is not always true, particularly in international commercial disputes. The nature of arbitration varies depending on the subject matter of the dispute and the interests of the disputants. A person familiar with labor arbitration does not necessarily know what to expect from commercial arbitration, and a person familiar with securities arbitration may be surprised to learn how arbitration works in the diamond industry. International and domestic arbitrations may look different from one another, and even international arbitration varies substantially depending on the context and location. The differences among the many forms of arbitration are crucial because the advantages and disadvantages of arbitration depend on the nature of the process.

Furthermore, the fact that the procedures in arbitration are the potential subject of customization by disputants does *not* necessarily mean arbitration procedures are simpler than those found in litigation. If you study, for example, even the default rules established under UNCITRAL, the American Arbitration Association, the International Institute for Conflict Prevention and Resolution, or the International Chamber of Commerce, you will find their complexity rivals the Federal Rules of Civil Procedure. Anticipating all of the possible ways that adverse parties may disagree about *how their dispute should be resolved* is no simple task.

A. ARBITRATION AS A DISPUTE RESOLUTION METHOD

1. Comparing Methods of Dispute Resolution

Arbitration is one among many different processes available to disputants. No single description can accurately and fully capture all of the different ways parties might negotiate, mediate, or litigate. However, in the interest of situating arbitration within the processes with which you are likely more familiar, we offer the following generalized summary of some of the key differences.

	Decision Maker	How It Starts	Role of the Third Party	Role of the Courts	Outcome
Litigation	Judge (and sometimes jury)	Plaintiff files a complaint with the court	Final decision maker	Comprehensive • Oversee all pretrial, trial, and enforcement.	Binding judgment, enforceable in court
Binding Arbitration	Arbitrator	Party files a claim pursuant to arbitration agreement procedures	Final decision maker	Minimal • Sometimes needed to compel parties to arbitration, to stay litigation. • Available to enforce arbitral award. • Rarely available for review or appeal.	Arbitral award, enforceable in court
Mediation	Parties	Either: Parties consent to meet in mediation Or: Parties are compelled to try mediation by rule or by court	Facilitator of negotiations	Minimal • Sometimes needed to compel mediation participation. • Available to enforce terms of agreement reached in mediation—whether through contract or consent order.	Either: An enforceable contract or a consent judgment Or: Parties go forward with another process
Negotiation	Parties	Parties consent to meet to negotiate	None	Minimal to none • Sometimes used to formalize an agreement. • Available to enforce terms of agreement in cases where the agreement is in a legal form.	

Figure 9.1[2]

2. Michael Moffitt & Andrea Schneider, Dispute Resolution: Examples & Explanations (4th ed. Aspen 2020).

2. Arbitration as a "Creature of Contract"

To a large extent, disputants can design the parameters of the process they want under the rubric of arbitration. Disputants who are primarily looking for a speedy, low-cost dispute resolution technique might meet these goals by making their arbitration informal and with virtually no opportunity for appeal. Disputants who want a decision-maker with a particular background or expertise can write those requirements into the arbitration agreement. If disputants want a private, non-published decision, they can call for that in their agreement, but if the disputants prefer a public process that results in a reasoned written award, that can also be arranged.

Parties could, if they chose, sit down and create an entire set of rules from whole cloth, negotiating every single aspect of the arbitration process. (Can you imagine sitting down to write the Rules of Civil Procedure, with your counterpart, from scratch?) In most cases, however, efficiency and commonsense urge parties to adopt a set of already-existing rules, either in whole or in part. Perhaps the most common source of default sets of rules comes from one of the prominent organizations providing arbitration administration.[3] For example, the American Arbitration Association suggests parties simply include a clause in commercial contracts reading, "Any controversy or claim arising out of or relating to this contract, or the breach thereof, shall be settled by arbitration administered by the American Arbitration Association under its Commercial Arbitration Rules and judgment on the award rendered by the arbitrator(s) may be entered in any court having jurisdiction thereof." Through incorporation by reference, such a clause answers the full range of questions that might arise about how an arbitration is to be commenced, conducted, and given effect.

Parties have the opportunity for customization, however, even when they refer to external sources for background arbitration rules. For example, parties could take an existing set of arbitration rules, but specify that a particular provision will be superseded by some other set of terms. They could make a rule restricting the professional backgrounds of those who can serve as arbitrators. They could specify different timetables. They could narrow the scope of the kinds of disputes subject to the arbitration clause. In some cases, parties will have so many particular interests about how an arbitration will unfold that their arbitration agreement will span many pages, rather than a single paragraph. The key thing to remember at this stage is that the parties' arbitration agreement (including any other provisions it incorporates by reference) will answer most procedural questions that normally arise. You may wish to visit AAA's ClauseBuilder tool to learn more about some of the most commonly customized aspects of arbitration agreements. The ClauseBuilder platform asks

3. See, e.g., those of the American Arbitration Association (www.adr.org/Rules), the CPR Institute for Conflict Resolution (www.cpradr.org), and the International Chamber of Commerce (iccwbo.org/dispute-resolution-services/arbitration).

a series of questions and provides a free, downloadable arbitration agreement. See www.clausebuilder.org

In this sense, many commentators and courts routinely refer to arbitration as a "creature of contract." For example, Tom Carbonneau describes "freedom of contract . . . [as being] at the very core of how the law regulates arbitration."[4] Tom Stipanowich suggests "the central and primary value of arbitration is not speed, or economy, or privacy, or neutral expertise, but rather the ability of users to make key process choices to suit their particular needs."[5] Stephen Ware argues, "Autonomy . . . is the value that transcends these other values," naming it as "arbitration's essential virtue."[6] The Supreme Court laid the foundation for these themes in the famous *Steelworkers* case, writing, "[T]he issue [before the Court] concerns the enforcement of but one promise—the promise to arbitrate in the context of an agreement dealing with a particular subject matter, the industrial relations between employers and employees. . . . And I emphasize this, for the arbitration promise is itself a contract. The parties are free to make that promise as broad or as narrow as they wish, for there is no compulsion in law requiring them to include any such promises in their agreement." Steelworkers v. American Mfg. Co., 363 U.S. 564 (1960).

However, not all are persuaded by the common characterization of arbitration as a "creature of contract." Consider Professor Aragaki's perspective, below.

Hiro N. Aragaki, ARBITRATION: CREATURE OF CONTRACT, PILLAR OF PROCEDURE

8 Y.B. on Arb. & Mediation 2 (2016)

. . . Merchants established arbitration associations and programs because they sought an alternative to the intolerable delay and injustice of courtroom procedure. Private ordering was an important means of achieving this goal, not least of which because legislative and judicial reform appeared well out of reach at the time the [Federal Arbitration Act] was enacted. But the goal was never a process that elevated efficiency and freedom of choice above all else, including fairness, legitimacy, or procedural integrity. Instead, the overriding goal was to achieve a process that was qualitatively superior to what could be obtained through public litigation.

. . . The upshot is that the history of arbitration in general, and the history of the FAA in particular, have been shaped just as much by ideals of procedure as

4. Thomas E. Carbonneau, The Exercise of Contract Freedom in the Making of Arbitration Agreements, 36 Vand. J. Transnat'l L. 1189, 1192-1193 (2003).

5. Thomas J. Stipanowich, Arbitration: The "New Litigation", 2010 Ill. L. Rev. 1, 51 (2010).

6. Stephen J. Ware, Vacating Legally-Erroneous Arbitration Awards, 6 Y.B. on Arb. & Mediation 56, 92 (2014) (quoting Stephen Ware, Comments of Professor Stephen Ware, in Edward Brunet et al., Arbitration Law In America: A Critical Assessment 327, 339 (2006)).

by ideals of contract. The point is not that freedom of contract was insignificant; rather, it is that we place undue importance on that theme each time we model arbitration after contract without also emphasizing that it is—and for centuries has been—a model of procedure.

. . . Contract is at best an awkward conceptual rubric for thinking about many of the procedural issues that arise in arbitration practice and that have become the subject of recent controversy. . . . [C]onsider the infamous case of Hooters v. Phillips [173 F.3d 933 (4th Cir. 1999)]. There, an employee brought a sexual harassment claim under Title VII. The district court denied Hooters' motion to compel arbitration because it held that the clause was unconscionable for a number of reasons. Among other things, the clause: (a) required the employee to provide notice of her claim but did not require the employer to answer or provide notice of its defenses; (b) required only the employee to provide notice of the witnesses she intended to call at the hearing; and (c) provided for a tripartite panel in which the chairperson and the employee's party-appointed arbitrator had to be selected from a list of arbitrators maintained by the employer, while the employer was free to select whomever it wished as its wing arbitrator—even its own managers. *Hooters* was essentially a case about procedural unfairness in arbitration rather than about contractual unfairness caused by things like asymmetric bargaining power or the diminished quality of consent.

. . . [T]he court could not deny Hooters's motion to compel for the simple reason that the arbitration clause flew in the face of basic norms of fair procedure. Instead, it had to reason (rather circuitously) that by promulgating such "egregiously unfair" rules, Hooters had "*materially breached* the arbitration agreement," which in turn warranted discharging Ms. Phillips of her duty to arbitrate.

From a legal realist perspective, the court's conclusion was undoubtedly influenced by concerns about fair procedure. The problem is that instead of engaging with those concerns directly and creating precedent about the type of procedures that will violate due process in arbitration, the court had to recast things in a way that would establish grounds for rescission of contract.

. . . And even if the contractual rubric ultimately yields the correct result in egregious cases such as *Hooters*, it is imperfect and will likely prove both over- and under-inclusive in cases where the procedural issues are more nuanced. It's a bit like trying to eat soup with a fork: You may manage to catch a piece of carrot here or a chunk of meat there, but you're not really getting the job done.

We will revisit Professor Aragaki's caution about the utility and limits of contract-based theories in assessing the enforceability of arbitration agreements later in Chapter 10.

3. Arbitration Timeline(s)

At the most basic level, binding arbitration happens only after two other things have happened: (1) the parties enter an agreement to submit a dispute to arbitration, and (2) a dispute arises. These two events can happen in either order. The most common is the one described above. The parties, typically while entering a larger contract, will include in the contract a provision contemplating the prospect of a future dispute, and they will include a clause that submits at least some category of those disputes to binding arbitration. Then, sometime later, a dispute arises that implicates the arbitration clause. These ex ante arbitration clauses are common—and in some contexts almost ubiquitous. It is unlikely, for example, that you have ever rented a car or purchased software without agreeing to submit future disputes to arbitration.

However, disputants who have no such pre-existing arbitration agreement can also benefit from the potential features of arbitration by agreeing to submit an existing dispute to arbitration. Such ex post arbitration agreements present some challenges for the drafters because the existence of a dispute may sharpen the strategic tradeoffs associated with each of the procedural differences in arbitration clauses. They also present some opportunities for disputants because they permit the crafting of even more narrowly tailored clauses.

The timelines within which arbitrations unfold vary tremendously. In some contexts, speed is critical, and efficiency is elevated above many other procedural interests. For example, in certain international sports arbitration contexts such as the Olympics, the time gap between claims and resolution is measured in hours or days. By contrast, some international commercial arbitration procedures provide for many months between the identification of a dispute and the filing of a claim, much less its eventual resolution. And public international arbitration processes commonly are measured in years.

As a general matter, if you are in doubt about any arbitration question—including questions about timelines—you should probably begin with: "It depends on what the arbitration clause provides . . ."

B. MODELS OF ARBITRATION

Arbitration can assume an almost limitless number of forms, based on the preferences of the parties who craft arbitration agreements. For this reason, arbitration has gained prominence as a dispute resolution mechanism in a number of different contexts, and in each of those the dispute context combines with the parties' interests have combined to create at least some "typical" forms of arbitration. In this section, we provide a brief snapshot of what arbitration often looks like in several different legal contexts. You will notice a great variety of practices—all within the framework of "arbitration." Please recall throughout this section that these descriptions are merely illustrative of arbitration processes.

1. Labor Arbitration

Arbitration has played a significant role in labor disputes for at least a century in the United States.[7] Arbitration plays a prominent role in at least two types of labor disputes: grievance arbitration and interest arbitration. The processes associated with each differ, so we provide examples of each below.

a. Grievance Arbitration

In the labor context, a grievance arbitration generally arises from a dispute in which an employee alleges an employer has taken an action not permitted by the existing contract or collective bargaining agreement (CBA). The vast majority of CBAs provide that arbitration will be used (and which procedures will be followed) to resolve any questions about the contract's meaning or the employer's alleged breach. Arbitrable disputes may arise concerning the alleged breach of the contract in other ways, but this is the most typical. Following are two examples of cases in which an arbitrator was called upon to judge whether the employer's actions were consistent with the relevant terms of the CBA.

EASTERN ASSOCIATED COAL CORP. v. UNITED MINE WORKERS OF AMERICA

531 U.S. 57 (2000)

. . . Petitioner, Eastern Associated Coal Corp., and respondent, United Mine Workers of America, are parties to a collective-bargaining agreement with arbitration provisions. The agreement specifies that, in arbitration, in order to discharge an employee, Eastern must prove it has "just cause." Otherwise the arbitrator will order the employee reinstated. The arbitrator's decision is final.

James Smith worked for Eastern as a member of a road crew, a job that required him to drive heavy trucklike vehicles on public highways. As a truck driver, Smith was subject to Department of Transportation (DOT) regulations requiring random drug testing of workers engaged in "safety-sensitive" tasks.

In March 1996, Smith tested positive for marijuana.

Eastern sought to discharge Smith. The union went to arbitration, and the arbitrator concluded that Smith's positive drug test did not amount to "just cause" for discharge. Instead the arbitrator ordered Smith's reinstatement, provided that

7. Under American law, the relationship between an employer and a group of employees represented by a union falls under the umbrella of "labor law." By contrast, when unions are not involved, contractual relationships between an employer and an individual employee fall under the umbrella of "employment law." We have overstated this distinction modestly. However, to understand how arbitration operates in each context, the distinction between contexts where a collective bargaining agreement is present and contexts in which the employment contract is directly between the employer and the employee is significant. We discuss arbitration of employment disputes later.

Smith (1) accept a suspension of 30 days without pay, (2) participate in a substance-abuse program, and (3) undergo drug tests at the discretion of Eastern (or an approved substance-abuse professional) for the next five years.

Between April 1996 and January 1997, Smith passed four random drug tests. But in July 1997 he again tested positive for marijuana. Eastern again sought to discharge Smith. The union again went to arbitration, and the arbitrator again concluded that Smith's use of marijuana did not amount to "just cause" for discharge, in light of two mitigating circumstances. First, Smith had been a good employee for 17 years. And, second, Smith had made a credible and "very personal appeal under oath . . . concerning a personal/family problem which caused this one time lapse in drug usage."

The arbitrator ordered Smith's reinstatement provided that Smith (1) accept a new suspension without pay, this time for slightly more than three months; (2) reimburse Eastern and the union for the costs of both arbitration proceedings; (3) continue to participate in a substance-abuse program; (4) continue to undergo random drug testing; and (5) provide Eastern with a signed, undated letter of resignation, to take effect if Smith again tested positive within the next five years. . . .

[The Supreme Court went on to hear an appeal arguing that the courts should refuse to enforce this arbitrator's ruling, citing public policy concerns. We return to this case and the Court's disposition of this appeal in Chapter 11.]

VULCAN IRON WORKS, INC., AND INTL. ASSOCIATION OF MACHINISTS AND AEROSPACE WORKERS, AFL-CIO, SUCCESS LODGE NO. 56

FMCS Arbn. No. 82K-05094 Grievance No. 2-81 (1982)

WILLIAMS, Arb.

The Company posted the following notice on November 16, 1981: [To] "All Production and Maintenance Employees: Years ago during a financially successful period, the Company, wishing to share such success with employees, decided to give employees a turkey at Thanksgiving and a ham at Christmas. The Company has continued this practice each year since that time. Unfortunately, this year has not been a particularly successful year. As a consequence, we regret to inform you that this year we will not provide a turkey at Thanksgiving. We will, however, give employees a ham at Christmas."

The issue is whether the Company violated the Agreement, or any binding past practice, or the National Labor Relations Act, when it failed to give Machinist bargaining unit employees a turkey for Thanksgiving 1981; and, if so, what shall be the remedy.

Employees have been given Thanksgiving turkeys by the Company since its relocation in Chattanooga [in 1960], and probably prior thereto while the plant was in Chicago. The exact year when turkeys were first given to employees at

Thanksgiving is unknown. The parties stipulated that they have been given annually at least since 1960, until Thanksgiving 1981.

[Section 15.1 of the CBA provides:] "This Agreement constitutes the entire agreement between the parties and . . . concludes all collective bargaining negotiations on any subject, whether specifically mentioned or not in this Agreement, for the term thereof. Any modifications of this Agreement shall be in writing and executed by both parties hereto. Neither party, however, is under any duty or obligation to bargain with respect to any changes, modifications or additions to the Agreement to take effect during its term."

Section 15.1 of the Agreement makes the Agreement the entire contract between the parties. This prevented the turkey bonus practice from becoming binding, and the Company was free to discontinue it. No past practice can bar the application of clear and unequivocal contractual provisions. The Arbitrator has no authority to engraft this practice upon the Agreement. . . .

This case is distinguishable on its facts from Jacobsen Mfg. Co. and Machinists, 81-1 ARB §8236, wherein Christmas cash bonuses to employees had been treated as income, with social security and income taxes withheld, and not as gratuities, and had therefore become an implied term of the wage agreement not subject to modification without consent of both parties. . . .

The grievance is denied.

---

b. Interest Arbitration

In each of the labor arbitrations above, the employer and employees were unambiguously bound to the terms of an existing CBA. Every labor contract expires after a certain number of years. What happens when a labor contract expires? In some contexts, unions may engage in strike activity, and management may engage in a lock-out or may impose terms of a contract in certain other conditions, subject to further proceedings. In some cases, however, the terms of the parties' *next* contract are the subject of arbitration—a type of arbitration called "interest arbitration."

Martin H. Malin, TWO MODELS OF INTEREST ARBITRATION

28 Ohio St. J on Disp. Resol. 145 (2013)

. . . [I]nterest arbitration may be viewed as a part of the parties' collective bargaining process or it may be viewed as a method for adjudicating disputes over terms and conditions of employment.

In other words, the interest arbitrator's task is to come up with the contract that the parties would have agreed to had their negotiation process not broken down. Of course, arbitrators are not mind readers. The best they can do is search for objective indicators. The indicator most commonly looked to by arbitrators is the agreements reached by comparable parties. Except where expressly modified by statute, comparability tends to drive interest arbitration awards, particularly with respect to wages and benefits.

A second major indicator of what agreement the parties would have reached had their negotiations not broken down is what agreements they reached in the past. It is often said that there are no breakthroughs in interest arbitration, that is that arbitrators are extremely reluctant to deviate from the status quo. As Kochan and colleagues observed:

> Experience demonstrates in New York and elsewhere that arbitrators are reluctant to break new ground in their awards and would prefer to leave innovative approaches to the parties. The conservative nature of arbitration suggests that only in rare cases will significant changes be achieved on critical contemporary issues if left to arbitrators to handle on a bargaining unit level. Thomas Kochan et al., The Long Haul Effects of Interest Arbitration: The Case of New York State's Taylor Law, 63 Indus. & Lab. Rel. Rev. 565, 582 (2010).

The conservative nature of interest arbitration may inhibit innovation in collective bargaining. A party resisting change may enter arbitration knowing that it is highly unlikely that an arbitrator will impose a change on an unwilling party. The inhibition may be exacerbated in final offer package arbitration where a party advocating a significant change may be likely to drop its proposals out of fear that including them could prompt the arbitrator to award the other party's package.

❖ TEAMSTERS LOCAL 726 v. CITY OF MARKHAM POLICE DEPT.

Ill. Labor Relations Bd. Interest Arbitration S-MA-01-232 (2003)

. . . The parties in this matter are the City of Markham, Illinois (hereinafter "the City"), and the State and Municipal Teamsters, Chauffeurs and Helpers Union, Local 726 (hereinafter "the Union"), which represents police officers and sergeants employed within the City's Police Department. The parties entered into collective bargaining negotiations over a successor agreement to their 1997-2001 contract. The parties engaged in extensive negotiations over the new agreement, and they were successful in resolving many of the issues between them. Because the parties were unsuccessful with regard to certain of the issues raised during negotiations, these unresolved issues were submitted for Compulsory Interest Arbitration with the Illinois Labor Relations Board. During the course of the arbitration proceedings, the parties settled additional open issues, leaving one issue unresolved. [The unresolved] issue presented here . . . revolves around the question of whether the City's police officers should be able to seek neutral arbitration of disputes over disciplinary matters. . . .

When the parties engaged in their current collective bargaining effort . . . [t]he Union propose[d] that the language awarded by [a previous arbitrator and included in two previous contracts] be included within their new collective bargaining agreement. The City essentially proposes that all disciplinary matters should be decided by the Board of Police and Fire Commission, and that there should be no contractual provision allowing for neutral arbitration of disputes over disciplinary matters. This history forms the backdrop for the analysis of the dispute presented here. . . .

[T]his is a mandatory subject of bargaining between these two parties. . . . [The relevant state statutes governing the relationship between the city and its police] demonstrates . . . that public policy is best served by allowing for bargaining on the issue of neutral arbitration of disciplinary disputes between [local] government[s] and labor organizations. This suggests that public policy also favors neutral arbitration of disciplinary disputes, even where there already exists a mechanism for handling disciplinary matters, such as the procedure before the City's Board of Police and Fire Commissioners. . . .

Neutral arbitration of disciplinary disputes has existed side-by-side with [state statutory] procedures for years, without any of the hypothetical difficulties associated with collateral estoppel and res judicata that the City asserts might occur. In fact, because the Union's proposal includes language that requires an aggrieved employee to expressly choose either the grievance and arbitration procedure or the Board of Police and Fire Commission procedures, but not both, collateral estoppel and res judicata do not come into play. Moreover, under the language proposed by the Union, which has appeared in the last two of the parties' collective bargaining agreements, a disciplinary grievance may be initiated only by the affected employee or by the Union on behalf of the affected employee, thereby eliminating the possible occurrence of at least one of the worst-case hypotheticals that the City described in its post-hearing brief.

Because neutral arbitration holds a well-established and widely accepted place as the primary means of resolving labor-management disputes, including disputes over discipline, it is evident that public policy considerations support the adoption of the Union's proposal in this proceeding. The City's police officers and sergeants deserve to have access to binding neutral arbitration as an alternative means of resolving disputes over disciplinary matters. I find that the City has failed to offer any valid, reasonable argument for changing the existing status quo by removing that option from the collective bargaining agreement, while the overwhelming weight of authority supports adoption of the Union's proposal on this issue.

Accordingly, this Arbitrator finds that the Union's final proposal on the issue of grievance and arbitration of disputes over disciplinary matters shall be adopted and incorporated into the parties' new collective bargaining agreement. . . .

In the case above, the interest arbitrator decided that the parties' contract should include a term related to the incorporation of a particular grievance procedure. Note that this involves the (re)distribution of public resources. Professor Raymond Horton, in a critique of public sector interest arbitration, calls it a "pragmatic adaptation to changing conditions that may not be consistent with traditional precepts." Raymond D. Horton, Arbitration, Arbitrators, and the Public Interest, 28 ILR Rev. 497 (1975). He goes so far as to say that "interest arbitration is inimical to a basic precept of political democracy, namely that authoritative political decisions should be reached by government officials who are accountable to the public." Even he notes, however, that "Arguments supporting interest arbitration are not wholly without merit. In certain situations, arbitration represents the only practical means of avoiding or terminating strikes that threaten vital public interests. . . . In addition, experience indicates that some third-party figures bring to negotiating disputes particular skill at resolving conflict on terms acceptable to both parties, and that acceptability of outcomes to the parties, whether decisions are reached by negotiators or imposed by arbitrators, is an important ingredient of labor relations stability." Id.

The process of interest arbitration may resemble hybrid processes discussed in more detail in Chapter 12. Interest arbitrators may have the authority to mediate prior to arbitrating. In many jurisdictions, the interest arbitrator must choose between proposals, rather than design their own awards. Public-sector unionized workplaces (such as education, public safety, etc.) may be governed by local law outlining the process and applicable deadlines for interest arbitration.

Problem 9-1. ***Interest Arbitration?***

Do you think the availability (or requirement) of interest arbitration systematically favors labor or management? Is it (should it be?) a necessary companion to any rule preventing certain public sector employees from going on strike?

2. Commercial Arbitration

Parties engaging in commercial transactions often foresee the possibility of disputes arising during the implementation of their agreements, and many parties include an arbitration clause in their commercial contracts, thus binding their future selves to resolve such issues through arbitration. Even in contexts in which no pre-commitment to arbitration exists, parties in commercial disputes may agree to submit those disputes to arbitration. *Hall Street Associates v. Mattel* presents a case illustrating the latter of these circumstances.

HALL STREET ASSOCIATES, LLC v. MATTEL, INC.

552 U.S. 576 (2008)

This case began as a lease dispute between landlord, petitioner Hall Street Associates, LLC, and tenant, respondent Mattel, Inc. The property was used for many years as a manufacturing site, and the leases provided that the tenant would indemnify the landlord for any costs resulting from the failure of the tenant or its predecessor lessees to follow environmental laws while using the premises. . . .

After Mattel gave notice of intent to terminate the lease in 2001, Hall Street filed this suit, contesting Mattel's right to vacate on the date it gave, and claiming that the lease obliged Mattel to indemnify Hall Street for costs of cleaning up the TCE [trichloroethylene], among other things. Following a bench trial before the United States District Court for the District of Oregon, Mattel won on the termination issue, and after an unsuccessful try at mediating the indemnification claim, the parties proposed to submit to arbitration. . . .

Arbitration took place, and the arbitrator decided for Mattel. In particular, he held that no indemnification was due, because the lease obligation to follow all applicable federal, state, and local environmental laws did not require compliance with the testing requirements of the Oregon Drinking Water Quality Act (Oregon Act); that Act the arbitrator characterized as dealing with human health as distinct from environmental contamination.

[The Supreme Court went on to hear a challenge to the arbitrator's decision in this case and issued an opinion clarifying parties' ability to contractually expand judicial review of arbitral awards. We return to this case in Chapter 11.]

---

3. International Arbitration

Disputes arise in the international context in at least three different forms. First, all of the disputants may be private actors. Two companies, for example, might form a joint venture across borders and might reasonably anticipate that disputes may arise. They might pre-commit to using a particular set of arbitration procedures to minimize transaction costs associated with such disputes. Awards resulting from such agreements, in many contexts, are easily enforced in domestic courts against the losing party.

A second kind of international dispute involves different states. In such cases, arbitration is sometimes used in state-to-state conflicts as a supplement or substitute for what might normally be characterized as the realm of diplomacy. For more than 150 years, ad hoc international arbitration panels have resolved state-to-state disputes in a wide variety of circumstances. For example, the Alabama Claims in 1871 stemmed from an allegation by the United States that Great Britain violated its neutrality during the U.S. Civil War by aiding the Confederacy. Those claims ultimately went through arbitration as part of the resolution process. In another example, the United States was party to a series of disputes surrounding the Bering Sea in the late 19th century, including a set of conflicts regarding fishing and fur seal hunting, all of which were addressed through multi-national arbitration. More recently, the Indus Waters Kishenganga arbitrations have resolved (or sought to resolve) a series of disputes between India and Pakistan arising in the decades since the Indus Water Treaty.

A dispute between France and New Zealand in the 1980s over the *Rainbow Warrior* incident provides a good illustration of how this second type of international arbitration can unfold. The activist organization Greenpeace dispatched the ship *Rainbow Warrior* to observe nuclear testing being conducted on French South Pacific islands. In 1985, France sent two spies to New Zealand, where the *Rainbow Warrior* was in port being repaired. The spies blew up the ship, and in the process, killed a Dutch national who was on board at the time. The ensuing dispute between France and New Zealand was ultimately brought to then-U.N. Secretary-General Pérez de Cuellar to arbitrate. In 1986, the Secretary-General issued an award requiring France to provide an unqualified apology, pay $7 million in compensation to New Zealand, withdraw economic sanctions it had previously imposed on New Zealand, and require its two spies to spend three years in a French military facility on the French island of Hao, in the South Pacific, with the express provision that "they should be prohibited from leaving the island for any reason, except with the mutual consent of the two Governments." The decision also required both countries to agree to arbitrate any future disputes arising out of the resolution. Less than two years later, France withdrew both its agents from Hao, saying they required medical attention. New Zealand did not consent to the withdrawal and initiated arbitration. In 1990, an arbitral tribunal issued an award holding France had violated the 1986 agreement, but the panel could not order the agents be returned to Hao. Instead, the tribunal ordered France to pay $2 million into a France-New Zealand friendship fund.[8]

A third form of international dispute includes those in which one of the parties is a state actor and another is a private actor. The most common contemporary example in the arbitration context involves investor-state disputes. This form of arbitration has grown increasingly common, in part because arbitration is thought to encourage investment. Without arbitration clauses, private foreign investors might not be willing to bear the risks associated with using domestic courts in the event of subsequent disputes. Yet, as the case below shows, the intersection of commercial interests and the national interests of the government can become complicated.

BG GROUP PLC v. REPUBLIC OF ARGENTINA

134 S. Ct. 1198 (2014)

Article 8 of an investment treaty between the United Kingdom and Argentina contains a dispute-resolution provision, applicable to disputes between one of those nations and an investor from the other. The provision authorizes either party to submit a dispute "to the decision of the competent tribunal of the Contracting Party in whose territory the investment was made," i.e., a local court. And [Article 8 of that treaty] provides for arbitration "(i) where, after a period of eighteen months has elapsed from the moment when the dispute was submitted to

8. See Rainbow Warrior Arbitration (New Zealand v. France), 82 I.L.R. 499 (1990).

the competent tribunal . . . , the said tribunal has not given its final decision; [or] (ii) where the final decision of the aforementioned tribunal has been made but the Parties are still in dispute." . . .

In the early 1990s, the petitioner, BG Group PLC, a British firm, belonged to a consortium that bought a majority interest in an Argentine entity called MetroGAS. MetroGAS was a gas distribution company created by Argentine law in 1992, as a result of the government's privatization of its state-owned gas utility. Argentina distributed the utility's assets to new, private companies, one of which was MetroGAS. It awarded MetroGAS a 35-year exclusive license to distribute natural gas in Buenos Aires, and it submitted a controlling interest in the company to international public tender. BG Group's consortium was the successful bidder. At about the same time, Argentina enacted statutes providing that its regulators would calculate gas "tariffs" in U.S. dollars, and that those tariffs would be set at levels sufficient to assure gas distribution firms, such as MetroGAS, a reasonable return.

In 2001 and 2002, Argentina, faced with an economic crisis, enacted new laws. Those laws changed the basis for calculating gas tariffs from dollars to pesos, at a rate of one peso per dollar. The exchange rate at the time was roughly three pesos to the dollar. The result was that MetroGAS' profits were quickly transformed into losses. BG Group believed that these changes (and several others) violated the Treaty; Argentina believed the contrary. . . .

The [arbitration] panel pointed out that in 2002, the President of Argentina had issued a decree staying for 180 days the execution of its courts' final judgments (and injunctions) in suits claiming harm as a result of the new economic measures. In addition, Argentina had established a "renegotiation process" for public service contracts, such as its contract with MetroGAS, to alleviate the negative impact of the new economic measures. But Argentina had simultaneously barred from participation in that "process" firms that were litigating against Argentina in court or in arbitration. These measures, while not making litigation in Argentina's courts literally impossible, nonetheless "hindered" recourse "to the domestic judiciary" to the point where the Treaty implicitly excused compliance with the local litigation requirement. Requiring a private party in such circumstances to seek relief in Argentina's courts for 18 months, the panel concluded, would lead to "absurd and unreasonable result[s]."

On the merits, the arbitration panel agreed with Argentina that it had not "expropriate[d]" BG Group's investment, but also found that Argentina had denied BG Group "fair and equitable treatment." It awarded BG Group $185 million in damages. . . .

The arbitration panel made three relevant determinations:

(1) "As a matter of treaty interpretation," the local litigation provision "cannot be construed as an absolute impediment to arbitration,"
(2) Argentina enacted laws that "hindered" "recourse to the domestic judiciary" by those "whose rights were allegedly affected by the emergency measures," that sought "to prevent any judicial interference with the emergency legislation," and that "excluded from the renegotiation process" for public service contracts "any licensee seeking judicial redress," [and]

(3) under these circumstances, it would be "absurd and unreasonable" to read Article 8 as requiring an investor to bring its grievance to a domestic court before arbitrating.

[The Supreme Court went on to affirm the arbitration panel's award, unpersuaded by the suggestion that the panel lacked jurisdiction or that the arbitrators deviated from their duties so egregiously that the award was rendered unenforceable.]

---

4. Sports Arbitration

For some people, cases involving athletes provide the most visible glimpse into the operation of arbitration as a dispute resolution mechanism.

In some circumstances, the disputes and the arbitrations that follow are not terribly different from many traditional legal contexts. For example, many professional athletes in the United States operate within the constraints of CBAs. Disputes arising out of the application and interpretation of those contracts are often matters sent to arbitration, just as they are for a wide range of different (if significantly less well-compensated and famous) employee groups. For example, former all-star Alex Rodriguez was accused of taking performance-enhancing drugs, in violation of the Major League Baseball (MLB) CBA. The contract, like many labor contracts, contains an arbitration clause. After the MLB sought to impose a 211-game suspension, an arbitrator reduced the suspension to 162 games (still, at that time, the longest such suspension for a drug violation in league history), citing the CBA's language and precedent in other cases. Aside from the relative fame associated with the grievant, note the similarities between the structures of the arbitrations for Alex Rodriguez and for James Smith (the truck driver facing discipline for failed drug tests in the *Eastern Associated Coal* case). Many athletic coaches have arbitration agreements in their non-union employment contracts. In a highly publicized case, the NFL successfully petitioned the federal court for an order to arbitrate many of head coach Brian Flores's claims of racial discrimination in hiring. Florez v. NFL, 658 F. Supp. 198 (S.D.N.Y. 2023).

Similarly, those engaged in "fantasy sports," like many who engage in commercial transactions, might reasonably anticipate that disputes may arise and might choose to include an arbitration clause in the body of the agreements, which bind the parties together. For example, the first sentence in the user agreement for FanDuel, a popular fantasy sports platform reads: "IMPORTANT NOTICE: THIS AGREEMENT IS SUBJECT TO BINDING ARBITRATION AND A WAIVER OF CLASS ACTION RIGHTS AS DETAILED IN SECTION 15." The FanDuel contract goes on to detail an arbitration process, which includes the Commercial Arbitration Rules of the American Arbitration Association. Sometimes, fantasy sports enthusiasts set up their own leagues, not administered through a fee-for-services company. Not surprisingly, disputes sometimes arise between members of these leagues. Companies such as sportsjudge.com, fantasyjudgment.com, and fantasysupremecourt.com offer to resolve these disputes through an online arbitration process. Although these fantasy sports disputes have a particular substantive background, they are not fundamentally different from commercial disputes in a range of other commercial settings, and not surprisingly, the arbitration processes used to resolve them are fairly typical of the processes used elsewhere.

In some sporting contexts, however, disputes present distinct opportunities and challenges. Consider, for example, the need for speedy resolution of eligibility or doping disputes arising during the Olympic Games. Multi-stage processes, with months or years of discovery, motion practice, trial, and appeal would be inconsistent with any of the parties' needs. As Professor Maureen Weston has written,

> The timing and nature of international sporting competition often necessitates swift resolution of eligibility disputes. [The Court of Arbitration for Sport] is logically designed to respond. With the viability of judicial recourse extremely limited, athletes with disciplinary and eligibility disputes must submit to CAS arbitration. But with the power to test, sanction, and deny an athlete of his or her sporting career, comes the obligation to provide a fair hearing process, including assurances of impartiality, access to information, and to legal advisors. It is about the athletes. It is about playing and judging true, clean, and fair.[9]

5. Adhesion Contracts

Certain forms of contracts are treated as "adhesion contracts,"[10] and these present particular challenges to fairness and enforceability. These challenges are particularly acute when it comes to contracts containing arbitration clauses. As you will read below in Chapter 10, arbitration clauses were not included in many adhesion clauses until a few decades ago, but the law in this area has shifted, and as a result, they are now commonplace in consumer, employment, health care, and other contexts in which adhesion contracts are the norm.

For example, in Nitro-Lift Technologies v. Howard, 568 U.S. 17 (2012), the Supreme Court heard an appeal of disputes from two former employees who had signed an employment agreement containing, among other things, an arbitration clause reading, "Any dispute, difference or unresolved question between Nitro-Lift and the Employee (collectively the 'Disputing Parties') shall be settled by arbitration by a single arbitrator mutually agreeable to the Disputing Parties in an arbitration proceeding conducted in Houston, Texas in accordance with the rules

9. Maureen A. Weston, Doping Control, Mandatory Arbitration, and Process Dangers for Accused Athletes in International Sports, 10 Pepp. Disp. Resol. L.J. 5 (2009).

10. The typical description of adhesion contracts includes reference to them being drafted by one party, as though it were a standard form, and presented as a take-it-or-leave-it proposition. This definition is not entirely satisfactory, though, because many contracts could meet this definition without raising the same adhesion contract concerns. For a fuller description, see Todd Rakoff, Contracts of Adhesion: An Essay in Reconstruction, 96 Harv. L. Rev. 1173 (1983) (outlining seven important characteristics of adhesion contracts).

existing at the date hereof of the American Arbitration Association." The Court held the former employees were bound by this clause and, therefore, had to bring their claims to an arbitrator rather than a court.

As you read in Section A, many of the foundational conceptions of arbitration hinge on the notion of party consent. Such consent is relatively easy to assume in contexts (like most of those described in Sections 1-4 above) in which both of the parties are relatively sophisticated, represented by counsel, and made a choice about the inclusion of an arbitration clause.

What should you make of arbitration clauses appearing in adhesion contracts? In the passage below, Jeff Sovern describes a study he and his colleagues undertook to examine the degree to which average consumers understand the meaning of average arbitration clauses. They reasoned that if a consumer cannot understand such a clause, then the extent of the consumer's "consent" is up for question.

❖ *Jeff Sovern*, CONSUMER UNDERSTANDING OF ARBITRATION CLAUSES IN CONTRACTS: "WHIMSY LITTLE CONTRACTS" WITH UNEXPECTED CONSEQUENCES

Forced Arbitration and the Fate of the 7th Amendment, Report of the 2014 Forum for State Appellate Court Judges (2014)

[W]e showed [study participants] a credit card contract. Ours was seven pages which sounds like a lot but if you look at the depository of credit cards that the Consumer Financial Protection Bureau maintains on the web, you'll see that some run over 20 pages, and, in fact, ours was pretty typical for credit card contracts. As for the arbitration clause . . . [t]here was a bold face reference to ours on the second page of the contract, saying, "It is important that you read the entire arbitration provision section carefully." The arbitration clause itself appeared on pages six and seven of the contract, again in bold, with key parts printed in italics and all caps. So all together the arbitration clause in our contract was either referred to or appeared on three of the seven pages. Our clause was also slightly more readable than the typical credit card arbitration clause, which doesn't mean it was all that readable. They typically still require two years of college to understand, but ours was better than average.

We wanted to find out if consumers actually understand four key aspects of typical arbitration clauses. Those four key aspects are that the clause bars suit in non-small claims courts, blocks class actions, prohibits jury trials, and provides that the arbitrator's decision is final. . . .

So how'd they do? Only two respondents out of 663 answered all eight questions correctly; 117 did not answer any of the questions correctly, which is more than answered at least half the questions right. I don't know about you, but when I was in high school a passing grade on a test was 65 percent. By that standard, 96 percent of our respondents would have failed.

What about the individual questions? Not one of the eight questions elicited a majority of correct answers; although, on one, a majority of the respondents gave wrong answers.

Before we conducted the survey, we expected to find that consumers would not really know what these arbitration clauses provided. So that piece of it may not be such a big surprise. What has surprised me, at least, is how many consumers think they do know, but what they think they know is simply wrong. . . .

And that suggests that when a company crafts its arbitration clause or decides whether to include it or not, it doesn't have to worry about how consumers will respond. It might have to worry about how the courts . . . will respond, but it doesn't have to worry about how consumers will respond, because this is not something that consumers are thinking about. . . .

We have people giving up their legal rights—their Constitutional rights, the right to a jury trial—without knowing it, all the while thinking that they're doing something completely different.

But let me talk about what I think of as the key takeaways from our study. Remember that you have to have consent for arbitration. So our study I think raises real questions about whether we have consent. Almost none of the respondents understand arbitration clauses. Only two out of 663 remember got all eight questions right. On top of that, more than half thought the clause didn't do what it did or even thought that "a whimsy little contract" can't do what it does. They have misconceptions about arbitration clauses. So we have people giving up their legal rights, their Constitutional rights, the right to a jury trial, giving up their ability to get effective redress without knowing it, all the while thinking that they're doing something completely different—and that's if they're thinking about this at all. I think that raises serious questions about how meaningful their consent to arbitration is, and even how valid that consent is.

Another research group similarly reports the public's general lack of knowledge of arbitration and what the process entails. See Kristen M. Blankley et al., ADR is Not a Household Term: Considering the Ethical and Practical Consequences of the Public's Lack of Understanding of Mediation and Arbitration, 99 Neb. L. Rev. 797 (2020). In their study, Professor Blankley and co-authors report that while upwards of 79% of community respondents knew the term "arbitration," follow-up questions indicated they lacked substantive knowledge of essential features of the process.

Problem 9-2. ***That Time You Agreed to Arbitration . . . ?***

Consider the contracts you have entered over the past two years and look for one that includes an arbitration agreement. We are confident you can find at least one. Your lease? A rental car agreement? Employment contract? Your credit card company? Your phone service or Internet provider? Computer or software? Your student loans or tuition? Find the exact clause and see what it provides for—rules, site of arbitration, choice of arbitrators, etc.

6. Nonbinding Arbitration

All of the arbitration processes we have described up until now have been *binding* arbitration processes—ones in which the arbitrator's decision is designed to resolve the dispute fully and finally. As you will see in the next chapter, in some contexts parties may nevertheless challenge the validity of the arbitrator's decision. However, unless there is either some flaw in the arbitration contract or some flaw in the conduct of the arbitration, the assumption is that the outcome will be the last word on the subject of the dispute.

In some contexts, however, a non-binding version of arbitration has become prominent. Described in more detail elsewhere in this book, non-binding arbitration involves a process in which a third party renders a decision following an adversarial, adjudicative process, but the opinion does not necessarily bind the parties. In its mildest form, non-binding arbitration is merely advisory, aimed at helping the parties reach a consensual resolution of their dispute.

Sometimes, non-binding arbitration occurs in a statutory context in which the parties are "encouraged" to agree to the terms of the arbitrator's decision through the threat of fee-shifting or other penalties. For example, in Oregon, most civil claims below $50,000 are subject to *mandatory non-binding* arbitration. See O.R.S. Ch. 36. The parties typically split the arbitration fees equally, and after a hearing, the chosen arbitrator issues a ruling. The parties can choose to accept the award as the final resolution of the case, and it will be entered as a judgment of the court. However, if one of the parties is unhappy with the arbitrator's ruling, she or he can object, pay an additional fee, and receive a trial *de novo* in the courts. However, if the appealing party does not achieve a more favorable outcome in the *de novo* trial, that party loses their deposit, loses any award they may have had for attorney fees and costs incurred after the arbitration, and will be liable for the other party's attorney fees and costs following the arbitration. See O.R.S. 36.425(4). Framed by some as a "penalty" for frivolous appeals, this fee-shifting structure creates a strong incentive for some disputants to "accept" the arbitrator's non-binding decision.

C. ARBITRATORS' POWERS

Illustrating the potentially breathtaking scope of the parties' ability to define virtually all aspects of the nature of the arbitration proceedings, Judge Posner once colorfully wrote,

> Short of authorizing trial by battle or ordeal or, more doubtfully by a panel of three monkeys, parties can stipulate to whatever procedures they want to govern the arbitration of their disputes; parties are as free to specify idiosyncratic terms of arbitration as they are to specify any other terms in their contract.

Baravati v. Josephthal, Lyon & Ross, Inc., 28 F.3d 704, 709 (7th Cir. 1994).

The breadth of arbitrators' powers can illustrate an ongoing debate about the appropriate role of third parties in adjudicative processes.

Lon L. Fuller, COLLECTIVE BARGAINING AND THE ARBITRATOR

1963 Wis. L. Rev. 3, 3-4

One conception of the role of the arbitrator is that he is essentially a judge. His job is to do justice according to the rules imposed by the parties' contract, leaving the chips to fall where they may. He decides the controversy entirely on the basis of arguments and proofs presented to him "in open court" with the parties confronting one another face to face. He does not attempt to mediate or conciliate, for to do so would be to compromise his role as an adjudicator. He will strictly forego any private communication with the parties after the hearing. . . .

The opposing conception expects the arbitrator to adapt his procedures to the case at hand. Indeed, in its more extreme form it rejects the notion that his powers for good should be restrained at all by procedural limitations. By this view the arbitrator has a roving commission to straighten things out, the immediate controversy marking the occasion for, but not the limits of, his intervention. If the formal submission leaves fringes of dispute unsettled, he will gladly undertake to tidy them up. If the arguments at the hearing leave him in doubt as to the actual causes of the dispute, or as to what the parties really expect of him, he will not scruple to hold private consultations for his further enlightenment. If he senses the possibility of a settlement, he will not hesitate to step down from his role as arbitrator to assume that of mediator. If despite his conciliatory skill negotiations become sticky, he will follow Harry Shulman's advice and—with an admonitory glance toward the chair just vacated—"exert the gentle pressure of a threat of decision" to induce agreement.[11]

Organizations that administer arbitrations often specify certain powers for arbitrators, and also provide catch-all provisions, empowering the arbitrator to make other decisions as she or he deems necessary for the proper conduct of the arbitration process. For example, Rule 23 of the American Arbitration Association's Commercial Arbitration Rules provides, "The arbitrator shall have the authority to issue any orders necessary to enforce the provisions of [the AAA] rules and to otherwise achieve a fair, efficient and economical resolution of the case. . . ." Statutory frameworks underlying arbitration rules often have similar default provisions. For example, Revised Uniform Arbitration Act, §15(a), provides "[a]n arbitrator may conduct an arbitration in such manner as the arbitrator

11. Harry Shulman, Reason, Contract, and Law in Labor Relations, 68 Harv. L. Rev. 999, 1023 (1955).

considers appropriate for a fair and expeditious disposition of the proceeding," subject to the specifics of the parties' agreement.

Parties contemplating a new arbitration agreement, however, typically focus on several specific aspects of arbitration—most of which deal with the arbitrator's powers. In this section, we survey some of the most important of decisions about arbitral powers. Recall that virtually anything may, at least in some contexts, be subject to the parties' contractual preferences.

1. Arbitrators' Power to Determine the Meaning and Validity of Contracts and Arbitration Clauses

Adverse parties find no shortage of things to disagree about. In the context of arbitration, the opportunity for conflict encompasses not only the underlying dispute, but also questions such as whether the contract containing an arbitration clause is valid, whether the arbitration clause applies to the dispute in question, and who should decide such questions.

a. Who Decides Whether a Contract that Contains an Arbitration Clause Is Valid?

Arbitration clauses are typically contained in larger contracts, which include a variety of terms. What happens if one of the parties argues the "container contract" (the document containing both an arbitration clause and whatever the original purpose of the contract was) is void or voidable? Should a judge or an arbitrator resolve that question? The Supreme Court has repeatedly stated when disputants challenge the larger container contract, and not the validity of the arbitration clause, the arbitrator, rather than a judge, should decide whether the contract is valid.

In Prima Paint Corp. v. Flood & Conklin Mfg. Co., 388 U.S. 395 (1967), a contract dispute arose between Prima Paint and its consultant, Flood & Conklin. The agreement between the two companies included a broad arbitration provision. However, Prima Paint argued it should not be bound to arbitrate the case because the entire agreement—including the arbitration clause—was, in Prima Paint's view, fraudulently induced. The Supreme Court held the arbitrator must resolve the question, writing "[I]f the claim is fraud in the inducement of the arbitration clause itself—an issue which goes to the 'making' of the agreement to arbitrate—the federal court may proceed to adjudicate it. But the statutory language [of the FAA] does not permit the federal court to consider claims of fraud in the inducement of the contract generally." 388 U.S. at 400-401. Critics were puzzled how a contract, which is ultimately deemed entirely invalid, could give rise to a valid arbitration provision. The majority's explanation, however, was that the parties wanted an arbitrator to resolve any disputes about the contract, and they could have excluded such disputes from the arbitrators' powers if they had preferred.

The Court has reiterated the standard set in *Prima Paint* multiple times. In Buckeye Check Cashing Inc. v. Cardegna, 546 U.S. 440 (2006), for example, consumers sued Buckeye in state court, arguing the entire Buckeye contract was unenforceable because it included a usurious interest rate, in violation of state civil and criminal laws. Buckeye filed a motion to compel arbitration, pointing to an arbitration agreement in the contract signed by the plaintiffs. In an 8-1 decision, the Court sided with Buckeye, holding that under the *Prima Paint* logic, an arbitrator should resolve any disputes about the validity of the container agreement.

b. Who Decides the Validity and Applicability of an Arbitration Clause?

The Supreme Court has consistently written, over the last several decades, in support of the federal policy favoring arbitration. In Granite Rock Co. v. International Brotherhood of Teamsters, 561 U.S. 287, 130 S. Ct. 2847 (2010), however, the Court made clear:

> [W]e have never held that this policy overrides the principle that a court may submit to arbitration only those disputes that the parties have agreed to submit. . . . It is well settled in both commercial and labor cases that whether parties have agreed to submit a particular dispute to arbitration is typically an issue for judicial determination. . . . It is similarly well settled that where the dispute at issue concerns contract formation, the dispute is generally for courts to decide . . . [C]ourts should order arbitration of a dispute only where the court is satisfied that neither the formation of the parties' arbitration agreement *nor* . . . its enforceability or applicability to the dispute is in issue.

The Court in *Granite Rock* went on to hold that a court, rather than an arbitrator, should determine the parties' dispute over the effective ratification date for the CBA, even though the CBA contained an arbitration clause.

The Supreme Court has explained that certain default rules give courts or arbitrators the power to make decisions, but parties can also draft their arbitration agreement to provide decisions ordinarily expected to be made by courts instead be made by arbitrators. When an issue under dispute is plainly covered by the scope of a valid arbitration agreement, the issue is said to be "arbitrable"—one that is expected to be resolved through arbitration. In First Options of Chicago, Inc. v. Kaplan, 514 U.S. 938 (1950), writing for the Court, Justice Breyer stated: "Just as the arbitrability of the merits of a dispute depends upon whether the parties agreed to arbitrate that dispute, so the question 'who has the primary power to decide arbitrability' turns upon what the parties agreed about *that* matter." However, Justice Breyer explained, "[c]ourts should not assume that the parties agreed to arbitrate arbitrability unless there is "clea[r] and unmistakabl[e]" evidence that they did so. . . ." The Court concluded "because the [parties]. . . . did not clearly agree to submit the question of arbitrability to arbitration, the Court of Appeals was correct in finding that the arbitrability of the Kaplan/First Options dispute was subject to independent review by the courts." That is, the court rather than the arbitrator should decide whether the issue of contractual applicability should be decided by a court or by an arbitrator.

Subsequently, in Rent-a-Center West v. Jackson, 130 S. Ct. 2772 (2010), the Supreme Court addressed the question of whether an arbitration agreement could delegate the power to decide whether the arbitration agreement itself was unconscionable to the arbitrator. Mr. Jackson, an employee, sought to have his employment discrimination claim heard by a court rather than an arbitrator, and argued the discovery limits and fee-splitting provisions made the arbitration clause unconscionable. In a 5-4 decision, Justice Scalia, writing for the Court, found the unconscionability decision could be delegated, so long as the *delegation clause itself* was not unconscionable. The Court in *Jackson* found the delegation of the unconscionability decision to the arbitrator valid because the plaintiff didn't argue the delegation clause itself was unconscionable. Justice Scalia recognized it would typically be more difficult to show a delegation provision is unconscionable than to show the arbitration clause itself is unconscionable. Dissenting, Justice Stevens insisted parties should not have the power to take unconscionability decisions away from the court, given that Section 2 of the FAA assigns arbitrability issues to the courts. The Supreme Court affirmed this holding in the 2019 case Henry Schein, Inc. v. Archer and White Sales, 586 U.S. 63 (2019), when it held that an arbitrator should determine arbitrability questions, even when the likelihood that the dispute is arbitrable is low.

None of the relevant Supreme Court opinions in this area prevents parties from having arbitrators be the locus of decision for such questions. These cases simply stand for the proposition that the parties' intention to resolve such disputes through arbitration must be "clear and unmistakable." The Commercial Arbitration Rules for the American Arbitration Association provide that "The arbitrator shall have the power to rule on his or her own jurisdiction, including any objections with respect to the existence, scope, or validity of the arbitration agreement or to the arbitrability of any claim or counterclaim." Such language is considered clear and unmistakable enough to override the presumption that these issues are for judicial determination.[12]

c. *Who Decides the Meaning of an Arbitration Clause?*

Under existing Supreme Court jurisprudence, if there has been a determination (by either a court or an arbitrator, depending on the relevant provisions) that an arbitration clause is valid and that it applies to the dispute in question, any questions about the meaning of the arbitration clause should be determined by an arbitrator. Thus, in Howsam v. Dean Witter Reynolds, Inc., 537 U.S. 79 (2002), the Court found that the question of whether a claim was time-barred by an arbitration provider's rule should be resolved by the arbitrator, not the court. The Court explained that this kind of issue involves "procedural" rather than "substantive" arbitrability, and that parties would expect such decisions to be made by arbitrators. The Court similarly stated that arbitrators should typically be the ones

12. *See also* Oracle America, Inc. v. Myriad Group A.G., 724 F.3d 1069 (9th Cir. 2013) (AAA language and the UNCITRAL arbitration rules); Belnap, M.D. v. Iasis Healthcare, 844 F.3d 1272 (10th Cir. 2017) (JAMS rules).

to decide questions pertaining to notice, laches, estoppel, and other conditions precedent.

> **Problem 9-3.** ***Desirable Delegation?***
> Assume you are general counsel for a professional services firm, and you have decided to include an arbitration clause in your standard engagement letter with your clients. What, if anything, would you want to include in your arbitration clause's "delegation clause"? Would your answer be different if you were general counsel for a big-box retailer?

2. Discovery, Injunctive & Provisional Relief, and Dispositive Motions

As an adjudicative procedure, arbitrations involve (or at least may involve) many aspects of the litigation system to which you were introduced in a Civil Procedure course. In most contexts, judges are able to exercise control over discovery and evidentiary matters. Judges are able to grant provisional or temporary relief, pending the final resolution of a case. Judges are able to hear and rule on dispositive motions. What about arbitrators? As you might imagine, arbitrators may enjoy many of these powers—but only if such powers are consistent with the parties' arbitration agreement, or the relevant statutory frameworks within which the arbitration is taking place.

a. Discovery and Witnesses

Section 7 of the FAA grants an arbitrator the power to "summon in writing any person to attend before them or any of them as a witness and in a proper case to bring with him or them any book, record, document, or paper which may be deemed material as evidence in the case." If a person summoned fails to obey the summons, then the federal district court is empowered to compel their attendance, and the court may use its contempt power to enforce the summons.

Many arbitration associations give arbitrators the discretion to decide what evidence is necessary to determine the outcome of the case. Rule 34 of the American Arbitration Association gives arbitrators the power to "determine the admissibility, relevance, and materiality of the evidence offered and . . . may exclude evidence deemed by the arbitrator to be cumulative or irrelevant." These rules have often been interpreted to mean that less discovery is available in arbitration than might be available in court.

Although arbitrators have the power to subpoena witnesses, questions still remain about whether an arbitrator can compel non-parties to produce documents.[13]

13. See Hay Group, Inc. v. E.B.S. Acquisition Corp., 360 F.3d 404 (3d Cir. 2004).

b. Provisional and Injunctive Relief

Although arbitration is often touted as being more efficient and speedy than litigation, some dispute contexts are so time-sensitive that the parties (or the arbitrator) might see a need to issue preliminary, provisional, or interim relief. Section 8 of the Revised Uniform Arbitration Act supports this as a possibility, providing "a party to an arbitration proceeding may move the court for a provisional remedy only if the matter is urgent and the arbitrator is not able to act timely or the arbitrator cannot provide an adequate remedy." Courts have generally affirmed this authority for arbitrators. See, e.g., Saturday Evening Post Co. v. Rumbleseat Press, Inc., 816 F.2d 1191, 1194 (7th Cir. 1987) (affirming the confirmation of an arbitration award enjoining company from making or selling porcelain dolls covered by copyright). In provisions related to emergency relief, many providers also provide for streamlined appointments of the arbitrators themselves—often within 24 hours.

Permanent injunctive relief raises somewhat greater legal challenges. In many contexts, injunctions issued by arbitrators could be more difficult to enforce than injunctions issued by courts because unlike courts, arbitrators do not retain jurisdiction over cases once arbitration ends. Still, many arbitration agreements explicitly provide for the prospect of arbitrators awarding equitable relief in some form, including through the issuance of injunctions. See, e.g., American Arbitration Association Rule 47(a) ("The arbitrator may grant any remedy or relief that the arbitrator deems just and equitable and within the scope of the agreement of the parties, including, but not limited to, specific performance of a contract.").

What if the parties' arbitration agreement does *not* provide arbitrators with the authority to issue injunctive relief? In many cases, this would not create any complication. After all, the arbitrator's authority is created and limited by the parties' agreement in most contexts. However, some claims have, embedded within them, the prospect of injunctive relief. For example, certain California consumer protection laws include the prospect of injunctive relief (in order to assure that a company engaged in unfair competition or false advertising cannot continue to do so). If such "statutory remedies" are unavailable in arbitration, to what extent is arbitration a viable forum for dispute resolution?

MCGILL v. CITIBANK

2 Cal. 5th 945, 961 (2017)

. . . The question we address in this case is the validity of a provision in a predispute arbitration agreement that waives the right to seek this statutory remedy in any forum. We hold that such a provision is contrary to California public policy and is thus unenforceable under California law. We further hold that the Federal Arbitration Act . . . does not preempt this rule of California law or require enforcement of the waiver provision. . . .

In 2001, plaintiff Sharon McGill opened a credit card account with defendant Citibank, N.A. (Citibank), and purchased a "credit protector" plan (Plan). Under the Plan, Citibank agreed to defer or to credit certain amounts on McGill's credit card account when a qualifying event occurred, such as long-term disability, unemployment, divorce, military service, or hospitalization. Citibank charged a monthly premium for the Plan based on the amount of McGill's credit card balance.

McGill's original account agreement did not contain an arbitration provision . . . [but it was subsequently amended to include a binding arbitration clause covering] "any claim, dispute, or controversy between you and us." . . . "The arbitrator will not award relief for or against anyone who is not a party. If you or we require arbitration of a Claim, neither you, we, nor any other person may pursue the Claim in arbitration as a class action, private attorney general action or other representative action, nor may such Claim be pursued on your or our behalf in any litigation in any court." . . .

In 2011, McGill filed this class action based on Citibank's marketing of the Plan and the handling of a claim she made under it when she lost her job in 2008. The operative complaint alleges claims under the UCL [Unfair Competition Law], the CLRA [Consumer Legal Remedies Act], and the false advertising law, as well as the Insurance Code. For relief, it requests, among other things, an injunction prohibiting Citibank from continuing to engage in its allegedly illegal and deceptive practices.

Pursuant to the arbitration provision, Citibank petitioned to compel McGill to arbitrate her claims on an individual basis. . . .

During oral argument in the Court of Appeal, McGill asserted that the arbitration agreement is unenforceable because it purports to prohibit her from pursuing claims for public injunctive relief, not just in arbitration, but *in any forum*. . . .

The Legislature enacted the CLRA "to protect consumers against unfair and deceptive business practices and to provide efficient and economical procedures to secure such protection." . . . [T]he CLRA authorizes any consumer who has been damaged by an unlawful method, act, or practice to bring an action for various forms of relief, including "[a]n order enjoining the methods, acts, or practices." The CLRA also expressly declares that "[a]ny waiver by a consumer" of the CLRA's provisions "is contrary to public policy and shall be unenforceable and void." . . .

[Similarly,] "the primary form of relief available under the UCL to protect consumers from unfair business practices is an injunction." . . . The false advertising law makes unlawful "untrue or misleading" statements designed to "induce the public to enter into any obligation" to purchase various goods and services. Like the UCL, the false advertising law allows an action for relief to be brought by specified government officials and "by any person who has suffered injury in fact and has lost money or property as a result of a violation." It also authorizes injunctive relief. . . .

In *Broughton* and *Cruz*, this court discussed the nature of the injunctive relief available under these statutes. It distinguished between private injunctive relief—i.e., relief that primarily "resolve[s] a private dispute" between the parties and "rectif[ies] individual wrongs" and that benefits the public, if at all, only incidentally—and public injunctive relief—i.e., relief that "by and large" benefits the general public and that benefits the plaintiff, "if at all," only "incidental[ly]" and/or as "a member of the general public" For example, the court explained in *Broughton*, an injunction under the CLRA against a defendant's deceptive methods, acts, and practices "generally benefit[s]" the public "directly by the elimination of deceptive practices" and "will . . . not benefit" the plaintiff "directly," because the plaintiff has "already been injured, allegedly, by such practices and [is] aware of them." "[E]ven if a CLRA plaintiff stands to benefit from an injunction against a deceptive business practice, it appears likely that the benefit would be incidental to the general public benefit of enjoining such a practice." Likewise, the court explained in *Cruz*, an injunction under the UCL or the false advertising law against deceptive advertising practices "is clearly for the benefit of . . . the general public"; "it is designed to prevent further harm to the public at large rather than to redress or prevent injury to a plaintiff." . . .

In answering this question, we first conclude that McGill's complaint does, in fact, appear to seek the type of public injunctive relief that *Broughton* and *Cruz* identified. The UCL claim alleges in part that Citibank's "advertising and marketing" of the Plan "is unfair, deceptive, untrue and misleading" in various respects, and that Citibank "continue[s] to violate" the UCL by selling the Plan "with advertising that includes false, misleading or deceptive information, and material omissions." For relief, it asks, among other things, for an order requiring Citibank "to immediately cease such acts of unfair competition and enjoining [Citibank] from continuing to conduct business via the unlawful, fraudulent or unfair business acts and practices complained of herein and from failing to fully disclose the true nature of its misrepresentations." . . .

Having determined that public injunctive relief remains a remedy available to private plaintiffs under the UCL and the false advertising law, as well as under the CLRA, we next conclude that the arbitration provision here at issue is invalid and unenforceable under state law insofar as it purports to waive McGill's statutory right to seek such relief. Civil Code section 3513 provides: "Any one may waive the advantage of a law intended solely for his benefit. But a law established for a public reason cannot be contravened by a private agreement." Consistent with this provision, we have explained that "a party may waive a statutory provision if a statute does not prohibit doing so [citation], the statute's 'public benefit . . . is merely incidental to [its] primary purpose,' and 'waiver does not seriously compromise any public purpose that [the statute was] intended to serve.'" By definition, the public injunctive relief available under the UCL, the CLRA, and the false advertising law, as discussed in *Broughton* and *Cruz*, is primarily "for the benefit of the general public." Its "evident purpose," the court said in *Broughton*, is "to remedy a public wrong," "not to resolve a private dispute," and any benefit to the plaintiff requesting such relief "likely . . . would be incidental to the general public benefit of enjoining such a practice." Accordingly, the waiver in a predispute arbitration agreement of the right to seek public injunctive relief under these statutes would seriously compromise the public purposes the statutes were intended to serve. Thus, insofar as the arbitration provision here purports to waive McGill's right to request in any forum such public injunctive relief, it is invalid and unenforceable under California law.

[The California Supreme Court went on to reject Citibank's assertion that the preemptive reach of the Federal Arbitration Act precludes the court from reaching this conclusion.]

Our invalidation of the arbitration provision insofar as it purports to waive McGill's statutory right to seek public injunctive relief in any forum gives rise, under the terms of the parties' agreement, to the following question: Is the rest of the provision enforceable? The arbitration provision contained in the 2001 Notice stated: "If any portion of the arbitration provision is deemed invalid or unenforceable, the entire arbitration provision shall *nevertheless* remain in force." However, the arbitration provision set forth in the 2005 Notice and the 2007 account agreement states: "If any portion of the arbitration provision is deemed invalid or unenforceable, the entire arbitration provision shall *not* remain in force." Because the parties have not mentioned, let alone discussed, this language, we do not decide whether, in light of our holding, it renders the remainder of the arbitration provision unenforceable. But because our holding raises this question, we need not detail each respect in which McGill's injunctive relief request constitutes a request for public injunctive relief. We leave these issues to the Court of Appeal on remand, should the parties raise them and should the court find it necessary to decide them.

---

3. Arbitrators' Awards

In one form of arbitration, an arbitrator is bound to make a simple, binary choice between two possible options: the final proposal of one party, or the final proposal of the other party. (We saw an example of this in *Teamsters Local 726 v. City of Markham Police Dept.* case from the previous section.) In such a process, the arbitrator cannot split the difference between the two, cannot award more or less, cannot add or delete terms, and cannot revise either of the final offers. Instead, the arbitrator weighs the evidence and judges which of the final offers most closely aligns with the merits of the dispute. This form of arbitration is often called "baseball arbitration" because it is used in certain kinds of salary arbitrations in professional baseball. One of the justifications for baseball-style arbitration is that it creates an incentive for settlement. Each party wants to be more reasonable than the other (although admittedly, only barely more reasonable.) In the process of arriving at their final offers, the parties often arrive at a consensual resolution because they fear that the arbitrator might impose the (awful!) final offer from the other side. Indeed, in many years, despite the availability of baseball arbitration to resolve a large number of contract disputes, virtually none proceeded through to a final arbitral award. Final offer arbitration has also been adopted by countries such as Canada in resolving disputes between transportation companies and companies using transportation to ship goods. See Murray A. Clemens, Final Offer Arbitration: Baseball, Boxcars & Beyond, Continuing Legal Education Society of British Columbia (2011) (Can.). This form of arbitration is discussed in more detail in Chapter 12.

On the other (more common) end of the spectrum, arbitrators' powers are not constrained, and arbitrators can award whatever they deem to be consistent with the law or equities of the dispute in front of them. This broad view of arbitrators' powers is reflected in Section 21 of the Revised Uniform Arbitration Act, for example:

> (a) An arbitrator may award punitive damages or other exemplary relief if such an award is authorized by law in a civil action involving the same claim and the evidence produced at the hearing justifies the award under the legal standards otherwise applicable to the claim.
>
> (b) An arbitrator may award reasonable attorney's fees and other reasonable expenses of arbitration if such an award is authorized by law in a civil action involving the same claim or by the agreement of the parties to the arbitration proceeding.

Similarly, the rules of the American Arbitration Association (AAA) allow an arbitrator to "grant any remedy that the arbitrator deems just and equitable and within the scope of the agreement of the parties."

In between these two extremes, parties are free to craft limits on the authority of an arbitrator to award certain types of relief. As you saw in the *McGill* case above, the opportunity to craft limits on arbitrators' award powers could create conditions in which plaintiffs have no realistic opportunity for relief that would otherwise be available to them under various statutory and common law causes of action.

Problem 9-4. ***Arbitrator Powers?***

Assume you are general counsel for a software company entering into a joint venture with an engineering firm. You plan to include an arbitration clause in the joint venture agreement.

(a) Provide your CEO with an explanation of the powers you would (and would not) want an arbitration panel to have, along with your reasoning.
(b) Draft an arbitration provision including/excluding those powers.

Would your answer be different if you were drafting the consumer arbitration agreement that you plan to include in the next release of your software?

D. ARBITRATOR SELECTION AND IDENTITIES

Some visions of Justice suggest a blindfolded decision-maker, presumably signaling that she (or he, although in most artistic interpretations, Justice presents as feminine) is not swayed by factors other than those dictated by the circumstance. In most cases, the suggestion is that she applies the law. Whether this image is descriptively accurate, or even desirable, is a question beyond the scope of this book. But notice that even in simplistic images of adjudication, who the decision maker is, and how she does her job, makes a huge difference. The same is at least as true—and probably more so—with respect to arbitration, given the broad and generally unreviewable powers arbitrators have in deciding disputes.

1. Number of Arbitrators

Most commonly, in litigation in the United States, a single judge presides over the trial and a panel of judges hears the appeal. Parties have the ability to structure their arbitration clauses, and therefore the arbitration process, according to their particular interests. If the parties prefer to have multiple arbitrators hear and rule on their disputes, they can contractually arrange for that process. Multi-arbitrator panels are more common in some contexts, such as international arbitration, than in others. In most cases, the parties' agreement will specify whether the arbitration will be conducted by a single arbitrator or by a panel of arbitrators. Consider, for example, the ICC and AAA rules excerpted below.

International Chamber of Commerce Arbitration Rules (2017)

Article 12

Number of Arbitrators

1. The disputes shall be decided by a sole arbitrator or by three arbitrators.

2. Where the parties have not agreed upon the number of arbitrators, the Court shall appoint a sole arbitrator, save where it appears to the court that the dispute is such as to warrant the appointment of three arbitrators. . . .

Sole Arbitrator

3. Where the parties have agreed that the dispute shall be resolved by a sole arbitrator, they may, by agreement, nominate the sole arbitrator for confirmation. If the parties fail to nominate a sole arbitrator within 30 days from the date when the claimant's Request for Arbitration has been received by the other party . . . the sole arbitrator shall be appointed by the Court.

Three Arbitrators

4. Where the parties have agreed that the dispute shall be resolved by three arbitrators, each party shall nominate in the Request and the Answer, respectively, one arbitrator

for confirmation. If a party fails to nominate an arbitrator, the appointment shall be made by the Court.

5. Where the dispute is to be referred to three arbitrators, the third arbitrator, who will act as president of the arbitral tribunal, shall be appointed by the Court, unless the parties have agreed upon another procedure for such appointment. . . .

6. Where there are multiple claimants or multiple respondents, and where the dispute is to be referred to three arbitrators, the multiple claimants, jointly, and the multiple respondents, jointly, shall nominate an arbitrator for confirmation pursuant to Article 13.

7. Where an additional party has been joined, and where the dispute is to be referred to three arbitrators, the additional party may, jointly with the claimant(s) or with the respondent(s), nominate an arbitrator for confirmation pursuant to Article 13.

8. In the absence of a joint nomination pursuant to Articles 12(6) or 12(7) and where all parties are unable to agree to a method for the constitution of the arbitral tribunal, the Court may appoint each member of the arbitral tribunal and shall designate one of them to act as president. . . .

American Arbitration Association Commercial Arbitration Rules and Mediation Procedures

Rule 16. Number of Arbitrators

(a) If the arbitration agreement does not specify the number of arbitrators, the dispute shall be heard and determined by one arbitrator, unless the AAA, in its discretion, directs that three arbitrators be appointed. A party may request three arbitrators in the Demand or Answer, which requests the AAA will consider in exercising its discretion regarding the number of arbitrator appointed to the dispute.

(b) Any request for a change in the number of arbitrators as a result of an increase or decrease in the amount of a claim of a new or different claim must be made to the AAA and other parties to the arbitration no later than seven calendar days after receipt of the R-6 required notice of change of claim amount. If the parties are unable to agree with respect to the request for a change in the number of arbitrators, the AAA shall make that determination.

What if the parties' agreement does not specify the number of arbitrators, or there is a dispute about the interpretation of the arbitration clause on this point? Some states have provided background statutory provisions to guide the disputants. See, e.g., Oregon Revised Statute 36.472 ("The parties may agree on the number of arbitrators. If the parties do not agree, the number of arbitrators shall be one."). But in some cases, the question becomes like a matryoshka doll—the sets of wooden dolls of decreasing size, stacked one inside the other. A case in which the original question ("Who should prevail in this business dispute?") can easily turn into a procedural question ("How many arbitrators should decide who wins?"), and that, in turn, into a preliminary procedural question ("Who should decide how many arbitrators should decide this case?").

2. Selection Criteria for Arbitrators

As a part of the customization associated with arbitration, disputants often have an opportunity to choose their decision-makers to a degree far beyond that which is afforded to litigants. Litigants do, of course, try to forum-shop, and one part of their interest in doing so is to secure decision makers they believe will be favorable to their side. But random judicial panels, limitations on venue transfers, and other procedures serve to limit litigants' ability to select judges at the granular level. Even if both sides to a piece of litigation wanted Judge Blankley to preside over their case, they would have no mechanism for guaranteeing she would be assigned to hear the case. By contrast, nothing would necessarily prevent parties from entering a contract specifying Judge Blankley will serve as the arbitrator in their dispute. As long as she agreed to serve in this capacity, they could have their choice of decision maker.

What are the practical, ethical, and legal implications of being able to choose your own arbitrator? Among other things, the ability to define the pool of people from whom arbitrators will be selected creates the risk that one of the parties (for example, the party who drafted the arbitration clause—particularly in an adhesion contract context) will name criteria for arbitrator selection that are biased in favor of that party (even if they are facially neutral).

❖ Chavarria v. Ralphs Grocery Co.

733 F.3d 916 (9th Cir. 2013)

Judge Clifton.

. . . The district court found that several terms rendered Ralphs' arbitration policy substantively unconscionable. First, the court noted that Ralphs' arbitrator selection provision would always produce an arbitrator proposed by Ralphs in employee-initiated arbitration proceedings. Second, the court cited the preclusion of institutional arbitration administrators, namely AAA or JAMS, which have established rules and procedures to select a neutral arbitrator. Third, the court was troubled by the policy's requirement that the arbitrator must, at the outset of the arbitration proceedings, apportion the arbitrator's fees between Ralphs and the employee regardless of the merits of the claim. The court identified this provision as "a model of how employers can draft fee provisions to price almost any employee out of the dispute resolution process." The combination of these terms created a policy, according to the court, that "lacks any semblance of fairness and eviscerates the right to seek civil redress. . . . To condone such a policy would be a disservice to the legitimate practice of arbitration and a stain on the credibility of our justice system."

Ralphs contests the district court's conclusion and argues that the policy is not unconscionable. Indeed, Ralphs goes a step further and argues that the provisions relied upon by the district court actually disadvantage Ralphs and are intended to benefit the employee. Ralphs' strained construction of its policy is unpersuasive. In fact, the policy includes further provisions that add to its unconscionability.

Regarding the arbitrator selection provision, Ralphs does not deny that its policy precludes the selection of an arbitrator proposed by the party demanding arbitration. Nor does it deny that the party selecting the arbitrator gains an advantage in subsequent proceedings. Ralphs' opening brief affirmatively acknowledges as much: "Section 7 of the [arbitration policy] disadvantages the party seeking arbitration in the arbitrator selection process, by ensuring that the party resisting arbitration is guaranteed an arbitrator of its choosing." Ralphs simply argues that it won't always be the party that is guaranteed an arbitrator of its choosing.

In particular, Ralphs argues that the district court erred in assuming that an employee will always be the party that demands arbitration. Ralphs contends that the opposite is true. In Ralphs' view, Chavarria, the employee in this case, will wind up with an arbitrator of her choosing because it is Ralphs that demanded arbitration. Ralphs' logic is thus: (1) Chavarria brought a claim in federal court; (2) Ralphs filed a motion to compel arbitration; (3) If the court grants the motion, then the case will go to arbitration; and (4) Ralphs will have "demanded" arbitration and thereby relinquished the first strike to Chavarria. Chavarria will, under Ralphs' scenario, strike all three of the arbitrators on Ralphs' list, and the last remaining arbitrator will necessarily be from Chavarria's list.

It doesn't take a close examination of Ralphs' argument to reveal its flaws. To begin with, Ralphs' argument invites an employee to disregard the arbitration policy and to file a lawsuit in court, knowing that the claim is subject to arbitration. Even if Ralphs is willing to waste its time and money for that detour, it is not one that makes any sense for the court. We cannot endorse an interpretation that encourages the filing of an unnecessary lawsuit simply to gain some advantage in subsequent arbitration.

Perhaps more to the point, Ralphs' argument relies on a fanciful interpretation of its arbitration policy. Ralphs' motion to compel arbitration does not constitute a "demand for arbitration" as provided in the policy. Paragraph 9 of the arbitration policy provides that "[a] demand for arbitration . . . must be made in writing, comply with the requirements for *pleadings* under the [Federal Rules of Civil Procedure] and be served on the other party." (emphasis added). Ralphs' motion to compel arbitration is not a demand for arbitration under the terms of Ralphs' policy because it does not comply with the Federal Rules of Civil Procedure requirements governing pleadings. See Fed. R. Civ. P. 7(a) (providing that "[o]nly these pleadings are allowed" before listing types of pleadings); Fed. R. Civ. P. 8 (stating the general rules of pleading).

A fair construction of the agreement suggests that an employee, even after filing a frivolous claim in federal court, nonetheless must serve on Ralphs a demand for arbitration that complies with the Federal Rules. Accordingly, as the district court found, Ralphs gets to pick the pool of potential arbitrators every time an employee brings a claim.

Even if it were the case that Ralphs' policy does not guarantee that Ralphs will always be the party with the final selection, the selection process is not one designed to produce a true neutral in any individual case. As noted above, Ralphs has not argued that the selection process is fair, acknowledging that the process "disadvantages the party seeking arbitration." Ralphs simply argues that sometimes the process may work to its disadvantage. But that is no consolation to the individual employee who is disadvantaged in her one and only claim. Forcing her into an arbitration process where Ralphs has an advantage cannot be justified by the possibility that some other employee might someday get the upper hand in that employee's arbitration against Ralphs.

Ralphs also argues that there is nothing of concern in its cost allocation provision because it simply follows the "American Rule" that each party shall bear its own fees and costs. Ralphs misses the point. The troubling aspect of the cost allocation provision relates to the arbitrator fees, not attorney fees.

The policy mandates that the arbitrator apportion those costs on the parties up front, before resolving the merits of the claims. Further, Ralphs has designed a system that requires the arbitrator to apportion the costs equally between Ralphs and the employee, disregarding any potential state law that contradicts Ralphs' cost allocation. Only a decision of the United States Supreme Court that directly addresses the issue can alter Ralphs' cost allocation term. . . . There is no justification to ignore a state cost-shifting provision, except to impose upon the employee a potentially prohibitive obstacle to having her claim heard. Ralphs' policy imposes great costs on the employee and precludes the employee from recovering those costs, making many claims impracticable.

The significance of this obstacle becomes more apparent through Ralphs' representation to the district court that the fees for a qualified arbitrator under its policy would range from $7,000 to $14,000 per day. Ralphs' policy requires that an employee pay half of that amount—$3,500 to $7,000—for each day of the arbitration just to pay for her share of the arbitrator's fee. This cost likely dwarfs the amount of Chavarria's claims. . . .

The district court focused its substantive unconscionability discussion on these terms, and it was correct in doing so because the terms lie far beyond the line required to render an agreement invalid. We therefore need not discuss at length the additional terms in Ralphs' arbitration policy, such as the unilateral modification provision, which we have previously held to support a finding of substantive unconscionability.

---

3. Arbitrator Identities

Embedded in the discussion above about the parties' ability to select their own arbitrators strategically is the assumption that it matters to individual disputants who their arbitrator is. Given the large number of disputes resolved through arbitration, might it also matter to society who the pool of people are who serve as arbitrators?

Yves Dezaley & Bryant G. Garth, Dealing in Virtue: International Commercial Arbitration and the Construction of a Transnational Legal Order

34-39 (U. of Chi. Press, 1996)

GRAND OLD MEN AND TECHNOCRATS

The starting point of the generational warfare is diverging ideas of arbitral competence—the characteristics that qualify one to be an arbitrator. For the pioneers of arbitration, exemplified especially, but not only, by very senior European professors imbued with the traditional values of the European legal elites, the dominant opinion has been that arbitration should not be a profession: "Arbitration is a duty, not a career." For true independence of judgment, in the words of another senior insider, "The person who goes into this business as an arbitrator to make a living should not be encouraged." Arbitrators, they insist, should render an occasional service, provided on the basis of long experience and wisdom acquired in law, business, or public service. Those who hold this opinion are, indeed, individuals who have risen to the top of their national legal professions and gained financial independence before being asked to serve as arbitrators. . . .

To the aura or the charisma of their elders, these new arrivals oppose their specialization and technical competence. In the words of a Swiss member of the new generation, "Arbitration was characterized by a limited, small group of impeccable, outstanding professionals—characters known around the world. . . . Today I have difficulty in seeing the outstanding personality [among] a big crowd of people." Put in more aggressive terms by a member of the same cohort, an arbitrator cannot now just step in "with all . . . [the] glorious past" and provide the "great old man's opinion." Indeed, charisma is said even to be a source of error. In the words of an ICC insider, "Some of the biggest problems that we see are probably with some of the big names." Why? "They're probably just more full of themselves than other people." Furthermore, "Sometimes an eminent arbitrator feels he doesn't have to explain things." A leading figure of the younger generation thus describes his generation as "technically better equipped in procedure and substance."

They present themselves in this new generation as international arbitration professionals, and also as entrepreneurs selling their services to business practitioners, contrasting their qualities to the "amateurism" or "idealism" of their predecessors. . . .

Indeed, now that arbitration has become accepted in commercial international mores, they assert, even citing Max Weber in one instance, that the time has come for the "routinization of charisma" essential to the transition from the stage of artisans to that of mass production. This transition requires the "rationalization" of arbitration know-how.

These technocrats play key roles now in institutions like the International Chamber of Commerce, which they not only have come to direct but also have used for their education in arbitration. The quick route to arbitration expertise is through the major institutions, which hire young lawyers to administer the arbitrations. These organizations, which the pioneers used for evangelical purposes to promote arbitration, now have added a more technical involvement in the administration of the arbitrations themselves.

The large Anglo-American law firms, which dominate the international market of business law, are also central to this conflict between grand old men and technocrats. With the growth of trade and the success of the pioneers in building international arbitration, they now consider it important to include this specialty in the gamut of services that they put at the disposition of their multinational clients. The attitude of the large law firms has been to favor overtly this "banalization" and rationalization of arbitration, which permits them to introduce themselves into the closed "club" and to introduce the legal techniques that are at the basis of their preeminence. . . .

This opposition between grand old men and young technocrats—supported by Anglo-American firms—is one of the keys that permits decoding a great number of the debates and the fights—in scholarship as well as in institutions—that affect this field of practice. One controversy . . . is whether the major institutions, the ICC notably, are now too involved in the actual work of the arbitrators. A second is whether arbitration is becoming too much like litigation. The perspective of the senior generation is highly critical of both of these trends. . . .

But beyond the contest between generations about what and whose characteristics should be at the center of international commercial arbitration, this fight for power contains the true transformation that is taking place—the passage from one mode to another for the production of arbitration and the legitimation of arbitrators. As is the case for the entire field of business law, the Anglo-American model of the business enterprise and merchant competition is tending to substitute itself for the Continental model of legal artisans and corporatist control over the profession. In the same way, international commercial arbitration is moving from a small, closed group of self-regulating artisans to a more open and competitive business.

Beyond what Dezaley and Garth refer to as the distinction between "grand old men" and "technocrats," what other characteristics might you expect to have an impact on how arbitrators make their decisions, on how they might be selected, or on how their opinions might be viewed? Which of the following might matter to how an arbitrator interprets evidence, reads contracts, judges witnesses, weighs equities, crafts outcomes, or articulates reasoning: Age? Education? Gender? Race? Ethnicity? Religion? Professional experience? Political party? Unconscious or implicit biases? Height? Birth order? Astrological sign?

Social science has not provided definitive answers to all of the questions above, but far more is known now than was once known about decision science. Pat Chew, for example, found that an arbitrator's gender had no effect on decisions in sex discrimination arbitrations, even though a judge's gender had a significant effect in similar lawsuits. See Pat Chew, Comparing the Effects of Judges' Gender and Arbitrators' Gender in Sex Discrimination Cases and Why It Matters, 32 Ohio St. J. on Disp. Resol. 195 (2017). The intersection of gender, political views, and the particular dispute context may have an impact on arbitrators' decisions. Biernat and Lamin, for example, experimentally created conditions in which arbitrators were faced with workplace disputes in which a grievant (either a man or a woman) was disciplined for absenteeism and later claimed one of two reasons (either child-care or elder-care responsibilities) for their absences. They then studied which features had the greatest effect on arbitrators' decisions, and found that the

> sex of the grievant affected decisions differently for liberal and conservative arbitrators, but only when they considered grievants with child care difficulties (in elder care scenarios, grievant sex and arbitrator politics had no effect). In the child care scenarios, increased conservatism was associated with increased favoring of the male grievant and with a trend toward disfavoring the female grievant. Relatively liberal arbitrators showed bias in favor of female grievants with child care problems over male grievants, and conservative arbitrators showed nonsignificant trend in the converse directions.[14]

Simpson and Martocchio determined that the work history of the "arbitrator heterogeneity does not appear to have biased the results" in industrial and labor relation arbitrations. See Patricia A. Simpson & Joseph J. Martocchio, The Influence of Work History Factors on Arbitration Outcomes, 50 Indus. & Lab. Rel. Rev. 252, 260 (1997). However, Girvan, Deason, and Borgida found that professional arbitrators' responses to questionnaires designed to measure gender attitudes ("benevolent sexism," for example, or "protective paternalism") were strongly correlated with those arbitrators' actual arbitration decisions involving women complaining of unlawful termination. See Erik J. Girvan, Grace Deason & Eugene Borgida, The Generalizability of Gender Bias: Testing the Effects of Contextual, Explicit, and Implicit Sexism on Labor Arbitration Decisions, 39 Law and Hum. Behavior 525 (2015). And Hoyman notes that "arbitrators with more education are less likely to reinstate grievants compared to arbitrators with lower levels of education (masters or law degree)." Id. at 181.

In some contexts, discrimination on at least some of the bases explored above, would be unconstitutional. In most contexts, the Constitution only protects against discriminatory behavior that constitutes "state action." Should arbitrator selection and subsequent procedural enforcement of arbitrators' awards be treated as wholly private matters between private disputants (such that many constitutional protections would not attach) or as state actions, such that the Constitution would prohibit many forms of discrimination, absent sufficient justification? As something in between? Sarah Cole writes,

> According to Supreme Court jurisprudence, private conduct becomes state action in [two situations potentially relevant to arbitration]. First, state action exists when the government becomes excessively entangled with private behavior and encourages or causes the unconstitutional behavior. Second, state action exists when a private entity performs what is traditionally an exclusively public function. . . . [But] there is no state action in contractual arbitration. Applying current Supreme Court jurisprudence, private party use of a private dispute

14. M. Biernat & M.H. Malin, Political Ideology and Labor Arbitrators' Decision Making in Work-Family Conflict Cases, 34 Personality & Soc. Psychol. Bull. 888, 895 (2008).

> resolution system does not create state action. Nor is state action present when one arbitral party seeks to enforce an arbitration agreement or award. The FAA, which provides the mechanism by which such enforcement actions proceed, is a neutral regulatory scheme. No race-based decision making takes place when a court decides whether to enforce an arbitration agreement or award. Moreover, even if such enforcement has a disproportionate impact on protected groups, courts still cannot find state action because the Supreme Court has repeatedly held that judicial enforcement of neutral laws is not state action even when the result disadvantages protected groups. . . . Court-ordered arbitration and agency-initiated arbitration, in contrast to contractual arbitration, [however,] do involve state action.[15]

In recent years, a number of initiatives have begun to address the issue of diversity of dispute resolution professionals, notably arbitrators. Among the most visible initiatives is a program known as the Ray Corollary Initiative (RCI); see https://raycorollary.org/. Law firms, organizations, and ADR provider organizations that use rosters to obtain dispute resolution professionals can publicly pledge to "include at least 30% of diverse neutral candidates (defined as Black, Hispanic, Latino/a/x, Indigenous, Asian American Pacific Islander ('AAPI'), other people of color, women, persons of differing sexual orientations and gender identities, and persons living with disabilities)" on each roster provided to parties.

Problem 9-5. *Arbitrator Selection Criteria*

You are counsel for a union representing professional nurses in a group of hospitals. The contract has always included an arbitration clause but has never specified anything about the backgrounds of potential arbitrators. What, if any, professional or other characteristics would you want to propose that management consider in the next contract?

Problem 9-6. *Identifying a Pool of Potential Arbitrators*

Your client, a real estate developer, is considering an arbitration clause for an upcoming major project. Among other things, the draft clause specifies that any arbitrators must have at least ten years of construction experience and must have arbitrated at least ten previous cases. Before you decide whether to agree to this clause, do some online research to identify what the pool of potential arbitrators might look like. See if you can find the backgrounds of at least five potential arbitrators matching that background within 25 miles of where you are going to law school.

Based on your research, what advice might you be able to provide your client regarding the potential arbitrator pool?

15. Sarah Cole, Arbitration and State Action, 2005 BYU L. Rev. 1.

Further Reading

Roger I. Abrams. (2000). The Money Pitch: Baseball Free Agency and Salary Arbitration. Philadelphia, PA: Temple University Press.

Hiro Aragaki, Constructions of Arbitration's Informalism: Autonomy, Efficiency, and Justice, 2016 J. Disp. Resol. 141.

Jerold S. Auerbach. (1983). Justice Without Law? New York: Oxford University Press.

Lisa Bernstein, Opting Out of the Legal System: Extralegal Contractual Relations in the Diamond Industry, 21 J. Legal Stud. 115 (1992).

Gary B. Born. (2009). International Commercial Arbitration. Alphen aan den Rijn: Kluwer Law International.

Pat K. Chew, Opening the Red Door to Chinese Arbitrations: An Empirical Analysis of Cietac Cases 1990-2000, 22 Harv. Negot. L. Rev. 241 (2017).

Sarah Cole, Arbitrator Diversity: Can It Be Achieved?, 98 Wash. U. L. Rev 965 (2021).

Yves Dezaley & Bryant G. Garth. (1996). Dealing in Virtue: International Commercial Arbitration and the Construction of a Transnational Legal Order. Chicago, IL: University of Chicago Press.

Christopher R. Drahozal, Contracting Out of International Law: An Empirical Look at the New Law Merchant, 80 Notre Dame L. Rev. 523 (2005).

Julius G. Getman, Labor Arbitration and Dispute Resolution, 88 Yale L.J. 916 (1979).

Stephen Hayford, Unification of the Law of Labor Arbitration and Commercial Arbitration: An Idea Whose Time Has Come, 52 Baylor L. Rev. 781 (2000).

Morton J. Horowitz. (1977). The Transformation of American Law, 1780-1860. Cambridge, MA: Harvard University Press.

William Catron Jones, Three Centuries of Commercial Arbitration in New York, 1956 Wash. U. L.Q. 193 (1956).

Ethan Katsh & Janet Rifkin. (2001). Online Dispute Resolution: Resolving Conflicts in Cyberspace. San Francisco: Jossey-Bass Publishers.

George Khoukaz, Sharia Law and International Commercial Arbitration: The Need for an Intra-Islamic Arbitral Institution, 2017 J. Disp. Resol. 181.

Bruce H. Mann, The Formalization of Informal Law Arbitration Before the American Revolution, 59 NYU L. Rev. 443 (1984).

Soia Mentschikoff, Commercial Arbitration, 61 Colum. L. Rev. 846 (1961).

Colin Rule. (2002). Online Dispute Resolution for Business: B2B, ECommerce, Consumer, Employment Insurance, and Other Commercial Conflicts. San Francisco: Jossey-Bass Publishers.

Harry Shulman, Reason, Contract, and Law in Labor Relations, 68 Harv. L. Rev. 999, 1004-1005 (1955).

Thomas Stipanowich, Arbitration: "The New Litigation," 2010 Ill. L. Rev. 1 (2010).

Maureen A. Weston, Doping Control, Mandatory Arbitration, and Process Dangers for Accused Athletes in International Sports, 10 Pepperdine Disp. Res. L.J. 5 (2009).

Chapter 10 Arbitration: Law and Policy

"Our lives are not dependent on whether or not we have conflict. It is what we do with conflict that makes the difference."

—Thomas Crum

A. ENFORCING ARBITRATION CLAUSES

In the case of pre-dispute arbitration clauses—those drafted before a particular dispute has arisen—one of the parties to the agreement may subsequently wish to avoid having the dispute resolved through arbitration. Perhaps they see arbitration as not being to their strategic advantage. Perhaps they believe the specific dispute in question as lying beyond the scope of the arbitration clause to which they previously agreed. Perhaps they did not pay adequate attention to the pre-dispute arbitration clause and now understand its implications for the first time. Perhaps intervening developments have occurred since the time of the pre-dispute arbitration clause's drafting, such that it is arguably illegal or impractical. Whatever the reason, courts are frequently confronted with circumstances in which a party seeks to avoid arbitration.

1. Frameworks for Enforcing (or Avoiding) Arbitration

Historically, the relationship between courts and arbitration was fraught. At one point, English courts treated arbitration agreements as unenforceable on the theory that they improperly "ousted" courts of their jurisdiction.

> Commentators have advanced two primary reasons for the existence of what has come to be known as the "ouster doctrine." The first of these has suggested that judges were wary of arbitration thinking it would result in miscarriages of justice. Judges believed the process could easily lead to many different forms of abuse because it did not include procedural safeguards to prevent bias in the determination

> of rights and duties. A more cynical theory, however, pinned judicial reluctance to enforce arbitration agreements on greed, arguing that private arbitration was seen as an economic threat to English judges, whose incomes often depended on fees from disputants. In any case, Parliament responded to commercial interests by enacting in 1684 an arbitration statute that authorized judicial enforcement of agreements to arbitrate as rules of court. This made properly executed agreements irrevocable and enforceable through the courts' contempt powers. . . . The ouster doctrine remained the common law rule in the United States until the early twentieth century, when the nation's established commercial and legal communities united to bring down the doctrine through legislative means.[1]

Today, the Federal Arbitration Act (FAA), enacted in 1925, provides the basic statutory framework for understanding the relationship between the courts and parties to an arbitration contract. State laws often parallel the FAA, sometimes also filling in certain gaps. In order to understand the basic mechanisms available to disputants, it is important to understand the mechanisms in the Federal Arbitration Act.

Given the FAA's history and its basic purpose, it should be no surprise that the FAA is primarily drafted from the perspective of a party who is seeking to enforce, rather than avoid, arbitration. FAA §4 provides a mechanism by which a party can seek a court "order directing the parties to proceed to arbitration." FAA §3 provides the mechanism by which a party can apply to a court for an order "stay[ing] the trial of the action until such arbitration has been had in accordance with the terms of the agreement. . . ." These two clauses cover the two basic avoidance contingencies: a party who refuses to proceed with arbitration, and a party who files suit in court instead. Review FAA §§3-4 in detail.

Section 2 of the Federal Arbitration Act provides the only explicitly stated basis for avoiding arbitration. The precise wording is important to read with care: "A written provision . . . to settle by arbitration a controversy thereafter arising out of such contract or transaction . . . shall be valid, irrevocable, and enforceable, save upon such grounds as exist at law or in equity for the revocation of any contract." As you will see below, the last portion of this provision, "save upon such grounds as exist in law or in equity for the revocation of any contract," commonly referred to as the "savings clause," has been the subject of considerable Supreme Court litigation in recent decades.

On its face, the savings clause plainly intends that arbitration clauses will not be enforceable in circumstances in which no other contract would be enforceable. A drunk eleven-year-old cannot be bound to the terms of an employment contract she signed, a real estate purchase agreement she signed, or an arbitration clause she signed. State contract law about capacity or the age of majority makes this outcome obvious. Perhaps less obvious is the line-drawing about whether unconscionability laws, jury waiver restrictions, or class action waiver restrictions under state law are "grounds as exist . . . for the revocation of any contract."

1. Richard Reuben, Public Justice: Toward a State Action Theory of Alternative Dispute Resolution, 87 Cal. L. Rev. 577 (1997). See also Tobey v. County of Bristol, 23 F. Cas. 1313 (D. Mass 1845).

As you will see, virtually any state law falling beyond the scope of the savings clause will be deemed preempted by the FAA under the Supreme Court's current jurisprudence.

Problem 10-1. *Treatment of Arbitration in Other Countries*

You have been retained to represent Widget, Inc., a U.S. corporation that sells its products in many countries around the world. The company has instructed you to use arbitration agreements in the company's contracts whenever possible, but you want to make sure the contracts would be enforceable. Many countries' laws and public policies provide that certain kinds of claims are not subject to arbitration, even if the parties seemingly contracted for arbitration. That is, "some disputes are treated as non-arbitrable or not objectively arbitrable, relieving states from otherwise applicable obligations to recognize and enforce agreements to arbitrate such disputes." Gary B. Born, International Commercial Arbitration Vol. 1, 767 (2009). Some claims that are commonly exempted include labor and employment, antitrust, and domestic relations. Also, within the European Union, companies are not permitted to require consumers to arbitrate their claims. See Jean R. Sternlight, Is the U.S. Out on a Limb? Comparing the U.S. Approach to Mandatory Consumer and Employment Arbitration to That of the Rest of the World, 56 Miami L. Rev. 831 (2002). How would you go about researching when it would be possible to include arbitration clauses in Widget's contracts?

2. The Evolution Toward "Favoring" Arbitration

The Supreme Court's 1953 decision in Wilko v. Swan, 346 U.S. 427, excerpted below, provides an example of the courts' historical failure to embrace commercial arbitration of statutory claims. However, it is critical to note that Rodriguez de Quijas v. Shearson/American Express, Inc., 490 U.S. 477 (1989), overruled *Wilko*'s holding in 1989, as part of the Supreme Court's current embrace of arbitration. Today the Supreme Court's view seems to be that all types of disputes are potentially arbitrable, unless Congress specifies that a particular type of dispute should not be arbitrated.

WILKO v. SWAN

346 U.S. 427, 430-438 (1953)

Mr. Justice Reed delivered the opinion of the Court. Mr. Justice Frankfurter and Mr. Justice Minton, dissented.

[Plaintiff, a securities brokerage customer, brought suit in federal court under §12(2) of the Securities Act of 1933 against the partners of the brokerage firm for securities fraud. He claimed the firm made various misrepresentations and omissions about stock that he purchased. Defendant responded by seeking a stay of the litigation under §3 of the FAA, pointing out that the margin agreement required the customer to arbitrate all disputes with the brokerage. The district court denied the stay on the ground that the arbitration agreement deprived plaintiff of the advantageous court remedy afforded by the Securities Act. The court of appeals reversed.]

The question is whether an agreement to arbitrate a future controversy is a "condition, stipulation, or provision binding any person acquiring any security to waive compliance with any provision" of the Securities Act which section 14 declares "void."[2] . . .

In response to a Presidential message urging that there be added to the ancient rule of caveat emptor the further doctrine of "let the seller also beware," Congress passed the Securities Act of 1933. Designed to protect investors, the Act requires issuers, underwriters, and dealers to make full and fair disclosure of the character of securities sold in interstate and foreign commerce and to prevent fraud in their sale. To effectuate this policy, section 12(2) created a special right to recover for misrepresentation which differs substantially from the common-law action in that the seller is made to assume the burden of proving lack of scienter. The Act's special right is enforceable in any court of competent jurisdiction—federal or state—and removal from a state court is prohibited. . . .

The United States Arbitration Act[3] establishes by statute the desirability of arbitration as an alternative to the complications of litigation. The reports of both Houses on that Act stress the need for avoiding the delay and expense of litigation, and practice under its terms raises hope for its usefulness both in controversies based on statutes or on standards otherwise created. This hospitable attitude of legislatures and courts toward arbitration, however, does not solve our question as to the validity of petitioner's stipulation by the margin agreements, set out below, to submit to arbitration controversies that might arise from the transactions.

Petitioner argues that section 14 [n.2, supra] shows that the purpose of Congress was to assure that sellers could not maneuver buyers into a position that might weaken their ability to recover under the Securities Act. He contends that arbitration lacks the certainty of a suit at law under the Act to enforce his rights. He reasons that the arbitration paragraph of the margin agreement is a stipulation that waives "compliance with" the provision of the Securities Act, set out in the margin, conferring jurisdiction of suits and special powers.

Respondent asserts that arbitration is merely a form of trial to be used in lieu of a trial at law, and therefore no conflict exists between the Securities Act and the United States Arbitration Act either in their language or in the congressional purposes in their enactment. Each may function within its own scope, the former

---

2. 48 Stat. 84, 15 U.S.C. §77n (2003). Section 14 provides: "Any condition, stipulation, or provision binding any person acquiring any security to waive compliance with any provision of this subchapter or of the rules and regulations of the Commission shall be void."

3. In early decisions, the FAA is usually referred to as the United States Arbitration Act.

to protect investors and the latter to simplify recovery for actionable violations of law by issuers or dealers in securities. . . .

The words of section 14 void any "stipulation" waiving compliance with any "provision" of the Securities Act. This arrangement to arbitrate is a "stipulation," and we think the right to select the judicial forum is the kind of "provision" that cannot be waived under section 14 of the Securities Act. . . . While a buyer and seller of securities, under some circumstances, may deal at arm's length on equal terms, it is clear that the Securities Act was drafted with an eye to the disadvantages under which buyers labor. Issuers of and dealers in securities have better opportunities to investigate and appraise the prospective earnings and business plans affecting securities than buyers. It is therefore reasonable for Congress to put buyers of securities covered by that Act on a different basis from other purchasers.

When the security buyer, prior to any violation of the Securities Act, waives his right to sue in courts, he gives up more than would a participant in other business transactions. The security buyer has a wider choice of courts and venue. He thus surrenders one of the advantages the Act gives him and surrenders it at a time when he is less able to judge the weight of the handicap the Securities Act places upon his adversary.

Even though the provisions of the Securities Act, advantageous to the buyer, apply, their effectiveness in application is lessened in arbitration as compared to judicial proceedings. Determination of the quality of a commodity or the amount of money due under a contract is not the type of issue here involved. This case requires subjective findings on the purpose and knowledge of an alleged violator of the Act. They must be not only determined but applied by the arbitrators without judicial instruction on the law. As their award may be made without explanation of their reasons and without a complete record of their proceedings, the arbitrators' conception of the legal meaning of such statutory requirements as "burden of proof," "reasonable care" or "material fact," . . . cannot be examined. Power to vacate an award is limited. While it may be true, as the Court of Appeals thought, that a failure of the arbitrators to decide in accordance with the provisions of the Securities Act would "constitute grounds for vacating the award pursuant to section 10 of the Federal Arbitration Act," that failure would need to be made clearly to appear. In unrestricted submission, such as the present margin agreements envisage, the interpretations of the law by the arbitrators in contrast to manifest disregard are not subject, in the federal courts, to judicial review for error in interpretation. The United States Arbitration Act contains no provision for judicial determination of legal issues such as is found in the English law. As the protective provisions of the Securities Act require the exercise of judicial direction to fairly assure their effectiveness, it seems to us that Congress must have intended section 14 to apply to waiver of judicial trial and review.

. . . By the terms of the agreement to arbitrate, petitioner is restricted in his choice of forum prior to the existence of a controversy. While the Securities Act does not require petitioner to sue, a waiver in advance of a controversy stands upon a different footing.

Two policies, not easily reconcilable, are involved in this case. Congress has afforded participants in transactions subject to its legislative power an opportunity generally to secure prompt, economical and adequate solution of controversies through arbitration if the parties are willing to accept less certainty of legally correct adjustment. On the other hand, it has enacted the Securities Act to protect the rights of investors and has forbidden a waiver of any of those rights. Recognizing the advantages that prior agreements for arbitration may provide for the solution of commercial controversies, we decide that the intention of Congress concerning the sale of securities is better carried out by holding invalid such an agreement for arbitration of issues arising under the Act.

Reversed.

Beginning in the early 1980s, the Supreme Court's attitude toward commercial arbitration changed substantially from suspicion or even hostility to enthusiasm. In Moses H. Cone Memorial Hosp. v. Mercury Constr., 460 U.S. 1 (1983), a case involving antitrust claims, the Court considered the validity of an arbitration provision that was part of a construction contract. The party opposing arbitration argued that its opponent waived any right it would have had to arbitrate by delaying the dispute resolution process. In the course of the opinion, Justice Brennan and the majority opined:

> [Q]uestions of arbitrability must be addressed with a healthy regard for the federal policy favoring arbitration. . . . The Arbitration Act establishes that, as a matter of federal law, any doubts concerning the scope of arbitrable issues should be resolved in favor of arbitration, whether the problem at hand is the construction of the contract language itself or an allegation of waiver, delay, or a like defense to arbitrability.

460 U.S. at 24-25.

Although the Court presented a policy "favoring" commercial arbitration as if it were a longstanding judicial philosophy, in fact, the policy had never previously been enunciated. Jean Sternlight characterizes the Court's announcement of this new philosophy as the espousal of a "myth that commercial arbitration served a substantial public purpose and should be favored regardless of the parties' intentions."[4] She explains:

> Significantly, the Court did not provide an explicit rationale for why arbitration should be favored over litigation. Most of the lower court cases it cited as favoring arbitration also provided no rationale for this favoritism. . . . In the absence of any other rationale, it appears that the Court was swayed or at least influenced by a desire to conserve judicial resources.[5]

Sternlight notes at least two of the Justices, Burger and Rehnquist, were writing articles and giving talks praising arbitration for being cost-effective and reducing court delay at the time.[6]

---

4. Jean R. Sternlight, Panacea or Corporate Tool?: Debunking the Supreme Court's Preference for Binding Arbitration, 74 Wash. U. L.Q. 637 (1996).

5. Id. at 660-661.

6. Id. at 660 n.126, citing Warren E. Burger, Isn't There a Better Way?, 68 A.B.A. J. 274 (1982), and William Rehnquist, A Jurist's View of Arbitration, Arb. J., Mar. 1 (1977).

In subsequent cases, the Court has frequently referred to the federal policy of "favoring" arbitration, although it has never explicitly explained whether this policy means only that arbitration agreements are looked upon with favor, or whether it means arbitration is to be favored over litigation. For example, in Scherk v. Alberto-Culver, 417 U.S. 506, 518-519 (1974), the Court held that a securities claim, which might not be ordered to arbitration if brought domestically, would be ordered to arbitration if the contract had international implications because arbitration is favored in the international context. In Mitsubishi Motors Corp. v. Soler Chrysler-Plymouth, Inc., 473 U.S. 614, 629 (1985), the Court similarly held that even if arbitration of antitrust claims could not be compelled domestically it could be compelled in the context of international transactions, where arbitration is favored. Subsequently, building on these cases, the Court began to issue decisions rejecting one purported public policy exception to the enforcement of arbitration agreements after another. See Shearson/American Express, Inc. v. McMahon, 482 U.S. 220 (1987) (holding that a consumer could be compelled to arbitrate claims against a brokerage under both §10(b) of the Securities Exchange Act of 1934 and RICO). Ultimately, in Rodriguez de Quijas v. Shearson/American Express, Inc., 490 U.S. 477 (1989), the Court explicitly overruled *Wilko* and held that a brokerage customer could be compelled to arbitrate claims brought under the Securities Act of 1933.

a. The FAA, State Courts, Interstate Commerce, and Preemption

The Supreme Court has clearly held, now on multiple occasions, that the FAA was intended to apply in state as well as federal courts so long as the relevant transaction involves interstate commerce. The Court first faced the issue in Southland v. Keating, 465 U.S. 1 (1984), and ruled 6-3 that Section 2 applies in state court. Justice O'Connor penned a highly critical dissent, and most academics who have opined on the issue share her view that the language and legislative history of the FAA should be interpreted to limit the scope of the statute to federal court. In subsequent decisions, several sitting Justices have expressed skepticism towards the *Southland* decision.[7] Twenty state attorneys general signed an amicus brief urging the Court to reverse itself. Nonetheless, despite dissents and criticism, in Allied-Bruce Terminix Cos. v. Dobson, 513 U.S. 265, 281 (1995), and Circuit City Stores v. Adams, 532 U.S. 105, 122 (2001), the Court proclaimed again and again that Section 2 of the FAA applies to state court proceedings.

In *Terminix*, the Supreme Court found that the FAA should be interpreted to apply to the broadest possible definition of interstate commerce, specifically all "commerce in fact." 513 U.S. at 278. The effect of the Court's ruling was to severely limit the scope of an Alabama statute providing that no pre-dispute arbitration agreements could be specifically enforced. Ala. Code Section 8-1-41 (2009).

Terminix involved Alabama homeowners who had hired the local Terminix termite extermination company to spray their home for termites. When the

---

7. See David S. Schwartz, Correcting Federalism Mistakes in Statutory Interpretation: The Supreme Court and the Federal Arbitration Act, 67 Law & Contemp. Probs 5 (2004). But see Christopher R. Drahozal, In Defense of *Southland*: Reexamining the Legislative History of the Federal Arbitration Act, 78 Notre Dame L. Rev. 101 (2002).

treatment proved unsuccessful, and substantial damage resulted, the homeowners asserted that the Alabama law quoted above trumped their arbitration agreement and gave them the right to bring a claim in court rather than arbitration. However, Terminix successfully argued that the FAA preempted the Alabama statute. The arbitration clause had a "written provision in . . . a contract evidencing a transaction involving commerce" and thus was covered by Sections 1 and 2 of the FAA. Therefore, regardless of whether parties believe their transaction involves interstate commerce or want the FAA to apply, the FAA applies to any transaction Congress would have the power to regulate directly under its commerce power. In light of this decision, almost no transactions have been found so purely local that the FAA does not apply. Although one Supreme Court decision, Volt Information Sciences, Inc. v. Board of Trustees of Leland Stanford Junior University, 489 U.S. 468 (1989), seemingly allows parties to choose to be governed by state rather than federal arbitration law, so long as the two do not conflict, the case has not exempted many transactions from FAA coverage.

In light of *Southland, Terminix*, and their progeny, it is clear the FAA has a very broad application, and the Supreme Court's subsequent decision in Doctor's Assocs. v. Casarotto, 517 U.S. 681 (1996), shows the FAA preempts rather than coexists with much state arbitration law. In *Casarotto*, an 8-1 majority held the FAA preempted a Montana statute requiring arbitration clauses in franchise agreements be "typed in underlined capital letters on the first page of the contract." Id. at 683. The Justices explained "[c]ourts may not . . . invalidate arbitration agreements under state laws applicable only to arbitration provisions." Id. at 687. Some might have argued the Montana Code ought to be permitted to coexist with the FAA because it merely ensured franchisees be afforded adequate notice as to arbitration. Instead, the Court found such a requirement was inconsistent with, and preempted by, the FAA.

It is also clear states cannot require disputes be resolved administratively, rather than through arbitration. In Preston v. Ferrer, 552 U.S. 346 (2008), the Court ruled a dispute between television judge Alex Ferrer and his attorney must be resolved through arbitration, as provided in their contract, even though California law provided disputes pertaining to entertainment contracts should be resolved by the California Labor Commissioner.

In 2011, the Court overruled a California common law test for unconscionability for contracts involving class action waivers in AT&T Mobility v. Concepcion, 563 U.S. 333 (2011). Although *Concepcion* is discussed more below, the case demonstrates that the Supreme Court will preempt state law in any form (statute, regulation, or common law) conflicting with the FAA.

Problem 10-2. ***State Legislation—Bar in Consumer Cases***

You work for a state legislator who believes that pre-dispute arbitration agreements should be unenforceable in typical consumer settings. The legislator has asked you about what, if any, legislation she could introduce during the upcoming legislative session. What advice would you give her?

Problem 10-3. ***Federal Legislation—Bar in Consumer Cases***

You work for a U.S. Congressman who believes that pre-dispute arbitration agreements should be unenforceable in typical consumer settings. The Representative has asked you about what, if any, legislation he could introduce during the upcoming legislative session. What advice would you give him?

Problem 10-4. ***Arbitrator Disclosures & State Law***

Does federal law preempt state rules requiring particular disclosures by arbitrators and arbitration providers? What about the regulation of arbitrator ethics generally? (See, e.g., Cal. Code Civ. Proc. Section 1281.5.)

Problem 10-5. ***If You Want to Do Business with Our State. . .***

Assume one state legislature passed a statute prohibiting any of that state's agencies from contracting or doing business with any companies that use mandatory pre-arbitration clauses in consumer contracts. If your client were a nationwide company doing business in that state, and some of your consumer contracts contain arbitration clauses, what arguments would you make to try to avoid the effects of the state law?

3. Arbitrating Statutory Claims

One early question about arbitration's reach emerged with respect to statutory claims. In short, even though it was plain that arbitration agreements were enforceable in contractual disputes, many wondered whether an arbitration clause's reach could include statutory claims and other claims based on public policy.

❖ GILMER v. INTERSTATE/JOHNSON LANE CORP.

500 U.S. 20, 22-35 (1991)

WHITE, J., delivered the opinion of the Court.

The question presented in this case is whether a claim under the Age Discrimination in Employment Act of 1967 (ADEA) . . . can be subjected to compulsory arbitration pursuant to an arbitration agreement in a securities registration application. The Court of Appeals held that it could, and we affirm. . . .

Interstate terminated Gilmer's employment in 1987, at which time Gilmer was 62 years of age. After first filing an age discrimination charge with the Equal Employment Opportunity Commission (EEOC), Gilmer subsequently brought suit in . . . [court] alleging that Interstate had discharged him because of his age, in violation of the ADEA. In response to Gilmer's complaint, Interstate filed . . . a motion to compel arbitration of the ADEA claim. . . .

The FAA was originally enacted in 1925. . . . Its purpose was to reverse the long-standing judicial hostility to arbitration agreements that had existed at English common law and had been adopted by American courts, and to place arbitration agreements upon the same footing as other contracts . . . Its primary substantive provision states that "[a] written provision in any maritime transaction or a contract evidencing a transaction involving commerce to settle by arbitration a controversy thereafter arising out of such contract or transaction . . . shall be valid, irrevocable, and enforceable, save upon such grounds as exist at law or in equity for the revocation of any contract." 9 U.S.C. §2. . . . The FAA . . . manifest[s] a "liberal federal policy favoring arbitration agreements." Moses H. Cone Memorial Hospital v. Mercury Construction Corp., 460 U.S. 1, 24 (1983).

Although all statutory claims may not be appropriate for arbitration, "[h]aving made the bargain to arbitrate, the party should be held to it unless Congress itself has evinced an intention to preclude a waiver of judicial remedies for the statutory rights at issue." In this regard, we note that the burden is on Gilmer to show that Congress intended to preclude a waiver of a judicial forum for ADEA claims. . . . If such an intention exists, it will be discoverable in the text of the ADEA, its legislative history, or an "inherent conflict" between arbitration and the ADEA's underlying purposes. . . . Throughout such an inquiry, it should be kept in mind that "questions of arbitrability must be addressed with a healthy regard for the federal policy favoring arbitration." *Moses H. Cone.*

Gilmer concedes that nothing in the text of the ADEA or its legislative history explicitly precludes arbitration. He argues, however, that compulsory arbitration of ADEA claims pursuant to arbitration agreements would be inconsistent with the statutory framework and purposes of the ADEA. Like the Court of Appeals, we disagree.

Gilmer contends, the ADEA is designed not only to address individual grievances, but also to further important social policies. . . . We do not perceive any inherent inconsistency between those policies, however, and enforcing agreements to arbitrate age discrimination claims. It is true that arbitration focuses on specific disputes between the parties involved. The same can be said, however, of judicial resolution of claims. Both of these dispute resolution mechanisms nevertheless also can further broader social purposes. The Sherman Act, the Securities Exchange Act of 1934, RICO, and the Securities Act of 1933 all are designed to advance important public policies, but, as noted above, claims under those statutes are appropriate for arbitration. "[S]o long as the prospective litigant effectively may vindicate [his or her] statutory cause of action in the arbitral forum, the statute will continue to serve both its remedial and deterrent function." *Mitsubishi.*

We also are unpersuaded by the argument that arbitration will undermine the role of the EEOC in enforcing the ADEA. An individual ADEA claimant subject to an arbitration agreement will still be free to file a charge with the EEOC, even though the claimant is not able to institute a private judicial action. Indeed, Gilmer filed a charge with the EEOC in this case. In any event, the EEOC's role in combating age discrimination is not dependent on the filing of a charge; the agency may receive information concerning alleged violations of the ADEA "from any source," and it has independent authority to investigate age discrimination. Moreover, nothing in the ADEA indicates that Congress intended that the EEOC be involved in all employment disputes. Such disputes can be settled, for example, without any EEOC involvement. . . . Finally, the mere involvement of an administrative agency in the enforcement of a statute is not sufficient to preclude arbitration.

Gilmer also argues that compulsory arbitration is improper because it deprives claimants of the judicial forum provided for by the ADEA. Congress, however, did not explicitly preclude arbitration or other nonjudicial resolution of claims, even in its recent amendments to the ADEA. "If Congress intended the substantive protection afforded [by the ADEA] to include protection against waiver of the right to a judicial forum, that intention will be deducible from text or legislative history." *Mitsubishi.* Moreover, Gilmer's argument ignores the ADEA's flexible approach to resolution of claims. The EEOC, for example, is directed to pursue "informal methods of conciliation, conference, and persuasion," which suggests that out-of-court dispute resolution, such as arbitration, is consistent with the statutory scheme established by Congress. . . .

In arguing that arbitration is inconsistent with the ADEA, Gilmer also raises a host of challenges to the adequacy of arbitration procedures. Initially, we note that in our recent arbitration cases we have already rejected most of these arguments as insufficient to preclude arbitration of statutory claims. Such generalized attacks on arbitration "res[t] on suspicion of arbitration as a method of weakening the protections afforded in the substantive law to would-be complainants," and as such, they are "far out of step with our current strong endorsement of the federal statutes favoring this method of resolving disputes." *Rodriguez de Quijas.*

An additional reason advanced by Gilmer for refusing to enforce arbitration agreements relating to ADEA claims is his contention that there often will be unequal bargaining power between employers and employees. Mere inequality in bargaining power, however, is not a sufficient reason to hold that arbitration agreements are never enforceable in the employment context. Relationships between securities dealers and investors, for example, may involve unequal bargaining power, but we nevertheless held in *Rodriguez de Quijas* and *McMahon* that agreements to arbitrate in that context are enforceable. . . .

In addition to the arguments discussed above, Gilmer vigorously asserts that our decision in Alexander v. Gardner-Denver Co., 415 U.S. 36 (1974), and its progeny . . . preclude arbitration of employment discrimination claims. Gilmer's reliance on these cases, however, is misplaced. . . .

We conclude that Gilmer has not met his burden of showing that Congress, in enacting the ADEA, intended to preclude arbitration of claims under that Act. Accordingly, the judgment of the Court of Appeals is Affirmed.

Following *Gilmer*, most lower courts held that agreements to arbitrate statutory claims arising out of the employment context are arbitrable (provided the disputes fit within the arbitration agreement). Three exceptions exist under this rule. Two of these exceptions are based on the text of the FAA. First, in 2022, Congress amended the FAA to exclude from enforcement a pre-dispute agreement to arbitrate a case relating to a "sexual assault dispute" or a "sexual harassment dispute." 9 U.S.C. §401.

Second, the text of FAA Section 1 does not "apply to contracts of employment of seamen, railroad employees, or any other class of workers engaged in foreign or interstate commerce." Recently, the Supreme Court clarified the scope of this exception, gradually broadening it. For example, in 2019, the Court noted that this exception applies to all workers engaged in interstate commerce, no matter if the workers are classified as independent contractors or employees. New Prime Inc. v. Oliveira, 586 U.S. 105 (2019). Thereafter, the Supreme Court held in Southwest Airlines Co. v. Saxon, 596 U.S. 450 (2022), that cargo loaders are engaged in interstate commerce, even if they do not travel with the cargo across state lines. In 2024, the Court held that the Section 1 exemption applies to transportation workers, even if their employer's primary business—in this case, a bakery—is outside of the transportation industry. Bissonnette v. LePage Bakeries, Park St., LLC, 601 U.S. 246 (2024). These cases may exempt a large number of employment contracts for workers for companies such as Walmart or Amazon from the FAA's reach.

The third exception arises from apparent conflicts between the FAA and other statutes providing causes of action for violations thereof. The Supreme Court held that statutory claims are generally arbitrable, unless a "contrary congressional command" exists in the substantive statute. The Supreme Court's application of this exception, as illustrated in CompuCredit Corp. v. Greenwood, 565 U.S. 95 (2012), is quite limited. The *CompuCredit* Court suggests that the text of the statute must explicitly exclude claims arising from the statute from an arbitral resolution.

Cases such as *Gilmer, Saxon, and Bissonnette* arose in the context of an individual's employment contract, rather than a collective bargaining agreement involving a union. As you have seen previously, labor contracts commonly include arbitration clauses, and those plainly cover disputes about the alleged breach of the union contract. Do such clauses also cover disputes in which employees allege the employer has breached federal or state laws (in addition to, or instead of, breaching the terms of the contract itself)? The Supreme Court, in 14 Penn Plaza v. Pyett, 129 S. Ct. 1456 (2009), held that union members, like non-unionized employees, can be contractually required to arbitrate statutory as well as contractual claims. However, the decision did not fully address a situation where an employee might be deprived of the right either to arbitrate or litigate the claim, rather leaving such factual and legal issues for another day. 129 S. Ct. at 1474. *Pyett* gave employers the right to use collective bargaining agreements to require unionized workers to resolve all statutory discrimination claims through arbitration, so long as the worker is given the opportunity to arbitrate the claim.

4. Arbitration, Unconscionability, Public Policy, and Other Grounds for Objections Based in State Law

As a reminder, the savings clause of the FAA says that an arbitration provision must be enforced, "save upon such grounds as exist at law or in equity for the revocation of any contract." FAA Section 2. In the almost two decades since *Gilmer*, courts have wrestled with questions about whether state laws such as the doctrine of unconscionability can be used to invalidate arbitration clauses.

In some cases, courts have found arbitration clause terms were so egregious and one-sided they were unconscionable and therefore unenforceable. Recall, for example, the *Hooters* case described in Professor Aragaki's article in Chapter 9. There, the court called the arbitration provision imposed by the employer on its employees "a sham system unworthy even of the name of arbitration," noting it was "so one-sided that their only possible purpose is to undermine the neutrality of the proceeding." Hooters of Am., Inc. v. Phillips, 173 F.3d 933, 938-940 (4th Cir. 1999). Similarly, in a suit by a patient alleging medical malpractice, the court refused to enforce an arbitration agreement that limited the arbitral panel to licensed obstetricians and gynecologists. See Broemmer v. Abortion Services of Phoenix, 840 P.2d 1013 (Ariz. 1992). The financial implications of an arbitration clause may even render a clause unconscionable. See Green Tree Fin. Corp. Ala. v. Randolph, 531 U.S. 79 (2000) ("where, as here, a party seeks to invalidate an arbitration agreement on the ground that arbitration would be prohibitively expensive, that party bears the burden of showing the likelihood of incurring such costs."); but see Am. Express Co. v. Italian Colors Restaurant, 570 U.S. 288 (2013) (limiting the *Randolph* decision to costs associated with the arbitral tribunal, and excluding from consideration costs, such as expert witness expenses, to prove or defend a claim).

In many circumstances, however, state statutes and judicial opinions limiting the enforceability of arbitration clauses have been struck down as preempted by the FAA.

❖ MARMET HEALTH CARE CENTER, INC., ET AL. v. CLAYTON BROWN ET AL.

565 U.S. 530 (2012)

Per Curiam.

State and federal courts must enforce the Federal Arbitration Act (FAA) with respect to all arbitration agreements covered by that statute. Here, the Supreme Court of Appeals of West Virginia, by misreading and disregarding the precedents of this Court interpreting the FAA, did not follow controlling federal law implementing that basic principle. The state court held unenforceable all predispute arbitration agreements that apply to claims alleging personal injury or wrongful death against nursing homes. In each of the three cases, a family member of a patient who had died sued the nursing home in state court, alleging that negligence caused injuries or harm resulting in death.

The decision of the state court found the FAA's coverage to be more limited than mandated by this Court's previous cases. The decision of the State Supreme Court of Appeals must be vacated. When this Court has fulfilled its duty to interpret federal law, a state court may not contradict or fail to implement the rule so established.

This litigation involves three negligence suits against nursing homes in West Virginia. The suits were brought by Clayton Brown, Jeffrey Taylor, and Sharon Marchio. In each case, a family member of a patient requiring extensive nursing care had signed an agreement with a nursing home on behalf of the patient. The relevant parts of the agreements in Brown's case and Taylor's case were identical. The contracts included a clause requiring the parties to arbitrate all disputes, other than claims to collect late payments owed by the patient. The contracts included a provision holding the party filing the arbitration responsible for paying a filing fee in accordance with the Rules of the American Arbitration Association fee schedules. The agreement in Marchio's case also included a clause requiring arbitration but made no exceptions to the arbitration requirement and did not mention filing fees.

In each of the three cases, a family member of a patient who had died sued the nursing home in state court, alleging that negligence caused injuries or harm resulting in death. A state trial court dismissed the suits by Brown and Taylor based on the agreements to arbitrate. The Supreme Court of Appeals of West Virginia consolidated those cases with Marchio's, which was before the court on other issues.

In a decision concerning all three cases, the state court held that "as a matter of public policy under West Virginia law, an arbitration clause in a nursing home admission agreement adopted prior to an occurrence of negligence that results in a personal injury or wrongful death, shall not be enforced to compel arbitration of a dispute concerning the negligence." The state court considered whether the state public policy was pre-empted by the FAA. The state court found unpersuasive this Court's interpretation of the FAA, calling it "tendentious," and "created from whole cloth." It later concluded that "Congress did not intend for the FAA to be, in any way, applicable to personal injury or wrongful death suits that only collaterally derive from a written agreement that evidences a transaction affecting interstate commerce, particularly where the agreement involves a service that is a practical necessity for members of the public." The court thus concluded that the FAA does not pre-empt the state public policy against predispute arbitration agreements that apply to claims of personal injury or wrongful death against nursing homes.

The West Virginia court's interpretation of the FAA was both incorrect and inconsistent with clear instruction in the precedents of this Court. The FAA provides that a "written provision in . . . a contract evidencing a transaction involving commerce to settle by arbitration a controversy thereafter arising out of such contract or transaction . . . shall be valid, irrevocable, and enforceable, save upon such grounds as exist at law or in equity for the revocation of any contract." The statute's text includes no exception for personal-injury or wrongful-death claims. It "requires courts to enforce the bargain of the parties to arbitrate." Dean Witter Reynolds Inc. v. Byrd, 470 U. S. 213, 217 (1985). It "reflects an emphatic federal policy in favor of arbitral dispute resolution." KPMG LLP v. Cocchi, 565 U.S. 18, 21 (2011).

As this Court reaffirmed last Term, "[w]hen state law prohibits outright the arbitration of a particular type of claim, the analysis is straightforward: The conflicting rule is displaced by the FAA." AT&T Mobility LLC v. Concepcion. That rule resolves these cases. West Virginia's prohibition against predispute agreements to arbitrate personal-injury or wrongful-death claims against nursing homes is a categorical rule prohibiting arbitration of a particular type of claim, and that rule is contrary to the terms and coverage of the FAA.

The West Virginia court proposed an "alternativ[e]" holding that the particular arbitration clauses in Brown's case and Taylor's case were unconscionable. It is unclear, however, to what degree the state court's alternative holding was influenced by the invalid, categorical rule discussed above, the rule against predispute arbitration agreements. For example, in its discussion of the alternative holding, the state court found the arbitration clauses unconscionable in part because a predispute arbitration agreement that applies to claims of personal injury or wrongful death against nursing homes "clearly violates public policy."

On remand, the West Virginia court must consider whether, absent that general public policy, the arbitration clauses in Brown's case and Taylor's case are unenforceable under state common law principles that are not specific to arbitration and pre-empted by the FAA.

The petition for certiorari is granted. The judgment of the Supreme Court of Appeals of West Virginia is vacated, and the cases are remanded for proceedings not inconsistent with this opinion.

---

5. Arbitration and the Special Case of Class Action Waivers

Given the enormous stakes involved in class actions and other collective or mass-joinder proceedings, one can easily imagine why companies have sought to use arbitration clauses as a potential mechanism to discourage or even prohibit such claims. A number of states passed statutes seeking to prohibit class action waivers, whether embedded within arbitration clauses or otherwise. The AT&T v. Concepcion case and the Viking River Cruises v. Moriana case, below, arose in that context.

❖ AT&T MOBILITY LLC v. CONCEPCION

563 U.S. 333, (2011)

Justice SCALIA delivered the opinion of the Court.

Section 2 of the Federal Arbitration Act makes agreements to arbitrate "valid, irrevocable, and enforceable, save upon such grounds as exist at law or in equity for the revocation of any contract." 9 U.S.C. §2. We consider whether the FAA prohibits States from conditioning the enforceability of certain arbitration agreements on the availability of classwide arbitration procedures.

In February 2002, Vincent and Liza Concepcion entered into an agreement for the sale and servicing of cellular telephones with AT&T Mobility LLC (AT&T). The contract provided for arbitration of all disputes between the parties, but required that claims be brought in the parties' "individual capacity, and not as a plaintiff or class member in any purported class or representative proceeding." . . . The agreement authorized AT&T to make unilateral amendments, which it did to the arbitration provision on several occasions. The version at issue in this case reflects revisions made in December 2006, which the parties agree are controlling.

The Concepcions purchased AT&T service, which was advertised as including the provision of free phones; they were not charged for the phones, but they were charged $30.22 in sales tax based on the phones' retail value. In March 2006, the Concepcions filed a complaint against AT&T in [court]. The complaint was later consolidated with a putative class action alleging, among other things, that AT&T had engaged in false advertising and fraud by charging sales tax on phones it advertised as free.

In March 2008, AT&T moved to compel arbitration under the terms of its contract with the Concepcions. The Concepcions opposed the motion, contending that the arbitration agreement was unconscionable and unlawfully exculpatory under California law because it disallowed classwide procedures. The District Court denied AT&T's motion. . . . [R]elying on the California Supreme Court's decision in Discover Bank v. Superior Court, 36 Cal. 4th 148 (2005), the court found that the arbitration provision was unconscionable because AT&T had not shown that bilateral arbitration adequately substituted for the deterrent effects of class actions. . . .

The Ninth Circuit affirmed, also finding the provision unconscionable under California law . . . It also held that the *Discover Bank* rule was not preempted by the FAA because that rule was simply "a refinement of the unconscionability analysis applicable to contracts generally in California. . . ." [T]he Ninth Circuit rejected the contention that "'class proceedings will reduce the efficiency and expeditiousness of arbitration'" and noted that "'*Discover Bank* placed arbitration agreements with class action waivers on the exact same footing as contracts that bar class action litigation outside the context of arbitration.'" . . .

We have described [§2 of the FAA] as reflecting both a "liberal federal policy favoring arbitration," *Moses H. Cone*, and the "fundamental principle that arbitration is a matter of contract," Rent-A-Center, West, Inc. v. Jackson, 561 U.S.

63, 67 (2010). In line with these principles, courts must place arbitration agreements on an equal footing with other contracts, Buckeye Check Cashing, Inc. v. Cardegna, 546 U.S. 440, 443 (2006), and enforce them according to their terms, Volt Information Sciences, Inc. v. Board of Trustees of Leland Stanford Junior Univ., 489 U.S. 468, 478, (1989).

The final phrase of §2, however, permits arbitration agreements to be declared unenforceable "upon such grounds as exist at law or in equity for the revocation of any contract." This saving clause permits agreements to arbitrate to be invalidated by "generally applicable contract defenses, such as fraud, duress, or unconscionability," but not by defenses that apply only to arbitration or that derive their meaning from the fact that an agreement to arbitrate is at issue. . . . The question in this case is whether §2 pre-empts California's rule classifying most collective-arbitration waivers in consumer contracts as unconscionable. We refer to this rule as the *Discover Bank* rule.

In *Discover Bank*, the California Supreme Court applied . . . [this] framework to class-action waivers in arbitration agreements and held as follows:

> "[W]hen the waiver is found in a consumer contract of adhesion in a setting in which disputes between the contracting parties predictably involve small amounts of damages, and when it is alleged that the party with the superior bargaining power has carried out a scheme to deliberately cheat large numbers of consumers out of individually small sums of money, then . . . the waiver becomes in practice the exemption of the party 'from responsibility for [its] own fraud, or willful injury to the person or property of another.' Under these circumstances, such waivers are unconscionable under California law and should not be enforced."

California courts have frequently applied this rule to find arbitration agreements unconscionable. . . .

The Concepcions argue that the *Discover Bank* rule, given its origins in California's unconscionability doctrine and California's policy against exculpation, is a ground that "exist[s] at law or in equity for the revocation of any contract" under FAA §2. Moreover, they argue that even if we construe the *Discover Bank* rule as a prohibition on collective-action waivers rather than simply an application of unconscionability, the rule would still be applicable to all dispute-resolution contracts, since California prohibits waivers of class litigation as well. . . .

When state law prohibits outright the arbitration of a particular type of claim, the analysis is straightforward: The conflicting rule is displaced by the FAA. . . . But the inquiry becomes more complex when a doctrine normally thought to be generally applicable, such as duress or, as relevant here, unconscionability, is alleged to have been applied in a fashion that disfavors arbitration. . . .

Although §2's saving clause preserves generally applicable contract defenses, nothing in it suggests an intent to preserve state-law rules that stand as an obstacle to the accomplishment of the FAA's objectives. . . . As we have said, a federal statute's saving clause "cannot in reason be construed as [allowing] a common law right, the continued existence of which would be absolutely inconsistent with the provisions of the act. In other words, the act cannot be held to destroy itself."

The overarching purpose of the FAA, evident in the text of §§2, 3, and 4, is to ensure the enforcement of arbitration agreements according to their terms so as to facilitate streamlined proceedings. Requiring the availability of classwide arbitration interferes with fundamental attributes of arbitration and thus creates a scheme inconsistent with the FAA. . . . The point of affording parties discretion in designing arbitration processes is to allow for efficient, streamlined procedures tailored to the type of dispute. . . .

California's *Discover Bank* rule similarly interferes with arbitration. Although the rule does not require classwide arbitration, it allows any party to a consumer contract to demand it ex post. The rule is limited to adhesion contracts, but the times in which consumer contracts were anything other than adhesive are long past. . . .

Although we have had little occasion to examine classwide arbitration, our decision in *Stolt-Nielsen* is instructive. In that case we held that an arbitration panel exceeded its power under §10(a)(4) of the FAA by imposing class procedures based on policy judgments rather than the arbitration agreement itself or some background principle of contract law that would affect its interpretation. . . . The conclusion follows that class arbitration, to the extent it is manufactured by *Discover Bank* rather than consensual, is inconsistent with the FAA. . . .

First, the switch from bilateral to class arbitration sacrifices the principal advantage of arbitration—its informality—and makes the process slower, more costly, and more likely to generate procedural morass than final judgment. . . . Second, class arbitration requires procedural formality. The AAA's rules governing class arbitrations mimic the Federal Rules of Civil Procedure for class litigation. . . . We find it unlikely that in passing the FAA Congress meant to leave the disposition of these procedural requirements to an arbitrator. Indeed, class arbitration was not even envisioned by Congress when it passed the FAA in 1925; as the California Supreme Court admitted in *Discover Bank*, class arbitration is a "relatively recent development." And it is at the very least odd to think that an arbitrator would be entrusted with ensuring that third parties' due process rights are satisfied. . . . Third, class arbitration greatly increases risks to defendants. Informal procedures do of course have a cost: The absence of multilayered review makes it more likely that errors will go uncorrected. Defendants are willing to accept the costs of these errors in arbitration, since their impact is limited to the size of individual disputes, and presumably outweighed by savings from avoiding the courts.

States cannot require a procedure that is inconsistent with the FAA, even if it is desirable for unrelated reasons. Moreover, the claim here was most unlikely to go unresolved. As noted earlier, the arbitration agreement provides that AT&T will pay claimants a minimum of $7,500 and twice their attorney's fees if they obtain an arbitration award greater than AT&T's last settlement offer. The District Court found this scheme sufficient to provide incentive for the individual prosecution of meritorious claims that are not immediately settled, and the Ninth Circuit admitted that aggrieved customers who filed claims would be "essentially guarantee[d]" to be made whole . . . Indeed, the District Court concluded that the Concepcions were better off under their arbitration agreement with AT&T than they would have been as participants in a class action, which "could take months, if not years, and which may merely yield an opportunity to submit a claim for recovery of a small percentage of a few dollars. . . ."

Because it "stands as an obstacle to the accomplishment and execution of the full purposes and objectives of Congress," Hines v. Davidowitz, 312 U.S. 52, 67, (1941), California's *Discover Bank* rule is pre-empted by the FAA. The judgment of the Ninth Circuit is reversed, and the case is remanded for further proceedings consistent with this opinion.

VIKING RIVER CRUISES, INC. v. MORIANA

596 U.S. 639 (2022)

Alito, J., delivered the opinion of the Court.

The California Legislature enacted the Labor Code Private Attorneys General Act (PAGA) to address a perceived deficit in the enforcement of the State's Labor Code. California's Labor and Workforce Development Agency (LWDA) had the authority to bring enforcement actions to impose civil penalties on employers for violations of many of the code's provisions. But the legislature believed the LWDA did not have sufficient resources to reach the appropriate level of compliance, and budgetary constraints made it impossible to achieve an adequate level of financing. The legislature thus decided to enlist employees as private attorneys general to enforce California labor law, with the understanding that labor-law enforcement agencies were to retain primacy over private enforcement efforts.

By its terms, PAGA authorizes any "aggrieved employee" to initiate an action against a former employer "on behalf of himself or herself and other current or former employees." California precedent also interprets the statute to . . . allow a party to unite multiple claims against an opposing party in a single action. An employee who alleges he or she suffered a single violation is entitled to use that violation as a gateway to assert a potentially limitless number of other violations as predicates for liability. This mechanism radically expands the scope of PAGA actions.

Petitioner Viking River Cruises, Inc. (Viking), is a company that offers ocean and river cruises around the world. When respondent Angie Moriana was hired by Viking as a sales representative, she executed an agreement to arbitrate any dispute arising out of her employment. The agreement contained a "Class Action Waiver" providing that in any arbitral proceeding, the parties could not bring any dispute as a class, collective, or representative PAGA action. After leaving her position with Viking, Moriana filed a PAGA action against Viking in California court [for a variety of wage and hour claims. Under California law, notably Iskanian v. CLS Transp. Los Angeles, LLC, 327 P.3d 129 (Cal. 2014), PAGA claims were not subject to arbitration].

We think a conflict between PAGA's procedural structure and the FAA does exist, and that it derives from the statute's built-in mechanism of claim joinder. As we noted at the outset, that mechanism permits "aggrieved employees" to use the Labor Code violations they personally suffered as a basis to join to the action any claims that could have been raised by the State in an enforcement proceeding. Iskanian's secondary rule prohibits parties from contracting around this joinder device because it invalidates agreements to arbitrate only "individual PAGA claims for Labor Code violations that an employee suffered."

This prohibition on contractual division of PAGA actions into constituent claims unduly circumscribes the freedom of parties to determine "the issues subject to arbitration" and "the rules by which they will arbitrate," and does so in a way that violates the fundamental principle that "arbitration is a matter of consent." The most basic corollary of the principle that arbitration is a matter of consent is that "a party can be forced to arbitrate only those issues it specifically has agreed to submit to arbitration." This means that parties cannot be coerced into arbitrating a claim, issue, or dispute "absent an affirmative 'contractual basis for concluding that the party agreed to do so.'"

For that reason, state law cannot condition the enforceability of an arbitration agreement on the availability of a procedural mechanism that would permit a party to expand the scope of the arbitration by introducing claims that the parties did not jointly agree to arbitrate. Rules of claim joinder can function in precisely that way. Modern civil procedure dispenses with the formalities of the common-law approach to claim joinder in favor of almost-unqualified joinder. Wright & Miller §1581. Federal Rule of Civil Procedure 18(a), which permits a party to "join, as independent or alternative claims, as many claims as it has against an opposing party," is typical of the modern approach. But the FAA licenses contracting parties to depart from standard rules "in favor of individualized arbitration procedures of their own design," so parties to an arbitration agreement are not required to follow the same approach. And that is true even if bifurcated proceedings are an inevitable result.

A state rule imposing an expansive rule of joinder in the arbitral context would defeat the ability of parties to control which claims are subject to arbitration. Such a rule would permit parties to superadd new claims to the proceeding, regardless of whether the agreement between them committed those claims to arbitration. Requiring arbitration procedures to include a joinder rule of that kind compels parties to either go along with an arbitration in which the range of issues under consideration is determined by coercion rather than consent, or else forgo arbitration altogether. Either way, the parties are coerced into giving up a right they enjoy under the FAA.

The effect of Iskanian's rule mandating this mechanism is to coerce parties into withholding PAGA claims from arbitration. PAGA departs from the norm by granting the power to enforce a subset of California public law to every employee in the State. This combination of standing to act on behalf of a sovereign and mandatory freeform joinder allows plaintiffs to unite a massive number of claims in a single-package suit. But as we have said, "[a]rbitration is poorly suited to the higher stakes" of massive-scale disputes of this kind. The absence of "multilayered review" in arbitral proceedings "makes it more likely that errors will go uncorrected." And suits featuring a vast number of claims entail the same "risk of 'in terrorem' settlements that class actions entail." As a result, Iskanian's indivisibility rule effectively coerces parties to opt for a judicial forum rather than "forgo[ing] the procedural rigor and appellate review of the courts in order to realize the benefits of private dispute resolution." This result is incompatible with the FAA. . . .

We hold that the FAA preempts the rule of Iskanian insofar as it precludes division of PAGA actions into individual and non-individual claims through an agreement to arbitrate. This holding compels reversal in this case. The agreement between Viking and Moriana purported to waive "representative" PAGA claims. Under our holding, Viking is entitled to compel arbitration of Moriana's individual claim.

The remaining question is what the lower courts should have done with Moriana's non-individual claims. Under our holding in this case, those claims may not be dismissed simply because they are "representative." Iskanian's rule remains valid to that extent. But as we see it, PAGA provides no mechanism to enable a court to adjudicate non-individual PAGA claims once an individual claim has been committed to a separate proceeding. Under PAGA's standing requirement, a plaintiff can maintain non-individual PAGA claims in an action only by virtue of also maintaining an individual claim in that action. When an employee's own dispute is pared away from a PAGA action, the employee is no different from a member of the general public, and PAGA does not allow such persons to maintain suit. As a result, Moriana lacks statutory standing to continue to maintain her non-individual claims in court, and the correct course is to dismiss her remaining claims.

It is so ordered.

Among scholars, the initial reaction to AT&T v. Concepcion and *Viking River Cruises* was largely negative. Jean Sternlight, for example, wrote

> By permitting companies to use arbitration clauses to exempt themselves from class actions, *Concepcion* will provide companies with free rein to commit fraud, torts, discrimination, and other harmful acts without fear of being sued. In many contexts, if plaintiffs cannot join together in a class action, lack of knowledge, lack of resources, or fear of retaliation will prevent them from bringing any claims at all. As one plaintiffs' lawyer specializing in consumer claims stated, "The ruling opens the door for companies to pickpocket $10 at a time from millions of consumers."[8]

8. Jean Sternlight, Tsunami: *AT&T Mobility v. Concepcion* Impedes Access to Justice, 90 Or. L. Rev. 703 (2012). But see Ryan H. Nelson, An Employment Discrimination Class Action By Any Other Name, 91 Fordham L. Rev. 1429 (2023) (questioning whether states could enact legislation allowing claims to be brought and bypassing the FAA entirely); Christopher Drahozal, FAA Preemption After *Concepcion*, 35 Berk. J. Empl. & Lab. L. 153 (2014) (arguing that "the courts (largely) have it right").

Perhaps not surprisingly, among companies potentially facing class or representative suits from customers, arbitration clauses with class action waivers have been significantly more common. For example, Elizabeth Chika Tippett and Bridget Schaaff analyzed contracts from dozens of companies in the sharing economy (for example Uber, Lyft, AirBNB, etc.), and found that between 2012 and 2016, the percentage of contracts containing an arbitration clause more than doubled, and that almost all of them now include class waivers.[9]

6. Arbitration and Other Federal Laws

Even accepting the scope of the Federal Arbitration Act, it is clear Congress could restrict its application in certain contexts—either by amending the FAA or by creating statutory carve-outs in areas of particular concern. Although rare, examples exist under both of these occurrences. Congress passed the Ending Forced Arbitration of Sexual Assault and Sexual Harassment Act of 2021 (EFAA), prohibiting the enforcement of pre-dispute agreements to arbitrate sexual assault disputes and sexual harassment disputes. 9 U.S.C. §401 et seq. The statute also prohibits enforcement of class-action waivers in these types of cases. EFAA is a response to the #metoo movement and passed Congress with bipartisan support.

Since the passage of EFAA, courts have enforced its provisions and denied motions to compel arbitration involving or relating to claims of sexual assault or harassment. See Turner v. Tesla, 686 F. Supp. 3d 917 (N.D. Cal. 2023) (refusing to sever claims directly relating to sexual harassment and those intertwined with the harassment claims and denying motion to compel); Johnson v. Everyrealm, Inc., 657 F. Supp. 3d 535 (S.D.N.Y. 2023) (denying motion to compel an entire case involving sexual harassment when only some of the individual claims were labeled explicitly so). At least one published decision differentiated between claims involving sexual harassment and those that "do not relate in any way to the sexual harassment dispute," and ordering the latter to arbitration. Mera v. SA Hosp. Grp., LLC, 675 F. Supp. 3d 442 (S.D.N.Y. 2023). Note the limitation of the statute. The EFAA, on its face, only applies to sexual assault and sexual harassment disputes, and it does not cover claims based on other types of protected classifications.

In other instances, Congress prohibits the use of arbitration to resolve disputes under specific federal law. For example, the Dodd-Frank Wall Street Reform and Consumer Financial Protection Act of 2010 and subsequent regulations prohibited the enforcement of pre-dispute arbitration agreements in residential mortgages. 18 U.S.C. §1514A(e)(2); 12 C.F.R. §1026.36(h). Similarly, federal legislation protects members of the military from arbitration imposed by payday lenders. It is "unlawful for any creditor to extend consumer credit to a covered member or a dependent of such member with respect to which . . . the

9. Elizabeth Chika Tippett and Bridget Schaaff, How *Concepcion* and *Italian Colors* Affected Terms of Service Contracts in the Gig Economy, 70 Rutgers L. Rev. 101 (2018).

creditor requires the borrower to submit to arbitration or imposes onerous legal notice provisions in the case of a dispute." 10 U.S.C. §987(e)(3) (2000).

How does the Federal Arbitration Act sit alongside other federal statutes? Consider, for example, the National Labor Relations Act, which provides much of the law governing collectively bargained employment contacts. How ought courts to handle circumstances in which certain arbitration terms in a collectively-bargained-for contract arguably contradict some of the protections encompassed in the National Labor Relations Act? The Supreme Court addressed this question in Epic Systems v. Lewis, 584 U.S. (2018).

❖ EPIC SYSTEMS, CORP. v. LEWIS

584 U.S. 497 (2018)

GORSUCH, J., delivered the opinion of the Court.

Should employees and employers be allowed to agree that any disputes between them will be resolved through one-on-one arbitration? Or should employees always be permitted to bring their claims in class or collective actions, no matter what they agreed with their employers?

As a matter of policy these questions are surely debatable. But as a matter of law the answer is clear. In the Federal Arbitration Act, Congress has instructed federal courts to enforce arbitration agreements according to their terms—including terms providing for individualized proceedings. Nor can we agree with the employees' suggestion that the National Labor Relations Act (NLRA) offers a conflicting command. It is this Court's duty to interpret Congress's statutes as a harmonious whole rather than at war with one another. And abiding that duty here leads to an unmistakable conclusion. The NLRA secures to employees rights to organize unions and bargain collectively, but it says nothing about how judges and arbitrators must try legal disputes that leave the workplace and enter the courtroom or arbitral forum. This Court has never read a right to class actions into the NLRA—and for three quarters of a century neither did the National Labor Relations Board. Far from conflicting, the Arbitration Act and the NLRA have long enjoyed separate spheres of influence and neither permits this Court to declare the parties' agreements unlawful.

. . . Ernst & Young and one of its junior accountants, Stephen Morris, entered into an agreement providing that they would arbitrate any disputes that might arise between them. The agreement stated that the employee could choose the arbitration provider and that the arbitrator could "grant any relief that could be granted by . . . a court" in the relevant jurisdiction. The agreement also specified individualized arbitration, with claims "pertaining to different [e]mployees [to] be heard in separate proceedings."

After his employment ended, and despite having agreed to arbitrate claims against the firm, Mr. Morris sued Ernst & Young in federal court. He alleged that the firm had misclassified its junior accountants as professional employees and violated the federal Fair Labor Standards Act (FLSA) and California law by paying them salaries without overtime pay. Although the arbitration agreement provided for individualized proceedings, Mr. Morris sought to litigate the federal claim on behalf of a nationwide class under the FLSA's collective action provision, 29 U.S.C. §216(b). He sought to pursue the state law claim as a class action under Federal Rule of Civil Procedure 23.

Ernst & Young replied with a motion to compel arbitration. The district court granted the request, but the Ninth Circuit reversed this judgment. The Ninth Circuit recognized that the Arbitration Act generally requires courts to enforce arbitration agreements as written. But the court reasoned that the statute's "saving clause," see 9 U.S.C. §2, removes this obligation if an arbitration agreement violates some other federal law. And the court concluded that an agreement requiring individualized arbitration proceedings violates the NLRA by barring employees from engaging in the "concerted activit[y]," 29 U.S.C. §157, of pursuing claims as a class or collective action. . . .

Although the Arbitration Act and the NLRA have long coexisted—they date from 1925 and 1935, respectively—the suggestion they might conflict is something quite new. Until a couple of years ago, courts more or less agreed that arbitration agreements like those before us must be enforced according to their terms. . . . But recently things have shifted. In 2012, the Board—for the first time in the 77 years since the NLRA's adoption—asserted that the NLRA effectively nullifies the Arbitration Act in cases like ours. In the last two years, though, some circuits have either agreed with the Board's conclusion or thought themselves obliged to defer to it under Chevron U.S.A. Inc. v. Natural Resources Defense Council, Inc., 467 U.S. 837, 104 S. Ct. 2778, 81 L. Ed. 2d 694 (1984). More recently still, the disagreement has grown as the Executive has disavowed the Board's (most recent) position, and the Solicitor General and the Board have offered us battling briefs about the law's meaning. We granted certiorari to clear the confusion. . . .

Congress adopted the Arbitration Act in 1925 in response to a perception that courts were unduly hostile to arbitration. No doubt there was much to that perception. Before 1925, English and American common law courts routinely refused to enforce agreements to arbitrate disputes. But in Congress's judgment arbitration had more to offer than courts recognized—not least the promise of quicker, more informal, and often cheaper resolutions for everyone involved. So Congress directed courts to abandon their hostility and instead treat arbitration agreements as "valid, irrevocable, and enforceable." 9 U.S.C. §2. The Act, this Court has said, establishes "a liberal federal policy favoring arbitration agreements." Moses H. Cone Memorial Hospital v. Mercury Constr. Corp., 460 U.S. 1, 24, 103 S. Ct. 927, 74 L. Ed. 2d 765 (1983) (citing Prima Paint Corp. v. Flood & Conklin Mfg. Co., 388 U.S. 395, 87 S. Ct. 1801, 18 L. Ed. 2d 1270 (1967)). . . .

Not only did Congress require courts to respect and enforce agreements to arbitrate; it also specifically directed them to respect and enforce the parties' chosen arbitration procedures. See §3 (providing for a stay of litigation pending arbitration "in accordance with the terms of the agreement"); §4 (providing for "an order directing that . . . arbitration proceed in the manner provided for in such agreement"). Indeed, we have often observed that the Arbitration Act requires courts "rigorously" to "enforce arbitration agreements according to their terms, including terms that specify with whom the parties choose to arbitrate their disputes and the rules under which that arbitration will be conducted." American Express Co. v. Italian Colors Restaurant, 570 U.S. 228, 233, 133 S. Ct. 2304, 186 L. Ed. 2d 417 (2013).

On first blush, these emphatic directions would seem to resolve any argument under the Arbitration Act. The parties before us contracted for arbitration. They proceeded to specify the rules that would govern their arbitrations, indicating their intention to use individualized rather than class or collective action procedures. And this much the Arbitration Act seems to protect pretty absolutely. See AT&T Mobility LLC v. Concepcion, 563 U.S. 333, 131 S. Ct. 1740, 179 L. Ed. 2d 742 (2011); *Italian Colors*, supra; DIRECTV, Inc. v. Imburgia, 577 U.S., 136 S. Ct. 463, 193 L. Ed. 2d 365 (2015). You might wonder if the balance Congress struck in 1925 between arbitration and litigation should be revisited in light of more contemporary developments. You might even ask if the Act was good policy when enacted. But all the same you might find it difficult to see how to avoid the statute's application. . . .

The saving clause recognizes only defenses that apply to "any" contract. In this way the clause establishes a sort of "equal-treatment" rule for arbitration contracts. Kindred Nursing Centers L.P. v. Clark, 581 U.S., 137 S. Ct. 1421, 197 L. Ed. 2d 806, 812 (2017). The clause "permits agreements to arbitrate to be invalidated by 'generally applicable contract defenses, such as fraud, duress, or unconscionability.'" *Concepcion*, 563 U.S., at 339. At the same time, the clause offers no refuge for "defenses that apply only to arbitration or that derive their meaning from the fact that an agreement to arbitrate is at issue." Ibid. Under our precedent, this means the saving clause does not save defenses that target arbitration either by name or by more subtle methods, such as by "interfer[ing] with fundamental attributes of arbitration." Id., at 344; see *Kindred Nursing,* 137 S. Ct. 1421, 197 L. Ed. 2d 806, 814.

This is where the employees' argument stumbles. They don't suggest that their arbitration agreements were extracted, say, by an act of fraud or duress or in some other unconscionable way that would render any contract unenforceable. Instead, they object to their agreements precisely because they require individualized arbitration proceedings instead of class or collective ones. And by attacking (only) the individualized nature of the arbitration proceedings, the employees' argument seeks to interfere with one of arbitration's fundamental attributes.

We know this much because of *Concepcion*. . . . The employees' efforts to distinguish *Concepcion* fall short. They note that their putative NLRA defense would render an agreement "illegal" as a matter of federal statutory law rather than "unconscionable" as a matter of state common law. But we don't see how that distinction makes any difference in light of *Concepion*'s rationale and rule. Illegality, like unconscionability, may be a traditional, generally applicable contract defense in many cases, including arbitration cases. But an argument that a contract is unenforceable just because it requires bilateral arbitration is a different creature. A defense of that kind, *Concepcion* tells us, is one that impermissibly disfavors arbitration whether it sounds in illegality or unconscionability. The law of precedent teaches that like cases should generally be treated alike, and appropriate respect for that principle means the Arbitration Act's saving clause can no more save the defense at issue in these cases than it did the defense at issue in *Concepcion*. At the end of our encounter with the Arbitration Act, then, it appears just as it did at the beginning: a congressional command requiring us to enforce, not override, the terms of the arbitration agreements before us. . . .

When confronted with two Acts of Congress allegedly touching on the same topic, this Court is not at "liberty to pick and choose among congressional enactments" and must instead strive " 'to give effect to both.' " Morton v. Mancari, 417 U.S. 535, 551, 94 S. Ct. 2474, 41 L. Ed. 2d 290 (1974). A party seeking to suggest that two statutes cannot be harmonized, and that one displaces the other, bears the heavy burden of showing " 'a clearly expressed congressional intention' " that such a result should follow. The intention must be " 'clear and manifest.' " *Morton*, supra, at 551. And in approaching a claimed conflict, we come armed with the "stron[g] presum[ption]" that repeals by implication are "disfavored" and that "Congress will specifically address" preexisting law when it wishes to suspend its normal operations in a later statute. United States v. Fausto, 484 U.S. 439, 452, 453, 108 S. Ct. 668, 98 L. Ed. 2d 830 (1988).

These rules exist for good reasons. Respect for Congress as drafter counsels against too easily finding irreconcilable conflicts in its work. More than that, respect for the separation of powers counsels restraint. Allowing judges to pick and choose between statutes risks transforming them from expounders of what the law is into policymakers choosing what the law should be. Our rules aiming for harmony over conflict in statutory interpretation grow from an appreciation that it's the job of Congress by legislation, not this Court by supposition, both to write the laws and to repeal them.

Seeking to demonstrate an irreconcilable statutory conflict even in light of these demanding standards, the employees point to Section 7 of the NLRA. That provision guarantees workers "the right to self-organization, to form, join, or assist labor organizations, to bargain collectively through representatives of their own choosing, and to engage in other concerted activities for the purpose of collective bargaining or other mutual aid or protection." 29 U.S.C. §157. From this language, the employees ask us to infer a clear and manifest congressional command to displace the Arbitration Act and outlaw agreements like theirs. But that much inference is more than this Court may make. . . .

The dissent sees things a little bit differently. In its view, today's decision ushers us back to the *Lochner* era when this Court regularly overrode legislative policy judgments. The dissent even suggests we have resurrected the long-dead "yellow dog" contract. But like most apocalyptic warnings, this one proves a false alarm.

Our decision does nothing to override Congress's policy judgments. As the dissent recognizes, the legislative policy embodied in the NLRA is aimed at "safeguard[ing], first and foremost, workers' rights to join unions and to engage in collective bargaining." Those rights stand every bit as strong today as they did yesterday. And rather than revive "yellow dog" contracts against union organizing that the NLRA outlawed back in 1935, today's decision merely declines to read into the NLRA a novel right to class action procedures that the Board's own general counsel disclaimed as recently as 2010.

Instead of overriding Congress's policy judgments, today's decision seeks to honor them. This much the dissent surely knows. Shortly after invoking the specter of *Lochner*, it turns around and criticizes the Court for trying too hard to abide the Arbitration Act's " 'liberal federal policy favoring arbitration agreements,' " Howsam v. Dean Witter Reynolds, Inc., 537 U.S. 79, 83, 123 S. Ct. 588, 154 L. Ed. 2d 491 (2002), saying we " 'ski' " too far down the " 'slippery slope' " of this Court's arbitration precedent. But the dissent's real complaint lies with the mountain of precedent itself. The dissent spends page after page relitigating our Arbitration Act precedents, rehashing arguments this Court has heard and rejected many times in many cases that no party has asked us to revisit. . . .

The respective merits of class actions and private arbitration as means of enforcing the law are questions constitutionally entrusted not to the courts to decide but to the policymakers in the political branches where those questions remain hotly contested. Just recently, for example, one federal agency banned individualized arbitration agreements it blamed for underenforcement of certain laws, only to see Congress respond by immediately repealing that rule. This Court is not free to substitute its preferred economic policies for those chosen by the people's representatives. That, we had always understood, was *Lochner's* sin.

The policy may be debatable but the law is clear: Congress has instructed that arbitration agreements like those before us must be enforced as written. While Congress is of course always free to amend this judgment, we see nothing suggesting it did so in the NLRA—much less that it manifested a clear intention to displace the Arbitration Act. Because we can easily read Congress's statutes to work in harmony, that is where our duty lies. The judgments in Epic, No. 16-285, and *Ernst & Young*, No. 16-300, are reversed, and the cases are remanded for further proceedings consistent with this opinion. The judgment in *Murphy Oil*, No. 16-307, is affirmed.

Justice Ginsburg, with whom Justice Breyer, Justice Sotomayor, and Justice Kagan join, dissenting.

The employees in these cases complain that their employers have underpaid them in violation of the wage and hours prescriptions of the Fair Labor Standards Act of 1938 (FLSA), and analogous state laws. Individually, their claims are small, scarcely of a size warranting the expense of seeking redress alone. But by joining together with others similarly circumstanced, employees can gain effective redress for wage underpayment commonly experienced. To block such concerted action, their employers required them to sign, as a condition of employment, arbitration agreements banning collective judicial and arbitral proceedings of any kind. The question presented: Does the Federal Arbitration Act (Arbitration Act or FAA), permit employers to insist that their employees, whenever seeking redress for commonly experienced wage loss, go it alone, never mind the right secured to employees by the National Labor Relations Act (NLRA) "to engage in . . . concerted activities" for their "mutual aid or protection"? The answer should be a resounding "No."

In the NLRA and its forerunner, the Norris-LaGuardia Act (NLGA), Congress acted on an acute awareness: For workers striving to gain from their employers decent terms and conditions of employment, there is strength in numbers. A single employee, Congress understood, is disarmed in dealing with an employer. The Court today subordinates employee-protective labor legislation to the Arbitration Act. In so doing, the Court forgets the labor market imbalance that gave rise to the NLGA and the NLRA, and ignores the destructive consequences of diminishing the right of employees "to band together in confronting an employer." Congressional correction of the Court's elevation of the FAA over workers' rights to act in concert is urgently in order.

To explain why the Court's decision is egregiously wrong, I first refer to the extreme imbalance once prevalent in our Nation's workplaces, and Congress' aim in the NLGA and the NLRA to place employers and employees on a more equal footing. I then explain why the Arbitration Act, sensibly read, does not shrink the NLRA's protective sphere. . . .

The end of the 19th century and beginning of the 20th was a tumultuous era in the history of our Nation's labor relations. Under economic conditions then prevailing, workers often had to accept employment on whatever terms employers dictated. Aiming to secure better pay, shorter workdays, and safer workplaces, workers increasingly sought to band together to make their demands effective.

Employers, in turn, engaged in a variety of tactics to hinder workers' efforts to act in concert for their mutual benefit. Notable among such devices was the "yellow-dog contract." Such agreements, which employers required employees to sign as a condition of employment, typically commanded employees to abstain from joining labor unions. Many of the employer-designed agreements cast an even wider net, "proscrib[ing] all manner of concerted activities." As a prominent United States Senator observed, contracts of the yellow-dog genre rendered the "laboring man . . . absolutely helpless" by "waiv[ing] his right . . . to free association" and by requiring that he "singly present any grievance he has." 75 Cong. Rec. 4504 (remarks of Sen. Norris).

Early legislative efforts to protect workers' rights to band together were unavailing. . . .

In the 1930's, legislative efforts to safeguard vulnerable workers found more receptive audiences. As the Great Depression shifted political winds further in favor of worker-protective laws, Congress passed two statutes aimed at protecting employees' associational rights. First, in 1932, Congress passed the NLGA, which regulates the employer-employee relationship indirectly. . . . [I]n 1935, . . .

it enacted the NLRA. Relevant here, §7 of the NLRA guarantees employees "the right to self-organization, to form, join, or assist labor organizations, to bargain collectively through representatives of their own choosing, and to engage in other concerted activities for the purpose of collective bargaining or other mutual aid or protection." 29 U.S.C. §157 (emphasis added).

Despite the NLRA's prohibitions, the employers in the cases now before the Court required their employees to sign contracts stipulating to submission of wage and hours claims to binding arbitration, and to do so only one-by-one. . . .

In resisting enforcement of the group-action foreclosures, the employees involved in this litigation do not urge that they must have access to a judicial forum. They argue only that the NLRA prohibits their employers from denying them the right to pursue work-related claims in concert in any forum. If they may be stopped by employer-dictated terms from pursuing collective procedures in court, they maintain, they must at least have access to similar procedures in an arbitral forum.

Because I would hold that employees' §7 rights include the right to pursue collective litigation regarding their wages and hours, I would further hold that the employer-dictated collective-litigation stoppers, i.e., "waivers," are unlawful. As earlier recounted, §8(a)(1) makes it an "unfair labor practice" for an employer to "interfere with, restrain, or coerce" employees in the exercise of their §7 rights. 29 U.S.C. §158(a)(1). Beyond genuine dispute, an employer "interfere[s] with" and "restrain[s]" employees in the exercise of their §7 rights by mandating that they prospectively renounce those rights in individual employment agreements. The law could hardly be otherwise: Employees' rights to band together to meet their employers' superior strength would be worth precious little if employers could condition employment on workers signing away those rights. Properly assessed, then, the "waivers" rank as unfair labor practices outlawed by the NLRA, and therefore unenforceable in court.

Today's decision rests largely on the Court's finding in the Arbitration Act "emphatic directions" to enforce arbitration agreements according to their terms, including collective-litigation prohibitions. Nothing in the FAA or this Court's case law, however, requires subordination of the NLRA's protections. . . .

Even assuming that the FAA and the NLRA were inharmonious, the NLRA should control. Enacted later in time, the NLRA should qualify as "an implied repeal" of the FAA, to the extent of any genuine conflict. Moreover, the NLRA should prevail as the more pinpointed, subject-matter specific legislation, given that it speaks directly to group action by employees to improve the terms and conditions of their employment. . . .

The inevitable result of today's decision will be the underenforcement of federal and state statutes designed to advance the well-being of vulnerable workers. . . . The probable impact on wage and hours claims of the kind asserted in the cases now before the Court is all too evident. Violations of minimum-wage and overtime laws are widespread. . . . Because of their limited resources, however, government agencies must rely on private parties to take a lead role in enforcing wage and hours laws. . . . If employers can stave off collective employment litigation aimed at obtaining redress for wage and hours infractions, the enforcement gap is almost certain to widen. Expenses entailed in mounting individual claims will often far outweigh potential recoveries. . . . Fear of retaliation may also deter potential claimants from seeking redress alone. . . . The upshot: Employers, aware that employees will be disinclined to pursue small-value claims when confined to proceeding one-by-one, will no doubt perceive that the cost-benefit balance of underpaying workers tips heavily in favor of skirting legal obligations.

If these untoward consequences stemmed from legislative choices, I would be obliged to accede to them. But the edict that employees with wage and hours claims may seek relief only one-by-one does not come from Congress. It is the result of take-it-or-leave-it labor contracts harking back to the type called "yellow dog," and of the readiness of this Court to enforce those unbargained-for agreements. The FAA demands no such suppression of the right of workers to take concerted action for their "mutual aid or protection." Accordingly, I would reverse the judgment of the Fifth Circuit in No. 16-307 and affirm the judgments of the Seventh and Ninth Circuits in Nos. 16-285 and 16-300.

Problem 10-6. *Multiple Claims . . . How Many Lawsuits or Arbitrations?*

You represent a transgender employee who is also an immigrant from Mexico. The employee has been subject to rude comments at work, and they receive the most undesirable shifts and work assignments compared to other employees. After extensive interviews with your client, you have concluded that the facts support claims against the company for both sexual and racial harassment. The employer and employee have a broad arbitration clause requiring that "all claims arising out of or relating to this employment, including statutory claims of harassment, are subject to arbitration." Given the provisions of the EFAA, what are your chances of litigating the sexual harassment claim? What about the racial harassment claim?

7. Preemption and Sovereign Immunity

Much of this section's content has focused on the relationship between the FAA and state or federal law. The over-simplified conclusion regarding such clashes is that the FAA almost always wins those preemption battles. However, what if one of the parties enjoys sovereign immunity?

❖ C & L ENTERPRISES, INC. v. CITIZEN BAND POTAWATOMI INDIAN TRIBE OF OKLAHOMA

532 U.S. 411 (2001)

Justice GINSBURG delivered the opinion of the Court.

In Kiowa Tribe of Okla. v. Manufacturing Technologies, Inc., 523 U.S. 751 (1998), this Court held that an Indian tribe is not subject to suit in a state court—even for breach of contract involving off-reservation commercial conduct—unless "Congress has authorized the suit or the tribe has waived its immunity." This case concerns the impact of an arbitration agreement on a tribe's plea of suit immunity. The document on which the case centers is a standard form construction contract signed by the parties to govern the installation of a foam roof on a building, the First Oklahoma Bank, in Shawnee, Oklahoma. The building and land are owned by an Indian Tribe, the Citizen Potawatomi Nation (Tribe). The building is commercial, and the land is off-reservation, nontrust property. The form contract, which was proposed by the Tribe and accepted by the contractor, C & L Enterprises, Inc. (C & L), contains an arbitration clause.

The question presented is whether the Tribe waived its immunity from suit in state court when it expressly agreed to arbitrate disputes with C & L relating to the contract, to the governance of Oklahoma law, and to the enforcement of arbitral awards "in any court having jurisdiction thereof." We hold that, by the clear import of the arbitration clause, the Tribe is amenable to a state-court suit to enforce an arbitral award in favor of contractor C & L.

Respondent Citizen Potawatomi Nation is a federally recognized Indian Tribe. In 1993, it entered into a contract with petitioner C & L for the installation of a roof on a Shawnee, Oklahoma, building owned by the Tribe. The building, which housed the First Oklahoma Bank, is not on the Tribe's reservation or on land held by the Federal Government in trust for the Tribe.

The contract at issue is a standard form agreement copyrighted by the American Institute of Architects. The Tribe proposed the contract; details not set out in the form were inserted by the Tribe and its architect. Two provisions of the contract are key to this case. First, the contract contains an arbitration clause:

"All claims or disputes between the Contractor [C & L] and the Owner [the Tribe] arising out of or relating to the Contract, or the breach thereof, shall be decided by arbitration in accordance with the Construction [I]ndustry Arbitration Rules of the American Arbitration Association currently in effect unless the parties mutually agree otherwise. . . . The award rendered by the arbitrator or arbitrators shall be final, and judgment may be entered upon it in accordance with applicable law in any court having jurisdiction thereof." The American Arbitration Association Rules to which the clause refers provide: "Parties to these rules shall be deemed to have consented that judgment upon the arbitration award may be entered in any federal or state court having jurisdiction thereof."

Second, the contract includes a choice-of-law clause that reads: "The contract shall be governed by the law of the place where the Project is located." Oklahoma has adopted a Uniform Arbitration Act, which instructs that "[t]he making of an agreement . . . providing for arbitration in this state confers jurisdiction on the court to enforce the agreement under this act and to enter judgment on an award thereunder." The Act defines "court" as "any court of competent jurisdiction of this state."

After execution of the contract but before C & L commenced performance, the Tribe decided to change the roofing material from foam (the material specified in the contract) to rubber guard. The Tribe solicited new bids and retained another company to install the roof. C & L, claiming that the Tribe had dishonored the contract, submitted an arbitration demand. The Tribe asserted sovereign immunity and declined to participate in the arbitration proceeding. It notified the arbitrator, however, that it had several substantive defenses to C & L's claim. On consideration of C & L's evidence, the arbitrator rendered an award in favor of C & L for $25,400 in damages (close to 30% of the contract price), plus attorney's fees and costs.

Several weeks later, C & L filed suit to enforce the arbitration award in the District Court of Oklahoma County, a state court of general, first instance, jurisdiction. The Tribe appeared specially for the limited purpose of moving to dismiss the action on the ground that the Tribe was immune from suit. The District Court denied the motion and entered a judgment confirming the award.

The Oklahoma Court of Civil Appeals affirmed, holding that the Tribe lacked immunity because the contract giving rise to the suit was "between an Indian tribe and a non-Indian" and was "executed outside of Indian Country." The Oklahoma Supreme Court denied review, and the Tribe petitioned for certiorari in this Court.

While the Tribe's petition was pending here, the Court decided *Kiowa*, holding: "Tribes enjoy immunity from suits on contracts, whether those contracts involve governmental or commercial activities and whether they were made on or off a reservation." *Kiowa* reconfirmed: "[A]n Indian tribe is subject to suit only where Congress has authorized the suit or the tribe has waived its immunity." Thereafter, we granted the Tribe's petition in this case, vacated the judgment of the Court of Civil Appeals, and remanded for reconsideration in light of *Kiowa*.

On remand, the Court of Civil Appeals changed course. It held that, under *Kiowa*, the Tribe here was immune from suit on its contract with C & L, despite the contract's off-reservation subject matter. The court then addressed whether the Tribe had waived its immunity. "The agreement of [the] Tribe to arbitration, and the contract language regarding enforcement in courts having jurisdiction," the court observed, "seem to indicate a willingness on [the] Tribe's part to expose itself to suit on the contract." But, the court quickly added, "the leap from that willingness to a waiver of immunity is one based on implication, not an unequivocal expression." Concluding that the Tribe had not waived its suit immunity with the requisite clarity, the appeals court instructed the trial court to dismiss the case. The Oklahoma Supreme Court denied C & L's petition for review. . . .

Kiowa, in which we reaffirmed the doctrine of tribal immunity, involved an off-reservation, commercial agreement (a stock purchase) by a federally recognized Tribe. The Tribe signed a promissory note agreeing to pay the seller

$285,000 plus interest. The note recited: "Nothing in this Note subjects or limits the sovereign rights of the Kiowa Tribe of Oklahoma." The Tribe defaulted, the seller sued on the note in state court, and the Tribe asserted sovereign immunity. We upheld the plea. Tribal immunity, we ruled in *Kiowa*, extends to suits on off-reservation commercial contracts. The Kiowa Tribe was immune from suit for defaulting on the promissory note, we held, because "Congress ha[d] not abrogated [the Tribe's] immunity, nor ha[d] petitioner waived it."

Like *Kiowa*, this case arises out of the breach of a commercial, off-reservation contract by a federally recognized Indian Tribe. The petitioning contractor, C & L, does not contend that Congress has abrogated tribal immunity in this setting. The question presented is whether the Tribe has waived its immunity.

To abrogate tribal immunity, Congress must "unequivocally" express that purpose. Santa Clara Pueblo v. Martinez, 436 U.S. 49, 58 (1978) (citing United States v. Testen, 424 U.S. 392, 399 (1976)). Similarly, to relinquish its immunity, a tribe's waiver must be "clear." Oklahoma Tax Comm'n v. Citizen Band Potawatomi Tribe of Okla., 498 U.S. 505, 509 (1991). We are satisfied that the Tribe in this case has waived, with the requisite clarity, immunity from the suit C & L brought to enforce its arbitration award.

The construction contract's provision for arbitration and related prescriptions lead us to this conclusion. The arbitration clause requires resolution of all contract-related disputes between C & L and the Tribe by binding arbitration; ensuing arbitral awards may be reduced to judgment "in accordance with applicable law in any court having jurisdiction thereof." For governance of arbitral proceedings, the arbitration clause specifies American Arbitration Association Rules for the construction industry, and under those Rules, "the arbitration award may be entered in any federal or state court having jurisdiction thereof."

The contract's choice-of-law clause makes it plain enough that a "court having jurisdiction" to enforce the award in question is the Oklahoma state court in which C & L filed suit. By selecting Oklahoma law ("the law of the place where the Project is located") to govern the contract, the parties have effectively consented to confirmation of the award "in accordance with" the Oklahoma Uniform Arbitration Act, ("judgment may be entered upon [the arbitration award] in accordance with applicable law").

The Uniform Act in force in Oklahoma prescribes that, when "an agreement . . . provid[es] for arbitration in this state," i.e., in Oklahoma, jurisdiction to enforce the agreement vests in "any court of competent jurisdiction of this state." On any sensible reading of the Act, the District Court of Oklahoma County, a local court of general jurisdiction, fits that statutory description.

In sum, the Tribe agreed, by express contract, to adhere to certain dispute resolution procedures. In fact, the Tribe itself tendered the contract calling for those procedures. The regime to which the Tribe subscribed includes entry of judgment upon an arbitration award in accordance with the Oklahoma Uniform Arbitration Act. That Act concerns arbitration in Oklahoma and correspondingly designates as enforcement forums "court[s] of competent jurisdiction of [Oklahoma]." C & L selected for its enforcement suit just such a forum. In a case involving an arbitration clause essentially indistinguishable from the one to which the Tribe and C & L agreed, the Seventh Circuit stated:

> There is nothing ambiguous about th[e] language [of the arbitration clause]. The tribe agrees to submit disputes arising under the contract to arbitration, to be bound by the arbitration award, and to have its submission and the award enforced in a court of law.

"The [tribal immunity] waiver . . . is implicit rather than explicit only if a waiver of sovereign immunity, to be deemed explicit, must use the words 'sovereign immunity.' No case has ever held that." *Sokaogon*, 86 F.3d, at 659-660. That cogent observation holds as well for the case we confront.

The Tribe strenuously urges, however, that an arbitration clause simply "is not a waiver of immunity from suit." The phrase in the clause providing for enforcement of arbitration awards "in any court having jurisdiction thereof," the Tribe maintains, "begs the question of what court has jurisdiction." As counsel for the Tribe clarified at oral argument, the Tribe's answer is "no court," on earth or even on the moon. No court—federal, state, or even tribal—has jurisdiction over C & L's suit, the Tribe insists, because it has not expressly waived its sovereign immunity in any judicial forum; cf. *Sokaogon*, 86 F.3d, at 660 (facing a similar argument, Seventh Circuit gleaned that counsel meant only a statement to this effect will do: "The tribe will not assert the defense of sovereign immunity if sued for breach of contract.").

Instead of waiving suit immunity in any court, the Tribe argues, the arbitration clause waives simply and only the parties' rights to a court trial of contractual disputes; under the clause, the Tribe recognizes, the parties must instead arbitrate. The clause no doubt memorializes the Tribe's commitment to adhere to the contract's dispute resolution regime. That regime has a real world objective; it is not designed for regulation of a game lacking practical consequences. And to the real world end, the contract specifically authorizes judicial enforcement of the resolution arrived at through arbitration.

The Tribe also asserts that a form contract, designed principally for private parties who have no immunity to waive, cannot establish a clear waiver of tribal suit immunity. In appropriate cases, we apply "the common-law rule of contract interpretation that a court should construe ambiguous language against the interest of the party that drafted it." Mastrobuono v. Shearson Lehman Hutton, Inc., 514 U.S. 52, 62 (1995) (construing form contract containing arbitration clause). That rule, however, is inapposite here. The contract, as we have explained, is not ambiguous. Nor did the Tribe find itself holding the short end of an adhesion contract stick: The Tribe proposed and prepared the contract; C & L foisted no form on a quiescent Tribe.

For the reasons stated, we conclude that under the agreement the Tribe proposed and signed, the Tribe clearly consented to arbitration and to the enforcement of arbitral awards in Oklahoma state court; the Tribe thereby waived its sovereign immunity from C & L's suit. The judgment of the Oklahoma Court of Civil Appeals is therefore reversed, and the case is remanded for further proceedings not inconsistent with this opinion.

B. ARBITRATION POLICY

1. Mandatory Pre-Dispute Arbitration Clauses

In the United States, the key policy issue that has arisen with respect to binding arbitration is whether, and if so, how and when, companies should be permitted to use form contracts to require consumers and employees to resolve future disputes with the company through binding arbitration, rather than through litigation. Both critics and defenders of mandatory arbitration agree that the practice has become increasingly common in the United States. Using small-print contracts, envelope stuffers, and computer click-through agreements, companies now often require customers and employees to agree in advance to arbitrate future disputes.

Indeed, you should empirically investigate the prevalence of mandatory arbitration by checking the extent to which providers of goods and services in your own life (e.g., credit cards, phones, apps, computers, leases, and contracts with doctors, gyms, nursing homes) require you to resolve future disputes through arbitration rather than litigation. One study conducted in Los Angeles with respect to a hypothetical "average Joe" showed that one-third of the consumer transactions in his life were covered by arbitration clauses. See Linda J. Demaine & Deborah R. Hensler, "Volunteering" to Arbitrate Through Predispute Arbitration Clauses: The Average Consumer's Experience, 67 Law & Contemp. Probs. 55 (2004). Indeed, some major law firms are now seeking to require their associates and other employees to agree to arbitrate rather than litigate any disputes they may have with the firm, although this practice appears to be waning. See Davis v. O'Melveny & Myers, 485 F.3d 1066 (9th Cir. 2007) (holding a particular clause unconscionable and thus unenforceable).

Critics of "mandatory" or "cram-down" arbitration assert that such clauses are unfair to individuals and bad as a matter of public policy. In brief, the critics argue that companies are using arbitration not merely to change the procedural venue of claims, but also, for example by proscribing class actions, to prevent consumers or employee from bringing claims at all. The critics argue that arbitration clauses are often drafted in an overreaching manner that is stacked against the "little guy" consumers and employees. Critics point to particular clauses that have required consumers to appear in front of biased arbitrators; forced them to pay high fees or travel to distant locations; deprived them of such remedies as attorney's fees and compensatory or punitive damages; shortened their statute of limitations; or eliminated their right to bring class claims. From the public perspective, critics complain that private arbitration will prevent the public-at-large from learning about defective products or widespread discrimination, and that the lack of public precedent will impede the development of law.

Defenders of the practice typically reject the "mandatory" label for the label "pre-dispute," urging that consumers and employees accept arbitration voluntarily, even if it is contained in form contracts. Such defenders point out that most contracts in our complex economy are form contracts, and that form contracts are routinely enforced by courts. Pointing to the high cost and slow speed of our litigation system, the defenders of "pre-dispute" arbitration assert that binding arbitration is beneficial not only for the companies that impose it, but also for individual consumers, employees, and society as a whole. They argue that when companies include arbitration in form contracts, they help consumers and employees by providing them with a forum that is cheaper, quicker, and more accessible than litigation. Such defenders also argue that to the extent companies reduce their own dispute resolution costs, market forces will ensure that they pass on such savings to their workers in the form of higher wages and to their customers in the form of lower prices. They contend that while it may be appropriate to proscribe egregiously unfair mandatory arbitration, it would be a mistake to prohibit the practice altogether.

In 2015, following the Dodd-Frank Wall Street Reform and Consumer Protection Act, the Consumer Financial Protection Bureau delivered a study of arbitration outlining a number of these concerns. The conclusion of its report was to publish a rule banning arbitration in certain contexts. Below, you will see that Congress subsequently overrode the rule entirely.

Consumer Financial Protection Bureau, CFPB ARBITRATION AGREEMENTS

12 C.F.R. § 1040 (2017)

Pursuant to section 1028(b) of the Dodd-Frank Wall Street Reform and Consumer Protection Act (Pub. L. 111-203), on July 10, 2017, the Bureau issued a final rule titled Arbitration Agreements to regulate pre-dispute arbitration agreements in contracts for specified consumer financial products and services. The Bureau published the arbitration agreements rule in the Federal Register on July 19, 2017 (82 FR 33210), establishing 12 CFR part 1040. As required by section 1028(a) of the Dodd-Frank Act, the arbitration agreements rule followed the publication and delivery to Congress of the Bureau's March 2015 study concerning the use of pre-dispute arbitration agreements. The arbitration agreements rule would have imposed two sets of limitations on the use of pre-dispute arbitration agreements by providers of certain consumer financial products and services. First, the arbitration agreements rule would have prohibited providers from using a pre-dispute arbitration agreement to block consumer class actions in court and would have required providers to include a provision reflecting this limitation in arbitration agreements they entered into. Second, the arbitration agreements rule would have required providers to redact and submit to the Bureau certain records relating to arbitral proceedings and relating to the use of pre-dispute arbitration agreements in court, and would have required the Bureau to publish these records on its Web site. While the arbitration agreements rule became effective on September 18, 2017, the arbitration agreements rule would have applied only to pre-dispute arbitration agreements entered into after March 19, 2018.

The United States House of Representative passed House Joint Resolution 111 disapproving the arbitration agreements rule under the Congressional Review Act (5 U.S.C. 801 et seq.) on July 25, 2017. The United States Senate passed the joint resolution on October 24, 2017. President Donald J. Trump signed the joint resolution into law as Public Law 115-74 on November 1, 2017. Under the joint resolution and by operation of the Congressional Review Act, the arbitration agreements rule has no force or effect. Accordingly, the Bureau is hereby removing the final rule titled Arbitration Agreements from the CFR . . .

---

2. Arbitration Confidentiality

Richard Reuben, CONFIDENTIALITY IN ARBITRATION: BEYOND THE MYTH

54 Kan. L. Rev. 1255 (2006)

A crucial distinction . . . must be drawn between the "privacy" of the arbitral proceeding and the "confidentiality" of the proceeding. The privacy of the proceeding refers to the ability of uninvited third parties—such as former spouses, business partners, and the media—to access and observe the proceedings, and perhaps disclose those observations, without the consent of the disputing parties, and possibly the arbitrator. The confidentiality of the proceeding, however, refers to the ability of the disputing parties, the arbitrator, witnesses, and others who attended the arbitration to disclose publicly oral statements made in arbitration, documents tendered in arbitration, or observations of conduct by parties, witnesses, and arbitrators during the course of the arbitration.

When considering confidentiality of arbitration communications, yet another important distinction must be drawn between disclosures to third persons in the general public and disclosures to institutions in the context of formal legal proceedings. Disclosures to third persons in the general public include a wide range of possibilities—from disclosures to spouses, family members and friends to business partners and competitors, and students in classrooms and training sessions. Since these disclosures are in the private realm, the law historically has permitted parties to regulate them through the law of contract, and that law is generally well-developed. Disclosures in the context of formal legal proceedings can also take many forms, such as disclosure pursuant to a deposition or in response to a discovery request, testimony during a trial, as well as the work of other public bodies, such as investigations and hearings by administrative agencies, legislatures, and grand juries. Unlike disclosures to third persons generally, which implicate private interests, disclosures in formal legal proceedings implicate public interests—specifically, the public's interest in accessing the information pursuant to governmental fact-finding, adjudication, or policy development and legal regulation. . . .

Arbitration is an important vehicle for the resolution of disputes, supported by a strong national policy favoring the arbitration of disputes. One of the potential advantages of the process is that it is private. Third parties can be prevented from observing the proceedings. Parties to the arbitration can contract to prevent each other from disclosing arbitration communications to third parties. And arbitrators are ethically bound to preserve this confidentiality unless otherwise required by law.

Less clear is whether the law can require the disclosure of those arbitration communications for purposes of discovery and admission in another legal proceeding. The emerging view of the courts appears to be that such disclosures may be compelled—a position that would undermine congressional intent to endorse a private alternative to public adjudication because once they are introduced, such communications would become public records that may be disseminated freely as a general matter. The continuation of this trend would undermine the national policy favoring arbitration by frustrating the parties' reasonable expectations with respect to the confidentiality of arbitration, ultimately chilling use of the arbitration process.

The law's expectation of access to these materials is not trivial, however, and proper legal policy must reflect a balance of these competing public and private interests. This balance may be struck by raising the burden of proof for the admission of evidence sought from arbitration proceedings by requiring the proponent of such evidence to demonstrate that it is otherwise unavailable and necessary for the resolution of the case. . . .

❖ *Amy Schmitz*, UNTANGLING THE PRIVACY PARADOX IN ARBITRATION

54 Kan. L. Rev. 1211 (2006)

Arbitration is private but not confidential. This is a paradox to the extent that it is seemingly contradictory, but states a truth. Arbitration is private in that it is a closed process, but it is not confidential because information revealed during the process may become public. This has caused misperceptions and confusion regarding the arbitration process. Contracting parties often assume that arbitration's privacy denies the public access to not only arbitration hearings, but also information revealed during the hearings. These parties may then accept arbitration agreements without contracting for confidentiality. This, in turn, may negatively impact corporate parties expecting arbitration to shield their business information, as well as individuals who assume that personal information revealed in arbitration will remain secret.

It is true that arbitration proceedings generally are private and do not produce published opinions that courts infuse into public law. It is not correct, however, to assume that information revealed in arbitration is automatically confidential. In other words, United States law does not guarantee such secrecy of arbitration information, and institutional rules parties incorporate in their arbitration agreements generally do not provide broad confidentiality protections. Furthermore, third-party participants who do not agree to any confidentiality agreement or rules remain free to talk about the arbitration proceedings.

Confusion regarding privacy and confidentiality in arbitration therefore fosters misguided contracting, as well as simplistic assumptions regarding the value of secrecy in the arbitration process. Privacy and confidentiality may be good and bad for the parties. Both may allow parties to save resources and reputation costs by arbitrating disputes outside the public purview. This may be especially true for "repeat players" that routinely incorporate arbitration clauses in their form contracts. Such routine arbitration may allow these players to enjoy efficiency benefits, which they may pass on by offering lower prices, higher wages, and better-quality products. Corporate parties sometimes misperceive benefits of arbitration's privacy, however, by assuming it will automatically ensure the secrecy of their trade and business information.

In contrast, consumer and employee advocates often focus only on drawbacks of arbitration's privacy without considering how individuals could benefit from increased confidentiality in the process. They complain that arbitration's privacy unduly benefits repeat players by allowing them to hide unfavorable information about their discriminatory practices, product defect and safety concerns, and other legal violations. This hinders future claimants in proving cases of repeat offenses. Some also claim that the lack of published opinions in arbitration thwarts development of the law in areas affecting public interests, such as civil rights and product defect[s].

These critics often overlook, however, how privacy and confidentiality in arbitration may benefit individuals with cases involving sensitive personal information. Indeed, individuals would be wise to contractually protect the confidentiality of their personal information. Without such contractual protection, consumers may become subject to arbitration provisions in form credit card contracts that block public access to awards revealing the financial companies' misconduct, but neglect to protect the confidentiality of consumers' personal financial information. Similarly, sexual harassment claimants may be dismayed when they cannot prevent witnesses from gossiping regarding what they learn while participating in arbitration hearings. Moreover, increased transparency in arbitration may dissuade sexual harassment claimants and those with poor financial histories from asserting their claims.

These multi-textured transparency issues raise thorny questions and complications. Do we want more or less transparency in arbitration? Should this vary in domestic versus international arbitration, or in arbitration pursuant to contract versus proceedings per statutory or administrative rule? Should different standards apply in arbitrations involving public parties, or in the proceedings consumers or employees must pursue under form agreements?

Problem 10-7. *The Ethics of Clauses They Won't Read*

Recall Jeff Sovern's study, described in Chapter 9. What ethical questions or obligations arise if a company's attorney is reasonably certain that consumers/employees will not read and/or understand the company's binding arbitration provision?

Problem 10-8. *Voluntary Post-Dispute Arbitration*

Critics of mandatory arbitration assert that if arbitration were truly better, quicker, and cheaper for all concerned, the disputants would agree to it voluntarily on a post-dispute basis. Defenders of mandatory arbitration claim that this position is naïve at best, or perhaps just a rhetorical ploy. Such defenders assert that although binding arbitration might seem desirable to all pre-dispute, on a post-dispute basis, one side or the other will often prefer litigation, thus making post-dispute agreements unlikely. For example, represented plaintiffs with strong claims and the potential for high damages would purportedly prefer litigation, and companies opposing plaintiffs with weaker or smaller value claims would prefer litigation, because they know litigation would not be viable for such a plaintiff. How viable do you think post-dispute arbitration is? Considering that litigation is a default process, how easy or difficult would it be to convince parties to alter that default to arbitration once a dispute arises?

Further Reading

Gary Born. (2020). International Commercial Arbitration: Commentary and Materials (3d ed). The Hague, The Netherlands: Kluwer Law International.

Edward Brunet, Richard E. Speidel, Jean R. Sternlight & Stephen J. Ware. (2006). Arbitration Law in America: A Critical Assessment. New York: Cambridge U. Press.

Thomas E. Carbonneau. (2004). The Law and Practice of Arbitration. Huntington, NY: JurisNet, LLC.

Pat K. Chew, Comparing the Effects of Judges' Gender and Arbitrators' Gender in Sex Discrimination Cases and Why It Matters, 32 Ohio St. J. on Disp. Resol. 195 (2017).

Pat K. Chew, Contextual Analysis in Arbitration, 70 SMU L. Rev. 837 (2017).

Rachel Childres, Arbitration Class Waivers, Independent Contractor Classification, and the Blockade of Workers' Rights in the Gig Economy, 69 Ala. L. Rev. 533 (2017).

Laura J. Cooper, Dennis Nolan, Richard A. Bales, Stephen F. Befort, Lise Gelernter & Michael Z. Green. (2020). ADR in the Workplace (4th ed). St. Paul, MN: The West Group.

Christopher R. Drahozal. (2013). Commercial Arbitration: Cases and Problems (3d ed). Durham, NC: Carolina Academic Press.

John T. Dunlop & Arnold M. Zack. (1997). Mediation and Arbitration of Employment Disputes. San Francisco: Jossey-Bass Publishers.

Cynthia Estlund, The Black Hole of Mandatory Arbitration, 96 NC L. Rev. 679 (2018).

Christopher Leslie, Conspiracy to Arbitrate, 96 NC L. Rev. 381 (2018).

David A. Noll, Regulating Arbitration, 105 Cal. L. Rev. 985 (2017).

Judith Resnik, Diffusing Disputes: The Public in the Private of Arbitration, the Private in Courts, and the Erasure of Rights, 124 Yale L.J. 2804 (2015).

Imri Szalai. (2013). Outsourcing Justice: The Rise of Modern Arbitration Laws in America. Durham, NC: Carolina Academic Press.

Chapter 11 Arbitration: Practice and Ethics

I've always felt that a person's intelligence is directly reflected by the number of conflicting points of view he can entertain simultaneously on the same topic.

—Abigail Adams

Even a sheet of paper has two sides.

—Japanese Proverb

A. ARBITRATION AGREEMENTS

The previous two chapters illustrated how arbitration often serves as a complete substitute for litigation and its associated protections, costs, and trappings. Additionally, you have seen that the availability of this adjudicative alternative to litigation hinges almost entirely on the particulars of the disputants' agreement containing an arbitration clause. This chapter begins, therefore, with the important question of what an arbitration clause contains, focusing in on two provisions in particular: the scope clause and the governing law clause.

1. Broad Scope Clauses

Arbitrators generally have the power not only to conduct arbitrations (and therefore can decide on evidentiary matters, create schedules, compel participation or discovery, and interpret the arbitration) but also to render a decision in order to resolve substantive disputes. The question arises, however: *Which disputes?* In other words, something must define the scope of disputes on which the arbitrator may render decisions. And in almost all cases, a clause in the parties' arbitration agreement (often called the "scope clause") will create those boundaries. Arbitration need not be a binary matter ("Either we arbitrate everything, or we arbitrate nothing."). Parties can specify precisely the kinds of disputes they want to send to arbitration.

In some cases, parties may want to bind themselves to use arbitration to resolve *every* possible dispute they can imagine in their relationship. In that case, they would want to craft an agreement that is broad enough to encompass everything (and therefore legally empower the arbitrator to act) while still being specific and clear enough to satisfy the requirement that a contract be enforceable. Consider, for example, standard clauses suggested by two major arbitration providers in the United States:

JAMS—Standard Engineering and Construction Arbitration Clause: Any dispute, claim or controversy arising out of or relating to this Agreement or the breach, termination, enforcement, interpretation or validity thereof, including the determination of the scope or applicability of this agreement to arbitrate, shall be determined by arbitration in (insert the desired place of arbitration), before (one) (three) arbitrator(s). The arbitration shall be administered by JAMS pursuant to its (Engineering and Construction Arbitration Rules & Procedures) (Engineering and Construction Arbitration Rules & Procedures for Expedited Arbitration). Judgment on the Award may be entered in any court having jurisdiction. This clause shall not preclude parties from seeking provisional remedies in aid of arbitration from a court of appropriate jurisdiction.

AAA—Standard General Commercial Transactions Clause: Any controversy or claim arising out of or relating to this contract, or the breach thereof, shall be settled by arbitration administered by the American Arbitration Association in accordance with its Commercial [or other] Arbitration Rules, and judgment on the award rendered by the arbitrator(s) may be entered in any court having jurisdiction thereof.

Problem 11-1. ***Scope Clauses***

Can you construct an example of a dispute that might arise between signatories to a contract containing either the JAMS clause or the AAA clause listed immediately above that would not fall within their scope?

Courts interpreting a broadly-worded arbitration scope clause will, consistent with the broad policy favoring arbitration, generally give clauses an expansive reach and resolve doubts about arbitrability in favor of arbitration. But as with any legal term, parties must take care in the precise drafting of scope clauses' language. See, e.g. Am. Recovery Corp. v. Computerized Thermal Imaging, Inc., 96 F.3d 88, 93 (4th Cir. 1996) (distinguishing between a scope clause encompassing any disputes "arising out of or relating to" and a clause encompassing "any disputes arising hereunder," with the latter being treated as a restrictive, limited arbitration clause).

2. Defined or Narrow Scope Clauses

As you have seen already, one of the principal benefits of arbitration is the degree to which it is customizable by the disputants. The scope clause provides another opportunity for disputants—or contracting parties who anticipate the prospect of a dispute—to specify that they want arbitration to be the method used to resolve *some*, but not all, of the kinds of disputes that might arise. Consider the following examples.

❖ CUMMINGS v. FEDEX GROUND PACKAGE SYSTEMS, INC.

404 F.3d 1258 (10th Cir. 2005)

. . . Plaintiffs entered into separate, but for all relevant purposes identical, contracts with FedEx to serve as package delivery contractors. Plaintiffs allege in their complaint that, prior to the execution of any agreement, FedEx made oral representations to them concerning the amount of income plaintiffs would earn based on their workload and assigned delivery route, as well as the assistance that FedEx would provide them. Each plaintiff alleges that, in response to FedEx advertisements, he met with a FedEx regional recruiter to inquire about acquiring a FedEx delivery route. The complaint alleges a FedEx recruiter told each plaintiff he would be assigned a route and that, if he worked between ten and twelve hours a day, he would earn approximately $1,500 a week, plus bonuses, on that route. Plaintiffs also allege the FedEx recruiter told them they were required to purchase a truck, but that FedEx would assist them in reselling their route and the truck if they left FedEx. Each plaintiff later signed FedEx's form Pick-Up and Delivery Contractor Operating Agreement (the "Operating Agreement"), and, as required, purchased a FedEx truck. Each was assigned a delivery route, originating from a Colorado FedEx facility. The plaintiffs allege that, despite working in excess of the recommended hours per day, they were never able to earn close to the amount of money represented by FedEx on their assigned route; Cummings and Bittle allege they were unable to earn more than $400 a week, despite working more than twelve hours a day. All of the plaintiffs resigned from FedEx in 2001. They allege that FedEx refused to assist them in selling their trucks.

In its motion to compel arbitration, FedEx cites the following arbitration clause contained in each Operating Agreement:

> Arbitration of Asserted Wrongful Termination. In the event FedEx Ground acts to terminate this Agreement (which acts shall include any claim by [plaintiff] of constructive termination) and [plaintiff] disagrees with such termination or asserts that the actions of [defendant] are not authorized under the terms of this Agreement, then each such disagreement (but no others) shall be settled

> by arbitration in accordance with the Commercial Arbitration Rules of the American Arbitration Association (AAA). . . .

In rejecting FedEx's argument that [any of plaintiffs'] claims were subject to arbitration, the district court first noted that the clause is a narrow one, which limits arbitration to very specific types of disputes. See McDonnell Douglas Fin. Corp. v. Pennsylvania Power & Light Co., 858 F.2d 825, 832 (2d Cir. 1988) (discussing the difference between broad and narrow arbitration clauses). By its terms, the arbitration clause in the Operating Agreement only covers acts by FedEx to terminate the Operating Agreement or acts claimed by plaintiffs to constitute a constructive termination of the Operating Agreement. . . .

Under a narrow arbitration clause, a dispute is subject to arbitration only if it relates to an issue that is on its face within the purview of the clause, and collateral matters will generally be beyond its purview. The arbitration clause in this case manifests an obvious intent to be narrowly construed. Thus, a dispute that is merely collateral to the Operating Agreement is beyond the purview of this narrow arbitration clause.

We agree with the district court that plaintiffs do not allege that FedEx actually or constructively terminated the Operating Agreement, which, according to its unambiguous terms, are the only disputes subject to arbitration. The subject matter of the claims—oral representations and implied agreements concerning income and truck resale assistance made prior to the execution of the Operating Agreement—is not reasonably factually related to a dispute over the termination, direct or otherwise, of the Operating Agreement. . . . In summary, given the narrow scope of the arbitration clause, we conclude that the district court correctly ruled [that the] plaintiffs' [claims] are not disputes within the scope of the arbitration agreement.

Parties might want to limit the scope of an arbitration award in a number of different ways. The example above limits the subject matter of the disputes that the parties seek to send to arbitration. The parties could also limit cases, for example, according to the amount in controversy:

> Any controversy or claim arising out of this agreement if less than or equal to $5,000 shall be resolved by an action in small claims court of the Municipal Court of the City of and County of Lancaster Pennsylvania. If a claim regarding fees charged by us exceeds $5,000, it shall be resolved by arbitration in the City of Lancaster Pennsylvania, administered by the American Arbitration Association in accordance with its Arbitration Rules for Adoption Agencies and Related Services Disputes, such arbitration shall be binding and final, and judgment upon the award rendered by the arbitrator(s) may be entered in any court having jurisdiction. In agreeing to arbitration, we both acknowledge that, in the event of a dispute over fees charged by us, each party is giving up the right to have the dispute decided in a court of law before a judge or jury and instead we are accepting the use of arbitration for resolution of this matter. In any such dispute, whether resolved by arbitration or lawsuit, the prevailing party will be entitled to attorney's fees and costs.

Turi v. Main St. Adoption Services, LLP, 633 F.3d 496, 506 (6th Cir. 2011) (plaintiffs' allegations that the adoption service violated racketeering laws, "as well as state-law claims for unjust enrichment, conversion, civil conspiracy, fraudulent misrepresentation, innocent misrepresentation, intentional infliction of emotional distress, and negligent infliction of emotional distress" are not claims "regarding fees" and are therefore not arbitrable).

Recall, however, that although an arbitration provision's scope clause may be specific, it may nonetheless have an expansive reach. Consider the clause in the following case.

HATEMI v. M & T BANK

633 Fed. Appx. 47 (2d Cir. 2016)

Defendant M & T Bank ("M & T") appeals from the district court's denial of its motion to compel arbitration and to dismiss the complaint of plaintiff Lachin Hatemi, who alleges that he was improperly subscribed to M & T's overdraft protection plan and assessed fees thereunder. . . .

We first look to the existence of an arbitration clause. It is uncontested that, upon opening an account with M & T, Hatemi signed an agreement (the "Account Agreement") containing the following arbitration clause:

> Each dispute or controversy that arises out of or is related to your account with us, or any service we provide in connection with your account, or any matter relating to your or our rights and obligations provided for in this agreement or any other agreement between you and us relating to your account or a service provided by us in connection with your account, whether based on statute, contract, tort, fraud, misrepresentation or any other legal or equitable theory, including any claim for interest and attorney's fees, where applicable (any "Claim") must be determined on an individual basis by binding arbitration in accordance with the Federal Arbitration Act ("FAA"—Title 9 of the United States Code) under the auspices of the American Arbitration Association ("AAA").

The agreement therefore mandates the determination by arbitration of any disputes or controversies arising out of or related to (1) Hatemi's account; (2) any service provided by M & T in connection with Hatemi's account; (3) any matter relating to Hatemi's or M & T's obligations provided for in the Account Agreement; or (4) any matter relating to Hatemi's or M & T's obligations provided for in any other agreement relating to his account.

Absent any dispute over the existence of this arbitration agreement, we "then consider whether the dispute falls within the scope of the arbitration agreement." Hatemi argues that there is a factual dispute as to (1) whether any valid overdraft protection agreement exists or was signed by him and, if so, (2) whether it was incorporated into the Account Agreement containing the arbitration clause. These arguments put the cart before the horse. Without affirmative opt-in, the existence or propriety of any overdraft protection agreement is indeed a factual issue, but it does not affect the validity of the Account Agreement's arbitration clause or its application to each dispute or controversy related to Hatemi's M & T account or any service provided in connection with that account. Because the issues of overdraft protection and accompanying fees are indisputably related to Hatemi's account and to a service provided in connection with his account, which results in a fee obligation connected to the account, the Account Agreement's arbitration clause extends to the instant dispute regardless of whether the disputed overdraft protection agreement is incorporated into the Account Agreement or even exists. The district court therefore erred in denying M & T's motion to compel arbitration. To be sure, in such arbitration, factual disputes as to the existence or terms of any overdraft protection and fee obligations can be raised and resolved.

Should the distinction between "broad" and "narrow" arbitration scope clauses have significance for courts seeking to interpret them? Many courts have suggested that this distinction matters, and at least creates a set of rebuttable presumptions. Then-Judge (now Justice) Gorsuch previously called this distinction into question in a concurring opinion.

HATEMI v. M&T BANK

633 Fed. Appx. 47 (2d Cir. 2016)

GORSUCH, Circuit Judge, concurring [with majority decision reviewing the substance of an arbitration clause and ruling some, but not all, of the plaintiff's claims to be arbitrable under the terms of the scope clause]:

I write separately only to question this business of classifying arbitration clauses as "broad" or "narrow." As the majority opinion notes, [according to] Cummings v. FedEx Ground Package Sys., Inc., 404 F.3d 1258 (10th Cir. 2005), the first thing a court must do when deciding the arbitrability of a claim under the Federal Arbitration Act (FAA) is to classify the parties' arbitration clause as either "broad" or "narrow." If the clause is thought to be "broad" then "there arises a presumption of arbitrability and arbitration of even a collateral matter will be ordered." But if we deem a clause "narrow," we are required to "take care to carry out the specific and limited intent of [the] parties" and a dispute will be subject to arbitration "only if it relates to an issue that is on its face within the purview of the clause, and collateral matters will generally be beyond its purview." Under this regime, the strength of the presumption of arbitrability thus depends on a critical classification of the parties' clause: the presumption is strong if the clause is deemed "broad," but weaker if the clause is deemed "narrow."

As a panel of this court we are bound to abide our precedent compelling this taxonomic task, but respectfully I question its appropriateness and utility. On the first of these scores, the relevant statute, the FAA, admits no distinction between "broad" and "narrow" clauses. All arbitration clauses, Congress has told us, are equally "valid, irrevocable, and enforceable." 9 U.S.C. §2. There is nothing in the language of the Act that suggests some clauses are more equal than others—a sort of four legs good, two legs bad. In Moses H. Cone Mem'l Hosp. v. Mercury Constr. Corp., 460 U.S. 1 (1983), the Supreme Court recognized precisely this point, holding that the FAA embodies "a liberal federal policy favoring arbitration agreements" applicable to *all* agreements within the Act's purview. Id. at 24. Neither Congress nor the Court, then, has suggested that we should engage in the scholastic task of classifying the parties' clause according to some abstract taxonomy, let alone as a first and necessary step in any arbitration dispute. Nor have they given us leave to vary the strength of the presumption of arbitrability based on the results of such a classification. It seems to me that we ought not be in the business of burdening a statute with words Congress has not written or inventing a test the Supreme Court has not endorsed. . . .

Not only is this categorization business and its resulting effect on the presumption of arbitration without a basis in the FAA or Supreme Court precedent, the utility of such an undertaking . . . "is dubious at best." The question of arbitrability is simply and always a matter of straightforward contract interpretation. See First Options of Chicago, Inc. v. Kaplan, 514 U.S. 938, 943 (1995) (arbitration is a "matter of contract"); Gilmer v. Interstate/Johnson Lane Corp., 500 U.S. 20, 24 (1991) (purpose of FAA was "to place arbitration agreements on the same footing as other contracts"). No additional taxonomies or tests are needed for this long familiar enterprise. When the arbitrability of a particular matter is plain on the face of the parties' agreement, the agreement is enforceable according to its terms—whether the arbitration clause is "broad" or "narrow" or somewhere in between (where, if we are to be frank, many clauses will fall). If and to the degree an agreement contains some residual ambiguity, that's when the *Moses Cone* presumption of arbitrability applies—and applies evenhandedly. We are told by the Supreme Court, again categorically, that "any doubts concerning the scope of arbitrable issues should be resolved in favor of arbitration, whether the problem at hand is the construction of the contract language itself or an allegation of waiver, delay, or a like defense to arbitrability." *Moses Cone.* An artificial dichotomy should not replace reasoned analysis of the parties' contractual agreement. It ought not be the case that, simply because we hold an arbitration clause to be "broad," we automatically have license, as *Cummings* suggests, to send "collateral matters" to arbitration even if those matters plainly fall outside the boundaries of the parties' arbitration clause. Neither ought it be the case that we "take care to carry out the specific and limited intent of [the] parties," only when faced with a "narrow" agreement, as *Cummings* implies. Our job is always to enforce the parties' intent and, absent such clear intent, apply the presumption of arbitrability.

Though the result in this case is the same whether or not we apply *Cummings,* and thus the judgment reached by the court today is surely right, it seems to me we have made more and needless work for ourselves in arbitration cases in having to peg clauses "broad" or "narrow." Conventional tools of contract interpretation are sufficient to the task of deciding these cases, the only ones authorized by statute or the Supreme Court, and in no need of adornment.

Problem 11-2. ***Categorizing Scope Clauses***

Do you agree with the majority in Hatemi v. M&T Bank? With then-Judge Gorsuch? Or would you urge the application of a different decision principle in assessing arbitration clauses such as the one in this case?

Should it matter whether the arbitration clause includes a class action waiver?

3. Disputes over Scope Clauses

What happens if the parties cannot agree whether a particular factual circumstance represents a dispute that falls within the scope of the parties' arbitration agreement? Who decides such questions (commonly referred to as "arbitrability"[1] questions)?

"[A]rbitration is a matter of contract and a party cannot be required to submit to arbitration any dispute which he has not agreed so to submit." Howsam v. Dean Witter Reynolds, Inc., 537 U.S. 79, 83 (2002). The threshold question of arbitrability, is generally to be decided by the court, not the arbitrator, unless the parties "clearly and unmistakably provide otherwise." Id. (quoting AT&T Tech., Inc. v. Comm. Workers of Am., 475 U.S. 643, 649 (1986)).

Consider the American Arbitration Association's Commercial Arbitration Rule 7:

> (a) The arbitrator shall have the power to rule on his or her own jurisdiction, including any objections with respect to the existence, scope, or validity of the arbitration agreement or to the arbitrability of any claim or counterclaim.
>
> (b) The arbitrator shall have the power to determine the existence or validity of a contract of which an arbitration clause forms a part. Such an arbitration clause shall be treated as an agreement independent of the other terms of the contract. A decision by the arbitrator that the contract is null and void shall not for that reason alone render invalid the arbitration clause.

Do you consider the AAA rule to satisfy the *Howsam v. Dean Witter Reynolds* standard?

---

1. The term "arbitrability" is not self-defining. "Arbitrability can mean anything from whether the contract compels arbitration to whether the contract is enforceable. For purposes of clarity, we intend to limit our usage of the term 'arbitrability' in this section to whether the contract compels parties into arbitration, but you should be aware that the term operates almost as a chimera in this area of the law." Michael Moffitt & Andrea Kupfer Schneider, Dispute Resolution: Examples & Explanations 218 (2014).

4. Governing Law Clauses

Like many commercial contracts, arbitration agreements often specify the law(s) under which the contract is to be interpreted and the arbitration clause is to be assessed. The parties might accomplish this with a simple clause, such as, "This Agreement is governed by and shall be construed in accordance with the laws of [New York] [Singapore] [etc.]." Somewhat more encompassing, and aimed at precluding future disputes over preemption and federal jurisdiction, JAMS suggests a choice of law clause reading:

> This Agreement and the rights of the parties hereunder shall be governed by and construed in accordance with the laws of the State of [], exclusive of conflict or choice of law rules. The parties acknowledge that this Agreement evidences a transaction involving interstate commerce. Notwithstanding the provision in the preceding paragraph with respect to applicable substantive law, any arbitration conducted pursuant to the terms of this Agreement shall be governed by the Federal Arbitration Act (9 U.S.C., Secs. 1-16).[2]

As you may have already encountered in your course on Contracts or Conflicts of Laws, courts routinely have to sort through the implications of parties residing or doing business in different locations in answering choice-of-law questions.

Two particular questions arise in the arbitration context, however. First, what happens if the laws specified in the parties' contract include provisions that are in tension (or even in conflict) with existing federal arbitration laws? Second, how do United States courts give effect to parties' contractual preferences that laws from other countries be used (as to the substance of the dispute and/or as to the arbitration-specific questions related to the dispute)?

Choice of law might create important distinctions in a wide variety of different circumstances. The question of the availability of class actions or class-wide arbitrations (which we discussed in the previous chapter) presents perhaps the highest stakes of these contexts. Consider the following two cases:

DIRECTV v. IMBURGIA

136 S. Ct. 463 (2015)

DIRECTV, Inc., the petitioner, entered into a service agreement with its customers, including respondents Amy Imburgia and Kathy Greiner. Section 9 of that contract provides that "any Claim either of us asserts will be resolved only by binding arbitration." It then sets forth a waiver of class arbitration, stating that

2. JAMS Clause Workbook: A Guide to Drafting Dispute Resolution Clauses for Commercial Contracts—Governing Law, available at https://jamsadr.com/files/uploads/Documents/JAMS-Rules/JAMS-ADR-Clauses.pdf (last visited June 20, 2018).

"[n]either you nor we shall be entitled to join or consolidate claims in arbitration." It adds that if the "law of your state" makes the waiver of class arbitration unenforceable, then the entire arbitration provision "is unenforceable." Section 10 of the contract states that §9, the arbitration provision, "shall be governed by the Federal Arbitration Act."

In 2008, the two respondents brought this lawsuit against DIRECTV in a California state court. They seek damages for early termination fees that they believe violate California law. After various proceedings not here relevant, DIRECTV, pointing to the arbitration provision, asked the court to send the matter to arbitration. The state trial court denied that request, and DIRECTV appealed.

The California Court of Appeal thought that the critical legal question concerned the meaning of the contractual phrase "law of your state," in this case the law of California. Does the law of California make the contract's class-arbitration waiver unenforceable? If so, as the contract provides, the entire arbitration provision is unenforceable. Or does California law permit the parties to agree to waive the right to proceed as a class in arbitration? If so, the arbitration provision is enforceable.

At one point, the law of California would have made the contract's class-arbitration waiver unenforceable. In 2005, the California Supreme Court held in *Discover Bank v. Superior Court*, that a "waiver" of class arbitration in a "consumer contract of adhesion" that "predictably involve[s] small amounts of damages" and meets certain other criteria not contested here is "unconscionable under California law and should not be enforced." But in 2011, this Court held that California's *Discover Bank* rule "stands as an obstacle to the accomplishment and execution of the full purposes and objectives of Congress" embodied in the Federal Arbitration Act. AT&T Mobility LLC v. Concepcion, 563 U.S. 333, 352 (2011).

The California Court of Appeal subsequently held in this case that, despite this Court's holding in *Concepcion*, "the law of California would find the class action waiver unenforceable." The court noted that *Discover Bank* had held agreements to dispense with class-arbitration procedures unenforceable under circumstances such as these. It conceded that this Court in *Concepcion* had held that the Federal Arbitration Act invalidated California's rule. But it then concluded that this latter circumstance did not change the result—that the "class action waiver is unenforceable under California law.". . .

The court reasoned that just as the parties were free in their contract to refer to the laws of different States or different nations, so too were they free to refer to California law as it would have been without this Court's holding invalidating the *Discover Bank* rule. The court thought that the parties in their contract had done just that. And it set forth two reasons for believing so.

First, §10 of the contract, stating that the Federal Arbitration Act governs §9 (the arbitration provision), is a general provision. But the provision voiding arbitration if the "law of your state" would find the class-arbitration waiver unenforceable is a specific provision. The court believed that the specific provision "is paramount to" and must govern the general.

Second, the court said that "a court should construe ambiguous language against the interest of the party that drafted it." DIRECTV had drafted the language; to void the arbitration provision was against its interest. Hence the arbitration provision was void. The Court of Appeal consequently affirmed the trial court's denial of DIRECTV's motion to enforce the arbitration provision. . . .

No one denies that lower courts must follow this Court's holding in *Concepcion.* The fact that *Concepcion* was a closely divided case, resulting in a decision from which four Justices dissented, has no bearing on that undisputed obligation. Lower court judges are certainly free to note their disagreement with a decision of this Court. But the "Supremacy Clause forbids state courts to dissociate themselves from federal law because of disagreement with its content or a refusal to recognize the superior authority of its source." Howlett v. Rose, 496 U.S. 356, 371 (1990).

While all accept this elementary point of law, that point does not resolve the issue in this case. As the Court of Appeal noted, the Federal Arbitration Act allows parties to an arbitration contract considerable latitude to choose what law governs some or all of its provisions, including the law governing enforceability of a class-arbitration waiver. In principle, they might choose to have portions of their contract governed by the law of Tibet, the law of pre-revolutionary Russia, or (as is relevant here) the law of California including the *Discover Bank* rule and irrespective of that rule's invalidation in *Concepcion.* The Court of Appeal decided that, as a matter of contract law, the parties did mean the phrase "law of your state" to refer to this last possibility. Since the interpretation of a contract is ordinarily a matter of state law to which we defer, Volt Information Sciences, Inc. v. Board of Trustees of Leland Stanford Junior Univ., 489 U.S. 468, 474 (1989), we must decide not whether its decision is a correct statement of California law but whether (assuming it is) that state law is consistent with the Federal Arbitration Act.

Although we may doubt that the Court of Appeal has correctly interpreted California law, we recognize that California courts are the ultimate authority on that law. While recognizing this, we must decide whether the decision of the California court places arbitration contracts "on equal footing with all other contracts." Buckeye Check Cashing, Inc. v. Cardegna, 546 U.S. 440, 443 (2006). And in doing so, we must examine whether the Court of Appeal's decision in fact rests upon "grounds as exist at law or in equity for the revocation of any contract." 9 U.S.C. §2. That is to say, we look not to grounds that the California court might have offered but rather to those it did in fact offer. . . .

We recognize, as the dissent points out, that when DIRECTV drafted the contract, the parties likely believed that the words "law of your state" included California law that then made class-arbitration waivers unenforceable. But that does not answer the legal question before us. That is because this Court subsequently held in *Concepcion* that the *Discover Bank* rule was invalid. Thus, the underlying question of contract law at the time the Court of Appeal made its decision was whether the "law of your state" included invalid California law. We must now decide whether answering that question in the affirmative is consistent with the Federal Arbitration Act. After examining the grounds upon which the Court of Appeal rested its decision, we conclude that California courts would not interpret contracts other than arbitration contracts the same way. Rather, several considerations lead us to conclude that the court's interpretation of this arbitration contract is unique, restricted to that field.

[W]e do not believe that the relevant contract language is ambiguous. The contract says that "[i]f . . . the law of your state would find this agreement to dispense with class arbitration procedures unenforceable, then this entire Section 9 [the arbitration section] is unenforceable." Absent any indication in the contract that this language is meant to refer to invalid state law, it presumably takes its ordinary meaning: valid state law. Indeed, neither the parties nor the dissent refer us to any contract case from California or from any other State that interprets similar language to refer to state laws authoritatively held to be invalid. While we recognize that the dissent believes this phrase to be "ambiguous," or "anomalous," we cannot agree with that characterization. . . .

[W]ere the phrase "law of your state" ambiguous, surely some court would have construed that term to incorporate state laws invalidated by, for example, federal labor law, federal pension law, or federal civil rights law. Yet, we have found no such case. Moreover, the reach of the canon construing contract language against the drafter must have limits, no matter who the drafter was. The fact that we can find no similar case interpreting the words "law of your state" to include invalid state laws indicates, at the least, that the anti-drafter canon would not lead California courts to reach a similar conclusion in similar cases that do not involve arbitration.

Taking these considerations together, we reach a conclusion that, in our view, falls well within the confines of (and goes no further than) present well-established law. California's interpretation of the phrase "law of your state" [in this case] does not place arbitration contracts "on equal footing with all other contracts," *Buckeye Check Cashing, Inc.* For that reason, it does not give "due regard . . . to the federal policy favoring arbitration." *Volt Information Sciences*, 489 U.S., at 476. Thus, the Court of Appeal's interpretation is pre-empted by the Federal Arbitration Act. Hence, the California Court of Appeal must "enforc[e]" the arbitration agreement. 9 U.S.C. §2.

The judgment of the California Court of Appeal is reversed, and the case is remanded for further proceedings not inconsistent with this opinion.

CAPE FLATTERY LTD. v. TITAN MARITIME LLC

647 F.3d 914 (9th Cir 2011)

BACKGROUND

On February 2, 2005, the M/V Cape Flattery ran aground on a submerged coral reef off Barbers Point, Oahu, Hawai'i. . . . Cape Flattery, as the vessel's owner, was liable for the cost of removing the vessel from the reef. Cape Flattery entered into an agreement with Titan Maritime to salvage the vessel (the "Agreement"). . . . The Agreement also contains an arbitration clause. The clause, titled "Arbitration," provides:

> Any dispute arising under this Agreement shall be settled by arbitration in London, England, in accordance with the English Arbitration Act 1996 and any amendments thereto, English law and practice to apply.

Titan succeeded in removing the M/V Cape Flattery from the reef and eliminating the threat of oil discharge. At some point in the M/V Cape Flattery's grounding or removal, however, serious damage was inflicted on the reef. Cape Flattery is liable to the United States government for all damage to natural resources resulting from the grounding. On August 8, 2008, the government informed Cape Flattery that it would likely be liable for damages in excess of $15 million. On October 24, 2008, Cape Flattery filed a complaint in the federal district court for the District of Hawai'i against Titan, seeking indemnity and/or contribution based on the damage Titan allegedly caused through gross negligence in removing the M/V Cape Flattery from the reef. The complaint also sought to enjoin Titan from requesting arbitration. On December 17, 2008, Titan filed a motion to compel arbitration based on the arbitration clause in the Agreement.

On March 19, 2009, after several rounds of briefing and a hearing, the district court denied the motion. The court first rejected Titan's argument that English law governed the arbitrability of the dispute. The court concluded that under Mitsubishi Motors Corp. v. Soler Chrysler-Plymouth, Inc., 473 U.S. 614, 626 (1985), federal arbitrability law applies to determine arbitrability. The court noted the legal uncertainty concerning whether federal arbitrability law allows parties to agree to apply non-federal arbitrability law. It concluded that even if parties are allowed to contract out of federal arbitrability law, the parties in this case had not done so. The district court then concluded that under federal arbitrability law, the current dispute did not "aris[e] under" the Agreement. It first concluded that under our [9th Circuit precedent,] the "arising under" language in the Agreement signifies a narrow arbitration agreement. Under these cases, claims that relate "only peripherally" to the Agreement are not arbitrable. The district court then held that because Titan's duty to prevent foreseeable damage to the coral reef is based on a federal statute and is thus "separate from and above and beyond Defendant's duties under the Agreement," Cape Flattery's tort claims against Titan are not arbitrable. . . .

DISCUSSION

Titan argues that the district court erred in deciding that federal arbitrability law applies, and in its application of that law. We address Titan's arguments in turn.

A. Choice of Arbitrability Law

The first issue is what law applies to determine the arbitrability of the dispute. Titan argues that the Agreement's provision that "[a]ny dispute arising under this

Agreement shall be settled by arbitration in London, England, in accordance with the English Arbitration Act 1996 and any amendments thereto, English law and practice to apply" constitutes an agreement that English law applies to determine the arbitrability of a dispute. Cape Flattery argues that parties cannot contract out of federal arbitrability law, and that even if they can, the parties did not do so in the Agreement.

The Federal Arbitration Act ("FAA"), 9 U.S.C. §1 et seq., creates "a body of federal substantive law of arbitrability, applicable to any arbitration agreement within the coverage of the Act." Moses H. Cone Mem'l Hosp. v. Mercury Const. Corp., 460 U.S. 1, 24 (1983). Neither the Supreme Court nor this court has decided whether federal arbitrability law allows contracting parties to agree to apply a non-federal law of arbitrability to interpret a given arbitration agreement. If the parties can agree to apply a non-federal arbitrability law, it is also undecided how courts should determine whether the parties have so agreed.

1. Parties' Power to Agree to Non-Federal Arbitrability Law

In defending their respective positions regarding the power of contracting parties to agree to a non-federal arbitrability law, Cape Flattery and Titan rely on different Supreme Court decisions. Cape Flattery relies on *Mitsubishi Motors.* Mitsubishi and Soler entered into a sales agreement that included the following arbitration clause: "All disputes, controversies or differences which may arise between [Mitsubishi] and [Soler] out of or in relation to . . . this Agreement or for the breach thereof, shall be finally settled by arbitration in Japan in accordance with the rules and regulations of the Japan Commercial Arbitration Association." When a dispute arose, Soler sued Mitsubishi alleging, among other things, violations of the Sherman Act. In determining whether the dispute was arbitrable, the Supreme Court stated: "[T]he first task of a court asked to compel arbitration of a dispute is to determine whether the parties agreed to arbitrate that dispute. The court is to make this determination by applying the 'federal substantive law of arbitrability, applicable to any arbitration agreement within the coverage of the [FAA].'" Id. at 626 (quoting *Moses H. Cone,* 460 U.S. at 24).

Cape Flattery argues that because *Mitsubishi* does not suggest any exception to the application of federal arbitrability law, courts should always apply federal arbitrability law to determine the arbitrability of a given dispute. It notes that district courts, including the district court in this case, have suggested, without directly holding, that federal arbitrability law may apply despite an agreement to apply non-federal arbitrability law.

Titan does not contest that federal arbitrability law applies generally, but argues that federal arbitrability law requires courts to enforce contracting parties' agreement to apply non-federal arbitrability law. Titan relies primarily on Volt Information Sciences, Inc. v. Board of Trustees, 489 U.S. 468 (1989). In *Volt,* the parties agreed to arbitrate any disputes pursuant to the arbitration rules in the California Arbitration Act ("CAA"). The question before the Court was whether the FAA preempts the CAA and requires that, in disputes subject to the FAA, federal rules of arbitration apply. The Court noted that the FAA preempts state laws that render arbitration agreements entirely unenforceable. It held, however, that the FAA does not mandate certain rules of arbitration. "There is no federal policy favoring arbitration under a certain set of procedural rules; the federal policy is simply to ensure the enforceability, according to their terms, of private agreements to arbitrate." *Volt*, 489 U.S. 476, 109 S. Ct. 1248. Titan argues that just as federal law will enforce an agreement to arbitrate pursuant to non-federal rules of arbitration, federal law should enforce an agreement to determine arbitrability based on non-federal arbitrability law.

We agree with Titan that, based on *Volt,* contracting parties have the power to agree to apply non-federal arbitrability law. The Court stated in *Mitsubishi* that courts should determine arbitrability "by applying the federal substantive law of arbitrability, applicable to any arbitration agreement within the coverage of the Act." *Mitsubishi,* 473 U.S. at 626 (citation and internal quotation marks omitted). But neither party in *Mitsubishi* argued that anything other than federal arbitrability law applied to the dispute. Thus, although *Mitsubishi* states that federal arbitrability law applies to disputes under the FAA, it does not address whether federal arbitrability law allows the parties to agree to a non-federal arbitrability law. *Volt*'s statement that the federal policy is "to ensure the enforceability, according to their terms, of private agreements to arbitrate," strongly suggests that courts should respect contracting parties' agreement to be governed by non-federal arbitrability law. . . .

We therefore hold that courts should enforce contracting parties' agreement to have arbitrability governed by non-federal arbitrability law.

2. *Parties' Choice of Arbitrability Law*

The more difficult question is how courts should decide whether the parties have agreed to apply non-federal arbitrability law. The general rule in interpreting arbitration agreements is that courts "should apply ordinary state-law principles that govern the formation of contracts." First Options of Chicago, Inc. v. Kaplan, 514 U.S. 938, 944 (1995). The general rule "would require the court to see whether the parties objectively revealed an intent to" apply non-federal arbitrability law. If we were to apply the general rule in this case, it may well be that English law would apply to determine arbitrability.

There are, however, some situations concerning the determination of arbitrability in which courts require a higher showing of intent. In *Kaplan,* the Supreme Court held that courts should be cautious in determining whether the parties have agreed to arbitrate arbitrability. The Court held that "[c]ourts should not assume that the parties agreed to arbitrate arbitrability unless there is clear and unmistakable evidence that they did so." Under *Kaplan,* the usual presumption that exists in favor of the arbitrability of merits-based disputes is replaced by a presumption *against* the arbitrability of arbitrability. The Court reasoned that the question of whether a given merits-based dispute is arbitrable arises when the parties have a contract that provides for arbitration of some issues. In such circumstances, the parties likely gave at least some thought to the scope of arbitration. And, given the law's permissive policies in respect to arbitration, one can understand why the law would insist upon clarity before concluding that the parties did *not* want to arbitrate a related matter. On the other hand, the [question of] "who (primarily) should decide arbitrability" . . . is rather arcane. A party often might not focus upon that question. . . . And, given the principle that a party can be forced to arbitrate only those issues it specifically has agreed to submit to arbitration, one can understand why courts might hesitate to interpret silence or ambiguity on the "who should decide arbitrability" point as giving the arbitrators that power, for doing so might too often force unwilling parties to arbitrate a matter they reasonably would have thought a judge, not an arbitrator, would decide. . . .

Like the question of who should decide arbitrability, the question of what law governs arbitrability is "rather arcane." In negotiating an agreement, parties are just as unlikely to give thought to the applicable arbitrability law as they are to give thought to the person determining arbitrability. Thus, if courts were to interpret silence or ambiguity concerning the applicable arbitrability law as providing for a non-federal arbitrability law, parties could be subjected to a foreign arbitrability law when they reasonably thought that federal arbitrability law would apply. We therefore conclude, following *Kaplan,* that courts should apply federal arbitrability law absent "clear and unmistakable evidence" that the parties agreed to apply non-federal arbitrability law.

In this case, there is no clear and unmistakable evidence that the parties agreed to apply English arbitrability law. The arbitration provision states that "[a]ny dispute arising under this Agreement shall be settled by arbitration in London, England, in accordance with the English Arbitration Act 1996 and any amendments thereto, English law and practice to apply." Under this provision, English arbitration law clearly applies to disputes that are subject to arbitration, and English law and practice are to be applied by the arbitrator. However, the agreement is ambiguous concerning whether English law also applies to determine whether a given dispute is arbitrable in the first place. Faced with such ambiguity, we conclude that federal law applies to determine arbitrability.

B. Federal Arbitrability Law

Applying federal arbitrability law, we conclude that this case is not arbitrable. The Agreement provides for arbitration of "[a]ny dispute arising under this Agreement." Our interpretation of the phrase "arising under" is controlled by [prior 9th Circuit decisions in which] we held that the phrase "arising under" in an arbitration agreement should be interpreted narrowly. . . .

Applying [9th Circuit precedent], we have no difficulty concluding that the present dispute is not arbitrable. . . . The present dispute does not turn on an interpretation of any clause in the contract. As the district court noted, "[t]he parties point to no Agreement provision that Defendant allegedly breached—the Agreement is silent regarding what tow lines Defendant must use, how precisely Defendant must salve the Vessel, and whether Defendant must take precautions to prevent harm to the coral reef." Nor does the dispute turn on Titan's performance under the contract. Instead the dispute involves a tort claim based on Hawaii and maritime tort law, incorporated as part of the Oil Pollution Act of 1990, and limited by that federal statute to grossly negligent acts.

We therefore conclude that under the narrow interpretation of "arising under" . . . the present dispute is not arbitrable.

Problem 11-3. ***Choice of Law Clause***

In the *DirecTV* decision, Justice Breyer suggested that parties might properly contract for the law of Tibet to govern the interpretation of their contract. In light of *DirecTV* and *Cape Flattery*, draft a choice of law provision to be included in a broader arbitration provision that would have the laws of Tibet govern all potential questions that may arise.

Exercise 11-4. ***Analyzing a Complete Arbitration Agreement***

Go online and find an example of an actual, complete arbitration agreement. Number its provisions and annotate each, with an explanation of the function each of the provisions serves.

If it does not specifically contain a provision regarding governing law, can you identify which law(s) would govern?

Exercise 11-5. ***Full Arbitration Agreement***

Imagine that you and one of your classmates share an apartment and that you have mutually decided to enter a pre-dispute arbitration clause, with the thought that disputes related to your shared living arrangement will be resolved through binding arbitration. (Neither of you is aware of any existing disputes, but it is early in the semester, and you are not naïve enough to believe that no issues could ever arise.) Negotiate the terms of a complete, binding arbitration agreement with your classmate.

B. ARBITRAL AWARDS

1. Drafting Arbitration Awards

Throughout your studies in law school, you have become accustomed to reading judicial opinions in which the judge, or panel of judges, provides not only an outcome ("the Plaintiff wins" or "Affirmed"), but also the outcome's *explanation.* At least two policy interests support this as a default practice. First, litigants have some interest in understanding why they won (or perhaps even more importantly, why they lost, since the articulation of the ruling's reasoning may be critical to form the basis of an appeal). Second, the public at large has an interest in having courts articulate their reasoning, as this supports the development of the common law.

To what extent do these same principles apply in arbitration? Arbitration has more limited opportunities for appeal.[3] Arbitration does not necessarily serve the same law-articulation function as courts because their awards have little to no precedential value. Arbitrators also have strict deadlines, often thirty days, to issue an award. Further, the parties to the arbitration must pay the costs associated with the arbitration, which can multiply significantly if the arbitrator(s) must write a detailed set of findings.[4] Perhaps as a result of these differences, arbitrators in the United States have no default legal presumption requiring them to explain their reasoning.[5] See United Steelworkers v. Enterprise Wheel & Car Corp., 363 U.S. 593 (1960) ("Arbitrators have no obligation to the court to give their reasons for an award."). But note that this presumption is not shared in all countries. See, e.g., UK Public General Acts Arbitration Act (1996) Section 52 ("The award must contain reasons.").

Three basic options present themselves regarding the question of the logic associated with the arbitrator's award: (1) a "standard" award, in which the arbitrator simply announces the result, (2) a "reasoned" award, and (3) a set of "findings of fact and conclusions of law." As you might imagine, however, parties are free to provide whatever they wish in their arbitration agreements regarding the form of the arbitral award. Not every arbitration provider uses the same language to describe the options for award form. For example, baseline rules from JAMS Rule 24(h) provide that "[t]he Award shall consist of a written statement signed by the Arbitrator regarding the disposition of each claim and the relief, if any, as to each claim. Unless all Parties agree otherwise, the Award shall also contain a concise written statement of the reasons for the Award." And in the FINRA context, the Rules similarly default against any level of reasoning, but use different phraseology. See FINRA Rule 12904(g) ("An 'explained decision' is a fact-based award stating the general reason(s) for the arbitrators' decision. Inclusion of legal

3. As Professor Blankley has written, "Parties who wish for the courts to have a more meaningful judicial review of their [arbitral] award will invariably have to require the arbitrator to actually provide a written, reasoned award." Kristen Blankley, Be More Specific! Can Writing a Detailed Arbitration Agreement Expand Judicial Review Under the Federal Arbitration Act? 2 Seton Hall Cir. Rev. 391 (2005).

4. Deborah Rothman, Trends in Arbitration Compensation, 8 Disp. Resol. Mag. (2017). Little concrete information exists about the market for arbitrators and the rates they charge for their services. See Trends in Arbitrator Compensation, DRM 2017 ("A rule of thumb is that the most in-demand arbitrators' rates tend to mirror the rates of the most skilled litigators in their respective jurisdictions.").

5. Although no legal presumption exists, expectations and norms may exist within the industry, based on the type of dispute. For example, standard awards with little to no explanation by the arbitrators are common in securities disputes. John Burritt McArthur, Parties Usually Benefit from Reasoned Awards, Not Standard Awards, 38 Alt. High Cost Litig. 44 (2022). Complex commercial arbitration awards may span dozens of pages to over a hundred pages.

authorities and damage calculations is not required . . . [An explained decision is required] only when all parties jointly request [it]").

Parties often elect to require that the arbitrator provide a "reasoned award," but this term is not self-defining, leading to the prospect of post-arbitration disputes. If an arbitrator provided an award with less reasoning than the losing party had hoped for, would the form of the award create a basis for challenging the award under FAA §10? In ARCH Dev. Corp. v. Biomet, Inc., 02 C 9013, 2003 WL 21697742 (N.D. Ill. July 30, 2003), the parties had entered a contract providing for arbitration under the American Arbitration Association rules. After the arbitrator issued an award in an ensuing intellectual property licensing dispute involving artificial knees, Biomet (the losing party) sought to have it vacated, in part on the grounds that the award was not "reasoned," as required under the relevant AAA rules. Rejecting this argument, the court wrote

> [T]he AAA scheduling form, to which Biomet points as evidence of the agreement as to a reasoned award, provides three award alternatives: "Standard Award," "Reasoned Award," and "Findings of fact and conclusions of law." This is the order in which the alternatives are listed, and I interpret this arrangement to be a spectrum of increasingly reasoned awards. In other words, "Standard Award" is the option least involving reasoning whereas "Findings of fact and conclusions of law" is the option most involving reasoning. Logically, a "Reasoned Award" is therefore something short of findings and conclusions but more than a simple result. The question then becomes whether the Arbitration Award falls within this somewhat vague range. Here, the Arbitrator did more than simply state who wins and who loses in the form of a "bare" award. He cited the relevant contractual provisions and definitions. He explained that the License Agreement has not terminated because it "was not restricted to a three-plane knee, which Biomet was not selling" and thus plainly rejected Biomet's main argument. Finally, he listed eight findings and conclusions that he made. In sum, it cannot be said that the September Award was devoid of explanation and thus not a reasoned award. Accordingly, I find that the Arbitrator has not exceeded his authority on this basis.

Id. at *4 (N.D. Ill. July 30, 2003). See also Cat Charter, LLC v. Schurtenberger, 646 F.3d 836 (11th Cir. 2011) (a "reasoned" award is an award that is provided with or marked by the detailed listing or mention of expressions or statements offered as a justification of an act—the "act" here being, of course, the decision of the Panel."); Tully Const. Co./A.J. Pegno Const. Co., J.V. v. Canam Steel Corp., 13 CIV. 3037 PGG, 2015 WL 906128 (S.D.N.Y. Mar. 2, 2015) (remanding to the arbitrator for clarification of an award that included multiple pages of "financial breakdown," indicating the prevailing party as to each of the relevant costs and claims, on the grounds that the award did not constitute a "reasoned award"). Might this question be answered differently under state law and the Uniform Arbitration Act? Dept. of Health & Hum. Serv. V. Neb. Assoc. of Pub. Employees, 984 N.W.2d 103 (Neb. 2023) (holding that an arbitrator did not exceed his authority when he issued a reasoned award, rather than findings of facts and conclusions of law, as required by the contract).

Problem 11-6. *Form of Award*

Your client is a small business owner specializing in custom-built tandem bicycles. Most of her employees are highly skilled mechanics, and her business uses a proprietary process during assembly that makes the bikes popular among high-end customers demanding the most exacting performance. Business is expanding, and your client has raised the possibility of adding an arbitration clause into employees' contracts as they are renewed next year. As you draft a clause for her consideration, would you include a provision requiring the arbitrator to provide a reasoned opinion? More? Less? Why? Is there a client for whom you would provide the opposite advice about reasoned opinions?

Problem 11-7. *Reviewing Reasoned Awards*

Look online for an arbitrator's award in a recent case. Why do you think the parties opted for the award to be reasoned? Public?

2. Enforcing Arbitral Awards

In the previous chapter, we explored how parties' agreements to arbitrate are given effect, at least in most cases. As you now know, parties who agree to use arbitration to resolve their disputes will usually be bound to use arbitration to resolve those disputes, unless all of the parties involved in that arbitration agreement mutually consent either to some voluntary resolution of the dispute (a settlement) or to some other dispute resolution process (thereby revising the arbitration agreement). Agreements to arbitrate would hold more modest attraction if they did not compel disputants to arbitrate disputes.

Similarly, parties would be less interested in using arbitration as a dispute resolution process if the arbitrator's final decision or award were not given effect. If the arbitrator's award were merely advisory, for example, then arbitration would be relegated to the position of an adjunct to consensual dispute resolution processes. Although such processes can be of great value, parties to arbitration agreements presumably want the arbitration to provide finality. Therefore, parties need some ability to enforce an arbitrator's award. In this Section, we survey the mechanisms available for such enforcement.

In typical litigation, courts retain jurisdiction over a dispute in the sense that failure to comply with a court's order or judgment leads clearly to an enforcement mechanism. As you have seen earlier in this book, arbitrators have broad powers in how an arbitration is conducted. Once they issue an award, however, most arbitration processes treat the arbitrator as *functus officio* (having performed her or his office) and therefore done with the task at hand. In many cases, parties then simply comply with the arbitrator's award—even when it is adverse to the outcome they sought—but this is certainly, in part, at least, because they know that mechanisms exist by which they can be forced to comply with the arbitration's outcome. In some cases, however, the question of enforcement becomes relevant.

In the simplest (somewhat overstated) terms, arbitrator's awards are enforced through roughly the same mechanisms by which courts' orders are enforced. This requires, though, the additional step of having the arbitrator's award converted into a judgment, such that it triggers existing judicial enforcement mechanisms.

Many standard form arbitration agreements include a clause designed to create contract-based consent to having the arbitrator's award enforced through the courts. For example, the American Arbitration Association's standard clause for commercial arbitration includes the clause, ". . . and judgment on the award rendered by the arbitrator(s) may be entered in any court having jurisdiction thereof." This language aims to preclude a party from subsequently arguing against the power of a court being used to enforce an arbitral award, but it leaves open the question of which courts have proper jurisdiction.

The Federal Arbitration Act specifically provides for enforcement, allowing:

> any party to the arbitration [to] apply to the court so specified for an order confirming the award, and thereupon the court must grant such an order unless the award is vacated, modified, or corrected as prescribed in [FAA §§10 and 11]. If no court is specified in the agreement of the parties, then such application may be made to the United States court in and for the district within which such award was made. Notice of the application shall be served upon the adverse party, and thereupon the court shall have jurisdiction of such party as though he had appeared generally in the proceeding.

FAA §9. It then provides for the entry of judgment pursuant to an arbitral award and concludes that a "judgment so entered shall have the same force and effect, in all respects, as, and be subject to all the provisions of law relating to, a judgment in an action; and it may be enforced as if it had been rendered in an action in the court in which it is entered." FAA §13.

Generally speaking, states have similar mechanisms for enforcing arbitration awards in state courts. Forty-nine states adopted variants on the Uniform Arbitration Act, and 17 have adopted the Revised Uniform Arbitration Act, both of which make allowances for confirming and enforcing arbitration awards.

Revised Uniform Arbitration Act (2000)

SECTION 22. Confirmation of Award.

After a party to an arbitration proceeding receives notice of an award, the party may make a [motion] to the court for an order confirming the award at which time the court shall issue a confirming order unless the award is modified or corrected [or] vacated. . .

SECTION 25. Judgment on Award. . .

(a) Upon granting an order confirming, vacating without directing a rehearing, modifying, or correcting an award, the court shall enter a judgment in conformity therewith. The judgment may be recorded, docketed, and enforced as any other judgment in a civil action.

Between the Federal Arbitration Act and the various state acts allowing for the enforcement of arbitral awards, the picture is relatively straightforward for domestic cases. But what if one or more of the parties is not from the United States? What if the dispute arose outside of the United States? What if the arbitration took place outside of the United States? As you likely learned in your Civil Procedure course, litigation involving multi-national parties or disputes raises a number of complicated questions. The international enforcement landscape for arbitration is, in many ways, actually simpler than the landscape for litigation.

Recognizing the increasing frequency of international commercial exchanges (and the corresponding increase in frequency of international commercial disputes), many nations joined in the New York Convention of 1958. Among the important impacts of the New York Convention is the ease with which arbitral awards can be enforced across borders.

United Nations Convention on the Recognition and Enforcement of Foreign Arbitral Awards

"The New York Convention" 330 U.N.T.S (1958), ratified U.S. 1970

Article II

1. Each Contracting State shall recognize an agreement in writing under which the parties undertake to submit to arbitration all or any differences which have arisen or which may arise between them in respect of a defined legal relationship, whether contractual or not, concerning a subject matter capable of settlement by arbitration

2. The term "agreement in writing" shall include an arbitral clause in a contract or an arbitration agreement, signed by the parties or contained in an exchange of letters or telegrams.

3. The court of a Contracting State, when seized of an action in a matter in respect of which the parties have made an agreement within the meaning of this article, shall, at the request of one of the parties, refer the parties to arbitration, unless it

United States of America

The United States of America will apply the Convention, on the basis of reciprocity, to the recognition and enforcement of only those awards made in the territory of another Contracting State. The United States of America will apply the Convention only to differences arising out of legal relationships, whether contractual or not, which are considered as commercial under the national law of the United States.

finds that the said agreement is null and void, inoperative or incapable of being performed.

Article III

Each Contracting State shall recognize arbitral awards as binding and enforce them in accordance with the rules of procedure of the territory where the award is relied upon, under the conditions laid down in the following articles. There shall not be imposed substantially more onerous conditions or higher fees or charges on the recognition or enforcement of arbitral awards to which this Convention applies than are imposed on the recognition or enforcement of domestic arbitral awards.

More than 170 countries have now signed on to the New York Convention, some as recently as January 2023 (Timor-Leste), creating a global enforcement framework. As you may have learned in a course on International Law, when countries contemplate the adoption of a treaty, they sometimes include reservations, declarations, and other statements that amount to caveats or otherwise seek to limit the basic terms of the treaty to which they otherwise agree. Beside are some examples of the reservations and statements from countries that have adopted the New York Convention.

Norway

[The Government of Norway] will apply the Convention only to the recognition and enforcement of awards made in the territory of one of the Contracting States[, and] will not apply the Convention to differences where the subject matter of the proceedings is immovable property situated in Norway, or a right in or to such property.

Canada

The Government of Canada declares that it will apply the Convention only to differences arising out of legal relationships, whether contractual or not, which are considered as commercial under the laws of Canada, except in the case of the Province of Quebec where the law does not provide for such limitation.

Kuwait

The State of Kuwait will apply the Convention to the recognition and enforcement of awards made only in the territory of another Contracting State. It is understood that the accession of the State of Kuwait to the Convention on the Recognition and Enforcement of Foreign Arbitral Awards, done at New York, on the 10th of June 1958, does not mean in any way recognition of Israel or entering with it into relations governed by the Convention thereto acceded by the State of Kuwait.

3. Challenges to Awards and Appeals

Just as litigants are sometimes disappointed with a judicial decision, parties to an arbitration are sometimes disappointed with an arbitrator's decision. What opportunities do parties have to challenge the arbitrator's award? By this point, following this book's treatment of arbitration, you should have the instinct to answer, "It depends what the parties' arbitration agreement says on this topic." And to some extent, that answer is exactly correct. But as you will see, there are limits to what parties can contractually provide by way of review of arbitral decisions.

Parties may contractually create an arbitration process in which one or more other *arbitrators* are empowered to hear appeals challenging the first arbitrator's decisions. For example, the American Arbitration Association provides an optional set of appellate procedures parties can invoke in their arbitration agreements. These include precisely the sorts of things you would imagine—procedures for giving notice of an appeal, jurisdiction for appeals, the makeup of appellate tribunals, briefing and argument timelines, etc. But, importantly, these appellate procedures bring the appeal to one or more other *arbitrators*. Once any available appeals are exhausted, the procedures described in the section immediately above come into force and the courts generally become involved only with enforcement questions. In practice, however, appeals to other arbitrators are rare.

Can parties bring appeals or challenges before a court? Yes, but the grounds upon which a court can vacate an arbitrator's award are specific and narrow. See FAA §10.

> **Problem 11-8.** ***Enforcing an Award?***
>
> Assume your client recently prevailed in an arbitration hearing in your jurisdiction, and under the terms of the arbitrator's award, is entitled to recover $200,000 from her former business partner. Draft the motion(s) you must file on behalf of your client and/or describe the next steps you must take in order to recover the funds from the losing party, in the event he refuses to pay.

Federal Arbitration Act §10

9 U.S.C. §10 (1925)

In any of the following cases the United States court in and for the district wherein the award was made may make an order vacating the award upon the application of any party to the arbitration—

(1) where the award was procured by corruption, fraud, or undue means;

(2) where there was evident partiality or corruption in the arbitrators, or either of them;

(3) where the arbitrators were guilty of misconduct in refusing to postpone the hearing, upon sufficient cause shown, or in refusing to hear evidence pertinent and material to the controversy; or of any other misbehavior by which the rights of any party have been prejudiced; or

(4) where the arbitrators exceeded their powers, or so imperfectly executed them that a mutual, final, and definite award upon the subject matter submitted was not made.

Although the FAA lists multiple grounds upon which courts may vacate arbitral awards, each of these four has been consistently interpreted narrowly. Moreover, you should note that nowhere in this list of four is "mistake of law" or "erroneous interpretation of the facts." FAA §10 concerns itself principally with whether there were intolerable flaws in the process by which the arbitration was conducted. In many cases, therefore, courts considering a motion under FAA §10 will not even delve into the factual allegations of a case. Even when they do, as illustrated in the *Industrial Steel Construction, Inc.* case immediately below, courts are far more reluctant to second-guess arbitrators than they would be in reviewing a trial court's decisions during the course of litigation.

INDUSTRIAL STEEL CONSTR., INC. v. LUNDA CONSTR. CO.

33 F.4th 1038 (8th Cir. 2022)

This case arises out of a contract related to the construction of a bridge across the Mississippi River between Bettendorf, Iowa, and Moline, Illinois. In 2017, the Iowa Department of Transportation (IADOT) hired Lunda as the general contractor for the project. Lunda then contracted with Industrial Steel Construction, Inc. (ISC) to fabricate structural steel for the bridge. In August 2020, ISC filed suit against Lunda alleging breach of contract, promissory estoppel, unjust enrichment, quantum meruit, and negligent misrepresentation. The district court compelled the parties to arbitration pursuant to their contract and stayed the court proceedings. The arbitrator held a hearing and issued a final award. In the final award, the arbitrator found no merit to ISC's claims. He found that Lunda was entitled to reimbursement for the costs of repairing ISC's defective work and awarded Lunda $84,977.19 for those repair costs. The arbitrator also awarded Lunda its attorney's fees and expert costs.

Lunda then moved to reopen proceedings before the district court and sought confirmation of the final award. ISC moved to vacate in part or modify the award, challenging the arbitrator's authority to award Lunda attorney's fees and expert costs. The district court agreed with ISC that the arbitrator exceeded his authority in awarding fees and expert costs to Lunda, vacated that portion of the award, and confirmed the rest. Lunda timely filed this appeal.

In their contract, Lunda and ISC agreed that disputes arising between them would be resolved in arbitration and that the American Arbitration Association (AAA) Construction Industry Rules would "govern all procedural matters not specified" in the contract. Regarding attorney's fees, the contract provided, "In the event ISC is required to bring an action to recover any amount owed to it, ISC shall be entitled to recover all costs, including reasonable attorneys' fees." The word "reasonable" in this provision is added in red handwritten text to the typed document and initialed. The paragraph addressing Lunda's right to seek damages from ISC provides that ISC "shall be liable for incidental and consequential damages (including attorney's fees and liquidated damages) resulting from delays caused solely by Seller in delivery, from the breach of any warranties, from defective goods and from any other breach of the term and conditions." The stricken and underlined portions appear in a different font color, and the bottom of the page bears two sets of initials.

The AAA Construction Industry Rules also speak to the issue of fees and costs. Rule 48(d)(ii) provides that the "award of the arbitrator may include . . . an award of attorneys' fees if all parties have requested such an award or it is authorized by law or their arbitration agreement." . . .

In their filings and presentations to the arbitrator, both Lunda and ISC requested attorney's fees and costs should they prevail. ISC pointed out that while the parties' contract explicitly stated that ISC could recover attorney's fees, the parties had agreed to strike the provision that would have allowed Lunda to recover fees. Lunda took the position that the contract did not directly address the issue of Lunda's attorney's fees but entitled it to generalized damages, and the arbitrator could award fees and costs under the AAA Construction Industry Rules. . . .

In seeking vacatur of the attorney's fee and expert costs, ISC relies on Section 10(a)(4). . . . Because the parties bargained for the arbitrator's construction of their agreement, an arbitral decision even arguably construing or applying the contract must stand, regardless of a court's view of its (de)merits. Therefore, the "sole question" for the court is "whether the arbitrator (even arguably) interpreted the parties' contract, not whether he got its meaning right or wrong." An arbitrator does not "exceed his powers" by making an error of law or fact, even a serious one.

Here, the arbitrator at least arguably construed the parties' agreement in awarding attorney's fees and expert costs to Lunda. The final award expressly relies on the AAA Construction Industry Rules in awarding attorney's fees and expert costs to Lunda, stating, "[T]he Arbitrator has reviewed R-48 of the Construction Industry Rules of the AAA and finds that an award of attorney's fees and costs is appropriate in this matter." The parties' agreement provided that those rules would govern any procedural matters not otherwise specified in the contract. And the mention of ISC's liability for Lunda's attorney's fees was stricken from the parties' agreement. Thus, we can conclude that the arbitrator at least arguably construed the agreement not to address Lunda's fees, determined liability for fees to be a "procedural matter not specified" in the agreement, and applied the Construction Industry Rules to fill in the gap, as provided by the contract.

ISC disagrees with the arbitrator's conclusion, but whether the arbitrator's interpretation is correct is not a question before this court. "[C]onvincing a court of an arbitrator's error—even his grave error—is not enough. . . . The potential for those mistakes is the price of agreeing to arbitration." Oxford Health, 569 U.S. 564, 572-73 (2013). ICS may wish that the arbitrator had explained his reasoning in greater detail, but it does not offer any basis to conclude that "the arbitrator based his decision on some body of thought, or feeling, or policy, or law that is outside the contract." Because there is a basis for this court to infer that the arbitrator reached his decision to award Lunda attorney's fees and expert costs by construing the parties' agreement, we must affirm the final award and may not examine the accuracy of the arbitrator's decision. . . .

We therefore vacate the judgment of the district court and remand with instructions to confirm the final award in full.

The question for courts reviewing arbitrators' decisions is typically not whether the courts would have decided things the same way as the arbitrator. Instead, the question is whether the courts are satisfied that the arbitrator was performing the job for which she or he was hired by the parties. In the *Eastern Associated Coal* case below, you will see the Supreme Court's articulation of the breadth of the court's deference to arbitrators' interpretation of the parties' agreements.

Recall from when this case was introduced in Chapter 9 that Eastern Associated Coal had dismissed James Smith, a truck driver, for failing a drug test. An arbitrator overturned this dismissal and reinstated Smith, ruling that the company did not have "just cause" (as required by the collective bargaining contract) for the dismissal. Later, Smith failed a second drug test, and the company again sought to dismiss him. In arbitration, Smith was again reinstated, this time with a number of penalties, including an undated letter of resignation, in the event Smith failed a third drug test. The employer sought to challenge the arbitrator's ruling as being contrary to public policy, and therefore unenforceable.

❖ EASTERN ASSOCIATED COAL CORP. v. UNITED MINE WORKERS OF AMERICA

531 U.S. 57 (2000)

Eastern claims that considerations of public policy make the arbitration award unenforceable. In considering this claim, we must assume that the collective-bargaining agreement itself calls for Smith's reinstatement. That is because both employer and union have granted to the arbitrator the authority to interpret the meaning of their contract's language, including such words as "just cause." See Steelworkers v. Enterprise Wheel & Car Corp., 363 U.S. 593, 599 (1960). They have "bargained for" the "arbitrator's construction" of their agreement. And courts will set aside the arbitrator's interpretation of what their agreement means only in rare instances. Of course, an arbitrator's award "must draw its essence from the contract and cannot simply reflect the arbitrator's own notions of industrial justice." Paperworkers v. Misco, 484 U.S. 29, 38 (1987). "But as long as [an honest] arbitrator is even arguably construing or applying the contract and acting within the scope of his authority," the fact that "a court is convinced he committed serious error does not suffice to overturn his decision." Eastern does not claim here that the arbitrator acted outside the scope of his contractually delegated authority. Hence we must treat the arbitrator's award as if it represented an agreement between Eastern and the union as to the proper meaning of the contract's words "just cause." For present purposes, the award is not distinguishable from the contractual agreement.

We must then decide whether a contractual reinstatement requirement would fall within the legal exception that makes unenforceable "a collective-bargaining agreement that is contrary to public policy." W.R. Grace & Co. v. Rubber Workers, 461 U.S. 757, 766 (1983). The Court has made clear that any such public policy must be "explicit," "well defined," and "dominant." It must be "ascertained 'by reference to the laws and legal precedents and not from general considerations of supposed public interests.'" And, of course, the question to be answered is not whether Smith's drug use itself violates public policy, but whether the agreement to reinstate him does so. To put the question more specifically, does a contractual agreement to reinstate Smith with specified conditions, run contrary to an explicit, well defined, and dominant public policy, as ascertained by reference to positive law and not from general considerations of supposed public interests? . . .

[T]he public policy exception is narrow and must satisfy the principles set forth in *W.R. Grace* and *Misco.* Moreover, in a case like the one before us, where two political branches have created a detailed regulatory regime in a specific field, courts should approach with particular caution pleas to divine further public policy in that area.

Eastern asserts that a public policy against reinstatement of workers who use drugs can be discerned from an examination of that regulatory regime, which consists of the Omnibus Transportation Employee Testing Act of 1991 and DOT's implementing regulations. The Testing Act embodies a congressional finding that "the greatest efforts must be expended to eliminate the . . . use of illegal drugs, whether on or off duty, by those individuals who are involved in [certain safety-sensitive positions, including] the operation of . . . trucks." It adds that "increased testing" is the "most effective deterrent" to "use of illegal drugs." It requires the Secretary of Transportation to promulgate regulations requiring "testing of operators of commercial motor vehicles for the use of a controlled substance." It mandates suspension of those operators who have driven a commercial motor vehicle while under the influence of drugs. And DOT's implementing regulations set forth sanctions applicable to those who test positive for illegal drugs.

In Eastern's view, these provisions embody a strong public policy against drug use by transportation workers in safety sensitive positions and in favor of random drug testing in order to detect that use. Eastern argues that reinstatement of a driver who has twice failed random drug tests would undermine that policy—to the point where a judge must set aside an employer-union agreement requiring reinstatement.

Eastern's argument, however, loses much of its force when one considers further provisions of the Act that make clear that the Act's remedial aims are complex. The Act says that "rehabilitation is a critical component of any testing program," that rehabilitation "should be made available to individuals, as appropriate," and that DOT must promulgate regulations for "rehabilitation programs." The DOT regulations specifically state that a driver who has tested positive for drugs cannot return to a safety-sensitive position until (1) the driver has been evaluated by a "substance abuse professional" to determine if treatment is needed; (2) the substance-abuse professional has certified that the driver has followed any rehabilitation program prescribed; and (3) the driver has passed a return-to-duty drug test. In addition, (4) the driver must be subject to at least six random drug tests during the first year after returning to the job. Neither the Act nor the regulations forbid an employer to reinstate in a safety-sensitive position an employee who fails a random drug test once or twice. The congressional and regulatory directives require only that the above-stated prerequisites to reinstatement be met.

Moreover, when promulgating these regulations, DOT decided not to require employers either to provide rehabilitation or to "hold a job open for a driver" who has tested positive, on the basis that such decisions "should be left to management/driver negotiation." That determination reflects basic background labor law principles, which caution against interference with labor management agreements about appropriate employee discipline.

We believe that these expressions of positive law embody several relevant policies. As Eastern points out, these policies include Testing Act policies against drug use by employees in safety-sensitive transportation positions and in favor of drug testing. They also include a Testing Act policy favoring rehabilitation of employees who use drugs. And the relevant statutory and regulatory provisions must be read in light of background labor law policy that favors determination of disciplinary questions through arbitration when chosen as a result of labor-management negotiation.

The award before us is not contrary to these several policies, taken together. The award does not condone Smith's conduct or ignore the risk to public safety that drug use by truck drivers may pose. Rather, the award punishes Smith by suspending him for three months, thereby depriving him of nearly $9,000 in lost wages, it requires him to pay the arbitration costs of both sides; it insists upon further substance-abuse treatment and testing; and it makes clear (by requiring Smith to provide a signed letter of resignation) that one more failed test means discharge.

The award violates no specific provision of any law or regulation. It is consistent with DOT rules requiring completion of substance-abuse treatment before returning to work, for it does not preclude Eastern from assigning Smith to a non-safety-sensitive position until Smith completes the prescribed treatment program. It is consistent with the Testing Act's 1-year and 10-year driving license suspension requirements, for those requirements apply only to drivers who, unlike Smith, actually operated vehicles under the influence of drugs. The award is also consistent with the Act's rehabilitative concerns, for it requires substance abuse treatment and testing before Smith can return to work.

The fact that Smith is a recidivist—that he has failed drug tests twice—is not sufficient to tip the balance in Eastern's favor. The award punishes Smith more severely for his second lapse. And that more severe punishment, which included a 90-day suspension, would have satisfied even a "recidivist" rule that DOT once proposed but did not adopt—a rule that would have punished two failed drug tests, not with discharge, but with a driving suspension of 60 days. Eastern argues that DOT's withdrawal of its proposed rule leaves open the possibility that discharge is the appropriate penalty for repeat offenders. That argument fails, however, because DOT based its withdrawal, not upon a determination that a more severe penalty was needed, but upon a determination to leave in place, as the "only driving prohibition period for a controlled substances violation," the "completion of rehabilitation requirements and a return-to-duty test with a negative result."

Regarding drug use by persons in safety-sensitive positions, then, Congress has enacted a detailed statute. And Congress has delegated to the Secretary of Transportation authority to issue further detailed regulations on that subject. Upon careful consideration, including public notice and comment, the Secretary has done so. Neither Congress nor the Secretary has seen fit to mandate the discharge of a worker who twice tests positive for drugs. We hesitate to infer a public policy in this area that goes beyond the careful and detailed scheme Congress and the Secretary have created.

We recognize that reasonable people can differ as to whether reinstatement or discharge is the more appropriate remedy here. But both employer and union have agreed to entrust this remedial decision to an arbitrator. We cannot find in the Act, the regulations, or any other law or legal precedent an "explicit," "well defined," "dominant" public policy to which the arbitrator's decision "runs contrary." *Misco*; *W.R. Grace*. We conclude that the lower courts correctly rejected Eastern's public policy claim. The judgment of the Court of Appeals [and, therefore, the arbitrator's ruling] is Affirmed.

What if the parties, as they are drafting their arbitration clause, prefer to use arbitration as their initial dispute resolution mechanism, but want any party to the arbitration to have the right to appeal to the courts on bases all of the parties specify? What if, for example, they want courts to be empowered to, on review, overturn an arbitrator's award if that court determines that the arbitrator made a mistake of law? Or if the court determines that the arbitrator's findings of fact are not supported by the evidence presented? The Hall Street Associates v. Mattel case we examined earlier in this book raised these questions before the Supreme Court.

HALL STREET ASSOCIATES, LLC v. MATTEL, INC.

552 U.S. 576 (2008)

[The parties to this case had previously entered an arbitration agreement, providing in part that "[t]he United States District Court for the District of Oregon may enter judgment upon any award, either by confirming the award or by vacating, modifying or correcting the award. The Court shall vacate, modify or correct any award: (i) where the arbitrator's findings of facts are not supported by substantial evidence, or (ii) where the arbitrator's conclusions of law are erroneous."]

The Federal Arbitration Act (FAA or Act), 9 U.S.C. §1 et seq., provides for expedited judicial review to confirm, vacate, or modify arbitration awards. §§9-11 (2000 ed. and Supp. V). The question here is whether statutory grounds for prompt vacatur and modification may be supplemented by contract. We hold that the statutory grounds are exclusive. . . .

Congress enacted the FAA to replace judicial indisposition to arbitration with a "national policy favoring [it] and plac[ing] arbitration agreements on equal footing with all other contracts." Buckeye Check Cashing, Inc. v. Cardegna, 546 U.S. 440, 443 (2006). As for jurisdiction over controversies touching arbitration, the Act does nothing, being "something of an anomaly in the field of federal-court jurisdiction" in bestowing no federal jurisdiction but rather requiring an independent jurisdictional basis. Moses H. Cone Memorial Hospital v. Mercury Constr. Corp., 460 U.S. 1, 25, n.32 (1983); see, e.g., 9 U.S.C. §4 (providing for action by a federal district court "which, save for such [arbitration] agreement, would have jurisdiction under title 28"). But in cases falling within a court's jurisdiction, the Act makes contracts to arbitrate "valid, irrevocable, and enforceable," so long as their subject involves "commerce." §2. And this is so whether an agreement has a broad reach or goes just to one dispute, and whether enforcement be sought in state court or federal. See ibid.; Southland Corp. v. Keating, 465 U.S. 1, 15-16 (1984).

The Act also supplies mechanisms for enforcing arbitration awards: a judicial decree confirming an award, an order vacating it, or an order modifying or correcting it. §§9-11. An application for any of these orders will get streamlined treatment as a motion, obviating the separate contract action that would usually be necessary to enforce or tinker with an arbitral award in court. §6. Under the terms of §9, a court "must" confirm an arbitration award "unless" it is vacated, modified, or corrected "as prescribed" in §§10 and 11. Section 10 lists grounds for vacating an award, while §11 names those for modifying or correcting one. . . .

Hall Street makes two main efforts to show that the grounds set out for vacating or modifying an award are not exclusive, taking the position, first, that expandable judicial review authority has been accepted as the law since Wilko v. Swan, 346 U.S. 427 (1953). This, however, was not what *Wilko* decided, which was that §14 of the Securities Act of 1933 voided any agreement to arbitrate claims of violations of that Act, see id., at 437-438, a holding since overruled by Rodriguez de Quijas v. Shearson/American Express, Inc., 490 U.S. 477, 484 (1989). Although it is true that the Court's discussion includes some language arguably favoring Hall Street's position, arguable is as far as it goes. . . .

Second, Hall Street says that the agreement to review for legal error ought to prevail simply because arbitration is a creature of contract, and the FAA is "motivated, first and foremost, by a congressional desire to enforce agreements into which parties ha[ve] entered." Dean Witter Reynolds Inc. v. Byrd, 470 U.S. 213, 220 (1985). But, again, we think the argument comes up short. Hall Street is certainly right that the FAA lets parties tailor some, even many features of arbitration by contract, including the way arbitrators are chosen, what their qualifications should be, which issues are arbitrable, along with procedure and choice of substantive law. But to rest this case on the general policy of treating arbitration agreements as enforceable as such would be to beg the question, which is whether the FAA has textual features at odds with enforcing a contract to expand judicial review following the arbitration.

To that particular question we think the answer is yes, that the text compels a reading of the §§10 and 11 categories as exclusive. To begin with, even if we assumed §§10 and 11 could be supplemented to some extent, it would stretch basic interpretive principles to expand the stated grounds to the point of evidentiary and legal review generally. Sections 10 and 11, after all, address egregious departures from the parties' agreed-upon arbitration: "corruption," "fraud," "evident partiality," "misconduct," "misbehavior," "exceed[ing] . . . powers," "evident material miscalculation," "evident material mistake," "award[s] upon a matter not submitted"; the only ground with any softer focus is "imperfect[ions]," and a court may correct those only if they go to "[a] matter of form not affecting the merits." Given this emphasis on extreme arbitral conduct, the old rule of ejusdem generis has an implicit lesson to teach here. Under that rule, when a statute sets out a series of specific items ending with a general term, that general term is confined to covering subjects comparable to the specifics it follows. Since a general term included in the text is normally so limited, then surely a statute with no textual hook for expansion cannot authorize contracting parties to supplement review for specific instances of outrageous conduct with review for just any legal error. "Fraud" and a mistake of law are not cut from the same cloth.

That aside, expanding the detailed categories would rub too much against the grain of the §9 language, where provision for judicial confirmation carries no hint of flexibility. On application for an order confirming the arbitration award, the court "must grant" the order "unless the award is vacated, modified, or corrected as prescribed in sections 10 and 11 of this title." There is nothing malleable about "must grant," which unequivocally tells courts to grant confirmation in all cases, except when one of the "prescribed" exceptions applies. This does not sound remotely like a provision meant to tell a court what to do just in case the parties say nothing else. . . .

If appellate review is limited, or even unavailable, in most arbitration contexts, what other mechanisms exist to assure arbitration parties of the quality of the arbitrator's services? Michael Moffitt has suggested, with reference to mediators, that there are four fundamental mechanisms to provide assurance to consumers: (1) public front-end mechanisms, such as a license or control over the pool of service providers; (2) private front-end mechanisms, such as reputational markets; (3) public back-end mechanisms, such as the threat of fines or the removal of licenses in the event of malpractice; and (4) private back-end mechanisms, such as the threat of malpractice liability. See Michael Moffitt, The Four Ways to Assure Mediator Quality (and why none of them work), 24 Ohio St. J. on Disp. Resol. 191 (2009). As to the first, no licensure regime exists for arbitrators, as parties can, broadly speaking, hire whomever they want to serve as an arbitrator. However, many arbitrators associate with a provider organization, such as the AAA or JAMS, and those organizations reserve the right to remove arbitrators from their rosters. As to the second, there are certainly repeat players in the arbitration market. Whether the dynamics are such that sub-standard arbitrators are filtered out may be up for debate. As to the third, because there is no license one can threaten to rescind, this option would largely be limited to the prospect of public fines. However, as to this and to the fourth option, the prospect of an arbitrator having personal exposure to liability is exceptionally limited. Most jurisdictions, either by statute or common law, afford arbitrators the same scope of immunity to which judges are entitled. Section 14(a) of the Revised Uniform Arbitration Act affords judicial immunity not only to arbitrators but also to arbitral organizations ("An arbitrator or an arbitration organization acting in that capacity is immune from civil liability to the same extent as a judge of a court of this State acting in a judicial capacity."). Whether the current immunity system strikes the proper policy balance has been the subject of ongoing debate. See, e.g., Maureen A. Weston, Reexamining Arbitral Immunity in an Age of Mandatory and Professional Arbitration, 88 Minn. L. Rev. 449 (2004); Peter Rutledge, Toward a Contractual Approach to Arbitral Immunity, 39 U. Ga. L. Rev. 151 (2004); Jenny Brown, The Expansion of Arbitral Immunity: Is Absolute Immunity a Foregone Conclusion?, 2009 J. Disp. Resol. 225.

Problem 11-9. ***Appeals from Arbitration?***

Can you think of a context in which a client might want, ex ante, to preserve contractually the possibility of appellate review from an arbitration? What would such a clause look like? (Keep in mind that your client will want the clause to be enforceable.) Some of the major international arbitration institutions now provide for some form of arbitral appeal by a different panel of arbitrators; see, e.g., JAMS, CIDR (ABA).

C. ARBITRATION ETHICS

Carrie Menkel-Meadow, ETHICS ISSUES IN ARBITRATION AND RELATED DISPUTE RESOLUTION PROCESSES: WHAT'S HAPPENING AND WHAT'S NOT

56 U. Miami L. Rev. 949, 951-953 (2002)

The use of arbitration presents a variety of different kinds of ethical issues, ranging from the particular ethical behavioral choices made by the actors inside an arbitration, including the arbitrators, lawyers (or other representatives), parties and witnesses, to the institutions who choose, administer and promote arbitration (such as courts, the American Arbitration Association, the Center for Public Resources, the International Chamber of Commerce, and many other "provider" organizations), to the parties or entities who place arbitration clauses in contracts of sale, or provision of services, sometimes without fully knowing what they are drafting. In addition to behavioral choices in the conduct of arbitration there are larger, macro or systemic justice issues in how arbitral choices and decisions are made in conjunction with other possible methods of dispute resolution (comparisons to formal legal justice in courts, foregoing conflict), whether disputing should be public or private, how real or deep the consent in consensual dispute resolution should be and what kind of formal governmental or other scrutiny there ought to be of privately arranged dispute resolution. . . .

I have come to use a simple mnemonic device to delineate the ethics issues presented by the use of arbitration as a device for dispute resolution: the 10 C's of dispute resolution ethics. I present them below, more or less in order of their current importance and controversy:

(1) choice/consent/coercion (Is it ethically improper to impose arbitration on persons who have not really chosen it?);
(2) courts or contracts (Is it ethical for courts to mandate arbitration and if so, what ethical rules apply?);
(3) conflicts of interest (Do arbitrators face improper conflicts of interest to the extent they are trying to please repeat-player clients or serve as party-appointed arbitrator advocates?);
(4) confidentiality (Although parties may seek confidentiality, is it ethical from a public perspective?);
(5) competence and credentialing (Should competency and credentials be governed by an ethical code?);
(6) corporate-organizational liability (To what extent should arbitration providers be governed by ethical rules?);
(7) communication and counseling (Should lawyers be ethically required to counsel their clients about arbitration or other forms of ADR?);
(8) costs and fees (Do the costs and fees associated with arbitration raise ethical concerns?);
(9) complaints and grievance systems (From an ethical standpoint, should parties be provided with a forum in which they can complain about alleged arbitration improprieties?); and
(10) conflicts of laws (Whether and, if so, how should the many sometimes conflicting statutes, rules, and codes of arbitration ethics be reconciled).

Menkel-Meadow identifies many ethical issues that arise with respect to arbitration. However, as her tenth "C" emphasizes, no single set of ethical rules applies to all arbitrators, disputants, representatives, or arbitration organizations. Indeed, some might suggest that because arbitration is a private process, the state should not seek to regulate the ethics of the process, but rather should leave such regulation to private parties and the marketplace.

The ethical regulation of arbitration can be seen as a glass that is either half-full or half empty. On the one hand, no single set of ethical rules applies to any of the many participants in arbitration. Neither arbitrators nor arbitration organizations are regulated or certified to the same extent as lawyers, accountants, or even hairdressers. While attorneys are, of course, regulated, no rules apply specifically to their conduct as representatives in arbitration. Yet, on the other hand, there is an abundance of statutes, rules, and codes that have at least precatory authority in these areas.

In the international realm, the ethical regulation of arbitration is even more problematic. Background differences among various countries' approach to litigation, for example, distinctions among adversarial and inquisitorial emphases, lead countries to take vastly different approaches to such issues as the propriety of ex parte conversations with judges, whether parties can testify, the degree of zeal attorneys should use to represent their clients, the extent to which attorneys should prepare their clients to testify, and whether parties can hear each other's testimony. These and other differences in litigation lead to great ethical confusion in the world of international arbitration. See Catherine Rogers, Ethics in International Arbitration (2014) and Carrie Menkel-Meadow, Ethical Ordering in Transnational Legal Practice?, 29 Geo. J. Legal Ethics 207 (2016).

Both domestically and internationally, the problem is often less a dearth of regulation than a conflict of regulations.

1. Arbitral Bias and the Duty to Disclose

Ethical challenges may arise at any stage of an arbitration and may involve any number of different decisions by an arbitrator. Still, because of the broad scope of arbitrators' powers once they are in place, questions of bias, conflicts of interest, disclosure and impartiality may represent the most important category of ethical duties for arbitrators.

❖ COMMONWEALTH COATINGS CORP. v. CONTINENTAL CASUALTY CO.

393 U.S. 145 (1968)

Mr. Justice Black delivered the opinion of the Court.

At issue in this case is the question whether elementary requirements of impartiality taken for granted in every judicial proceeding are suspended when the parties agree to resolve a dispute through arbitration.

The petitioner, Commonwealth Coatings Corporation, a subcontractor, sued the sureties on the prime contractor's bond to recover money alleged to be due for a painting job. . . . Pursuant to th[e] agreement [to arbitrate] petitioner appointed one arbitrator, the prime contractor appointed a second, and these two together selected the third arbitrator. This third arbitrator, the supposedly neutral member of the panel, conducted a large business in Puerto Rico, in which he served as an engineering consultant for various people in connection with building construction projects. One of his regular customers in this business was the prime contractor that petitioner sued in this case. This relationship with the prime contractor was in a sense sporadic in that the arbitrator's services were used only from time to time at irregular intervals, and there had been no dealings between them for about a year immediately preceding the arbitration. Nevertheless, the prime contractor's patronage was repeated and significant, involving fees of about $12,000 over a period of four of five years, and the relationship even went so far as to include the rendering of services on the very projects involved in this lawsuit. An arbitration was held, but the facts concerning the close business connections between the third arbitrator and the prime contractor were unknown to petitioner and were never revealed to it by this arbitrator, by the prime contractor, or by anyone else until after an award had been made. Petitioner challenged the award on this ground, among others. . . .

Section 10 [of the FAA] . . . sets out the conditions upon which awards can be vacated. The two courts below held, however, that §10 could not be construed in such a way as to justify vacating the award in this case. We disagree and reverse. Section 10 does authorize vacation of an award where it was "procured by corruption, fraud, or undue means" or "[w]here there was evident partiality . . . in the arbitrators." These provisions show a desire of Congress to provide not merely for any arbitration but for an impartial one. It is true that petitioner does not charge before us that the third arbitrator was actually guilty of fraud or bias in deciding this case, and we have no reason, apart from the undisclosed business relationship, to suspect him of any improper motives. But neither this arbitrator nor the prime contractor gave to petitioner even an intimation of the close financial relations that had existed between them for a period of years. We have no doubt that if a litigant could show that a foreman of a jury or a judge in a court of justice had, unknown to the litigant, any such relationship, the judgment would be subject to challenge. This is shown beyond doubt by Tumey v. State of Ohio, 273 U.S. 510 (1927), where this Court held that a conviction could not stand because a small part of the judge's income consisted of court fees collected from convicted defendants. Although in *Tumey* it appeared the amount of the judge's compensation actually depended on whether he decided for one side or the other, that is too small a distinction to allow this manifest violation of the strict morality and fairness Congress would have expected on the part of the arbitrator and the other party in this case. Nor should it be at all relevant, as the Court of Appeals apparently thought it was here, that "[t]he payments received were a very small part of (the arbitrator's) income. . . ." For in *Tumey* the Court held that a decision should be set aside where there is "the slightest pecuniary interest" on the part of the judge, and specifically rejected the State's contention that the compensation involved there was "so small that it is not to be regarded as likely to influence improperly a judicial officer in the discharge of his duty. . . ." Since in the case of courts this is a constitutional principle, we can see no basis for refusing to find the same concept in the broad statutory language that governs arbitration proceedings and provides that an award can be set aside on the basis of "evident partiality" or the use of "undue means.". . . It is true that arbitrators cannot sever all their ties with the business world, since they are not expected to get all their income from their work deciding cases, but we should, if anything, be even more scrupulous to safeguard the impartiality of arbitrators than judges, since the former have completely free rein to decide the law as well as the facts and are not subject to appellate review. We can perceive no way in which the effectiveness of the arbitration process will be hampered by the simple requirement that arbitrators disclose to the parties any dealings that might create an impression of possible bias. . . .

[A]ny tribunal permitted by law to try cases and controversies not only must be unbiased but also must avoid even the appearance of bias. We cannot believe that it was the purpose of Congress to authorize litigants to submit their cases and controversies to arbitration boards that might reasonably be thought biased against one litigant and favorable to another.

Did the Court in *Commonwealth Coatings* hold that arbitrators cannot have any financial interests associated with the case brought before them, or did it hold that any such interests must be disclosed? Justice White, in his concurrence to this opinion, made it clear that he would guard against the former construction, writing, "The Court does not decide today that arbitrators are to be held to the standards of judicial decorum of Article III judges, or indeed of any judges. It is often because they are men of affairs, not apart from but of the marketplace, that they are effective in their adjudicatory function. . . . This does not mean the judiciary must overlook outright chicanery in giving effect to their awards; that would be an abdication of our responsibility. But it does mean that arbitrators are not automatically disqualified by a business relationship with the parties before them if both parties are informed of the relationship in advance, or if they are unaware of the facts but the relationship is trivial. I see no reason automatically to disqualify the best informed and most capable potential arbitrators."

Justice Fortas, in his dissent in the same case, believes the Court went too far even with a per se disclosure requirement. He notes that in the *Commonwealth Coatings* case, all three arbitrators ruled the same way, and he argued instead that "failure of an arbitrator to volunteer information about business dealings with one party will, prima facie, support a claim of partiality or bias. But where there is no suggestion that the nondisclosure was calculated, and where the complaining party disclaims any imputation of partiality, bias, or misconduct, the presumption clearly is overcome."

Problem 11-10. ***Arbitrator Bias, Disclosure, and Disqualification***

Which of the three Justices' approaches in *Commonwealth Coatings* is most persuasive?

In Caperton v. A.T. Massey Coal Co., 556 U.S. 868 (2009), the Supreme Court held that the Due Process Clause requires a judge who had received a very substantial campaign contribution from one of the parties to recuse himself from the case. The Court reasoned that even if there was no actual bias, there was at least an appearance of impropriety in that the circumstances were such as to pose a temptation to the average judge "not to hold the balance nice, clear and true." The Court explained that "fears of bias can arise when—without the other parties' consent—a man chooses the judge in his own cause." Does the Supreme Court's logic in *Caperton* support its conclusion in *Commonwealth Coatings*? For arbitrators, some courts hold that the "evident partiality" standard is not met regarding small contributions to an arbitrator's unsuccessful campaign for judge because the contributions are matters of public record. Freeman v. Pittsburg Glass Works, 709 F.3d 240 (3d Cir. 2013). In *Freeman*, both sides made campaign contributions to the arbitrator—the party on one side, and the attorney on the other. Does that fact matter?

Section 12 of the Revised Uniform Arbitration Act provides:

> (a) Before accepting appointment, an individual who is requested to serve as an arbitrator, after making a reasonable inquiry, shall disclose to all parties . . . and to any other arbitrators any known facts that a reasonable person would consider likely to affect the impartiality of the arbitrator in the arbitration proceeding, including
>
> (1) a financial or personal interest in the outcome of the arbitration proceeding; and
>
> (2) an existing or past relationship with any of the parties to the agreement to arbitrate or the arbitration proceeding, their counsel or representatives, a witness, or another [arbitrator].
>
> (b) An arbitrator has a continuing obligation to disclose to all parties . . . and to any other arbitrators any facts that the arbitrator learns after accepting appointment which a reasonable person would consider likely to affect the impartiality of the arbitrator.
>
> (c) If an arbitrator discloses a fact required by subsection (a) or (b) to be disclosed and a party timely objects to the appointment or continued service of the arbitrator based upon the fact disclosed, the objection may be a ground . . . for vacating an award made by the arbitrator.
>
> (d) If the arbitrator did not disclose a fact as required by subsection (a) or (b), upon timely objection by a party, the court . . . may vacate an award.
>
> (e) An arbitrator appointed as a neutral arbitrator who does not disclose a known, direct, and material interest in the outcome of the arbitration proceeding or a known, existing, and substantial relationship with a party is presumed to act with evident partiality. . . .
>
> (f) If the parties to an arbitration proceeding agree to the procedures of an arbitration organization or any other procedures for challenges to arbitrators before an award is made, substantial compliance with those procedures is a condition precedent to a [motion] to vacate an award on that ground. . . .

Problem 11-11. ***Arbitration Providers' Disclosures***

Recognizing the potential FAA preemption challenges associated with imposing particular requirements on arbitration clauses, the National Consumer Law Center has proposed the following model state language:

> Any private company that administers five or more arbitrations a year in this State involving a consumer or employee shall collect and publish the following information about each of its arbitrations for at least five years after the arbitration has completed:
>
> The names of the parties to the arbitration;
>
> The party that filed the arbitration claim;
>
> The type of dispute involved, including goods or services, insurance, credit, debt collection, or employment;
>
> The prevailing party;
>
> Whether the consumer or employee was represented by an attorney;
>
> The date the company administering the arbitration received the demand for arbitration, the date the arbitrator was appointed, and the date of the arbitration's disposition;
>
> Whether the arbitration resulted in an in-person hearing;
>
> Whether the parties provided each other with any pre-hearing discovery;
>
> The amount of the claim, the amount of the award, and any other relief granted, if any;
>
> The name of the arbitrator, his or her total fee for the case, and the percentage of the arbitrator's fee paid by each party; and
>
> The arbitrator's professional affiliations.

Do you think the NCLC's proposed language would withstand FAA preemption challenge? Do you think the language, if adopted, would alleviate any of the concerns about arbitrator ethics?

2. Party-Appointed Non-Neutral Arbitrators

In the United States, in both commercial and labor contexts, parties sometimes elect a process in which each party selects one or more non-neutral arbitrators to be part of an arbitration panel. These party-appointed arbitrators then select a neutral arbitrator who serves as the Chair of the panel. In some cases, the non-neutral arbitrator may confer ex parte with the appointing party, may educate the other arbitrators about evidence that has been presented, and may even, in some sense, serve as an advocate for the appointing party. A party-appointed arbitrator may ultimately rule against the party that appointed her, but as you might imagine, such outcomes are uncommon.

Comment 5 to §12 of the RUAA discusses the phenomenon of non-neutral party-appointed arbitrators, stating that:

> The integrity of the process demands that the non-neutral arbitrators chosen by the parties, like neutral arbitrators, disclose pertinent interests and relationships to all parties as well as other members of the arbitration panel. It is particularly important for the neutral arbitrator to know the interest of the arbitrator selected by each of the parties if, for example, such non-neutral arbitrator is being paid on a contingent-fee basis.

The practice of appointing non-neutral arbitrators has been controversial, particularly outside the United States. Although the 2004 AAA/ABA Code of Ethics for Arbitrators in Commercial Disputes allows the practice, it clearly states a preference against it, and even promulgates a set of ethical rules specifically targeting non-neutral arbitrators. The CPR Rules go even further, providing that arbitrators shall be "independent and impartial" and prohibiting ex parte communications. See International Institute for Conflict Prevention & Resolution, CPR Procedures & Clauses Non-Administered Arbitration Rules 7.1 and 7.4 (2007). Also, Article 12 of the Rules of Arbitration of the International Chamber of Commerce (2017) states: "Every arbitrator must be and remain independent of the parties involved in the arbitration."

3. Arbitral Provider Ethics

The scope of provider ethical responsibilities under current law is not clear. Nor is it clear how any such responsibilities can be enforced. Providers often argue that they, like arbitrators, should have quasi-judicial immunity, and this argument has often been accepted. See, e.g., International Medical Group, Inc. v. American Arbitration Ass'n, Inc., 312 F.3d 833 (7th Cir. 2002). Section 14(a) of the RUAA provides that "(a) An arbitrator *or an arbitration organization* acting in that capacity is immune from civil liability to the same extent as a judge of a court of this State acting in a judicial capacity." (Emphasis added). The Reporter's Notes to Section 14 explain:

> Section 14(a) also provides the same immunity as is provided to an arbitrator to an arbitration organization. Extension of judicial immunity to those arbitration organizations is appropriate to the extent that they are acting "in certain roles and with certain responsibilities" that are comparable to those of a judge. Corey v. New York Stock Exch., 691 F.2d 1205, 1209 (6th Cir. 1982). This immunity to neutral arbitration organizations is appropriate because the duties that they perform in administering the arbitration process are the functional equivalent of the roles and responsibilities of judges administering the adjudication process in a court of law. There is substantial precedent for this conclusion.

Immunity also helps curb collateral attacks on awards and promotes finality. Yet, the practice of providing broad immunity to arbitral providers can be critiqued by those who believe the analogy between judges (who are afforded full immunity) and arbitrators breaks down. Such critics note that arbitration may lack the procedural safeguards of court (such as full appeal), arbitrations are conducted out of the public eye, arbitrators are often sufficiently compensated that they could purchase malpractice insurance, arbitration may be mandatorily imposed, and that some enforcement mechanisms, such as suits against arbitrators, are needed in order that ethical restrictions have teeth.

4. Ethics for Attorney Representatives in Arbitration

Do lawyers who represent clients in arbitration have the same ethical responsibilities as lawyers representing clients in litigation? In negotiation? In mediation? Unfortunately, policy makers have not provided substantial guidance regarding whether attorney advocates in arbitration must follow the same rules as attorney advocates in other contexts. For the most part, attorneys' rules of professional conduct do not contain clear rules for those engaged as advocates in arbitration. Internationally, the ethical rules governing advocates' conduct in arbitration are even fuzzier.

In most jurisdictions, attorneys owe the same duty of candor to an arbitrator in a binding arbitration as they would to a judge. Model Rule 1.0(m) now includes binding arbitration in the definition of "tribunal." So, Model Rule 3.3's requirements that attorneys be truthful with respect to tribunals apply to attorneys' conduct as representatives in binding arbitration. (Note that the term "tribunal" does not cover mediation.)

Rule 3.3 Candor Toward the Tribunal

(a) A lawyer shall not knowingly:

(1) make a false statement of fact or law to a tribunal or fail to correct a false statement of material fact or law previously made to the tribunal by the lawyer; (2) fail to disclose to the tribunal legal authority in the controlling jurisdiction known to the lawyer to be directly adverse to the position of the client and not disclosed by opposing counsel; or (3) offer evidence that the lawyer knows to be false. If a lawyer, the lawyer's client, or a witness called by the lawyer, has offered material evidence and the lawyer comes to know of its falsity, the lawyer shall take reasonable remedial measures, including, if necessary, disclosure to the tribunal. A lawyer may refuse to offer evidence, other than the testimony of a defendant in a criminal matter, that the lawyer reasonably believes is false.

5. Non-Attorney Representatives

As noted earlier, in the collective bargaining context, it is quite common for both sides to be represented by non-lawyers in arbitration hearings. Although such representatives have no formal legal training, they often have a great deal of familiarity with the union contract and company work rules, as well as substantial experience serving as an advocate in arbitration hearings. Outside of the labor context, however, Bar Associations have increasingly taken the view that such representation constitutes the practice of law and must, therefore, be undertaken only by licensed members of the Bar. See, e.g., Supreme Court of Florida, Florida Bar re: Advisory Opinion on Nonlawyer Representation in Securities Arbitration, 696 So. 2d 1178, 1183 (Fla. 1997) ("[N]onlawyer representatives give specific legal advice and perform the traditional tasks of the lawyer at every stage of the arbitration proceeding in an effort to protect the investor's important legal and financial interests. We cannot ignore such a situation. Because such activities—when performed by nonlawyers—are wholly unregulated and non-sanctionable, we further agree with the proposed opinion that these activities must be enjoined. In these circumstances, the public faces a potential for harm from incompetent and unethical representation by compensated nonlawyers which cannot otherwise be remedied."). In 2024, the Securities and Exchange Commission approved a proposed FINRA rule prohibiting the use of compensated non-attorney representatives in FINRA arbitrations. 89 Fed. Reg. 3481 (2024).

Further Reading

Harold I. Abramson, Protocols for International Arbitrators Who Dare to Settle Cases, 10 Am. Rev. Int'l Arb. 1 (1999).

Neal Blacker, Drafting the Arbitration/ADR Clause: A Checklist for Practitioners, 46 Prac. Law 55 (2000).

Kristen M. Blankley, Lying, Stealing, and Cheating: The Role of Arbitrators as Ethics Enforcers, 52 U. Louis. L. Rev. 443 (2014).

Wayne D. Brazil, When Getting It Right Is What Matters Most, Arbitrations Are Better than Trials, 18 Cardozo J. Conflict Resol. 277 (2017).

Sarah R. Cole, Blurred Lines: Are Non-Attorneys Who Represent Parties in Arbtration Involving Statutory Claims Practicing Law?, 48 U.C. Davis L. Rev. 921 (2015).

John W. Cooley & Steven Lubet. (2003). Arbitration Advocacy. Notre Dame, IN: National Institute for Trial Advocacy.

Susan Frank, et al., Inside the Arbitrator's Mind, 66 Emory L.J. 1115 (2017).

Peter Halprin & Stephen Wah, Ethics in International Arbitration, 2018 J. Disp. Resol. 87.

Marvin F. Hill, Jr., Anthony V. Sinicropi & Amy L. Evenson. (1997). Winning Arbitration Advocacy. Washington, DC: Bureau of National Affairs.

David Horton, Arbitration About Arbitration, 70 Stan. L. Rev. 363 (2018).

Carrie Menkel-Meadow, Ethical Ordering in Transnational Legal Practice? A Review of Catherine A. Rogers's *Ethics In International Arbitration*, 29 Geo. J. Legal Ethics 207 (2016).

Catherine A. Rogers. (2011). Ethics in International Arbitration. New York: Oxford University Press.

Kathleen M. Scanlon. (2002). CPR Institute for Dispute Resolution, Drafter's Deskbook for Dispute Resolution Clauses. New York: CPR Institute.

Alec Stone Sweet & Florian Grisel. (2017). The Evolution of International Arbitration: Judicialization, Governance, Legitimacy. New York: Oxford University Press.

Nelson Edward Timkin, A Proposal to Establish an International Commercial Arbitration Ethics Panel and Hotline to Resolve Disclosure and Conflicts Issues, 24 Cardozo J. Confl. Resol. 303 (2023).

Terry L. Trantina, How to Design ADR Clauses That Satisfy Clients' Needs and Minimize Litigation Risk, 19 Altern. High Cost Litig. 137 (2001).

PART III PROCESS PLURALISM: ADAPTATIONS AND VARIATIONS OF PROCESSES

We have now studied the three foundational processes used as alternatives to litigation in resolving disputes: negotiation, mediation, and arbitration. The fourth foundational process, litigation, is the focus of your studies in Civil Procedure and most of the rest of your law school courses. As the uses of mediation, negotiation, and arbitration have increased in both the private and public sectors, they have altered preexisting adjudicative and administrative processes to the point that it is no longer so clear where one process ends and another begins. In addition, while traditional thinking about legal disputes separates disputants into plaintiff and defendant, modern life often presents situations that involve multiple issues in which there are more than two parties and sides to a dispute.

As the result of these developments, the foundational processes of negotiation, mediation, arbitration, and adjudication have been modified, expanded, and transformed. Nonlitigation processes now resolve disputes referred by courts and administrative agencies, sometimes on a mandatory basis. Mediators are increasingly asked to make evaluations, and judges and arbitrators increasingly try to settle disputes. New processes are invented to deal with complex issues of multiple causation and responsibility, pre-dispute negotiation, and public policy making.

Part III of this book explores multiple aspects of these new forms of dispute resolution. Chapter 12 examines the ways in which the foundational processes are combined or adapted to create variations on original themes. This chapter looks first at how private parties sometimes choose to blend dispute resolution processes and then moves on to examine how public entities adopt new forms of dispute resolution. Chapter 13 focuses on multiparty disputes, looking at how the foundational processes must be adjusted as disputes become more complex, both in number of parties and numbers of issues. This chapter also considers how dispute resolution systems should be designed for those with complex disputes or those in ongoing relationships and organizations. We also take a look at how dispute resolution methods can be useful in transaction planning and negotiation. Finally, having provided you with substantial information about each of these processes, the final chapter of the book, Chapter 14, helps you to understand where the field of dispute resolution is heading in the future, what are some of its promises and some of its limits, how you can help clients to choose between and among processes, and what processes you might help design in the future that meet your clients' needs. You will see that, in the design of conflict handling, "one size *does not* fit all."

Chapter 12 Private and Public Hybrid Processes

Can the whole be greater than the sum of its parts?

—Anonymous

The foundational processes of negotiation, mediation, arbitration, and litigation are often combined or modified to reflect the demands and desires of private individuals, organizations, and policy makers seeking to create or redesign transactions and relationships of many kinds. Whether creating new legal arrangements, preventing disputes, or resolving disputes, these mixed processes rely on the negotiation principle of direct engagement in problem-solving, and on the use of third-party neutrals to create new forms of conflict resolution and multiparty decision-making. This chapter first examines hybrid processes in private settings. It then moves on to public hybrids offered or mandated by court rules, government agencies, regulations. Most importantly, the uses of technology for dispute resolution have produced the field of "Online Dispute Resolution" or ODR, used in both private (e.g., customer service) and public (online courts) settings. And, while we often associate ADR processes with civil matters, alternative processes are also used in criminal cases, including "restorative justice" efforts, mediated victim-offender "healing," community and specialized courts (such as drug courts), and "sentencing circles." Such processes typically yield new conceptions of remedial possibilities such as rehabilitation and restitution. You will see, however, that this private/public line is no clearer in this context than it is in many others. Also, you will note how many ideas flow from the private sector to the public and vice versa. The final section of the chapter examines problems posed by the institutionalization of ADR processes.

As you examine how these processes are redesigned to deal with particular kinds of disputes, conflicts, decision-making processes, and policy issues, consider the following questions:

1. What foundational (primary) processes are used? How have these processes been modified? With what effects?
2. Can multiple processes be combined without sacrificing the special "morality" or "integrity" of each process?
3. What is the role of third-party neutrals? Facilitative, evaluative, or decisional?

4. Who has designed the particular hybrid process? The parties themselves? A process expert? Another party or institution, such as a court or an administrative agency?
5. Is this ADR process *ad hoc* (designed for a particular dispute, transaction, rulemaking, or other "event") or more formal, permanent, or institutionalized (contractual, rule-based, common practice)?
6. What is the "authority" for creation of this particular process? A contract (private ADR)? A court rule, judge's recommendation or suggestion, law, or administrative regulation (public ADR)?
7. Is entrance to this process consensual or more directed or "coerced"?
8. What are the goals or intended purposes of this process, and how might it differ from other possible processes?
9. What special areas of concern apply to the use of this process (for example, notice, fairness, ethics, inclusion, publicity, confidentiality)?
10. What other adaptations or variations of this process might be available?

A. PRIVATE HYBRIDS

One of the most attractive aspects of various forms of ADR is that they can be crafted to meet the particular needs and interests of the disputants. The sections that follow discuss some particular combinations that are now common, but remember that the potential variations are really infinite. You may be asked to design your own special processes someday for particular client needs.

1. Variations on Arbitration

In Chapters 9, 10, and 11 we looked at conventional arbitration processes in a variety of settings. What makes arbitration "conventional" is its reliance on a binding decision by a third-party decision maker, backed up by the force of court enforcement through either the Federal Arbitration Act (domestic) or the New York Convention for Recognition and Enforcement of Foreign Arbitral Awards (international). But arbitration itself has become a much-hybridized process, in both public and private spheres, as variations have developed with respect to how awards are reached ("final offer") and whether they are binding or not, depending on how parties tailor the processes to their needs.

a. Binding Offer Arbitration

Although binding offers can be structured in many ways, two variations warrant special attention: *final-offer* and *high-low arbitration.*

Final-offer arbitration is also known as *baseball arbitration* because it is used to resolve salary disputes among many baseball players and their teams. However, this form of arbitration is also used outside the baseball or sports context. With final-offer arbitration, the arbitrator does not have unbounded power to reach whatever conclusion she wants. Instead, the two opposing parties submit sealed offers or requests to the arbitrator, and the arbitrator must choose only one or the other of these offers.

The goal of limiting arbitrators' discretion through the final-offer process is to encourage disputants to take more reasonable positions. When arbitrators are free to select whatever result they think is best, parties have some incentive to take extreme positions in arguing their case to the arbitrator. This is particularly true to the extent one believes arbitrators typically reach compromise or "split the baby" results. In contrast, if the arbitrator is permitted to select only the offer of one side or the other, each side has an incentive to be reasonable. If the plaintiff is too greedy, the arbitrator will feel compelled to select the defendant's offer; if the defendant is too stingy, the arbitrator will select the plaintiff's offer. Thus, the final-offer process encourages both sides to be reasonable and, in a sense, to bid against themselves. The final-offer process also proves very effective as a means to encourage settlement. As each side fears that the arbitrator may choose the other side's offer, the two parties often opt for settlement to avoid that risk, usually moving closer and closer to a "mid-point" evaluation of the real value. In real baseball arbitration this is made "easier" or more predictable with the use of statistics of comparable players' "worth" based on playing history—batting, fielding and other measures of baseball value.[1] Of course, final-offer arbitration does not always result in settlement—for example, when the parties stay firmly rooted to their assessment of value; or the actual "value" is more mixed with uneven data; or the parties do not fear the extra costs of the arbitration itself; or when, in some cases, they actually prefer a third party, like an arbitrator, to make the decision and distance themselves from the outcome (such as by avoiding a precedent for an offer). In baseball arbitration (and entertainment arbitration, too) egos and personalities can get in the way of negotiated settlement. Going to arbitration, rather than a negotiated settlement, can be a problem, though, if the costs are high, if relationships are damaged, and if opportunities to create more detailed and tailored packages of compensation and other benefits are lost with simple salary arbitration.

Another variation on final-offer arbitration is sometimes called "*night baseball*" arbitration. Here, the arbitrator holds a hearing and makes a tentative ruling without having reviewed either side's offer. However, the arbitrator examines the offers submitted previously by both sides and is required to select whichever offer is closest to her own tentative ruling. The purported advantage of this approach is that although the arbitrator makes a tentative decision she thinks is fair—without being influenced by the parties' offers—her actual decision is reined in by the parties' reasonable positions. Note that night baseball arbitration, in particular, risks creating a challenge in cases in which the nature of the dispute in question is not easily confined to easily-compared numerical offers. It is easy to determine which simple dollar figure is closest to the arbitrator's tentative ruling, and

1. Roger I. Abrams, Inside Baseball's Salary Arbitration Process, 6 U. Chi. L. Sch. Roundtable 55 (1999).

potentially more challenging in a case in which the award has multiple variables, along multiple timeframes, with different payout structures.

High-low contracts, which can be used in litigation as well as arbitration, are another means of constraining the decision makers' discretion and limiting the parties' exposure to risk. With high-low agreements, parties agree in advance that no matter what the fact finder's actual award is, plaintiff will not receive more than X or less than Y. That is, the award is bracketed between a minimum and a maximum figure. Such agreements can be attractive to plaintiffs because they are assured at least a set minimum award, and they can be attractive to defendants because defendants can limit their maximum exposure. In addition, high-low agreements can save both sides time and expense because less time needs to be devoted to arbitrating the damages portion of the case, and no appeal of the amount of the award is permitted. Unlike high-low agreements in the context of public litigation (the legal enforceability of which is the subject of some debate), high-low arbitration processes are readily enforceable, provided all parties agree to the constraints in their agreement to arbitrate.

b. Nonbinding Arbitration

Another and quite different type of arbitration is nonbinding arbitration, which sounds a bit like an oxymoron given how we have defined arbitration in earlier chapters. Yet this, too, shows how the processes are flexible. Here, the arbitrator's award becomes binding only if it is accepted voluntarily by the disputants. The purpose of this type of arbitration is not to guarantee a final resolution of the dispute, but rather to give the disputants a good prediction of how the claim would be resolved if it went to trial. The hope is that once the disputants learn this prediction and have the opportunity to go through a process that is similar to what they might obtain in court, they will voluntarily abide by the arbitrator's decision. Although nonbinding arbitration sometimes is agreed to contractually, most nonbinding arbitration that takes place in the United States occurs pursuant to court order, rule, or statute.

In addition, many courts have adopted nonbinding arbitration programs with the hope that they will provide a quicker, cheaper form of justice than litigation. We will look at these arbitration programs in Section B.7 below.

Problem 12-1. ***What Type of Arbitration?***

If you were drafting a contractual arbitration clause mandating arbitration, what variations of arbitration might you consider? What kinds of matters would lend themselves to different kinds of treatments in arbitration? Would it matter if the parties were disputing only monetary amounts or had other issues? Would it be advisable to specify the form of arbitration in advance, or let the parties choose at the time of the dispute? Why?

2. Med-Arb

One of the first-used types of hybrid processes was med-arb—mediation, followed by arbitration if the parties fail to reach agreement. This practice began in labor contexts, but it has spread to family (child custody conciliation) and commercial matters. In the original form of med-arb, the parties select an individual to facilitate the negotiation of their dispute (using all the usual ground rules of mediation, such as confidentiality and private caucusing). If that process fails, the mediator is empowered to turn into an arbitrator who then makes a decision. Med-arb can be varied in a number of interesting ways, each of which has its own advantages and disadvantages. In one alternative version of med-arb, two different neutrals are used. If the mediation fails to result in agreement, the mediator is replaced by a second neutral who arbitrates the dispute. In another version of med-arb, the arbitrator issues a nonbinding rather than a binding determination.[2]

Sometimes the order of the processes is reversed in a process known as arb-med. Here an arbitrator hears the parties' presentations on the legal merits and then tries to help settle, rather than decide the case. In some cases, the arbitrator may make a sealed award before or during settlement discussions, which is revealed only after mediation or negotiation fails. Arb-med has become common practice in many settings, including labor, employment and commercial cases. Alternatively, the arbitrator can issue a nonbinding award and then allow the parties to shift to a mediation process to try to "improve" on the award.[3]

Some argue that combining arbitration and mediation blends the best aspects of each process. The speed, efficiency, and consensual aspects of mediation are combined with the efficient finality of arbitration. For example, some labor arbitrators find it beneficial to use mediation in situations that were formerly allocated to arbitration, such as "grievances" under collective bargaining agreements, because of the greater flexibility of mediation and the possibility of resolving more than a single issue at once.[4]

However, the question of whether the same person ought to perform both the mediator and arbitrator roles is controversial. It is certainly more efficient to have the same person hear the facts and interests of the case so as to avoid duplication of effort, time, and information disclosure. Yet critics assert that the practice is problematic because mediators typically urge parties to be forthcoming and honest about their needs, interests, and facts, in settings where the disputants are assured the mediators have no power over them. If the mediators then turn into decision-makers, unwary parties may find their confidences used against them.

---

2. Sherry Landry, Med-Arb: Mediation with a Bite and an Effective ADR Model, 63 Def. Couns. J. 263 (1996).

3. See Lawrence D. Connor, How to Combine Facilitation with Evaluation, 14 Alternatives High Cost Litig. 15 (1996).

4. Stephen B. Goldberg, Grievance Mediation: A Successful Alternative to Labor Arbitration, 5 Negotiation J. 9, 11 (1989) (urging that two different persons perform the mediation and arbitration roles).

One example of this occurs in California, where family court conciliators (mediators) transform into decision-advising probation officers who sometimes reveal facts told to them in confidence during the mediation and who make arbitral-like recommendations to the court. This role switching may undermine participant trust in the whole system. At the same time, knowledge that the mediator may change roles allows savvy parties to rethink what they tell mediators, potentially undermining the effectiveness of the mediation. Similarly, critics of arb-med argue that the parties may resent the arbitrator's effort to force a "compromise" of the dispute, when what the parties seek is a clear-cut decision, assignment of liability or blame, enforcement of a rule, precedential value, or one of the other underlying reasons for choosing arbitration.

The classic work discussing "role confusion" when mediation and arbitration are combined was written by Lon Fuller.

Lon L. Fuller, COLLECTIVE BARGAINING AND THE ARBITRATOR

in Collective Bargaining and the Arbitrator's Role: Proceedings of the Fifteenth Annual Meeting, National Academy of Arbitrators 8, 29-30, 32-33 (Mark L. Kahn ed., 1962)

Mediation and arbitration have distinct purposes and hence distinct moralities. The morality of mediation lies in optimum settlement, a settlement in which each party gives up what he values less, in return for what he values more. The morality of arbitration lies in a decision according to the law of the contract. The procedures appropriate for mediation are those most likely to uncover that pattern of adjustment which will most nearly meet the interests of both parties. The procedures appropriate for arbitration are those which most securely guarantee each of the parties a meaningful chance to present arguments and proofs for a decision in his favor. Thus, private consultations with the parties, generally wholly improper on the part of an arbitrator, are an indispensable tool of mediation.

Not only are the appropriate procedures different in the two cases, but the facts sought by those procedures are different. [There] is no way to define "the essential facts" of a situation except by reference to some objective. Since the objective of reaching an optimum settlement is different from that of rendering an award according to the contract, the facts relevant in the two cases are different, or, when they seem the same, are viewed in different aspects. If a person who has mediated unsuccessfully attempts to assume the role of arbitrator, he must endeavor to view the facts of the case in a completely new light, as if he had previously known nothing about them. This is a difficult thing to do. It will be hard for him to listen to proofs and arguments with an open mind. If he fails in this attempt, the integrity of adjudication is impaired. . . .

What, then, are the objections to an arbitrator's undertaking mediative efforts after the hearing and before rendering the award, this being often so advantageous a time for settlement? Again, the objection lies essentially in the confusion of role that results. In seeking a settlement, the arbitrator turned mediator quite properly learns things that should have no bearing on his decision as an arbitrator. For example, suppose a discharge case in which the arbitrator is virtually certain that he will decide for reinstatement, though he is striving to keep his mind open until he has a chance to reflect on the case in the quiet of his study. In the course of exploring the possibilities of a settlement he learns that contrary to the position taken by the union at the hearing, respectable elements in the union would like to see the discharge upheld. Though they concede that the employee was probably innocent of the charges made by the company, they regard him as an ambitious troublemaker the union would be well rid of. If the arbitrator fails to mediate a settlement, can he block this information out when he comes to render his award?

Problem 12-2. ***Med-Arb or Arb-Med?***

To what extent are Fuller's criticisms of combining mediation and arbitration valid when two different persons perform the mediation and arbitration roles? As noted in the beginning of this section, mediation and arbitration are sometimes combined in different orders. What advantages and disadvantages do you see with how the order is established—med-arb or arb-med? What kinds of disputes lend themselves to the use of med-arb or arb-med?

3. The Mini-Trial

In 1977, a group of creative lawyers were faced with a complex and expensive patent infringement lawsuit that threatened to cost millions of dollars and to publicly reveal trade secrets.[5] These lawyers designed a special new legal process called the "mini-trial." The parties in Telecredit, Inc. v. TRW, Inc. engaged in expedited discovery for several months, deposed key witnesses, and exchanged a limited number of documents. During the two-day proceeding, counsel presented, in structured but abbreviated time, their "best case" in arguments, along with their supporting evidence, to the top management of both companies. The proceeding was presided over by a former Federal Court of Claims, Judge James Davis, an expert in patent infringement matters. His official duties, as negotiated by the parties, were to moderate the proceedings and to keep order, but not to rule in any way on the outcome. As the parties agreed in advance, if they did not reach a negotiated agreement at the end of the information exchange, Judge Davis was to supply a nonbinding opinion discussing the strengths and weaknesses of

---

5. This description of the process is taken from The CPR Legal Program Mini-Trial Handbook, in 1982 CPR Corporate Dispute Management, at MH-5 (Eric D. Green et al., eds., 1982). For further analysis of *Telecredit* by some of the lawyers involved, see Eric D. Green, Jonathan B. Marks & Ronald L. Olsen, Settling Large Case Litigation: An Alternative Approach, 11 Loy. L.A. L. Rev. 493 (1978).

each party's case and predict how a court might rule on the merits. The parties agreed that everything exchanged during this special proceeding would be inadmissible at any subsequent trial. After the information exchange, the top management officials negotiated directly without their lawyers. And, in fact, the case resolved within 30 minutes of the completion of the process.

For some years after this first mini-trial, the process was used often in high stakes cases. It was particularly attractive in cases where the parties sought to avoid the high costs of litigation; get informal advice from noted experts; keep the subject matter of their disputes private; or avoid the inevitable vagaries of having issues resolved by "lay" juries or judges who were presumed not to know enough about complex business disputes or complicated legal issues.

Over time, however, use of the mini-trial has diminished, perhaps because of the expense after taking into account attorney's fees, high neutral advisor fees, and lost work time for key corporate or government officials.

4. Private Judges and Juries

Some private disputants are attracted by many aspects of the public litigation system but put off by others, such as its public nature, high cost, or slow speed. Thus, both bench and jury trials have been recreated as private dispute resolution processes.

a. Private Judges

A number of states permit "referral" or "reference" to private (often retired) judges who have the full authority of public judges, either by authorizing statute or by constitutional provision. While similar to arbitration, private judging uniquely treats the judge's determination just like a public judge's award. That is, the private judgment can be enforced and executed like any other judgment and appealed through regular public processes, when authorized by statute or other legal authority. In contrast, as you will recall, there is usually no effective appeal from binding arbitration awards. In addition, parties may choose the private judge and arrange fees, timing, and scheduling on their own, as in a private dispute resolution process. Of all the states, California probably has the most well-developed private judging program.[6]

From the disputants' standpoint, private judging offers many potential advantages over public litigation: privacy (no public courtrooms), speed (self-scheduled), and choice of decision maker. For example, many corporations and celebrities have chosen private judging to keep matters out of the public eye (as in divorces and claims of corporate misfeasance). Costs in private judging can be higher (with private judges receiving fees much higher than public judges and fees for facilities,

---

6. See Cal. Civ. Proc. Code §§638-645. Florida has also adopted a private judging program, known as "voluntary trial resolution." Fla. Stat. Ann. §44.104.

etc.), but the process can also be more efficient, since parties can control scheduling better than with public dockets.

Although quite popular in some states, private judging is criticized by many as introducing a system of tiered justice in which those who can afford it are able to buy their way out of the public justice system, which often takes longer, and to choose their own decision-makers.[7] Because of increased scrutiny of this form of ADR by consumer advocates and others, the California Judicial Council has promulgated rules that attempt to regulate some aspects of the process of "compensated judges."

Private judging has had an interesting impact on the career of some sitting judges. One of the first private provider organizations of dispute resolution services, JAMS,[8] was founded in 1979 by a retiring California judge, Warren Knight. Other judges soon joined the organization and offered arbitration and mediation services privately for a fee. JAMS now has offices in over 30 cities worldwide and is a multimillion-dollar-a-year business. Indeed, some say that the career of private judging has become so attractive that it is hard to keep public judges from retiring at a young age to go private.

b. Private Juries

Private jury trials can be attractive to disputants who want lay fact finders but don't want to wait or pay for the expensive, time-consuming, public version of the jury trial. In response to this need, some private dispute resolution providers offer their own private jury trials. The private jurors, recruited through help-wanted advertisements, are paid a daily fee to perform typical juror duties. The disputants and their lawyers have the opportunity to use typical voir dire procedures to choose among the potential jurors. To the extent the parties agree, the demographics of the jury pool can be adjusted to meet their particular needs, such as for a more- or less-highly-educated jury. The parties can agree, by contract, to be bound by the jury's verdict. Or, with the acquiescence of the court, private jury verdicts can be appealed on the same grounds as regular jury verdicts.

Some critics of the private jury trial argue that it is inappropriate to decide matters of public concern (such as police abuse, for which private juries have been used) outside the view of the public eye. Some complain of the "vanishing civil jury trial" in the public system, the result of which has been the privatization of civil justice and the reduction in lay decision-making and fact-finding.[9] It can

7. See, e.g., Barlow F. Christensen, Private Justice: California's General Reference Procedure, 1982 Am. B. Found. Res. J. 79; Ann S. Kim, Note: Rent-a-Judges and the Cost of Selling Justice, 44 Duke L.J. 166 (1994). But see Richard Chernick, Helen I. Bendix & Robert C. Barrett, Private Judging: Privatizing Civil Justice (1997), for a defense of this process.

8. "JAMS" originally stood for Judicial Arbitration and Mediation Services, but the organization is now known only by its acronym.

9. See, e.g., ADR and the Vanishing Trial, Disp. Resol. Mag. 3-21 (Summer 2004); Symposium, The Vanishing Trial, 1 (3) J. of Empirical Stud. (2004); see also Carrie Menkel-Meadow, Is the Adversary System Really Dead? Dilemmas of Legal Ethics as Legal Institutions and Roles Evolve, in Current Legal Problems (Jane Holder, C. O'Cinneide & M. Freeman, eds., 2005).

also be argued that it is inappropriate to tamper with the natural demographics of the jury pool, and that using this private tool may erode public confidence in the public jury trial.[10]

Problem 12-3. *Are Private Processes Good for the Public?*

Should private parties be able to recreate the public justice system on a private basis? Does this recreation harm the public in any way? Does your answer depend on whether the parties recreate bench or jury trials? Would you be willing to serve on a private jury? Why or why not?

What downsides, if any, are there to allowing private judicial determinations to be enforced and appealed as if they had been made by public judges? Should parties who have filed formal court proceedings be permitted to agree on any kind of private process they want to resolve their dispute? In a divorce case? In a personal injury case? In a stockholder derivative suit? Explain your answer.

Problem 12-4. *What Difference Depending on Who Uses?*

In litigation, parties often use the services of private consultants, jury experts, mock juries, and focus groups so they can evaluate the quality of their presentations and evidence. What difference does it, or should it, make if only one side to a dispute uses these techniques? What should we think about these private processes when both or all sides to a dispute use them?

5. Dispute Resolution and Large Organizations: Ombuds

Private organizations such as corporations and universities have long looked for ways to resolve disputes efficiently within their own structures to avoid the fees, and often the publicity and complexity, of public courts.

One tool that private organizations have used is the Ombuds (formerly known as ombudsman), meaning, from the original Swedish, "agent." Ombuds serve as counselors, problem solvers, and mediators of issues and disputes involving persons employed by or working with companies or organizations. Disputes handled by Ombuds may be internal (such as employment) or external (involving clients, students, or customers of the organization). The concept of the Ombuds

10. Margaret A. Jacobs, Legal Beat: Private Jury Trials: Cheap, Quick, Controversial, Wall St. J., July 7, 1997, at B1.

was originally distilled from a form of neutral public office, used in Scandinavia, to which citizens could seek individualized redress with respect to government action. Today the role of Ombuds has taken many forms in modern American life, in both the public and private sectors. There are many tensions in defining the position, and even Ombuds themselves disagree on such issues as the extent to which the Ombuds must be independent of management; whether the Ombuds is an advocate for citizen-claimants or instead a counselor or a mediator; and whether the Ombuds possesses legal protections, such as confidentiality, that apply to others in similar professional roles. Today, Ombuds worry about whether their primary responsibility is to the grievants who seek them out for advice and help, or to the organization for whom they work. Some Ombuds are working to use their casework experience to document patterns of problems that may then be used to improve organizational policies and practices.[11]

The House of Delegates of the American Bar Association, in February 2004, approved standards for appropriate behavior for public and private Ombuds. These standards emphasize three key characteristics of the Ombuds: impartiality, independence, and confidentiality. The standards also distinguish between three different types of Ombuds: classical (within government), organizations (in educational and private corporate settings), and advocacy (giving advice and counseling to grievants). These standards are reproduced on the Web site of the ABA Section of Dispute Resolution, *http://www.abanet.org/dispute.* In 2017, the ABA House of Delegates adopted Resolution 103 to encourage "the greater use and development of ombuds programs that comply with generally recognized standards of practice, as an effective means of preventing, managing, and resolving individual and systemic conflicts and disputes."

Note that whether the Ombuds treats the information acquired in the course of his work as confidential may differ in traditional and legal understandings of the Ombuds role. In Carman v. McDonnell Douglas Corp., 114 F.3d 790 (8th Cir. 1997), the plaintiff in a civil rights claim sought to obtain notes and documents in possession of a corporate Ombuds; the company claimed that the documents were protected by an "ombudsman privilege." The Eighth Circuit found that the district court lacked sufficient justification for creating an ombudsman privilege and therefore reversed and remanded the district court's denial of plaintiff's discovery request. The appellate court explained that the company failed to make the factual showing necessary to justify a new evidentiary privilege. It stated:

> First, McDonnell Douglas has failed to present any evidence, and indeed has not even argued, that the ombudsman method is more successful at resolving workplace disputes than other forms of alternative dispute resolution, nor has it even pointed to any evidence establishing that its own ombudsman is especially successful at resolving workplace disputes prior to the commencement of litigation. . . . Second, McDonnell Douglas has failed to make a

11. Susan Sturm and Howard Gadlin, Conflict Resolution and Systemic Change, 2007 J. of Disp. Resol. 2; Cathy Costantino, Second Generation Organizational Conflict Management Systems Design: A Practitioner's Perspective on Emerging Issues, 14 Harvard. Negot. L. Rev. 81, 93-96 (2009).

> compelling argument that most of the advantages afforded by the ombudsman method would be lost without the privilege. Even without a privilege, corporate ombudsmen still have much to offer employees in the way of confidentiality, for they are still able to promise to keep employee communications confidential from management. Indeed, when an aggrieved employee or an employee-witness is deciding whether or not to confide in a company ombudsman, his greatest concern is not likely to be that the statement will someday be revealed in civil discovery. More likely, the employee will fear that the ombudsman is biased in favor of the company, and that the ombudsman will tell management everything that the employee says. The denial of an ombudsman privilege will not affect the ombudsman's ability to convince an employee that the ombudsman is neutral, and creation of an ombudsman privilege will not help alleviate the fear that she is not. We are especially unconvinced that "no present or future [McDonnell Douglas] employee could feel comfortable in airing his or her disputes with the Ombudsman because of the specter of discovery." . . . McDonnell Douglas also argues that failure to recognize an ombudsman privilege will disrupt the relationship between management and the ombudsman's office. In cases where management has nothing to hide, this is unlikely.

Carman, 114 F.3d at 793-794 (citation omitted).

Note that several courts have gone the other way and sustained an Ombuds privilege. Is development of a uniform definition or uniform rules desirable? Should states adopt statutes affording legal confidentiality or an evidentiary privilege to work undertaken by Ombuds? See Chapter 8 for a discussion of confidentiality and privilege with respect to mediation. To protect information given to Ombuds or mediators, should it make a difference whether the case is in the private sector or the public sector (where other rules, like the Freedom of Information Act, sunshine laws, or criminal prohibitions might apply)?

Problem 12-5. ***Confidentiality and the Ombuds***

An Ombuds has been asked by a member of an organization to investigate a claim of fraudulent use of funds by her supervisor. The employee asks the Ombuds to hold her identity confidential for fear she will be retaliated against, and the Ombuds assures her that everything she says will be kept confidential. Shortly after the internal meeting occurs, a criminal investigation is launched by public authorities. The court subpoenas the records of the Ombuds. The Ombuds refuses to turn over the records on the ground that he has promised confidentiality to the employee, and he claims an evidentiary privilege on this basis. How should the court rule on a motion to quash the subpoena? See In re Grand Jury Subpoena dated December 17, 1996, 148 F. 3d 487 (5th Cir. 1998).

6. Online Dispute Resolution Mechanisms

As we discussed in the chapters on mediation, some of the most innovative forms of dispute resolution are those developed for use on the Internet. Variously called EDR (electronic dispute resolution), Technology Mediated Dispute Resolution, or ODR (online dispute resolution), these online processes vary enormously. Some ODR directly involves the Internet (such as claims relating to sales made on the Internet or relating to rights over Web site addresses). Other ODR resolves disputes having nothing to do with the Internet, such as automobile accidents. Sometimes the ODR consists simply of taking conventional forms of mediation or arbitration and conducting the process through words and e-mails rather than face-to-face. At other times, more unusual methods are used, including auctions, blind-bidding, or a "behind the screen" mediation conducted by an unseen moderator, either in real time or with sequential discussion. ODR will change quickly as technology changes. For example, as Web-based cameras become more common, the line between online and live hearings may become fuzzier. For an excellent overview of ODR, see *http://www.odr.info* (The Center for Information Technology and Dispute Resolution).

Some of the best-known online providers include *http://www.squaretrade.com* (which handles many disputes relating to eBay); *http://www.cybersettle.com* (which uses a double-blind bidding system to resolve many personal injury claims involving insurance); *http://www.hamaar.com* (which handles insurance and other commercial disputes); and the World Intellectual Property organization, *http://arbiter.wipo.int* (which handles intellectual property disputes). You can view decisions pertaining to conflicts over domain name ownership at *http://www.icann.org/udrp*.

The use of ODR raises unique issues of both over- and under-use of the technology. Does the absence of a "real" person, whether neutral or participant, incite parties to more conflict, or does the necessity of using written words slow down communication and require people to think before they write, encouraging more rational discourse than might occur in person? Does this particular medium encourage parties to overemphasize narrowly defined aspects of the dispute? Can an electronic written dispute really ever be confidential, even with encryption and other protections? Does this form of communication prevent significant "human connection" from occurring? Do some prefer to deal through "texting" and words and machines, without dealing directly with real people? Does dispute resolution on the Web make resources for creative solutions more immediately available to a broader audience? Will parties participate more actively in the drafting of their agreements when they can easily see and draft each other's words? Will middlemen and brokers, such as lawyers and agents, become less useful when people use the Internet to communicate with each other directly? How or why should ODR be regulated when the rest of the Web is largely unregulated? Are there particular issues in ODR that are *sui generis* to technology, or are the issues essentially the same as in other forms of dispute resolution?

Carrie Menkel-Meadow, IS ODR ADR?: REFLECTIONS OF AN ADR FOUNDER FROM 15TH ODR CONFERENCE AT THE HAGUE

3(1) International J. of Online Disp. Resol. 4-6 (2016)

I am left asking the question, do ODR and "A" DR (now "appropriate," not "alternative") dispute resolution have the same goals? Access to justice? Efficiency and transparency of dispute resolution? Quality of solutions? Satisfaction with dispute resolution? Justice?. . .

Online Dispute Resolution is just a bit younger than the ADR movement. Twenty years ago, founders of ODR, Ethan Katsh, Janet Rifkin and Colin Rule, all had a hand in online dispute system design by creating and working with eBay's online dispute resolution system, which now handles over 60 million disputes a year between online vendors and buyers of goods by a private innovative company that wanted to create a world-wide network with a quality reputation. Imagine if all those cases went to court!

. . . [P]arts of the private sector have advanced with uses of online complaint systems and customer service (Amazon is reported to have better customer service than any bricks and mortar business, but recent newspaper reports suggest that is due to exploitation of Amazon workers—if the customer is always right, maybe it is the employee who is making it possible!). . . .

The caseloads of modern life cannot be sustained in a paper-filled legal system. Courts, unlike, hospitals, businesses and even schools, have resisted change in design and function as we move to an electronically based communication society. Lord Fulford (Lord Chancellor of the UK) suggested we could dispense with buildings and consumers and complainants would indeed have access to computers, smartphones and could go to local community libraries to get online to deal with their cases, as physical courts move into "Virtual" courts of streamlined case management and document filing and access, and decisions. . . .

I still have my doubts. The digital divide is still profound—language, both linguistic and computer logic language, age (sight and typing and comprehension for the elderly or those alone), income, access to equipment and learning of constant updates and an inability to talk to a real person to give and get advice about legal matters that don't lend themselves to tick boxes are issues that continue to worry me.

I am most impressed by the Dutch Rechtwijzer divorce platform, which combines great computer design and human interfaces—parties will be able to file for divorce and then use financial and calendar programs to figure out support and child custody schedules on their own, but also to access a counselor or mediator if they prefer some real-life human interaction. Watching how this program can work has converted me somewhat to thinking the future of ODR is a combination of a well-designed computer platform where some interactive possibilities still allow human and more flexible and tailored advice and information to come through. . . .

As one who has been studying the challenges of regulating the new platform economies of Uber and Airbnb as they both offer new access to services, but also challenge labor, health and safety regulations, and tax payments, I wonder how the regulation of advice giving online will play out in different legal regimes—much will depend on the power of that great profession of monopolization—the lawyers.

. . . Nancy Welsh and Leah Wing [reminded us] of the importance of "procedural justice" and ethics of online dispute resolution design. In my personal interviews of several of the platform developers it is clear that ethics and quality is a concern of many. But, what about those entrepreneurial outliers who seek to make money without participating in these voluntary meetings of sharing the state of the art and knowledge at the cutting edge of the field? . . . But what about those who weren't there to hear these exchanges and proposed codes of conduct in an unregulated field?

. . . What I wonder about is what drove me to ADR in the first place—where in the tick boxes and the email communications will there be room to brainstorm and create a different solution, give an apology, come to understand someone else's perspective and improve, rather than just "resolve," relations and disputes. For me Online Dispute Resolution may be one tool for some "access" to dispute resolution of some kind, but I wouldn't over-claim the "justice" part. I recently resolved an ongoing dispute with one of my airlines online—what I felt was relief it was over and done, not any sense that 'justice' had been served and it was very clear that at the other end of my computer was not someone with the power or discretion of a mediator or judge to consider a more creative and tailored solution. I got what the tick boxes or company policy allowed. Will we be getting small claims or civil justice in a programmed set of legally required tick boxes? I thought the common law allowed more flexible rulings and mediators and negotiators working in the "shadow of the law" could still fashion new and creative remedies that looked to the parties' futures, as well as past conflicts.

Problem 12-6. ***Try It Out Yourself!***

The next time you make a less-than-pleasing purchase on the Internet, try contacting one of the ODR services and keep a record of your interactions. Does dispute resolution over the Internet feel different from in-person dispute resolution? Do you have any way of knowing how many people were involved in the dispute?

B. PUBLIC HYBRIDS

The line between ADR and more purportedly "traditional" forms of dispute resolution (litigation and administrative agency processes) has never been as sharp as some might think. There have always been judges and lawyers who encouraged settlement.

Still, it is clear that the recent emphasis on alternatives to litigation has brought these alternatives right into the traditional litigation system and into governmental and administrative processes that were once handled on a more adversarial basis. This institutionalization of ADR can be linked to the 1976 Pound Conference, discussed in Chapter 1, in which Frank Sander urged the development of a public system of justice that would allow disputants to choose among various forms of dispute resolution (often called "the Multidoor Courthouse").

The institutionalization of alternative approaches can also be linked to several important pieces of federal legislation. First, the Civil Justice Reform Act of 1990 encourages all federal courts to reduce cost and delay. As part of this effort, the Act authorizes each district court to "refer appropriate cases to alternative dispute resolution programs that . . . have been designated for use in a district court; or the court may make available, including mediation, minitrial, and summary jury trial." 28 U.S.C. §473(a)(6). Two other important pieces of legislation were also passed in 1990 to encourage the use of ADR approaches in the administrative context. The Negotiated Rulemaking Act of 1990, 5 U.S.C. §§561-570, permits federal agencies to bring together public and private entities and individuals to draft federal regulations. The Administrative Dispute Resolution Act of 1990, 5 U.S.C. §§571-584, permits and encourages federal agencies to use mediation, arbitration, and other alternative processes to resolve disputes quickly and informally. Finally, the Alternative Dispute Resolution Act of 1998, 28 U.S.C. §§651-658, focuses again on the courts, but this time mandates, rather than encourages, the use of alternative processes. In particular, the Act requires "[e]ach United States district court . . . to authorize, by local rule . . . the use of alternative dispute resolution processes in all civil actions. . . ." 28 U.S.C. §651(b).

This portion of the book traces the development of alternative processes in public spheres—that is, in courts and government agencies. One of the key questions to examine is whether the use of these processes is mandatory in either of two senses. First, *can* the judge or administrative agency require disputants to use the alternative process? Second, *must* the judge or administrative agency require disputants to use the alternative process?

1. Mandatory Judicial Settlement Conferences

Even prior to the passage of the laws outlined above, many federal and state judges sought to require disputants to attend settlement conferences or use ADR processes. In issuing such orders, judges often relied on Rule 16 of the Federal Rules of Civil Procedure and its state equivalents. The initial version of Rule 16, entitled "Pre-Trial Procedures; Formulating Issues," authorized courts to require attorneys to appear before them for pretrial conferences. In 1983, the rule was amended to specify that such conferences might "facilitat[e] the settlement of the case." Fed. R. Civ. P. 16(a)(5). The current version of the rule makes even clearer that judges may "take appropriate action, with respect to . . . settlement and the use of special procedures to assist in resolving the dispute when authorized by statute or local rules." Fed. R. Civ. P. 16(c)(9). It specifically allows courts to "require that a party or its representative be present or reasonably available by telephone in order to consider possible settlement of the dispute." Fed. R. Civ. P. 16(c).

The institutionalization of settlement and other forms of dispute resolution is controversial. Judges have authority and experience that make them particularly expert in predicting probable outcomes in an evaluative context, and they are usually well-respected as "wise neutrals" because of their selection process and the formal rules that govern judicial neutrality, recusals, and conflicts of interest. On the other hand, some analysts argue that judges, who are supposed to perform adjudicatory roles, should not be involved in the settlement process—most certainly, when the judge at the settlement conference might be the same one to ultimately find the facts or rule on the legal issues. Judges, these critics argue, are not trained to act as facilitative mediators, and adjudication (with rules of evidentiary admissibility) should be separated from efforts to settle the case—often on grounds different from the legal merits. See Ellen Deason, Beyond "Managerial Judges": Appropriate Roles in Settlement," 78 Ohio St. L. Rev. 74 (2017). A second controversy surrounds the question of whether institutionalizing settlement or other forms of dispute resolution actually serve the intended purpose of saving time and money. Further, questions have been raised about what legal duty lawyers might have to participate in mandatory settlement conferences (and other court required or suggested forms of ADR)—what would it mean to require "good faith participation?"[12] Carrie Menkel-Meadow discusses some of these issues below.[13]

❖ *Carrie Menkel-Meadow*, FOR AND AGAINST SETTLEMENT: USES AND ABUSES OF THE MANDATORY SETTLEMENT CONFERENCE

33 UCLA L. Rev. 490-494, 497-498, 503-504, 506-511, 513-514 (1985)

THE EVIDENCE ON SETTLEMENT CONFERENCES: WHAT DO THE DATA DEMONSTRATE?

. . . The first systematic study of the pretrial conference was undertaken by Maurice Rosenberg on mandatory conference, voluntary conference, and nonconference cases in New Jersey. That study reported findings, as yet uncontradicted, that mandatory pretrial conferences improved the quality of trial proceedings, but actually reduced the efficiency of the court by consuming judges' time in handling conferences, rather than in trying cases. Plaintiff "victories" were as

12. John Lande, Using Dispute System Design Methods to Promote Good-Faith Participation in Court-Connected Mediation Programs, 50 UCLA L. Rev. 69 (2002).

13. See also, Carrie Menkel-Meadow and Bryant Garth, Courts and Civil Procedure in Oxford Handbook of Empirical Legal Research (2010).

frequent (all cases were personal injury cases) in mandatory conference cases as in other cases, though pretried cases were likely to result in higher recoveries. Most significantly, cases submitted to mandatory pretrial conferences were no more likely to result in settlements than those that were not. . . . In addition to quantitative analysis of the data collected, the Rosenberg study also consisted of interviews with and observations of judges with a variety of views on the judicial role in settlement conferences. Some judges participated as passive, neutral referees of the dispute; others were actively engaged in case management (i.e., issue clarification); still others saw settlement as one of their most useful functions. One of the most interesting and seldom noted implications of the Rosenberg study is that if parties achieve settlement with equal frequency in mandatory, voluntary, and nonconference cases, judicial settlement management may indeed be an inefficient use of judicial time. . . .

THE ROLE FOR SETTLEMENT CONFERENCES IN PROVIDING SUBSTANTIVE JUSTICE: WHEN SETTLEMENT?

Those who criticize the role of the judge in settlement functions assume the judge's proper role is purely adjudicative. Owen Fiss has stated starkly: "Courts exist to give meaning to public values, not to resolve disputes." Judith Resnik has argued that judges are required to provide reasoned explanations for their decisions, are supposed to rule without concern for the interests of particular constituencies, are required to act with deliberation, and are to be disinterested and disengaged from the dispute and disputants. Those who criticize the settlement function, I fear, have enshrined the adjudicative function based on an unproven, undemonstrated record of successful performance, just as the efficiency experts have exalted settlement conferences relying on unconvincing statistics. For me, the more fruitful inquiry is to ask under what circumstances adjudication is more appropriate than settlement, or vice-versa. In short, when settlement?. . .

THE FUNCTIONS AND PURPOSES OF THE MANDATORY SETTLEMENT CONFERENCE: THE HOW AND WHY OF SETTLEMENT PRACTICES

As greater numbers of judges and courts use settlement conferences, our information about particular practices increases. . . . What emerges from the data is a variety of role conceptions that parallel the various conceptions of the goals of settlement. For some, efficient case management is the primary role; for others, the primary role is the facilitation of substantive or procedural justice. For others still, the primary role is simple brokering of what would occur anyway in bilateral negotiations. Some judges avoid active settlement activity because they view adjudication as their primary role.

A. The Dangers of Efficiency-Seeking Settlement Techniques

For those who seek to use the settlement conference as a docket-clearing device, the conference becomes most problematic in terms of the substantive and process values (i.e., *quality* of solution) previously discussed. Judges see their role as simplifying the issues until the major issue separating the parties (usually described as money) is identified and the judge can attempt to "narrow the gap." In one study judges and lawyers were asked to report on judicial settlement activity. Seventy-two percent of the lawyers reported that they participated at least once in settlement conferences in which the judge requested the parties to "split the difference." The same study noted that when local rules require settlement conferences judges tend to be more assertive in their settlement techniques (using several techniques that some of the lawyers considered to be unethical). According to the study, jurisdictions with mandatory settlement conferences took more time in moving cases toward trial. This confirms the findings of earlier studies.

A much touted settlement technique is the use of the "Lloyds of London" formula: The settlement judge asks the parties to assess the probabilities of liability and damages and, if the figures are within reasonable range, to split the difference. The difficulty with such settlement techniques is that they tend to monetarize and compromise all the issues in the case. Although some cases are reducible to monetary issues, an approach to case evaluation on purely monetary grounds may decrease the likelihood of settlement by making fewer issues available for trade-offs. Furthermore, a wider definition of options may make compromise unnecessary. . . . The irony is that settlement managers, who think they are making settlement easier by reducing the issues, may in fact be increasing the likelihood of deadlock by reducing the issues to one. Furthermore, as I have argued at length elsewhere, using money as a proxy for other interests the parties may have, may thwart the possibilities for using party interests for mutual gain.

In addition to foreclosing a number of possible settlements, the efficiency-minded settlement officer seems prone to use coercive techniques such as suggesting a particular result, making threats about taking the case off the docket, directing meetings with clients or parties. Lawyers find these techniques problematic. Thus, the quest for efficiency may in fact be counterproductive. . . .

To the extent that settlement procedures are used to achieve substantive outcomes that are better than court-defined remedies, they have implications for how the settlement conference should be conducted and who should conduct it. First, those with knowledge about the larger implications of the litigation—the parties—should be present (this is the principle behind the mini-trial concept with business personnel in attendance) to offer or accept solutions that involve more than simple money settlements. Second, such conferences should be managed by someone other than the trial judge so that interests and considerations that might affect a settlement but would be inadmissible in court will not prejudice a later trial. Some argue for a separate "settlement officer" because the skills required for guiding negotiations are different from those required for trying cases. Third, some cases in which issues should not be traded off should not be subjected to the settlement process at all. For example, in employment discrimination cases, parties should not be asked to accept monetary settlements in lieu of a job for which they are qualified. Finally, a more traditional mediator's role may be more appropriate when the substantive process (i.e., direct communication between the parties) may be more important than the substantive outcome (i.e., employer-employee disputes, some civil rights cases).

CONCLUSION

. . . The settlement conference is a process that can be used to serve a number of different ends. How we evaluate its utility depends on whether we are looking at the individual dispute being settled, the numbers of cases on the docket, the quality of the results (measured against cases that would have settled anyway and cases that would have gone on to trial), the effect of the number and types of settlements on the number and types of cases that remain in the system, or the alternatives available. These considerations do not all point in the same direction. The evaluation of settlement conferences is something we will have to keep watching. . . .

Problem 12-7. ***Uniformity or Variety***

Do you think there should be uniformity in how judges and courts approach settlement and other ADR practices, or is it appropriate for there to be local variation and discretion (whether at the level of court or individual judge)? See John Maull, ADR in the Federal Courts: Would Uniformity Be Better?, 34 Duq. L. Rev. 245 (1996).

In a variant on the settlement conference, some courts use a special form of ADR known as "settlement week." During a specified period of time, regular trial assignments are suspended for an entire courthouse, and judges, magistrates, and often volunteer lawyers spend the entire period meeting with lawyers and parties in "settlement conferences" that may resemble either mediation, in its facilitative or evaluative forms, or nonbinding arbitration. As you might imagine, some argue that this suspension of the trial docket for judges to perform other roles is *ultra vires* judicial roles and is unauthorized by statutes or court rules. Despite such objections, many courts (mostly at the state level) still pursue this settlement device in an effort not only to settle particular cases and reduce court caseloads (the efficiency criterion), but also to educate lawyers and parties about negotiation, mediation, and other settlement techniques and theories (the qualitative approach). What do you think of the practice? What advantages and disadvantages do you see?

2. Special Masters

Just as settlement conferences have long been part of the traditional judicial repertoire, so too have "special masters," appointed by judges to assist them in resolving cases. In 1983, as judges began to experiment in broadening their procedural approaches, Fed. R. Civ. P. 53 was amended to permit individual judges, rather than whole courts, to appoint a "master" to serve as a "referee, an auditor, an examiner [or] an assessor." Fed. R. Civ. P. 53(a) (1983, amended 2003). In 2003, Rule 53 was "revised extensively" because special masters had come to perform a "variety of pretrial and post-trial functions." Fed. R. Civ. P. 53, Advisory Committee's Note on 2003 Amendments. While many special masters simply assist in gathering data or organizing discovery in complex cases, some judges have used special masters far more creatively, bringing in ADR concepts. Some special masters have served as mediators (Kenneth Feinberg in the Agent Orange litigation), developed data for rationalized grids of predictable settlement awards, or made factual or legal findings that helped disputants reach an amicable agreement.

The role of special masters, like that of the judge in settlement conferences, is controversial. Some question the propriety of using non-Article III court personnel to affect the legal rights and remedies of parties before the courts. Others criticize the wide-ranging and essentially unregulated nature of special masters' activities, despite the fact that they are supervised by the appointing judge. Although proponents justify the use of special masters on both efficiency and case management grounds, critics are concerned about whether special masters are sufficiently sensitive to justice and legal-rights issues, and question how they are appointed and held accountable. In the reading below, Francis McGovern examines one judge's creative use of the special master provision.

❖ *Francis E. McGovern*, TOWARD A FUNCTIONAL APPROACH FOR MANAGING COMPLEX LITIGATION

53 U. Chi. L. Rev. 440, 456-463, 465-468 (1986)

In 1979 Judge Fox of the Eastern District of Michigan ruled that the Treaty of 1836 between the United States and the Ottawa and Chippewa peoples reserved to the tribes the right to fish in the treaty waters of the Great Lakes unfettered by regulation by the State of Michigan. The U.S. Department of the Interior subsequently ceased regulating Great Lakes fishing, leaving two independent sovereigns to govern a common natural resource. The tribal commercial fishers and other Michigan commercial and sport fishers competed for fish in most of the Michigan waters of Lakes Superior, Huron, and Michigan.

This competition triggered significant resource depletion and violence among the competitors. In an attempt to save the basic stocks of fish, the tribes, the state, and the United States agreed to close the fishery each year as soon as a certain amount of fish had been caught. As the competition increased, closure occurred earlier and earlier each year, and the tribes took a smaller and smaller percentage of the catch. The tribes could not compete technologically with the state commercial fishers, nor were they numerous enough to compete with the burgeoning state sport fishers. . . .

The treaty itself contained little guidance for resolving the allocation issue.

Given the paucity of precedent for any allocation scheme, the parties' wildly differing approaches, the extreme volatility of the situation, the complexity of any allocation process, and institutional weaknesses associated with continuing judicial management, Judge Enslen decided that if allocation was appropriate, the parties preferably should do it. He also believed that an expeditious decision was necessary to minimize the potential for violence in the uncertain situation. Judge Enslen appointed a special master to prepare the case for trial within eight months and explore the possibilities for settlement. The master's duties did not include ruling on substantive issues, and all his decisions were subject to de novo review by the judge.

Under this view of the lawsuit, its big issues were polycentric, not susceptible to the yes-or-no answers or mutually exclusive inquiries typical of special interrogatories posed to juries. The solution to any given question concerning resource division was dependent upon the solutions reached on the other questions: no issues were independent. This complex interrelationship of issues created difficulties which were compounded by the lack of any—much less clear—legal standards. The court was being asked to make extremely complex management decisions by using policy differences unreflected in the substantive law—"reasonable living standards," "subsistence," "maximizing value," and "equal distribution." Because of the continuing relationship among the parties, any court-imposed solution would probably generate future conflict. Even under optimal conditions, changes in the resource itself would breed future controversies.

Judge Enslen concluded that these characteristics begged for an allocation plan developed by the parties themselves. It was a classic case for integrative bargaining. The parties could identify their respective interests, share information concerning how they valued those interests, and reach for a combination of trade-offs that would maximize each side's use of the resource. Under an economic analysis of integrative bargains, they could seek superior allocations, reduce conflicts of interest, and possibly achieve an optimal solution. Given constraints on a court's ability to gather and evaluate this type of information, the parties would be in a superior position to locate an optimal allocation plan. A party-developed plan would also eliminate any dislocation that could accompany a court-ordered resolution. . . .

The first task was to determine the likelihood of success for any bargain at all. In conjunction with the Program on Negotiation at Harvard, the master attempted to develop a scorable game that would mimic the actual dispute. The task involved identifying each party's interests, selecting all feasible elements to any allocation plan, stating the parties' priorities, and determining the variety of systems that could be used to organize those interests and elements. Each priority was then quantified in regard to each issue. The negotiation theory applied to the game was so-called differences orientation. For example, each party might value the same portion of Lake Michigan differently. The tribes living in the northern Michigan peninsula would probably prefer unlimited access to waters close to their homes. In contrast, the sports fishers generally lived in southern Michigan and would value the southern waters more highly. Differences orientation was particularly valuable here because of the economic and cultural disparities among the parties: what appeared in the litigation context to be a major problem of fundamental value differences was actually an asset in developing a mutually acceptable allocation plan. Once relative differences had been identified, they were entered into a computer.

A program was run to determine if any scenario would satisfy each party's minimum priorities. When the game was limited to the case's legal issues, no negotiated outcome seemed possible. If, however, the issues were expanded to include other items that might be subject to negotiation, some solutions might satisfy the hypothetical minimum interests of the parties. A court, for example, was limited to interpreting the treaty in perpetuity; an agreement by the parties could be for a term of years. A negotiated disposition, unlike a typical court decision, could also include provisions for plantings of fish, monetary payments, and market development. When these and other issues were added to the computer, there emerged combinations of components which indicated different possible solutions where agreement was feasible. . . .

The court then assigned the special master to mediate among the named parties and the litigating amici. Because the case would eventually be tried to the judge, his ability to facilitate negotiation was limited by his strong ethical constraints against prejudging the outcome of the case. Therefore, the master performed this role while insulating the judge from the details of any bargaining. As a part of the mediation role, the master also kept the parties' critical decision makers aware of the progress of the litigation and the negotiations. He met with the leaders and sometimes virtually all the members of the tribes, officials of the U.S. Department of the Interior, and Michigan's Governor, Attorney General, and the Director of its Department of Natural Resources.

. . . After three days of negotiations the parties reached a settlement on March 28, four weeks before the scheduled trial. The settlement agreement closely paralleled one of the scorable game solutions that indicated possible areas of compromise. The court approved the settlement, but one of the tribes overruled its leaders on a subsequent 31-29 vote and decided to proceed with the litigation. All the other parties ratified the negotiated agreement. The judge severed the two alternative management plans for trial, conducted a trial, and ruled on the merits in favor of the negotiated plan. . . .

Problem 12-8. ***Games Instead of Trials?***

What do you think of the appointment of a special master in a complex case like this? Is this appropriate under the Federal Rules of Civil Procedure? Is this an abdication of judicial authority by the judge or the proper use of a court to facilitate a more lasting, pleasing settlement to all parties? Was it appropriate for the special master to use a scorable game (or simulation or economic model) to help the parties quantify their preferences and priorities and to rationalize the negotiation process, as you have studied it here? Explain your answer.

Were the deviations from the traditional trial model—the special master, scorable game, abbreviated discovery schedule, computer-assisted negotiations, and presentation from United States v. Washington—justified? Would the parties have settled anyway? Was the settlement "better" than an adjudicated outcome? Given the stated criteria, an ex post analysis suggests that the intervention was worthwhile. Ex ante, however, with the extremely high risk of no settlement, the answers are less clear.

Perhaps the most dramatic use of a Special Master was the appointment of private attorney mediator and arbitrator, Kenneth Feinberg, to allocate government funds to victims and survivors of the attack on the World Trade Center on September 11, 2001, pursuant to special statutory authority and subsequent authorizing regulations, see 28 C.F.R. §§104.2 et seq. (2003). Acting relatively alone and *pro bono publico* (without pay but with assistance from his firm and members of the Department of Justice), Mr. Feinberg allocated millions of dollars on behalf of the government to compensate those who no longer had the legal ability to sue airlines and the government (though a few lawsuits are still pending). Mr. Feinberg used a special master-arbitral process in which parties presented documents of their claims and were allocated amounts based on a regularized grid of death benefits, injury, pain and suffering, and some remit for secondary coverage and other benefits. Those who requested a personal hearing with Mr. Feinberg were granted one and could tell the story of the harm they had suffered, though this rarely, or seldom, changed the amount they received. In a subsequent memoir about the experience, Special Master Feinberg suggested that perhaps a more mediative, rather than arbitral, process would have been appropriate, given the extreme pain and suffering, and need for expression and catharsis expressed by the claimants. He also opined that the government should never again provide for a special compensation scheme (based on tort principles of recovery) in extreme catastrophes like this one. Instead, he would favor something closer to equal payments for all victims.[14] Is Special Master Feinberg feeling the "weight" of judicial authority in allocating funds, without the full structure of adjudication, or is he suggesting something else is troubling about the process?

In more recent years, this particular field has been trying to move away from the terminology "special master" and replace it with the term "court-appointed neutral," or CAN. In 2023, the American Bar Association adopted Resolution 516, which amends the term in ABA documents encouraging the use of CANs. The resolution also "supports rule and legislative changes designed to replace the term 'master' or 'special master' with 'court-appointed neutral.'" The leading organization of CANs, the Academy of Court-Appointed Neutrals ("ACAN") has created initiatives to diversify the field and create pathways for more diverse attorneys to engage in this work.

---

14. Kenneth Feinberg, What Is Life Worth? The Unprecedented Effort to Compensate the Victims of 9/11 (2006). In fact, Feinberg did act as Special Master again in the Deepwater Horizon oil spill compensation program and in a variety of other mass compensation programs (e.g., Virginia Tech school shootings and Boston Marathon bombings), as well as serving as a consultant to governments facing aggregative compensation situations (e.g., the London bombings of July 7, 2007).

3. Administrative Law Judges

Many federal and state agencies have used "quasi" judicial officers to hold hearings in a variety of regulatory matters, both involving individual rights and to rule on agency actions., such as enforcement of regulations. In a recent Supreme Court case, *SEC v. Jarkesy,* 603 U.S.___ (2024), the Court ruled that where civil penalties could be at stake in an enforcement of securities regulations, the party being assessed was entitled to a civil jury trial under the Seventh Amendment. Consider what implications this decision has for a variety of "alternative" adjudicative processes in formal proceedings. What kinds of arguments can you imagine parties making in other contexts based on this case? Is the claim for a right to a jury trial in mandatory arbitration settings (see Chapter 10) up for grabs again? Why or why not?

4. Disputes Involving Groups: Aggregate Claims and Class Actions

Disputes involving groups offer unique problems and opportunities. In this section, we examine some of the hybrid processes that have been developed to handle such disputes. As we discuss hybrid processes for resolving group claims, we explore both claims that begin with litigation and group disputes that have not yet been, and might never be, filed in a court. Alternative procedural processes can be useful in both contexts. (Chapter 13, on multiparty processes, further examines some of the unique aspects of disputes involving groups.)

From the litigation standpoint, group claims are sometimes desirable but potentially are difficult to handle. The class action was developed in the United States as one means of handling special aspects of group claims. Under Rule 23 of the Federal Rules of Civil Procedure and its state law equivalents, one or more named plaintiffs can bring claims on behalf of other unnamed, often unidentified, class members. Compared to individual litigation, proponents of the class action believe it is more efficient, improves access to the litigation system, and serves the public interest.[15] At the same time, class actions can be slow and expensive. Questions also arise as to whether class representatives or their lawyers adequately represent absent class members.

The increasing recognition that mass torts can be handled as group claims has increased the pressure on courts to find alternative means to handle such claims. Hundreds and sometimes thousands of people claim to have been injured in natural disasters, through the mass production of defective products, or by actions taken against large groups (as in employment discrimination, securities litigation, antitrust, and consumer protection actions). Courts need to find ways to manage

---

15. The American Law Institute has completed a review of legal guidelines for mass and group litigation, in both class action and other aggregative forms; see ALI, Principles of the Law of Aggregate Litigation (Samuel Issacharoff, Robert H. Klonoff, Richard Nagareda, and Charles Silver, Reporters, 2010).

these complex suits.[16] Sometimes alternative processes are used in conjunction with litigation of mass claims; at other times the alternative processes take the place of litigation. This section provides examples of several of these different approaches, starting with those most closely connected to litigation. First, it examines uses of ADR in connection with mass personal injury litigation. Second, it considers how ADR has been used in connection with employment class actions.

As you read these excerpts, consider that managing group claims has itself become a subfield of dispute resolution professionals who help courts, government agencies, or private institutions design dispute resolution systems for mass claims. These processes raise special concerns and often engender controversy as they try to balance such interests as efficiency, equity, fairness, justice, and the desire for individualized treatment. Note that more informal versions of ADR can be devised to resolve group disputes.

Deborah R. Hensler, A GLASS HALF FULL, A GLASS HALF EMPTY: THE USE OF ALTERNATIVE DISPUTE RESOLUTION IN MASS PERSONAL INJURY LITIGATION

73 Tex. L. Rev. 1587, 1596, 1598-1600, 1606-1609, 1612-1616, 1619-1623 (1995)

Although mass torts may constitute only a small fraction of the total national civil caseload in any given year, litigation arising out of the use of—or exposure to—mass-marketed products has accounted for as much as one-fourth of civil money suits in some courts.

In addition to their sheer numbers, these cases challenge the civil justice system because of the grave significance of their results to the plaintiffs—who often seek compensation for alleged life-threatening and other severe injuries—and to the defendants—whose financial viability may ride on the outcome of the litigation. Moreover, because the costs of this type of litigation are measured in the billions of dollars and because a large fraction of these dollars are attributable to "transaction costs"—that is, legal fees and expenses—the management of the litigation by judges and attorneys attracts considerable attention. . . .

Mass torts involve a common set of injuries that occurred in the same or similar circumstances—for example, a hotel fire, a building collapse, or widespread product use—and that are allegedly linked to the actions of a single or small number of defendants. Plaintiffs and defendants are represented by a

16. See Eric D. Green, What Will We Do When Adjudication Ends? We'll Settle in Bunches: Bringing Rule 23 into the Twenty-First Century, 44 UCLA L. Rev. 1773 (1997); Francis E. McGovern, Settlement of Mass Torts in a Federal System, 36 Wake Forest L. Rev. 871 (2001); Carrie Menkel-Meadow, Ethics and the Settlements of Mass Torts: When the Rules Meet the Road, 80 Cornell L. Rev. 1159 (1995).

small number of law firms (relative to the magnitude of the litigation), and a single or small number of judges frequently manage the litigation because of aggregative procedures such as multidistricting and class action certification. . . .

In addition to numerosity, commonality, and interdependence of case values, many mass personal injury torts share three other features: controversy over scientific evidence of causation, emotional or political heat, and higher than average potential for claiming by allegedly injured parties. . . .

Mass personal injury litigation also appears to stimulate a higher rate of claiming than is associated with ordinary personal injuries. Contrary to conventional wisdom, most Americans do not bring legal claims when they are injured in accidents. . . .

These distinguishing features of mass tort litigation—numerosity, commonality, interdependence of case values, scientific controversy, heated emotional atmosphere, and increased propensity to claim—set the conditions for the resolution of all mass torts. They create the incentives for plaintiffs' attorneys to invest in mass litigation, for defendants to settle cases, and for judges to adopt novel disposition practices. . . .

Courts have responded to the challenges posed by mass personal injury litigation by devising streamlined procedures to resolve individual cases, informally aggregating and formally consolidating cases for settlement or trial, facilitating global settlements, and facilitating the design and implementation of administrative processes for delivering compensation to individual claimants. These approaches have been used alone in some litigation, but many mass tort cases have involved the use of two or more of these approaches concurrently or sequentially. These techniques have resolved litigation in trial courts, bankruptcy courts, and private fora. Over time, courts, and some attorneys, appear to have developed a preference for collective mechanisms, such as consolidation and aggregate settlements, over streamlining individual case disposition, and for global settlements resolving all current and future cases. . . .

1. Settlement Strategies

Many judges have tried to settle, rather than adjudicate, the cases that have been consolidated before them. In some instances, judges have played a strong role in developing the settlement plan; in others, judges have relied heavily on a special master appointed to help the attorneys shape the plan. The attorneys in turn are usually organized into committees either appointed by the judge or formed voluntarily. . . .

2. Elements of Global Settlement Plans

Judges, special masters, and attorneys have fashioned settlement strategies that have three central components.

a. ***Aggregate settlement amounts that cap defendants' damages exposure*** —The aggregate value of the settlement fund (and the allocation of shares among defendants) is a negotiated amount, which is sometimes determined more by what defendants are willing to pay and plaintiffs' attorneys are willing to accept than by any systematic data on the total size of the claimant population and the severity of their injuries.

b. ***Rules for allocating the settlement fund among claimants.*** The allocation of dollars from a fund is determined by a grid or matrix—also arrived at through negotiation—that assigns potential claimants to categories with different cash values on the basis of evidence of causation, disease, or injury severity. The development of compensation grids is closely linked to the concept of a limited fund, which seems to lend itself to a rule-based system for allocating compensation. The criteria that underlie compensation grids or matrices are derived from an amalgam of scientific or medical information about the nature of injuries and their appropriate treatment, information about the factors that have determined settlement or trial value before the aggregate settlement, and the amount for which negotiators will settle.

In some early global settlements of mass toxic torts, the details of the grid were not worked out until after the attorneys had agreed on the total value of the settlement. In the Agent Orange litigation, special master Kenneth Feinberg suggested criteria for distributing compensation funds in a draft settlement plan that was shared with attorneys before the $180 million settlement was reached, but the final distribution plan was apparently devised subsequently. . . . The Dalkon Shield bankruptcy plan laid out a framework for allocating compensation that included four options—or tracks—for obtaining payment, but did not indicate what injuries would be compensated or what amounts would be paid under each option. It was left to the trustees of the fund established under the plan to develop specific eligibility criteria and payment levels. Perhaps in response to criticism of the operation of the Dalkon Shield Claimants' Trust, more recent global settlement plans have laid out detailed injury and disease categories and specified exact payments or payment ranges for each category. . . .

c. ***Procedures for distributing compensation.*** Once global settlements are finalized, the daunting task of distributing funds to claimants begins. Most global settlement plans have established a claimants' trust facility to manage the corpus of funds and a claims resolution facility to distribute compensation to claimants. These facilities differ from case to case in many respects, including the options they offer for dispute resolution. Some payment schemes, such as those devised by the DDT settlement and the Agent Orange settlement, are wholly administrative. Recognizing the essentially administrative task of claims payment under the Agent Orange scheme, Judge Weinstein contracted with the Aetna insurance company to distribute compensation. At the other extreme, the first Manville Trust, although intended to rely primarily on negotiation, mediation, and arbitration to decide payment amounts, found itself embroiled in litigation and sank under the pressure of an unanticipated number of filings and size of damage awards. . . .

In an effort to balance efficiency and equity concerns, the Dalkon Shield Claims Facility offered claimants a combination of administrative processes, for no injury and minor injury claims, and ADR processes, for more serious claims, with trial available for those who rejected other options. Under Option 1 of the bankruptcy plan, claimants could receive a flat amount of $725 simply for filing an affidavit that they were Shield users and had sustained injury. More than half of the claimants availed themselves of this option. Under Option 2 of the plan, claimants who presented minimal medical evidence of use and injury could receive scheduled damages ranging from $850 to $5500, depending on the nature of the injury. Under Option 3, claimants who thought they had stronger evidence of causation and damages above the Option 2 cap could enter into more traditional negotiations, including a settlement conference, with the Trust. Plaintiffs' lawyers expected that Option 3 offers would be in line with historical settlement values of Dalkon Shield legal claims. Finally, under Option 4, claimants could elect binding arbitration or trial. To implement the Option 4 portion of the plan, the Trust contracted with the Duke University Private Adjudication Center [to provide arbitration services] . . . .

Creative dispute resolution techniques are also used in the context of employment discrimination class actions. The settlement agreements in such class actions often create special procedures for awarding relief to class members. Some settlements cap the monetary awards made available; other settlements simply consider class members' individual claims. Of course, the process of designing these systems leads to interesting dispute resolution problems. Dispute resolution professionals often help design these systems, although given the adversarial nature of the conflict, their role may be more to facilitate than to serve as experts in process design.[17]

Problem 12-9. ***What's the Best Process?***

Where many people are hurt or injured at the same time, do you think ADR can deal appropriately with legal damages, the need for catharsis, and other forms of redress—or should claimants retain their rights to go to trial? Does it depend on the kind of case—death or bodily injury? Employment discrimination or civil rights violations? Economic harm? Opioid addiction?

Another way of dealing with mass tort claims has been through bankruptcy, as in the Dalkon Shield case. Similarly, a major settlement of the opioid claims was negotiated through the bankruptcy process, providing some individual monetary compensation, but also providing billions of dollars in aid for states, cities and communities to provide medical services and education for opioid addicts. The

17. See Lisa Bingham, Cynthia J. Hallberlin, Denise A. Walker & Won-Tae Chung, Dispute System Design and Justice in Employment Dispute Resolution: Mediation at the Workplace, 14 Harvard Negot. L. Rev. 1 (2009); Margaret L. Shaw & Lynn P. Cohn, Employment Class Actions Provide Unique Context for ADR, 5 Disp. Resol. Mag. 10 (Summer 1999), for further discussion of these processes and of the role neutrals can play in helping to devise ADR systems in this special context. For a recent survey of comparative approaches to dispute resolution in employment discrimination, see Jean R. Sternlight, In Search of the Best Procedure for Enforcing Employment Discrimination Laws: A Comparative Analysis, 78 Tulane L. Rev. 1401 (2004).

Supreme Court rejected this settlement in Harrington v. Purdue Pharma, 603 U.S. ___, holding that a settlement with the bankrupt company, Purdue Pharma, could not "release" the Sackler family (owners of Purdue, but not included in the bankruptcy plan formally, even though they had contributed about $6 billion to the settlement fund). Though the decision was on a formal reading of the bankruptcy statute, consider what this means for involving "all" the parties in dispute-resolution processes. After this decision, many new lawsuits have now been filed against the Sacklers; see Chapter 13.

For the view that some claimants may find it more cathartic and therapeutic to have a hearing, see Carrie Menkel-Meadow, Taking the Mass Out of Mass Torts: Reflections of a Dalkon Shield Arbitrator on Alternative Dispute Resolution, Judging, Neutrality, Gender, and Process, 31 Loy. L.A. L. Rev. 513-550 (1998).

In addition to efforts to develop class action, global settlements, and institutional settlement facilities at the national level, there have also been international efforts to construct programs for compensating people when there are mass injuries or many claims arising out of the same events. For example, the UN established a United Nations Compensation Commission in 1991 to compensate people who were injured in the Iraqi invasion of Kuwait in 1990.[18] And for many years, a compensation program, primarily using arbitration, that adjudicated claims arising out of the hostage-taking by Iran of Americans (and the subsequent freezing of Iranian assets in the United States) operated out of a special tribunal in The Hague. For many years until relations deteriorated again, Israel and Lebanon maintained a public arbitral body (outside of formal courts) to adjudicate and order compensation for claims arising out of border disputes between citizens of both countries.[19]

Problem 12-10. *ADR for Aggregate Harm?*

Should the government have provided for an ADR process for claims arising out of the harm caused by the Hurricane Katrina in New Orleans? Was the government responsible for any of the harm? What kind of substantive compensatory program, with what kind of process, would have been appropriate? Do you think the government will ever again provide this kind of substantive relief or civil process for aggregate claims of this sort?

Should the government develop an ADR program for resolving the mass mortgage foreclosure and home finance issues arising out of the 2008 recession? Is this a different kind of mass or group dispute? Is it "private" or "public"? Is it a "mass" dispute or a series of private individual disputes? Who is responsible? Who should "resolve" these disputes? See Symposium, 11 Nev. L. J. 2010.

18. Francis McGovern, Dispute System Design: The United Nations Compensation Commission, 14 Harvard Negot. L. Rev. 171 (2009).

19. Gabriella Blum, Islands of Agreement: Managing Enduring Armed Rivalries (2007).

5. The Summary Jury Trial

As the ADR movement gained momentum, judges began to use new procedural techniques more creatively. The private mini-trial was so successful in the late 1970s and early 1980s that federal judge Thomas Lambros of Ohio imported aspects of it for use in federal courts. The practice spread to state courts as well.[20]

In summary jury trials, used in jury cases containing contested factual or legal liability questions, lawyers present shortened versions of their cases (usually no more than part of a day), drawing on argument, testimony, or summarized depositions and documentary evidence. The audience—members of a regular jury venire who don't actually serve as jurors—deliberates and offers what is ultimately only an advisory verdict. The verdict is then communicated to the parties to encourage more realistic negotiations. This process was credited with providing lodestar damage assessments in some kinds of repeat cases (such as those involving asbestos); reducing caseloads; and offering individualized assessments in cases with conflicting lawyer or party demands. However, this process also creates controversy because of its mandatory nature, its unorthodox use of jurors (who often don't know they are not "real" jurors), and its use of public courtrooms to facilitate private settlements. Retired federal judge Richard Posner (and the founder of the law and economics school) criticized this process in The Summary Jury Trial and Other Methods of Alternative Dispute Resolution: Some Cautionary Observations, 53 U. Chi. L. Rev. 366 (1986), and the process is not much used anymore. Can you see any places where it might still be useful?

6. Early Neutral Evaluation

Instead of using jurors or judges to help facilitate a settlement within the court system, some courts have developed hybrids that draw on mediation, arbitration, and case management and valuation practices. Early Neutral Evaluation (ENE) uses volunteer or paid lawyers to help parties assess the value of a case before trial and, in some cases, assist in fact development and discovery issues. ENE was first developed in the federal courts in the Northern District of California (San Francisco), while a similar system, called "Michigan mediation," was developed in the state trial courts in Michigan. In both settings, the practice involves shortened case presentations (with varying degrees of documentary or witness evidence, discovery completion, and argumentation) to either a single lawyer (California federal practice) or panel of three lawyers (in Michigan), who then evaluate the case. The evaluation may suggest either substantive strengths or weaknesses in the case or attach a numerical value to what a likely verdict would be. This nonbinding

20. Thomas D. Lambros, The Summary Jury Trial and Other Alternative Methods of Dispute Resolution: A Report to the Judicial Conference of the United States Committee on the Operation of the Jury System, 103 F.R.D. 461 (1984).

evaluation is then used to facilitate settlement negotiations by the parties and their lawyers. In some cases, if the evaluation does not result in a settlement, the neutral evaluators may assist the parties with other matters, such as developing a discovery schedule, streamlining issues for trial, or planning other settlement events.

The Federal District Court for the Northern District of California sets out its process on its Web site, *https://www.cand.uscourts.gov/localrules/ADR* (last updated 5/19/18). It explains that the goals of ENE are to:

> Enhance direct communication between the parties about their claims and supporting evidence
> Provide an assessment of the merits of the case by a neutral expert
> Provide a "reality check" for clients and lawyers
> Identify and clarify the central issues in dispute
> Assist with discovery and motion planning or with an informal exchange of key information
> Facilitate settlement discussions, when requested by the parties.

The district court Web site explains that "settlement is not the major goal of ENE, but the process can lead to settlement." Under the district court's plan, the evaluator provides a written assessment (samples are provided on the Web site), and parties are given the opportunity to negotiate a resolution either prior or subsequent to hearing the evaluation. The neutral may also help facilitate these negotiations. Attendance at the ENE is mandatory not only by the lead trial attorney for each side, but also by "clients with settlement authority and knowledge of the facts" and by "insurers of parties," if their agreement would be necessary for a settlement to occur. Id.[21]

Some jurisdictions use the ENE process in family-law cases. In Hennepin County, Minnesota (home of Minneapolis), parents can present their case to a male-female pair of evaluators who provide an evaluation of the likely outcome of a contested custody case. The parents are asked to set aside up to three hours total to make their presentations to the evaluators. Do you think this is a beneficial way to handle disputed custody cases?

7. Court-Connected Mediation and Nonbinding Arbitration

Other than settlement conferences, the most prevalent forms of court-connected ADR are mediation and nonbinding arbitration. In nonbinding arbitration, the award usually only becomes final if it is voluntarily accepted by the parties. The primary

21. For further discussion of the ENE process, see Stephanie Smith and Jan Martinez, An Analytic Framework for Dispute System Design, 14 Harvard Negot. L. Rev. 123, 146-151 (2009); W.D. Mich. L. Civ. R. 16.4; Wayne D. Brazil, A Close Look at Three Court-Sponsored ADR Programs: Why They Exist, How They Operate, What They Deliver, and Whether They Threaten Important Values, 1990 U. Chi. Legal F. 303; Robert J. Niemic, Donna Stienstra & Randall E. Ravitz, Guide to Judicial Management of Cases in ADR (2001); Elizabeth Plapinger & Donna Stienstra, ADR and Settlement in the Federal District Courts: A Sourcebook for Judges & Lawyers (1996).

purpose of this form of arbitration would be, like summary jury trials or mini-trials, to give the parties (and their lawyers) some prediction of how a claim would be resolved if it went to trial. The hope would be that once the disputants learn this prediction and have an opportunity to go through a process that is much like court litigation, they would abide by the arbitrator's decision. Although nonbinding arbitration is sometimes agreed to voluntarily, as we explored in Chapters 9, 10, and 11 and in the first part of this chapter, most "nonbinding" arbitration now takes place in both federal and state courts, which, by statute, court order, or procedural rule, assign certain classes of cases (usually by monetary amount) to an arbitration proceeding. This is nonbinding in the sense that often a de novo appeal is possible, but court fees and bonds often "tax" such awards to make them feel more "binding." Nevertheless, so far, most challenges to this form of "nonbinding" arbitration as infringing on the Seventh Amendment right to civil jury trial have failed.[22]

Many courts have adopted nonbinding arbitration programs with the hope that they will provide a quicker, cheaper form of justice than litigation. Certain jurisdictions, such as Pennsylvania, have used mandatory court-supervised nonbinding arbitration for a long time in both their state and federal courts. Other state and federal jurisdictions adopted mandatory nonbinding arbitration programs during the 1980s and 1990s. Many of the federal programs were established in response to the Civil Justice Reform Act of 1990. Over half of the states had rules allowing or requiring nonbinding arbitration. About a quarter of the federal district courts had a nonbinding arbitration program, with ten of them requiring nonbinding arbitration.[23] However, a number of federal court programs have replaced their mandatory nonbinding arbitration programs with mediation.[24] Court-connected arbitration programs require that certain categories of disputes be heard by arbitrators before they can be aired in court. For example, Local Rule 53.2 of the Eastern District of Pennsylvania requires that virtually all suits brought for less than $150,000 proceed initially to nonbinding arbitration. Nevada Arbitration Rule 3 provides that, with certain exceptions, all civil cases brought for $50,000 or less must be handled first through nonbinding arbitration.

In most programs, the arbitrators are local attorneys or retired judges, but the ways in which they are chosen and conduct the arbitration may vary substantially. Some programs assign the arbitrators to a case and afford the litigants little or no opportunity to choose or even reject arbitrators, whereas other programs allow disputants to select their own arbitrators. In some programs, as in Pennsylvania,

22. Jean Sternlight, Mandatory Binding Arbitration and the Demise of the Seventh Amendment Right to Jury Trial, 16 Ohio St. J. on Disp. Res. 669 (2001); Dwight Golann, Making Alternative Dispute Resolution Mandatory: The Constitutional Issues, 68 Oregon L. Rev. 487 (1989). See also Zamaro v. Price, 213 P.3d 490 (2009) (finding no right to trial by jury violated even though arbitrator's decision was shown to the jury in a "de novo" hearing).

23. Amy J. Schmitz, Nonconsensual + Nonbinding = Nonsensical? Reconsidering Court-Connected Arbitration Programs, 10 Cardozo J. Conflict Resol. 587 (2009).

24. Wayne Brazil, Should Court Sponsored ADR Survive? 21 Ohio St. J. on Disp. Resol. 241 (2006); Lisa B. Bingham, Why Suppose? Let's Find Out: A Public Policy Research Program on Dispute Resolution, 2002 J. Disp. Resol. 101, 120.

arbitrators sit in panels and hear several cases in a day. But in Nevada, court-annexed arbitrators hear cases individually and typically hear only a single matter in a day.

The economics of court-annexed arbitration also varies quite a bit. In some jurisdictions, the program is provided free to disputants, and the arbitrators serve on a volunteer basis or receive merely a small honorarium, such as $100 per case. But in other jurisdictions, such as Nevada, the disputants are required to pay for court-annexed arbitration. The Nevada Arbitration Rules require disputants to pay arbitrators $100 per hour up to a maximum of $1,000 per case (unless otherwise authorized by the ADR commissioner), and further require payment of up to $250 in costs to the arbitrator. These fees and costs are to be shared among the disputants.

Most court-annexed arbitration rules provide that the ordinary rules of evidence may be "relaxed," and that the arbitrators have discretion to modify the types and timing of discovery that are permitted in court. These rules are intended to make the process speedier and cheaper than litigation.

The nonbinding arbitration rules of many jurisdictions provide that the arbitration award becomes final and binding unless either party demands a trial de novo within a short period of time, often 30 days. Thus, although the award is nonbinding, it can easily become binding. Some jurisdictions seek to discourage parties from seeking a trial de novo by providing that a party who seeks trial de novo and secures a result less favorable than the arbitrator's award must pay a significant amount. In California, a party who is unsuccessful on appeal must pay opposing party's court costs and expert fees, and also reimburse the county or opposing party for fees paid to arbitrator. In Nevada, if the party requesting the trial de novo fails to obtain a judgment that exceeds the arbitration award by at least 20 percent of the award, the non-requesting party is entitled to its attorney's fees and costs associated with the proceedings following the request for trial de novo. In other jurisdictions, the risk is far less, since the party who unsuccessfully pursues a trial de novo loses only the arbitrator fees of $100 or so. E.D. Pa. Local Rule 53.2(7)(E).

Although court-mandated nonbinding arbitration remains popular in some jurisdictions, it is unclear whether these programs meet the goal of resolving disputes more cheaply and quickly than through a combination of litigation and negotiation.[25]

---

25. Some books and articles discussing nonbinding arbitration include Amy Schmitz, supra note 23; Jane W. Adler et al., Simple Justice: How Litigants Fare in the Pittsburgh Court Arbitration Program (1983); Lisa Bernstein, Understanding the Limits of Court-Connected ADR: A Critique of Federal Court-Annexed Arbitration Programs, 141 U. Pa. L. Rev. 2169 (1993); Deborah Hensler, What We Know and Don't Know About Court-Administered Arbitration, 69 Judicature 270 (1986); Judge William P. Lynch, Problems with Court-Annexed Mandatory Arbitration: Illustrations from the New Mexico Experience, 32 N.M. L. Rev. 181 (2002); Barbara S. Meierhoefer, Court-Annexed Arbitration in Ten District Courts (1990); and Note, L. Christopher Rose, Nevada's Court-Annexed Mandatory Arbitration Program: A Solution to Some of the Causes of Dissatisfaction with the Civil Justice System, 36 Idaho L. Rev. 171 (1999).

Interestingly, nonbinding arbitration was originally more popular, but today more jurisdictions opt for mediation. Can you explain this trend? When mediation and nonbinding arbitration are handled through the courts rather than privately, several interesting policy issues inevitably arise. Not surprisingly, similar issues arise with respect to other court-connected processes that we have already discussed:

- Should the process be voluntary or mandatory from the perspective of the parties?
- Should the judge have discretion concerning which cases to order to mediation or arbitration, or should there be a set rule?
- Should mediation or arbitration be free, or should the parties pay a fee?
- What qualifications should be required of the mediators and arbitrators, and how should these be monitored?
- If mediation or arbitration is mandatory, who should be required to attend? Attorneys? Parties?
- Should the parties be required to participate in good faith? If so, how should good faith be determined?
- Should the proceedings be protected by rules regarding confidentiality or privilege?
- Should the practice of having volunteer neutrals in court-sponsored programs continue, or should neutrals be compensated like other professionals?

8. Restorative Justice: ADR in Criminal Contexts

Although most people think of using ADR only with respect to civil disputes, it is also used to handle conflicts arising in the criminal context. "Victim-offender" mediation and "restorative justice" aim to make the victim whole (or at least more whole), to instill some sense of remorse and responsibility in the offender, and, more generally, to heal the conflict and restore the fabric of communities torn apart by crime. While some programs focus on caseload reduction, most programs focus on broader themes of forgiveness and reconciliation, with reconciliation being sought not only for its own sake but to prevent vengeance and vigilantism. These forms of ADR are used in settings ranging from neighborhood disputes and minor misdemeanors all the way up the criminal ladder to serious felonies and murder. Proponents of restorative justice advocate approaching crime and punishment from more than just a legalistic perspective. Some programs are used as pre-trial and diversionary (agreements and apologies can result in dismissal of charges), while others focus more on post-conviction rehabilitation or reconciliation involving injured parties and the community. Though over the last decade many restorative justice programs have focused on youth offenders, programs exist for both juveniles and adults.

Marty Price, PERSONALIZING CRIME: MEDIATION PRODUCES RESTORATIVE JUSTICE FOR VICTIMS AND OFFENDERS

7 Disp. Resol. Mag. 8-11 (2000)

Our traditional criminal justice system is a system of retributive justice—a system of institutionalized vengeance. The system is based on the belief that justice is accomplished by assigning blame and administering pain. If you do the crime, you do the time. If you do the time, then you've paid your debt to society and justice has been done. But justice for whom?

In our system, crime is defined as an act against the state (e.g., State v. John Jones) rather than an act against individuals and their community. The prosecutor is the attorney for the state, not the harmed individuals. Victims may be viewed, at worst, as impediments to the prosecutorial process—at best, as valuable witnesses for the prosecution of the state's case. Only the most progressive prosecutor's offices view crime victims as their clients and prioritize the needs of victims.

The criminal justice system is offender-centered, placing its emphasis upon guilt, punishment and the rights of the accused. Crime victims' so-called rights are violated as often as they are honored. In most victims' rights amendments and statutes, these are rights without remedies.

Incarceration may be said to serve functions other than retribution: incapacitation, deterrence and rehabilitation. Public safety requires incapacitation of the minority of incarcerated offenders who are violent and dangerous. Intuitively, incarceration (or the threat of incarceration) may seem like a deterrent, but its proven deterrent effects are extremely limited. It is generally agreed that some rehabilitation programs work (notably, drug treatment), but rehabilitation as a goal of imprisonment has been widely abandoned by the corrections system in the United States since the 1970s. Although it is difficult to justify empirically on a broad scale, punishment appears to be a societal value in and of itself. Politicians cry out for more and longer prison terms; the building of prisons has become a major growth industry. In some states, the corrections budget exceeds the education budget.

PUNISHMENT OFTEN UNSATISFYING FOR MANY VICTIMS OF CRIME

Because our society defines justice in terms of guilt and punishment, crime victims often seek the most severe possible punishment for their offenders. Victims believe this will bring them justice, but it often leaves them feeling empty and unsatisfied. Retribution cannot restore their losses, answer their questions, relieve their fears, help them make sense of their tragedy, or heal their wounds. And punishment cannot mend the torn fabric of the community that has been violated.

FOCUS ON INDIVIDUALS, HEALING

Restorative justice has emerged as a social movement for justice reform. Virtually every state is implementing restorative justice at state, regional and/or local levels. A growing number of states that have officially adopted restorative justice principles and policies require any justice program that receives state funding to adhere to these principles.

Instead of viewing crime as a violation of law, restorative justice emphasizes one fundamental fact: crime damages people, communities and relationships. Retributive justice asks three questions: who did it, what laws were broken and what should be done to punish or treat the offender? Contrast a restorative justice inquiry, in which three very different questions receive primary emphasis. First, what is the nature of the harm resulting from the crime? Second, what needs to be done to "make it right" or repair the harm? Third, who is responsible for the repair?

Traditionally, accountability has been viewed as compliance with program rules or as taking one's punishment. But accepting punishment is passive, requiring nothing from the offender. A restorative justice system holds the offender accountable by facilitating and enforcing reparative agreements, including restitution. Restorative justice recognizes that we must give offenders the opportunity to right their wrongs and redeem themselves, in their own eyes and in the eyes of the community.

A DIFFERENT PARADIGM

Restorative justice is not any one program. It is a different paradigm for understanding and responding to issues of crime and justice. Restorative justice takes its most familiar forms in victim-offender mediation (VOM) programs and victim-offender reconciliation programs (VORP). Other restorative justice responses to crime include family group conferencing, community sentencing circles, neighborhood accountability boards, reparative probation, restitution programs, restorative community service, victim and community impact statements and victim awareness panels.

As the most common application of restorative justice principles, VOM/VORP programs warrant examination in detail. These programs bring offenders face to face with the victims of their crimes, with the assistance of a trained mediator, usually a community volunteer. Victim participation is always voluntary; offender participation is voluntary in most programs.

In mediation, crime is personalized as offenders learn the human consequences of their actions, and victims have the opportunity to speak their minds and their feelings to the one who most ought to hear them, contributing to the victim's healing. Victims get answers to haunting questions that only the offender can answer. The most commonly asked questions are "Why did you do this to me? Was this my fault? Could I have prevented this? Were you stalking or watching me?" Victims commonly report a new peace of mind, even when the answers to their questions were worse than they had feared.

Offenders take meaningful responsibility for their actions by mediating a restitution agreement with the victim to restore the victims' losses in whatever ways possible. Restitution may be monetary or symbolic; it may consist of work for the victim, community service or other actions that contribute to a sense of justice between the victim and offender. . . .

At their best, mediation sessions focus upon dialogue rather than the restitution agreement (or settlement), facilitating empathy and understanding between victim and offender. Ground rules help assure safety and respect. Victims typically speak first, explaining the impact of the crime and asking questions of the offender. Offenders acknowledge and describe their participation in the offense, usually offering an explanation and/or apology. The victim's losses are discussed. Surprisingly, a dialogue-focused (rather than settlement-driven) approach produces the highest rates of agreement and compliance.

DIFFERENT CONCEPT OF NEUTRALITY

. . . VOM requires specialized training beyond the basic skills of conflict resolution. Mediators are trained to guide the sensitive process of preparing victims and offenders to come face to face. Further advanced training is needed to mediate in crimes involving severe violence. Most victim-offender programs limit their service to juvenile offenses, crimes against property and minor assaults, but a growing number of experienced programs have found that a face-to-face encounter can be invaluable even in heinous crimes.

A number of programs have now mediated violent assaults, including rapes, and mediations have taken place between murderers and the families of their victims. Mediation has been helpful in repairing the lives of surviving family members and the offender in drunk-driving fatalities. In severe crime mediations, case development may take a year or more before the mediation can take place.

VOM may be useful at any stage of the criminal justice process. For young offenders and first- or second-time offenders, mediation may provide diversion from prosecution. In these cases, charges may be dismissed if the offender mediates an agreement with the victim and complies with its terms. After a guilty plea or a conviction, a court may refer an offender to VOM as a part of the sentence or as a term of probation. In cases of severely violent crime, VOM has not been a substitute for a prison sentence, and prison terms have seldom been reduced following mediation. Mediations have even taken place in prison. Impending release of an offender may motivate victims to seek mediation, and mediations have taken place after release from prison.

WHAT CAN WE LEARN?

The most important lesson learned from restorative justice practice may be the realization that the key to justice is found not in laws but in the recognition and honoring of human relationships. If the application of restorative justice principles can bring justice and healing to some of the most grievous losses that human beings can suffer, the potential for more effective conflict resolution in other arenas must be considered. If crimes or disputes are not resolved with relationship values guiding the process, it is predictable that all parties may walk away feeling like losers or like victims—feeling that justice has not been done.

When lawyers are viewed as healers of conflicts, it will be a clear indicator that our justice system has become restorative in its assumptions, goals and priorities. Regrettably, there will always be a need for adversarial processes for resolution of the situations where, sadly, the conflicts cannot be healed restoratively. In these intractable cases, we will employ the adversarial contest as the means for "alternative dispute resolution."

Problem 12-11. ***Integrating Restorative Justice***

Are there particular kinds of cases that you think are appropriate or inappropriate for this form of dispute resolution? Why? Is restorative justice possible in a world of determinate sentencing? ADR and restorative justice require discretion, flexibility, and degrees of "softness" in the system, qualities that determinate sentencing seeks to remove for reasons of justice and equity. How do we resolve these tensions?

Who should be involved in the decision(s) about using Restorative Justice? In a specific case? As a general policy matter?

9. Problem Solving Courts

With the success of restorative justice programs and the increasing emphasis on legal problem solving, some courts in the late 1980s and early 1990s developed new "multidisciplinary" or "multijurisdictional" courts to deal with and supervise more rehabilitative systems of justice. Recognizing that criminal activity often has its roots in other social problems such as drug addiction, homelessness, and family violence, such courts sentence offenders to community service rather than to jail and provide each defendant with a detailed assessment on matters that include substance use, work record, health, and homelessness. These specialty or "unified" courts have been used in family matters (such as child abuse, neglect, delinquency, child custody, divorce, or a combination of these); gun violations; drug violations; and victimless crimes such as prostitution. Judge Judith Kaye, of the New York Court of Appeals, reported that preliminary evaluations of such programs in the criminal and family court contexts show signs of decreasing recidivism and changing behavior.[26] What are some of the advantages and disadvantages of courts that seek to do more than "merely" adjudicate? Has ADR come full circle when judges attempt to co-opt methods that were designed to be used outside of the courts? Can judges be remedial problem solvers, looking toward the future, as well as adjudicating the past? Note that many criminal defense and juvenile lawyers have

---

26. Judith S. Kaye, Changing Courts in Changing Times: The Need for a Fresh Look at How Courts Are Run, 48 Hastings L.J. 851 (1997).

been somewhat critical of problem-solving courts, which are seen as extensions of state power without the full protection of conventional legal rights.[27] Moreover, when defendants fail the requirements of the court, they are often punished more severely than other similarly-situated defendants who do not participate in the problem-solving court. On other hand, where defendants opt to accept a diversion to "rehab" and thereby regain their sobriety, or fulfill whatever the requirements of the court were, depending on the conditions imposed by the particular form of problem solving court, both the individual and society are winners.

C. CONCLUDING THOUGHTS ON HYBRID PROCESSES

Modifications of the four foundational processes are limited only by the imaginations of the users and designers, and we have not covered all of the possibilities here. Among other existing processes are appellate mediation/settlement conferences (now used in every federal circuit court of appeals, as well as in many state courts) and consensus-building fora for public policy disputes (discussed more fully in the next chapter).

In concluding this chapter, let us recapitulate a few themes of this book by asking these questions: If "appropriate" or "alternative" forms of dispute resolution are suggested to compensate for or supplement problematic aspects of the conventional legal system, what happens when the alternatives present problems of their own? Should we revert back to traditional litigation or seek to fix the problems with alternative processes? Or should we create new alternatives? Are there some basic fault lines we should continue to observe between private and public institutions? Between consensual and mandated processes? In respecting the neutrality of the third party? Carrie Menkel-Meadow raises below the question of whether the hybrid blending and institutionalization of ADR processes may, in fact, jeopardize the values underlying the ADR processes.

❖ *Carrie Menkel-Meadow*, PURSUING SETTLEMENT IN AN ADVERSARY CULTURE: A TALE OF INNOVATION CO-OPTED OR "THE LAW OF ADR"

19 Fla. St. U. L. Rev. 1, 13-14, 16-17, 32-33, 35-39 (1991)

What has this "institutionalization" meant? Has the growth and expansion of alternative dispute resolution institutions changed the consciousness of those

27. Anthony C. Thompson, Courting Disorder: Some Thoughts on Community Courts, 10 Wash. U. J.L & Pol'y. 63 (2002). For an eloquent description and defense of these courts, see Greg Berman, John Feinblatt and Sarah Glazer, Good Courts: The Case for Problem Solving Justice (2005).

whose job it is to solve legal problems? In my view, the qualified answer to these questions is no. This is illustrated by the cases which are now beginning to deal with some of the difficult legal issues raised by the uses of ADR. As we survey some of these developments, I suggest that attempts to innovate have been partly, if not totally, "captured" and co-opted by the uses to which advocates have put these new procedures. At the same time, advocates "attacking" or "manipulating" ADR may tell us something about its limits and abuses in the court system and alert us to the regulatory boundaries that may be necessary to keep each process working within its proper sphere.

I was first struck by the omnipresence of the adversary model when, as a mediator for the Asbestos Claim Facility, I received a copy of a letter in which one party had "filed an ADR proceeding *against*" the other party. The fact that the process had been labeled a mediation process did nothing to move the parties away from their adversarial perceptions of each other. The ADR proceeding of "mediation" was just a condition precedent to be attended to on the way to litigation. As the parties engaged in more disputing about the rules of the proceedings, it became clear that ADR was just another stop in the "litigation" game which provides an opportunity for the manipulation of rules, time, information, and ultimately, money.

As ADR has been increasingly used by courts and by private institutions of dispute resolution, it has been increasingly "legalized"—made the subject of legal regulation, in both private and public rules systems. Skillful lawyers are raising legitimate claims regarding the constitutionality of some of the aspects of ADR—such as infringements of the right to a jury trial, separation of powers, due process, and equal protection. Other claims which may not be as legitimate—such as refusing to participate in arbitration by claiming that it is coerced discovery—demonstrate that ADR has become just another battleground for adversarial fighting rather than multi-dimensional problem-solving.

In an important sense, the ADR movement represents a case study in the difficulties of legal reform when undertaken by different groups within the legal system. At the beginning were the *conceptualizers*—academics and judicial activists who developed both the critique of the adversary system and, in some cases, the design of alternative systems of dispute resolution. The *implementers* developed the concrete forms these innovations took when they moved into the legal system. Some of the *conceptualizers*—Frank Sander and several of the judges—were also *implementers*. In addition, other judges and judicial administrators principally concerned about caseload management, and about the quality of solutions or decisions, became *implementers*. Support for the implementation of these ADR programs came from the principal foundation and government funding sources, as well as from groups of change-oriented practicing lawyers who played an important catalytic role in supporting and using some of the first alternative procedures.

Finally, the *constituents* of these ADR systems—lawyers and their clients as consumers—were "acted upon," sometimes somewhat consensually, by the force of court rules or judicial encouragement. We are just beginning to see some of their reactions in the litigation developing from ADR innovation and in evaluation research.

Each of these groups of actors within the ADR legal reform movement inhabit different cultural worlds—academia, the judiciary, law practice, the business world, and everyday life. Each group uses, transforms, and "colonizes" the work of the others. The research of academics is ignored or simplified; judges move cases along and adopt the language of case management rather than justice; lawyers "infect" clients with a desire for adversarial advantage, or in other cases clients do the same to lawyers; and professionals argue about credentialing and standards for the new profession.

Problem 12-12. ***Multi-Doors Under One Courthouse Roof?***

To what extent will courts lose their legitimacy as courts if they perform too many other kinds of case processing within their walls? If the "other" processes are not considered legitimate within public institutions, they may be legally challenged and transformed into watered-down versions of court adjudication. No longer "alternatives," these watered-down versions may violate the legal rights and rules our courts are intended to safeguard. Can theorists, practitioners, and citizens change our views of what courts should do? What forms of ADR should or shouldn't be institutionalized?

Further Reading

Cynthia Alkon & Andrea Kupfer Schneider (2019). Negotiating Crime: Plea Bargaining, Problem Solving and Dispute Resolution in the Criminal Context. Durham, North Carolina: Carolina Press.

James J. Alfini, Summary Jury Trials in State and Federal Courts: A Comparative Analysis of the Perceptions of Participating Lawyers, 4 Ohio St. J. on Disp. Resol. 213 (1989).

Greg Berman, John Feinblatt & Sarah Glazer. (2005). Good Courts: The Case for Problem Solving Justice. New York: New Press.

Robert C. Bordone, Electronic Online Dispute Resolution: A Systems Approach—Potential Problems, and a Proposal, 3 Harvard Negot. L. Rev. 175 (1998).

Wayne D. Brazil, A Close Look at Three Court-Sponsored ADR Programs: Why They Exist, How They Operate, What They Deliver, and Whether They Threaten Important Values, 1990 U. Chi. Legal F. 303.

Wayne D. Brazil. (2013). Early Neutral Evaluation. Washington, DC: ABA Press.

CPR Corporate Dispute Management (E. Green, Ed.). (1982). The CPR Legal Program Mini-Trial Handbook. New York: CPR.

Dispute Resolution Magazine, Ombuds, 23 (1) Disp. Res. Mag. 6 (Fall 2016).

Noam Ebner. (2017). Negotiating via Text Messaging, in Christopher Honeyman & Andrea Kupfer Schneider (Eds.), The Negotiator's Desk Reference. St. Paul, MN: DRI Press.

Kenneth Feinberg. (2005). What Is Life Worth?: The Unprecedented Effort to Compensate Victims of 9/11. New York: Public Affairs.

Harvard Negotiation Law Review, Symposium on Dispute System Design, 14 Harv. Negot. L. Rev. 1-342 (2009).

Charles L. Howard. (2010). The Organizational Ombudsman. Washington, DC: ABA Press.

Kenneth Feinberg. (2012). Who Gets What: Fair Compensation After Tragedy and Financial Upheaval. New York, New York: PublicAffairs.

James S. Kakalik, Terence Dunworth, Laural Hill, Daniel McCaffrey, Marian Oshiro, Nicolas Pace & Mary E. Vaiana (1996). An Evaluation of Mediation and Early Neutral Evaluation Under the Civil Justice Reform Act. Santa Monica, CA: Rand.

Ethan Katsh & Janet Rifkin. (2001). Online Dispute Resolution: Resolving Conflicts in Cyberspace. San Francisco: Jossey-Bass Publishing.

Ethan Katsh & Orna Rabinovitz-Einy. (2017). Digital Justice. Oxford: Oxford University Press.

David Allen Larson, Amy J. Schmitz & Alan Wiener, The American Bar Association Section of Dispute Resolution Adopts Guidance for Online Dispute Resolution, 38 Ohio St. J. on Disp. Resol. 235 (2023).

John Maull, ADR in the Federal Courts: Would Uniformity Be Better?, 34 Duq. L. Rev. 245 (1996).

Carrie Menkel-Meadow. (2007). Restorative Justice: What Is It and Does It Work?, in Annual Review of Law and Social Science. Palo Alto, Cal.: Annual Reviews.

Carrie Menkel-Meadow, Unsettling the Lawyers: Other Forms of Justice in Indigenous Claims of Expropriation, Abuse and Injustice, 64 University of Toronto L. J. 620 (2014).

Carrie Menkel-Meadow. (2018). Hybrid and Mixed Processes: Integrities of Process Pluralism. In Maria Moscati, Michael Palmer & Marion Roberts (Eds.), Comparative Dispute Resolution Research Handbook. UK: Elgar Publishing.

Carrie Menkel-Meadow & Robert Dingwall. (2017). Scripts: What to Do When Big Bad Companies Won't Negotiate. In Andrea Kupfer Schneider & Christopher Honeyman (Eds.), The Negotiator's Desk Reference. St Paul, MN: DRI Press.

Michael L. Moffitt & Robert C. Bordone (Eds.). (2005). Handbook of Dispute Resolution. San Francisco: Jossey-Bass Publishing.

Mayo Moran, Cardinal Sins: How the Catholic Church Sexual Abuse Crisis Changed Private Law. XXI Georgetown J. of Gender & the Law (2019).

Orna Rabinovich-Einy & Ethan Katsh. (2017). Lawyers and Online Negotiation, in Andrea Kupfer Schneider & Christopher Honeyman (Eds.), The Negotiator's Desk Reference. St. Paul, MN: DRI Press.

Mary Rowe, The Ombudsman's Role in a Dispute Resolution System, 7 Negotiation J. 353 (1991).

Elizabeth Plapinger & Donna Stienstra. (1996). ADR and Settlement in the Federal District Courts. Washington, DC: Federal Judicial Center.

Lionel M. Schooler and Luke Gilman, Private Juries Within the Arbitration Framework: A Third Path in Dispute Resolution, 21 Pepp. Disp. Resol. L.J. 457 (2021).

Jeffrey M. Senger. (2003). Federal Dispute Resolution: Using ADR with the U.S. Government. San Francisco: Jossey-Bass Publishing.

Thomas J. Stipanowich, Arbitration, Mediation, and Mixed Modes: Seeking Workable Solutions and Common Ground on Med-Arb, Arb-Med, and Settlement-Oriented Activities by Arbitrators, 26 Harv. Negot. L. Rev. 265 (2021).

Richard Susskind. (2019). Online Courts and the Future of Justice. Oxford: Oxford University Press.

William Ury, Jeanne Brett & Stephen B. Goldberg. (1988). Getting Disputes Resolved: Designing Systems to Cut the Cost of Conflict. San Francisco: Jossey-Bass Publishing.

Douglas H. Yarn. (1999). Dictionary of Conflict Resolution. San Francisco: Jossey-Bass Publishing.

Chapter 13 Multiparty Dispute Resolution and Dispute System Design

If two heads are better than one, are more than two always better?

—Anon.

Many disputes involve more than just one issue (money) and two parties (a plaintiff and a defendant). Even disputes that risk appearing like they are "just about money" involve many issues: how much money, in what form, with what assurances, in exchange for what release, when, with what level of publicity, etc. And even a seemingly simple personal injury case often involves multiple parties, including those who are not formally part of any lawsuit—the injured party, his or her family members, insurance companies, employers, manufacturers, or retailers. Complex cases or disputes such as class actions, mass torts, civil rights cases, environmental matters, corporate cases, and regulatory matters always involve more than two parties. Sometimes the number, complexity, and importance of issues and parties call for different approaches to dispute resolution.

Increasingly, those who study dispute resolution analyze how what they know about negotiation, mediation, arbitration, and adjudication might have to be adapted when there are more than two parties and more than a few issues. How do we know when we have agreement or consent for dispute resolution? Must all parties agree? Most? What are the decision rules? Many forms of conflict resolution are specially designed to deal with multiparty processes, both in public or governmental settings, and in private disputes. Negotiated rule making ("reg-neg") in the administrative context, class actions in litigation, and consensus-building fora for public policy disputes (such as in environmental siting or community disputes) are some examples. This chapter will introduce concepts and principles for multiparty contexts. The formation of coalitions and alliances between some parties and "defections" by others change the dynamics of negotiation. With more people and complexity, organizational challenges are compounded, calling for more formal management of dispute resolution processes. At an institutional level, the field of Dispute System Design seeks to develop organizational, systematic, and rationalized means of handling conflict in complex and iterated settings. Applying dispute resolution theory and skills to complex transactions is another emerging field that is addressed in this chapter.

Particular practice and skill sets are required for managing meetings and facilitating group process. The "appropriateness" of particular processes must be considered. Do they work? Are they ethical? For example, who decides who participates? What sort of discourse is permitted or encouraged? What is the relationship between our democratic principles and the processes we create?

Consider these additional questions as you read this chapter:

1. Are all relevant interested parties able to participate in the particular form of multiparty dispute resolution? How are participants/representatives at the table chosen? Are any interested parties excluded?
2. How does this form of dispute resolution fit within our constitutional framework of government?
3. When might these new or different processes be "better" at solving some legal, political, or human problems than the processes we are currently using?

A. MULTIPARTY DISPUTE PROCESSES: HOW ARE THEY DIFFERENT?

The readings in this section suggest some of the ways in which multiparty dispute resolution may differ from dyadic (negotiation) or triadic (mediation or arbitration) processes. See if you can think of particular ways in which adding more parties changes some of the basic principles of negotiation, mediation, and arbitration practices, processes, and law.

This first section explores differences in two-party versus more-than-two-party negotiations. These excerpts provide guidance for thinking about and making choices in situations where the numbers of negotiators matters and coalitions are likely to form. This section then presents some of the problems that can develop in group negotiations (including the two extremes of groupthink, or more divergent and extreme positions). It then presents some of the ways in which multiparty negotiations have been organized and institutionalized in different settings, and considers their legitimacy in legal and constitutional terms.

1. Negotiating with More Than Two Parties: Coalitions and Groups

❖ *Carrie Menkel-Meadow*, INTRODUCTION

in Multi-Party Dispute Resolution, Democracy and Decision-Making: Volume II (Conflict Resolution) xiii-xvi (Carrie Menkel-Meadow ed., 2012)

THE PROBLEM OF NUMBERS: NEW THEORY

The outpouring of both intellectual and practical work in this new field of negotiation and conflict resolution produced a canon of new concepts to be explored and tested in both laboratories and real-world situations. It was not long before Howard Raiffa, a mathematician turned decision scientist and negotiation theorist, and others, began to notice that *numbers matter.* And numbers matter in important and different ways. The *number of parties* quickly challenged some of the basic canonical concepts in conflict resolution theory and practice:

- What happens to *BATNAs* (best alternatives to negotiated agreements) or WATNAs (worst alternatives to negotiated agreements) when there are more than two parties and there may be many more possible alternative arrangements (with some, but not all, of the parties involved)?
- How can *ZOPAs* (zones of possible agreements) be mapped on a two-dimensional playing field (or piece of paper) when adding parties to the mix makes many multi-dimensional zones possible?
- What happens when those *ZOPAs* do not overlap with all of the parties, but only with some?
- While two-party negotiations can be successfully accounted for by the concept of "*consent*" or agreement when there is, by definition, no agreement if one party refuses to agree, what happens in a multi-party setting when some, but not all, consent? By what measure (or voting or *decision rule*) do we determine if there is "an" agreement in a multi-party setting? (*Consensus*, all, most, majority, plurality?)
- What are the dangers to any agreement reached by only a few of the parties when others seek to sabotage the agreement (vetoes, "*holdouts*," saboteurs, defectors)?
- How is *enforcement* of or *compliance* with a multi-party agreement to be achieved? How might this be different from a two-party agreement?
- What happens when parties form *coalitions* or *alliances* to engage in group action and what happens when, after agreements to cooperate in such alliances are defected on, there is *betrayal* or *defection?* How are coalitions and alliances disciplined? How do we measure *trust* in multi-party situations? How *stable* are alliances and coalitions in multi-party settings?
- How are *information sharing* strategies complexified when there are more than two parties asking for or giving information? What if information is distributed differentially to the parties?
- Power imbalances are difficult enough to manage in two-party settings, what happens when there are *power differentials* among numbers of parties? (Consider, in international negotiations, the developed and developing nations, the oil-rich and resource-poor, coastal versus inland nations, etc. And, within nations, consider indigenous groups vs. settlers or colonizers or multi-ethnic/religious or other "cultural" differences. Within more conventional lawsuits, consider the differences between those who can afford representation with resources and those who have none, labor and management, differently endowed partners in partnership dissolutions, creditors and debtors, etc.).
- How does the *role of third-party facilitators* or helpers (mediators, arbitrators, even judges) change in conflicts or disputes with more than two parties?

(Consider the management of group or class litigation now allowed in many legal systems; mediation of multi-party environmental, community or regulatory disputes; facilitation of complex policy formation and implementation.)

- Does it matter if the parties have *iterative* (on-going, repeat) *relationships* with each other or are simply dealing with a one-shot issue?
- What are different groups and parties like *internally*? Who makes decisions for each party? A single leader? A constituency with or without clear voting procedures?
- Who is the "*representative*" or *agent* of each party and what are they authorized to do? How do we know when a party or group has "agreed" to something? What happens when a party or group has *internal dissension*? How can even single parties become multiple parties with negotiations that are both "across the table" and "behind the table" (with constituents) (Mnookin et al. 2000)?
- Who talks when? How are complex multi-party or group negotiations structured? What *processes* are possible? Helpful, destructive?

Howard Raiffa, along with his colleagues at Harvard's innovative Program on Negotiation, including Nobel laureate Thomas Schelling, began (but never quite finished) an evocative questioning of how numbers of parties in negotiation might help us develop a fully elaborated theory (and practice) related to how many participants exist in a negotiation. Beginning with the *intrapersonal* negotiations we all have with ourselves (should I do x or not? What happens when I want to do x, but instead do y? ["cognitive dissonance"]), we can look at different conditions of negotiation when there is an *n of 2* (conventional two-party negotiation), *n of 3* (two negotiators with a mediator or other third-party assistant), *n of 5* (parties, lawyers or other representatives and a third party), *more than 5,* and ultimately *more than 100* (most international negotiations, like most treaty negotiations now, may include as many as 200 negotiators; and more if one considers, as we do later in this volume, the negotiations of a full polity in democratic deliberation, or even larger, "global" negotiations). Raiffa (and almost all of us who labor practically in these fields) has concluded that there are some sharp breaking points in the conduct and process of conflict resolution with different numbers of negotiators. Beyond about 100 people in a room people do not really listen to each other without clear process management and amplification of attention, and any group over about 30 suffers a reduction in individual participation (ask any teacher!). The numbers of participants in a group affects consensus building, dissent, and disciplining of both individual and group behavior as some of the articles here demonstrate.

The *number of issues* may further complicate the questions above. In some situations, the *more issues the merrier* (more issues means that *trades* are more likely to forge more integrative agreements); in other cases if there are too many issues it might be more difficult to trade, especially if valuation is different about those issues for different parties. Though some have suggested complex metrics for quantifying preferences in complex negotiations, the number of issues tends to increase (not always) with the numbers of parties and makes negotiation structure and management of both process and outcome more difficult:

- Should one start with the easiest issues or the most difficult?
- Should all parties be present for all discussions of all issues? When are private caucuses appropriate/dangerous? Is transparency in negotiation always advantageous? When not?
- Should one go to parties in agreement first (those who are "with us")? Or, should we try to win over our most difficult "enemies" first? What are more optimal ways of sequencing multi-party negotiations?
- Is trading or "log-rolling" with some, but not all, of the parties permissible?
- Can issues not formally on the "agenda" be used privately or with just a few parties, without involving everyone? How public or transparent should the agenda for multi-party negotiations be?
- Must there be agreement on all contested issues for there to be an agreement at all?
- Are all issues equally important? How should priorities be established with differential utilities or valuations by different parties in "mixed" "co-opetition" situations? . . .
- How can parties assure "fair divisions" among many parties when allocating values (especially when the parties may have differential endowments and/or needs)? Are all issues for division quantifiable? Divisible? Commensurable? What do we do with "non-material" issues?
- How are *monetary and material issues* to be compared to (traded with) *non-material* desiderata (e.g., identity, respect, dignity needs and values)? (the problem of *incommensurability*).

All of these issues (and more) suggest that much of the theory developed with two-party negotiation, even with the assistance of third-party facilitators (like mediators), may have to be re-examined in the different contexts of more than two or three parties. The complexities of these issues has led to the development of other new applied fields of research, study and practice—decision sciences, deliberative democracy, strategic planning and group facilitation.

THE CHALLENGES OF GROUP NEGOTIATIONS

When negotiations occur in settings of groups (even when there are only two groups in a more conventional, "two-party, one issue" distributional setting) there are issues of group behavior ("groupthink") . . . which can be enacted in different ways and affect the processes and outcomes of negotiation. Groups can come closer to each other or move each other to more extreme positions. They can fracture and cease to be a single cohesive group at all. Or, while remaining a group for negotiation or conflict resolution purposes (imagine a labor and management dispute, for example) they can have several sub-groups or issue-related constituencies. Representation of group interests is quite complex in even the simplest of negotiation settings, but all of this becomes even more complex when there are many groups in a negotiation, as is the case in all international negotiations, whether about war and peace, general diplomacy, trade, environmental issues, cooperation in joint ventures to eliminate or reduce threats (e.g. like terrorism and health), and joint efforts to engage in positive human endeavors (poverty reduction, resource exploration, cultural exchanges.)

Groups must decide how they will proceed in a conflict resolution setting —how to select representatives, how to hold them accountable, how to decide when and how concessions, offers, and proposals are to be made and agreements to be reached. Thus, every negotiation or conflict setting which involves groups contains negotiations within the group, as well as with whatever parties the group is negotiating with. Though human beings need to work in collectivities to accomplish many of their aims, work in groups is difficult and clearly requires theory, management and feedback through study and adjustment. . . .

As scholarship and practice in negotiation and conflict resolution became more sophisticated and argued for a "scaling up" of insights from the basic dyadic negotiation to group decision making and deliberation about policy in the larger polity, the field of conflict resolution joined with developments in political science to form a new applied (and theoretical) field of deliberative democracy [see Section A.2 below]. The questions, first framed by political and social philosophers like Jürgen Habermas, Stuart Hampshire, Amy Gutmann & Dennis Thompson, and Amartya Sen, seek to explore how knowledge about conflict resolution, group and aggregated decision making, can be employed to provide for the best possible (not the "best" or "perfect" (Elster)) processes for policy formation and decision making in democratic societies.

Robert H. Mnookin, STRATEGIC BARRIERS TO DISPUTE RESOLUTION: A COMPARISON OF BILATERAL AND MULTILATERAL NEGOTIATIONS

159 J. Institutional & Theoretical Econ. 200-201, 219 (2003)

I suggest that Pareto-criterion[1] may not provide an appropriate standard to evaluate issues of efficiency in multiparty bargaining. In a two-party case, any negotiated deal presumably better serves the parties than the *status quo.* The same could be said in a multiparty negotiation only if the consent of *every party* were necessary. A requirement of unanimity in multilateral negotiation, however, creates potential holdout problems that may pose severe strategic barriers to resolution. This problem can be mitigated if the consent of less than all the parties can permit action. But other problems may arise. If conditions of less than all are able to

1. The Pareto-criterion is that gains or improvements to negotiated outcomes should be pursued that continue to cause benefit for one party without harm to the other. This criterion may assume only two parties. Gains and harms may become more difficult to hold constant or without affecting other parties if there are more than two parties.

change the *status quo*, this necessarily means that a party left out of a coalition may potentially be made worse off.

A variety of procedural rules may permit decision-making without unanimity in multiparty negotiations. Majority voting is but one of many possible mechanisms to allocate decision-making authority. The outcome of any multilateral negotiation can be profoundly affected by these procedural rules and various decisions concerning agenda. [Another part of this paper] briefly explores the application of an unusual procedural rule—the "sufficient consensus" standard—that was employed in the multiparty "constitutional" negotiations in South Africa and in Northern Ireland. . . .

Carrie Menkel-Meadow, COMPLEX MULTI-PARTY MULTI-ISSUE NEGOTIATIONS

Very Short Introduction to Negotiation, Oxford University Press, 97-98; 98-103

Coalitions, Alliances, Commitments, Defections and Holdouts

Consider the tragedy of World War I, where "the enemy of my enemy is my friend" politics linked two alliances of the Austro-Hungarian and Ottoman empires with Germany against France, England and Russia (with their own prior conflicts), ending with its own disastrous negotiation, The Treaty of Versailles. This in turn led to a new war (WWII) also with temporary alliances (US, France, United Kingdom and Soviet Union) which in turn transformed into new and dangerous alliances in the Cold War West (NATO) vs. Soviet Bloc (Warsaw Pact). Consider also how that Warsaw Pact in turn crumbled when, after challenges to the internal reforms in the Soviet Union, one country after another defected from the Pact by declaring independence from both the Soviet Union and then the Warsaw Pact itself.

In any alliance or coalition there is the problem of commitments (signed, collateralized, pledges or writing) and defections (simple exits or moves to other alliances or deals). Once the numbers of negotiators increases from two, almost any agreement can be unstable without clear undertakings and enforcement provisions. This is not to say that two-party negotiated agreements are not breached, but more-than-two-party negotiations tend to be more unstable and may require additional terms of penalty, incentive or enforcement.

Related to the problem of *defection* is the issue of *vetoes or holdouts* if there are agreements about how a coalition or alliance will decide its moves. If groups of negotiators form sub-groups and there are customs, rules or procedures for agreement for both process and substantive outcome, any single member may sabotage or prevent agreement by holding out for what it wants or vetoing what the rest of the group wants. In practical terms this is an *internal negotiation* within the group and may turn on who has *power* within any alliance. Consider how

President George W. Bush constituted a "coalition of the willing" in the wars in Afghanistan and Iraq in the early 2000s (by using both carrots and sticks of granting or withholding of American aid). Groups that negotiate within themselves and then with other groups will want to consider how decisions are made about both process and substantive matters. In any negotiation where one of the parties is a group (e.g., trade union, organizational departments, factions within a dispute, or different allegiances within a political party, class action lawsuit, country or other grouping) getting and keeping the parties sufficiently aligned to negotiate with "other" parties is itself a complex multi-party negotiation of coordination.

Process and Groundrules

When there are many parties and many issues in a negotiation it is often useful for an official agenda and a set of groundrules for deliberation to be separately negotiated. In the negotiation of the Northern Ireland Easter Peace Accords close to one and a half years were spent developing rules of engagement including de-commissioning of arms, speaking and talking rules, permitted participants (prohibiting violent individuals), representation rules and some rules and customs about separate meetings (caucuses) and sanctions for process rule violations. In the three-month deliberations which formed the United States Constitution in 1787 two full days were spent on process rules. These rules included: total confidentiality of the deliberations, attendance rules (voting only when all were present in the plenary sessions) and speaking rules (only two comments per delegate per issue and could not speak second time until all who wanted to speak on the issue could). In addition, the delegates developed task groups and committees to work on specific issues (rather than full plenary deliberations on each issue), assignment of roles of a recorder (James Madison), a "neutral" leader of the meeting (George Washington, who spoke only once on a matter of substance) and a process commentator (Benjamin Franklin, who often appealed to prayer to calm heated negotiations and an attempt to keep the focus on the desired end of the negotiation). The delegates also used voting rules that included no attribution to particular individuals (now known as *Chatham House* rules), votes to allow reconsideration of previously agreed to items, in order to encourage *linkage, trades, contingent agreements,* and *compromise,* and finally, an agreement that the final document would be voted on *in toto* (preparing the way for seeking the legitimacy of the finished agreement for a contested ratification process). As is common in so many large number negotiations, it was assumed that a majority vote of states (12 in attendance out of 13) and delegates (55 present) would control decision making.

In modern complex negotiations it is often useful to have a combination of George Mitchell, George Washington and Benjamin Franklin—what we call *process experts* (facilitators, mediators and consensus builders) to help frame and manage the process of difficult negotiations seeking to accomplish a particular outcome, such as in urban planning, environmental regulations, community relations, budget allocations, legislation, and international treaties. Professional process experts can help groups negotiate their own ground rules in an effort to help legitimacy and enforcement of those self-imposed ground rules. They may use a template of ground rules which have been used with other groups (e.g., no interruptions, use of a "talking stick" to rotate turns of speaking, contingency or revision rules, and prohibitions on violence, insults, threats or other counter-productive actions in the deliberations).

Decision Rules and Voting

When negotiating with multiple parties, how do we know an agreement has been reached? In complex settings it is useful to agree on *decision rules for the substantive terms* of any agreement. This is a complicated issue and is affected by mathematics, game theory and strategic voting theory. How we vote has enormous consequences for what agreements can be reached. All negotiators should understand the implications of each possible method of voting.

Consider that in Western democracies the default voting rules for most decisions is *majority* rule (50% + 1 of all voters). This assumes all voters are equal, which sometimes they are not. The European Union, the World Bank and many other organizations allocate percentage of voting powers by financial contributions, size of population, GNP or some other "weighted" expression of a particular member's power within the group so that some members have a greater "share" of votes. The majority voting rule is often effective and efficient for reaching a decision which has some strong support (but not total consensus), but it also means that a very large minority (49.99%) might not be happy with final decisions. All voting rules are also subject to "rules within the rules" that affect outcomes. Is it a majority of votes cast (including abstentions)? Of those eligible to vote? Those present at the meeting? Some groups and organizations use more demanding voting rules for greater legitimacy of the decision—some form of *super-majority* voting rule such as a 2/3 or 3/4 or even total *unanimity* of those voting. Where a single entity can veto the will of the majority (such as in the United Nations Security Council) even a super-majority rule will not authorize an agreement.

Consider the different effects of different voting rules. Simple majority of votes cast are easier to obtain but also potentially unstable with a strong dissenting minority. Larger super majority votes may be harder to obtain (taking more time to bring more people along) but once achieved may have greater acceptance. Seeking total *consensus* or close to it can motivate the parties to seek more creative solutions to meet more of the needs and preferences of all parties (constantly seeking "improvement" of what is being voted on). Or more problematically, searching for unanimous agreement or total consensus can lead to "satisficing" (not optimal) compromises or the "lowest common denominator."

An example can illustrate what difference voting rules make. Hiring appointments to university faculties can use any of these rules. A majority vote means most, but not all, agree on a candidate. But not requiring everyone to agree may yield greater diversity of successful candidates. For many years at least one university department required unanimity—total consensus for appointment, assuming that was a high standard for the quality of candidate. Alas, it resulted in a faculty of people with very similar views about conflictual issues in the field and not much diversity. The 2/3 and 3/4 rules provide a middle point, where most, but not all, agree on an appointment so some dissent is permitted, but a greater degree of acceptability to "most" is also assured. In the university setting this has consequences for a possible second vote (later in time) for tenure or promotion. With a strong dissent at appointment (minority within majority rule) there may be a greater chance of a later negative vote. Stronger numbers of initial vote (2/3 or 3/4) may signal greater consensus and a greater likelihood of a positive vote at the second stage. Note that these voting rules and their consequences are true in any situation of groups of people voting on decisions and are especially important when groups of people vote on many things, so that there may be *linkages* or *history of voting patterns* that affect each vote (whether on each issue, each candidate or even total "packages" of agreements). Another form of voting issue here is *logrolling* or trading of votes to affect particular outcomes—if you vote for my candidate now, I will vote for yours next time (without others knowing such "side deals" have been made). Some political systems now use ranked choice or sequential preference voting with several rounds to determine intensity of support and to create several elimination rounds.

Voting on preferences for a negotiation (especially when deciding among and between possible options) is complicated by a variety of mathematical paradoxes. The *Condorcet paradox* tells us that how people will vote may turn on the order in which options are presented. Consider that there are three parties and three options from which to choose. When preferences differ among the parties rankings 1, 2 and 3, the parties may decide to vote on each sequentially. When this is done option A defeats B, and B ranked against C might be first, but what happens when C defeats A? In sequential voting those options that come later will tend to do better than those that come first (seeming to be a better comparison!) Compare this to anchor effects with a single proposal or offer. Clever negotiators in multiparty and multi-issue settings will know how to manipulate presentations of proposals to affect the vote they desire. When individuals vote (and have equal votes) in group settings, with different preferences, ranked when there are multiple issue options, it might be impossible (the *impossibility theorem)* to ever determine a single *stable preference of the whole group for all the issues.* In these settings votes may be taken on single issues to determine preferences but when multiple issues are combined to create a "package" proposal preferences may differ and aggregation of different issues will provide what is called an intransitive (unstable) preference. This may be exacerbated when new proposals (linked or seriatim) are presented by the other parties to the negotiation and parties have different preferences with respect to different elements of the proposal.

A serious problem in any voting situation is *strategic voting*, which is the misrepresentation of true preferences in order to block other proposals or manipulation of the voting rules. Returning to the example of faculty voting, if we have a limited number of jobs to offer and we have to have a ranking of candidates for a preference vote, people can put last those candidates whom they think others will favor in order to move them to the bottom of aggregate voting.

Some of these (and other) voting problems have no simple or mathematical solutions but they can be managed by having the parties fully understand how voting rules may actually affect the substance of what they are deciding. Professional mediators and facilitators can help manage such processes by explaining both process rules and decision rules before any substantive negotiations occur. In the international negotiations for what became the Kyoto Environmental Clean Air Accords, professionals were engaged to provide negotiation instructions to the diplomatic negotiators present so that power imbalances in negotiation expertise might be reduced and everyone could be subject to the same process and decision rules. Part of such pre-negotiation training can also help advise parties that are representatives of larger groups to develop protocols for assessing client preferences and communication rules for sharing (public transparency and press relations) or keeping confidential interim proposals. Remember that although transparency often sounds like a good value, making public commitments can hinder more creative solutions and constrict what negotiators may be authorized to do.

The question of how people behave in groups, whether forming coalitions or seeking to achieve something as a group, has long been the subject of study by sociologists and social psychologists. Not surprisingly, scholars have differed on whether people within a group become more solidified in their views,[2] especially as "against" other groups, or whether individuals within groups resist collective thinking. This has important implications for forming coalitions among individuals and is even more complex when one tries to bring groups, organizations, or nations together for multiple-party negotiations in the political, commercial, policy, or international arenas. Legal scholar Cass Sunstein explores some of the implications of this research next.

Cass R. Sunstein, DELIBERATIVE TROUBLE? WHY GROUPS GO TO EXTREMES

110 Yale L.J. 71, 73-78, 82, 85-86, 88-90, 105-106, 113-116 (2000)

Every society contains innumerable deliberating groups. Church groups, political parties, women's organizations, juries, legislative bodies, regulatory commissions, multimember courts, faculties, student organizations, those participating in talk radio programs, Internet discussion groups, and others engage in deliberation. It is a simple social fact that sometimes people enter discussions with one view and leave with another, even on moral and political questions. Emphasizing this fact, many recent observers have embraced the traditional American aspiration to "deliberative democracy," an ideal that is designed to combine popular responsiveness with a high degree of reflection and exchange among people with

2. Irving L. Janis, Groupthink (2d ed. 1982); Robert B. Cialdini, Influence: The Psychology of Persuasion (rev. ed. 1993).

competing views. But for the most part, the resulting literature has not been empirically informed. It has not dealt much with the real-world consequences of deliberation, and with what generalizations hold in actual deliberative settings, with groups of different predispositions and compositions.

The standard view of deliberation is that of Hamilton and Rawls . . . Group discussion is likely to lead to better outcomes, if only because competing views are stated and exchanged. Aristotle spoke in similar terms, suggesting that when diverse people

> all come together . . . they may surpass—collectively and as a body, although not individually—the quality of the few best. . . . [W]hen there are many [who contribute to the process of deliberation], each has his share of goodness and practical wisdom. . . . Some appreciate one part, some another, and all together appreciate all.

But an important empirical question is whether and under what circumstances it is really true that "some appreciate one part, some another, and all together appreciate all."

My principal purpose in this Essay is to investigate a striking but largely neglected statistical regularity—that of group polarization—and to relate this phenomenon to underlying questions about the role of deliberation in the "public sphere" of a heterogeneous democracy. In brief, group polarization means that members of a deliberating group predictably move toward a more extreme point in the direction indicated by the members' predeliberation tendencies. "Like polarized molecules, group members become even more aligned in the direction they were already tending." . . . Notably, groups consisting of individuals with extremist tendencies are more likely to shift, and likely to shift more; the same is true for groups with some kind of salient shared identity (like Republicans, Democrats, and lawyers, but unlike jurors and experimental subjects). When like-minded people are participating in "iterated polarization games"—when they meet regularly, without sustained exposure to competing views—extreme movements are all the more likely.

Two principal mechanisms underlie group polarization. The first points to social influences on behavior and in particular to people's desire to maintain their reputation and their self-conception. The second emphasizes the limited "argument pools" within any group, and the directions in which those limited pools lead group members. An understanding of the two mechanisms provides many insights into deliberating bodies. Such an understanding illuminates a great deal, for example, about likely processes within multimember courts, juries, political parties, and legislatures—not to mention ethnic groups, extremist organizations, criminal conspiracies, student associations, faculties, institutions engaged in feuds or "turf battles," workplaces, and families. At the same time, these mechanisms raise serious questions about deliberation from the normative point of view. If deliberation predictably pushes groups toward a more extreme point in the direction of their original tendency, whatever that tendency may be, is there any reason to think that deliberation is producing improvements?. . .

HOW AND WHY GROUPS POLARIZE

There have been two main explanations for group polarization. Both of these have been extensively investigated and supported. The first explanation of group polarization—social comparison—begins with the claim that people want to be perceived favorably by other group members and also to perceive themselves favorably. . . .

The second explanation is based on the commonsense intuition that any individual's position on an issue is partly a function of which arguments presented within the group seem convincing. The choice therefore moves in the direction of the most persuasive position defended by the group, taken as a whole. Because a group whose members are already inclined in a certain direction will have a disproportionate number of arguments going in that same direction, the result of discussion will be to move people further in the direction of their initial inclinations. The key is the existence of a limited argument pool, one that is skewed (speaking purely descriptively) in a particular direction. Hence there will be a shift in the direction of the original tilt.

There is a related possibility, not quite reducible to either of the two standard arguments, but incorporating elements of each. In their individual judgments, people are averse to extremes; they tend to seek the middle of the relevant poles. It is possible that when people are making judgments individually, they err on the side of caution, expressing a view in the direction that they really hold, but stating that view cautiously, for fear of seeming extreme. Once other people express supportive views, the relevant inhibition disappears, and people feel free to say what, in a sense, they really believe. There appears to be no direct test of this hypothesis, but it is reasonable to believe that the phenomenon plays a role in group polarization and choice shifts. . . .

DELIBERATIVE TROUBLE?

The central problem is that widespread error and social fragmentation are likely to result when like-minded people, insulated from others, move in extreme directions simply because of limited argument pools and parochial influences. As an extreme example, consider a system of one-party domination, which stifles dissent in part because it refuses to establish space for the emergence of divergent positions; in this way, it intensifies polarization within the party while also disabling external criticism.

In terms of institutional design, the most natural response is to ensure that members of deliberating groups, whether small or large, will not isolate themselves from competing views—a point with implications for multi-member courts, open primaries, freedom of association, and the architecture of the Internet. Here, then, is a plea for ensuring that deliberation occurs within a large and heterogeneous public sphere, and for guarding against a situation in which like-minded people wall themselves off from alternative perspectives. . . .

It is important to ensure social spaces for deliberation by like-minded persons, but it is equally important to ensure that members of the relevant groups are not isolated from conversation with people having quite different views.

The goal of that conversation is to promote the interests of those inside and outside the relevant enclaves, by subjecting group members to competing positions, by allowing them to exchange views with others and to see things from their point of view, and by ensuring that the wider society does not marginalize, and thus insulate itself from, views that may turn out to be right or at least informative. . . .

Problem 13-1. ***Design a Process!***

From these descriptions of the complexities of multiparty decision-making processes, including negotiation for consensual agreements or voting to resolve conflicts, imagine how you might structure processes to facilitate the following, depending on whether you are designing a process for a town hall meeting, a class action settlement discussion, or an international negotiation:

a. The best possible process for an "efficient" decision;
b. The best possible process for "maximum stakeholder participation";
c. The best possible process to avoid bad "group polarization" and promote optimal heterogeneity in participation.

Are these processes all the same, or do different values suggest different process design?

2. Organizing and Legitimizing Group Negotiations: New Processes and Deliberative Democracy

As complex legal and social problems have increased, many participants and decision makers have used dispute resolution processes in official governmental, private, and hybrid settings. Those who have designed these processes are hoping to broaden party participation, achieve better substantive solutions, and create greater legitimacy, compliance with, and acceptance of the outcomes reached. In many cases, parties agree to "contingent" solutions that can be revisited, using these new multiparty processes, variously called consensus building, deliberative democracy, or public policy fora.

The excerpts below explore the use of some of these new "deliberative democracy" enhancing processes to resolve political and policy issues, by looking at different kinds of deliberations (principled argument, bargaining, and appeals to emotions, ethics, and values) that can be organized into different forms of processes. Consider how these processes could be used to deal with such issues as land use, water allocation, community disputes, budget decisions, and highly conflictual policy disputes, such as health care, abortion, and gun control.

❖ *Carrie Menkel-Meadow*, THE LAWYER'S ROLE(S) IN DELIBERATIVE DEMOCRACY

5 Nev. L.J. 347 (2005)

To the extent that participation remains a cornerstone of democratic theory, new forms of participation may require the creation of new institutions or modifications of old forms to permit optimum and appropriate levels of participation for effective and legitimate outcomes. Whether tied to traditional constitutional and legal institutions, like courts, legislatures, and administrative agencies, or created new out of the particularities of specific situations, lawyers have knowledge, skills, craft and wisdom . . . to help craft and manage such institutions. . . .

The terrain has shifted to what kinds of processes or procedures may best facilitate either partial or more global "agreements" about the good and the just. What is fair becomes the principal concern in these process-oriented theories. Thus, some political theorists look to "reasoned deliberation" focused on rationality, principled and rational discourse, others on explicit models of bargaining and interest or preference trading or negotiation, and still others, on the recognition of emotional or subjective sensibilities (such as empathy and "imaginative identification") in the processes by which modern political actors must get things done. Some insist that foundational principles like American constitutionalism are essential to the legitimacy and fairness of any dispute resolution and political governance system, while others suggest that constitutionalism is too rigid and prevents important procedural flexibility from letting process rules be negotiated along with substantive outcomes, as particular parties and problems require. Modern political theorists seek to describe, elaborate and in some cases, prescribe "ideal speech conditions," "ideal proceduralism," "procedural justice," "fairness in procedure as an invariable value" or "discourse ethics" at various levels of theoretical complexity. Others have focused on "new institutions" or new understandings or reconfigurations of existing governmental institutions or structures, like courts, legislatures and agencies, often by focusing on new public and private collaborations. Still others suggest that new forms of participation will themselves generate new substantive solutions or at least contingent accommodations, recognizing that the tools used to solve problems may influence the resolutions that may be recognized. . . .

Those that describe such processes don't always agree about their purposes, structures or operation. Thus, for some "consensus," or some form of agreement by participants, beyond a majority, is an essential part of the commitment, for others, consensus may never be possible or desirable (especially about pre-deliberation commitments) and thus new democratic institutions are "pragmatic" because they may develop issue specific resolutions or develop collaboration out of necessity, rather than "real" and deep agreement. For still others, democratic discourse doesn't even produce policy or decisional "outcomes," just the possibility of increased conversation and "understanding."

In the world of politics, different kinds of problems call up different kinds of participants who may speak in different "languages" (for example, appeals to principles, reasons, logic, emotions, utilitarian interests or preferences, moral, ethical, or religious persuasion). To make conflict resolution legitimate and effective in a wide variety of public and private settings, we have to marry conflict resolution theory and its process pluralism to political theory. Political scientist Jon Elster compares the processes of public-open and plenary processes, which employ highly principled and politicized rhetoric (as was used in the French constitutional process) to the more "secret," committee-based, and "pragmatic bargaining" rhetoric of the American constitutional process, suggesting that sometimes "second-best processes" (less transparent, more compromising, and less "principled") make for more robust outcomes or conclusions. (The American Constitution, even with its Civil War and amendments, has lasted far longer than the French.[3]) Drawing on Elster's work, Carrie Menkel-Meadow has elaborated a taxonomy of different modes of processes to use in conflict resolution and political deliberation. Her chart below describes and separates modes of discourse with different structures of process and different kinds of parties. She then provides examples of different kinds of group process and decision-making.

❖ *Carrie Menkel-Meadow*, INTRODUCTION: FROM LEGAL DISPUTES TO CONFLICT RESOLUTION AND HUMAN PROBLEM SOLVING

in Dispute Processing and Conflict Resolution xi, xxxi (2003)

MODES OF CONFLICT RESOLUTION

MODE OF DISCOURSE	**PRINCIPLED (REASONS) (appeals to law, rules, universals)**	**BARGAINING (INTERESTS) (trades of interests, preferences, compromises)**	**PASSIONS (NEEDS/ EMOTIONS/ RELIGION)**
FORMS OF PROCESS:			
Closed (Confidential)	Some court proceedings; arbitration	Negotiation-U.S. Constitution; diplomacy	Mediation (e.g., divorce)
Open (Public)	French Constitution; courts; arbitration	Public negotiations; some labor	Dialogue movement
Plenary	French Constitution	Reg-Neg	Town meetings
Committees	Faculty committees; task groups	U.S. Constitution/ U.S. Congress	Caucuses—interest groups

3. Jon Elster, Strategic Uses of Argument, in Barriers to Conflict Resolution (Kenneth J. Arrow et al. eds., 1995).

Expert/Facilitator	Consensus building	Mini-trial	Public conversations
Naturalistic (Leaderless)			Grassroots organizing/ WTO protests
Permanent	Government, institutions	Business organizations, unions	Religious organizations, Alcoholics Anonymous, Weight Watchers
Constitutive	UN, national constitutions	National constitutions/ professional associations	Civil justice movements, peace
Temporary/Ad Hoc	Issue organizations/ social justice	Interest groups	Occupy Wall Street, vigilantes

---

B. STRUCTURES, SKILLS, AND PRACTICES FOR MULTI-PARTY PROCESSES

The complexity of multi-party and multi-issue dispute resolution calls for more formal management and conceptualization of the processes to be used. In this section we look at how some successful facilitators and multi-party negotiators have designed processes and developed ideas for organizing such processes. Professor Sebenius suggests that a process of "backward mapping" helps organize complex processes to get to agreement by looking at paths of influence and decision. Philip Harter describes how negotiated rule-making is structured in administrative negotiations, and Professor Lawrence Susskind outlines a more streamlined form of process and decision making, now called Consensus Building, that can substitute for the more cumbersome "Robert's Rules of Order" for public policy formation, decision making and meeting management.

❖ *James K. Sebenius,* MAPPING BACKWARD: NEGOTIATING IN THE RIGHT SEQUENCE?

Negotiation 7, No. 6 (June 2004). Reprinted as "A Better Way to Negotiate: Backward" in Working Knowledge, July 26, 2004

How often have you heard that, when entering a negotiation, you should get your allies onboard first? Conventional wisdom, but not always the best advice. When the United States sought to build a global anti-Iraq coalition following Iraq's 1990 invasion of Kuwait, for instance, Israel appeared to be its strongest regional ally.

Yet because Israel's formal membership might have kept numerous Arab states from joining the coalition, the U.S. government pointedly excluded the Israelis, starting negotiations elsewhere. Careful sequencing plus tacit Israeli membership avoided a potential setback.

Here's another bit of conventional wisdom on proper sequencing: "Get your own house in order first." Yet this was not the path that President George H. W. Bush followed in preparing for the first Gulf War. Instead of approaching Congress first, Bush committed U.S. troops to the region, built international political and military coalitions, and negotiated a U.N. Security Council Resolution authorizing "all necessary means" to eject Iraq from Kuwait. Only after these steps were taken did the Bush administration begin negotiating in earnest for congressional approval to use force in the Gulf.

Had Bush first approached a deeply skeptical Congress, agreement on the use of force would have been unlikely. A negative vote would have stymied any subsequent American efforts to build an international coalition. Getting the right players involved at the right moment opened the door to success. Getting the sequence wrong could have led to failure.

Though often overlooked, sequencing matters greatly in negotiation. Whether you're trying to get the "right" people to attend a charity event, invest in a new venture, or sign onto a complex deal, you'll face elaborate sequencing choices. With whom should you speak first? Whom next? Rules of thumb such as "allies first" or "negotiate internally, then externally" are unreliable guides. Yet a more effective approach, the logic of backward mapping, can help you choose your partners wisely—and negotiate in the right order.

SORTING OUT THE POSSIBILITIES

When Steve Perlman was preparing to launch WebTV in 1996, he faced a critical sequencing dilemma. He had obtained seed funding, developed the technology to bring the Internet to ordinary television sets, created a prototype, and hired core technical and management team members. Now running desperately low on cash, Perlman had to contend with many potential deal partners, including VCs, angels, and industrial partners (as potential sources of cash); consumer electronics firms, Internet service providers (ISPs), and content providers (for possible alliances and partnerships); manufacturers (for manufacturing set-top boxes); non-U.S. licensees; and wholesale and retail distributors (for sales). With his promising venture running on fumes, Perlman's next obvious negotiation might have been with venture capital firms for funding. Yet Perlman knew that, while VCs might have been willing to make small investments in his new firm, they were, at the time, quite wary of making major financial commitments to consumer electronics plays such as WebTV.

Instead, Perlman mapped backward from his VC target, reasoning that WebTV's appeal and value to the VCs would be greatly enhanced by partnership with a prominent consumer electronics firm. Perlman started by pitching his product to Sony, his first choice, which initially turned him down. But he then negotiated successfully with Philips and used the agreement to forge a complementary deal with Sony. With Sony and Philips onboard, Perlman was able to negotiate for VC money—at a far higher valuation. With this additional funding, Perlman had little difficulty threading a path of supporting agreements through manufacturers, wholesale and retail distribution channels, content providers, ISPs, and alliance partners abroad—and ultimately sold his young but thriving business to Microsoft for $425 million.

THE LOGIC OF BACKWARD MAPPING

When you map a negotiation backward, you envision your preferred outcome and think in reverse about how to get there. Here are the basic steps:

1. Draw a "map" of the parties who are currently involved and those who might potentially get onboard, along with their interests and their no-deal options.
2. Estimate the difficulty and cost of gaining agreement with each party as well as the value of having that person or group onboard.
3. Identify key relationships among the parties: who influences whom, who tends to defer to whom, who owes something to whom, and so on.
4. Focus on the most-difficult-to-persuade player—your ultimate target or someone else who's critical to the deal. Ask these questions: Which *prior* agreement or agreements among which set of the other players—if such agreements were in place—would maximize the chances of the target saying yes on your terms? Whom would you like to have onboard when you initiate negotiations with the target?
5. Ask analogous questions about the player(s) at this next-to-final stage: Whom would you ideally like to have onboard to maximize the chances of the most difficult player at this stage saying "yes"? How can you win that party over? Map backward in this fashion until you have found the most promising path through the cloud of possibilities.

To better understand the logic of backward mapping, consider the logic of project management. When deciding how to undertake a complex project, you focus first on your endpoint, and then develop a critical path and a timeline by working backward to the present. A successfully completed project is comparable to a value-creating agreement supported by a sustainable coalition.

Once you begin applying the logic of backward mapping, you'll find yourself facing a number of questions: How can you identify critical players? Should your negotiations be secret or open, separate or collective? How can you avoid being harmed by the sequencing tactics of others?

HERE'S SOME ADVICE:

Study patterns of influence and deference. Would-be coalition builders learn quickly that approaching the most difficult—and perhaps most critical—party first may offer slim chances for a deal. To improve the odds, try to discern who influences the target player and to whom that player defers. In a 1993 *New Yorker* article, Sidney Blumenthal described how Bill Daley, then President Clinton's key strategist for congressional approval of the North American Free Trade Agreement, went about securing buy-in: "News might arrive that a representative who had been leaning toward yes had come out as a no. . . . When he heard the bad news, [Daley went into action]. . . . 'Can we find the guy who can deliver the guy? We have to call the guy who calls the guy who calls the guy. . .' ".

Careful sequencing can help manage sensitive information. For a building developer worried about being squeezed on price if her intentions become public, the property acquisition sequence may depend on the likelihoods of different paths. Other factors involve the physical relationship of the parcels acquired to those remaining. Rather than waiting for a later acquisition, can the developer use parcels already obtained to push forward some version of the project?

The answer to this question might drive the order of approach. Similar sequencing calculations face investors who seek to quietly purchase a series of blocks of stock for a possible acquisition or take positions in various debt securities to improve their position in a bankruptcy negotiation.

BEWARE SNEAKY SEQUENCERS

Be cautious: others may try to pull devious sequencing moves on you. Most parents quickly wise up to the household version of this gambit: to get Dad to say "yes," Junior will claim that "Mom said it was OK," then scurry to tell Mom that Dad has given the green light. Some children grow up to use these time-honored tactics in the workplace. For example, when a private equity firm negotiates with a major institutional investor, the investor might informally commit capital, relying on the supposed commitments of another investor known to be savvy. Knowing of this reliance, a less than scrupulous firm may be tempted to keep the two negotiations separate, using Party A's alleged agreement as a reason for Party B to close—and vice versa. Advice: explicitly verify the assertions of anyone who claims to have secured a prior commitment from another negotiator—who may be under the false impression that you've already said "yes."

OPENING UP THE PROCESS

The secrecy that surrounds some sequenced deals can make them appear manipulative. By contrast, a group of negotiators who know and trust one another and who are skilled at joint problem solving may find that an open, collective process generates better, more creative options than a separated, sequential approach. Open negotiations can also enhance feelings of legitimacy and group ownership of an eventual agreement.

Yet relying on inclusive meetings can be risky. Interests and agendas may surface that are better dealt with privately in a careful order. Large, open meetings may help opponents to identify each other, meet, join forces, and thus mount a more powerful combined challenge.

With each negotiation, you should consider whether to create a private or public sequential strategy, launch a group process, or opt for a hybrid. When sequencing appears to have an advantage—in coalition building, managing sensitive information, and dealing with potential opponents—the logic of backward mapping will help guide your path.

Problem 13-2. *Drawing a "Backward Map"*

Think of a current multiparty dispute (either domestic or international) and see if you can draw a "backward map" of the "deference patterns" of the parties.

Philip Harter combined the insights of problem-solving dispute resolution theory with the formal governmental processes used in multiparty disputes and public policy settings to devise a process called negotiated rule making ("reg-neg"). Reg-neg uses negotiation by the regulated and regulators, rather than top-down rulemaking, to produce new government regulations. Following Harter's publication of "Negotiating Regulations: A Cure for Malaise," 71 Geo.L. J. 1 (1982), Congress permitted these processes in the Negotiated Rulemaking Act of 1990, 5 U.S.C. §§561-570, and multiparty negotiations in the form of reg-neg began to be employed in a variety of regulatory settings (occupational health and safety, food and drug administration, and environmental, to name a few). In 1996, these processes were more formally legitimated in the Administrative Dispute Resolution Act, 5 U.S.C. §§571-584. Though Harter's pathbreaking work has been primarily influential in federal policymaking, many states have employed these processes as well.[4] Variations on this multiparty participation in negotiated rulemaking have also been used in private disputes, such as those over land use or development and racial or ethnic conflicts.

❖ *Philip J. Harter*, NEGOTIATING REGULATIONS: A CURE FOR MALAISE

71 Geo. L.J. 1, 28-31, 33-34, 42, 82-86, 112-113 (1982)

This article proposes that a form of negotiation among representatives of the interested parties, including administrative agencies, would be an effective alternative procedure to the current rulemaking process. Although virtually every rulemaking includes some negotiation, it is almost never the group consensus envisioned

4. For some examples, see Consensus Building Institute, http://www.cbuilding.org, and Policy Consensus Institute, http://www.policyconsensus.org.

here. Negotiations among directly affected groups, conducted within both the existing policies of the statute authorizing the regulation and the existing policies of the agency, would enable the parties to participate directly in the establishment of the rule. . . .

THE ADVANTAGES OF RULEMAKING BY NEGOTIATION

Negotiating has many advantages over the adversarial process. The parties participate directly and immediately in the decision. They share in its development and concur with it, rather than "participate" by submitting information that the decision maker considers in reaching the decision. Frequently, those who participate in the negotiation are closer to the ultimate decision-making authority of the interest they represent than traditional intermediaries that represent the interest in an adversarial proceeding. Thus, participants in negotiations can make substantive decisions, rather than acting as experts in the decision-making process. In addition, negotiation can be a less expensive means of decision making because it reduces the need to engage in defensive research in anticipation of arguments made by adversaries.

Undoubtedly, the prime benefit of direct negotiations is that it enables the participants to focus squarely on their respective interests. They need not advocate and maintain extreme positions before a decision maker. Therefore, the parties can develop a feel for the true issues that lie within the advocated extremes and attempt to accommodate fully the competing interests. An example of this benefit occurred when a group of environmentalists opposed the construction of a dam because they feared it would lead to the development of a nearby valley. The proponents of the dam were farmers in the valley who were adversely affected by periodic floods. Negotiations between the two groups, which were begun at the behest of the governor, revealed a common interest in preserving the valley. Without the negotiations the environmentalists would have undoubtedly sued to block construction, and necessarily would have employed adversarial tactics. Negotiations, however, demonstrated the true interests of the parties and permitted them to work toward accommodation. . . .

Rulemaking by negotiation can reduce the time and cost of developing regulations by emphasizing practical and empirical concerns rather than theoretical predictions. In developing a regulation under the current system, an agency must prove a factual case, at least preliminarily, and anticipate the factual information that will be submitted in the record. Because the agency lacks direct access to empirical data, the information used is often of a theoretical nature derived from models. In negotiations, the parties in interest decide together what information is necessary to make a reasonably informed decision. . . .

Overarching all the other benefits of negotiations is the added legitimacy a rule would acquire if all parties viewed the rule as reasonable and endorsed it without a fight. Affected parties would participate in the development of a rule by sharing in the decisions, ranking their own concerns and needs, and trading them with other parties. . . .

NEGOTIATING REGULATIONS

1. Establishing the Groundrules

Because the parties are unlikely to have previously engaged in negotiations among themselves, they need to establish the groundrules that will govern, or at least guide, the negotiations. . . . Therefore, defining the rules of acceptable conduct and the procedures under which negotiations will be conducted is important if the benefits of negotiation are to be realized. Although creative problem-solving can develop only with time, the rules can foster that process.

2. Rule of Reason

Milton R. Wessel has developed a set of dispute resolution principles that he calls the "Rule of Reason." Perhaps the fundamental application of the guidelines to negotiations is to remind the participants periodically that their purpose is to reach a mutually acceptable agreement when possible, not to seek victory for their positions. The parties should keep in mind that they must sort out, weigh, and accommodate conflicting interests. Thus, they need to be reminded of the give and take and good faith of the negotiation process.

3. Confidentiality

One significant issue the participants must face at the outset of negotiations is the extent to which the process will be open to public inspection. Under current theories agencies are accountable for reaching rational results based on the neutral exercise of their discretion. Thus, the rulemaking process is subject to public scrutiny at virtually every stage. For example, ex parte rules prohibit discussions and transmittal of data unavailable to others; advisory committees are open to public attendance; the Sunshine Act requires that meetings of collegial agencies be open to the public, and the Freedom of Information Act requires agencies to provide the public with many of their internal documents. In short, the current political climate distrusts meetings and other communications between agency officials and members of the private sector unless they are open to all. Therefore, confidential exchanges are frowned upon, if not banned outright. In keeping with this theory, the parties to a regulatory negotiation may agree to conduct their affairs in public.

Several experts, however, believe that negotiation is a process best carried on in private. Several examples demonstrate the benefits of privacy. First, the negotiators must make concessions on different issues to permit maximization of their own goals. Moreover, negotiators must be able to explain the results of their negotiations to their constituents and the reasons for conceding a particular issue that the negotiator believes is not of central importance. Second, a party may be reluctant to yield confidential data that can be useful to negotiations, if doing so will destroy its confidentiality. Third, a party reasonably could be reluctant to engage in the give and take of the negotiation process if it thought that a tentative position it raised in the negotiations subsequently would be held against it in another forum, such as litigation or an ensuing rulemaking process. Finally, and perhaps most significantly, a public forum may cause some of the parties to continue to posture and to take a hard, unyielding position. In short, public scrutiny could mean that the detrimental aspects of the adversarial process result without the correlative benefits of a neutral decisionmaker.

The negotiators therefore should be able to close their meetings in appropriate circumstances. The procedures of the negotiation process itself provide the safeguards that accrue from public meetings. The political legitimacy of the resulting rule derives from the acceptance of the rule by the parties in interest, and not on the public procedures by which it was developed. Further, the parties should feel no inhibition from meeting on a confidential basis with the mediator or other parties to the negotiation.

Since Harter's original suggestion, many reg-negs have occurred. However, these reg-neg processes have inspired heated academic and evaluative debate about their effectiveness and how that effectiveness should be measured.[5]

Because multiparty processes occur in so many different contexts, it is hard to specify in advance what a particular multiparty process does or should do. A new field within dispute resolution has formed to develop structures, procedures, rules, protocols, and training models to guide both formal and informal multiple-party negotiations called Consensus Building or Public Policy Facilitation.

Problem 13-3. ***How Well Does It Work?***

What evaluative criteria would you use to assess whether stakeholder negotiations, held before formal rulemaking, are more or less successful than the more conventional draft rule, publish notice and comments, promulgation of regulation, and litigation model of administrative law (see Administrative Procedure Act, 5 U.S.C. §§551 et seq.)? How can we evaluate different kinds of processes when the subject matter of each process may be different and, unlike experimental evaluation, we cannot assign the same "issue" to several different treatments simultaneously for evaluation?

One of the founders of this new field, Lawrence Susskind, professor of urban planning at MIT and founder of the Consensus Building Institute, has pioneered the development of facilitated processes in complex public policy matters and

---

5. See, e.g., Cary Coglianese, Assessing Consensus: The Promise and Performance of Negotiated Rulemaking, 46 Duke L.J. 1255 (1997); Jody Freeman, Collaborative Governance in the Administrative State, 45 UCLA L. Rev. 1 (1997); Jody Freeman & Laura I. Langbein, Regulatory Negotiation and the Legitimacy Benefit, 9 N.Y.U. Envtl. L.J. 60 (2000); Philip J. Harter, Assessing the Assessors: The Actual Performance of Negotiated Rulemaking, 9 N.Y.U. Envtl. L.J. 32 (2000).

disputes. In a handbook for this new practice, Susskind and several colleagues develop guidelines for conducting facilitated processes in both formal and ad hoc settings. The protocols and processes described below are intended to replace the more complex Robert's Rules of Order for parliamentary and other organized meetings.

Lawrence Susskind, AN ALTERNATIVE TO ROBERT'S RULES OF ORDER FOR GROUPS, ORGANIZATIONS, AND AD HOC ASSEMBLIES THAT WANT TO OPERATE BY CONSENSUS

in The Consensus Building Handbook: A Comprehensive Guide to Reaching Agreement 3, 3-13, 20-35, 55-56 (Lawrence Susskind, Sarah McKearnan & Jennifer Thomas-Larmer eds., 1999)

Let's compare what this "Short Guide" has to say with what *Robert's Rules of Order* requires. Assume that a few dozen people have gotten together, on their own, at a community center because they are upset with a new policy or program recently announced by their local officials. After several impassioned speeches, someone suggests that the group appoint a moderator to "keep order" and ensure that the conversation proceeds effectively. Someone else wants to know how the group will decide what to recommend after they are done debating. "Will we vote?" this person wants to know. At this point, everyone turns to Joe, who has had experience as a moderator. Joe moves to the front of the room and explains that he will follow *Robert's Rules of Order.* From that moment on, the conversation takes on a very formal tone.

Instead of just saying what's on their mind, everyone is forced to frame suggestions in the cumbersome form of *motions.* These have to be *seconded.* Efforts to *move the question* are proceeded by an explanation from Joe about what is and isn't an acceptable way of doing this. Proposals to *table* various items are considered, even though everyone hasn't had a chance to speak. Ultimately, all-or-nothing votes are the only way the group seems able to make a decision.

As the hour passes, fewer and fewer of those in attendance feel capable of expressing their views. They don't know the rules, and they are intimidated. Every once in a while, someone makes an effort to restate the problem or make a suggestion, but the person is shouted down ("You're not following *Robert's Rules*!"). No one takes responsibility for ensuring that the concerns of everyone in the room are met, especially the needs of those individuals who are least able to present their views effectively. After an hour or so, many people have left. A final proposal is approved by a vote of 55 percent to 45 percent of those remaining.

If the group had followed the procedures spelled out in this "Short Guide to Consensus Building," the meeting would have been run differently and the result would probably have been a lot more to everyone's liking. The person at the front of the room would have been a trained facilitator or mediator—a person adept at helping groups build consensus—not a moderator with specialized knowledge about how motions should be made or votes should be taken. His or her job would have been to get agreement at the outset on how the group wanted to proceed. Then, the facilitator would have focused on producing an agreement that could meet the underlying concerns of everyone in the room: no motions, no arcane rituals, and no vote at the end. Instead, the facilitator might have pushed the group to brainstorm (e.g., "Can anyone propose a way of proceeding that meets all the interests we have heard expressed thus far?"). After as thorough a consideration of options as time permitted, the facilitator would ask, "Is there anyone who can't live with the last version of what has been proposed? If so, what improvement or modification can you suggest that will make it more acceptable to you, while continuing to meet the interests of everyone else with a stake in the issue?" The group would have likely developed a proposal that everyone—or nearly everyone—in the, room could support. And participants would leave satisfied that their opinions and needs had been heard, understood, and taken into account.

DEFINITIONS

Consensus Building (An Agreement-Seeking Process)

Consensus building is a process of seeking unanimous agreement. It involves a good-faith effort to meet the interests of all stakeholders. Consensus has been reached when everyone agrees they can live with whatever is proposed after every effort has been made to meet the interests of all stakeholding parties. Thus, consensus building requires that someone frame a proposal after listening carefully to everyone's concerns. Participants in a consensus building process have both the right to expect that no one will ask them to undermine their interests and the responsibility to propose solutions that will meet everyone else's interests as well as their own.

Most consensus building efforts set out to achieve unanimity. Along the way, however, there are sometimes *holdouts*: people who believe that their interests are better served by remaining outside the emerging agreement. Should the rest of the group throw in the towel? No, this would invite blackmail (i.e., outrageous demands by the holdouts that have nothing to do with the issues under discussion). Most dispute resolution professionals believe that groups or assemblies should seek unanimity, but settle for overwhelming agreement that goes as far as possible toward meeting the interests of all stakeholders. This effort to meet the interests of all stakeholders should be understood to include an affirmative responsibility to ensure that those who are excluded really are holdouts and are rejecting the proposal on reasonable grounds that would seem compelling to anyone who found themselves in the holdouts' shoes. It is absolutely crucial that the definition of success be clear at the outset of any consensus building process.

Facilitation (A Way of Helping Groups Work Together in Meetings)

Facilitation is a meeting management skill. When people are face-to-face, they need to talk and to listen. When there are several people involved, especially if they don't know each other or they disagree sharply, getting the talking-listening-deciding sequence right is hard. Often, it is helpful to have someone who has no stake in the outcome assist in managing the conversation. Of course, a skilled group member can, with the concurrence of the participants, play this role, too. As the parties try to collect information, formulate proposals, defend their views, and take account of what others are saying, a facilitator reminds them of the ground rules they have adopted and, much like a referee, intervenes when someone violates the ground rules. The facilitator is supposed to be nonpartisan or neutral.

There is some disagreement in various professional circles about the extent to which an effective facilitator needs to be someone from outside the group. Certainly in a corporate context, work teams have traditionally relied on the person "in charge" to play a facilitative role. The concept of facilitative leadership is growing in popularity. Even work teams in the private sector, however, are turning more and more to skilled outsiders to provide facilitation services. In the final analysis, there is reason to worry that a stakeholder might use facilitative authority to advance his or her own interests at the expense of the others. . . .

Before the parties in a consensus building process come together, mediators (or facilitators) can play an important part in helping to identify the right participants, assist them in setting an agenda and clarifying the ground rules by which they will operate, and even in "selling" recalcitrant parties on the value of participating. Once the process has begun, mediators (and facilitators) try to assist the parties in their efforts to generate creative resolution of differences. During these discussions or negotiations, a mediator may accompany a representative back to a meeting with his or her constituents to explain what has been happening. The mediator might serve as a spokesperson for the process if the media are following the story. A mediator might (with the parties' concurrence) push them to accept an accord (because they need someone to blame for forcing them to back off some of the demands they made at the outset). Finally, the mediator may be called on to monitor implementation of an agreement and reassemble the parties to review progress or deal with perceived violations or a failure to live up to commitments.

Facilitation and *mediation* are often used interchangeably. We think the key distinction is that facilitators work mostly with parties once they are at the table, while mediators do that as well as handle the prenegotiation and postnegotiation tasks described above. Also, mediators tend to be called on in particularly conflictual situations. In addition, some facilitators do not necessarily strive for agreement as mediators always do, but rather seek to ensure productive deliberation. Some professionals have both sets of skills; many do not. Neither form of consensus building assistance requires stakeholders to give up their authority or their power to decide what is best for them.

Recording (Creating a Visual Record of What a Group Has Discussed and Decided)

Recording involves creating a visual record that captures the key points of agreement and disagreement during a dialogue. Some facilitators (and mediators) work in tandem with a recorder. Recording can be done on large sheets of paper, often called flip charts, tacked up in front of a room. With the introduction of new computer and multimedia technologies, this can be done electronically as well. The important thing is to have an ongoing visual representation of what the group has discussed and agreed. Unlike formal minutes of a meeting, this "group memory" may use drawings, illustrations, maps, or other icons to help people recall what they have discussed. Visual records prepared by a recorder ultimately need to be turned into written meeting summaries. Like minutes, these summaries must be reviewed in draft by all participants to ensure that everyone agrees with the review of what happened.

Convening (Bringing Parties Together)

Convening, or the gathering together of parties for a meeting or a series of meetings, is not a skill that depends on training. An agency or organization that has decided to host a consensus building process (and wants to encourage others to participate) can play an important convening role. In a private firm, for example, a senior official might be the convener. In the public arena, a regulatory agency might want to convene a public involvement process. There is some disagreement about whether or not the convener or the convening organization is obliged to stay at the table as the conversation proceeds. In general, convening organizations want to be part of the dialogue, but we do not feel they must commit to ongoing participation in a consensus building process.

Someone has to finance a consensus building process. When it takes place inside an existing organization, financial arrangements are reasonably straightforward. When consensus building involves a wide range of groups in an ad hoc assembly, it is much less obvious who can and will provide the financial support. If costs are not shared equally by the parties, for example, and if they are covered by the convening organization, special steps must be taken to ensure that the facilitator or mediator has a contract with the entire group, and not just the convener, and that the organization(s) providing the financing do not use that sponsorship to dictate the outcome.

Conflict Assessment (An Essential Convening Step)

A conflict assessment is a document that spells out what the issues are, who the stakeholding interests are, where they disagree, and where they might find common ground. It is usually prepared by a neutral outsider based on confidential interviews with key stakeholders. There is some disagreement over whether the same neutral who prepared the conflict assessment should then be the one to facilitate or mediate, if the process goes forward. Typically, after interviewing a wide range of stakeholders, a neutral party will suggest whether or not it makes sense to go forward with a consensus building process and, if so, how the process ought to be structured. . . .

Circles of Stakeholder Involvement (A Strategy for Identifying Representative Stakeholders)

Stakeholders are persons or groups likely to be affected by (or who think they will be affected by) a decision—whether it is their decision to make or not. When we talk about "circles of stakeholders," we are talking about individuals or groups that want or ought to be involved in decision making, but at different levels of intensity. Some stakeholders may be involved in a core negotiating team, others may have their interests represented on that team, and still others may choose to observe the process from the sidelines.

Some stakeholders are very hard to represent in an organized way. Think about "future generations," for example. Who can represent them in a dialogue about sustainable development? In the law, various strategies have evolved so that surrogates or stand-ins can represent hard-to-represent groups (such as the members of a class of consumers who have been hurt by a certain product or children who have no capacity to speak for themselves in a court proceeding).

Sometimes, it is necessary to caucus all the groups or individuals who think they represent a certain set of stakeholders for the purposes of selecting a representative for a particular dialogue or problem-solving purpose. Such meetings typically need to be facilitated by an outside party. Finally, there are various statutes that govern who may and who must be invited to participate in various public and private dialogues. Ad hoc consensus building processes must take these laws into account.

Problem 13-4. ***Who Makes the Ground Rules?***

Consider whether, in Susskind's view, participants or facilitators should set ground rules. Does he believe rules should be "laid down" by facilitators or themselves be negotiated by the participants? What might be the consequences (both on the process and on ultimate outcomes) of ground-rule setting by the parties versus the facilitators? Are Susskind's rules flexible enough for use in a number of different contextual settings?

What, if anything, would you add to these guidelines?

These excerpts contemplate a very particular kind of process, a relatively formal multiparty negotiation or policy-setting consensus-building environment. There are many other ways to organize multiparty negotiations, running from no rules at all to very formal rules of speaking and participation. Similarly, there are many schools of thought about how to be an effective third-party neutral in facilitating such meetings, depending on whether a decision or action is required at the end or whether a group is being convened for different purposes, such as to foster understanding across divisive value differences.

C. DISPUTE SYSTEM DESIGN: PLANNING AND STRUCTURING REPEATED DISPUTE RESOLUTION

As dispute resolution processes and possibilities have become more complex, an entire new field, Dispute System Design, has developed to help organizations create processes to help prevent conflicts and manage disputes before they ripen into full-scale grievances or lawsuits. Organizations face both internal disputes and grievances involving their own employees, and external disputes, with either one-shot or repeat customers, suppliers, vendors, or constituents. For some organizations, these disputes are now referred to as "streams of disputes" because they involve large numbers of people (for example, in matters of defective products, employment discrimination, and price fixing). Claimants may experience one-shot or repeat disputes (such as when an operation fails to fix something adequately). The challenge is to create processes that treat individual complaints non-bureaucratically and also fairly and efficiently deal with repetitive issues. The principles and skills used in Dispute System Design are now relevant in a number of different contexts—organizational, administrative, class action and aggregate litigation, and in a variety of international claims settings.

Good Dispute System designers recognize that "one size does not fit all" and that a tiered system is often optimal. Tiered systems may begin with informal conversation and negotiation, then use consensual mediation with a third party, and finally offer a system for hearing arguments and legal rights claims, with appropriate remedial possibilities (for example, non-binding arbitration). Of course, dispute mechanisms vary, according to the relationship between the disputants and the issues that arise.

The excerpts that follow explore the basic principles of Dispute System Design.

William L. Ury, Jeanne M. Brett & Stephen B. Goldberg, GETTING DISPUTES RESOLVED: DESIGNING SYSTEMS TO CUT THE COSTS OF CONFLICT

41-45, 52-56, 58-64 (1988)

DESIGNING AN EFFECTIVE DISPUTE RESOLUTION SYSTEM

Two oil companies, about to engage in a joint venture, agree in advance on a dispute resolution system. They will try to resolve all disputes in a partnership committee. Failing that, they will refer disputes to two senior executives, one from each company, both uninvolved in the joint venture. The executives' task is to study the problem and, in consultation with their respective companies, to negotiate a settlement. They thus act as mediators as well as negotiators. If the "wise counselors" cannot reach an agreement, the dispute will be sent to arbitration. Litigation will be avoided.

A statewide fire fighters union and an organization of cities and towns in the state are unhappy with the delay, unsatisfactory outcomes, and damaged relationships resulting from state-mandated arbitration to resolve disputes about the terms of fire fighters' collective bargaining contracts. They consult a dispute systems designer, who proposes that a joint committee of labor and management officials use mediation to break impasses. Both groups accept his proposal and successfully lobby the state legislature to add mediation to the statute. Arbitration remains available for disputes that cannot otherwise be resolved, but the favored procedure is to be mediation.

At the Catholic Archdiocese of Chicago, school administrators, looking for better ways to resolve disputes about teacher dismissals and student suspensions, designed a multistep dispute resolution procedure that requires negotiation between disputing parties; provides advice from a school conflict management board composed of teachers, parents, and principals from other schools; and offers the services of a trained mediator.

[A] dispute resolution system is designed to reduce the costs of handling disputes and to produce more satisfying and durable resolutions. . . . [H]ow to design such a system—how to create an interests-oriented system, starting from a diagnosis of the existing system. . .—[involves] six basic principles of dispute systems design:

PRINCIPLE 1: PUT THE FOCUS ON INTERESTS. . .

In multistep procedures, a dispute that is not resolved at one level of the organizational hierarchy moves to progressively higher levels, with different negotiators involved at each step. One example is the contractual grievance procedure in the coal industry: step 1 is negotiation between the miner and his foreman, step 2 is negotiation between the mine committee and mine management, and step 3 is negotiation between the district union representative and senior management.

Multistep negotiation procedures, common in the labor-management context, are increasingly being used by parties to long-term business contracts. . . . In adding more negotiation steps, however, the designer needs to be careful. In some cases, the easy availability of a higher-level person will simply discourage people from reaching agreement at a lower level and will thus make lower-level negotiation a *pro forma* step. . . .

PRINCIPLE 2: BUILD IN "LOOP-BACKS" TO NEGOTIATION

Interests-based procedures will not always resolve disputes, yet a rights or power contest can be excessively costly. The wise designer will thus build in procedures that encourage the disputants to turn back from such contests to negotiation. These are what we call "loop-back" procedures. It is useful to distinguish such procedures on the basis of whether they encourage disputants to "loop back" from a rights contest or from a power contest. . . .

In recent years, thousands of claims against asbestos manufacturers have flooded the judicial system. Some innovative designers, working as agents of the court, have set up data bases containing information about the characteristics and results of asbestos claims that have been resolved either by trial or by settlement. When a new claim is filed, the designers identify similar claims in the data base and use the information about the outcomes of previously resolved cases to determine the range within which the new case is likely to be resolved. This information reduces uncertainty about the likely outcome of the case and provides an independent standard that can help the lawyers settle the case. . . .

Rarely does a negotiated agreement look so attractive as when the parties are on the verge of a costly power contest or are in the midst of one. One simple procedure designed to take advantage of this receptivity is a cooling-off period—a specified time during which the disputants refrain from a power contest. The Taft-Hartley Act and the Railway Labor Act both provide for cooling-off periods before strikes that threaten to cause a national emergency. During the cooling-off period, negotiations, while not required, normally take place. Cooling-off periods are also useful in small-scale disputes. In the Noel Coward play Private Lives, a bickering couple agree that, whenever an argument threatens to get out of control, one person will shout "Solomon Isaacs," which will bring all conversation to a halt for five minutes while each tries to calm down. . . .

PRINCIPLE 3: PROVIDE LOW-COST RIGHTS AND POWER BACKUPS

A key part of an effective dispute resolution system is low-cost procedures for providing a final resolution based on rights or power. Such procedures serve as a backup should interests-based negotiation fail to resolve the dispute.

Low-Cost Procedures to Determine Rights

A less costly alternative to court is arbitration—in other words, private adjudication. Like court, arbitration is a rights procedure in which the parties (or their representatives) present evidence and arguments to a neutral third party who makes a binding decision. Arbitration procedures can be simpler, quicker, and less expensive than court procedures. Formal rules need not be followed, strict time limits can be agreed to, and restrictions can be placed on the use of lawyers and of expensive evidence discovery procedures. . . .

Sometimes, even when interests and rights-based procedures are available, agreement is impossible because one or both parties believes it is more powerful than the other, and can obtain a more satisfactory resolution through a power contest. The designer, anticipating this situation, should consider building into the system a low-cost power procedure to be used as a backup to all other procedures. Getting the parties to accept such a procedure may be difficult, since each party is likely to oppose any new procedure that appears to give an advantage to the other. As a result such a design effort is likely to succeed only when the use of power procedures imposes high costs on all parties. There are a variety of relatively low-cost power contests including voting, limited strikes, and rules of prudence. . . .

Before the National Labor Relations Act (NLRA) of 1935, disputes about workers right to engage in collective bargaining were handled through bitter strikes and violence. Some workers were killed; many were seriously injured. The NLRA did a great deal to end the violence by setting up a low-cost power contest—the union election—and by requiring employers to bargain in good faith with a union elected by a majority of the employees. . . .

PRINCIPLE 4: BUILD IN CONSULTATION BEFORE, FEEDBACK AFTER

A fourth design principle is to prevent unnecessary conflict and head off future disputes. This may be done through notification and consultation, as well as through post-dispute analysis and feedback. . . . Some disputes are symptomatic of a broader problem that the disputants or their organizations need to learn about and deal with. The wise designer builds into the system procedures for post-dispute analysis and feedback. At some manufacturing companies, lawyers and managers regularly analyze consumer complaints to determine what changes in product design might reduce the likelihood of similar disputes in the future. At the Massachusetts Institute of Technology, ombudsmen identify university practices that are causing disputes and suggest changes in those practices.

Where a broader community interest is at stake, the designer may include a different sort of feedback: a procedure for aggregating complaints and taking action to protect the community. For example, some consumer mediation agencies keep records of complaints against each merchant and alert the appropriate state authorities when repeated complaints are lodged against the same merchant. . . .

PRINCIPLE 5: ARRANGE PROCEDURES IN A LOW-TO-HIGH-COST SEQUENCE

The design principles above suggest creating a sequence of procedures from interests-based negotiation to loop-back procedures to low-cost rights and power backups. The sequence can be imagined as a series of steps up a "dispute resolution ladder." . . . The sequence used in the oil companies' joint venture contains three successive steps: first, try to catch disputes early by resolving them in the partnership committee; if that fails, bring in two uninvolved senior executives to negotiate; and, if that fails, turn to low-cost arbitration rather than to expensive litigation.

> **Problem 13-5.** ***Designing Systems for Different Contexts***
>
> What role does context play in designing a system? Design a dispute resolution system for (1) grade disputes at your school, (2) employment grievances at your workplace, (3) disputes within your living unit or family. How do your systems differ? Why? What values are expressed in each? Who are the decision makers or third-party neutrals in each system? How much direct negotiation or interaction have you designed for the principal disputants?

PRINCIPLE 6: PROVIDE THE NECESSARY MOTIVATION, SKILLS, AND RESOURCES

A final principle cuts across all others: Make sure the procedures work by providing the motivation to use them, the relevant skills, and the necessary resources. In designing a system, for example, to deal with disputes over the location of hazardous waste treatment facilities, as described earlier . . . one state legislature makes negotiation mandatory and provides resources in the form of technical assistance to aid the negotiation process. Without the necessary motivation, skills, and resources, procedures might well fail.

Dispute system design professionals Janet Martinez and Stephanie Smith (working with Maude Pervere) have developed a template for consideration of the key issues in dispute system design planning:

Stephanie Smith and Janet Martinez, AN ANALYTIC FRAMEWORK FOR DISPUTE SYSTEM DESIGN

14 Harvard Neg. L. Rev. 123, 133 (2009)

THE ANALYTIC FRAMEWORK

1. Goals

a) Which types of conflicts does the system seek to address?
b) What does the system's designer seek to accomplish?

2. Processes and Structure

a) Which processes are used to prevent, manage and resolve disputes?
b) If there is more than one process, are they linked or integrated?
c) What are the incentives and disincentives for using the system?
d) What is the system's interaction with the formal legal system?

3. Stakeholders

a) Who are the stakeholders?
b) What is their relative power?
c) How are their interests represented in the system?

4. Resources

a) What financial resources support the system?
b) What human resources support the system?

5. Success and Accountability

a) How transparent is the system?
b) Does it include an evaluation component?
c) Is the system successful?

For a discussion of the particular ethical challenges facing dispute system designers, see Carrie Menkel-Meadow, "Are There Systemic Ethics Issues in

Dispute System Design? And What We Should (Not) Do About It: Lessons from International and Domestic Fronts, 14 Harv. Negot. L. Rev. 195 (2009).

If mediators, facilitators, and other third-party neutrals help disputing parties find solutions to their conflicts, or facilitate the making of complex public policy decisions, why shouldn't they also devote their skills to crafting good deals or transactions at the beginning of relationships? Increasingly, business lawyers and clients are seeing the benefits of inviting in a third party to create value, prevent waste, or remove strategic barriers to information asymmetries, as well as to deal with emotional, cognitive, and other barriers to agreement and to facilitate Pareto-efficient (most gain with least harm to parties) and relationally satisfying arrangements in complex transactions. This creative use of ADR-like techniques to prevent disputes and create new transactions and entities is gaining more and more attention, especially in complex deals involving partnerships of venture capitalists in the private sector, public funding sources, governments, insurers, lenders, suppliers, developers, and consumers. This kind of managed transactional dispute resolution can be used in multiparty business deals, siting and design issues, major construction projects, and in the development of new projects (land use, joint fundraising) and entities (joint public and private agencies, such as Redevelopment and Stadium Authorities in many localities). See e.g., Frank Carr, Kim Hurtado, Charles Lancaster, Charles Markert & Paul Taylor, Partnering in Construction: A Practical Guide for Project Success (1999) and Scott Peppet, Contract Formation in Imperfect Markets: Should We Use Mediators in Deals? 19 Ohio St. J. on Disp. Resol. 283 (2004).

D. LEGAL ISSUES IN THE USE OF CONSENSUS BUILDING AND GROUP NEGOTIATIONS

As government agencies, whether federal or state, legislative, executive or administrative, use more of these consensus-building and negotiated processes, there are many legal questions about when and how negotiated solutions actually become legal enactments with binding legal authority. These are complicated questions involving how the negotiation or consensus-building event was convened, who participates, and whether processes must be open to the public or can be conducted in private. The following excerpt explores some of these legal issues.

Dwight Golann & Eric E. Van Loon, LEGAL ISSUES IN CONSENSUS BUILDING

in The Consensus Building Handbook: A Comprehensive Guide to Reaching Agreement 495, 495-497 (Lawrence Susskind, Sarah McKearnan & Jennifer Thomas Larmer eds., 1999)

. . . With so many state legislatures, courts, and systems of legal rules in the United States, it is impossible to offer a single answer to most legal questions. Responses are likely to depend on the state(s) in which a consensus building effort takes place and the terms of the ground rules that govern a process. Precise answers are also difficult for the more fundamental reason that lawmakers themselves are sometimes unclear; the laws they pass and the rules they write often create more ambiguities than they resolve. For some issues, no statute or regulation exists, forcing individual courts to make law on an ad hoc basis. As a result, it can take decades before a particular issue is addressed in the legal system—and even then, the answer may vary from one place to another.

Despite these limitations, it *is* possible to provide general guidance on legal challenges that may arise in the course of consensus building. We have identified six categories of challenges. Many of the issues within these categories proceed from the fact that consensus processes often involve public officials, who are subject to special constraints because of their role in government.

1. Relationship to government agencies and the courts. Disputes that are the subject of consensus building are sometimes simultaneously the focus of legal proceedings before agencies or courts. This raises the question of how the two processes should be coordinated.

2. Procedural requirements imposed by laws and regulations. Government employees often must follow specific procedures, which may prevent them from making binding commitments during a negotiation. For example, agency officials usually cannot commit to change regulations as part of a settlement, because they must first consider comments from the general public.

3. Substantive restrictions on the power of government representatives. Some limitations on government negotiators cannot be resolved even by following the right procedures because they arise from fundamental constraints embedded in the U.S. system of government. An example is the concept of separation of powers. The head of a federal agency, for example, cannot make commitments that bind Congress to take action. Similarly, state agencies are limited in how they can control the activities of municipalities on topics such as education or zoning.

4. Disclosure requirements and confidentiality protections. Participants in sensitive negotiations often prefer to hold their discussions in private, and many states bar participants from revealing what was said during a mediation process. Other statutes, however, require that meetings in which public officials participate be open to citizens and the press. Because consensus building is a mediative process that often involves public officials, both sets of laws may apply, creating confusion.

5. Liability considerations. Mediators and facilitators can be held legally liable for their actions in a consensus-based process and should therefore take appropriate precautions. Certain risky behaviors should be avoided, for example, and liability insurance should be obtained.

6. Implementation concerns. Once an agreement has been reached, everyone involved presumably wants to see it carried out. Nonetheless, implementation problems may arise over time, prompting two legal questions. One concerns the minimum requirements for a contract to be legally binding. For instance, must an agreement be written in "legalese" to be enforceable? The other question involves how to structure the terms of an agreement so that, if necessary, it can be enforced by court order. . . .

You have now seen many of the creative ways in which dispute resolution processes are being expanded, modified, and adapted to facilitating human action in a variety of contexts, including private and public dealings and decision making. In the final chapter that follows, we ask you to think about what new uses might be made of these processes that you have studied. What are some of the opportunities and challenges presented by the use of these different methods of dispute resolution and problem solving in the wide variety of contexts in which they might be employed?

Further Reading

Max Bazerman (Ed.). (2005). Negotiation, Decision Making and Conflict Management. International Critical Library on Business and Management.

Ingrid Bens. (2005). Facilitating With Ease! San Francisco: Jossey-Bass Publishers.

Lisa Blomgren Amsler, Janet Martinez & Stephanie Smith. (2020). Dispute System Design: Preventing, Managing and Resolving Conflict. Stanford: Stanford University Press.

Lisa Blomgren Bingham, Cynthia J. Halberlin, Denise Walker & Won-Tae Chung, Dispute System Design and Justice in Employment Dispute Resolution: Mediation in the Workplace, 14 Harv. Negot. L. Rev. 1-50 (2009).

Susan L. Carpenter & W.L.D. Kennedy. (2001). Managing Public Disputes: A Practical Guide for Professionals in Government, Business and Citizen Groups. San Francisco: Jossey-Bass Publishers.

Center for Conflict Resolution (1977). Manual for Group Facilitators.

Cathy Costantino & Christina Sickles Merchant. (1996). Designing Conflict Management Systems. San Francisco: Jossey-Bass Publishers.

E. Franklin Dukes, Marina A. Piscolish & John B. Stephens. (2000). Reaching for Higher Ground in Conflict Resolution: Tools for Powerful Groups and Communities. San Francisco: Jossey-Bass Publishers.

John Forester. (2009). Dealing with Differences: Dramas of Mediating Public Disputes. New York: Oxford University Press.

Ronald Gilson & Robert H. Mnookin (eds.), Business Lawyers and Value Creation for Clients, 74 Oregon L. Rev. 1-13 (1995).

L. Michael Hager & Robert Pritchard, Deal Mediation: How ADR Techniques Can Help Achieve Durable Agreements in Global Markets, 14 ICSID Rev. Foreign Investment L.J. 1 (1999).

Harvard Negotiation Law Review, Symposium on Dispute System Design, 14 Harvard Negot. L. Rev. 1-342 (2009).

Tim Hindle. (1998). Managing Meetings. New York: DK Publishing.

Sam Kaner. (2014). Facilitator's Guide to Participatory Group Decision Making. San Francisco: Jossey-Bass Publishers.

Carrie Menkel-Meadow, Are There Systemic Ethics Issues in Dispute System Design? And What We Should [Not] Do About It: Lessons from International and Domestic Fronts, 14 Harv. Negot. L. Rev. 195-231 (2009).

Carrie Menkel-Meadow (Ed.). (2011). Complex Dispute Resolution. New York: Ashgate Press.

Hallum Movius & Lawrence Susskind. (2009). Built to Win: Creating a World Class Negotiating Organization. Boston: Harvard Business School.

Public Conversations Project (now Essential Partners). Constructive Conversations about Challenging Times: A Guide to Community Dialogues. Available at: http://www.publicconversations.org/pcp/UploadDocsCommunityGuide3.0.pdf.

Nancy Rogers, Robert C. Bordone, Frank E.A. Sander & Craig A. McEwen. (2019). Designing Systems and Processes for Managing Disputes (2d ed). New York: Wolters Kluwer.

Roger Schwartz. (2002). The Skilled Facilitator (2d ed). San Francisco: Jossey-Bass Publishers.

Stephanie Smith & Jan Martinez, An Analytic Framework for Dispute Systems Design, 14 Harv. Negot. L. Rev. 123-170 (2009).

Lawrence Susskind, Sarah McKearnan & Jennifer Thomas Larmer. (1999). The Consensus Building Handbook: A Comprehensive Guide to Reaching Agreement. Thousand Oaks, CA: Sage Publications.

Lawrence Susskind & Jeffrey Cruickshank. (2006). Breaking Robert's Rules: The New Way to Run Your Meeting, Build Consensus and Get Results. New York: Oxford Univ. Press.

Chapter 14 Choosing an Appropriate Process: For Your Clients and the Future of ADR as Systems of Dispute Resolution

Never underestimate the power of a small group of committed people to change the world. In fact, it is the only thing that ever has.

—Margaret Mead

Justice cannot be for one side alone but must be for both.

—Eleanor Roosevelt (and engraved in the Supreme Court of the United Kingdom)

You have now studied a wide variety of processes used to resolve conflicts and solve problems in many different settings. These processes offer opportunities and challenges. Existing processes may offer the opportunity to enhance autonomy, creativity, efficiency, and justice in some combination. And the landscape of ADR processes continues to grow as policymakers, disputants, and their attorneys craft novel variations aimed at particular circumstances or policy objectives.

As you have seen in Chapter 13, an important part of the field of dispute resolution, called Dispute System Design, focuses on developing appropriate processes for different kinds of disputes in a variety of repetitive and organizational settings. While the modern dispute resolution processes have grown out of dissatisfactions with the cost, duration, rigidity, and complexity of conventional litigation processes, some worry that those processes also have limitations and difficulties, such as in "privatizing" justice or reinforcing party inequalities. In this final chapter we ask you to reflect on how we should evaluate and assess the effectiveness of particular processes and to try to imagine what new processes might be developed in the future. Assessing and evaluating which process is appropriate for a particular legal matter or problem has at least two important components:

1. How to advise your own client about what process is appropriate for his or her particular matter, some of which we have already previewed in Chapters 2 (counseling your client) and 3 (choosing among different negotiation approaches in particular settings). In a sense, this can be labeled the "private" side of ADR—lawyers assisting their clients with choices about which process is most likely to help the client achieve his or her goals and objectives.
2. As a matter of public policy, which processes are best for achieving societal or institutional goals? Which processes should public institutions like courts, legislatures, and administrative agencies encourage and support?

> When should public institutions control private problem solving? In what circumstances should legal, political, or social disputes remain in the public eye for transparency, political debate, and formal resolution?

Both of these questions require us to think about parties' goals and what public interests are involved. Considering these questions requires us to be rigorous in how we evaluate the processes, empirically, strategically, and jurisprudentially. We will examine these issues in this chapter, looking first at how lawyers help clients evaluate particular processes, then at how these processes have been studied and evaluated so far. Finally, we return to the issues with which we began in Chapter 1. As we contemplate a future of further ADR use and development, what are the basic values we hope to express in our process designs and choices?

You are the next generation of dispute resolution professionals. We hope, through the learning you have done with this book, and in this course, you will rise to the possibilities of adapting existing processes and creating new processes for the resolution of new problems and conflicts that we cannot even imagine today.

A. CHOOSING AMONG DISPUTE RESOLUTION PROCESSES: PRIVATE INTERESTS

1. Comparing the Processes

The following excerpt from two founders of the modern dispute resolution movement is considered "a classic" in how to advise clients about the variety of dispute resolution options and how to ensure that clients' problems are addressed in the most appropriate process.

❖ *Frank E.A. Sander & Stephen B. Goldberg*, FITTING THE FORUM TO THE FUSS: A USER-FRIENDLY GUIDE TO SELECTING AN ADR PROCEDURE

10 Negotiation J. 49 (1994)

CLIENT GOALS

In the hypothetical [sexual harassment] case with which we began this article, how do you, as [her] attorney, prepare for your initial interview with your client? Is she eager to remain at the company (perhaps because alternative employment opportunities are scarce) and hence wants to resolve this situation with the least disruption and fuss? Or is she so angry that she is determined to have some outside neutral pronounce her "right," and thus vindicate her position?

Answers to questions like these are critical in determining what dispute resolution procedure is appropriate in this case. The fact that [she] has decided to come to an attorney indicates that she is dissatisfied with the present posture of the dispute. But should she file a lawsuit or seek some other way of resolving the problem? If she has an emotional need for vindication, she will have to resort to some form of adjudication, either in court or—if the company is willing—through private means, such as arbitration or private judging. Private adjudication, in addition to assuring confidentiality, is often faster and cheaper than a court decision. In arbitration and private judging, there is also an opportunity to participate in the selection of the adjudicator and thus to obtain particular expertise. In addition, arbitration almost guarantees finality, since a reviewing court will hardly ever overturn an arbitrator's decision. If [she] wants public vindication, however, or a binding precedent, only court will do. . . .

These, then, are some of the considerations that lawyers and clients must examine with regard to processes that might meet client objectives. The value of various procedures in meeting specific client objectives is set forth in Table 1.

An important point to note is that the values assigned to each procedure in Table 1 . . . are not based on empirical research but rather upon our own experience, combined with the views of other dispute resolution professionals. Moreover, the numerical values assigned to each procedure are not intended to be taken literally, but rather as a shorthand expression of the extent to which each procedure satisfies a particular objective. . . .

The next step in the analysis is to list the client's goals in order of priority. If the client is primarily interested in a prompt and inexpensive resolution of the dispute that also maintains or improves the parties' relationship—which is typical of most clients in most business disputes—mediation is the preferred procedure. Mediation is the only procedure to receive maximum scores on each of these dimensions—cost, speed, and maintain or improve the relationship—as well as on assuring privacy, another interest which is present in many business disputes. It is only when the client's primary interests consist of establishing a precedent, being vindicated, or maximizing (or minimizing) recovery that procedures other than mediation are more likely to be satisfactory. . . .

	PROCEDURES					
	NONBINDING				BINDING	
	MEDIATION	MINITRIAL	SUMMARY JURY TRIAL	EARLY NEUTRAL EVALUATION	ARBITRATION/ PRIVATE JUDGING	COURT
OBJECTIVES						
Minimize costs	3	2	2	3	1	0
Speed	3	2	2	3	1	0
Privacy	3	3	2	2	3	0
Maintain/improve relationship	3	2	2	1	1	0
Vindication	0	1	1	1	2	3
Neutral opinion	0	3	3	3	3	3
Precedent	0	0	0	0	2	3
Maximizing/ minimizing recovery	0	1	1	1	2	3

0 = Unlikely to satisfy objective
1 = Satisfies objective somewhat
2 = Satisfies objective substantially
3 = Satisfies objective very substantially

One final point concerning client goals: Some contend that ADR should be avoided altogether when one party will be sure to win if the matter is litigated. We disagree. First, the likely loser may be persuaded, through the use of one of the evaluative ADR procedures, to concede, thus sparing both parties the costs of litigation. An agreed-upon outcome is also more likely to be fully complied with than a court order. Alternatively, the likely loser may offer, in ADR, a settlement that is better in non-monetary terms than what could be achieved in litigation; such a settlement preserves, and often enhances, the parties' relationship. Thus, the prospect of a victory in litigation is not reason enough for avoiding ADR.

IMPEDIMENTS TO SETTLEMENT AND WAYS OF OVERCOMING THEM

In some circumstances, a settlement is not in the client's interest. For example, the client may want a binding precedent or may want to impress other potential litigants with its firmness and the consequent costs of asserting claims against it. Alternatively, the client may be in a situation in which there are no relational concerns; the only issue is whether it must pay out money; there is no pre-judgment interest; and the cost of contesting the claim is less than the interest earned on the money. In these and a small number of other situations, settlement will not be in the client's interest.

Still, a satisfactory settlement typically is in the client's interest. It is the inability to obtain such a settlement, in fact, that impels the client to seek the advice of counsel in the first place. The lawyer must consider not only what the client wants but also why the parties have been unable to settle their dispute, and then must find a dispute resolution procedure that is likely to overcome the impediments to settlement. . . .

Poor Communication

The relationship between the parties and/or their lawyers may be so poor that they cannot effectively communicate. Neither party believes the other, and each searches for hidden daggers in all proposals put forth by the other. An inability to communicate clearly and effectively, which impedes successful negotiations, is often, but not always, the result of a poor relationship. . . .

The Need to Express Emotions

At times, no settlement can be achieved until the parties have had the opportunity to express their views to each other about the dispute and each other's conduct. . . .

Different Views of Facts

Did the defendant engage in the conduct that forms the basis of the plaintiff's complaint? Whose version of the facts is the finder of fact likely to believe? The greater the parties' disagreement on these matters, the more difficult settlement is likely to be. . . .

Different Views of Legal Outcome if Settlement Is Not Reached

Disputants often agree on the facts but disagree on their legal implications. The plaintiff asserts that, on the basis of the agreed-upon facts, he has a 90 percent likelihood of success in court; the defendant, with equal fervor, asserts that she has a 90 percent chance of success. While there may be a legitimate dispute over the likely outcome, both these estimates cannot be right. . . .

Issues of Principle

If each of the disputing parties is deeply attached to some "fundamental" principle that must be abandoned or compromised in order to resolve the dispute, then resolution is likely to be difficult. Two examples: a suit challenging the right of neo-Nazis to march in a town where many Holocaust survivors live; and a suit by a religious group objecting to the withdrawal of life support systems from a comatose patient. . .

Constituency Pressures

If one or more of the negotiators represents an institution or group, constituency pressures may impede agreement in two ways: different elements within the institution or group may have different interests in the dispute, or the negotiator may have staked her political or job future on attaining a certain result. . . .

Linkage to Other Disputes

The resolution of one dispute may have an effect on other disputes involving one or both parties. If so, this linkage will enter into their calculations, and may so complicate negotiations as to lead to an impasse. . . .

Multiple Parties

When there are multiple parties, with diverse interests, the problems are similar to those raised by diverse constituencies and by issue linkages. . . .

Different Lawyer/Client Interests

Lawyers and clients often have divergent attitudes and interests concerning settlement. This may be a matter of personality (one may be a fighter, the other a problem solver) or of money. An attorney who is paid on an hourly basis stands to profit handsomely from trial, and may be less interested in settlement than the client. On the other hand, an attorney paid on a contingent fee basis is interested in a prompt recovery without the expense of preparing for or conducting a trial, and may be more interested in settlement than is the client. It is in part because of this potential conflict of interest that most processes that seek to promote settlement provide for the client's direct involvement. . . .

The "Jackpot" Syndrome

An enormous barrier to settlement often exists in those cases where the plaintiff is confident of obtaining in court a financial recovery far exceeding its damages, and the defendant thinks this is highly unlikely. . . .

The Public Perspective

For either a judge or a court employee responsible for recommending an ADR procedure, the question regarding barriers to settlement and how they can be overcome is the same as it is for individual disputants. The other question concerning goals is similar, but with a broader perspective. In lieu of asking what are the objectives one party wishes to achieve, as would counsel, the question is what both parties want to achieve. . . .

When a process selection is made from a public perspective, the public interest must also be considered. If the dispute is one in which a trial is likely to be lengthy, and so consume precious court time, there may be a public interest in referring the dispute to some form of ADR. Beyond that, one must ask if there is a public interest in having the dispute resolved pursuant to a particular procedure. For example, the referral of child custody disputes to mediation is required by law in several jurisdictions. The disputing parents may believe that they have no interest in a better relationship, but only in vindication, and hence prefer court to mediation. However, many states believe that a better relationship between the parents serves the public interest by improving the life of the child, and so mandate that child custody disputes go first to mediation.

The final question that must be asked in the public context is whether the public interests will be better served by a court decision than by a private settlement. If, for example, the dispute raises a significant question of statutory or constitutional interpretation, a court resolution might be preferable to a private settlement. While a court normally has no power to prevent parties from settling their own dispute, it does not follow that the court, as a public agency, should encourage or assist settlement in such a case.

Litigation may also serve the public interest better than mediation in cases of consumer fraud, which are often handled by the consumer protection division of an attorney general's office. Here not only the issue of precedent, but also the related issue of recurring violations, is key. The establishment of a general principle or a class remedy, by means of a class action, is clearly preferable to a series of repetitive and inconsistent mediations. . . .

Finally, two more situations may militate against any use of ADR. First, one or more of the parties may be incapable of negotiating effectively. An unsophisticated pro se litigant, for example, may be vulnerable to exploitation in an ADR process. (On the other hand, such an individual, if not represented by a lawyer, may not fare better in court.) Second, court process may be required for some other reason: for example, when serious issues of compliance or discovery are anticipated.

CONCLUSION

In addressing the problem of "fitting the forum to the fuss," we have suggested two lines of inquiry: What are the disputants' goals in making a forum choice? And, if the disputants are amenable to settlement, what are the obstacles to settlement, and in what forum might they be overcome?

The fact that these inquiries rarely lead to a clear answer to the question of forum selection does not, we think, indicate that the analysis is faulty. Rather, it indicates that the question of forum selection ultimately turns on the extent to which the interests of the disputing parties (and sometimes of the public) will be met in various forums. Thus, the most that analysis can offer is a framework that clarifies the interests involved and promotes a thoughtful weighing and resolution of those interests.

Moreover such an inquiry concerning goals and impediments is often independently helpful in clarifying the dimensions of the basic dispute. When it then comes to exploring the ADR implications of that analysis, a sophisticated ADR user might well ask: "If these are my goals and my impediments, what kinds of third-party help do I need, and how can I design a procedure that provides that kind of help?"

Problem 14-1. ***Counseling a Client About Process Choice***

Considering the case type Professors Sander and Goldberg use at the beginning of this excerpt,—sexual harassment—how would you counsel: (a) a plaintiff and, (b) a defendant in such a matter about which processes might be most appropriate for their needs and objectives?

Do you think the authors' analysis is correct? Complete?

Do you think they might have arrived at a different framework or set of overall conclusions if their starting case had been a dispute over a commercial lease? An estate contested by multiple family members? A workplace accident? A divorce?

2. Assessing the Impact of Processes on Clients

Professor Andrea Kupfer Schneider adds the dimension of therapeutic jurisprudence into dispute process choice, arguing that lawyers should consider the emotional and mental impact of legal processes on their clients. Professor Schneider encourages attorneys to examine the emotional or therapeutic impact of each dispute resolution process in addition to narrower legal concerns, arguing that this broader approach is more consistent with the ideals of dispute resolution itself. This advice also builds on the counseling concepts discussed in Chapter 2—specifically, that lawyers should seek to understand a client's non-legal concerns.

Andrea Kupfer Schneider, BUILDING A PEDAGOGY OF PROBLEM-SOLVING: LEARNING TO CHOOSE AMONG ADR PROCESSES

5 Harv. Negot. L. Rev. 113 (2000)

A NEW MODEL FOR CHOOSING AMONG THE ADR PROCESSES

Therapeutic jurisprudence and preventive law [TJPL] provide a coherent methodology for choosing among the ADR processes of negotiation, mediation and arbitration. Given that ADR was developed with the goal of increasing parties' satisfaction, ADR practitioners should be advising their clients on that basis. An intellectual framework for choosing the process could achieve the qualitative-justice advantages that ADR's founders intended. This approach adds a needed layer to the current analysis of ADR choices by explicitly adding emotional and psychological concerns to that of the traditional legal and financial analysis. TJPL can help us look at additional factors in order to make a fully educated and beneficial choice for the client.

Finally, lawyers must examine the result of the ADR process for the impact on the client. Again, TJPL provides a framework for this analysis that is comprehensive and informative.

PROCESS/CLIENT INTEREST	NEGOTIATION	MEDIATION	ARBITRATION
Emotional (stress, speed, relationship, vindication)			
Legal (precedent,neutral opinion)			
Financial (costs, speed, recovery)			

APPLYING THE MODEL

To demonstrate the usefulness of applying TJPL, [we assume the following facts, outlined in Leonard Riskin, James Westbrook & James Levin, Instructor's Manual to Accompany Dispute Resolution and Lawyers 119 (1998)]. . . .

Dr. John Roark sued the Daily Bugle, its editor, and reporter Terry Ives for defamation. Terry Ives wrote a front page article about a fire in slum housing owned by Dr. John Roark. The article reports that a source in the Fire Marshal's office has indicated that the office is not ruling out the possibility of arson. The article also alleges that it is not uncommon for owners of tenements to intentionally burn their properties to collect insurance. When Roark called to complain, the editor said he stood by the story.

Roark insists that the reporter was negligent because property records show that Roark was only a limited partner in a group owning the property. Roark also believes that the reporter acted with malice because Ives had once before written a story about Roark's youngest son when the son was arrested for drug possession.

Roark seeks $250,000 in actual damages for harm to his reputation, lost income in his medical practice, aggravation of a serious health problem, and mental anguish. He also seeks punitive damages of $1 million.

A. Step One: Counseling & Interviewing—Identifying Emotional Concerns

As part of the initial meeting with Roark, the lawyer should discuss, in addition to legal and financial concerns, the emotional impact of various dispute resolution processes. These concerns could range from broad issues applicable to every client to the more specific concerns that Roark might have in this case. The lawyer should first determine general issues such as how much Roark would like to participate in resolving the dispute, whether he is comfortable in formal settings, and how at ease he is with the legal process in general. The lawyer should review Roark's desire to tell his story and determine whether he (a) wishes to confront the other side; (b) wants to tell his story to a neutral third party; (c) would want to testify (and would be good at testifying) in a courtroom; or (d) would like to detach from the process as much as possible.

The lawyer should also look for emotional concerns particular to this client. In a defamation case with a claim of mental anguish, these issues should not be ignored. . . .

First, Roark's feelings of anger at the paper and hurt at his subsequent treatment need to be considered. . . . Second, this event has aggravated Roark's medical condition. . . . Finally, Roark could have more general emotional concerns. He might be worried about the impact of this situation on his reputation. He might be concerned about the impact that dealing with this situation would have on his quality of work and his quality of life. . . .

B. Step Two: Choosing a Process—Determining Legal Procedures That Would Be Therapeutic

In light of Roark's emotional concerns, each of the ADR processes should be assessed in terms of their ability to provide therapeutic, or emotionally beneficial, results. They should also be judged by whether any of these processes could also have nontherapeutic, or emotionally harmful, effects.

Again, this analysis is intended to augment, not supplant, traditional consideration of legal and financial ramification. Indeed, given the facts of this particular claim, it is plausible that only litigation would vindicate Dr. Roark's desires. Defamation is a complex legal claim and he might trust a court to better apply the relevant standards. . . .

1. Negotiation Negotiation has the advantage of allowing clients to be more detached from legal proceedings because most negotiations occur solely between the lawyers outside the presence of the clients. Thus, if the client is relatively uninterested in participating, negotiation [without clients present] may provide the most therapeutic effects.

A problem-solving approach to negotiation can also have therapeutic effects on both lawyers and the clients. Since problem solving focuses on the interests of the client, the client must be more involved in the preparation of the case. . . .

2. Mediation Mediation can have excellent therapeutic effects for clients. Numerous articles on mediation have discussed the value of being heard or meeting face-to-face to resolve disputes. The strength of mediation lies in providing the client the opportunity to tell her story in a setting that is safe and helpful. The opportunity to be heard is cathartic for many clients. Also, simply sitting across from the person whom the client perceives as having wronged him can be helpful in resolving and overcoming the dispute. Mediation allows parties the opportunity to face one another and to have a true conversation together. In addition, the ability to hear the plaintiff's story, perhaps even apologize, and to tell the other side of the dispute can be important for the defendant as well. . . .

In the Daily Bugle example, mediation would allow Roark to tell his story. A face-to-face meeting with the editor who ignored him could be of great psychological benefit. It might also provide the opportunity for the editor or reporter to apologize. Nevertheless, an unproductive mediation could be even more aggravating to Roark. If the editor is intransigent or the reporter admits no fault, Roark could leave even more infuriated.

3. Arbitration Arbitration provides a different array of therapeutic advantages and disadvantages. Roark might want the whole world to know what has happened. If Roark feels that the paper has a history of sloppy reporting, he might opt for litigation to obtain a public ruling condemning their actions.

He might, however, be content with a private adjudication of his rights. In arbitration, a decision is made on the merits of the case, but with more speed and confidentiality than litigation. This might be a great benefit to him and his family given the situation between Roark and his son, as well as the family's general desire to keep its name out of the paper. . . .

C. Step Three: Looking to Settlement—Implementing Preventive Law for Therapeutic Outcomes

1. Negotiation & Mediation Negotiation and mediation . . . can implement ideas from preventive law by looking beyond the specific litigation issue. If the goal is to prevent further disputes between the parties, then the ability of mediation to deal with these issues is more likely to work to clients' benefit than litigation. Settlements can be structured so that all of the elements of the dispute are discussed, evaluated, and dealt with in a final agreement. . . .

In Roark's case, the settlement agreement should be written with an eye toward the future. If payment is agreed upon, the settlement should specify how and when that payment will arrive. What if payment does not occur? If a public apology or retraction is part of the settlement, the settlement should include details such as timing and placement of such retraction. Is the apology on behalf of the paper, or will the apology come from the reporter? The settlement might include internal changes within the paper—a punishment for the reporter or new procedures for fact-checking. The where, when, and how of each of these elements should be covered in the settlement agreement. By dealing with these issues as part of the ADR process and settlement, Roark's lawyer can help him avoid disturbing legal problems down the road.

2. Arbitration Arbitration can provide different preventive law opportunities, although there is often little opportunity to do so in the process. Frequently, individual arbitrators feel constrained to keep to the dispute at hand and not look down the road. This, however, should not prevent the parties from doing so. The parties can do this in two ways. First, they can agree to widen the scope of the questions presented to the arbitrator or perhaps give the arbitrator broader remedial powers. This would allow the arbitrator to employ preventive law ideas in crafting the decision by examining future interactions between the parties.

Problem 14-2. ***Is the Therapeutic Model Always Appropriate?***

In what ways does the author suggest that the Therapeutic Jurisprudence approach is consistent with dispute resolution principles? What, if any, disadvantages or risks do you see in including this kind of approach in client counseling? Do you think lawyers need additional training to engage in this kind of counseling?

3. Counseling Clients About Appropriate Processes

Many jurisdictions require, in their ethics codes (see, e.g., Ark. Code Ann. Sect. 16-7-204) or in court rules (see, e.g., Missouri Supreme Court Rule 17.02), procedural rules, or cases, that lawyers advise their clients about "the dispute resolution options available to them" and to suggest what might be "reasonably pursued to attempt to resolve the legal dispute to reach the legal objective sought." Different jurisdictions use different language to connote responsibilities to counsel, including "must," "shall," "should," or "suggest," and some courts now go so far as to require lawyers to check boxes on pleadings or other documents to certify that such counseling has, in fact, occurred. See, e.g., Mass. Supreme Court Rule 1:18 and U.S. Bankr. Ct. R. S.D. Cal. LBR 7 0 16-4. See Marshall Breger, Should An Attorney Be Required to Advise a Client of ADR Options?, 13 Geo. J. Leg. Ethics 427 (2000); Robert F. Cochran, Jr., Educating Clients on ADR Alternatives: The Rules of Professional Conduct Should Require Lawyers to Inform Clients About ADR,

L.A. Law., Oct. 2002, at 52. See in earlier sections of this book (Chapters 2, 5 and 8) references to Model Rules of Professional Conduct, Rules 1.2, 1.4, 2.1 and 3.2. A few states now even sanction lawyers for not consulting clients about what process to use, and some states have found malpractice liability in situations where lawyers have failed to adequately consult with their clients about what process to pursue in particular cases.

Problem 14-3. ***There Oughta Be a Law?***

Do you think advising clients about the varieties of dispute resolution processes available should be mandatory? In all cases? Try drafting such a rule. Where would you put it? Any exceptions? How should compliance be documented? What sanction(s) should be available, in the event a lawyer failed to comply?

B. EVALUATING AND ASSESSING ADR PROCESSES: PUBLIC INTERESTS

How well does a dispute resolution process "work?" At a theoretical level, one can argue about the alignment between a particular process (litigation or some alternative) and a particular set of policy goals. In the articles above, Professors Sander, Goldberg, and Schneider each invite this kind of analysis. But beyond theoretical alignment, there are important empirical questions on which policy ought to rely. And the truth is that there is not yet an empirical consensus on the strengths and weaknesses of the various processes, including adjudication.

Think about how you would design a study to test whether particular processes are meeting the needs of the parties or the interests of the public. Would you need different techniques to study whether a process was appropriate for the users (the parties), or for the larger system (the court system, society, a particular industry, or type of dispute)?

One study indicates that litigants (parties) don't know what ADR options are available to them through the courts—even when they are represented by lawyers. The same study indicates that parties tend to be more satisfied when court programs offer some mediation (but not arbitration) options. See Donna Shestowksy, When Ignorance Is Not Bliss: An Empirical Study of Litigants' Awareness of Court-Sponsored Alternative Dispute Resolution Programs, 22 Harv. Neg. L. Rev. 189 (2017).

The next two articles summarize a variety of studies that have empirically tested certain claims made about both "alternative" forms of dispute resolution and adjudication. After you read these articles, think about what methods and variables might be used to evaluate the performance of different forms of process for different audiences. Different kinds of clients and different institutions may value different things in processes for dispute resolution, so it may be hard to use single or simple measures.

Carrie Menkel-Meadow, DISPUTE RESOLUTION

in Oxford Handbook of Empirical Legal Research (Peter Cane & Herbert Kritzer eds., 2010)

Stark political, practical, and policy debates about the appropriate uses of various forms of "non-litigative," "non-adversarial," or "alternative-to-court" processes have led to heated debates about definitions, categorizations, methodologies, measurements, and conclusions from a wide range of studies attempting to "settle the scores" on practical issues of cost, fairness, efficiency, consumer satisfaction, and more jurisprudential issues such as voice, democracy, self-determination, rule of law, and the "justice" produced by the use of different processes. There are a variety of contested issues such as:

- whether there should be voluntary or mandatory assignment to a particular form of dispute resolution,
- whether the privacy of the parties is more important than or should be measured against the transparency to others of both processes and outcomes,
- whether vesting of power in privately paid professionals, rather than state officials, for dispute decisions is desirable,
- whether some forms of dispute resolution are more likely to serve the empowerment of parties, communities, and other non-elites, rather than those in the more expensive and elite controlled litigation systems,
- whether the resources invested in alternative systems are justified or improve compliance and enforcement of outcomes over commanded litigation results, and
- whether institutional design of alternative justice systems at very advanced stages of legal development can serve as a model in more newly created legal systems and political orders.

All of this has led to a serious "baseline" problem in empirical analysis of dispute resolution processes. With so many issues about how processes deliver fairness and justice being so hotly contested, it is difficult, if not impossible, to know what is being compared to what. Litigation varies as much in different venues (e.g., civil law versus common law, or federal versus state courts) as mediation does in private or court-annexed settings or, as arbitration does in domestic and international settings. Whenever I read any attempt to "compare" and "contrast" the efficacy or quality of different processes, I always ask, "compared to what?" Close scrutiny of virtually any comparison will dampen one's confidence in the conclusions reached. Put simply, truly experimental methods are virtually impossible in this field; one cannot submit the same actual dispute to two treatments. At best, so-called "like" cases in one "treatment" are compared to "like (similar) cases" in another "treatment" and therein lies the problem.

In large aggregate studies, such as in the "Vanishing Trial" statistics demonstrating decreasing uses of full civil trials,[1] we can see general trends in processes used and in variations in gross outcomes. But when the focus is more on "internal" experiences of fairness of process and outcomes in particular cases, it is much harder to match totally homologous case types. Processes with the same name are practiced differently; different private ADR institutions and providers use different rules, standards, procedures, and definitions. Even in the public sector, when courts or administrative agencies use various forms of ADR, they do so with different intentions, different requirements, and different effects such as whether or not negotiated agreements can serve as public outcomes without formal governmental ratification.

. . . [M]y theme is one of skepticism that we can ever truly determine with any degree of confidence whether one particular process is "better" or "worse" than another in a specific case.

This is related to another theme illustrated here. In some cases there are "communities" of interest in promoting particular forms of ADR. It is often argued that big business prefers the control and economic efficiency of arbitration against individual employees, consumers, and investors, and that some courts prefer to deflect "smaller" cases to arbitration or mediation. Yet it is also often true that individual disputants might have very different motivations for seeking a particular kind of process. Thus, we have an additional measurement problem of aggregating individual preferences when those preferences may not be uniform, either for individuals or for organizations.

Those engaged in design of dispute-resolution institutions (whether in courts or private organizations) often ask instrumental questions, wanting to know what forms of process are "better" in terms of factors such as efficiency or fairness for a particular type of conflict. Existing studies seldom provide clear answers to such questions. In ADR some criteria of quality measurement for some factors such as efficiency can be quantitative, while other factors—fairness, availability of tailored and flexible solutions, and the degree of self-determination in such processes—resist quantitative measurement and must be assessed in a more qualitative fashion. Thus, the core question is not "which process is better?" but "which process is better for what and for whom?" Some form of "process pluralism" and choice is usually the answer.

To summarize, as we try to understand the meaning of many attempts to weigh and evaluate the successes and failures of ADR processes it is useful to always ask—what is the baseline—compared to what? In assessing what we know, don't know, and should know about ADR's actual empirical practices, it

1. Marc Galanter, The Vanishing Trial: An Examination of Trials and Related Matters in Federal and State Courts, 1 Journal of Empirical Legal Studies 459-570 (2004).

is important to recognize that ADR is itself variable, and it may be difficult, if not impossible, to specify with any degree of reliability what is going on inside particular processes and how particular processes can be compared to each other. But many have tried.

As the field of ADR has grown to include more kinds of disputes and a greater variety of processes, other structural and policy issues have been raised. Early on, one of the most important claims made against ADR was that compared with formal adjudication, it was likely to cause unfair or unequal outcomes for subordinated or disempowered parties (especially women, and various racial and ethnic minority groups). A variety of studies have been designed to test whether there are systematic biases and structural inequalities in how different parties and groups experience various dispute resolution processes, including arbitration, and mediation in court and in private settings.

Related to claims about the effects of differences in power or resources between the parties, debates in the ADR literature have focused on the "repeat player effect." The argument is that parties who participate often in the same process (e.g., company-controlled arbitration) or third-party neutrals (whether arbitrators or mediators) who work often for the same parties produce unfair or structurally biased outcomes. . . . [T]he many recent attempts to evaluate this assertion have produced decidedly mixed and contested results.

In studies which attempt to evaluate ADR processes there is always the question of what the yardstick of "measurement" of fairness, justice or efficiency should be, which has given rise to another important dispute: Should the outcomes of all dispute resolution conform to legal rules or precedents or are the parties free to resolve their disputes in creative, tailored ways that might provide fair or just outcomes for particular parties but might depart from formal legal rules or precedents (without themselves constituting unlawful outcomes)? This important jurisprudential question is not easily studied in direct form but some surrogates of measurement, such as compliance with agreements as opposed to commanded or law-based rulings, are increasingly the subject of evaluation in some areas such as in environmental and land-use, divorce and family, and labor and employment matters.

A variety of other controversial claims about the comparative value of different processes have also spawned inconclusive and contradictory studies. Cary Coglianese has long questioned whether the use of negotiated-rule making or public policy consensus building processes has in fact decreased the cost of administrative rulemaking or bolstered its "consensual" and non-contested quality, against continuing claims by its proponents that well managed multi-party negotiation processes can provide rulemaking in administrative contexts that is less likely to be challenged in post-hoc litigation. Jody Freeman has provided one of the most in-depth empirical case studies of several collaborative rule-making efforts, but her work is challenged by Coglianese who insists on the need for more aggregate data and for comparisons with more conventional rule-making administrative processes before drawing conclusions about relative costs, compliance, and other post-hoc effects. In my own view, attempts to study and compare these particular uses of ADR are even more problematic than attempts to match aggregate cases in traditional litigation settings. Rule-making proceedings in front of different U.S. federal agencies (Environmental Protection Agency, Federal Drug Administration, Departments of Labor, Interior, etc.) are so factually, scientifically, legally and historically complex that comparisons across case types and are quite resistant to rigorous comparisons.

In my view, one of the few rigorously successful studies of comparability of process is the Metro Court study of outcomes and satisfaction rates among adjudication and mediation users in New Mexico state courts. In an attempt to test Delgado, et al.'s thesis that private processes would be adversely experienced by minority litigants, Michelle Hermann and her colleagues found far more complex relationships in the mix of process used, demographics of litigants and third-party neutrals, and case types. Some women, for example, fared "better" in mediation outcomes, but were more skeptical of that process, and somewhat distrusting of its informal quality. Hispanics and some Blacks preferred mediation, even when their outcomes were relatively inferior to what they might have achieved in litigation, demonstrating some distrust of formal justice systems (particularly among immigrants who carry memories of corrupt courts from their native lands). This study generally refuted Delgado's "informality" hypotheses by demonstrating that factors other than race, gender and ethnicity such as case-type, repeat player effects, and whether parties had representatives or not, accounted for more of the differences in both outcomes and satisfaction rates. One important finding was that, in general, parties were more satisfied with processes in which the third-party neutral, whether a judge or mediator, "matched" their own ethnicity.

Recent extensions of ADR to "online dispute resolution," truth and reconciliation commissions, transactional mediation in contract formation, not to mention such conventional uses of various forms of dispute resolution in diplomacy, market transactions, family relations, and ordinary day-to-day disputes and conflicts, suggest that the domain of dispute-resolution research is far more capacious than assessing how disputes are managed in formal legal arenas such as lawsuits or courts. These new domains of dispute resolution suggest a number of new and interesting research questions, combined with the still unresolved "older" research questions explored in this essay—some descriptive, others comparative, still others relevant to normative or prescriptive issues:

1. Must dispute resolution be conducted face-to-face to be effective? What will the role of new technologies be in dispute resolution?
2. When can disputing "culture" be changed? Can people be taught to "collaborate" or is the assumption of scarcity and competition the human default? What difference would it make in lawyering behavior if legal rules allowed "apologies" to be admitted as evidence? Can publicity about alternative forms of dispute resolution (e.g. South Africa's Truth and Reconciliation Commission) change political or disputing cultures?
3. Do particular domains (e.g., transnational and inter-organizational) or subject matters (e.g. on-going relationships) require particular forms of

dispute processing? In other words, is "trans-substantive" process a misconceived or impossible notion?
4. What factors influence party choice in dispute processes?
5. Does any form of dispute resolution require particular expertise?
6. When should dispute processing be public and transparent and when should parties be permitted to resolve disputes privately? Does a legal system require totally public dispute processes for all of its conflicts?

Finally, as this essay began, can we ever fully study and know whether particular structural patterns of parties, case types, and processes are "better" for the parties or for outsiders than any other set of process structures or choices?

❖ *Bobbi McAdoo, Nancy A. Welsh & Roselle L. Wissler,* INSTITUTIONALIZATION: WHAT DO EMPIRICAL STUDIES TELL US ABOUT COURT MEDIATION?

Disp. Resol. Mag. 8-9 (Winter 2003)

This article focuses on the lessons that seem to be emerging from the available empirical data regarding best practices for programs that mediate non-family civil matters. Throughout the article, we consider the answers provided by research to three questions: (1) How does program design affect the success of the institutionalization of mediation? (2) In what ways do design choices affect the likelihood of achieving settlement of cases? and (3) Which program design choices affect litigants' perceptions of the procedural justice provided by court connected mediation? Because these issues of institutionalization, settlement and justice are so important to the success and quality of court-connected mediation, they must be considered carefully in deciding both how to structure new court-connected mediation programs and how to improve existing programs.

DESIGN AND INSTITUTIONALIZATION

Most court-connected mediation programs seek successful institutionalization, which we define here as regular and significant use of the mediation process to resolve cases. Voluntary mediation programs rarely meet this goal because they suffer from consistently small caseloads. In contrast, programs that make mediation mandatory (at the request of one party or on a judge's own initiative) have dramatically higher rates of utilization. Significantly, mandatory referral does not appear to adversely affect either litigants' perceptions of procedural justice or, according to most studies, settlement rates. Further, judicial activism in ordering parties into mediation triggers increased voluntary use of the process, as lawyers begin to request it themselves in anticipation of court referral. An additional benefit of exposing lawyers to mediation is that they are more likely to discuss and recommend the process to their clients.

Another program design option involves requiring lawyers to consider mediation as an integral part of their usual litigation planning. For example, some courts require lawyers to discuss the potential use of mediation or other ADR processes and report the results of that discussion to the court early in the life of a case. Other courts require lawyers to discuss ADR with their clients. These court rules face less lawyer opposition than mandatory case referral and can give lawyers more control over the logistics of mediation (e.g., choice of mediator and timing). Adopting these rules (combined with active judicial support and willingness to order mediation when deemed appropriate) tends to increase requests to use mediation. . . .

WHICH CASES SHOULD MEDIATE

Although it has been suggested that certain general categories of civil cases (e.g., employment, contract) are "best" handled by mediation, there is no empirical support for this notion. Neither settlement rates nor litigants' perceptions of the procedural justice provided by mediation vary with case type. (There is some limited evidence, however, that medical malpractice and product liability cases may be somewhat less likely to settle than other types of tort cases.) Interestingly, the level of acrimony between the litigants in non-family civil cases does not seem to affect the likelihood of settlement in mediation. Not surprisingly, the cases most likely to settle in mediation are those in which the litigants' positions are closer together, the issues are less complex, or the issue of liability is less strongly contested. Litigants' perceptions of procedural justice do not seem to vary with the tenor of the relationship between the litigants or with these other case characteristics. Thus, because no case characteristics have been identified for which mediation has detrimental effects, mediation programs do not need to exclude certain types of cases. Some programs may be tempted to exclude the cases that seem likely to reach settlement on their own, without the assistance of a mediator. This choice, however, is likely to limit not only the rate of settlement achieved but also the opportunity to improve litigants' perceptions of the procedural justice of the settlement process and to enhance their views of the courts. . . .

WHO THE MEDIATORS SHOULD BE

Mediation is most likely to be successfully institutionalized if the mediators are drawn from the pool that is preferred by lawyers: litigators with knowledge in the substantive areas being mediated. But neither mediators' knowledge of the subject matter of the dispute nor the number of years they have practiced law has proved to be related to settlement or to litigants' perceptions of procedural justice. One characteristic of the mediators, namely having more mediation experience, is related to more settlements. However, several aspects of mediator training, such as the number of hours of training or whether it included role play, tend not to affect settlement. None of these mediator characteristics seem to be related to litigants' perceptions of the procedural justice of mediation. . . .

WHAT THE MEDIATORS SHOULD DO

The approach that mediators ought to use (facilitative, evaluative, transformative) has been the subject of much debate. Both active facilitation and some types of evaluative interventions tend to produce more settlements as well as heighten perceptions of procedural justice. For example, when mediators disclose their views about the merits or value of a case, cases are more likely to settle and litigants are more likely to assess the mediation process as fair. By contrast, when mediators keep silent about their views of the case, cases are less likely to settle and litigants' views of procedural justice are not enhanced. But when mediators recommend a particular settlement, litigants' ratings of the procedural fairness of the process suffer, notwithstanding an increased rate of settlement. When litigants or their lawyers participate more during mediation, cases are more likely to settle than when they participate less. Moreover, the litigants evaluate the mediation process as more fair. In addition, when the lawyers behave more cooperatively during mediation sessions, both the likelihood of settlement and litigant perceptions of procedural fairness increase.

Controversies abound about how to collect data, how to categorize inputs and outputs, how to define program and process objectives (cost savings to systems versus party satisfaction or self-determination for individuals), and how to find appropriate baseline comparisons of alternative treatments. It is difficult to measure ultimate consequences for parties inside a dispute, as well as the impacts on larger systems or societies in which particular disputes or dispute processing systems are located.

Because the evaluation of "success" of such processes entails both objective and quantitative measures (time and cost savings, transaction costs of systems used, number of cases settled) and qualitative and more subjective assessments (client satisfaction, better ongoing relationships, greater worker productivity, self-determination, and development of better human skill-sets for communication), it is difficult to reach agreement on appropriate metrics. The lack of consensus surrounding metrics is not merely an academic curiosity. In a contested policy space in which resources are limited, claims about "effectiveness" are (and should be) central to decision-making.

Below is a list of possible metrics that various studies have used to measure these aspects of dispute resolution processes. Developing a sound evaluation and research protocol requires some conceptualization of more "composite" formulas and measurement tools in order to capture both the quantitative and qualitative richness of what conflict resolution processes both promise and actually deliver.

QUANTITATIVE OR "OBJECTIVE" MEASURES

- Number of conflicts or disputes in relevant "universe" (which, and how many, form into formal claim or complaint)
- Number of contacts or cases (in a particular process, as compared to the full "universe" of possible cases or comparable cases in another process)

- Numbers of issues
- Number of cases resolved/settled/closed/disposed of ("settlement rates")
- Number of cases referred to another process
- Number of cases dropped
- Case types (categories within systems, e.g., employment promotion, dismissal, communication, etc.)
- Numbers of parties
- Types of agreements, resolutions, outcomes
- Time to process case
- Cost of processing case—to complainant, to (third-party neutral), to program or system
- Comparisons (where possible) of all of above of comparable cases in different systems
- Comparisons of pre-conflict resolution program claiming (grievance systems, litigation) or violence with post-programmatic claiming
- Comparisons of rates of compliance with agreements, judgments, or orders
- Durability/longevity of outcomes
- Longitudinal comparisons of changes in usage, time for processing, case types, etc.
- Demographic data on users, third-party neutrals, and other facilitators or professionals
- Variations in usage, outcomes, solutions by demographics
- Differential characteristics of disputants and third-party neutrals, e.g., "experience" ratings
- Awareness of ability to choose different processes (an attitudinal measure)

QUALITATIVE OR SUBJECTIVE MEASURES

- Client satisfaction
- Criteria for selecting particular processes
- Improved relationships (post-conflict societies, families, workplaces, commercial relations)
- Improved communication
- Enhanced workplace productivity
- Learned conflict resolution/communication/relational skills ("transformative" mutual intersubjective understandings or learned use of new processes, e.g., lawyers using mediation and other forms of problem solving)
- "Better" outcomes (more creative, individually tailored, deeper solutions)
- Perceived self-determination/autonomy/control over decision making
- Compliance with national, systemic, family, company, workplace, contractual norms/rules when legitimacy less questioned
- Perceptions of fairness, justice, and legitimacy of process
- Trust in institutions, both dispute processing and others

- Resolution of systemic issues (proactive conflict resolution, policy changes)
- "Value added" to organization or institution

> **Problem 14-4.** ***What Metrics for ADR Evaluations?***
>
> Can you think of any other measures in addition to those above? How would you combine both quantitative and qualitative measures to develop an accurate assessment of how a particular process is working (in comparison to others)?
>
> Choose a particular form of dispute resolution you are familiar with and design a study to evaluate its effectiveness. What measures will you choose? How will you collect data? For whom are you conducting your evaluation? The users? An organization? A client deciding what process to use in a particular dispute?

C. FUTURE USES OF DISPUTE RESOLUTION PROCESSES: PEACE AND JUSTICE REDUX

This text focuses on the foundational forms and some hybrid forms of dispute resolution found primarily in the domestic American context. Currently, these primary forms of dispute resolution are being extended to various forms of deliberative democracy and policy decision making, borrowing from basic mediation and facilitation techniques. Beyond the United States, international and transnational forms of dispute resolution abound. These include formal courts; new special-jurisdiction international tribunals (like the World Trade Organization Appellate Body, and the International Criminal Courts for the former Yugoslavia and Rwanda); international arbitration, mediation, and new hybrid forms of conflict resolution and peacekeeping or nation building, such as Truth and Reconciliation Commissions in South Africa, Chile, Liberia, Guatemala, East Timor, and many other places where there have been civil wars, genocides, post-military dictatorships, and other major conflicts.

We have more recently seen reconciliation processes applied to contexts in which societies have sought to come to terms with brutal historical injustices, even when they are not more broadly characterized as "transitional." For example, the Truth and Reconciliation Commission of Canada has used similar processes regarding the Indian Residential Schools. The Maine-Wabanaki-State Child Welfare Truth and Reconciliation Commission is an example of similar processes adopted within the United States. The design and implementation of such processes, of course, represents contested policy space.

> It is evident that successfully establishing, designing, and implementing a transitional justice process is an uphill battle from the very start. Parties that oppose reconciliation, reparations, truth-seeking, or accountability for whatever reason

> will have multiple opportunities to derail, co-opt, limit, or declaw a transitional justice process. Meanwhile those hoping to see a transitional justice process to the finish line will need to grapple with targeted political attacks, waning public support, polarization, and inconsistent stakeholder buy-in. This is not said to discourage attempts to pursue transitional justice—quite the opposite. We hope that heightened awareness of and preparedness for such politicization risks in the United States will make those advocating for transitional justice better prepared to shepherd it successfully to its conclusion, providing those who need it with the redress, acknowledgement, truth, and remedy that is long overdue to them.

Erin Bloom & Lisa Dicker, The Politics of Justice: Analyzing the Politicization of Transitional Justice Processes, 38 Ohio St. J. on Disp. Resol. 303, 338-339 (2023).

In the years to come, ordinary legal conflicts will likely continue to proliferate, putting more stress on formal court systems. We have described many of the ways in which modern alternatives to litigation have evolved to address the needs of disputants, institutions, and society. To what extent have courts, too, adapted to the evolving landscapes in which they are called to act? Have courts "learned" anything from dispute resolution over the past decades? One might point to the evolution of Rule 16 (see Chapter 12) as evidence that the litigation system continues to evolve. To date, however, those reforms have simply changed the way in which litigants are introduced to the prospect of non-litigation alternatives.

Some have called upon courts to permit litigants to custom-craft litigation procedural rules, much as parties to arbitration routinely do. Should civil litigants be permitted to contractually limit discovery? Limit appeals? Enter high-low agreements? Alter jury unanimity requirements? Shorten relevant deadlines? See, e.g., Michael L. Moffitt, Customized Litigation: The Case for Making Civil Procedure Negotiable, 75 Geo. Wash. L. Rev. 461, 462 (2007); Henry S. Noyes, If You (Re)Build It, They Will Come: Contracts to Remake the Rules of Litigation in Arbitration's Image, 30 Harv. J.L. & Pub. Pol'y 579 (2007); Elizabeth Thornburg, Designer Trials, 2006 J. Disp. Resol. 181. Still, any of these proposals would do nothing to the default rules of litigation.

In the excerpt below, Professor Michael Moffitt points out ways in which modern litigation's rules seem crafted as though settlement were not the norm.

> Legal disputes begin with pleadings. Most legal disputes end with settlement. One might assume, therefore, that pleadings create conditions conducive to the private resolution of disputes—that pleadings help in some way to facilitate disputants' negotiations. Instead, the opposite appears to be true. Modern pleadings start legal disputes off in a way that makes it more difficult to find wise and efficient settlement.
>
> Modern pleadings principally contain only information that goes directly to an element of a legal claim or defense. The rules of pleading prohibit the inclusion of other information. Based on the principle of notice-giving, pleadings rules demand that plaintiffs provide only a "short and plain statement . . . showing that [they] are entitled to relief" under some legal theory. Defendants, similarly, are limited to stating defenses "in short and plain terms," and must respond to each of the plaintiff's individual averments with an admission, a denial, or a denial for want of information. Pleadings do not contain perceptions; they contain assertions

> framed as absolute statements of historical truth. Pleadings do not contain emotions and aspirations; they contain only the language of entitlement. Problems, if one is to trust most pleadings, boil down to, "Do you owe me money?"
>
> In an age when courts regularly encourage parties to resolve disputes extrajudicially, this system of pleading is flawed. A careful examination of the theories underlying modern pleadings and the dispute resolution literature shows a fundamental disconnect between what pleadings require and what negotiation theory suggests is helpful to parties at the outset of a dispute. A basic premise of much of the negotiation and mediation literature suggests that problems are resolved with greatest efficiency and satisfaction when problems are defined broadly, when disputants are able to move beyond backward-looking assertions of entitlement, and when disputants are able to address the full range of considerations motivating them in the dispute. The first step in a pleading-initiated sequence is to define the dispute in binary, backward-looking terms, limiting the scope of "the problem" significantly. Parties must then take a second step, however, if they hope to discover efficient settlement opportunities for most disputes. In settlement talks, they must try to broaden the scope of the dispute and the information relevant to it, essentially trying to undo the effects of the first step. Setting up the adjudicative system such that problem definition is a function assigned to pleadings, therefore, flies in the face of our contemporary understanding of beneficial bargaining practices.

Michael Moffitt, Pleadings in the Age of Settlement, 80 Ind. L.J. 727 (2005). Professor Moffitt then goes on to suggest that courts consider reforming pleadings in a way to require pre-pleading consultations between the parties, for example.

Problem 14-5. ***Who Influences Whom? Courts and ADR***

Can you think of other ways in which our court system has adapted based on its experiences with dispute resolution?

And what about the very act of policymaking or governance itself? The bargaining dynamics and the conflicts among various political actors share some of the same characteristics of other disputes we have studied in this book. To the extent we see impasse in government, for example, should we view that as a positive, as a design feature, or as a failure of some sort? What perspectives might ADR offer? See, e.g. Hannah Firestone, A Call for Compromise: Examining Polarization and the Potential Use of ADR Solutions in Congress Post-Trump Administration, 38 Ohio St. J. Disp. Resol. 667 (2023); James Freund, For the Election Season: Mediating Legislative Cliffs, 40 Alt. High Cost Litig. 152 (2022); Carrie Menkel-Meadow, Applying conflict resolution insights to hyper-polarization: "When will (we) ever learn?" 39 Conflict Resolution Quarterly (2022); Carrie Menkel-Meadow, Why We Can't 'Just All Get Along': Dysfunction in the Polity and Conflict Resolution and What We Might Do About It, 2018 J. Disp. Resol. 5; Nancy Rogers, One Idea for Ameliorating Polarization: Reviving Conversations About an American Spirit, 2018 J. Disp. Resol. 27 (2018).

> **Problem 14-6. *Dispute Resolution and Governance***
>
> Based on your understanding of ADR, what diagnoses would you offer about the dynamics you currently observe in Congress, in the Executive, or in their interactions? To the extent you wish it looked different, what prescriptions might you suggest? (Would you focus on individuals' skill-sets? On the information flow, the allocation of decision making, the systems in which they work? Something else?)

No forward-looking conclusion could responsibly ignore the potential, the promise, and the potential pitfalls resulting from technological development. At a minimum, changes in technology have the potential to affect three different aspects of the Dispute Resolution landscape. First, it will almost certainly continue to change the availability of information. To the extent more information is available to more people, this holds the promise of democratizing, of enhancing access to justice, and of reducing barriers. The history of access to information does not suggest that developments will necessarily lead to greater, cheaper access. But viewed over the long-term, one can hope this will be the case.

Second, technology will almost certainly continue to change the mechanisms through which we encounter each other. This means, most likely, a further increase in initial interactions that are not face-to-face, with the concomitant increase in the potential for both deal-making and dispute-creating. It likely also will mean that more disputants will seek to resolve their disputes in technology-assisted ways. Simple versions of this will involve continued use of technology to aid in communications. More sophisticated versions may change the actual nature of the communications themselves. Third and finally, technology may supplement or even replace some aspect of dispute resolution decision making. We are not yet convinced that generative artificial intelligence, for example, will replace the human actors who are currently part of the ADR landscape. But nor are we persuaded that we are done seeing the impacts of technological developments.

You will be the practitioners and designers of new forms of dispute resolution. Some of you will be handling local disputes in your communities, with your local, state, or federal governments, on behalf of institutions, whether for profit or non-profit, local or multinational, and on behalf of victims of crime, violence, war, or mal-distributions of wealth or other benefits. Some of you will represent individuals seeking some form of compensation, apology, or other relief for some forms of injustice or wrongs. Others of you will seek to form new entities or engage in transactions to produce more wealth, new products, or new social services. Some of you will seek positions in government, whether as politicians or civil servants, or on the larger world stage. Others of you may cease to practice law and become managers, entrepreneurs, teachers, or artists. Many of you will eventually become judges, arbitrators, mediators, or other forms of legal decision makers. Most of you will form new relationships and families in your professional and personal lives. All of you will be involved in conflicts or disputes of some sort. We hope you have learned enough about the different methods of conflict resolution that you will be able to assist your clients, constituencies, and loved ones in resolving their conflicts by employing a dispute resolution process.

We hope that you have learned to analyze some basic features of dispute resolution:

- Who are the parties to a conflict?
- What are their needs, interests, and goals?
- What is the substance of the conflict?
- Are there applicable precedents, rules, laws, or customs for resolving the conflict?
- What are the resource-expanding possibilities for solving the problem?
- How should scarce or divisible materials be allocated?
- Do the parties need help (from representatives or third-party neutrals) to resolve their conflicts?
- Are particular disputes unique or repetitive?
- Do the parties desire privacy to resolve their dispute?
- Does someone else (the "public") require transparency or precedents or other guidance from particular disputes?
- Is a possible "resolution" likely to be final or to need some contingency planning and reopening provisions?
- Is the conflict an ad hoc (one-shot) conflict, or is there a need for some more institutionalized dispute handling?
- What kind of process seems most appropriate for the particular dispute (consensual, party-controlled, command decision with enforcement, informal or formal, intimate or private setting or public transparent process)?

Whatever the conflicts, disputes, and problems you encounter, some of the themes and issues presented in this book will continually arise, even if the contexts change. When is there a need for public, authoritative, legal rulings? When can/should parties be allowed to create their own solutions to problems, with their own forms of justice? When should parties deal with each other directly and when through intermediaries or representatives? Are there only two sides to a dispute, or should all who are affected by a decision be able to participate in making that decision? Can conflict resolution operate effectively across cultural, class, religious, and political divides, or does it require some basic value agreements?

Below are some excerpts illustrating some of the possibilities for and concerns about the development of different forms of dispute resolution.

❖ *Jean Sternlight*, ADR IS HERE: PRELIMINARY REFLECTIONS ON WHERE IT FITS IN A SYSTEM OF JUSTICE

3 Nev. L.J. 289, 291, 293, 294, 296, 299, 300, 301, 303-304 (2002/2003)

For twenty-five years or more we have been debating the proper role of alternative dispute resolution (ADR) in our system of justice. While the birth of the modern ADR movement is often linked to the 1976 Pound Conference, heated discussions as to the desirability of ADR continued long after that date. . . . Today it is clear that far more disputes in the United States are resolved through negotiation, mediation, and arbitration, than through trial. But the arrival of ADR does not mean that the questioning and critiquing has ended or must end, but rather that it should take a different form. . . .

Reviewing some of the anthropological and other literature regarding other societies' resolution of disputes, I saw that historically many societies have placed far greater emphasis on harmony and healing, and far less emphasis on individualistic adversarial approaches, than we do in the United States today. I also saw that a society's approach to dispute resolution will depend on a number of geographic, historic and other factors, and that the emphasis on harmony and community has both positive and negative aspects.

In pondering the comments of the various participants, I find myself attracted to aspects of each analysis. I am searching for ways to synthesize their perspectives. This attempt at synthesis leads me to offer five insights regarding how a society should go about deciding what type of dispute resolution process it ought to establish:

A. It is a Mistake to Distinguish Litigation from other forms of Dispute Resolution in an Either/Or Fashion. . . .
B. Despite the Entanglement of Various Forms of Dispute Resolution, Significant Choices Must be Made Among the Forms of Dispute Resolution. . . .
C. More Research is Needed Regarding What Disputants Want in a Dispute Resolution System.

. . . Once this research has been conducted, I believe it will ultimately show that disputants are generally looking for three benefits from a dispute resolution system: (1) a system that provides them with a substantively fair/just result; (2) a system that meets the procedural justice criteria of voice, participation, and dignity. . . . and (3) a system that helps them to achieve other personal and emotional goals, such as reconciliation, or that at least does not leave them feeling worse, emotionally and psychologically.

D. We Need to Consider Societal as Well as Individual Interests in Setting Up a System of Justice. . . .
E. We Can Ask a System of Justice to Do More than Just Resolve Disputes or Enforce Rights. . . .

It may well be appropriate to have a procedural system with multiple components in order to serve our multiple goals. Of course, if we devise a system that contains multiple procedures (e.g. both litigation and mediation), we will also have to solve the additional problem of determining how and by whom the choice should be made as to which disputes should be handled under which process. . . . Who decides which disputes go where? . . . I have called this the problem of finding the appropriate "switching" mechanism, to choose between multiple dispute resolution tracks. . . . If we do not use pre-determined criteria, we must at least decide who will make these determinations, and on what basis. . . .

ADR is exciting in part because it allows and encourages us to move beyond our existing conceptions. Without abandoning what is precious about our legal system, we must also be open to new possibilities as we begin to rethink our approach to procedural justice.

❖ *Carrie Menkel-Meadow*, Alternative and Appropriate Dispute Resolution in Context: Formal, Informal, and Semiformal Legal Processes

in Handbook of Conflict Resolution 5-6 (Peter Coleman & Morton Deutsch, 3d ed. 2017)

In the United States, we now have more than formal or informal processes: we have many semiformal processes, and the question is, how shall we evaluate the efficacy, efficiency, and legitimacy of so many different kinds of process? In the United States, we have a very elaborate formal justice system of federal and state rules of procedure (both civil and criminal), as well as countless specialized tribunals with their own procedural rules, such as in bankruptcy, labor, family law, securities, technology, trade, patent and trademark, and taxes. We also have many informal forums for dispute resolution, including private uses of mediation, arbitration and related processes, religious courts and mediation agencies, specialized business and industry panels of dispute resolution (e.g., banking, insurance, franchise, construction, technology, sports, and energy, among others), using both mediation and arbitration techniques, community and neighborhood dispute resolution processes, online consumer forms of dispute resolution, internal organizational forms of dispute resolution (ombuds or internal dispute resolution, including grievance processes in large corporations, universities, trade unions, government agencies, and nongovernmental institutions), as well as dispute resolution forums even in illegitimate enterprises—gangs and organized crime. We now also have a more hybrid set of processes that can be called semiformal forms of dispute resolution, which use both private and public processes with increasingly structured and formal aspects of process, even if there is little to no recourse to more formal adjudication or appellate review. These include the ADR programs annexed to courts, with a great deal of federal and state variations in rules, and access to courts after use, mandatory arbitration clauses found in many consumer and business contracts, which obligate parties to use structured out-of-court arbitration tribunals, some with very detailed procedural rules, but little to no appeal to courts (under the Federal Arbitration Act's limited grounds for vacatur of an arbitration award), as well as the elaborate structure of international commercial arbitration that is now quite "formal" in its conduct, if still mostly unattached to formal courts. . . .

I use the term semiformal from American etiquette dressing requirements ("smart casual" is the British equivalent) to connote the attempt to locate dispute processes halfway between tuxedos and evening gowns of the bygone days of formal gatherings, and the totally informal or casual dress more common in today's variety of professional, family, and entertainment gatherings. To request semiformal dress is to ask the gentlemen to wear ties and jackets, if not tuxedos, and to hope the women will wear, if not dresses and skirts, then at least "fancy pants." The idea is to preserve some notion of order, elegance, solemnity, and seriousness to the social event. Thus, semiformal uses of mediation and arbitration in the courts suggest (sometimes falsely) that someone is looking over or supervising the choice of mediators or arbitrators and ensuring their competence and ethics, and in some cases, permitting a further appeal to the black-robed (and formal) adjudicator. . . .

Totally casual or informal forms of dispute resolution are now called "litigation-lite" (arbitration) or "mediation-heavy" (evaluative mediation where third-party neutrals decide or strongly suggest solutions to parties, rather than simply facilitating party negotiation); they occur without formal clarity about the procedural rules applied or what can happen if the process fails. The question here is whether semiformal processes can legitimately operate in a space between the transparency and presumed consistency of formal justice, and the confidentiality, flexibility, and self-determination of informal processes. Should we be subjecting different kinds of processes to different kinds of evaluative criteria, or should all process be judged by the same criteria?

This increasing complexification, segmentation, and differentiation of process that was intended to express and be justified by such important justice values as party choice, consent, self-determination, and party-tailored solutions to problems now potentially threatens other justice notions of consistency, transparency, true consent, and knowledge, as well as equity, equal treatment, clarity, and socially uniform and just solutions.

Carrie Menkel-Meadow, PEACE AND JUSTICE: NOTES ON THE EVOLUTION AND PURPOSES OF PLURAL LEGAL PROCESSES

94 Geo. L.J. 553, 555-556, 557, 576-579 (2006)

Process pluralism means paying attention to a variety of different systemic values (some of which may seem oppositional to each other) and party needs at the same time, and offering variegated possibilities of process for engagement and decision making. Such values include the attempt to achieve peace with justice, choice and self-determination of the individual with care and responsibility for others, and recognition of the harms of the past with hopes for reconciliation in the future. . . .

Some of the nettlesome issues to explore here include: (1) the relation of principle and social justice to compromise and consensus; (2) the need to include at least three forms of human discourse in human problem solving and legal decision making: principled argument, traded or bargained for preferences, and passionate commitments of emotion, religion, and moral values; (3) the tensions presented by needing rules of process and (perhaps different) rules of decision; and finally, (4) what I call the Oscar Wilde problem—if socialism takes up too many evenings, imagine what process pluralism and participatory democracy will do to our social lives. Do we have the time, desire, and commitment to fully participate in the processes of our polities and personal lives?. . .

The British social philosopher Stuart Hampshire, in what turned out to be his last major work, Justice Is Conflict, (2000) opined that because we are unlikely ever to reach any real, uniform consensus on what constitutes the "substantive good" in a deeply pluralist and divided world, perhaps we can, at best, arrive at some close-to-universal principles for processes that enable us to live together within these differences. For him, this process is *audi alterum partum* ("hear the other side," or the Anglo-American adversary principle). For me, . . . it is closer to "understand all sides" of our modern multi-partied and multi-issued disputes. So I substitute "understand" for Hampshire's "hear" (a deeper level of human engagement and empathy, as well as reason) and "all" sides for Hampshire's "other" or "two" sides. Modern social and legal life needs to get beyond the binary, adversarial idea that there are only two sides to an argument or the "truth." "Understanding" and "coexistence" as aspirational values of peace give us some goals and end-states but do not tell us much about how to get there. Political theorists and philosophers over the years have elaborated many theories of political and social organization, from Hobbes's Leviathan and Rawls's "veil of ignorance" to Habermas' "ideal speech conditions for uncoerced communicative action." Most recently, a movement and plea for "deliberative democracy" harkening back to Aristotelian notions of participatory democracy and argument have inspired much writing on how we can achieve legitimate and fair consensus and good decisions at all levels of human interaction and conflict, even when we have deep conflicts about facts and values. These recent efforts seek to provide a legitimating and explanatory framework for how to seek fair and "just" outcomes in highly conflictual situations of disputes, conflicts, policy, and law-making. It is my hope to marry this work on deliberative democracy to conflict resolution theory and practice so that we might seek peace and justice (always provisional and evolving in a postmodern world) simultaneously. . . .

THE WAY FORWARD

In the last ten years or so we have seen the flowering of process creativity in attempts to create whole new processes for human governance. Out of the horrors of apartheid, political oppression, genocide, and civil and ethnic wars, we, as a species, have created truth and reconciliation commissions and have adapted traditional community justice systems like *gacaca* in Rwanda, while using more traditional forms of adjudicated justice in the international war crimes tribunals of the former Yugoslavia, Rwanda, and other sites.

These new processes are intended to work on the levels of the most aspirational—of what could be best in our human species, often after what has been the worst—terrible violence. Intended to provide "truth" and "answers" for those who have been killed or seriously harmed (and their families), these processes "triage" cases so that the "least" serious can be dealt with by offering forgiveness, healing, and the possibility of reconciliation and the creation of a new and more peaceful society. These processes are the first I have seen to really take the emotional life of humans seriously. By use of narrative, storytelling, and some confrontation, victims and perpetrators meet head-on in a protected setting in which they are called to account on legal, emotional, and, ultimately, human levels.

These new processes are also quite controversial, and their successes and limits are being explored by participants and scholars. Nevertheless, political scientist James Gibson has concluded, after rigorous public opinion research, that those who participated in (or even only watched) the South African truth and reconciliation processes, even with all their weaknesses, were more likely to have internalized a "human rights consciousness" with an enhanced belief (or hope) in the rule of law to improve human relations and achieve justice. This is consistent with decades of research in what is called "procedural justice," by social psychologists Tom Tyler and Allan Lind, finding that people judge their satisfaction with legal processes by their participation in and perceptions of fairness of those processes, irrespective of the outcomes.

In many settings, these new processes of forgiveness, reconciliation, and new-constitution-drafting have come from new participants in the process design. Women and disempowered racial, ethnic, or religious groups are increasingly finding their voices, after great catastrophe, in the creation of new communities and governments, and seeking new processes to participate in, so that old factions and patterns of power domination will not be repeated. Those who are creating these new processes are interested in justice, but they also want peace—to live together with mutual respect, to have sufficient resources to be free from want or illness and to be able to seek their own forms of human flourishing. But many of these processes have still come too late—post hoc or after terrible conflict and violence and injustice. Can we imagine the use of such processes before the terrible conflict, violence, and injustice happens, preventing the Rwandan genocide, the Holocaust, Darfur, and more unnecessary killing in the Mideast? What processes can we develop for preventative dispute resolution, when our legal education and processes are so currently focused on the past (lawsuits and judicial decision making from past disputes)?. . .

The challenges for us are many in creating and sustaining new forms of processes with which to seek peace and justice:

1. What should the role of emotions/passions/beliefs be in our conflicts and deliberations with each other? Transformative empathy is among the most significant and important ways of grounding justice and moving people to new places. (Think Martin Luther King, Jr., the Civil Rights Movement, and parents of gays whose love for their children teaches them to change

their views; think contra the emotional appeals of fascists and demagogues that tap into the baser forms of group identity and values).

2. How do we reconcile the need to adjudicate and punish the past, with correction of injustice, with reintegration of the future with peace and forgiveness, if not forgetfulness?
3. Do we need "rules" of process and decision rules "laid down" in advance, or can we negotiate and deliberate about the very processes we will use to achieve peace and justice in different contexts (historically, geographically, and culturally)?
4. How do we deal with the tyranny of the majority in a democracy and the needs of minorities for recognition and fulfillment (whether temporary, by issue or politics, or more permanent, by group or other identification)?

Robert C. Bordone, Michael Moffitt & Frank Sander, THE NEXT THIRTY YEARS: DIRECTIONS AND CHALLENGES IN DISPUTE RESOLUTION

The Handbook Of Dispute Resolution (2005).

We have great hope that dispute resolution—both as an academic discipline and as a growing career opportunity for professionals—is here to stay. . . . And yet, the field's evolution is not complete. Over the next thirty years, important opportunities and challenges are sure to arise. . . . [Below,] we survey four questions that we expect will drive much of the agenda for those in the dispute resolution field:

- How can we best respond to those who have voiced concerns with the application of dispute resolution principles? Not everyone is enthusiastic about the recent expansion of dispute resolution. Consistent with the very principles underlying the effective management of differences, we need to understand better their concerns and develop appropriate responses.
- How can we best address private resistance to dispute resolution in the world of practice? For dispute resolution to fulfill its promise, scholars, practitioners, disputants, and the general public must benefit from effective transfer of knowledge. We must also identify and overcome the obstacles facing those who seek to apply the ideas in practice.
- How can we build bridges between the various disciplines working on questions of dispute resolution? The field is interdisciplinary by nature, and many of the most promising developments demand greater cross-disciplinary collaboration and greater cross-disciplinary utilization of knowledge and resources.
- How can we develop new knowledge about dispute resolution processes? Dispute resolution rests on an important set of hypotheses about how

disputants, dispute contexts, and various dispute resolution mechanisms interact. Yet we know less about each of these than we would prefer.

Problem 14-7. ***What Is Justice? What Is Peace?***

Imagine yourself a person grievously wronged.

What kind of process would you want to feel you had been "justly" dealt with? Would you want a public process to give testimony? A private ceremony of grief? Would you require compensation? An apology? Retribution? A formal determination of guilt with punishment?

Would it matter to you how those who injured you were coming to the process? (Does it matter if they are compelled to participate? If they have incentives to participate? If they are there purely voluntarily?)

Would you want to create your own process, or would you be willing to use the same process as other people who suffered the same wrongs? How likely do you think it will be that others who suffered the same or similar injuries would agree to the same process?

We conclude this chapter with a few last words on the conundrums presented by making such choices. When is the primary purpose of dispute resolution "justice"[2]—and for whom (just us, the parties? Or a larger constituency?)[3]—or peace, or can we have both? What are some of the opportunities (and limits) in creating new forms of dispute resolution? Should dispute resolution be formal and public, informal and private, something in-between—semi-formal—and who should decide, clients, lawyers or system designers?

As you go out into the world to ponder these questions in new settings, with new conflicts, problems, and disputes unimaginable to us, we hope you will remember the questions and issues that you have studied here. We wish you great wisdom and good luck in solving problems and resolving disputes.

Further Reading

Peter Adler. (2008). Eye of the Storm Leadership: 150 Stories, Quotes and Exercises on the Art and Politics of Managing Human Conflicts. Keystone: CO.

---

2. For a compelling account of the many forms of justice (with no realizable universal ideal), see Amartya Sen, The Idea of Justice (2009).

3. Carrie Menkel-Meadow, Whose Dispute Is It Anyway? A Philosophical and Democratic Defense of Settlement (in some cases), 83 Geo. L.J. 2663 (1995).

American Bar Association Center for Innovation, Online Dispute Resolution in the United States, Data Visualizations (2020).

Gilat J. Bachar & Deborah Hensler, Does Alternative Dispute Resolution Facilitate Prejudice and Bias: We Still Don't Know, 70 SMU L. Rev. 817-836 (2017).

Alyson Carrel & Noam Ebner, Mind the Gap: Bringing Technology to the Mediation Table, 2019 J. Disp. Resol. 1.

Cary Coglianese, Evaluating Regulatory Performance, 8 Penn. J. Law & Public Affairs 47 (2023).

Richard Freer, Exodus from and Transformation of American Civil Litigation, 65 Emory L.J. 1491 (2016).

Stuart Hampshire. (2000). Justice is Conflict. Princeton: Princeton University Press.

Priscilla Hayner. (2001). Unspeakable Truths: Confronting State Terror and Atrocity. Routledge.

Mariana Hernandez-Crespo Gonstead, Remedy without Diagnosis: How to Optimize Results by Leveraging the Appropriate Dispute Resolution and Shared Decision-Making Process, 88 Fordham L. Rev. 2165 (2020).

Ethan Katsh & Orna Rabinovich-Einy. (2017). Digital Justice. Oxford: Oxford University Press.

Michael King, Arie Freiberg, Becky Batagol & Ross Hyams. (2009). Non-Adversarial Justice. Sydney: Federation Press.

Carrie Menkel-Meadow. (2010). Dispute Resolution. In Peter Cane & Herbert Kritzer (Eds.), Oxford Handbook of Empirical Legal Research. Oxford: Oxford University Press.

Carrie Menkel-Meadow, Chronicling the Complexification of Negotiation Theory and Practice, 25 Negotiation J. 415-429 (2009).

Carrie Menkel-Meadow, Remembrance of Things Past? The Relationship of Past to Future in Pursuing Justice in Mediation, 5 Cardozo J. Conflict Resol. 97, 105 (2004).

Michael Moffitt, Truth. Regardless of Reconciliation? 24 Nev. L. J. 1071 (2024).

Nancy Rogers, One Idea for Ameliorating Polarization: Reviving Conversations About an American Spirit, 2018 J. Disp. Resol. 27 (2018).

Emily Rothkin, How to Create a Metter Mediation: Using Divorce Mediation Outcomes to Assess Gender's Effect on Mediation, 102 B.U. L. Rev. 631 (2022).

Frank Sander, The Future of ADR, 2000 J. Disp. Resol. 1 (2000).

Frank Sander, Ways of Handling Conflict: What We Have Learned, What Problems Remain, 25 Negotiation J. 533-537 (2009).

Amy J. Schmitz & Colin Rule. (2017). The New Handshake: Online Dispute Resolution and the Future of Consumer Protection. American Bar Association.

Andrea Kupfer Schneider, Bargaining in the Shadow of (International Law), 41 N.Y.U. J. Int'l L. & Pol. 789 (2009).

Andrea Kupfer Schneider, The Day After Tomorrow: What Happens Once a Middle East Peace Treaty Is Signed?, 6 Nev. L.J. 401 (2006).

Andrea Kupfer Schneider, How Does DSD Help Us Teach About Community Conflict (and How Can Community Conflict Help Illustrate DSD)?, 31 St. Thomas L.J. 370 (2017).

Amartya Sen. (2009). The Idea of Justice. Cambridge, MA: Belknap Press.

Donna Shestowsky, When Ignorance Is Not Bliss: An Empirical Study of Litigants' Awareness of Court-Sponsored Alternative Dispute Resolution Programs, 22 Harv. Negot. L. Rev. 189-239 (2017).

Felix Steffek, Hannes Unberath, Hazel Genn, Reinhard Greger & Carrie Menkel-Meadow (2013). Regulating Dispute Resolution: ADR and Access to Justice at the Crossroads. Oxford: Hart Publishing.

Jane Stromseth, David Wippman & Rosa Brooks. (2006). Can Might Make Rights? Cambridge and New York: Cambridge University Press.

Lawrence Susskind, Twenty-Five Years Ago and Twenty-Five Years from Now: The Future of Public Dispute Resolution, 25 Negotiation J. 551-557 (2009).

Nancy A Welsh, Symposium: Achieving Access to Justice Through ADR: Fact or Fiction? Bringing Transparency and Accountability (With a Dash of Competition) to Court-Connected Dispute Resolution, 88 Fordham L. Rev 2449 (2020).

Roselle L. Wissler, Representation in Mediation: What We Know from Empirical Research, 37 Fordham Urb. L.J. 419 (2010).

Roselle L. Wissler, Court-Connected Settlement Procedures: Mediation and Judicial Settlement Conferences, 26 Ohio St. J. on Disp. Resol. 2-3 (2011).

Craig Zelizer & Robert A. Rubenstein. (2009). Building Peace: Reflections from the Field. Kumarian Press.

Table of Online Resources

https://about.usps.com
http://arbiter.wipo.int
http://cbuilding.org
https://clausebuilder.org
https://implicit.harvard.edu
https://jamsadr.com
https://mediate.com
https://open.mitchellhamline.edu
https://raycorollary.org
http://www.abanet.org/dispute
http://www.adr.org
https://www.cand.uscourts.gov
http://www.cbi.org
http://www.cpradr.org
http://www.cybersettle.com
http://www.icann.org/udrp
http://www.iccwbo.org
http://www.odr.info
http://www.policyconsensus.org
http://www.publicconversations.org
http://www.squaretrade.com
https://www.ted.com
http://www.uscourts.gov

Table of Principal Cases

Collected References

AARON, Marjorie Corman (2013). *Client Science: Advice for Lawyers on Initial Client Interviews.* Retrieved from clientsciencecourse.com.

______ (2012). *Client Science: Advice for Lawyers on Counseling Clients Through Bad News and Other Legal Realities.* Oxford: Oxford University Press.

______ (1996). "ADR Toolbox: The Highwire Art of Evaluation," 14 *Alternatives to High Cost Litig.* 62.

ABRAMS, Roger I. (2000). *The Money Pitch: Baseball Free Agency and Salary Arbitration.* Philadelphia, PA: Temple University Press.

______ (1999). "Inside Baseball's Salary Arbitration Process," 6 *U. Chi. L. Sch. Roundtable* 55.

ABRAMSON, Hal (2018). "Fashioning an Effective Negotiation Style: Choosing Between Good Practices, Tactics, and Tricks," 23 *Harv. Negot. L. Rev.* 319.

ABRAMSON, Hal, ed. (2019). "Singapore Mediation Convention Reference Book," 20 *Cardozo J. Conflict Resol.* 1001.

ABRAMSON, Hal, Birgit Sambeth GLASNER, Bill MARSH, Bennett G. PICKER, and Jerry WEISS (2017). "Are Legal Disputes Just About Money? Answers from Mediators on the Front Line," 19 *Cardozo J. Conflict Resol.* 1.

ABRAMSON, Harold I. (2013). *Mediation Representation: Advocating in a Problem-Solving Process* (3d ed.). South Bend, IN: National Institute for Trial Advocacy.

______ (1999). "Protocols for International Arbitrators Who Dare to Settle Cases," 10 *Am. Rev. Int'l Arb.* 1.

ADLER, Jane W., Deborah R. HENSLER, and Charles E. NELSON (1983). *Simple Justice: How Litigants Fare in the Pittsburgh Court Arbitration Program.* Santa Monica, CA: Rand.

ADLER, Peter S. (2008). *Eye of the Storm Leadership: 150 Stories, Quotes and Exercises on the Art and Politics of Managing Human Conflicts.* Colorado: Keystone.

ALBIN, Cecilia (1993). "The Role of Fairness in Negotiation," 9 *Negot. J.* 223.

ALEXANDER, Nadja M., James R. COBEN, Sarah R. COLE, Craig A. McEWEN, Nancy H. ROGERS, and Peter N. THOMPSON (2024). *Mediation Law Policy and Practice.* Thomson Reuters Trial Practice Series.

ALFINI, James J. (1991). "Trashing, Bashing, and Hashing It Out: Is This the End of 'Good Mediation'?," 19 *Fla. St. U. L. Rev.* 47.

______ (1989). "Summary Jury Trials in State and Federal Courts: A Comparative Analysis of the Perceptions of Participating Lawyers," 4 *Ohio St. J. on Disp. Resol.* 213.

ALFINI, James, Sharon PRESS, and Joseph STULBERG (2013). *Mediation Theory and Practice* (3d ed.). Durham, NC: Carolina Academic Press.

ALKON, Cynthia, and Andrea Kupfer SCHNEIDER (2019). *Negotiating Crime: Plea Bargaining, Problem Solving and Dispute Resolution in the Criminal Context.* Durham, NC: Carolina Press.

AMERICAN BAR ASSOCIATION, AMERICAN ARBITRATION ASSOCIATION, and ASSOCIATION FOR CONFLICT RESOLUTION (2005). "Model Standards of Conduct for Mediators." Washington, DC: ABA. Retrieved from http://www.abanet.org/dispute/news/ModelStandardsofConductforMediatorsfinal05.pdf.

AMERICAN BAR ASSOCIATION (2017), *Report of the Task Force on Research on Mediator Techniques.* Washington, DC: ABA, Section of Dispute Resolution.

______ (2004). "Resolution on Good Faith Requirements for Mediators and Mediation Advocates in Court-Mandated Mediation Programs." Washington, DC: ABA, Section of Dispute Resolution. Retrieved from http://www.abanet.org/dispute/webpolicy.html#9/.

______ (2002). "Resolution on Mediation and the Unauthorized Practice of Law." Washington, DC: ABA, Section of Dispute Resolution. Retrieved from http://www.abanet.org/dispute/ resolution2002.pdf.

AMERICAN BAR ASSOCIATION CENTER FOR INNOVATION (2020). *Online Dispute Resolution in the United States: Data Visualizations.*

AMERICAN LAW INSTITUTE (1986). *Restatement of the Law Governing Lawyers (Third)* §22(3).

______ (1981). *Restatement of the Law of Contracts (Second)* §§161, 164.

______ (1977). *Restatement of the Law of Torts (Second)* §525.

AMSLER, Lisa Blomgren, Janet K. MARTINEZ, and Stephanie E. SMITH (2020). *Dispute System Design: Preventing, Managing and Resolving Conflict.* Stanford: Stanford University Press.

ANGIER, Natalie (2002). "Why We're So Nice: We're Wired to Cooperate," *N.Y. Times,* July 23, p. F1.

APPLBAUM, Arthur Isak (1999). *Ethics for Adversaries.* Princeton, NJ: Princeton University Press.

ARAGAKI, Hiro N. (2016). "Arbitration: Creature of Contract, Pillar of Procedure," 8 *Y.B. on Arb. & Mediation* 2.

______ (2016). "Constructions of Arbitration's Informalism: Autonomy, Efficiency, and Justice," 2016 *J. Disp. Resol.* 141.

ARNOLD, Tom (1995). "20 Common Errors in Mediation Advocacy," 13 *Alternatives to High Cost Litig.* 69.

AUERBACH, Jerold S. (1983). *Justice Without Law?* New York: Oxford University Press.

AXELROD, Robert (1984). *The Evolution of Cooperation.* New York: Basic Books.

AYRES, Ian (1995). "Further Evidence of Discrimination in New Car Negotiations and Estimates of Its Cause," 94 *Mich. L. Rev.* 109.

______ (1991). "Fair Driving: Gender and Race Discrimination in Retail Car Negotiations," 104 *Harv. L. Rev.* 817.

BABCOCK, Linda, and Sara LASCHEVER (2003). *Women Don't Ask: Negotiation and the Gender Divide.* Princeton, NJ: Princeton University Press.

BACHAR, Gilat J., and Deborah R. HENSLER (2017). "Does Alternative Dispute Resolution Facilitate Prejudice and Bias? We Still Don't Know," 70 *SMU L. Rev.* 817.

BARKAI, John (1984). "How to Develop the Skill of Active Listening," 30 *Prac. Law.* 73.

BARRETT, Jerome T., and Joseph BARRETT (2004). *A History of Alternative Dispute Resolution: The Story of a Political, Social and Cultural Movement.* San Francisco, CA: Jossey-Bass Publishers.

BARTOS, Otomar J. (1978). "Simple Model of Negotiation: A Sociological Point of View," in I. William Zartman, ed., *The Negotiation Process: Theories and Applications.* Beverly Hills, CA: Sage Publications.

BAUM, Simeon H. (2005). "Top 10 Things Not to Do in Mediation," *N.Y.L.J.*, Apr. 25, 2005, at 510.

BAZERMAN, Max H., ed. (2005). *Negotiation, Decision Making and Conflict Management.* International Critical Library on Business and Management.

BAZERMAN, Max H., and Margaret A. NEALE (1992). *Negotiating Rationally.* New York: The Free Press.

BENS, Ingrid (2005). *Facilitating with Ease!* San Francisco: Jossey-Bass Publishers.

BERMAN, Greg, John FEINBLATT, and Sarah GLAZER (2005). *Good Courts: The Case for Problem Solving Justice.* New York: New Press.

BERNARD, Phyllis, and Bryant GARTH, eds. (2002). *Dispute Resolution Ethics: A Comprehensive Guide.* Washington, DC: ABA Section of Dispute Resolution.

BERNSTEIN, Lisa (1993). "Understanding the Limits of Court-Connected ADR: A Critique of Federal Court-Annexed Arbitration Programs," 141 *U. Pa. L. Rev.* 2169.

______ (1992). "Opting Out of the Legal System: Extralegal Contractual Relations in the Diamond Industry," 21 *J. Legal Stud.* 115.

BEZANSON, Randall P., Gilbert CRANBERG, and John SOLOSKI (1987). *Libel Law and the Press: Myth and Reality.* New York: Free Press.

BIERNAT, M., and M.H. MALIN (2008). "Political Ideology and Labor Arbitrators' Decision Making in Work-Family Conflict Cases," 34 *Personality & Soc. Psychol. Bull.* 888.

BINDER, David A., Paul BERGMAN, Paul R. TREMBLEY, and Ian S. WEINSTEIN (2019). *Lawyers As Counselors: A Client-Centered Approach* (4th ed.). Egan, MN: West.

BINGHAM, Lisa B. (2002). "Why Suppose? Let's Find Out: A Public Policy Research Program on Dispute Resolution," 2002 *J. Disp. Resol.* 101.

BINGHAM, Lisa B., Cynthia J. HALLBERLIN, Denise A. WALKER, and Won Tae CHUNG (2009). "Dispute System Design and Justice in Employment Dispute Resolution: Mediation at the Workplace," 14 *Harv. Negot. L. Rev.* 1.

BIRKE, Richard, and Craig R. FOX (1981). "Psychological Principles in Negotiating Civil Settlements," *Acad. Mgmt. Rev.* 23 (Oct.).

BLACKER, Neal (2000). "Drafting the Arbitration/ADR Clause: A Checklist for Practitioners," 46 *Prac. Law.* 55.

BLAIR, H. Allen (2017). "Promise and Peril: Doctrinally Permissible Options for Calibrating Procedure Through Contract," 95 *Neb. L. Rev.* 787.

BLANKLEY, Kristen (2014). "Lying, Stealing, and Cheating: The Role of Arbitrators as Ethics Enforcers," 52 *U. Louisville L. Rev.* 443.

______ (2005). "Be More Specific! Can Writing a Detailed Arbitration Agreement Expand Judicial Review Under the Federal Arbitration Act?," 2 *Seton Hall Cir. Rev.* 391.

BLANKLEY, Kristen M., Ashley VOTRUBA, Logen M. BARTZ, and Lisa M. PytlikZillig (2021). "ADR Is Not a Household Term: Considering the Ethical and Practical Consequences of the Public's Lack of Understanding of Mediation and Arbitration," 99 *Neb. L. Rev.* No. 797.

BLOOM, Erin, and Lisa DICKER (2023). "The Politics of Justice: Analyzing the Politicization of Transitional Justice Processes," 38 *Ohio. St. J. on Disp. Resol.* 303.

BLUM, Gabriella (2007). *Islands of Agreement: Managing Enduring Armed Rivalries.* Cambridge, MA: Harvard University Press.

BONE, Robert G. (2012). "Party Rulemaking: Making Procedural Rules Through Party Choice," 90 *Tex. L. Rev.* 1329.

BORDONE, Robert C. (1998). "Electronic Online Dispute Resolution: A Systems Approach—Potential Problems, and a Proposal," 3 *Harv. Negot. L. Rev.* 175.

BORDONE, Robert C., and Michael MOFFITT (2006). "Create Value Out of Conflict," 9 *Negot.* 1.

BORDONE, Robert C., Michael MOFFITT, and Frank SANDER (2005). "The Next Thirty Years: Directions and Challenges in Dispute Resolution," in *The Handbook of Dispute Resolution*. New York: John Wiley & Sons.

BORN, Gary B. (2020). *International Commercial Arbitration: Commentary and Materials* (3d ed.). The Hague, The Netherlands: Kluwer Law International.

BOULLE, Laurence J., and Nadja ALEXANDER (2019). *Mediation: Skills and Techniques* (3d ed.). Chattswood, NSW: Lexis Nexis Butterworths.

BRAMS, Steven J., and Alan D. TAYLOR (1996). *Fair Division*. Cambridge, MA: Cambridge University Press.

BRAZIL, Wayne D. (2017). "When Getting It Right Is What Matters Most, Arbitrations Are Better than Trials," 18 *Cardozo J. Conflict Resol.* 277.

______ (2013). *Early Neutral Evaluation*. Washington, DC: ABA Press.

______ (2006). "Should Court Sponsored ADR Survive?," 21 *Ohio St. J. on Disp. Resol.* 241.

______ (1990). "A Close Look at Three Court-Sponsored ADR Programs: Why They Exist, How They Operate, What They Deliver, and Whether They Threaten Important Values," 1990 *U. Chi. Legal F.* 303.

BREGER, Marshall J. (2000). "Should an Attorney Be Required to Advise a Client of ADR Options?," 13 *Geo. J. Legal Ethics* 427.

BRETT, Jeanne M. (2001). *Negotiating Globally: How to Negotiate Deals, Resolve Disputes, and Make Decisions Across Cultural Boundaries*. San Francisco: Jossey-Bass Publishers.

BROWN, Jennifer Gerarda (2006). "Creativity and Problem-Solving," in Andrea Kupfer Schneider and Christopher Honeyman, eds., *The Negotiator's Fieldbook*. Washington, DC: ABA Section of Dispute Resolution.

______ (2004). "Creativity and Problem-Solving," 87 *Marq. L. Rev.* 697.

BROWN, Jenny (2009). "The Expansion of Arbitral Immunity: Is Absolute Immunity a Foregone Conclusion?," 2009 *J. Disp. Resol.* 225.

BRUNET, Edward, Richard E. SPEIDEL, Jean R. STERNLIGHT, and Stephen J. WARE (2006). *Arbitration Law in America: A Critical Assessment*. New York: Cambridge University Press.

BURGER, Warren E. (1982). "Isn't There a Better Way?," 68 *A.B.A. J.* 274.

______ (1971). "The Necessity for Civility," 52 *F.R.D.* 211.

BUSH, Robert A. Baruch (1990). "Mediation and Adjudication, Dispute Resolution and Ideology: An Imaginary Conversation," 3 *J. Contemp. Legal Issues* 1.

BUSH, Robert A. Baruch, and Joseph P. FOLGER (2005 rev. ed.). *The Promise of Mediation: The Transformative Approach to Conflict*. San Francisco: Jossey-Bass Publishers.

CARBONNEAU, Thomas E. (2004). *The Law and Practice of Arbitration*. Huntington NY: JurisNet, LLC.

______ (2003). "The Exercise of Contract Freedom in the Making of Arbitration Agreements," 36 *Vand. J. Transnat'l L.* 1189.

CARPENTER, Susan L., and W.L.D. KENNEDY (2001). *Managing Public Disputes: A Practical Guide for Professionals in Government, Business and Citizen Groups*. San Francisco: Jossey-Bass Publishers.

CARR, Albert H.Z. (1968). *Business as a Game*. New York: New American Library.

CARR, Frank, with Kim HURTADO, Charles LANCASTER, Charles MARKERT, and Paul TUCKER (1999). *Partnering in Construction: A Practical Guide for Project Success*. Chicago: Forum on the Construction Industry, ABA.

CARREL, Alyson, and Noam EBNER (2019). "Mind the Gap: Bringing Technology to the Mediation Table," 2019(2) *J. Disp. Resol.* 1.

CARTER, Alexandra (2020). *Ask for More*. New York: Simon & Schuster.

CENTER FOR CONFLICT RESOLUTION (1977). *Manual for Group Facilitators.* Madison, WI: Center for Conflict Resolution.

CENTER FOR PUBLIC RESOURCES (1995). "The ABC's of ADR: A Dispute Resolution Glossary," 13(11) *Alternatives to High Cost Litig.* 1.

CHERNICK, Richard, Helen I. BENDIX, and Robert C. BARRETT (1997). *Private Judging: Privatizing Civil Justice.* Washington, DC: National Legal Center for the Public Interest.

CHEW, Pat (2017). "Comparing the Effects of Judges' Gender and Arbitrators' Gender in Sex Discrimination Cases and Why It Matters," 32 *Ohio St. J. on Disp. Resol.* 195.

______ (2017). "Contextual Analysis in Arbitration," 70 *SMU L. Rev.* 837.

______ (2017). "Opening the Red Door to Chinese Arbitrations: An Empirical Analysis of Cietac Cases 1990-2000," 22 *Harv. Negot. L. Rev.* 241.

CHILDRES, Rachel (2017). "Arbitration Class Waivers, Independent Contractor Classification, and the Blockade of Workers' Rights in the Gig Economy," 69 *Ala. L. Rev.* 533.

CHRISTENSEN, Barlow F. (1982). "Private Justice: California's General Reference Procedure," 1982 *Am. B. Found. Res. J.* 79.

CIALDINI, Robert B. (1993). *Influence: The Psychology of Persuasion* (rev. ed.). New York: William Morrow.

CLEMENS, Murray A. (2011). *Final Offer Arbitration: Baseball, Boxcars & Beyond.* Canada: Continuing Legal Education Society of British Columbia.

CLINTON, William J. (2001). Acceptance Speech for the International Advocate for Peace Award, March 19. Benjamin N. Cardozo School of Law. Retrieved from http://www.cardozo.yu.edu/cojcr/final_site/IAP_Award/2001/clintpdf.pdf.

COBEN, James R. (2000). "Mediation's Dirty Little Secret: Straight Talk About Mediator Manipulation and Deception," 2 *J. Alternative Disp. Resol. Emp.* 4.

COBEN, James R., and Peter N. THOMPSON (2006). "Disputing Irony: A Systematic Look at Litigation About Mediation," 11 *Harv. Neg. L. Rev.* 43.

COBEN, James, Sarah COLE, Craig McEWEN, and Nancy ROGERS (2018). *Mediation Law Policy and Practice 2017-18 ed.* Thomson Reuters Trial Practice Series.

COCHRAN, Robert F., Jr. (2003). "Introduction: Three Approaches to Moral Issues in Law Office Counseling," 30 *Pepp. L. Rev.* 592.

______ (2002). "Educating Clients on ADR Alternatives: The Rules of Professional Conduct Should Require Lawyers to Inform Clients About ADR," L.A. Law., Oct., at p.52.

COGLIANESE, Cary (2023). "Evaluating Regulatory Performance," 8 *U. Pa. J.L. Pub. Aff.* 47.

______ (1997). "Assessing Consensus: The Promise and Performance of Negotiated Rulemaking," 46 *Duke L.J.* 1255.

COHEN, Jonathan R. (2003). "Adversaries? Partners? How About Counterparts? On Metaphors in the Practice and Teaching of Negotiation and Dispute Resolution," 20 *Conflict Resol. Q.* 433.

______ (2001). "When People Are the Means: Negotiating with Respect," 14 *Geo. J. Legal Ethics* 739.

COHEN, Taya R., Erik G. HELZER, and Robert A. CREO (2022). "Honesty Among Lawyers: Moral Character, Game Framing, and Honest Disclosures in Negotiation," 38 *Negot. J.* 199.

COLE, Sarah Rudolph (2021). "Arbitrator Diversity: Can It Be Achieved?," 98 *Wash. U. L. Rev.* 965.

______ (2015). "Blurred Lines: Are Non-Attorneys Who Represent Parties in Arbitration Involving Statutory Claims Practicing Law?," 48 *U.C. Davis L. Rev.* 921.

______ (2005). "Arbitration and State Action," 2005 *B.Y.U. L. Rev.* 1.

CONNOR, Lawrence D. (1996). "How to Combine Facilitation with Evaluation," 14 *Alternatives to High Cost Litig.* 15.

COOLEY, John W. (2005). *Creative Problem Solver's Handbook for Negotiators and Mediators* (Vol. 1 & 2). Washington, DC: ABA Section of Dispute Resolution.

______ (2000). *The Mediator's Handbook.* Notre Dame, IN: National Institute for Trial Advocacy.

COOLEY, John W., and Steven LUBET (2003). *Arbitration Advocacy* (2d ed.). Notre Dame, IN: National Institute for Trial Advocacy.

COOPER, Laura J., Dennis NOLAN, Richard A. BALES, Stephen F. BEFORT, Lise GELERNTER, and Michael Z. GREEN (2020). *ADR in the Workplace* (4th ed.). St. Paul, MN: The West Group.

COSTANTINO, Cathy (2009). "Second Generation Organizational Conflict Management Systems Design: A Practitioner's Perspective on Emerging Issues," 14 *Harv. Negot. L. Rev.* 81.

COSTANTINO, Cathy A., and Christina Sickles MERCHANT (1996). *Designing Conflict Management Systems: A Guide to Creating Productive and Healthy Organizations.* San Francisco: Jossey-Bass Publishers.

COVEY, Stephen R. (1989). *The Seven Habits of Highly Effective People: Restoring the Character Ethic.* New York: Simon and Schuster.

CPR CORPORATE DISPUTE MANAGEMENT (1982). E. Green ed., *The CPR Legal Program Mini-Trial Handbook.* New York: CPR.

CPR-GEORGETOWN (2002). *Model Rule 4.5.4: Conflicts of Interest.* Retrieved from http://www.cpradr.org.

CULBERT, Mary B. (2023). "Proposal: A New Unified Canon of Mediator Ethics," 29 *Ohio St. J. on Disp. Resol.* 1.

DAVIS, Kevin E., & Helen HERSHKOFF (2011). "Contracting for Procedure," 53 *Wm. & Mary L. Rev.* 507.

DAY, Barry, ed. (2000). *Oscar Wilde, A Life in Quotes.* London: Metro.

DE BONO, Edward (1999). *Six Thinking Hats* (rev. ed.). Boston: Little, Brown.

DE PALO, Giuseppe (2021). "Mediating Mediation Itself: The Easy Opt-Out Model Settles the Perennial Dispute Between Voluntary and Mandatory Mediation," 22 *Cardozo J. Conflict Resol.* 543.

de WAAL, Frans (2011). "Do Animals Have Morals?" *TED Talk.* Retrieved from https://www.ted.com/talks/frans_de_waal_do_animals_have_morals.

DEASON, Ellen E. (2017). "Beyond 'Managerial Judges': Appropriate Roles in Settlement," 78 *Ohio St. L. Rev.* 74.

______ (2004). "Procedural Rules for Complementary Systems of Litigation and Mediation—Worldwide," 80 *Notre Dame L. Rev.* 533.

______ (2001). "Enforcing Mediated Settlement Agreements: Contract Law Collides with Confidentiality," 35 *U.C. Davis L. Rev.* 33.

DEL GOBBO, Daniel (2018). "The Feminist Negotiator's Dilemma," 33 *Ohio St. J. on Disp. Resol.* 1.

DELGADO, Richard, Chris DUNN, Pamela BROWN, Helena LEE, and David HUBBERT (1985). "Fairness and Formality: Minimizing the Risk of Prejudice in Alternative Dispute Resolution," 1985 *Wis. L. Rev.* 1359.

DEMAINE, Linda J., and Deborah R. HENSLER (2004). "'Volunteering' to Arbitrate Through Predispute Arbitration Clauses: The Average Consumer's Experience," 67 *Law & Contemp. Probs.* 55.

DEUTSCH, Morton (1973). *The Resolution of Conflict: Constructive and Destructive Processes.* New Haven: Yale University Press.

DEUTSCH, Morton, and Peter T. COLEMAN, eds. (2000). *The Handbook of Conflict Resolution: Theory and Practice.* San Francisco: Jossey-Bass Publishers.

DEZALAY, Yves, and Bryant G. GARTH (1996). *Dealing in Virtue: International Commercial Arbitration and the Construction of a Transnational Legal Order.* Chicago: University of Chicago Press.

DICKENS, Charles (1853) *Bleak House* (1956 ed.). Boston: Houghton Mifflin.
DISPUTE RESOLUTION MAGAZINE (2016). "Ombuds," 23(1) *Disp. Resol. Mag.* 6 (Fall).
DODGE, Jaime (2011). "The Limits of Procedural Private Ordering," 97 *Va. L. Rev.* 723.
DRAHOZAL, Christopher R. (2013). *Commercial Arbitration: Cases and Problems* (3d ed.). Durham, NC: Carolina Academic Press.
______ (2014). "FAA Preemption After *Concepcion*," 35 *Berkeley J. Emp. & Lab. L.* 153.
______ (2005). "Contracting Out of International Law: An Empirical Look at the New Law Merchant," 80 *Notre Dame L. Rev.* 523.
______ (2002). "In Defense of *Southland*: Reexamining the Legislative History of the Federal Arbitration Act," 78 *Notre Dame L. Rev.* 101.
DRAHOZAL, Christopher R., and S. ZYONTZ (2009). "An Empirical Study of AAA Consumer Arbitration." SSRN. Retrieved from http://ssrn.com/abstract=1365435.
DUBLER, Nancy, and Carol LIEBMAN (2011). *Bioethics Mediation: A Guide to Shaping Shared Solutions.* New York: United Hospital Fund.
DUKES, E. Franklin, Marina A. PISCOLISH, and John B. STEPHENS (2000). *Reaching for Higher Ground in Conflict Resolution: Tools for Powerful Groups and Communities.* San Francisco: Jossey-Bass Publishers.
DUNLOP, John T., and Arnold M. ZACK (1997). *Mediation and Arbitration of Employment Disputes.* San Francisco: Jossey-Bass Publishers.
EBNER, Noam (2017). "Negotiating via Text Messaging," in Chris Honeyman and Andrea Kufper Schneider, eds., *The Negotiator's Desk Reference.* St. Paul, MN: DRI Press.
EBNER, Noam, Anita D. BHAPPU, Jennifer BROWN, Kimberlee K. KOVACH, and Andrea Kupfer SCHNEIDER (2009). "You've Got Agreement: Negoti@ting via email," in Christopher Honeyman, James Coben, and Giuseppe de Palo, eds, *Rethinking Negotiation Teaching: Innovations for Context and Culture.* St. Paul, MN: DRI Press.
ELLMAN, Stephen, Robert D. DINERSTEIN, Isabelle R. GUNNING, Katherine R. KRUSE, and Ann C. SHALLECK (2009). *Lawyers and Clients: Critical Issues in Interviewing and Counseling.* Eagan, MN: West.
ELLMAN, Stephen, Isabelle GUNNING, Robert DINERSTEIN, and Ann SHALLECK (2003). "Legal Interviewing and Counseling: An Introduction," 10 *Clinical L. Rev.* 281.
ELSTER, Jon (1995). "Strategic Uses of Argument," in Kenneth J. Arrow et al., eds., *Barriers to Conflict Resolution.* New York: W.W. Norton.
ESTLUND, Cynthia (2018). "The Black Hole of Mandatory Arbitration," 96 *N.C. L. Rev.* 679.
FALK, David B. (1992). "The Art of Contract Negotiation," 3 *Marq. Sports L.J.* 1.
FEINBERG, Kenneth (2012). *Who Gets What: Fair Compensation After Tragedy and Financial Upheaval.* New York, NY: PublicAffairs.
______ (2006). *What Is a Life Worth? The Unprecedented Effort to Compensate the Victims of 9/11.* New York: PublicAffairs.
FELSTINER, William L.F., Richard L. ABEL, and Austin SARAT (1980-81). "The Emergence and Transformation of Disputes: Naming, Blaming, Claiming . . . ," 15 *Law & Soc'y Rev.* 631.
FIRESTONE, Hannah (2023). "A Call for Compromise: Examining Polarization and the Potential Use of ADR Solutions in Congress Post-Trump Administration," 38 *Ohio St. J. Disp. Resol.* 667.
FISHER, Roger, Elizabeth KOPELMAN, and Andrea Kupfer SCHNEIDER (1996). *Beyond Machiavelli: Tools for Coping with Conflict.* New York: Penguin.
FISHER, Roger, William L. URY, and Bruce PATTON (2011). *Getting to YES* (3d ed.). New York: Penguin.
FISS, Owen M. (1984). "Against Settlement," 93 *Yale L.J.* 1073.
FOLGER, Joseph P., and Robert A. Baruch BUSH (1996). "Transformative Mediation and Third-Party Intervention: Ten Hallmarks of a Transformative Approach to Practice," 13 *Mediation Q.* 263.

FOLLETT, Mary Parker (1995). "Constructive Conflict," in Pauline Graham, ed., *Mary Parker Follett—Prophet of Management: A Celebration of Writings from the 1920s.* Boston: Harvard Business School Press.

FOREST, Heather (1996). "The Wise Master," in *Wisdom Tales from Around the World.* Little Rock, AR: August House Publishers.

FORESTER, John (2009). *Dealing with Differences: Dramas of Mediating Public Disputes.* New York: Oxford University Press.

FRANK, Susan, et al. (2017). "Inside the Arbitrator's Mind," 66 *Emory L.J.* 1115.

FREEMAN, Jody (1997). "Collaborative Governance in the Administrative State," 45 *UCLA L. Rev.* 1.

FREEMAN, Jody, and Laura I. LANGBEIN (2000). "Regulatory Negotiation and the Legitimacy Benefit," 9 *N.Y.U. Envtl. L.J.* 60.

FREER, Richard, "Exodus from and Transformation of American Civil Litigation," 65 *Emory L.J.* 1491.

FRENKEL, Douglas, and James STARK (2018). *The Practice of Mediation: A Video-Integrated Text.* Aspen Publishers.

FRESHMAN, Clark (1997). "Privatizing Same-Sex 'Marriage' Through Alternative Dispute Resolution: Community-Enhancing Versus Community-Enabling Mediation," 44 *UCLA L. Rev.* 1687.

FRESHMAN, Clark, Adele HAYES, and Greg FELDMAN (2002). "The Lawyer-Negotiator as Mood Scientist: What We Know and Don't Know About How Mood Relates to Successful Negotiation," 2002 *J. Disp. Resol.* 1.

FREUND, James (2022). "For the Election Season: Mediating Legislative Cliffs," 40 *Alternatives to High Cost Litig.* 152.

FRIEDMAN, Gary, and Jack HIMMELSTEIN (2009). *Challenging Conflict: Mediation Through Understanding.* Washington, DC: ABA Publishing.

______ (2008). "Nature Preserve: The Loop of Understanding," in *Challenging Conflict: Mediating Through Understanding.* Washington, DC: ABA Publishing.

______ (2004). *The Understanding-Based Approach to Mediation.* The Center for Mediation in Law. Retrieved from http://www.mediationinlaw.org/about.html.

______ (2003). "Memo, No. 2, Elements of Mediator-Parties Contract." The Center for Mediation in Law. Retrieved from http://www.mediationinlaw.org/about.html.

FULLER, Lon L. (2001). "The Forms and Limits of Adjudication," in Kenneth I. Winston, ed., *The Principles of Social Order: Selected Essays of Lon L. Fuller* (rev. ed.). Oxford, UK: Hart Publishing.

______ (1971). "Mediation —Its Forms and Functions," 44 *S. Cal. L. Rev.* 305.

______ (1963). "Collective Bargaining and the Arbitrator," 1963 *Wis. L. Rev.* 3.

______ (1962). "Collective Bargaining and the Arbitrator," in Mark L. Kahn, ed., *Collective Bargaining and the Arbitrator's Role: Proceedings of the Fifteenth Annual Meeting, National Academy of Arbitrators.* Washington, DC: BNA.

GABRIELI, Amos, Nourit ZIMERMAN, and Michal ALBERSTEIN (2018), "Authority-Based Mediation," 20 *Cardozo J. Conflict Resol.* 1.

GALANTER, Marc S. (2004). "The Vanishing Trial: An Examination of Trials and Related Matters in Federal and State Courts," 1 *J. Empirical Legal Stud.* 459.

______ (1983). "Reading the Landscape of Disputes: What We Know and Don't Know (and Think We Know) About Our Allegedly Contentious and Litigious Society," 31 *UCLA L. Rev.* 4.

GALTON, Eric, and Lela LOVE, eds. (2012). *Stories Mediators Tell.* Washington, DC: ABA Publishing.

GARDNER, Howard, Mihaly CSIKSZENTMIHALYI, and William DAMON (2001). *Good Work: When Excellence and Ethics Meet.* New York: Basic Books.

GARTH, Bryant G. (1992). "Privatization and the New Market for Disputes: A Framework for Analysis and a Preliminary Assessment," 12 *Stud. L. Pol. & Soc'y* 367.

GETMAN, Julius G. (1979). "Labor Arbitration and Dispute Resolution," 88 *Yale L.J.* 916.

GIBSON, James L. (2004). *Overcoming Apartheid: Can Truth Resolve a Divided Nation?* New York: Russell Sage Foundation.

GIFFORD, Donald G. (1985). "A Context-Based Theory of Strategy Selection in Legal Negotiation," 46 *Ohio St. L.J.* 41.

GILSON, Ronald J., and Robert H. MNOOKIN, eds. (1995). "Business Lawyers and Value Creation for Clients," 74 *Or. L. Rev.* 1.

GIRVAN, Erik J., Grace DEASON, and Eugene BORGIDA (2015). "The Generalizability of Gender Bias: Testing the Effects of Contextual, Explicit, and Implicit Sexism on Labor Arbitration Decisions," 39 *Law & Hum. Behav.* 525.

GOH, Bee Chen (2017). "Typical Errors of Westerners," in Chris Honeyman and Andrea Kupfer Schneider, eds., *The Negotiator's Desk Reference.* St. Paul, MN: DRI Press.

GOLANN, Dwight (2021). *Mediating Legal Disputes: Effective Strategies for Neutrals and Advocates* (2d ed.). ABA Book Publishing.

______ (2019). "Grieving Over Settlement: The Role of Loss in Settlement Negotiations," 34 *Ohio St. J. on Disp. Resol.* 333.

______ (1989). "Making Alternative Dispute Resolution Mandatory: The Constitutional Issues," 68 *Or. L. Rev.* 487.

GOLANN, Dwight, and Eric E. VAN LOON (1999). "Legal Issues in Consensus Building," in Lawrence Susskind, Sarah McKearnan, and Jennifer Thomas-Larmer, eds., *The Consensus Building Handbook: A Comprehensive Guide to Reaching Agreement.* Thousand Oaks, CA: Sage Publications.

GOLDBERG, Stephen B. (1989). "Grievance Mediation: A Successful Alternative to Labor Arbitration," 5 *Negot. J.* 9.

GOODPASTER, Gary (1996). "A Primer on Competitive Bargaining," 1996 *J. Disp. Resol.* 325.

GREEN, Eric D. (1997). "What Will We Do When Adjudication Ends? We'll Settle in Bunches, Bringing Rule 23 into the Twenty-First Century," 44 *UCLA L. Rev.* 1773.

GREEN, Eric D., et al., eds. (1982). "The CPR Legal Program Mini-Trial Handbook," in CPR *Corporate Dispute Management: A Manual of Innovative Corporate Strategies for the Avoidance and Resolution of Legal Disputes.* New York: CPR.

GREEN, Eric D., Jonathan B. MARKS, and Ronald L. OLSEN (1978). "Settling Large Case Litigation: An Alternative Approach," 11 *Loy. L.A. L. Rev.* 493.

GRILLO, Trina (1991). "The Mediation Alternative: Process Dangers for Women," 100 *Yale L.J.* 1545.

GULLIVER, Phillip H. (1979). *Disputes and Negotiations: A Cross-Cultural Perspective (Studies on Law and Social Control).* New York: Academic Press.

GUNNING, Isabelle R. (1995). "Diversity Issues in Mediation: Controlling Negative Cultural Myths," 1995 *J. Disp. Resol.* 55.

GUTMANN, Amy, and Dennis THOMPSON (1996). *Democracy and Disagreement.* Cambridge, MA: Belknap Press of Harvard University Press.

HABERMAS, Jürgen (1984). *A Theory of Communicative Action,* Trans. Thomas McCarthy. 2 vols. Boston: Beacon Press.

HAGER, L. Michael, and Robert PRITCHARD (1999). "Deal Mediation: How ADR Techniques Can Help Achieve Durable Agreements in the Global Markets," 14 *ICSID Rev.-Foreign Investment L.J.* 1.

HALPRIN, Peter, and Stephen WAH (2018). "Ethics in International Arbitration," 2018 *J. Disp. Resol.* 87.

HAMPSHIRE, Stuart (2000). *Justice Is Conflict.* Princeton, NJ: Princeton University Press.

HARTER, Philip J. (2000). "Assessing the Assessors: The Actual Performance of Negotiated Rulemaking," 9 *N.Y.U. Envtl. L.J.* 32.

______ (1982). "Negotiating Regulations: A Cure for Malaise," 71 *Geo. L.J.* 1.

HAYFORD, Stephen L. (2000). "Unification of the Law of Labor Arbitration and Commercial Arbitration: An Idea Whose Time Has Come," 52 *Baylor L. Rev.* 781.

HAYNER, Priscilla (2001). *Unspeakable Truths: Confronting State Terror and Atrocity.* New York: Routledge.

HAYNES, John M. (1993). *The Fundamentals of Family Mediation.* Albany, NY: State University of New York Press.

HEAVIN, Heather, & Michaela KEET (2021). "Client-Centered Communication: How Effective Lawyering Requires Emotional Intelligence, Active Listening, and Client Choice," 22 *Cardozo J. Conflict Resol.* 199.

HEEN, Shelia, and Douglas STONE (2017). "Perceptions and Stories," in Chris Honeyman and Andrea Kupfer Schneider, eds., *The Negotiator's Desk Reference.* St. Paul, MN: DRI Press.

HENSLER, Deborah R. (2002). "Suppose It's Not True: Challenging Mediation Ideology," 2002 *J. Disp. Resol.* 81.

______ (2000). "In Search of 'Good' Mediation: Rhetoric, Practice, and Empiricism," in Joseph Sanders and V. Lee Hamilton, eds., *Handbook of Justice Research in Law.* New York: Kluwer Academic/Plenum Publishers.

______ (1995). "A Glass Half Full, a Glass Half Empty: The Use of Alternative Dispute Resolution in Mass Personal Injury Litigation," 73 *Tex. L. Rev.* 1587.

______ (1986). "What We Know and Don't Know About Court-Administered Arbitration," 69 *Judicature* 270.

HERMAN, Cary (2021). *Client Interviewing, Counseling, and Decision-Making: A Practical Approach* (2d ed.). Durham, NC: Carolina Academic Press.

HERMANN, Michelle et al. (1993). *Metro Court Project Final Report.* Albuquerque, NM: University of New Mexico Center for the Study and Resolution of Disputes.

HERNANDEZ-CRESPO GONSTEAD, Mariana (2020). "Remedy Without Diagnosis: How to Optimize Results by Leveraging the Appropriate Dispute Resolution and Shared Decision-Making Process," 88 *Fordham L. Rev.* 2165.

HILL, Marvin F., Jr., Anthony V. SINICROPI, and Amy L. EVENSON (1997). *Winning Arbitration Advocacy.* Washington, DC: Bureau of National Affairs.

HINDLE, Tim (1998). *Managing Meetings.* New York: DK Publishing.

HINSHAW, Art (2016). "Regulating Mediators," 21 *Harv. Negot. L. Rev.* 163.

HINSHAW, Art, and Jess K. ALBERTS (2011). "Doing the Right Thing: An Empirical Study of Attorney Negotiation Ethics," 16 *Harv. Negot. L. Rev.* 95.

HINSHAW, Art, Peter REILLY, and Andrea Kupfer SCHNEIDER (2013). "Attorneys and Negotiation Ethics: A Material Misunderstanding?," 29 *Negot. J.* 265.

HOFFMAN, David (2013). *Mediation: A Practice Guide for Mediators, Lawyers, and Other Professionals.* MCLE New England.

HOFFMAN, Jan (2018). "Can This Judge Solve the Opioid Crisis?," *N.Y. Times,* Mar. 5.

HOFSTADTER, Douglas R. (1985). *Metamagical Themas: Questing for the Essence of Mind and Pattern.* New York: Basic Books.

HOLLANDER-BLUMOFF, Rebecca, and Tom R. TYLER (2008). "Procedural Justice in Negotiation: Procedural Fairness, Outcome Acceptance, and Integrative Potential," 33 *Law & Soc. Inquiry* 473.

HONEYMAN, Christopher, and Andrea Kupfer SCHNEIDER, eds. (2017). *The Negotiator's Desk Reference* (2d ed.). St. Paul, MN: DRI Press.

HOROWITZ, Morton J. (1977). *The Transformation of American Law, 1780-1860.* Cambridge, MA: Harvard University Press.

HORTON, David (2018). "Arbitration About Arbitration," 70 *Stan. L. Rev.* 363.

______ (1975). "Arbitration, Arbitrators, and the Public Interest," 28 *ILR Rev.* 497.

HOWARD, Charles L. (2010). *The Organizational Ombudsman.* Washington, DC: ABA Press.

HUANG, Jennie, and Corinne LOW (2017). "Trumping Norms: Lab Evidence on Aggressive Communication Before and After the 2016 US Presidential Election," 107 *Am. Econ. Rev.* 120.

HUGHES, Scott H. (2004). "Mediator Immunity: The Misguided and Inequitable Shifting of Risk," 83 *Or. L. Rev.* 107.

______ (2001). "The Uniform Mediation Act: To the Spoiled Go the Privileges," 85 *Marq. L. Rev.* 9.

HYMAN, Jonathan M., and Lela P. LOVE (2002). "If Portia Were a Mediator: An Inquiry into Justice in Mediation," 9 *Clinical L. Rev.* 157.

ISSACHAROFF, Samuel, Robert H. KLONOFF, Richard NAGAREDA, and Charles SILVER (Reporters) (2010). *Principles of the Law of Aggregate Litigation.* St. Paul, MN: American Law Institute Publishers.

IZUMI, Carol (2010). "Implicit Bias and the Illusion of Mediator Neutrality," 34 *Wash. U. J.L. & Pol'y* 71.

IZUMI, Carol L., and Homer C. LA RUE (2003). "Prohibiting 'Good Faith' Reports Under the Uniform Mediation Act: Keeping the Adjudication Camel Out of the Mediation Tent," 2003 *J. Disp. Resol.* 67.

JACOBS, Margaret A. (1997). "Legal Beat: Private Jury Trials: Cheap, Quick, Controversial," *Wall St. J.*, July 7, p. B1.

JAMS (2018). *JAMS Clause Workbook: A Guide to Drafting Dispute Resolution Clauses for Commercial Contracts—Governing Law.* Retrieved from https://jamsadr.com/files/uploads/Documents/JAMS-Rules/JAMS-ADR-Clauses.pdf.

JANIS, Irving L. (1982). *Groupthink: Psychological Studies of Policy Decisions and Fiascoes* (2d ed.). Boston: Houghton Mifflin.

JONES, William Catron (1956). "Three Centuries of Commercial Arbitration in New York: A Brief Survey," 1956 *Wash. U. L.Q.* 193.

KAKALIK, James S., Terence DUNWORTH, Laural A. HILL, Daniel McCAFFREY, Marian OSHIRO, Nicholas M. PACE, and Mary E. VAIANA (1996). *An Evaluation of Mediation and Early Neutral Evaluation Under the Civil Justice Reform Act.* Santa Monica, CA: Rand.

KANER, Sam (2014). *Facilitator's Guide to Participatory Group Decision Making.* San Francisco: Jossey-Bass Publishers.

KATSH, Ethan, and Orna RABINOVITZ-EINY (2017). *Digital Justice.* Oxford: Oxford University Press.

KATSH, Ethan, and Janet RIFKIN (2001). *Online Dispute Resolution: Resolving Conflicts in Cyberspace.* San Francisco: Jossey-Bass Publishers.

KAYE, Judith S. (1997). "Changing Courts in Changing Times: The Need for a Fresh Look at How Courts Are Run," 48 *Hastings L.J.* 851.

KELLY, Loretta (2006). "Indigenous Experiences in Negotiation," in Andrea Kupfer Schneider and Christopher Honeyman, eds., *The Negotiator's Fieldbook.* Washington, DC: ABA Section of Dispute Resolution.

KENTRA, Pamela A. (1997). "Hear No Evil, See No Evil, Speak No Evil: The Intolerable Conflict for Attorney-Mediators Between the Duty to Maintain Mediation Confidentiality and the Duty to Report Fellow Attorney Misconduct," 1997 *BYU L. Rev.* 715.

KHOUKAZ, George (2017). "Sharia Law and International Commercial Arbitration: The Need for an Intra-Islamic Arbitral Institution," 2017 *J. Disp. Resol.* 181.

KICHAVEN, Jeff (2003). "Apology in Mediation: Sorry to Say, It's Much Overrated." *Int'l Risk Mgmt. Inst.*

KIM, Anne S. (1994). Note, "Rent-a-Judges and the Cost of Selling Justice," 44 *Duke L.J.* 166.

KING, Michael, Arie FREIBERG, Becky BATAGOL, and Ross HYAMS (2009). *Non-Adversarial Justice.* Sydney, Australia: Federation Press.

KOLB & Associates (1997). *When Talk Works: Profiles of Mediators.* San Francisco, CA: Jossey-Bass Publishers.

KOROBKIN, Russell (2002). "Aspirations and Settlement," 88 *Cornell L. Rev.* 1.

______ (2000). "A Positive Theory of Legal Negotiation," 88 *Geo. L.J.* 1789.

KOROBKIN, Russell, and Chris GUTHRIE (2006). "Heuristics and Biases at the Bargaining Table," in Andrea Kupfer Schneider and Christopher Honeyman, eds., *The Negotiator's Fieldbook.* Washington, DC: ABA Section of Dispute Resolution.

______ (1994). "Psychological Barriers to Litigation Settlement: An Experimental Approach," 93 *Mich. L. Rev.* 107.

KOVACH, Kimberlee K. (2004). *Mediation: Principles and Practice* (3d ed.). St. Paul, MN: Thomson West.

______ (1997). "Good Faith in Mediation—Requested, Recommended, or Required? A New Ethic," 38 *S. Tex. L. Rev.* 575.

KOVACH, Kimberlee K., and Lela P. LOVE (1996). "'Evaluative' Mediation Is an Oxymoron," 14 *Alternatives to High Cost Litig.* 31.

KRIEGER, Stefan H., and Richard K. NEUMANN, Jr. (2015). *Essential Lawyering Skills: Interviewing, Counseling, Negotiation, and Persuasive Fact Analysis: Fifth Edition.* Philadelphia: Wolters Kluwer.

KRUSE, Katherine R. (2010). "Beyond Cardboard Clients in Legal Ethics." 23 *Geo. J. Legal Ethics* 1.

KURTZBERG, Joel, and Jamie HENIKOFF (1997). "Freeing the Parties from the Law: Designing an Interest and Rights Focused Model of Landlord/Tenant Mediation," 1997 *J. Disp. Resol.* 53.

LaFREE, Gary, and Christine RACK (1996). "The Effects of Participants' Ethnicity and Gender on Monetary Outcomes in Mediated and Adjudicated Civil Cases," 30 *Law & Soc'y Rev.* 767.

LAMBROS, Thomas D. (1984). "The Summary Jury Trial and Other Alternative Methods of Dispute Resolution: A Report to the Judicial Conference of the United States Committee on the Operation of the Jury System," 103 *F.R.D.* 461.

LANDAU, Sy, Barbara LANDAU, and Daryl LANDAU (2001). *From Conflict to Creativity: How Resolving Workplace Disagreements Can Inspire Innovation and Productivity.* San Francisco: Jossey-Bass Publishers.

LANDE, John (2002). "Using Dispute System Design Methods to Promote Good-Faith Participation in Court-Connected Mediation Programs," 50 *UCLA L. Rev.* 69.

LANDRY, Sherry (1996). "Med-Arb: Mediation with a Bite and an Effective ADR Model," 63 *Def. Couns. J.* 263.

LAO-TZU (1991). *Tao Te Ching.* Trans. Steven Mitchell. New York: Harper & Row.

LARSON, David Allen, Amy J. SCHMITZ, and Alan WIENER (2023). "The American Bar Association Section of Dispute Resolution Adopts Guidance for Online Dispute Resolution," 38 *Ohio St. J. on Disp. Resol.* 235.

LAX, David A., and James K. SEBENIUS (2006). *3D Negotiation.* Cambridge: Harvard Business Press.

______ (1986). *The Manager as Negotiator: Bargaining for Cooperation and Competitive Gain.* New York: Free Press.

LeBARON, Michelle, and Maged SENBEL (2022). "Conflicts with Religious or Worldview Dimensions: Why They Matter and How to Engage Them," 23 *Cardozo J. Conflict Resol.* 301.

LEHMAN, Warren (1979). "The Pursuit of a Client's Interest," 77 *Mich. L. Rev.* 1078.

LERMAN, Lisa (1984). "Mediation of Wife Abuse Cases: The Adverse Impact of Informal Dispute Resolution on Women," 7 *Harv. Women's L.J.* 57.

LESLIE, Christopher (2018). "Conspiracy to Arbitrate," 96 *N.C. L. Rev.* 381.

LEVIN, Murray S. (2001). "The Propriety of Evaluative Mediation: Concerns About the Nature and Quality of an Evaluative Opinion," 16 *Ohio St. J. on Disp. Resol.* 267.

LEWICKI, Roy J., and Barbara Benedict BUNKER (1995). "Trust in Relationships: A Model of Development and Decline," in Barbara Benedict Bunker, Jeffrey Z. Rubin, et al., eds., *Conflict in Cooperation and Justice.* San Francisco: Jossey-Bass Publishers.

LEWIS, Michael (1989). *Liar's Poker: Rising Through the Wreckage on Wall Street.* New York: W.W. Norton.

LIND, E. Allan, Robert J. MacCOUN, Patricia A. EBENER, William L.F. FELSTINER, Deborah R. HENSLER, Judith RESNIK, and Tom R. TYLER (1989). *The Perception of Justice: Tort Litigants' Views of Trial, Court-Annexed Arbitration, and Judicial Settlement Conferences.* Santa Monica, CA: Rand.

LIVNEH, Yair (2020). "Overcoming the Loss Aversion Obstacle in Negotiation," 25 *Harv. Negot. L. Rev.* 187.

LOBEL, Orly (2022). *The Equality Machine: Harnessing Digital Technology for a Brighter, More Inclusive Future.* New York, NY: PublicAffairs.

LOPEZ, Gerald (1984). "The Internal Structure of Lawyering: Lay Lawyering," 32 *UCLA L. Rev.* 1.

LOVE, Lela P. (2000). "Images of Justice," 1 *Pepp. Disp. Resol. L.J.* 29.

______ (2000). "Training Mediators to Listen: Deconstructing Dialogue and Constructing Understanding, Agendas, and Agreements," 38 *Fam. & Conciliation Cts. Rev.* 27.

______ (1997). "The Top Ten Reasons Why Mediators Should Not Evaluate," 24 *Fla. St. U. L. Rev.* 937.

______ (1993). "Glen Cove: Mediation Achieves What Litigation Cannot," 20 *Consensus* 1 (Oct.).

LOVE, Lela P., and John W. COOLEY (2005). "The Intersection of Evaluation by Mediators and Informed Consent: Warning the Unwary," 21 *Ohio St. J. on Disp. Resol.* 45.

LOVE, Lela P., and Kimberlee K. KOVACH (2000). "ADR: An Eclectic Array of Processes, Rather than One Eclectic Process," 2000 *J. Disp. Resol.* 295.

LOVE, Lela P., and Joseph B. STULBERG (2004). "Targets and Techniques to Generate Movement," in Training Materials (unpublished).

LOVE, Lela P., and Glenn PARKER, eds. (2017). *Stories Mediators Tell—World Edition.* Washington, DC: ABA Publishing.

LOVE, Lela P., and Thomas J. STIPANOWICH (2021). "Dear 1L: Five Guideposts for Your Future Professional Practice," 22 *Cardozo J. Conflict Resol.* 529.

LOWENTHAL, Gary (1982). "General Theory of Negotiation Process, Strategy and Behavior," 31 *Kan. L. Rev.* 96.

LUBAN, David (1988). *Lawyers and Justice.* Princeton, NJ: Princeton University Press.

______ (1986). "Some Greek Trials: Order and Justice in Homer, Hesiod, Aeschylus and Plato," 54 *Tenn. L. Rev.* 279.

LUBET, Steven (1996). "Notes on the Bedouin Horse Trade or 'Why Won't the Market Clear, Daddy?,'" 74 *Tex. L. Rev.* 1039.

LYNCH, William P. (2002). "Problems with Court-Annexed Mandatory Arbitration: Illustrations from the New Mexico Experience," 32 *N.M. L. Rev.* 181.

MACFARLANE, Julie (2008). *The New Lawyer.* Vancouver: UBC Press.

MALIN, Martin H. (2013). "Two Models of Interest Arbitration," 28 *Ohio St. J. on Disp. Resol.* 145.

MANN, Bruce H. (1984). "The Formalization of Informal Law Arbitration Before the American Revolution," 59 *N.Y.U. L. Rev.* 443.

MARCUS, Mary G., Walter MARCUS, Nancy A. STILWELL, and Neville DOHERTY (1999). "To Mediate or Not to Mediate: Financial Outcomes in Mediated Versus Adversarial Divorces," 17 *Conflict Resol. Q.* 143.

MARGALIT, Avishai (2010). *On Compromise and Rotten Compromises.* Princeton, NJ: Princeton University Press.

MAULL, John (1996). "ADR in the Federal Courts: Would Uniformity Be Better?," 34 *Duq. L. Rev.* 245.

MAUTE, Judith L. (1991). "Public Values and Private Justice: A Case for Mediator Accountability," 4 *Geo. J. Legal Ethics* 503.

McADOO, Barbara, Nancy A. WELSH, and Roselle L. WISSLER (2003). "Institutionalization: What Do Empirical Studies Tell Us About Court Mediation," *Disp. Resol. Mag.* 8 (Winter).

McARTHUR, John Burritt (2022). "Parties Usually Benefit from Reasoned Awards, Not Standard Awards," 38 *Alternatives to High Cost Litig.* 44.

McGOVERN, Francis E. (2009). "Dispute System Design: The United Nations Compensation Commission," 14 *Harv. Negot. L. Rev.* 171

______ (2001). "Settlement of Mass Torts in a Federal System," 36 *Wake Forest L. Rev.* 871.

______ (1986). "Toward a Functional Approach for Managing Complex Litigation," 53 *U. Chi. L. Rev.* 440.

MEIERHOEFER, Barbara S. (1990). *Court-Annexed Arbitration in Ten District Courts.* Washington, DC: Federal Judicial Center.

MELTSNER, Michael, and Philip G. SCHRAG (1974). "Negotiation," in *Public Interest Advocacy: Materials for Legal Education.* Boston: Little, Brown.

MENKEL-MEADOW, Carrie (2025). *Advanced Introduction to Alternative Dispute Resolution.* Cheltenham, UK; Northampton Mass: Edward Elgar.

______ (2022). "Applying Conflict Resolution Insights to Hyper-Polarization: 'When Will (We) Ever Learn?,'" 39 *Conflict Resol. Q.* 375.

______ (2022). "Complex Multi-Party Multi-Issue Negotiations," in *Very Short Introduction to Negotiation.* Oxford: Oxford University Press.

______ (2022). *Very Short Introduction to Negotiation.* Oxford: Oxford University Press.

______ (2018). "Hybrid and Mixed Processes: Integrities of Process Pluralism," in Michael Palmer, Marion Roberts, and Maria Moscati, eds., *Comparative Dispute Resolution Research Handbook.* Cheltenham, UK: Elgar Publishing.

______ (2018). "Why We Can't 'Just All Get Along': Dysfunction in the Polity and Conflict Resolution and What We Might Do About It," 2018 *J. Disp. Resol.* 5.

______ (2017). "Alternative and Appropriate Dispute Resolution in Context: Formal, Informal, and Semiformal Legal Processes," in Peter Coleman and Morton Deutsch, eds., *Handbook of Conflict Resolution* (3d ed.). San Francisco: Jossey-Bass Publishers.

______ (2017). "The Evolving Complexity of Dispute Resolution Ethics," 30 *Geo. J. Legal Ethics* 389.

______ (2016). "Ethical Ordering in Transnational Legal Practice? A Review of Catherine A. Rogers's Ethics in International Arbitration," 29 *Geo. J. Legal Ethics* 207.

______ (2016). "Is ODR ADR?: Reflections of an ADR Founder from 15th ODR Conference at The Hague," 3(1) *Int'l J. Online Disp. Resol.* 4.

______ (2016). *Mediation and Its Applications for Good Decision Making and Dispute Resolution.* Cambridge, Antwerp, Portland: Intersentia.

______ (2014). "Unsettling the Lawyers: Other Forms of Justice in Indigenous Claims of Expropriation, Abuse and Injustice," 64 *U. Toronto L. J.* 620.

______ (2013). "The Historical Contingencies of Conflict Resolution," 1(1) *Int'l J. Conflict Resol.* 32.

______ (2013). "Regulation of Dispute Resolution in the United States of America: From the Formal to the Informal to the Semi-Formal," in Felix Steffek, Hannes Unberath, Hazel Genn, Reinhard Greger, and Carrie Menkel-Meadow, eds., *Regulating Dispute Resolution: ADR and Access to Justice at the Crossroads.* Oxford and Portland: Hart Publishing.

______ (2012). "Introduction," in Carrie Menkel-Meadow, ed., *Multi-Party Dispute Resolution, Democracy and Decision-Making: Volume II (Conflict Resolution).* Farnham, UK: Ashgate Press.

______ (2011). "Scaling Up Dispute Resolution and Deliberative Democracy in Health Care Reform: A Work in Progress," 74(3) *Law & Contemp. Probs.* 1.

______ (2010). "Dispute Resolution" in Peter Cane and Herber Kritzer, eds., *Oxford Handbook of Empirical Legal Research*. Oxford: Oxford University Press.

______ (2009). "Are There Systemic Ethics Issues in Dispute System Design? And What We Should [Not] Do About It: Lessons from International and Domestic Fronts," 14 *Harv. Negot. L. Rev.* 195.

______ (2009). "Chronicling the Complexification of Negotiation Theory and Practice," 25 *Negot. J.* 415.

______ (2007). "Know When to Show Your Hand," 10 *Negot. Newsl.* 1.

______ (2007). "Restorative Justice: What Is It and Does It Work?," in *Annual Review of Law and Social Science* 3. Palo Alto, CA: Annual Reviews.

______ (2006). "Peace and Justice: Notes on the Evolution and Purposes of Plural Legal Processes," 94 *Geo. L.J.* 553.

______ (2005). "Is the Adversary System Really Dead? Dilemmas of Legal Ethics as Legal Institutions and Roles Evolve," in Jane Holder, C. O'Cinneide, and M. Freeman, eds., *Current Legal Problems* 57. New York: Oxford University Press.

______ (2005). "The Lawyer's Role(s) in Deliberative Democracy," 5 *Nev. L.J.* 347.

______ (2004), "Remembrance of Things Past? The Relationship of Past to Future in Pursuing Justice in Mediation," 5 *Cardozo J. Conflict Resol.* 97.

______ (2004), "What's Fair in Negotiation? What Is Ethics in Negotiation?," in Carrie Menkel-Meadow and Michael Wheeler, eds., *What's Fair: Ethics for Negotiators*. San Francisco: Jossey-Bass Publishers.

______ (2003). "Conflict Theory," in Karen Christensen and David Levinson, eds., 1 *Encyclopedia of Community: From the Village to the Virtual World*. 4 vols. Thousand Oaks, CA: Sage Publications.

______ (2003). *Dispute Processing and Conflict Resolution: Theory, Practice and Policy*. Aldershot, UK, and Burlington, VT: Ashgate Press.

______ (2003). "Introduction: From Legal Disputes to Conflict Resolution and Human Problem Solving," in Carrie Menkel-Meadow, ed., *Dispute Processing and Conflict Resolution: Theory, Practice and Policy*. Aldershot, UK: Ashgate/Dartmouth.

______ (2002). "Cross-cultural Disputes and Mediator Strategies," in *Routledge Handbook of Intercultural Mediation* (Dominic Busch, ed.). New York and London: Routledge Taylor Francis Group.

(2002). "Ethics Issues in Arbitration and Related Dispute Resolution Processes: What's Happening and What's Not," 56 *U. Miami L. Rev.* 949.

______ (2002). "Ethics, Morality and Professional Responsibility in Negotiation," in Phyllis Bernard and Bryant Garth, eds., *Dispute Resolution Ethics*. Washington, DC: ABA Section of Dispute Resolution.

______ (2002). "The Lawyer as Consensus Builder: Ethics for a New Practice," 70 *Tenn. L. Rev.* 63.

______ (2002). "Practicing 'In the Interests of Justice' in the Twenty-First Century: Pursuing Peace and Justice," 70 *Fordham L. Rev.* 1761.

______ (2001). "Aha? Is Creativity Possible in Legal Problem Solving and Teachable in Legal Education?," 6 *Harv. Negot. L. Rev.* 97.

______ (2001). "Ethics in ADR: The Many 'Cs' of Professional Responsibility and Dispute Resolution," 28 *Fordham Urb. L.J.* 979.

______ (2001). *Mediation: Theory, Policy, and Practice*. Farnham, U.K. and Burlington, VT: Ashgate Press.

______ (2000), "Mothers and Fathers of Invention: The Intellectual Founders of ADR," 16 *Ohio St. J. on Disp. Resol.* 1.

______ (1999). "Ethics and Professionalism in Non-Adversarial Lawyering," 27 *Fla. St. U. L. Rev.* 153.

______ (1999). "The Lawyer as Problem Solver and Third-Party Neutral: Creativity and Non-Partisanship in Lawyering," 72 *Temp. L. Rev.* 785.

______ (1998). "Taking the Mass Out of Mass Torts: Reflections of a Dalkon Shield Arbitrator on Alternative Dispute Resolution, Judging, Neutrality, Gender, and Process," 31 *Loy. L.A. L. Rev.* 513.

______ (1996). "Is Mediation the Practice of Law?," 14 *Alternatives to High Cost Litig.* 57.

______ (1996). "The Trouble with the Adversary System in a Postmodern, Multicultural World," 38 *Wm. & Mary L. Rev.* 5.

______ (1995). "Ethics and the Settlements of Mass Torts: When the Rules Meet the Road," 80 *Cornell L. Rev.* 1159.

______ (1995). "Whose Dispute Is It Anyway?: A Philosophical and Democratic Defense of Settlement (in Some Cases)," 83 *Geo. L.J.* 2663.

______ (1991). "Pursuing Settlement in an Adversary Culture: A Tale of Innovation Co-Opted or 'The Law of ADR,'" 19 *Fla. St. U. L. Rev.* 1.

______ (1985). "For and Against Settlement: Uses and Abuses of the Mandatory Settlement Conference," 33 *UCLA L. Rev.* 485.

______ (1985). "The Transformation of Disputes by Lawyers: What the Dispute Paradigm Does and Does Not Tell Us," 1985 *Mo. J. Dispute Res.* 25.

______ (1984). "Toward Another View of Legal Negotiation: The Structure of Problem Solving," 31 *UCLA L. Rev.* 754.

______ (1983). "Legal Negotiation: A Study of Strategies in Search of a Theory," 1983 *Am. B. Found. Res. J.* 905.

MENKEL-MEADOW, Carrie, ed. (2011). *Complex Dispute Resolution.* 3 vols. New York: Ashgate Press.

MENKEL-MEADOW, Carrie, and Robert DINGWALL (2017). "Scripts: What to Do When Big Bad Companies Won't Negotiate," in Chris Honeyman and Andrea Kupfer Schneider, eds., *The Negotiator's Desk Reference.* St. Paul, MN: DRI Press.

MENKEL-MEADOW, Carrie, and Bryant GARTH (2010). "Courts and Civil Procedure," in Peter Cane and Herbert Kritzer, eds., *Oxford Handbook of Empirical Legal Research.* New York: Oxford University Press.

MENKEL-MEADOW, Carrie, and Michael WHEELER (2004). *What's Fair? Ethics for Negotiators.* San Francisco: Jossey-Bass Publishers.

MENTSCHIKOFF, Soia (1961). "Commercial Arbitration," 61 *Colum. L. Rev.* 846.

MNOOKIN, Robert H. (2003). "Strategic Barriers to Dispute Resolution: A Comparison of Bilateral and Multilateral Negotiations," 159 *J. Institutional & Theoretical Econ.* 199.

______ (1993). "Why Negotiations Fail: An Exploration of Barriers to Conflict Resolution," 8 *Ohio St. J. on Disp. Resol.* 235.

MNOOKIN, Robert H., and Lewis KORNHAUSER (1979). "Bargaining in the Shadow of the Law: The Case of Divorce," 88 *Yale L.J.* 950.

MNOOKIN, Robert H., Scott R. PEPPET, and Andrew S. TULUMELLO (2000). *Beyond Winning: Negotiating to Create Value in Deals and Disputes.* Cambridge, MA: Belknap Press of Harvard University Press.

MOBERLY, Robert B. (1994). "Ethical Standards for Court-Appointed Mediators and Florida's Mandatory Mediation Experiment," 21 *Fla. St. U. L. Rev.* 701.

MOFFITT, Michael L. (2024). "Truth. Regardless of Reconciliation?," 24 *Nev. L.J.* 1071.

______ (2019). "Settlement Malpractice," 86 *Chi. L. Rev.* 1825.

______ (2009). "The Four Ways to Assure Mediator Quality (and why none of them work)," 24 *Ohio St. J. on Disp. Resol.* 191.

______ (2009). "Three Things to Be Against ('Settlement' Not Included)," 78 *Fordham L. Rev.* 1203.

______ (2007). "Customized Litigation: The Case for Making Civil Procedure Negotiable," 75 *Geo. Wash. L. Rev.* 461.

______ (2005). "Pleadings in the Age of Settlement," 80 *Ind. L.J.* 727.

______ (2003). "Suing Mediators," 83 *B.U. L. Rev.* 147.

______ (2003). "Ten Ways to Get Sued: A Guide for Mediators," 8 *Harv. Negot. L. Rev.* 81.

______ (1997). "Casting Light on the Black Box of Mediation: Should Mediators Make Their Conduct More Transparent?," 13 *Ohio St. J. on Disp. Resol.* 1.

MOFFITT, Michael L., and Robert C. BORDONE, eds. (2005). *The Handbook of Dispute Resolution.* San Francisco: Jossey-Bass Publishers.

MOFFITT, Michael L., and Andrea SCHNEIDER (2014). Examples & Explanations for Dispute Resolution (3d ed.). New York: Wolters Kluwer Law & Business.

MOORE, Christopher W. (2014). *The Mediation Process: Practical Strategies for Resolving Conflict* (4th ed.). San Francisco: Jossey-Bass Publishers.

______ (1996). *The Mediation Process.* San Francisco: Jossey-Bass Publishers.

MORAN, Mayo (2019). "Cardinal Sins: How the Catholic Church Sexual Abuse Crisis Changed Private Law," 21 *Geo. J. Gender & L.* 95.

MOVIUS, Hallum, and Lawrence SUSSKIND (2009). *Built to Win: Creating a World Class Negotiating Organization.* Boston, MA: Harvard Business School.

NADER, Laura (1984). "The Recurrent Dialectic Between Legality and Its Alternatives: The Limitations of Binary Thinking," 132 *U. Pa. L. Rev.* 621.

NALEBUFF, Barry, and Ian AYRES (2003). *Why Not? How to Use Everyday Ingenuity to Solve Problems Big and Small.* Boston: Harvard Business School Press.

NELSON, Ryan H. (2023). "An Employment Discrimination Class Action by Any Other Name," 91 *Fordham L. Rev.* 1429.

NEWELL, Lauren (2019). "Rebooting Empathy for the Digital Generation Lawyer," 34 *Ohio St. J. on Disp. Resol.* 1.

NIEMIC, Robert J., Donna STIENSTRA, and Randall E. RAVITZ (2001). *Guide to Judicial Management of Cases in ADR.* Washington, DC: Federal Judicial Center.

NISBETT, R., and L. ROSS (1980). *Human Inference: Strategies and Shortcomings of Social Judgment.* Englewood Cliffs, NJ: Prentice Hall.

NOLAN-HALEY, Jacqueline M. (1999). "Informed Consent in Mediation: A Guiding Principle for Truly Educated Decisionmaking," 74 *Notre Dame L. Rev.* 775.

NOLL, David A. (2017). "Regulating Arbitration," 105 *Cal. L. Rev.* 985.

NOYES, Henry S. (2007). "If You (Re)Build It, They Will Come: Contracts to Remake the Rules of Litigation in Arbitration's Image," 30 *Harv. J.L. & Pub. Pol'y* 579.

ORR, Dan, and Chris GUTHRIE (2006). "Anchoring, Information, Expertise, and Negotiation: New Insights from Meta-analysis," 2006 *Ohio St. J. on Disp. Resol.* 597.

PEPPET, Scott R. (2005). "Six Principles for Using Negotiating Agents to Maximum Advantage," in Michael Moffitt and Robert Bordone, eds., *The Handbook of Dispute Resolution.* San Francisco: Jossey-Bass Publishers.

______ (2004). "ADR Ethics," 54 *J. Legal Educ.* 72.

______ (2004). "Contract Formation in Imperfect Markets: Should We Use Mediators in Deals?," 19 *Ohio St. J. on Disp. Resol.* 283.

______ (2003). "Contractarian Economics and Mediation Ethics: The Case for Customizing Neutrality Through Contingent Fee Mediation," 82 *Tex. L. Rev.* 227.

PHILBIN, Donald R., Jr. (2008). "The One Minute Manager Prepares for Mediation: A Multidisciplinary Approach to Negotiation Preparation," 13 *Harv. Negot. L. Rev.* 249.

PLAPINGER, Elizabeth, and Donna STIENSTRA (1996). *ADR and Settlement in the Federal District Courts: A Sourcebook for Judges & Lawyers.* Washington, DC: Federal Judicial Center.

PLOUS, Scott (1993). *The Psychology of Judgment and Decision Making.* Philadelphia: Temple University Press.

POSNER, Richard A. (1986). "The Summary Jury Trial and Other Methods of Alternative Dispute Resolution: Some Cautionary Observations," 53 *U. Chi. L. Rev.* 366.

POU, Charles, Jr. (2003). "'Embracing Limbo': Thinking About Rethinking Dispute Resolution Ethics," 108 *Penn St. L. Rev.* 199.

POUNDSTONE, William (2003). *How Would You Move Mount Fuji?* Boston: Little, Brown.

PRESS, Sharon, and Ellen E. DEASON (2021). "Mediation: Embedded Assumptions of Whiteness?," 22 *Cardozo J. Conflict Resol.* 453.

PRICE, Marty (2000). "Personalizing Crime: Mediation Produces Restorative Justice for Victims and Offenders," 7 *Disp. Resol. Mag.* 8 (Fall).

PRUITT, Dean G. (1983). "Achieving Integrative Agreements," in Max H. Bazerman and Roy J. Lewicki, eds., *Negotiation in Organizations.* Beverly Hills, CA: Sage Publications.

PRUITT, Dean G., and Steven A. LEWIS (1977). "The Psychology of Interactive Bargaining," in Daniel Druckman, ed., *Negotiations: Social-Psychological Perspectives.* Beverly Hills, CA: Sage Publications.

PUBLIC CONVERSATIONS PROJECT (now Essential Partners) (2003). "Constructive Conversations About Challenging Times: A Guide to Community Dialogue" (version 3.0). Available at http://www.publicconversations.org/pcp/uploadDocs/CommunityGuide3.0.pdf.

PURCELL, Sandra E. (1985). "The Attorney as Mediator—Inherent Conflict of Interest?," 32 *UCLA L. Rev.* 986.

PUTNAM, Linda L. (2006). "Communication and Interaction Patterns," in Andrea Kupfer Schneider and Christopher Honeyman, eds., *The Negotiator's Fieldbook.* Washington, DC: ABA Section of Dispute Resolution.

RABINOVICH-EINY, Orna, and Ethan KATSH (2017). "Lawyers and Online Negotiation," in Chris Honeyman and Andrea Kupfer Schneider, eds., *The Negotiator's Desk Reference.* St. Paul, MN: DRI Press.

RAIFFA, Howard (1982). *The Art and Science of Negotiation.* Cambridge, MA: Belknap Press of Harvard University Press.

RAIFFA, Howard, with John RICHARDSON and David METCALFE (2007). *Negotiation Analysis: The Science and Art of Collaborative Decision Making.* Cambridge, MA: Belknap Press of Harvard University Press.

RAKOFF, Todd (1983). "Contracts of Adhesion: An Essay in Reconstruction," 96 *Harv. L. Rev.* 1173.

RAWLS, John (1971). *A Theory of Justice.* Cambridge, MA: Harvard University Press.

REHNQUIST, William H. (1977). "A Jurist's View of Arbitration," *Arb. J.* 1 (Mar.).

REILLY, Peter (2009). "Was Machiavelli Right? Lying in Negotiation and the Art of Defensive Self-Help," 24 *Ohio St. J. on Disp. Resol.* 3.

RELIS, Tamara (2009). *Perceptions in Litigation and Mediation: Lawyers, Defendants, Plaintiffs and Gendered Parties.* Cambridge, UK: Cambridge University Press.

RESNIK, Judith (2015). "Diffusing Disputes: The Public in the Private of Arbitration, the Private in Courts, and the Erasure of Rights," 124 *Yale L.J.* 2804.

______ (1995). "Many Doors? Closing Doors? Alternative Dispute Resolution and Adjudication," 10 *Ohio St. J. on Disp. Resol.* 211.

______ (1982). "Managerial Judges," 96 *Harv. L. Rev.* 374.

REUBEN, Richard C. (2018). "Rethinking the Law of Legal Negotiation: Confidentiality Under Federal Rule of Evidence 408 and Related State Laws," 59 *B.C. L. Rev.* 523.

______ (2006). "Confidentiality in Arbitration: Beyond the Myth," 54 *Kan. L. Rev.* 1255.

______ (1997). "Public Justice: Toward a State Action Theory of Alternative Dispute Resolution," 87 *Cal. L. Rev.* 577.

REYES, Robert M., William C. THOMPSON, and Gordon H. BOWER (1980). "Judgmental Biases Resulting from Differing Availabilities of Arguments," 39 *J. Personality & Soc. Psychol.* 2.

RHODE, Deborah L. (2000). *In the Interests of Justice: Reforming the Legal Profession.* New York: Oxford University Press.

RISKIN, Leonard L. (2003). "Decisionmaking in Mediation: The New Old Grid and the New New Grid System," 79 *Notre Dame L. Rev.* 1.

______ (1994). "Mediator Orientations, Strategies and Techniques," 12 *Alternatives to High Cost Litig.* 111.

______ (1984). "Toward New Standards for the Neutral Lawyer in Mediation," 26 *Ariz. L. Rev.* 329.

______ (1982). "Mediation and Lawyers," 43 *Ohio St. L.J.* 29.

RISKIN, Leonard L., and Nancy WELSH (2008). "Is That All There Is? 'The Problem' in Court-Oriented Mediation," 15 *Geo. Mason L. Rev.* 863.

RISKIN, Leonard L., James E. WESTBROOK, and James LEVIN (1998). *Instructor's Manual with Simulation and Problem Materials,* accompanying *Dispute Resolution and Lawyers* (2d abr. ed.). St. Paul, MN: West Group.

ROBBENNOLT, Jennifer K. (2003). "Apologies and Legal Settlement: An Empirical Examination," 102 *Mich. L. Rev.* 460.

ROGERS, Catherine A. (2011). *Ethics in International Arbitration.* New York: Oxford University Press.

ROGERS, Nancy (2018). "One Idea for Ameliorating Polarization: Reviving Conversations About an American Spirit," 2018 *J. Disp. Resol. 27.*

ROGERS, Nancy, Robert C. BORDONE, Frank E.A. SANDER, and Craig A. McEWEN (2019). *Designing Systems and Processes for Managing Disputes* (2d. ed.). New York: Wolters Kluwer.

ROSE, L. Christopher (1999). Note, "Nevada's Court-Annexed Mandatory Arbitration Program: A Solution to Some of the Causes of Dissatisfaction with the Civil Justice System," 36 *Idaho L. Rev.* 171.

ROSS, Lee (1995). "Reactive Devaluation in Negotiation and Conflict Resolution," in Kenneth J. Arrow, et al., eds., *Barriers to Conflict Resolution.* New York: W.W. Norton & Co.

ROTHKIN, Emily (2022). "How to Create a Better Mediation: Using Divorce Mediation Outcomes to Assess Gender's Effect on Mediation," 102 *B.U. L. Rev. 631.*

ROTHMAN, Deborah (2017). "Trends in Arbitration Compensation," *Disp. Resol. Mag.* 8.

ROWE, Mary P. (1991). "The Ombudsman's Role in a Dispute Resolution System," 7 *Negot. J.* 353.

RUBIN, Jeffrey Z., and Frank E.A. SANDER (1991). "Culture, Negotiation, and the Eye of the Beholder," 7 *Negot. J.* 249.

______ (1988). "When Should We Use Agents? Direct vs. Representative Negotiation," 4 *Negot. J.* 395.

RULE, Colin (2002). *Online Dispute Resolution for Business: B2B, Ecommerce, Consumer, Employment Insurance, and Other Commercial Conflicts.* San Francisco: Jossey-Bass Publishers.

RUSSO, J. Edward, and Paul J.H. SCHOEMAKER (1990). *Decision Traps: The Ten Barriers to Brilliant Decision-Making and How to Overcome Them.* New York: Simon & Schuster.

RUTLEDGE, Peter (2004). "Toward a Contractual Approach to Arbitral Immunity," 39 *U. Ga. L. Rev.* 151.

SALINAS, Oscar (2016). *A Short & Happy Guide to Effective Client Interviewing and Counseling.* Eagan, MN: West.

SANDER, Frank E.A. (2009). "Ways of Handling Conflict: What We Have Learned, What Problems Remain," 25 *Negot. J.* 533.

______ (2000). "The Future of ADR," 2000 *J. Dispute Resol.* 1.

______ (1976). "Varieties of Dispute Processing," 70 *F.R.D.* 111.

SANDER, Frank E.A., and Stephen B. GOLDBERG (1994). "Fitting the Forum to the Fuss: A User-Friendly Guide to Selecting an ADR Procedure," 10 *Negot. J.* 49.

SANDER, Frank E.A., and Jeffrey Z. RUBIN (1988). "The Janus Quality of Negotiation: Dealmaking and Dispute Settlement," 4 *Negot. J.* 109.

SCANLON, Kathleen M. (2002). *Drafter's Deskbook for Dispute Resolution Clauses.* New York: CPR Institute for Dispute Resolution.

SCARDILLI, Frank J. (1982). "*Sisters of the Precious Blood v. Bristol-Myers Co.*: A Shareholder-Management Dispute," Presentation at a Harvard Faculty Seminar on Negotiation on April 13, 1982.

SCHLITZ, Patrick J. (1999). "On Being a Happy, Healthy, and Ethical Member of an Unhappy, Unhealthy, and Unethical Profession," 52 *Vand. L. Rev.* 871.

SCHMITZ, Amy J. (2009). "Nonconsensual + Nonbinding = Nonsensical? Reconsidering Court-Connected Arbitration Programs," 10 *Cardozo J. Conflict Resol.* 587.

______ (2006). "Untangling the Privacy Paradox in Arbitration," 54 *Kan. L. Rev.* 1211.

SCHMITZ, Amy J., and Colin RULE (2017). *The New Handshake: Online Dispute Resolution and the Future of Consumer Protection.* American Bar Association.

SCHNEIDER, Andrea Kupfer (2017). "How Does DSD Help Us Teach About Community Conflict (and How Can Community Conflict Help Illustrate DSD)?," 31 *St. Thomas L.J.* 370.

______ (2017). "Negotiating While Female," 70 *SMU L. Rev.* 695.

______ (2017). "Productive Ambition," in Chris Honeyman and Andrea Kupfer Schneider, eds., *The Negotiator's Desk Reference.* St. Paul, MN: DRI Press.

______ (2012). "Teaching a New Negotiation Skills Paradigm," 39 *Wash. U. J.L. & Pol'y* 13.

______ (2009). "Bargaining in the Shadow of (International Law)," 41 *N.Y.U. J. Int'l L. & Pol.* 789.

______ (2006). "The Day After Tomorrow: What Happens Once a Middle East Peace Treaty Is Signed?," 6 *Nev. L.J.* 401.

______ (2002). "Shattering Negotiation Myths: Empirical Evidence on the Effectiveness of Negotiation Style," 7 *Harv. Negot. L. Rev.* 143.

______ (2000). "Building a Pedagogy of Problem-Solving: Learning to Choose Among ADR Processes," 5 *Harv. Negot. L. Rev.* 113.

SCHNEIDER, Andrea Kupfer, and Noam EBNER (2017). "Social Intuition," in Chris Honeyman and Andrea Kupfer Schneider, eds., *Negotiator's Desk Reference.* St. Paul, MN: DRI Press.

SCHNEIDER, Andrea Kupfer, and Christopher HONEYMAN (2017). *The Negotiator's Desk Reference* (2d ed.). St. Paul, MN: DRI Press.

SCHNEIDER, Andrea Kupfer, and David KUPFER (2017). *Smart & Savvy: Negotiation Strategies in Academia.* Park City, UT: Meadows Communications, LLC.

SCHNEIDER, Andrea Kupfer, and Sean McCARTHY (2017). "Choosing Among Modes of Communication," in Christopher Honeyman and Andrea Kupfer Schneider, eds., *The Negotiator's Desk Reference.* DRI Press.

SCHNEIDER, Andrea Kupfer, et al. (2010). "Likeability v. Competence: The Impossible Choice Faced by Female Politicians, Evaded by Lawyers," 17 *Duke J. Gender L. & Pol'y* 363.

SCHÖN, Donald A. (1983). *The Reflective Practitioner.* New York: Basic Books.

SCHOOLER, Lionel M., and Luke GILMAN (2021). "Private Juries Within the Arbitration Framework: A Third Path in Dispute Resolution," 21 *Pepp. Disp. Resol. L.J.* 457.

SCHUMACHER, E.F. (1977). *A Guide for the Perplexed.* New York: Harper & Row.

SCHWARTZ, David S. (2004). "Correcting Federalism Mistakes in Statutory Interpretation: The Supreme Court and the Federal Arbitration Act," 67 *Law & Contemp. Probs.* 5.

SCHWARZ, Roger (2002). *The Skilled Facilitator: A Comprehensive Resource for Consultants, Facilitators, Managers, Trainers, and Coaches* (2d ed.). San Francisco: Jossey-Bass Publishers.

SEBENIUS, James K. (2004). "Mapping Backward: Negotiating in the Right Sequence?," 7(6) *Negotiation*, June. Reprinted as "A Better Way to Negotiate: Backward," in *Working Knowledge*, July 26, 2004.

SEN, Amartya (2009). *The Idea of Justice.* Cambridge, MA: Belknap Press.

SENGER, Jeffrey M. (2004). "Decision Analysis in Negotiation," 87 *Marq. L. Rev.* 721.

______ (2003). *Federal Dispute Resolution: Using ADR with the U.S. Government.* San Francisco: Jossey-Bass Publishers.

SEUL, Jeff (2022). "Negotiating Across Worldviews," 38 *Negot. J.* 357.

SHAPIRO, Daniel L. (2006). "Untapped Power: Emotions in Negotiation," in Andrea Kupfer Schneider and Christopher Honeyman, eds., *The Negotiator's Fieldbook.* Washington, DC: ABA Section of Dispute Resolution.

SHAPIRO, Martin (1981). *Courts: A Comparative and Political Analysis.* Chicago: University of Chicago Press.

SHAW, Margaret L., and Lynn P. COHN (1999). "Employment Class Actions Provide Unique Context for ADR," 5 *Disp. Resol. Mag.* 10 (Summer).

SHELL, G. Richard (2006). *Bargaining for Advantage: Negotiation Strategies for Reasonable People* (2d ed.). New York: Viking.

______ (1999). *Bargaining for Advantage: Negotiation Strategies for Reasonable People.* New York: Viking.

SHERMAN, Edward F. (1993). "Court Mandated Alternative Dispute Resolution: What Form of Participation Should Be Required?," 46 *SMU L. Rev.* 2079.

SHESTOWSKY, Donna (2017). "Psychology and Persuasion," in Chris Honeyman and Andrea Kupfer Schneider, eds., *The Negotiator's Desk Reference.* St. Paul, MN: DRI Press.

______ (2017). "When Ignorance Is Not Bliss: An Empirical Study of Litigants' Awareness of Court-Sponsored Alternative Dispute Resolution Programs," 22 Harv. Negot. L. Rev. 189.

SHULMAN, Harry (1955). "Reason, Contract, and Law in Labor Relations," 68 *Harv. L. Rev.* 999.

SIMPSON, Patricia A., and Joseph J. MARTOCCHIO (1997). "The Influence of Work History Factors on Arbitration Outcomes," 50 *Indus. & Lab. Rel. Rev.* 252.

SMITH, Linda F. (2007). "Was It Good for You Too? Conversation Analysis of Two Interviews," 96 *Ky. L.J.* 579.

SMITH, Stephanie, and Janet MARTINEZ (2009). "An Analytic Framework for Dispute System Design," 14 *Harv. Negot. L. Rev.* 123.

SOVERN, Jeff (2014). "Consumer Understanding of Arbitration Clauses in Contracts: 'Whimsy Little Contracts' with Unexpected Consequences," in *Forced Arbitration and the Fate of the 7th Amendment, Report of the 2014 Forum for State Appellate Court Judges.*

STEFFEK, Felix, Hannes UNBERATH, Hazel GENN, Reinhard GREGER, and Carrie MENKEL-MEADOW, eds. (2013). *Regulating Dispute Resolution: ADR and Access to Justice at the Crossroads.* Oxford and Portland: Hart Publishing.

STEMPEL, Jeffrey W. (2000). "The Inevitability of the Eclectic: Liberating ADR from Ideology," 2000 *J. Disp. Resol.* 247.

STERNLIGHT, Jean R. (2012). "Tsunami: *AT&T Mobility v. Concepcion* Impedes Access to Justice," 90 *Or. L. Rev.* 703.

______ (2010). "Lawyerless Dispute Resolution: Rethinking a Paradigm," 37 *Fordham Urb. L.J.* 1.

______ (2004). "In Search of the Best Procedure for Enforcing Employment Discrimination Laws: A Comparative Analysis," 78 *Tul. L. Rev.* 1401.

______ (2003). "ADR Is Here: Preliminary Reflections on Where It Fits in a System of Justice," 3 *Nev. L.J.* 289.

______ (2002). "Is the U.S. Out on a Limb? Comparing the U.S. Approach to Mandatory Consumer and Employment Arbitration to That of the Rest of the World," 56 *U. Miami L. Rev.* 831.

______ (2001). "Mandatory Binding Arbitration and the Demise of the Seventh Amendment Right to a Jury Trial," 16 *Ohio St. J. on Disp. Resol.* 669.

______ (1999). "Lawyers' Representation of Clients in Mediation: Using Economics and Psychology to Structure Advocacy in a Nonadversarial Setting," 14 *Ohio St. J. on Disp. Resol.* 269.

______ (1996). "Panacea or Corporate Tool?: Debunking the Supreme Court's Preference for Binding Arbitration," 74 *Wash. U. L.Q.* 637.

STERNLIGHT, Jean R., and Jennifer ROBBENNOLT (2008). "Good Lawyers Should be Good Psychologists: Insights for Interviewing and Counseling Clients." 23 *Ohio St. J. on Disp. Resol.* 437.

STIPANOWICH, Thomas J. (2021). "Arbitration, Mediation, and Mixed Modes: Seeking Workable Solutions and Common Ground on Med-Arb, Arb-Med, and Settlement-Oriented Activities by Arbitrators," 26 *Harv. Negot. L. Rev.* 265.

______ (2010). "Arbitration: 'The New Litigation,'" 2010 *Ill. L. Rev.* 1.

STONE, Douglas, Bruce PATTON, and Sheila HEEN (1999). *Difficult Conversations: How to Discuss What Matters Most.* New York: Viking.

STROMSETH, Jane, David WIPPMAN, and Rosa BROOKS (2006). *Can Might Make Rights?* Cambridge and New York: Cambridge University Press.

STULBERG, Joseph B. (1998). "Fairness and Mediation," 13 *Ohio St. J. on Disp. Resol.* 909.

______ (1981). "The Theory and Practice of Mediation: A Reply to Professor Susskind," 6 *Vt. L. Rev.* 85.

STULBERG, Joseph B., and Lela P. LOVE (2019). *The Middle Voice: Mediating Conflict Successfully* (3d ed.). Durham, NC: Carolina Academic Press.

STURM, Susan, and Howard GADLIN (2007). "Conflict Resolution and Systemic Change," 2007 *J. Disp. Resol.* 2.

SUMMERS, Robert S. (1982). "The General Duty of Good Faith—Its Recognition and Conceptualization," 67 *Cornell L. Rev.* 810.

SUNSTEIN, Cass R. (2000). "Deliberative Trouble? Why Groups Go to Extremes," 110 *Yale L.J.* 71.

SUSSKIND, Lawrence (2009). "Twenty-Five Years Ago and Twenty-Five Years From Now: The Future of Public Dispute Resolution," 25 *Negot. J.* 551.

______ (1999). "An Alternative to *Robert's Rules of Order* for Groups, Organizations, and Ad Hoc Assemblies That Want to Operate by Consensus," in Lawrence Susskind, Sarah McKearnan, and Jennifer Thomas-Larmer, eds., *The Consensus Building Handbook: A Comprehensive Guide to Reaching Agreement.* Thousand Oaks, CA: Sage Publications.

______ (1981). "Environmental Mediation and the Accountability Problem," 6 *Vt. L. Rev.* 1.

SUSSKIND, Lawrence, and Jeffrey CRUICKSHANK (2006). *Breaking Robert's Rules: The New Way to Run Your Meeting, Build Consensus and Get Results.* New York: Oxford University Press.

SUSSKIND, Lawrence, Sarah McKEARNAN, and Jennifer Thomas LARMER (1999). *The Consensus Building Handbook: A Comprehensive Guide to Reaching Agreement.* Thousand Oaks, CA: Sage Publications.

SUSSKIND, Richard (2019). *Online Courts and the Future of Justice.* Oxford: Oxford University Press.

SWEET, Alec Stone, and Florian GRISEL (2017). *The Evolution of International Arbitration: Judicialization, Governance, Legitimacy.* Oxford: Oxford University Press.

SYMPOSIUM (2010). 11 *Nev. L. Rev.*

SYMPOSIUM (2009). "Dispute System Design." 14 *Harv. Negot. L. Rev.* 1.

SYMPOSIUM (2004). "ADR and the Vanishing Trial," *Disp. Resol. Mag.* 3-21 (Summer).

SYMPOSIUM (2004). "The Vanishing Trial," 3 *J. Empirical Stud.* 1.

SZALAI, Imri (2013). *Outsourcing Justice: The Rise of Modern Arbitration Laws in America.* Durham, NC: Carolina Academic Press.

TANNEN, Deborah (1998). *The Argument Culture: Moving from Debate to Dialogue.* New York: Random House.

THOMPSON, Anthony C. (2002). "Courting Disorder: Some Thoughts on Community Courts," 10 *Wash. U. J.L. & Pol'y* 63.

THOMPSON, Leigh L. (2001). *The Mind and Heart of the Negotiator* (2d ed.). Englewood Cliffs, NJ: Prentice Hall.

THORNBURG, Elizabeth G. (2006). "Designer Trials," 2007 *J. Disp. Resol.* 181.

TIMKIN, Nelson Edward (2023). "A Proposal to Establish an International Commercial Arbitration Ethics Panel and Hotline to Resolve Disclosure and Conflicts Issues," 24 *Cardozo J. Conflict Resol.* 303.

TIPPETT, Elizabeth Chika, and Bridget SCHAAFF (2018). "How *Concepcion* and *Italian Colors* Affected Terms of Service Contracts in the Gig Economy," 70 *Rutgers L. Rev.* 101.

TONN, Joan C. (2003). *Mary P. Follett: Creating Democracy, Transforming Management.* New Haven: Yale University Press.

TRANTINA, Terry L. (2001). "How to Design ADR Clauses That Satisfy Clients' Needs and Minimize Litigation Risk," 19 *Alternatives to High Cost Litig.* 137.

TREMBLAY, Paul R. (2006). "'Pre-Negotiation' Counseling: An Alternative Model," 13 *Clinical L. Rev.* 541.

TRUMP, Donald J. (1987). *The Art of the Deal.* New York: Random House.

URY, William L., Jeanne M. BRETT, and Stephen B. GOLDBERG (1988). *Getting Disputes Resolved: Designing Systems to Cut the Costs of Conflict.* San Francisco: Jossey-Bass Publishers.

WALDMAN, Ellen A. (1997). "Identifying the Role of Social Norms in Mediation: A Multiple Model Approach," 48 *Hastings L.J.* 703.

WALDMAN, Ellen, ed. (2011). *Mediation Ethics: Cases and Commentaries.* San Francisco: Jossey-Bass Publishers.

WARE, Stephen J. (2014). "Vacating Legally-Erroneous Arbitration Awards," 6 *Y.B. on Arb. & Mediation* 56.

______ (2006). "The Case for Enforcing Adhesive Arbitration Agreements—with Particular Consideration of Class Actions and Arbitration Fees," 5 *J. Am. Arb.* 251.

______ (2006). "Comments of Professor Stephen Ware," in Edward Brunet et al., *Arbitration Law in America: A Critical Assessment* 327.

WATSON, Lawrence M., Jr. (2002). *Effective Advocacy in Mediation: A Planning Guide to Prepare for a Civil Trial Mediation.* Upchurch Watson White & Max Mediation Group. Retrieved from http://www.uww-adr.com/2002/pdfs/effectiveadvocacy.pdf.

WEINSTEIN, Robyn, and Lance BOND (2021). "Visions for the Future: Diversity and Inclusion Initiatives in Court-Annexed ADR Program," 22 *Cardozo J. Conflict Resol.* 499.

WEINSTEIN, Janet, and Linda MORTON (2003). "Stuck in a Rut: The Role of Creative Thinking in Problem Solving and Legal Education," 9 *Clinical L. Rev.* 835.

WELSH, Nancy A. (2020). "Symposium: Achieving Access to Justice Through ADR: Fact or Fiction?, Bringing Transparency and Accountability (With a Dash of Competition) to Court-Connected Dispute Resolution," 88 *Fordham L. Rev.* 2449.

______ (2004). "Remembering the Role of Justice in Resolution: Insights from Procedural and Social Justice Theories," 54 *J. Legal Educ.* 49.

______ (2001). "The Thinning Vision of Self-Determination in Court-Connected Mediation: The Inevitable Price of Institutionalization?," 6 *Harv. Negot. L. Rev.* 1.

WESTON, Maureen A. (2009). "Doping Control, Mandatory Arbitration, and Process Dangers for Accused Athletes in International Sports," 10 *Pepp. Disp. Res. L.J.* 5.

______ (2004). "Reexamining Arbitral Immunity in an Age of Mandatory and Professional Arbitration," 88 *Minn. L. Rev.* 449.

______ (2001). "Checks on Participant Conduct in Compulsory ADR: Reconciling the Tension in the Need for Good-Faith Participation, Autonomy, and Confidentiality," 76 *Ind. L.J.* 591.

WHEELER, Michael (2013). *The Art of Negotiation: How to Improvise Agreement in a Chaotic World.* New York: Simon & Schuster.

WHITE, James J. (1980). "Machiavelli and the Bar: Ethical Limitations on Lying in Negotiation," 1980 *Am. B. Found. Res. J.* 926.

WILDE, Oscar (2000). Barry Day, ed., *A Life in Quotes*. London, UK: Metro Books.

______ (1983). *Legal Negotiation and Settlement*. St. Paul, MN: West Group.

WISSLER, Roselle L. (2011). "Court-Connected Settlement Procedures: Mediation and Judicial Settlement Conferences," 26 *Ohio St. J. on Disp. Resol.* 2.

______ (2010). "Representation in Mediation: What We Know from Empirical Research," 37 *Fordham Urb. L.J.* 419.

______ (2004). "The Effectiveness of Court-Connected Dispute Resolution in Civil Cases," 22 *Conflict Res. Q.* 55.

______ (1997). "The Effects of Mandatory Mediation: Empirical Research on the Experience of Small Claims and Common Pleas Courts," 33 *Willamette L. Rev.* 565.

WISSLER, Roselle L., and Art HINSHAW (2021). "The Initial Mediation Session: An Empirical Examination," 27 *Harv. Negot. L. Rev.* 1.

YARN, Douglas H. (1999). *Dictionary of Conflict Resolution*. San Francisco: Jossey-Bass Publishers.

YOUNG, Michael (2010). "Mediation Gone Wild: How Three Minutes Put an ADR Party Behind Bars," 25 *Alternatives to High Cost Litig.* 97.

ZELIZER, Craig, and Robert A. RUBENSTEIN (2009). *Building Peace: Reflections from the Field*. Sterling, VA: Kumarian Press.

Index